SACRAMENTO PUBLIC LIBRARY

S0-ASP-223

CENTRAL LIBRARY
828 "I" STREET
SACRAMENTO, CA 95814

AUG   - 1998

A. Lincoln

THE EVERY-DAY LIFE OF ABRAHAM LINCOLN

By Francis Fisher Browne

Introduction to the Bison Book Edition
by John Y. Simon

University of Nebraska Press
Lincoln and London

Introduction to the Bison Book Edition © 1995 by the University of
Nebraska Press
All rights reserved
Manufactured in the United States of America

⊗ The paper in this book meets the minimum requirements of American National Standard for Information Sciences—Permanence of
Paper for Printed Library Materials, ANSI Z39.48-1984.

First Bison Book printing: 1995
Most recent printing indicated by the last digit below:
10   9   8   7   6   5   4   3   2   1

Library of Congress Cataloging-in-Publication Data
Browne, Francis F. (Francis Fisher), 1843–1913.
The every-day life of Abraham Lincoln / by Francis Fisher Browne;
introduction to the Bison Book Edition by John Y. Simon.
p.   cm.
"Reprinted from the 1887 ed. published by Northwestern Pub. Co.,
Minneapolis, based on the original ed. published by N. D. Thompson
Pub. Co., N.Y., 1886"—CIP info.
ISBN 0-8032-6115-2 (pbk.: alk. paper)
1. Lincoln, Abraham, 1809–1865.   2. Presidents—United States—
Biography.   I. Title.
E457.B88   1995
973.7'092—dc20
[B]
94-45451   CIP

Reprinted from the 1887 edition published by Northwestern Publishing Co., Minneapolis, based on the original edition published by N. D.
Thompson Publishing Co., New York (1886)

INTRODUCTION

John Y. Simon

Francis Fisher Browne's 1886 biography of Abraham Lincoln, which began as hackwork, remains an indispensable source of information. Browne, editor of *The Dial*, a Chicago literary monthly, compiled *The Every-Day Life of Abraham Lincoln* with the aid of scissors and a large pot of paste. He ransacked Lincoln biographies, periodical literature, and newspapers. Most importantly, he corresponded with people who had known Lincoln. Although time has diminished the value of some of his sources, Browne's book retains significance in Lincoln literature because it contains so many personal recollections unavailable elsewhere.

Browne knew that he had created a rough and shaggy book. Errors in names and facts abounded. Despite such flaws, however, the book sold well, attracting an audience hungrier for personal reminiscence than for panegyric. Despite this popularity, Browne determined on considerable changes for the revised edition. Completed shortly before he died in 1913, the revised edition provides a benchmark in Lincoln historiography. Alterations in the Lincoln image become apparent by tracking what Browne decided to omit in his somewhat more compact revision.

Browne was born on 1 December 1843 in South Halifax, Vermont, the son of William Goldsmith Brown and Eunice Fisher Brown. (Browne later added an "e" to the end of his last name for reasons unknown.) Early in life, Browne was indoctrinated with the idea that his Puritan heritage demanded a life of austerity, integrity, and moral and intellectual endeavor. His father had taught school, then became involved in editing antislavery newspapers in Vermont and Massachusetts, and had a local reputation as a poet. At fourteen, after a minimal public school education, young Browne began to assist his father in editing and printing

the *Chicopee* (Massachusetts) *Journal*. While still a teenager in
fall 1862, Browne enlisted in the Forty-Sixth Massachusetts Volunteers, a militia regiment mustered for nine months of service,
most of the time along the North Carolina coast. When Robert E.
Lee invaded Pennsylvania in the summer of 1863, the regiment
embarked for Baltimore and participated in the half-hearted pursuit of the Confederates after the battle of Gettysburg. The regiment saw little action and lost one man killed and thirty-five who
succumbed to disease. Although Browne returned to a long and
productive career, he was never free of health problems that dated
to his military service.[1]

After discharge, Browne decided to study law. He spent some
time in a law office in Rochester, New York, and briefly attended
the University of Michigan, which he left either because of health
or money. Returning to Rochester, he worked as a printer, married, and moved to Chicago in 1867, where he established a
printshop. Two years later, he left printing to buy a partnership in
the ambitious literary magazine *Western Monthly*, of which he became editor. Under Browne, the magazine expanded, changed its
name to the *Lakeside Monthly*, abandoned its regional focus, and
won recognition as a leading literary journal. In 1870 fire destroyed
the office and equipment; a new building burned in the great Chicago fire of 1871. The magazine finally surrendered to the Depression of 1873. In 1875, plagued by poor health, Browne had to ask
his father for money. In 1878, Browne joined the Chicago publishing and book wholesaling firm of Jansen, McClurg, and Company,
which in 1880 launched *The Dial,* a monthly edited and partly
owned by Browne. In 1892, Browne bought out his partner, began
to publish twice each month, and continued as editor until his
death in 1913. *The Dial*, primarily a magazine of book reviews,
immediately became influential but not necessarily prosperous.[2]

Probably for economic reasons Browne became an anthologist,
editing *Golden Poems by British and American Authors* (1881),
*The Golden Treasury of Poetry and Prose: Choice Selections from
the Works of Leading British and American Authors for a Period
of Five Hundred Years* (1883), and *Bugle-Echoes: A Collection of
Poems of the Civil War, Northern and Southern* (1886). The last
and most successful of the anthologies was *The Every-Day Life of
Abraham Lincoln.* Publishers in New York and St. Louis, Hartford, and Philadelphia printed this book in 1886; a Minneapolis
publisher used an 1887 date. Another printing came from St. Louis

in 1896. Sold through subscription agents who went door-to-door, the book benefited from representation as the product of a local publisher. Selling books to the unbookish meant emphasizing illustrations, and Browne's book, which fell far short of the promised one hundred, was generously sprinkled with woodcuts, some perfunctory and others extremely crude.

What apparently made this book so successful was its "everyday" character. Instead of lingering over Lincoln's noble traits and political accomplishments, Browne presented story after story. Each chapter consisted of selections from such a wide variety of sources that 747 pages readily subdivided into relatively small and easily managed segments. Browne drew upon many Lincoln biographies, selecting their choicest passages and anecdotes, supplementing these with a variety of reminiscences, some drawn from newspapers and magazines, others solicited by Browne himself. The last class of material gives the book its enduring importance as an indispensable source of information about Lincoln.

When Browne published his Lincoln book, William H. Herndon, Lincoln's former law partner, had not yet published the long-planned biography of Lincoln that he had undertaken immediately after Lincoln's assassination. He had, however, sold copies of his accumulation of correspondence and interviews to another former Lincoln legal associate, Ward Hill Lamon, who produced a ghost-written biography in 1872 that told more than many thought seemly about Lincoln's parents, his backwoods upbringing, his love for Anne Rutledge, and his tempestuous marriage. Above all, Lamon's biography offended by emphasizing Lincoln's lack of conventional religious faith. In the fall of 1886, another Lincoln biography written by his former White House secretaries, John G. Nicolay and John Hay, began to appear serially in *The Century*. Nicolay and Hay's biography, drawing upon family papers supplied by Lincoln's son Robert and dependent upon Robert's approval of the text, presented a far more conventional and respectable Abraham Lincoln.[3] Browne's *Every-Day Life* fell somewhere in between. Both Herndon, responsible for several speeches and interviews, and Lamon, purveyor of the Herndon sources, furnished hefty chunks of source material. Yet Browne also drew upon material from more reverential former Lincoln associates.

Browne's *Every-Day Life* appeared in the same year as Allen Thorndike Rice's *Reminiscences of Abraham Lincoln by Distinguished Men of his Time*. Assembled by the editor of the *North*

American Review, Rice's book differed from Browne's in having by-lined chapters especially written for Rice by men who had known Lincoln, and Rice made no attempt to weave the individual chapters into a connected biography. The "distinguished men" assembled were far more likely to have known Lincoln as president than as an Illinoisan. Slightly more than half of Browne's book dealt with Lincoln before his presidency. In other respects, including length— 656 pages for Rice, 747 for Browne—the two books bore more similarities than differences. Rice's compilation also sold well, appearing in something labeled an eighth edition in 1889 and in a genuinely new and revised edition in 1909. Together, Rice and Browne affirmed the healthy market for Lincoln reminiscence.

Although Browne is best remembered as a Lincoln biographer, his interest in Lincoln apparently subsided as *The Dial* achieved greater success. He became an arbiter of genteel literary taste, somewhat old-fashioned in his own day. He worshipped Matthew Arnold, favored English writers over American, and preferred New England writers to those of the Midwest. A correspondent for *The Dial* found *The Red Badge of Courage* "utterly without merit."[4] When Hamlin Garland complained that conservative reviewers of *The Dial* dealt harshly with realistic western authors, Browne replied that western literature was "no longer a baby" and ought to be judged "by the standards of world-literature, rather than by the standards of the back settlement."[5] Although *The Dial* depended upon the advertisements of publishers, Browne refused to run any advertisement for a book in the same issue in which a favorable review appeared.

Browne admired both Lincoln and Ulysses S. Grant, yet voted for Democrats in 1872 and in six succeeding presidential elections. Although *The Dial* maintained political neutrality, outside his editorial office Browne took a passionate interest in issues of the day. In 1896 he wrote an article for a British magazine concerning Governor John P. Altgeld of Illinois, frequently denounced by Republican orators as a champion of anarchy. Browne rather carefully explained Altgeld's two most famous acts: his pardon in 1893 of three men convicted and imprisoned for complicity in the Haymarket affair of 1886 and his protest in 1894 of the use of federal troops to end the Pullman strike. Browne clearly admired Altgeld and carefully depicted him as responsible and judicious.[6] Indeed, Browne wanted to be regarded the same way. Browne had reacted to the Haymarket trial in verse, and his small collection of poems on various subjects was the only book of his own composition, other than an anthology, ever published.[7]

In 1907, Browne opened a bookstore in the Fine Arts Building adjacent to the offices of *The Dial*. Frank Lloyd Wright designed the store, which had such elegant touches as a fireplace surrounded by chairs to encourage the social gathering of booklovers. Widely admired for Wright's design and Browne's reverence for books, the bookstore failed to prosper, in part because nearby department stores sold popular books at discount prices, and closed in 1912.

By this time, Browne was approaching the end of his long and productive career. As early as 1887, he had spent part of the winter in California to avoid Chicago's weather, and in 1900 established a permanent winter home in Pasadena. Even avoiding icy winds blowing across Lake Michigan could not prolong his life quite to three score and ten. He died on 11 May 1913 while preparing the revised edition of *The Every-Day Life of Abraham Lincoln*, and the book appeared after the editor's death.

In his preface to the revised edition, Browne wrote that the earlier version had "been compressed into about two-thirds of its former compass," an assertion contradicted by comparing the two books. The 714 text pages of the 1886 edition had been reduced to 599 in 1913, but the revised edition had only three illustrations, none of them in the text, and the earlier had 60, some full-page, more half-page. The earlier text had frequent subheads throughout, an average of more than one per page, while the last edition compacted the text. These subheads vanished because Browne had previously presented his material as a series of anecdotes, reminiscences, or quotations from other sources, whereas later he strove to weave them into a connected narrative.

Such changes did not come without price. In 1886, Browne had written: "Nearly thirty years after Anne Rutledge was buried, Mr. Lincoln said, in talking with a boyhood friend: 'I have loved the name of Rutledge to this day. . . . I loved the woman dearly. . . .'" (129). In 1913, Browne revised the passage to read: "A long time afterward, when the grass had for nearly thirty years grown over the grave of Anne Rutledge, Lincoln was one day introduced to a man named Rutledge in the White House. He looked at him a moment, then grasped his hand and said to him with deep feeling: 'I love the name of Rutledge to this day. Anne was a lovely girl. . . .'"[8] In both cases Browne quoted Isaac Cogdal, a friend of Lincoln's from New Salem days, who had visited him in Springfield during the winter of 1860–1861 and asked about Anne Rutledge. Herndon later transcribed what Cogdal remembered of Lincoln's response. "I have loved the name of Rutledge to this day. . . . I loved the woman dearly & sacredly: she was a handsome girl—would have made a good loving wife. . . ."[9] Some have disputed whether Cogdal remembered accurately what Lincoln said, but Browne had reported far better the first time than the second.

In the same paragraph, Browne turned to another source. " 'The love and death of this girl,' said Mr. Herndon, 'shattered Lincoln's purposes and tendencies. He threw off his infinite sorrow only by leaping wildly into the political arena.' 'He needed,' said another, 'whip and spur to save him from despair'" (129). As revised in 1913: "Mr. Herndon has said that the love and death of this young girl shattered Lincoln's purposes and tendencies. 'He threw off his infinite sorrow only by leaping wildly into the political arena. He needed whip and spur to save him from despair.'"[10] For convenience, the person once simply labeled "another" disappears, his words belatedly flying into Herndon's mouth. Those interested in accurate quotations must turn from the revision to the original edition. In the 1886 edition, Lincoln says of Ulysses S. Grant: "The only evidence you have that he's in any place is that he makes things *git!* Wherever he is, things move" (612). In 1913, Lincoln said, "The only evidence you have that he's in any particular place is that he makes things move."[11] Even Lincoln's own correspondence received editorial emendation. Lincoln's ". . . it is this that induces me to advise," (195) became ". . . it is this that induces me to offer you this advice."[12]

Rather than diminish the overall wordage, Brown replaced older material with new in the 1913 edition. In the process, he abridged coverage of Lincoln's life before he entered the White House—originally more than half the book—in favor of lengthier treatment of the presidency. What Browne omitted often reflected rougher aspects of frontier life. He understandably deleted an ugly and tasteless anecdote about a Lincoln prank as New Salem postmaster (119). Nonetheless, Browne may have done himself and Lincoln a favor at history's expense. Space saved by paring coverage of the prairie years was used to enhance coverage of the war years. Time after time, occasionally at considerable length, Browne drew upon the diary of Gideon Welles, secretary of the navy in the Lincoln administration. Since the diary was published in full in 1911,

Browne frequently abandoned unique accounts for reprinted material.

By 1913, Browne could anticipate few additional reliable Lincoln reminiscences. What he had gathered by 1886 constituted his principle stock of contemporary anecdotes. In preparing a new edition, Browne sought to make his book more nearly a comprehensive Lincoln biography. In assessing Browne's success, Paul M. Angle, author of a magisterial survey of Lincoln literature, commended the revised edition to the general reader, the first edition to anyone seeking as much Lincoln information as possible.[13] He also should have warned that the revised edition did not always respect the integrity of sources gathered earlier.

When Lincoln died, biographers began to battle for the man they wanted known. Although the events of his presidency could be determined by abundant contemporary sources and living witnesses, his first half-century was relatively obscure. Some biographers tried to shape Lincoln's early life into a wholesome inspiration for posterity; others sought material for a true likeness, undeterred by complexity, contradiction or even crudity. None of the latter group believed that Lincoln's greatness would fade in the light of reality. Confident that those who knew Lincoln intimately would admire him more, Browne assembled his grab bag of yarns, anecdotes, and stories.

Indeed, he was correct. The unkempt book that Browne published in 1886 brought Lincoln the man to respectful readers. More than a century later, when so many of the contemporary books printed on wood-pulp have disintegrated, a new generation deserves the pleasure of reading Browne's assemblage of Lincoln reminiscences.

NOTES

1. For Browne's biography, see Chas. F. Lummis, "In Western Letters," *Land of Sunshine*, 12 (April 1900): 296–302; "Francis Fisher Browne, 1843–1913," *Dial*, 54 (1 June 1913): 437–43; "The 'Dial's' Puritan Editor," *American Review of Reviews* (July 1913): 115–16; Lloyd Lewis, "Francis Fisher Browne," *Newberry Library Bulletin* (Sept. 1945): 23–36; Frederic John Mosher, "Chicago's 'Saving Remnant': Francis Fisher Browne, William Morton Payne, and *The Dial* (1880–1892)," Ph.D. diss., University of Illinois, 1950; Henry Regnery, "A Prophet without Honor: Francis F. Browne and *The Dial*," *Modern Age*, 30 (Summer/Fall 1986):

267–73; Roger Cameron Lips, "Francis Fisher Browne," in *American Dictionary of Literary Biography,* Volume 79: *Magazine-Journalists, 1850–1900,* ed. Sam G. Riley (Detroit: Gale Research, 1989), 74–83.

2. For Browne's journalism, in addition to sources above, see "The Life-Story of a Magazine," *Dial,* 54 (16 June 1913): 489–92; Frank Luther Mott, *A History of American Magazines* (Cambridge, Mass.: Harvard University Press, 1938), 413–16; 539–43; Michael Hackenberg, "The Lakeside Monthly," in *American Literary Magazines: The Eighteenth and Nineteenth Centuries,* ed. Edward E. Chielens (Westport, Conn.: Greenwood, 1986), 199–203; Clarence Major, *"The Dial,"* American Literary *Magazines: The Twentieth Century,* ed. Edward E. Chielens (Westport, Conn.: Greenwood, 1992), 79–87; Nicholas Joost, *Years of Transition: The Dial 1912–1920* (Barre, Mass.: Barre Publishers, 1967).

3. Benjamin P. Thomas, *Portrait for Posterity* (New Brunswick, N.J.: Rutgers University Press, 1947); Merrill D. Peterson, *Lincoln in American Memory* (New York: Oxford, 1994), 83–135.

4. *Dial,* 20 (16 April 1896): 227.

5. Lewis, "Browne," 32.

6. "The Presidential Contest. I. Altgeld of Illinois," *National Review,* 28 (Dec. 1896): 452–73. Portions of this article were reprinted in *Dedicatory Exercises at the Unveiling of Bronze Tablets in Memory of John P. Altgeld at the Garrick Theatre, Chicago, Sunday, September 4, 1910* (n.p., n.d.), 23–38. Browne's son also drew on this article. Waldo R. Browne, *Altgeld of Illinois: A Record of His Life and Work* (New York: B. W. Huebsch, 1924), 275–79, 313–14.

7. *Volunteer Grain* (Chicago: Way & Williams, 1895).

8. Browne, *The Every-Day Life of Abraham Lincoln* ... (Chicago: Browne & Howell, 1913), 52.

9. John Y. Simon, "Abraham Lincoln and Anne Rutledge," *Journal of the Abraham Lincoln Association,* 11 (1990): 25.

10. Browne, *Every-Day Life* (1913), 52.

11. Ibid., 520.

12. Ibid., 105. The 1886 rendering is supported in Roy P. Basler et al., eds. *The Collected Works of Abraham Lincoln* (New Brunswick, N. J.: Rutgers University Press, 1953–55), 1: 498.

13. Paul M. Angle, *A Shelf of Lincoln Books: A Critical Selective Bibliography of Lincolniana* (New Brunswick: Rutgers University Press, 1946), 26–28.

PREFACE.

This book aims to give a view, clearer and completer than has been or could be given before, of the personality of Abraham Lincoln. A life so full of incident, and a character so many-sided as his, can be understood only with the lapse of time. A sense of the exhaustless interest of that life and character, and the inadequacy of ordinarily-constructed biographies to portray his many-sidedness, suggested the preparation of a work upon the novel plan here represented. Begun several years ago, the undertaking proved of such unexpected magnitude that its completion has been delayed beyond the anticipated time. The extensive correspondence with persons at a distance was an almost interminable task, in addition to the exploration of available sources of information in the books, pamphlets, magazines and newspapers of a quarter of a century, and in the scraps and papers of historical collections. The examination and sifting of this mass of material, its verification amidst often conflicting testimony, and its final moulding into shape, has involved time and labor that can be estimated only by those who have had similar experience.

Acknowledgements are heartily made to the many persons who have kindly furnished original contributions, and to others who have aided the work by valuable suggestions and information; also to earlier biographies of Lincoln—those of Raymond, Holland, Barrett, Lamon, Carpenter, and,

best and latest of all, that of Hon. I. N. Arnold.   Much that
was offered could not be used ; as in the choice of material,
from whatever source, the purpose has been to avoid mere
opinions and eulogies of Lincoln, and to give abundantly those
actual experiences, incidents, anecdotes, and reminiscences
which reveal the phases of his unique and striking personality.

It scarcely need be pointed out that this work does not attempt to give a connected history of the Civil War, but only
to sketch briefly those episodes with which Lincoln is personally identified, and of which some knowledge is essential to an
understanding of his acts and character.   Other characters are
brought into prominence only as they are associated with the
chief actor in that great drama.   Many of them are disappear-
ing—fading into the smoky and lurid background ; but that
colossal central figure, playing one of the grandest roles ever
set upon the stage of human life, becomes more impressive
as the scenes recede.

F. F. B.

TABLE OF CONTENTS.

PART I.

LINCOLN'S EARLY LIFE.

CHAPTER I.

CHAPTER II.

CHAPTER III.

CHAPTER IV.

CHAPTER V.

CHAPTER VI.

PART II.

LINCOLN AS LAWYER AND POLITICIAN.

CHAPTER I.

CHAPTER II.

CHAPTER III.

PART III.

LINCOLN AS PRESIDENT.

CHAPTER I.

CHAPTER II.

CHAPTER XI.

CHAPTER XII.

CHAPTER XIII.

PART IV.

MEMORIES OF LINCOLN.

ILLUSTRATIONS.

INDEX TO NAMES.

THE EVERY-DAY LIFE

OF

ABRAHAM LINCOLN

*A BIOGRAPHY OF THE GREAT AMERICAN PRESIDENT FROM
AN ENTIRELY NEW STANDPOINT, WITH FRESH
AND INVALUABLE MATERIAL.*

LINCOLN'S LIFE AND CHARACTER

PORTRAYED BY THOSE WHO KNEW HIM.

A SERIES OF PEN-PICTURES

BY FRIENDS, NEIGHBORS, AND DAILY ASSOCIATES, DURING HIS WHOLE CAREER.

ESTIMATES AND IMPRESSIONS OF DISTINGUISHED MEN,

WITH REMINISCENCES, INCIDENTS, AND TRIBUTES

FROM UNIVERSAL SOURCES.

A COMPLETE

PERSONAL DESCRIPTION AND BIOGRAPHY

OF HIM WHO WAS

*THE HUMBLEST AND GREATEST OF AMERICAN CITIZENS,
THE TRUEST AND MOST LOYAL OF MEN,
AND A CENTRAL FIGURE IN THE WORLD'S HISTORY*

WITH NEARLY 100 ORIGINAL ILLUSTRATIONS.

PREPARED AND ARRANGED BY

FRANCIS F. BROWNE,

Compiler of "The Golden Treasury of Poetry and Prose," " Poems of the Civil War," etc.

MINNEAPOLIS :

THE NORTHWESTERN PUBLISHING CO.

1887.

G. Washington

1796.

Your friend, as ever,
A. Lincoln

1863.

WASHINGTON AND LINCOLN—THE TWO GREAT FIGURES OF AMERICAN HISTORY.

PART I.

LINCOLN'S EARLY LIFE.

CHAPTER I.

THE TWO GREAT FIGURES OF AMERICAN HISTORY.——WASHINGTON AND LINCOLN.——LINCOLN'S LOWLY ORIGIN.——HIS ANCESTORS.——LINCOLN'S AUTOBIOGRAPHY.——THE LINCOLN FAMILY IN KENTUCKY.——A PICTURE OF THE WILDERNESS.——THE LINCOLNS AS PIONEERS.——KILLING OF LINCOLN'S GRANDFATHER.——MORDECAI LINCOLN.——AN ODD CHARACTER.——THE BIRTH OF PRESIDENT LINCOLN.——HIS PARENTS.

In speaking of the great men who have been native to the soil of the New World, who have been the natural outgrowth of our American civilization, and have grandly met all the requirements of their situation and of a critical epoch, the first name which springs to our lips is that of GEORGE WASHINGTON, and the second is that of ABRAHAM LINCOLN. The list is not long of our veritable heroes, but at its head stands, without question, the Father of Our Country, who led the forlorn hope of the American colonies throughout the desperate struggle of the Revolution; and next to him comes our martyred President, who held the helm of State during the more awful warfare of the Great Rebellion, who saved our glorious Republic from the ruin of a dissevered Union, and restored to a race of bondmen their God-given right of freedom.

Laying down his sword and the trappings of a soldier after the battle of Yorktown, Washington conducted the affairs of the nation during the grave trials of its infancy, guiding it to a point of comparative peace and safety, and then, rejecting the proposal of a "third term," retired to the seclusion of a private citizen. Lincoln bore the brunt of responsib'lity for

33

the success of the Federal army and the integrity of the United States for four terrible years; and, re-appointed to his arduous post by the voice of the people, was shot down by an assassin's bullet at the moment when the light of peace was breaking on the horizon, and a promise of rest and reward comforted the sore heart of him who had so faithfully sustained the people's trust.

Both men were patriots, sages, statesmen, and heroes. Both in their separate ways went through the hard school of adversity. Both were tried by the severest tests, and both came out victorious. The noblest virtues of humanity formed the basis of their characters: honesty, fidelity, courage, determination, fortitude, and sublime capacity for self-sacrifice. And both had, in a remarkable degree, judgment, foresight, purity of purpose, lofty ambition, love of country, and consideration for the feelings and the rights of their fellow-men.

The dignity of Washington was balanced by the tenderness of Lincoln; the polished manners and courtly bearing of the high-born Virginian, by the stainless life, in private and public, of the homely and lowly pioneer of the West. From his childhood, Lincoln revered the memory of Washington, keeping his image ever before him as a pattern to be imitated in his own life and conduct. As history advances, the generations will look back on the figure of Abraham Lincoln towering in the distance above the level of ordinary men as the statue of Liberty at the gateway of the American continent towers above the waves beating at its feet.

LINCOLN'S LOWLY ORIGIN.

The early life of Lincoln was doomed to unvarying hardship. He was born and nurtured in penury, and the coarse food and scanty clothing which barely served the necessities of existence were earned, after the age of infancy was past, by the labor of his own brave and willing hands. The story of his privations is full of pathos; yet when we consider the lofty career they led up to, we realize that the success of the man was gained through the discipline imposed on the youth—that the sterling and indomitable traits which made Lincoln a leader among all classes of people, owed much of their strength and steadfastness to the vicissitudes he had patiently endured. His spirit was tried as by fire; and, perfectly tempered and true, like the famous Damascus steel, it never failed to do the deed expected of it at the vital moment.

Abraham Lincoln was never ashamed of his lowly birth. He was a man of the people, a true citizen of the Republic; and he put a just estimate on the relative value of the advantages of wealth and position, and the achievements of enterprise and integrity. Not only the word but the teaching of his favorite poet (Burns) had sunk into his heart, and with quiet self-assurance he lived up to the text:

"The rank is but the guinea's stamp,
The man's the gowd for a' that."

The barefooted boy in the Western wilderness, wielding the axe or following the plough, the gaunt lad in homespun jean, steering the flat-boat on the Mississippi, and the inmate of the White House, the chief magistrate of a great nation, was the offspring of democratic institutions, and an illustration of the chance which the poor man has in America to rise to the summit of his ambition, and of the power of resolute will to lift the owner of respectable talents from the lowest grade to the highest station.

ANCESTORS OF LINCOLN.

The blood reddening the veins of Abraham Lincoln was good and pure, although it descended from obscure sources. His ancestors have been traced back with tolerable certainty through five generations, to Norfolk County, England. From this locality, Mordecai Lincoln emigrated to Hingham, Massachusetts, not long after the landing of the Mayflower at Plymouth, or about the year 1638. Later on, Mordecai left Hingham for Berks County, Pennsylvania; and a hint of the cause of this removal may be found in the statement that he belonged to the persecuted sect of Quakers. John Lincoln, a son of Mordecai, settled in Rockingham County, Virginia.

In an allusion to the incidents of his boyhood and youth, Mr. Lincoln once remarked to a friend, "My early history is perfectly characterized by a single line of Gray's Elegy:

'The short and simple annals of the poor.'"

At another time he drew up a statement of the leading events in his career, at the request of Hon. J. W. Fell, of Bloomington, Illinois.

LINCOLN'S AUTOBIOGRAPHY.

"I was born Feb. 12, 1809, in Hardin County, Kentucky. My parents were both born in Virginia, of undistinguishable families—second families, perhaps I should say. My mother, who died in my tenth year, was of a family of the name of Hanks, some of whom now reside in Adams, and others in Macon Counties, Illinois. My paternal grandfather, Abraham Lincoln, emigrated from Rockingham County, Virginia, to Kentucky, about 1781 or '2, where, a year or two later, he was killed by Indians, not in battle, but by stealth, when he was laboring to open a farm in the forest. His ancestors, who were Quakers, went to Virginia from Berks County, Pennsylvania. An effort to identify them with the New England family of the same name, ended in nothing more than a similarity of Christian names in both families, such as Enoch, Levi, Mordecai, Solomon, Abraham, and the like.

"My father, at the death of his father, was but six years of age, and he grew up literally without education. He removed from Kentucky to what is now Spencer County, Indiana, in my eighth year. We reached our new home about the time the State came into the Union. It was a wild region, with many bears and other wild animals still in the woods. There I grew up. There were some schools, so called, but no qualification was ever required of a teacher beyond 'readin,' writin' and cipherin' to the Rule of Three. If a straggler, supposed to understand Latin, happened to sojourn in the neighborhood, he was looked upon as a wizard. There was absolutely nothing to excite ambition for education. Of course when I came of age I did not know much. Still, somehow, I could read, write, and cipher to the Rule of Three, but that was all. I have not been to school since. The little advance I now have upon this store of education, I have picked up from time to time under the pressure of necessity.

"I was raised to farm work, which I continued till I was twenty-two. At twenty-one I came to Illinois, and passed the first year in Macon County. Then I got to New Salem, at that time in Sangamon, now in Menard County, where I remained a year as a sort of clerk in a store. Then came the Black Hawk war, and I was elected a Captain of Volunteers—a success which gave me more pleasure than any I have had since. I went through the campaign, was elated, ran for the Legislature the same year (1832), and was beaten—the only time I have ever been beaten by the people. The next, and three succeeding biennial elections, I was elected to the Legislature. I was not a candidate afterwards. During this legislative period I had studied law, and removed to Springfield to practice it. In 1846 I was once elected to the Lower House of Congress, but was not a candidate for re-election. From 1849 to 1854, both inclusive, practiced law more assiduously than ever before. Always a Whig in politics, and generally on the Whig electoral tickets, making active canvasses. I was losing interest in politics, when the repeal of the Missouri Compromise aroused me again. What I have done since then is pretty well known.

"If any personal description of me is thought desirable, it may be said, I am in height, six feet, four inches, nearly; lean in flesh, weighing, on an average, one hundred and eighty pounds; dark complexion, with coarse black hair, and gray eyes. No other marks or brands recollected.

Yours very truly,

A. LINCOLN."

THE LINCOLN FAMILY IN KENTUCKY.

The Lincolns seem to have had a strong liking for frontier life, certain members of the family in every generation moving westward to keep pace with the tide of civilization. In 1781 or 1782, while the last events of the war for Independence were in progress, a son of John Lincoln, named Abraham, moved into Kentucky and took up a tract of government land in Mercer County. It was a part of the territory comprised in the surveys of Daniel Boone, the famous Kentucky pioneer, who, in his "Field Book," now in the possession of the Wisconsin Historical Society, made the following note of the purchase: "Abraham Lincoln enters 500 acres of land, on a Treasury warrant, on the south side of Licking Creek or River, in Kentucky."

A PICTURE OF THE WILDERNESS.

At this date, Kentucky was included within the limits and jurisdiction of Virginia. It had been made a county by the Legislature of that State in 1776, but failed to become an independent territory until 1790. Its early settlers were chiefly emigrants from Virginia, who, in advancing into the border country, did not pass beyond the boundaries of the parent colony. In 1775 Daniel Boone built a fort at Boonesborough, on the Kentucky river; and it was not far from this site that Abraham Lincoln, President Lincoln's grandfather, located his claim and put up a rude log hut for the shelter of his

DANIEL BOONE, THE KENTUCKY PIONEER.

family. The pioneers who were now penetrating the wilderness of Kentucky and clearing small scattered spaces around their humble dwellings, had not only to contend with the wild forces of nature and defend themselves against the beasts of the forest, but they were subject to attack from the hostile Indians.

THE LINCOLNS AS PIONEERS.

The region, probably from its picturesque beauty and the abundance of wild game, had been a favorite hunting-ground of the Cherokees and other powerful and warlike tribes. From the frequent and bloody contests which these savages had waged with each other on this field, the country was named by them Kentucky, or "the dark and bloody ground." It retained its evil designation long after the white men ventured into it; but now the conflict was between the intruding race and the resisting natives. The settlers were haunted by terrors of their stealthy foe, and at home or abroad kept their guns ready for instant use by night and by day. Many a hard battle was fought between the Indians and the pioneers before the latter obtained secure possession of the State, and many an unguarded woodsman was shot down without warning while busy about his necessary work.

KILLING OF LINCOLN'S GRANDFATHER.

Abraham Lincoln, the President's grandfather, fell a victim to the murderous Indians within a year or two after his arrival in the new State. His sons, Mordecai, Josiah, and Thomas, were witnesses of the shocking tragedy, the circumstances of which are vividly told by Mr. I. N. Arnold. Thomas Lincoln was in the field with his father, when the savages suddenly burst upon them. "Mordecai and Josiah, his elder brothers, were near by in the forest. Mordecai, startled by a shot, saw his father fall, and, running to the cabin, seized the loaded rifle, rushed to one of the loop-holes cut through the logs of the cabin, and saw the Indian who had fired. He had just caught the boy, Thomas, and was running toward the forest. Pointing the rifle through the logs, and aiming at a silver medal on the breast of the Indian, Mordecai fired. The Indian fell, and the boy, springing to his feet, ran to the open arms of his mother, at the cabin door. Meanwhile Josiah, who had run to the fort for aid, returned with a party of settlers, who brought in the bodies of Abraham Lincoln and the Indian who had been shot. From this time throughout his life, Mordecai was the mortal enemy of the Indians, and it is said, sacrificed many in revenge for the murder of his father."

It was in the presence of such dangers crossing every step, that Thomas Lincoln spent his boyhood. His father's murder before his baby eyes was like a baptism of blood. He was born in 1778, so could not have been much more than four years old on that fatal day when the yell of the fierce Indians chilled the blood of the startled group, and in one swift moment his father lay dead beside him, and vengeance had been exacted by his resolute boy brother. Men of strong nature, who grow up amid such experiences, acquire habits of stern heroism. Their nerves turn to steel, their sinews become wiry, their senses are sharpened, and they grow alert, steady, prompt, and deft, in every crisis. The craft of the Indian is outwitted by the art of the frontiersman, who joins to the cunning of the savage the intelligence inherited from a superior race.

MORDECAI LINCOLN.—AN ODD CHARACTER.

So far as they are known, the Lincolns were all marked characters. Some reminiscences related of Mordecai, after he had reached manhood, give a welcome glimpse of the boy who exhibited such coolness and daring on the occasion which cost his father's life. "He was naturally a man of considerable genius," says one who knew him. "He was a man of great drollery, and it would almost make you laugh to look at him. I never saw but one other man whose quiet, droll look excited in me the same disposition to laugh, and that was Artemas Ward. He was quite a story-teller; and in this Abe resembled his 'Uncle Mord,' as we all called him. He was an honest man, as tender-hearted as a woman, and to the last degree charitable and benevolent. No one ever took offense at Uncle Mord's stories—not even the ladies. I heard him once tell a bevy of fashionable girls that he knew a very large woman who had a husband so small that in the night she often mistook him for the baby, and that upon one occasion she took him up and was singing to him a soothing lullaby, when he awoke and told her that she was mistaken, that the baby was on the other side of the bed. Abe Lincoln had a very high opinion of his uncle, and on one occasion remarked, 'I have often said that Uncle Mord had run off with all the talents of the family.' 'Old Mord,' as we sometimes called him, had been in his younger days a very stout man, and was quite fond of playing a game of fisticuffs with any one who was noted as a champion. He told a parcel of us once of a pitched battle

MORDECAI LINCOLN ("UNCLE MORD.")

he had fought with one of the champions of that day. He said they fought on the side of a hill or ridge; that at the bottom there was a rut or canal, which had been cut out by the freshets. He said they soon clinched, and he threw his man and fell on top of him. He said he always thought he had the best eyes in the world for measuring the distance to the bottom of the hill, and concluded that by rolling over and over till they came to the bottom, his antagonist's body would fill it, and he would be wedged in so tight that he could whip him at his leisure. So he let the fellow turn him, and over and over they went, when about the twentieth revolution brought Mord's back in contact with the bottom of the rut, and, said he, 'before fire could scorch a feather, I yelled out: 'Take him off!' "

THE BIRTH OF PRESIDENT LINCOLN.

Thomas Lincoln was twenty-eight years of age before he took a wife, his choice then falling on a young girl of twenty-three, named Nancy Hanks. She was of English descent, like her husband; and her ancestors had followed, like his, in the path of emigration from Virginia to Kentucky. The two were married by a Methodist minister, the Rev. Jesse Head, who was then located at Springfield, in Washington County, Ky. The young couple lived for a time in Elizabethtown, and after the birth of their first child, Sarah, removed to "Rock Spring Farm," on Nolin Creek, in Hardin County, afterward changed to La Rue County. It was a desolate spot, a strange and unlikely place for the birth of one who was to take a memorable part in the world's history; yet here, on the 12th of February, 1809, Abraham Lincoln came into the world. His brother Thomas, born later, died in infancy; but the two elder children had the tough fibre which endures the strain of continuous and severe hardship.

LINCOLN'S PARENTS.

The father was a rough, illiterate, and thriftless man, with peaceful, brave, social, and kindly disposition. He was of short and compact frame, with the dark coarse hair, gray eyes, brown complexion and brawny strength which Abraham inherited. The mother was cast in a finer mould, and, according to trustworthy accounts, was a woman whose gentle instincts and lovely virtues would have adorned any station. She is said to have been beautiful in her youth, with a face of the brunette type, "with dark hair, regular features, and soft, sparkling hazel eyes.'' Mr. Arnold states that ''she was by nature refined, and of far more than ordinary intellect. Her friends spoke of her as being a person of marked and decided character. She was unusually intelligent, reading all the books she could obtain. She was a woman of deep religious feeling, of the most exemplary character, and most tenderly and affectionately devoted to her family. Her home indicated a degree of taste and a love of beauty exceptional in the wild settlement in which she lived; and, judging from her early death, it is probable that she was of a physique less hardy than that of most of those by whom she was surrounded. But in spite of this she had been reared where the very means of existence were to be obtained but by a constant struggle, and she had learned to use the rifle and the tools of the backwoods farmer, as well as the distaff, the cards, and the spinning wheel. She could not only kill the wild game of the woods, but she could also dress it, make of the skins clothes for her family, and prepare the flesh for food. Hers was a strong, self-reliant spirit, which commanded the respect as well as the love of the rugged people among whom she lived.'' The tender and reverent spirit of Abraham Lincoln, and the pensive melancholy of his disposition, he no doubt inherited from his mother. He never ceased to cherish the memory of her life and teachings. Her death, and the sad and solemn rites of the funeral ''made an impression on the mind of the son as lasting as life. She had found time, amidst her weary toil and the hard struggle of her busy life, not only to teach him to read and to write, but to impress ineffaceably upon him that love of truth and justice, that perfect integrity and reverence for God, for which he was noted all his life. These virtues were ever associated in his mind with the most tender love and respect for his mother.'' Says Dr. Holland: '' Mr. Lincoln always looked back to her with an unspeakable affection. Long after her sensitive heart and weary hands had crumbled into dust, and had climbed to life again in forest flowers, he said to a friend, with tears in his eyes; 'All that I am, or hope to be, I owe to my angel mother.' ''

CHAPTER II.

REMOVAL OF THE LINCOLNS FROM KENTUCKY TO INDIANA.——EARLY DAYS IN INDIANA.——THE FIRST LOG CABIN.——UNCLE DENNIS HANKS.——UNCLE DENNIS' RECOLLECTIONS.——LINCOLN'S BOYHOOD DAYS.——LEARNING TO "READ, WRITE, AND CIPHER."——TURKEY-BUZZARD PENS AND BRIAR-ROOT INK.——WEBSTER'S SPELLER, THE "ARABIAN NIGHTS," AND SPEECHES OF HENRY CLAY.——ABE A "RASTLER" AT FIFTEEN.——EARLY RELIGIOUS EXPERIENCES.——CORN DODGERS, BACON, AND BLUE JEANS.——A VISIT TO LINCOLN'S INDIANA HOME.——REMINISCENCES BY ONE OF LINCOLN'S PLAYMATES.

A SPIRIT of restlessness, a love of adventure, a longing for new scenes, and possibly the hope of improving his condition, led Thomas Lincoln in the fall of 1816 to abandon the Rock Spring farm and begin life afresh in the wilds of southern Indiana. The wish to free himself from the despotic institutions of a slave State, which paralyzed the efforts and crushed the spirits of the poor white man, may have had its influence in determining this movement. At any rate, the farm was disposed of, their few personal possessions were packed upon a couple of horses, and the little household set out on the long and painful journey to their new home beyond the Ohio river.

Their march, leading through an unbroken country, was beset with difficulties from the beginning. Often the travellers were obliged to cut their road as they went. With the resolution of veteran pioneers they toiled on, sometimes being able to pick their way for a long distance without chopping, and then coming to a standstill in consequence of dense forests. Several days were occupied in going eighteen miles. It was a difficult, wearisome, trying journey, and Mr. Lincoln often said that he never passed through a harder experience than he did in going from Thompson's Ferry to Spencer County, Indiana. Mr. Barrett states that "after reaching the Indiana side of the Ohio river, the adventurers landed at or near the mouth of Anderson's Creek, now the boundary between the counties of Perry and Spencer, about one hundred and forty miles below Louisville, by the river, and sixty above Evansville. In a direct line across the country from their former residence, the distance is hardly one hundred miles. The place at which Lincoln settled, at the end of this journey, is some distance back from the Ohio river, near the present town of Gentryville."

The young Abraham, who is represented as bearing a manful share in the labors and fatigues of this arduous expedition, and who exercised his strength and skill in felling trees and clearing a track through the wilderness, and lent a willing hand in every needful service, was only seven years old. But he was unusually large and strong of his age, and already accustomed to the use of the axe and the rifle. Thus early begins the practical education of the child reared in the backwoods.

EARLY DAYS IN INDIANA.

The circumstances which surrounded the Lincolns on their arrival in Indiana, and which were but slowly bettered during the thirteen years of their residence in the State, are sketched with a graphic pen by Hon. O. H. Smith: "Indiana was born in the year 1816, with some 65,000 inhabitants. A few counties only were then organized. The whole middle, north, and northwest portions of the State were an unbroken wilderness, in the possession of the Indians. Well do I remember when there were but two families settled west of the Whitewater Valley,—one at Flat Rock, above where Rushville now stands, and the other on Brandywine, near where Greenfield was afterward located. When I first visited the ground on which Indianapolis now stands, the whole country, east to Whitewater and west to the Wabash, was a dense and unbroken forest. There were no public roads, no bridges over any of the streams. The traveler had literally to swim his way. No cultivated farms, no houses to shelter or feed the weary traveler or his jaded horse. The courts, years afterward, were

THE MARCH THROUGH THE WILDERNESS.—REMOVAL OF THE LINCOLN FAMILY FROM KENTUCKY TO INDIANA, IN 1816.

held in log huts, and the juries sat under the shade of the forest trees. I was Circuit Prosecuting Attorney at the time of the trials at the falls of Fall Creek, where Pendleton now stands. Four of the prisoners were convicted of murder and three of them hung, for killing Indians. The court was held in a double log cabin, the grand jury sat upon a log in the woods, and the foreman signed the bill of indictment which I had prepared, upon his knee; there was not a petit juror that had shoes on—all wore moccasins, and were belted around the waist, and carried side knives used by the hunter. The products of the country consisted of peltries, the wild game killed in the forest by the Indian hunters, the fish caught in the interior lakes, rivers and creeks, the pawpaw, wild plum, haws, and small berries gathered by the squaws in the woods. The travel was confined to the single horse and his rider, the commerce to the pack-saddle, and the navigation to the Indian canoe. Many a time and oft have I crossed our swollen streams, by day and by night, sometimes swimming my horse, and at others paddling the rude bark canoe of the Indian. Such is a mere sketch of our State when I traversed its wilds, and I am not one of its first settlers."

THE FIRST LOG CABIN.

The immediate duty of the emigrants, after reaching their final camping ground, was to provide a structure which should protect them from the weather. A shanty was quickly built of poles, and enclosed on three sides, the fourth remaining open. This served for a home during the first year, when a more comfortable cabin was built on a pleasant site. "It was on the top of an eminence which sloped gently away on every side. The landscape was beautiful, the soil rich, and in a short time some land was cleared and a crop of corn and vegetables raised. The struggle for life and its few comforts was in this wilderness a very hard one, and none but those of the most vigorous constitution could succeed. The trials, privations and hardships incident to clearing, breaking up and subduing the soil and establishing a home, so far away from all the necessaries of life, taxed the strength and endurance of all to the utmost. Bears, deer, and other sorts of wild game, were abundant, and contributed largely to the support of the family.''

From an official record, it appears that on the 18th of October, 1817, Thomas Lincoln entered a quarter-section of gov-

LINCOLN'S HOME IN BOYHOOD.

ernment land. This probably includes the place where he originally settled, which was eighteen miles north of the Ohio river and within a mile and a half of the present village of Gentryville.

UNCLE DENNIS HANKS.

Now that the Lincolns were settled securely in the wilderness of Indiana, they were followed by the family of Thomas

and Betsey Sparrow, relatives of Mrs. Lincoln, and old-time
neighbors on the "Rock Spring Farm" in Kentucky.   Dennis Hanks, one of the members of the Sparrow household,
and a cousin of Abraham Lincoln, is still living (1886), hale
and hearty in spite of his advanced age, at Paris, Illinois.   He
has lately furnished some entertaining recollections of the boy-
life of the President, which are richly worth recording.   "Un-

DENNIS HANKS IN HIS YOUNGER DAYS.

cle Dennis," as the old man is familiarly called, is himself a
striking character, exciting attention at once by his original
manners and racy conversation.   An impressive portrait of
him, as he appears in his later days, is thus given: "Uncle
Dennis is a typical Kentuckian, born in Hardin County, in
1799.   His face is sun-bronzed and ploughed with furrows of

time; he has a resolute mouth, with firm grip of the jaws, and a broad forehead above a pair of piercing eyes. The eyes seem out of place in the weary, faded face; they glow and flash like two diamond sparks, set in ridges of dull gold. The face is a serious one; but the play of light in the eyes, unquenchable by time, betrays the nature full of sunshine and elate with life. A side glance at the profile shows a face strikingly Lincoln-like—prominent cheek bones, temple, nose and chin; but best of all is that twinkling drollery in the eye that flashed in the White House during the dark days of the Civil War."

UNCLE DENNIS' RECOLLECTIONS.

Uncle Dennis' recollections go back to the birth of Abraham Lincoln, who was "about twenty-four hours old, hardly that," when his cousin first saw him. To repeat the words of the old man: "I rikkilect I run all the way, over two miles, to see Nancy Hanks' boy baby. Her name was Nancy Hanks before she married Thomas Lincoln. 'Twas common for connections to gather in them days to see new babies. I held the wee one a minute. I was ten years old, and it tickled me to hold the pulpy, red, little Lincoln."

LINCOLN'S BOYHOOD DAYS.

The Hanks family moved to Indiana, according to Uncle Dennis' recollection, "when Abe was about nine. Mr. Lincoln moved first, and built a camp of brush in Spencer County. We came out a year later, and he then had a cabin up, and he gave us the shanty. Abe killed a turkey the day we got there, and couldn't get through tellin' about it. ·The name was pronounced Linkhorn by the folks then. We was all uneducated. After a spell we learned better." The cabins occupied by the two families were about fifteen rods apart, and their children grew up together on the intimate terms of kinship. "I was the only boy in the place, all them years, and we were always together."

LEARNING TO "READ, WRITE, AND CIPHER."

Uncle Dennis claims to have taught his young cousin to read, write, and cipher. "He knew his letters pretty wellish; but no more. His mother taught him his letters. If ever there was a good woman on earth, she was one, a true christian of the Baptist church; but she died soon after we arrived, and left him without a teacher; his father couldn't read a word." The boy had "only about one quarter of schooling, scarcely that. I then set in to help him; I didn't know much, but I did the best I could."

TURKEY-BUZZARD PENS AND BRIAR-ROOT INK.

As to the materials with which the boy learned to write, Uncle Dennis says: "Sometimes he would write with a piece of charcoal, or the p'int of a burnt stick, on the fence or floor. We got a little paper at the country town, and I made ink out of blackberry briar-root and a little copperas in it. It was black, but the copperas would eat the paper after awhile. I made his first pen out of a turkey-buzzard feather. We had no geese them days. After he learned to write he was scrawlin' his name everywhere; sometimes he would write it on the white sand down by the crick bank, and leave it till the waves would blot it out."

It seems from his cousin's statement that young Lincoln did not take to books eagerly in the beginning. "We had to hire him at first. But when he got a taste on't it was the old story—we had to pull the sow's ears to get her to the trough, and pull her tail to get her away. He read a great deal and had a wonderful memory—wonderful. Never forgot anything."

WEBSTER'S SPELLER, THE "ARABIAN NIGHTS," AND SPEECHES OF HENRY CLAY.

His first reading book was Webster's speller. "When I got him through that, I only had a copy of Indiana statutes. Then he got hold of a book; I can't rikkilect the name. It told a yarn about a feller, a nigger or suthin', that sailed a flatboat up to a rock, and the rock was magnetized and drawed the nails out of his boat, an' he got a duckin' or drowned, or suthin, I forget now." (It was the "Arabian Nights"). "Abe would lay on the floor with a chair under his head, and laugh over them stories by the hour. I told him they was likely lies from end to end; but he learned to read right well in them. I borrowed for him the 'Life of Washington' and the 'Speeches of Henry Clay.' They had a powerful influence on him. He told me afterwards, in the White House, he wanted to live like Washington. His speeches show that; but the other book did the most amazing work. He was a Democrat, like his father and all of us, when he began to read it. When he closed it he was a Whig, heart and soul, and he went on step by step until he became leader of the Republicans."

ABE A "RASSLER" AT FIFTEEN.

Abe was at this time, says Uncle Dennis, "not grown, only six feet two inches high. He was six feet four and one-half inches when grown—tall, lathy, and gangling,—not much appearance, not handsome, not ugly, but peculiar. He was this kind of a fellow: If a man rode up on horseback, Abe would be the first one out, up on the fence and asking questions, till his father would give him a knock side o' the head; then he'd go throw at snowbirds or suthin,' but ponderin' all the while. I was ten years older, but I couldn't rassle him down. His legs was too long for me to throw him. He would fling one foot upon my shoulder and make me swing corners swift, and his arms was long and strong. My, how he would chop! His axe would flash and bite into a sugar-tree or sycamore, and down it would come. If you heard him fellin' trees in a clearin' you would say there were three men at work by the way the trees fell. But he never was sassy or quarrelsome. I've seen him walk into a crowd of sawin' row-

dies, and tell some droll yarn and bust them all up. It was
the same when he was a lawyer; all eyes whenever he riz
were on him; there was *suthin' peculiarsome* about him."

EARLY RELIGIOUS EXPERIENCE.

"Abe wasn't in early life a religious man. He was a moral
man strictly—never went to frolics, never drank liquor, never
used tobacco, never swore. In after life he became more
religious; but the Bible puzzled him, especially the miracles.
He often asked me in the timber, or sittin' around the fire-
place nights, to explain Scripture. He never joined any
church or any secret order."

Thomas Lincoln and wife were of strongly marked religious
character, and were members of the Baptist faith. Whenever
services were held in the log building a mile distant which passed
for a church, they and their two children were there. As an
illustration of the lad's remarkable memory, Uncle Dennis
relates that "he would come home from church, and put a
box in the middle of the cabin floor, and git on it and repeat
the sermint from text to doxology. I've heard him do it
often."

CORN-DODGERS, BACON, AND BLUE-JEANS.

As far as food and clothing were concerned, the boy had
plenty, "such as it was—corn-dodgers, bacon, and game, some
fish, and wild fruits. I've often seen him take a dodger to the
field, and gnaw at it when ploughing. We had very little
wheat flour. The nearest mill was eighteen miles. A boss
mill it was, with a plug pullin' a sweep around; and Abe used
to say his dog could stand and eat the flour as fast as it was
made, and then be ready for supper. For clothing he had
jeans. He was grown before he wore all-wool pants. It was
a new country, and he was a raw boy, rather a bright and likely lad; but the big world seemed far ahead of him. We were
all slow-goin' folks, but he had the stuff for greatness in him.
He got his rare sense and sterling principles from both par-

ents, but his strong will from his father. I'll tell you an incident: His father used to swear a little, and one day his baby girl picked up a foul oath and was bruisin' the bitter morsel in her sweet lips, when Nancy called 'Thomas !' and said 'Listen, husband.' He stopped that habit thar; never swore agin. But Abe's kindliness, humor, love of humanity, hatred of slavery, all came from her. I am free to say Abe was a mother's boy.

"I moved from Indiana to Illinois when Abe did. I bought a little improvement near him, six miles from Decatur. Here the famous rails were split that were carried around in the campaign. They were called his rails; but nobody can tell about that. I split some of 'em, and we had a rail frolic, and folks came and helped us split. He was a master hand maulin' rails. I heard him say in a speech one day about these rails: 'If I didn't make these, I made many just as good.' Then the crowd yelled."

A VISIT TO LINCOLN'S INDIANA HOME.

Every incident connected with the boyhood of Lincoln is precious for the help it gives toward a correct understanding of the influences which moulded his disposition and determined the bent of his mind. Some facts relating to the past and present appearance of his home in Indiana are related by one who lately visited the scene: "Being on a train one day, on the railway leading from Jasper to Rockport, in southwestern Indiana, a casual travelling acquaintance remarked that we would soon pass over the Lincoln farm. On seeking further information he informed me that it was the farm once owned and occupied by Thomas Lincoln, the father of President Lincoln, and where the latter passed most of his youthful years. This arrested my attention and decided me to stop at Lincoln Station (which takes its name from the farm), and pass a few hours amid the scenes and surroundings which had been so familiar to the martyred President. The place is in Carmen Township, Spencer County. Lincoln Station is located in the center of the Lincoln homestead, and is now a village of a dozen buildings or so, having the usual features of a store, blacksmith-shop, and saloon. Into this then wild and rough region, almost literally in the wilderness, Thomas Lincoln moved his family, composed of his wife and two children, Abraham and Sarah. He built his cabin on a knoll some fifteen rods from where the depot is now located. The cabin has been removed, and nothing remains to mark the spot where it stood, but the partly filled cellar, and a solitary cedar tree near by, planted by young Abraham.''

REMINISCENCES BY ONE OF LINCOLN'S PLAYMATES.

Of the reputation which Lincoln left behind him in the neighborhood where he passed much of his boyhood and youth, an aged man in the vicinity, who was Abe's playmate, furnishes much that is interesting in regard to his early habits, his earnest desire to learn, and his passion for books which he was not able to obtain. He read everything he could find in all the region about; it may have been that this deprivation of books and the means of learning threw him upon his own resources and led him into those modes of thought, of quaint and apt illustration and logical reasoning, so peculiar to him. He was about the only one in the vicinity who could read and write; he was noted for his kindness to everyone, and his services were frequently drawn upon by the settlers to write their letters, a kindness he always cheerfully rendered. Said the old man: "Abe was all'rs much given to larnin'." Whenever the court was in session he was a frequent attendant, as often as he could be spared from the labors of the farm, and especially when a lawyer of the name of John A. Breckenridge was to appear in any case. Breckenridge was the foremost lawyer in that region, widely famed as an advocate in criminal cases. Lincoln was sure to be present when he spoke. Doing his "chores" in the morning, he would walk to Booneville, the county seat of Warrick County, seventeen miles away, and then home again in time to do his "chores" at night, repeating this day after day. The lawyer soon came to know him. Years afterwards, when Lincoln was President, a venerable gentleman one day entered his office in the White House, and standing before him, said: "Mr. President, you don't know me." Mr. Lincoln eyed him sharply for a moment, then quickly replied, with a smile: "Yes, I do; you are John A. Breckenridge. I used to walk thirty-four miles a day to hear you plead law in Booneville, and listening to your speeches at the bar first inspired me with the determination to be a lawyer."

CHAPTER III.

DEATH OF LINCOLN'S MOTHER.——A SOLEMN AND TOUCHING SCENE.——LIN-
COLN'S STEP-MOTHER.——EARLY SCHOOLMASTERS, BIRNEY, HAZEL, DOR-
SEY, AND CRAWFORD.——THE BOOKS LINCOLN READ.——PERSONAL TESTI-
MONY TO THE VALUE OF HIS EARLY IMPRESSIONS.——"ALWAYS READING."
——ABE'S DISLIKE OF THE CRAWFORDS.——THE LONGEST AND STRONGEST
MAN IN THE SETTLEMENT.——DEATH OF LINCOLN'S ONLY SISTER.——EARLY
FONDNESS FOR ORATORY.——LINCOLN'S FIRST DOLLAR.——PRESENTIMENTS
OF FUTURE GREATNESS.——LINCOLN AT SEVENTEEN.——LEARNS SURVEYING.
——DOWN THE MISSISSIPPI.——A FIGHT WITH RIVER PIRATES.——"ABE,
WHAT A FOOL YOU ARE!"——LINCOLN'S WARM HEART.

THE touching story of Lincoln's love for his gentle mother, and of her untimely death, is thus told: "Lincoln always manifested the strongest affection for his mother, and ever strove to relieve her, as much as was in his power, of the cares and burdens of their hard life. Although her lot was cast in that humble sphere, it is evident that she was a superior woman, possessing all the traits of a true and noble mother, and that she left an impression for good upon her young son which he never threw off. But the fatal disease of consumption had fastened upon her, and her life was slowly wasting away. Day by day young Abraham sat by her bedside, and read to her for hours such portions of the Bible as she desired to hear. During the intervals in reading she talked to him of goodness and truth, and urged him to walk in the ways thereof. She portrayed to him the beauties of the Christian faith, the hope of the Christian life, and the joys of the Heavenly Kingdom to which she was going. The end was at hand; the faithful watchers at the bedside of the dying woman felt the shadow creeping upon the walls; it was the shadow of death; the light of the lowly cabin went slowly out—the mother had rest. Abraham gave way to grief that could not be consoled. They laid her tenderly away in an opening in the timber, an eighth of a mile away from the house. No minister could be procured at the time to perform the last sad rites, but sympathizing friends offered up sincere prayers over the dead. This simple service did not seem to the father and son to be a sufficient tribute to the memory of the true and exemplary wife and mother whose loss they so sorely felt; so when springtime came the boy wrote to Elder Elkin, who lived near the family when they were in Kentucky, appealing to him to come and preach a funeral sermon over his mother's grave, adding that granting this request would be to him and his father and sister a lasting favor. The good man cheerfully complied with the request, though it involved a journey of over a hundred miles on horseback.

A SOLEMN AND TOUCHING SCENE.

On a lovely day the people came from all the country around and gathered about the grave; the minister discoursed to them of the virtues and estimable qualities of the departed, and commended her worthy example for the emulation of all. As the last prayer was said the whole audience fell upon their knees on the ground around the grave, and this the last scene in the burial of his mother was ended. The grave is now inclosed with a high iron fence, and at its head stands a beautiful white marble stone, on which is inscribed the following:

"Nancy Hanks Lincoln, who died Oct. 5, 1818, aged 35 years. Erected in 1879 by a friend of her martyred son."

Dr. J. G. Holland gives some additional particulars of the services performed over the grave of Mrs. Lincoln. "As the appointed day approached, notice was given to the whole neighborhood, embracing every family within twenty miles. Neighbor carried the notice to neighbor. There was probably not a family that did not receive intelligence of the anxiously anticipated event. On a bright Sabbath morning, the settlers of the region started for the cabin of the Lincolns; and, as they gathered in, they presented a picture worthy the pencil of the ablest artist. Some came in carts of the rudest construction, their wheels consisting of sections of the huge boles of forest trees, and every other member the product of the axe and

A MEMORABLE SCENE.—FUNERAL OF LINCOLN'S MOTHER.

auger; some came on horseback, two or three upon a horse; others came in wagons drawn by oxen, and still others came on foot. Two hundred persons in all were assembled when Parson Elkin came out from the Lincoln cabin, accompanied by the little family, and proceeded to the tree under which the precious dust of a wife and mother was buried. The congregation received the preacher and the mourning family in a silence broken only by the songs of birds and the murmur of insects, or the creaking cart of some late comer. Taking his stand at the foot of the grave, Parson Elkin lifted his voice in prayer and sacred song, and then preached a sermon. The occasion, the eager faces around him, and all the sweet influences of the morning, inspired him with an unusual fluency and fervor; and the flickering sunlight, as it glanced through the wind-parted leaves, caught many a tear upon the bronzed cheeks of his auditors, while father and son were overcome by the revival of their great grief. He spoke of the precious Christian woman who had gone, with the warm praise which she deserved, and held her up as an example of true womanhood. Those who knew the tender and reverent spirit of Abraham Lincoln later in life, will not doubt that he returned to his cabin-home deeply impressed by all that he had heard. It was the winding-up for him of the influence of a Christian mother's life and teaching. It recalled her sweet and patient example, her assiduous efforts to inspire him with pure and noble motives, her simple instructions in divine truth, her devoted love for him, and the motherly offices she had rendered him during all his tender years. His character was planted in this Christian mother's love; and those that have wondered at the truthfulness and earnestness of his mature character have only to remember that the tree was true to the soil from which it sprang."

LINCOLN'S STEP-MOTHER.

The vacant place of wife and mother was sadly felt in the Lincoln cabin; but before the year 1819 had closed, it was

filled by a woman who nobly performed the duties of her trying position. Mr. Lincoln had known Mrs. Sarah Johnson
when both were young and living in Elizabethtown, Kentucky. They had married in the same year; and now, being
alike bereaved, he persuaded her to unite their broken house-
holds into one.

By this union, a son and two daughters, John, Sarah, and
Matilda, were added to the Lincoln family, and all dwelt to·

SARAH LINCOLN, THE PRESIDENT'S STEP-MOTHER.

gether in perfect harmony, the mother showing no difference
in the treatment of her own children and the two now committed to her charge. She exhibited a special fondness for the
little Abraham, whose precocious talents and enduring qualities she was quick to apprehend. Though he never forgot
the "angel mother" sleeping under the branching sycamore
on the forest-covered hill-top, the boy rewarded with a pro-

found and lasting affection the devoted care of her who proved a faithful friend and helper during the rest of his childhood and youth. In her later life the step-mother spoke of him always with the tenderest feeling. On one occasion she said: "He never gave me a cross word or look, and never refused, in fact or appearance, to do anything I requested of him." Where, in the history of great men, or of men of any degree, can this tribute of praise be paralleled? It was a wonderful testimony to the gentle, dutiful nature of the step-son.

EARLY SCHOOLMASTERS, BIRNEY, HAZEL, DORSEY, AND CRAWFORD.

The child had enjoyed a little irregular schooling while living in Kentucky, getting what instruction was possible of one Zachariah Birney, a Catholic, who taught for a time close by his father's house. He also attended, as convenience permitted, a school kept by Caleb Hazel, nearly four miles away, walking the distance back and forth with his sister. Soon after coming under the care of his step-mother, the lad was afforded some similar opportunities for learning. His first master in Indiana was Azel Dorsey; and the sort of education dispensed by him, and the circumstances under which it was given, are described by Mr. W. H. Lamon: "Azel Dorsey presided in a small house near the Little Pigeon Creek meeting-house, a mile and a half from the Lincoln cabin. It was built of unhewn logs, and had 'holes for windows,' in which 'greased paper' served for glass. The roof was just high enough for a man to stand erect. Here the boy was taught reading, writing, and ciphering. They spelt in classes, and 'trapped' up and down. These juvenile contests were very exciting to the participants; and it is said by the survivors that Abe was even then the equal, if not the superior, of any scholar in his class. The next teacher was Andrew Crawford. Mrs. Gentry says he began teaching in the neighborhood in the winter of 1822-3; whilst most of his other scholars are unable to fix an exact date. He 'kept' in the same little schoolhouse which had been the scene of Dorsey's labors, and the windows were still adorned with the greased leaves of old copybooks that had come down from Dorsey's time. Abe was now in his fifteenth year, and began to exhibit symptoms of gallantry toward the weaker sex. He was growing at a tremendous rate, and two years later attained his full height of six feet four inches. He was long, wiry and strong; while his big feet and hands, and the length of his legs and arms, were out of all proportion to his small trunk and head. His complexion was very swarthy, and Mrs. Gentry says that his skin was shrivelled and yellow even then. He wore low shoes, buckskin breeches, linsey-woolsey shirt, and a cap made of the skin of an opossum or a coon. The breeches clung close to his thighs and legs, but failed by a large space to meet the tops of his shoes. Twelve inches remained uncovered, and exposed that much of 'shin-bone, sharp, blue and narrow.' 'He would always come to school thus, good-humoredly and laughing,' says his old friend, Nat Grigsby. He was always in good health, never was sick, had an excellent constitution, and took care of it. Crawford taught 'manners.' This was a feature of backwoods education to which Dorsey had not aspired, and Crawford had doubtless introduced it as a refinement which would put to shame the humble efforts of his predecessor. One of the scholars was required to retire, and re-enter as a polite gentleman is supposed to enter a drawing-room. He was received at the door by another scholar, and conducted from bench to bench until he had been introduced to all the young ladies and gentlemen in the room. Abe went through the ordeal countless times. If he took a serious view of the business, it must have put him to exquisite torture; for he was conscious that he was not a perfect type of manly beauty, with his long legs and blue shins, his small head, his great ears, and shrivelled skin. If, however, it struck him as at all funny, it must have filled him with unspeakable mirth, and given rise to many antic tricks and sly jokes, as he was gravely led about, shamefaced and gawky, under the eye of the precise Crawford, to be introduced to the boys and girls of his acquaintance.''

Many years after Azel Dorsey wielded the birch in South-western Indiana, he was living in Schuyler County, Illinois, where he was ''looked up to with much respect by his neighbors, as one of those who had assisted in the early instruction of the then President of the United States. He told with great satisfaction how his pupil, who was then remarked for the diligence and eagerness with which he pursued his studies, came to the log-cabin school-house arrayed in buckskin clothes, a raccoon-skin cap, and provided with an old arithmetic which had somewhere been found for him to begin his investigations in the 'higher branches.' ''

While in Crawford's school, the lad made his first essay in writing compositions. The exercise was not required by the teacher, but ''he took it up on his own account,'' as Nat Grigsby has said. He first wrote short sentences against 'cruelty to animals,' and at last came forward with a regular composition on the subject. He was very much annoyed and pained by the conduct of the boys, who were in the habit of catching terrapins and putting coals of fire on their backs. ''He would chide us,'' says Nat, ''tell us it was wrong, and would write against it.''

One who has had the privilege of looking over some of the boyish possessions belonging to Lincoln at this period remarks : ''Among the most touching relics which I saw at Springfield was an old copy-book, in which, at the age of fourteen, Lincoln had taught himself to write and cipher. Scratched in his boyish hand on the first page were these lines :

> '' 'Tis Abraham Lincoln holds the pen,
> He will be good, but God knows when !''

Mr. Arnold says in regard to Lincoln's school training : ''The common free schools which now so closely follow the heels of the pioneer and settler in the western portions of the republic had not then reached Indiana. An itinerant teacher sometimes straggled into a settlement, and if he could teach readin', writin', and cipherin' to the rule of three, he was deemed qualified to set up a school. With teachers thus qualified, Lincoln attended school at different times; in all, about twelve months. An anecdote is told of an incident occurring at one of these schools, which indicates his kindness and his readiness of invention. A poor, diffident girl, who spelled definite with a "y," was threatened and frightened by the rude teacher. Lincoln, with a significant look, putting one of his long fingers to his eye, enabled her to change the letter in time to escape punishment. He early manifested the most eager desire to learn. He acquired knowledge with great facility. What he learned he learned thoroughly, and every-- thing he had once acquired was always at his command."

THE BOOKS LINCOLN READ.

The boy's thirst for learning was not to be satisfied with the meagre knowledge furnished in the miserable schools he was able to attend at long intervals. His step-mother says: "He read diligently. He read everything he could lay his hands on, and when he came across a passage that struck him, he would write it down on boards, if he had no paper, and keep it until he had got paper. Then he would copy it, look at it, commit it to memory, and repeat it. He kept a scrap-book, into which he copied everything which particularly pleased him." Mr. Arnold further states: "There were no libraries, and but few books in the 'back settlements' in which Lincoln lived. Among the few volumes which he found in the cabins of the illiterate families by which he was surrounded were the Bible, Bunyan's 'Pilgrim's Progress,' Weems' 'Life of Washington,' and the poems of Robert Burns. These he read over and over again, until they became as familiar as the alphabet. The Bible has been at all times the one book in every home and cabin in the republic; yet it was truly said of

Lincoln that no man, clergyman or otherwise, could be found so familiar with this book as he. This is apparent both in his conversation and his writings. There is hardly a speech or state paper of his in which allusions and illustrations taken from the Bible do not appear. Burns he could quote from end to end. Long afterwards he wrote a most able lecture upon this, perhaps next to Shakespeare, his favorite poet. Young Abraham borrowed of the neighbors and read every book he could hear of in the settlement within a wide circuit. If by chance he heard of a book that he had not read, he would walk many miles to borrow it. Among other volumes that he borrowed of Crawford was Weems' 'Life of Washington.' Reading it with the greatest eagerness, he took it to bed with him in the loft of the cabin, and read on until his 'nubbin' of tallow candle had burned out. Then he placed the book between the logs of the cabin, that it might be at hand as soon as there was light enough in the morning to enable him to read. But during the night a violent rain came on, and he awoke to find his book wet through and through. Drying it as well as he could, he went to Crawford and told him of the mishap, and, as he had no money to pay for it, offered to work out the value of the injured volume. Crawford fixed the price at three days' work; and the future President pulled corn three days, and thus became the owner of the fascinating book."

In addition to the books named above, Lincoln was fortunate enough to get the reading of "Æsop's Fables," "Pilgrim's Progress," and the lives of Benjamin Franklin and of Henry Clay. These were sterling books, and he made them his own by conning them over and over, and copying the more impressive portions until they were fixed indelibly in his memory. Commenting upon the value of this sort of mental training, Dr. Holland wisely remarks: "For those who have witnessed the dissipating effects of many books upon the minds of modern children, it is not hard to believe that

Abraham's poverty of books was the wealth of his life. These few books did much to perfect that which his mother's teachings had begun, and to form a character which, for quaint simplicity, earnestness, truthfulness and purity, has never been surpassed among the historic personages of the world. The Life of Washington, while it gave to him a lofty example of patriotism, incidentally conveyed to his mind a general knowledge of American history; and the Life of Henry Clay spoke to him of a living man who had risen to political and professional eminence from circumstances almost as humble as his own." The latter book undoubtedly did much to excite his taste for politics, to kindle his ambition, and to make him a warm admirer and partisan of Henry Clay, of whom, long afterwards, Mr. Lincoln said: "His example teaches us that one can scarcely be so poor but that, if he will, he can acquire sufficient education to get through the world respectably."

PERSONAL TESTIMONY TO THE VALUE OF HIS EARLY IMPRESSIONS.

A singular and beautiful testimonial to the influence of this early reading upon his childish mind was given by Mr. Lincoln himself, many years afterwards. While on his way to Washington to assume the duties of the Presidency, he passed through Trenton, New Jersey, and in a speech made in the Senate Chamber at that place, he said: "May I be pardoned if, upon this occasion, I mention that away back in my childhood, in the earliest days of my being able to read, I got hold of a small book, such a one as few of the younger members have seen, Weems' 'Life of Washington.' I remember all the accounts there given of the battle-fields and struggles for the liberties of the country; and none fixed themselves upon my imagination so deeply as the struggle here at Trenton. The crossing of the river, the contest with the Hessians, the great hardships endured at that time, all fixed themselves in my memory more than any single Revolutionary event; and you all know, for you have all been boys, how these early impressions last longer than any others. I recollect thinking then, boy even though I was, that there must have been something more than common that these men struggled for. I am exceedingly anxious that that thing which they struggled for, that something even more than National Independence, that something that held out a great promise to all the people of the world to all time to come, I am exceedingly anxious that this Union, the Constitution, and the liberties of the people, shall be perpetuated in accordance with the original idea for which that struggle was made.''

''ALWAYS READING.''

One of the companions of Lincoln's boyhood adds to the preceding statements that ''he was always reading, writing, ciphering, writing poetry.'' ''He would go to the store of an afternoon and evening, and his jokes and stories were so odd, so witty, so humorous, that all the people of the town would gather around him.'' ''He would sometimes keep a crowd about him until midnight.'' ''He was a great reader and a good talker.''

ABE'S DISLIKE OF THE CRAWFORDS.

It has been related in a previous connection, that Abraham gave three days' work as an equivalent for the book which had been injured while in his possession. It appears that he held something of a grudge against the owner for what he regarded as his unjust extortion. The incident is narrated by Mr. Lamon, with other anecdotes: ''For a long time there was only one person in the neighborhood for whom Abe felt a decided dislike; and that was Josiah Crawford, who had made him 'pull fodder,' to pay for the Weems' 'Washington.' On that score he was 'hurt' and 'mad,' and often declared he would 'have revenge.' But being a poor boy, a circumstance of which Crawford had already taken shameful advantage to extort three days' labor,—he was glad to get work at any place, and frequently hired out to his old adversary. Abe's first business in his employ was daubing his cabin, which was

built of logs, unhewn, and with the bark on.   In the loft of
this house, thus finished by his own hands, he slept for many
weeks at a time.   He spent his evenings as he did at home,—
writing on wooden shovels or boards with 'a coal, or keel,
from the branch.'   This family was rich in the possession of
several books, which Abe read through time and again, according to his usual custom.   One of the books was the 'Kentucky
Preceptor,' from which Mrs. Crawford insists that he 'learned
his school orations, speeches, and pieces to write.'   She tells
us also that 'Abe was a sensitive lad, never coming where he
was not wanted;' that he always lifted his hat, and bowed,
when he made his appearance; and that 'he was tender and
kind,' like his sister, who was at the same time her maid-of-
all-work.   His pay was twenty-five cents a day; 'and, when
he missed time, he would not charge for it.'   This latter remark of Mrs. Crawford reveals the fact that her husband was
in the habit of docking Abe on his miserable wages whenever
he happened to lose a few minutes from steady work.   The
time came, however, when Abe got his revenge for all this
petty brutality.   Crawford was as ugly as he was surly.   His
nose was a monstrosity,—long and crooked, with a huge mis-
shapen stub at the end, surmounted by a host of pimples, and
the whole as blue as the usual state of Mr. Crawford's spirits.
Upon this member Abe levelled his attacks, in rhyme, song,
and chronicle; and, though he could not reduce the nose, he
gave it a fame as wide as to the Wabash and the Ohio.   It is
not improbable that he learned the art of making the doggerel
rhymes in which he celebrated Crawford's nose from the study
of Crawford's own 'Kentucky Preceptor.' "

THE LONGEST AND STRONGEST MAN IN THE SETTLEMENT.

The same authority continues: "In the meantime, Abe
had become, not only the longest, but the strongest man in the
settlement.   Some of his feats almost surpass belief, and those
who beheld them with their own eyes stood literally amazed.
Richardson, a neighbor, declares that he could carry a load to

which the strength of three ordinary men would scarcely be equal. He saw him quietly pick up and walk away with 'a chicken-house, made of poles pinned together, and covered, that weighed six hundred, if not much more.' At another time the Richardsons were building a corn-crib; Abe was there, and seeing three or four men preparing 'sticks' upon which to carry some huge posts, he relieved them of all further trouble by shouldering the posts, single-handed, and walking away with them to the place where they were wanted. 'He could strike with a maul,' says old Mr. Wood, 'a heavier blow than any other man. He could sink an axe deeper into the wood than any man I ever saw.' "

DEATH OF LINCOLN'S ONLY SISTER.

The sister who is alluded to in the foregoing paragraphs was warmly attached to Abraham, but she was taken at an early age from his companionship. "It is said that her face somewhat resembled his. In repose it had the gravity which they both, perhaps, inherited from their mother; but it was capable of being lighted almost into beauty by one of Abe's ridiculous stories or rapturous sallies of humor. She was a modest, plain, industrious girl, and is kindly remembered by all who knew her. She was married to Aaron Grigsby at eighteen, and died a year after. Like Abe, she occasionally worked out at the houses of the neighbors. She lies buried, not with her mother, but in the yard of the old Pigeon Creek meeting-house."

EARLY FONDNESS FOR ORATORY.

Young Lincoln's taste for public speaking appeared to be natural and irresistible. His step-sister, Matilda Johnson, says he was an indefatigable preacher. "When father and mother would go to church, Abe would take down the Bible, read a verse, give out a hymn, and we would sing. Abe was about fifteen years of age. He preached, and we would do the crying. Sometimes he would join in the chorus of tears.

One day my brother, John Johnson, caught a land terrapin, brought it to the place where Abe was preaching, threw it against the tree, and crushed the shell. It suffered much, quivered all over. Abe then preached against cruelty to animals, contending that an ant's life was as sweet to it as ours to us.'' ''But this practice of preaching and political speaking,'' says Mr. Lamon, ''into which Abe had fallen, at length became a great nuisance. It distracted everybody, and sadly interfered with the work. If Abe had confined his discourses to Sunday preaching, while the old folks were away, it would not have been so objectionable. But he knew his power, and would be sure to set up as an orator wherever he found the greatest number of people together. When it was announced that Abe had taken the 'stump' in the harvest field, there was an end of work. The hands flocked around him, and listened to his curious speeches with infinite delight. 'The sight of such a thing amused us all,' says Abe's step-mother; though she admits that her husband was compelled to break it up with a strong hand; and poor Abe was many times dragged from the platform and hustled off to his work in no gentle manner.''

LINCOLN'S FIRST DOLLAR.

A story which belongs to this period was told by Mr. Lincoln to Mr. Seward and a few friends one evening in the Executive Mansion at Washington. The President said: ''Seward, you never heard, did you, how I earned my first dollar?'' ''No,'' rejoined Mr. Seward. ''Well,'' continued Mr. Lincoln, ''I belonged, you know, to what they call down South the 'scrubs.' We had succeeded in raising, chiefly by my labor, sufficient produce, as I thought, to justify me in taking it down the river to sell. After much persuasion, I got the consent of mother to go, and constructed a little flatboat, large enough to take a barrel or two of things that we had gathered, with myself and the bundle, down to the Southern market. A steamer was coming down the river. We have, you know, no wharves on the Western streams; and the custom was, if passengers were at any of the landings, for them to go out in a boat, the steamer stopping and taking them on board. I was contemplating my new flatboat, and wondering whether I could make it stronger or improve it in any particular, when two men came down to the shore in carriages, with trunks, and looking at the different boats, singled out mine, and asked, 'Who owns this?' I answered, somewhat modestly, 'I do.' 'Will you,' said one of them, 'take us and our trunks out to the steamer?' 'Certainly,' said I. I was very glad to have the chance of earning something. I supposed that each of them would give me two or three bits. The trunks were put on my flatboat, the passengers seated themselves on the trunks, and I sculled them out to the steamboat. They got on board, and I lifted up their heavy trunks, and put them on deck. The steamer was about to put on steam again, when I called out that they had forgotten to pay me. Each of them took from his pocket a silver half dollar and threw it on the bottom of my boat. I could scarcely believe my eyes as I picked up the money. Gentlemen, you may think it was a very little thing, and in these days it seems to me a trifle; but it was a most important incident in my life. I could scarcely credit that I, a poor boy, had earned a dollar in less than a day, that by honest work I had earned a dollar. The world seemed wider and fairer before me. I was a more hopeful and confident being from that time."

PRESENTIMENTS OF FUTURE GREATNESS.

Notwithstanding the limitations of every kind which hemmed in the life of young Lincoln, he had an instinctive feeling, probably growing out of his eager ambition, that he should some day attain an exalted position. The first betrayal of this curious premonition is indicated in an incident related by Mr. Arnold: "Lincoln attended court at Boonville, the county seat of Warrick county, to witness a trial for murder, at which one of the Breckenridges, from Kentucky, made a very eloquent speech for the defense. The boy was carried away with intense admiration, and was so enthusiastic that, although a perfect stranger, he could not refrain from expressing his admiration to Breckenridge. He wished he could be a lawyer, and went home and dreamed of courts, and got up mock trials, at which he would defend imaginary prisoners. Several of his companions at this period of his life, as well as those who knew him after he went to Illinois, declare that he was often heard to say, not in joke, but seriously, as if he were deeply impressed, rather than elated, with the idea: 'I shall some day be President of the United States.' It is stated by many of Lincoln's old friends, that he often said, while still an obscure man: 'Some day I shall be President.' He undoubtedly had, for years, some presentiment of this."

LINCOLN AT SEVENTEEN.

At seventeen, Lincoln wrote a clear, neat, legible hand, was quick at figures, and able to solve easily any arithmetical problem not going beyond the "Rule of Three." Mr. Arnold, noting these facts, says: "I have in my possession a few pages from his manuscript 'Book of Examples in Arithmetic.' One of these is dated March 1, 1826, and headed 'Discount,' and then follows, in his careful handwriting: 'A definition of Discount,' 'Rules for its computation,' 'Proofs and Various Examples,' worked out in figures, etc.; then 'Interest on money' is treated in the same way, all in his own handwriting. I doubt whether it would be easy to find among scholars of our common or high schools, or any school of boys of the age of seventeen, a better written specimen of this sort of work, or a better knowledge of figures than is indicated by this book of Lincoln's, written at the age of seventeen."

LEARNS SURVEYING.

It was about this time that the boy became interested in the theory of surveying. He pursued the study at odd hours, stolen from sleep or from the recreation which is regarded as essential to the happiness and health of youth. Mr. Simmons, an old Indiana friend, says : "Abe and I used to live and work together when we were young men. Many a job of woodcutting and rail-splitting have I done with him. Abe was the likeliest boy in God's world. He would work all day as hard as any of us, and study by firelight in the log house half the night; and in this way he made himself a thorough practical surveyor."

DOWN THE MISSISSIPPI.

In March, 1828, Abe went to work for old Mr. Gentry, the founder of Gentryville. "Early the next month the old gentleman furnished his son Allen with a boat and a cargo of bacon and other produce, with which he was to go to New Orleans, unless the stock should be sooner disposed of. Abe, having been found faithful and efficient, was employed to accompany the young man as a 'bow-hand,' to work the 'front oars.' He was paid eight dollars per month, and ate and slept on board." The entire business of the trip was placed in Abraham's hands. The fact tells its own story touching the young man's reputation for capacity and integrity. He had never made the trip, knew nothing of the journey, was unaccustomed to business transactions, had never been much upon the river; but his tact, ability and honesty were so far trusted that the trader was willing to risk the cargo in his care. The delight with which the youth swung loose from the shore upon his clumsy craft, with the prospect of a ride of eighteen hundred miles before him, and a vision of the great world, of which he had read and thought so much, may be imagined. At this time he had become a very tall and powerful young man. He had reached the height of six feet and four inches, a length of trunk and limb remarkable even among the tall race of pioneers to which he belonged.

A FIGHT WITH RIVER PIRATES.

The incidents of a trip like this were not likely to be exciting; but there were many passing chats with settlers and

THE TRIP TO NEW ORLEANS.—YOUNG LINCOLN AS A "BOW-HAND."

hunters along the banks of the Ohio and Mississippi, and occasional hailing of similar craft afloat. Arriving at a sugar plantation, somewhere between Natchez and New Orleans, the boat was pulled in and tied to the shore for purposes of trade; and here an incident occured which was sufficiently exciting, and one which, in the memory of recent events, reads somewhat strangely. Seven negroes attacked the life of the future liberator of their race; and it is not improbable that some of them have lived to be emancipated by his proclamation. Night had fallen, and the two tired voyagers had lain down upon their hard bed for sleep. Hearing a noise on shore, Abraham shouted out: "Who's there?" The noise continuing, and no voice replying, he sprang to his feet, and saw seven negroes, evidently bent on plunder. Abraham guessed their errand at once, and seizing a hand-spike, rushed toward them, and knocked one into the water the moment that he touched the boat. The second and third and fourth, who leaped on board, were served in the same rough way. Seeing that they were not likely to make headway in their thieving enterprise, the remainder turned to flee. Abraham and his companion, growing excited and warm with their work, leaped on shore and followed them. Both were too swift of foot for the negroes, and all of them received a severe pounding. The young men returned to their boat just as the others escaped from the water, but the latter fled into the darkness as fast as their feet could carry them. Abraham and his fellow in the fight were both injured, but not disabled. Not being armed, and unwilling to wait until the negroes procured reinforcements, they cut adrift, and floating down the river a mile or two, tied up to the bank again, and watched and waited for the morning.

The trip was brought at length to a successful end. The cargo, or "load" as they called it, was all disposed of for money, the boat itself sold, and the young men retraced the passage, partly at least, on shore and on foot, occupying several weeks in the difficult and tedious journey.

"ABE, WHAT A FOOL YOU ARE."

Just before this river expedition, Lincoln and the young girl whom he had years before befriended in her struggle with the school teacher over the failure to spell the word *definite* had an interview which, as related by his companion, is full of significance. "One evening," says she, "Abe and I were sitting on the banks of the Ohio, or rather on the boat spoken of. I said to Abe that the sun was going down. He said to me, 'That's not so; it don't really go down; it seems so. The earth turns from west to east, and the revolution of the earth carries us under; we do the sinking, as you call it. The sun, as to us, is comparatively still; the sun's sinking is only an appearance.' I replied, 'Abe, what a fool you are!' I know now that I was the fool, not Lincoln. I am now thoroughly satisfied that Abe knew the general laws of astronomy and the movements of the heavenly bodies. He was better read then than the world knows, or is likely to know exactly. No man could talk to me as he did that night, unless he had known something of geography as well as astronomy. He often and often commented or talked to me about what he had read,—seemed to read it out of the book as he went along; and he did so to others. He was the learned boy among us unlearned folks. He took great pains to explain; could do it so simply. He was diffident then, too."

Nat Grigsby bears similar testimony to Lincoln's instructive conversation, as follows: "When he appeared in company the boys would gather and cluster around him to hear him talk. Mr. Lincoln was figurative in his speeches, talks, and conversations. He argued much from analogy, and explained things, hard for us to understand, by stories, maxims, tales, and figures. He would point his lesson or idea by some story that was plain and near to us, that we might instantly see the force and bearing of what he said."

LINCOLN'S WARM HEART.

An incident showing the warm and generous heart beating in the breast of the rough backwoodsman, comes in place in this portion of his history. "One evening, while returning from a 'raising' in his neighborhood, with a number of companions, he discovered a stray horse, with saddle and bridle upon him. The horse was recognized as belonging to a man who was accustomed to excess in drink, and it was suspected at once that the owner was not far off. A short search only was necessary to confirm the suspicions of the young men. The poor drunkard was found in a perfectly helpless condition upon the chilly ground. Abraham's companions urged the policy of leaving him to his fate; but young Lincoln would not hear of the proposition. At his request the miserable sot was lifted to his shoulders, and he actually carried him eighty rods to the nearest house. Sending word to his father that he should not be back that night, he attended and nursed the man until the morning, and had the pleasure of believing he had saved his life."

CHAPTER IV.

A change in the scene of Abraham Lincoln's life occurred in 1830, when his father again set out on the emigrant's trail, which this time conducted them to a point ten miles west of Decatur, in Macon county, Illinois. The family had become dissatisfied with their situation in southern Indiana, and hearing favorable reports of the prairie lands in the new State on their western border, were encouraged to hope for better fortunes there. Mr. Lincoln parted with his farm, and preparations were made for the journey. Abraham visited all the neighbors and bade them an affectionate good-bye. When the morning of the day which **had** been selected for their departure arrived, he was found sitting and weeping upon his mother's grave, whither he had gone at an early hour in the morning. He said he could not bear the thought of leaving his mother behind.

The few household goods and utensils were loaded upon the farm wagon, the oxen yoked, and the family, getting aboard, young Lincoln took his place beside the oxen and drove away. An aged man who lived in Indiana at the time, and was a neighbor of the Lincoln family says that he remembers the scene when Abe started that morning, barefooted, with his pants coming down only half way between

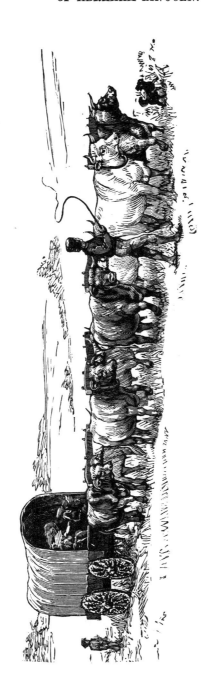

THE REMOVAL TO ILLINOIS.—ABE AS AN OX-DRIVER.—THE SCENE AS COMMONLY DESCRIBED.

his knees and his feet, and adds: "Little did I think he'd ever be President of the United States." In that ungainly six-foot-four youth, by the side of the ox team, went forth, seeking a new home in the west, the future President, the illustrious leader, the immortal emancipator.

According to the accounts usually given by Lincoln's biographers, this memorable journey was performed with four yoke of oxen and an ordinary "prairie-schooner," as shown in the accompanying illustration. But it seems hardly probable that this could have been the case. The Lincoln family were very poor when they left Indiana; indeed, it is doubtful if Thomas Lincoln's property, all told, would at any time have equalled the value of four good yoke of oxen. Later accounts of this event confirm the probability that the turn-out was a much more moderate affair.

THE ENTRY INTO ILLINOIS DESCRIBED BY AN OLD ACQUAINT-
ANCE.

A most interesting account of the entry of the Lincoln family into Illinois, with an excellent personal sketch of Thomas Lincoln, Abraham's father, is furnished by Mr. George B. Balch, who is still a resident of Lerna, Coles county, Illinois. This gentleman knew both the Lincolns, father and son; and from his accurate personal knowledge he is able to correct some important errors that have crept into the works of other biographers of Lincoln. Mr. Balch says: "Thomas Lincoln, the father of the great President, called 'Uncle Tommy' by near friends, and 'Old Tom Lincoln' by others, moved from Spencer county, Indiana, to Macon county, Illinois, in the year 1830. That part of Illinois now embraced in Coles, Shelby, and Macon counties, received its first installments of permanent settlers during and between the years 1828 and 1830. The greater portion of these settlers came from Tennessee, Kentucky and southern Indiana. As the streams were unbridged, and many of them were unfordable a considerable portion of the year, the emigrants crossed the Wabash river at points below the mouth of the Embarrass, or 'Ambraw' river, and travelled in a northwesterly direction, between the waters of the 'Ambraw' on the east and the waters of the Little Wabash and other streams on the west, passing through the western part of Coles county. It was along this winding trail—for such it was—that Thomas Lincoln, the 'Terah' of modern times, accompanied by his son Abraham, came into Illinois. Their outfit was doubtless far more rude than that of the ancient pilgrim who 'died at Haran;' for an old settler who is still living (in 1886), and who settled in Coles county in 1829, says the wagon was made entirely of wood, and that the wheels were solid, having been cut from a large oak log; the team was a small yoke of oxen, driven by the immortal Lincoln, who was then a barefooted youth. This story has been disputed by historians who never saw Thomas Lincoln, who are wholly unacquainted with the circumstances with which he was surrounded, and who have little knowledge of the customs of the people of those times. Their writings are traditional, and not trustworthy. The writer is personally acquainted with his informant, and knows him to be reliable; and although I did not not see the outfit spoken of, I saw like ones which came from North Carolina to Coles county.

"Thus we behold Abraham Lincoln, an unlettered, uncouth, barefooted boy, driving a pair of oxen across the unpeopled prairies of Illinois. No money, no friends, no opportunities, his mother in her grave, and his father incapable of rising above the lowest level,—how dark the picture, and yet how true! A little more than thirty years sweep by, and we behold him again. A million men, with all the appliances of war, are obeying his command; he is stamping, as it were, millions of money out of the earth; the shackles are falling from the hands and hearts of four millions of bondmen, and the whole world is looking on with wonder and astonishment."

RECOLLECTIONS OF LINCOLN'S FATHER.

Thomas Lincoln, continues Mr. Balch's narrative, "remained in Macon county only about two years; but his son, having engaged labor as a farm hand, never again lived beneath the parental roof. Therefore Abraham Lincoln never lived in Coles county. Returning to Coles county in the year 1832, Thomas Lincoln settled in a little log cabin in Pleasant Grove, at a point about nine miles from where the city of Mattoon is now located, and about one-half mile from my father's dwelling. His family consisted of his wife—a second one—and her son, John Johnson, a profligate and dissipated young man, who did not live out half his days. His property consisted of an old horse, a pair of oxen, and a few sheep—seven or eight head. My father bought two of the sheep, they being the first we owned after settling in Illinois. At that time all the people, both male and female, wore homespun; and the man who owned a few sheep, and whose wife knew how to manufacture their wool into wearing apparel, was considered lucky; and if he was able to buy a little indigo, so that she could color a part of the wool, and thus be enabled to make him a 'mixed jeans' suit, he was considered a little aristocratic. But Thomas Lincoln had no such aristocracy; his clothing was always a walnut brown. I never saw him wearing clothes of any other color. His outer garments consisted of brown jeans pants and 'roundabout,' which may be described as a dress-coat without any skirt to it.

"Thomas Lincoln was a large and bulky man, six feet tall, and weighing about two hundred pounds. He was large-boned, coarse-featured, had a large, blunt nose, a florid complexion, light sandy hair and whiskers. He was slow in speech and slow in gait, and his whole appearance denoted a man of small intellect and less ambition; and such he was.

"While living in the above described cabin, he built another about one mile south of it, and moved into it in the spring of 1834. By a 'cabin' I mean a small house built of unhewn logs. It was about sixteen feet square, with a fireplace and clay chimney at one end of it. The cooking, eating, sleeping, and entertaining were all done in the one room.

"During this period, Thomas Lincoln was occasionally visited by his son 'Abe.' On these occasions my father would usually go and sit of evenings and converse with the young man, whose talents he admired; and even then, as I well remember, he predicted that Abraham Lincoln would become a great political leader, of national reputation.

"The first time the writer ever saw Abraham Lincoln was in the fall of 1834; he was passing my father's house, going to visit his humble father, who at that time lived in the last-mentioned cabin.

> " 'Twas just a hut, with puncheon floor,
> And chimney rude and creaking door,
> Which stood beneath the forest shade;
> For 'round it, in their primal mood,
> The kingly oaks in grandeur stood
> Untouched by woodman's ruthless blade.
> But hither came on weary feet
> A son to whom that home was sweet,
> Although so lowly and obscure;
> For filial love, angelic guest,
> Had made her home within his breast,
> And woo'd him to a place so poor.

"As he was walking, and as this was long before the day of stage-coaches, we concluded he had walked the whole way from Springfield—a distance of one hundred miles. In fact, there is no doubt of it.

"Thomas Lincoln remained only about two years at the last-named place, and then moved on to land given him by his son. This place is on the south line of Coles county, and about fourteen miles southeast from Mattoon. It is now (1886) owned and occupied by a grandson of Thomas Lincoln's second wife. Here, the house he built, with its rude fireplace, and the trees that he planted, are still to be seen.

"It is generally supposed that Thomas Lincoln was a farmer; and such he was, if one who tilled so little land by such primitive modes could be so called. He never planted more than a few acres; and instead of gathering and hauling his crops in a wagon, he usually carried them in a basket or large tray. Sometimes he stowed a large portion of them under his bed. He was uneducated, illiterate, and contented with a 'from hand to mouth' living.

"At his death, which occurred on the 15th day of January, 1851, he was buried in a neighboring county graveyard, about one mile north of Janesville, Coles county. There was nothing to mark the place of his resting, except the mound and a small boulder, until February, 1861, when Abraham Lincoln paid a last visit to his grave just before leaving Springfield for Washington. At that time he cut the initial letters "T. L." on a bit of oak board, and placed it at the head of the grave. This board was afterwards—as was supposed—carried away by some relic-hunter; and the place remained with nothing to mark it, except the memory of the old settlers who laid him away, until the spring of 1876, when the writer, fearing the grave would become entirely unknown, succeeded in awakening an interest on the subject, and soon thereafter a plain marble shaft, twelve feet in height, was erected over the grave. It has on its western face a plain inscription in words and form as follows:

THOMAS LINCOLN,

Father of

THE MARTYRED PRESIDENT.

Born

Jan. 6th, 1778.

Died

Jan. 15th, 1851.

LINCOLN.

"And now I have given about all that can ever be known of Thomas Lincoln. I have written impartially, and with a strict regard to facts which can be substantiated by many old settlers who are still living in this county. Thomas Lincoln was an honest and a harmless man; beyond this, the biographer will search his character in vain to find any ancestral clue to the greatness of Abraham Lincoln.''

NOVEL METHODS OF BOOK-KEEPING.

William G. Greene furnishes the following: "In 1836 I was going to Kentucky, and at the request of Abe Lincoln I carried a letter to his father, who lived in Coles county, Illinois, at the head of the 'Ambraw' river. When I got to the place, the old man's house looked so small and humble that I felt embarrassed, until he received me with much heartiness, telling me what a handy house he had, and how conveniently it was arranged. It was a log house, and some of the logs

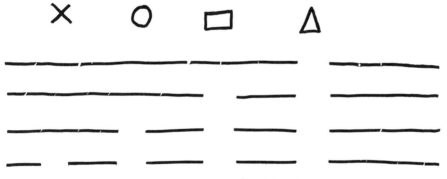

THOMAS LINCOLN'S LEDGER.

stuck out two or three feet from the wall at the corners. He said that he could dress his deer as he killed them, and hang them on the projecting logs, and could tie his horse to them. The old man inquired how his son was getting along. He said Abe was a good boy, but he was afraid he would never amount to much; he had taken a notion to study law, and these men were generally 'eddicated' to do wrong. 'Here now,' he said, 'I cannot read or write a bit; but I can beat any book-keeper I ever saw at making my accounts so easy and simple that anybody can understand them, just by taking

my forefinger and rubbing out that black mark.' In the little
cabin where he was living, the joists were about seven feet
from the floor, and were, of course, unfinished. The old
man had taken a fire-coal and drawn four black marks on the
face of a joist, something like the four bars of music. He
then explained that he had been 'tending mill' for a man
down the river; and when he sold a customer a peck of meal
he simply reached up and drew his fingers through the lower
line; for two pecks, he rubbed a hole through two of the lines;
for three pecks, three lines; and for a bushel, four lines were
erased. He put a mark to indicate the customer right over
his dues. 'The simplest thing in the world,' said he; and
added, 'if Abe don't fool away all his time on his books, he
may make something yet.' "

ABE AS A RAIL-SPLITTER.

After reaching the new home in Illinois, young Lincoln
worked with his father until things were put in train for comfortable living. He helped build the log cabin, break up the
new land, and fence it in, splitting the rails for this purpose
with his own skillful hands. It was these very rails, it may
be remarked in passing, over which so much sentiment was
expended years afterward at an important epoch in Lincoln's
political career. "During the sitting of the Republican State
Convention at Decatur, a banner, attached to two of these
rails, and bearing an appropriate inscription, was brought into
the assemblage, and formally presented to that body, amid a
scene of unparalleled enthusiasm. After that they were in
demand in every State of the Union in which free labor is
honored, where they were borne in processions of the people,
and hailed by hundreds of thousands of freeman as a symbol
of triumph and a glorious vindication of freedom and of the
rights and dignity of free labor. These, however, were far
from being the first or only rails made by Lincoln. He was
a practiced hand at the business." As a memento of this
special pioneer accomplishment, Mr. Lincoln preserved in

later years a cane carved from one of the rails he had split on his father's farm.

MAKING A "CRAP" OF CORN.

When the Lincolns moved to Illinois Abraham was twenty-one years old. "Up to this time, all his earnings, with the exception of his own very frugal support, had gone to the maintenance of his father and family. Ambitious to make his way in the world, he now asked permission to strike out for himself and to seek his own fortune." It is not known positively where he found employment during his first summer in Illinois, but a story told by a Mrs. Brown gives a clue to his whereabouts that season. "Mr. Linken worked with my old man thirty-four year ago," says Mrs. Brown, "and made a crap. We lived on the same farm where we live now, and he worked all the season, and made a crap of corn, and the next winter they hauled the crap all the way to Galena, and sold it for two dollars and a half a bushel. At that time there was no public houses, and travelers were obliged to stay at any house along the road that could take them in. One evening a right smart looking man rode up to the fence, and asked my old man if he could get to stay over night. 'Well,' said Mr. Brown, 'we can feed your crittur and give you something to eat, but we can't lodge you unless you can sleep on the same bed with the hired man.' The man hesitated, and asked, 'Where is he?' 'Well,' said Mr. Brown, 'you can come and see him.' So the man got down from his crittur, and Mr. Brown took him around to where, in the shade of the house, Mr. Lincoln lay full length on the ground, with an open book before him. 'There,' said Mr. Brown, pointing at him, 'there he is.' The stranger looked at him a minute, and said, 'Well, I think he'll do,' and he stayed and slept with the President of the United States."

LINCOLN AS A LOG-ROLLER.

Mr. Holland, of Tazewell county, who has resided in Illinois since 1815, and is still living (1886), narrates that he once asked young Lincoln to go down to his saw-mill and help roll logs. Lincoln was among the most active and useful of the company, giving directions and doing a large share of the work. After the log-rolling was completed, Mr. Holland invited the company to his orchard to eat apples. Mr. Lincoln replied: "Well, I don't believe I care for any apples, but I'll go along and reach down a few to the boys."

SECOND VOYAGE TO NEW ORLEANS.

The next important record of Lincoln's career connects him with Mr. Denton Offutt. The circumstances which brought him into this relation are thus narrated by Mr. J. H. Barrett: "While there was snow on the ground, at the close of the year 1830, or early in 1831, a man came to that part of Macon county where young Lincoln was living, in pursuit of hands to aid him in a flatboat voyage down the Mississippi. The fact was known that the youth had once made such a trip, and his services were sought for this occasion. As one who had his own subsistence to earn, with no capital but his hands, he accepted the proposition made him. Perhaps there was something of his inherited and acquired fondness for exciting adventure impelling him to this decision. With him were also employed his former fellow-laborer, John Hanks, and a son of his step-mother named John Johnson. In the spring of 1831 Lincoln set out to fulfill his engagement. The floods had so swollen the streams that the Sangamon country was a vast sea before him. His first entrance into that county was over these wide-spread waters in a canoe. The time had come to join his employer on his journey to New Orleans, but the latter had been disappointed by another person on whom he relied to furnish him a boat on the Illinois river. Accordingly all hands set to work, and themselves built a boat on that river, for their purposes. This done, they set out on their long trip, making a successful voyage to New Orleans and back."

Mr. Herndon says: "Mr. Lincoln came into Sangamon county, down the North Fork of the Sangamon river, in a frail canoe, in the Spring of 1831. I can see from where I write the identical place where he cut the timbers for his flatboat, which he built at a little village called Sangamon Town, seven miles northwest of Springfield. Here he had it loaded with corn, wheat, bacon, and other provisions, destined for New Orleans, at which place he landed in the month of May, 1831. He returned home in June of that year, and finally settled in another little village called New Salem, on the high bluffs of the Sangamon river, then in Sangamon county and now in Menard county, and about twenty miles northwest of Springfield."

It was midsummer when the flatboatman returned from this his second and last trip in that capacity. Some interesting facts relating to this adventure are furnished by Mr. Lamon: "In March, Hanks and Johnson and Lincoln went down the Sangamon in a canoe to Jamestown (then Judy's Ferry), five miles east of Springfield. Thence they walked to Springfield, and found Mr. Offutt comforting himself at Elliott's tavern, in Old Town. He had contracted to have a boat ready at the mouth of Spring creek, but, not looking after it himself, was disappointed. There was only one way out of the trouble: the three hands must build a boat. They went to the mouth of Spring creek, five miles north of Springfield, and there consumed two weeks cutting the timber from Congress land. In the meantime, Abe walked back to Judy's Ferry, by way of Springfield, and brought down the canoe which they had left at the former place. The timber was hewed and scored, and then 'rafted' down to Sangamon Town. At the mouth of Spring creek they had been compelled to walk a full mile for their meals; but at Sangamon Town they built a shanty, and boarded themselves. Abe was elected cook, and performed the duties of the office to the satisfaction of the party. The lumber for the boat was sawed at Kirkpatrick's mill, a mile and a half from the shanty. Laboring under many disadvantages like this, they managed to complete and launch the boat in about four weeks from the time of beginning. In those days Abe, as usual, is described as being 'funny, jokey, full of yarns, stories and rigs;' as being 'long, tall and green;' 'frequently quoting poetry and reciting orations.' The party had their own amusements. Abe extracted a good deal of fun out of the cooking; and played 'seven up' at night, at which he made a good game."

LINCOLN AS AN INVENTOR.

One of Mr. Lincoln's early friends, W. G. Greene, states that the first time he ever saw Mr. Lincoln, "he was in the Sangamon river, with his trousers rolled up five feet, more or less, trying to pilot a flatboat over a mill-dam. The boat was so full of water that it was hard to manage. Lincoln got the prow over, and then, instead of waiting to bail the water out, bored a hole through the projecting part and let it run out." The practical and ingenious character of Lincoln's mind is shown in the fact that several years after his river experience he invented and patented a device for overcoming some of the difficulties in the navigation of western rivers with which this trip had made him familiar. The following interesting account of this invention is given: "Occupying an ordinary and commonplace position in one of the show-cases in the large hall of the Patent Office, is one little model which, in ages to come, will be prized as one of the most curious and one of the most sacred relics in that vast museum of unique and priceless things. This is a plain and simple model of a steamboat, roughly fashioned in wood, by the hand of Abraham Lincoln. It bears date in 1849, when the inventor was known simply as a successful lawyer and rising politician of Central Illinois. Neither his practice nor his politics took up so much of his time as to prevent him from giving some attention to contrivances which he hoped might be of benefit to the world and of profit to himself. The design of this invention is suggestive of one phase of Abraham Lincoln's early life, when he went up and down the Mississippi as a flatboatman, and became familiar with some of the dangers and inconveniences attending the navigation of the western rivers. It is an attempt to make it an easy matter to transport vessels over shoals and snags and 'sawyers'. The main idea is that of an apparatus resembling a noiseless bellows, placed on each side of the hull of the craft, just below the water-line, and worked by an odd but not complicated system of ropes, valves, and pulleys. When the keel of the vessel grates against the sand or obstruction, these bellows are to be filled with air; and, thus buoyed up, the ship is expected to float lightly and gayly over the shoal, which would otherwise have proved a serious interruption to her voyage. The model, which is about eighteen or twenty inches long, and has the appearance of having been whittled with a knife out of a shingle and a cigar-box, is built without any elaboration or ornament, or any extra apparatus beyond that necessary to show the operation of buoying the steamer over the obstructions. Herein it differs from very many of the models which share with it the shelter of the immense halls of the Patent Office, and which are fashioned with wonderful nicety and exquisite finish, as if much of the labor and thought and affection of a lifetime had been devoted to their construction. This is a model of a different kind; carved as one might imagine a retired rail-splitter would whittle, strongly but not smoothly, and evidently made with a view solely to convey to the minds of the patent authorities, by the simplest possible means, an idea of the purpose and plan of the invention. The label on the steamer's deck informs us that the patent was obtained; but we do not learn that the navigation of the western rivers was revolutionized by this quaint conception. The modest little model has reposed here many years; and since it found its resting-place here on the shelf, the shrewd inventor has found it his task to guide the ship of state over shoals more perilous, and obstructions more obstinate, than any prophet dreamed of when Abraham Lincoln wrote his bold autograph on the prow of this miniature steamer.''

SPLITTING FOUR HUNDRED RAILS FOR A YARD OF CLOTH.

The personal appearance of young Lincoln at this date, and the shifts to which he was driven to secure a bare subsistence, are now hardly imaginable. Mr. George Cluse, who worked with Lincoln during his first years in Illinois, says that at that time Abe was the roughest-looking person he ever saw. "He was tall, angular and ungainly, wore trousers made of flax and tow, cut tight at the ankle and out at both knees." He was known to be very poor, but he was a welcome guest in every house in the neighborhood. Mr. Cluse speaks of splitting rails with Abraham, and reveals some very interesting facts concerning wages. Money was a commodity never reckoned upon. Lincoln split rails to get clothing, and he made a bargain with Mrs. Nancy Miller to split four hundred rails for every yard of brown jeans, dyed with white walnut bark, that would be necessary to make him a pair of trousers.

In those hard days, Lincoln used to walk five, six and seven miles to work. His poverty, though it depressed him, did not extinguish his spirits or blunt his faculties, and he was ready to engage in an intellectual or a physical encounter with a suitable antagonist, whenever circumstances warranted. John Hanks, his cousin and companion in his recent voyage, relates an anecdote in point: "After Abe got to Decatur, or rather to Macon, a man by the name of Posey came into our neighborhood and made a speech. It was a bad one, and I said Abe could beat it. I turned down a box or keg, and Abe mounted it and made a speech. The other man was a candidate; Abe wasn't. Abe beat him to death, his subject being the navigation of the Sangamon river. The man, after the speech was through, took Abe aside, and asked him where he had learned so much, and how he did so well. Abe replied, stating his manner and method of reading, and what he had read. The man encouraged him to persevere."

REMOVAL TO NEW SALEM.—LINCOLN AS A STOREKEEPER.

At the conclusion of his trip to New Orleans, Mr. Offutt, Lincoln's employer, entered into mercantile trade in a small way at New Salem, a settlement on the Sangamon river, in Menard county, two miles from Petersburg, the county seat. He opened a store of the class commonly supported in a little wayside town, and also ran a flouring mill. He had found out in his late expedition down the Mississippi the valuable qualities

THE COUNTRY STORE.

of young Lincoln, and was anxious to secure his help in his new enterprise. "For want of other immediate employment," says Mr. Barrett, "and in the same spirit which had heretofore actuated him, Abraham Lincoln now entered upon the duties of a clerk, having an eye to both branches of the business carried on by his employer. This connection continued for nearly a year, all the duties of his position being faithfully performed." It was to this year's humble but honorable service that Mr. Douglas tauntingly alluded in one of his speeches during the canvass of 1858, as "keeping a groggery." In his reply, Mr. Lincoln declared his adversary "wofully at fault" as to his ever having been a "groggery-keeper," and that he had "never kept a groggery anywhere in the world."

THIRST FOR KNOWLEDGE.

Abraham's habits of study were now again regularly resumed. "While engaged in the duties of Offutt's store he commenced the study of English grammar. There was not a text-book to be obtained in the neighborhood; but hearing that there was a copy of Kirkham's Grammar in the possession of a person seven or eight miles distant, he walked to his house and succeeded in borrowing it. L. M. Green, a lawyer of Petersburg, in Menard county, says that every time he visited New Salem, at this period, Lincoln took him out upon a hill and asked him to explain some point in Kirkham that had given him trouble. After having mastered the book he remarked to a friend that if that was what they called a science he thought he could 'subdue another.' Mr. Green says that Mr. Lincoln's talk at this time showed that he was beginning to think of a great life and a great destiny. Lincoln said to him, on one occasion, that all his family seemed to have good sense, but somehow none had ever become distinguished. He thought perhaps he might become so. He had talked, he said, with men who had the reputation of being great men, but he could not see that they differed much from others. During this year he was also much engaged with debating clubs, often walking six or seven miles to attend them. One of these clubs held its meetings at an old store-house in New Salem, and the first speech young Lincoln ever made was made there. He used to call the exercising 'practicing polemics.' As these clubs were composed principally of men of no education whatever, some of their 'polemics' are remembered as the most laughable of farces. Lincoln's favorite newspaper at this time was the Louisville Journal, a paper which he received regularly by mail, and paid for during a number of years when he had not money enough to dress decently. He liked its politics, and was particularly delighted with its wit and humor, of which he had the keenest appreciation.''

STUDYING UNDER DIFFICULTIES.

When out of the store Lincoln was always busy in the pursuit of knowledge. One gentleman who met him during this period says that the first time he saw him ''he was lying on a trundle-bed, covered with books and papers, and rocking a cradle with his foot. Of the amount of uncovered space between the extremities of his trousers and the top of his socks, which this informant observed, there shall be no mention. The whole scene, however, was entirely characteristic,—Lincoln reading and studying, and at the same time helping his landlady by quieting her child.'' Mr. Lamon says: ''Sometimes, when business was not particularly brisk, he would lie under a shade-tree in front of the store and pore over the book; at other times a customer would find him stretched on the counter intently engaged in the same way. But the store was a bad place for study; and he was often seen quietly slipping out of the village, as if he wished to avoid observation, when, if successful in getting off alone, he would spend hours in the woods 'mastering a book,' or in a state of profound abstraction. He kept up his old habit of sitting up late at night; but as lights were as necessary to his purpose as they were expensive, the village cooper permitted him to sit in his shop, where he burnt the shavings, and kept a blazing fire to read by, when every one else was in bed. The Greens lent him books; the schoolmaster gave him instructions in the store, on the road, or in the meadows; every visitor to New Salem who made the least pretension to scholarship was waylaid by Abe and required to explain something which he could not understand. The result of it all was that the village and the surrounding country wondered at his growth in knowledge, and he soon became as famous for his understanding as for his muscular power and his unfailing humor.''

LINCOLN'S FIRST OFFICIAL ACT.

This event happened in the summer of 1831. "On the day of the election, in the month of August," as Minter Graham, the school teacher, tells us, "Abe was seen loitering about the polling place. It must have been but a few days after his arrival in New Salem, for nobody knew that he could write. They were 'short of a clerk' at the polls ; and, after casting about in vain for some one competent to fill the office, it occurred to one of the judges that perhaps the tall stranger possessed the needful qualifications. He thereupon accosted him, and asked if he could write. He replied, 'Yes, a little.' 'Will you act as clerk of the election to-day?' said the judge. 'I will try,' returned Abe, 'and do the best I can, if you so request.'" He did try accordingly, and, in the language of the schoolmaster, "performed the duties with great facility, firmness, honesty, and impartiality. I clerked with him," says Mr. Graham, "on the same day and at the same polls. The election books are now in the city of Springfield, where they can be seen and inspected any day."

LINCOLN AS A WRESTLER.—THE "CLARY GROVE BOYS."

At this era, Lincoln was as famous for his skill in athletic sports as he was for his love of books. Mr. Offutt, who had a strong regard for him, according to Mr. Arnold, "often declared that his clerk, or salesman, knew more than any man in the United States, and that he could out-run, whip, or throw any man in the county. These boasts came to the ears of the 'Clary Grove Boys,' a set of rude, roystering, good-natured fellows, who lived in and around Clary's Grove, a settlement near New Salem. Their leader was Jack Armstrong, a great square-built fellow, strong as an ox, who was believed by his partisans to be able to whip any man on the Sangamon river. The issue was thus made between Lincoln and Armstrong as to which was the better man ; and although Lincoln tried to avoid such contests, nothing but an actual trial could settle the question among their partisans. And so they met and wrestled for some time, without any decided advantage on either side. Finally Jack resorted to some foul play, which roused Lincoln's indignation. Putting forth his whole strength, he seized the great bully by the neck, and holding him at arm's length shook him like a boy. The 'Clary Grove Boys,' who made up most of the crowd of lookers-on, were ready to pitch in on behalf of their companion, and a general onslaught upon Lincoln was threatened. Lincoln backed up against Offutt's store, and was ready, calmly awaiting the attack of the whole crowd. But his cool courage touched the manhood of Jack Armstrong. He stepped forward, seized Lincoln's hand and shook it heartily, as he declared: 'Boys, Abe Lincoln is the best fellow that ever broke into this settlement. He shall be one of us.' From that time on, Jack Armstrong was Lincoln's man and most willing thrall. His hand, his table, his purse, his vote, and that of the 'Clary Grove Boys,' belonged to Lincoln. Lincoln's popularity with them was unbounded, and his rule was just. He would have fair play, and he repressed the violence and brutality of these rough fellows to an extent which would have been impossible to another man. He could stop a fight and quell a riot among these rude neighbors when all others failed.''

FRIENDSHIPS THROUGH THRASHINGS.

·Under whatever circumstances Lincoln was forced into a fight, the end could be confidently predicted. He was sure to thrash his opponent, and gain his friendship afterwards by a generous use of his victory. Innumerable instances could be cited in proof of the statement. ''While showing goods to two or three women in Offutt's store one day, a bully came in and began to talk in an offensive manner, using much profanity, and evidently wishing to provoke a quarrel. Lincoln leaned over the counter, and begged him, as ladies were present, not to indulge in such talk. The bully retorted that the opportunity had come for which he had long sought, and he would like to see the man who could hinder him from saying anything he might choose to say. Lincoln, still cool, told him that if he would wait until the ladies retired, he would hear what he had to say, and give him any satisfaction he desired. As soon as the women were gone, the man became furious. Lincoln heard his boasts and his abuse for a time, and finding that he was not to be put off without a fight, said: 'Well, if you must be whipped, I suppose I may as well whip you as any other man.' This was just what the bully had been seeking, he said; so out of doors they went. Lincoln made short work of him. He threw him upon the ground, and held him there as if he had been a child, and gathering some 'smart-weed' which grew upon the spot, rubbed it into his face and eyes until the fellow bellowed with pain. Lincoln did all this without a particle of anger, and when the job was finished went immediately for water, washed his victim's face and did everything he could to alleviate his distress. The upshot of the matter was that the man became his life-long friend, and was a better man from that day.''

LINCOLN AND SMOOT.

The chief repute of a sturdy frontiersman is built upon his deeds of prowess, and the fame of the great, rough, strong-limbed, kind-hearted Titan was spread over all the country around. Says Mr. Lamon: "On one occasion while he was clerking for Offutt, a stranger came into the store, and soon disclosed the fact that his name was Smoot. Abe was behind the counter at the moment; but hearing the name he sprang over and introduced himself. Abe had often heard of Smoot, and Smoot had often heard of Abe. They had been as anxious to meet as ever two celebrities were; but hitherto they had never been able to manage it. 'Smoot,' said Lincoln, after a steady survey of his person, 'I am very much disappointed in you; I expected to see an old Probst of a fellow.' (Probst, it appears, was the most hideous specimen of humanity in all that country). 'Yes,' replied Smoot; 'and I am equally disappointed, for I expected to see a good-looking man when I saw you.' A few neat compliments like the foregoing laid the foundation of a lasting intimacy between the two men, and in his present distress Lincoln knew no one who would be more likely than Smoot to respond favorably to an application for money." "After he was elected to the Legislature," says Mr. Smoot, "he came to my house one day in company with Hugh Armstrong. Says he, 'Smoot, did you vote for me?' I told him I did. 'Well,' says he, 'you must loan me money to buy suitable clothing, for I want to make a decent appearance in the Legislature.' I then loaned him two hundred dollars, which he returned to me according to promise."

THE CHAMPION OF GOOSENEST PRAIRIE.

About this period Abraham paid a visit to his father, who, yielding to a fresh vagrant impulse, had transferred his family from Macon to a place near Goosenest Prairie, in Coles county. While there, Abraham had been compelled to try his strength with the "champion" of the region. Mr. Lamon thus describes their meeting: "Scarcely had Abe reached Coles county, when he received a visit from a famous wrestler, one Daniel Needham, who regarded him as a growing rival, and had a fancy to try a fall or two with him. He considered himself the 'best man' in the country, and the report of Abe's achievements filled his big breast with envious pains. His greeting was friendly and hearty, but his challenge was rough and peremptory. Abe valued his popularity among 'the boys' too highly to decline it, and met him by public appointment in the 'greenwood,' at Wabash Point, where he threw him twice with so much ease that Needham's pride was more hurt than his body. 'Lincoln,' said he, 'you have thrown me twice, but you can't whip me.'' Needham,' replied Abe, 'are you satisfied that I can throw you? If you are not, and must be convinced through a thrashing, I will do that, too, for your sake.' Needham had hoped that the youngster would shrink from a fight with the acknowledged 'bully of the patch;' but finding him willing, and at the same time magnanimously inclined to whip him solely for his own good, he concluded that a bloody nose and a black eye would be the reverse of soothing to his feelings, and therefore surrendered the field with such grace as he could command.''

THE FIRST MEETING BETWEEN LINCOLN AND RICHARD YATES.

Lincoln's old friend, W. G. Greene, tells us that while he was a student at the Illinois College at Jacksonville, he became acquainted with Richard Yates, also a student. On one occasion, while Yates was a guest of Greene's during a vacation, the latter took him up to Salem to make him acquainted with Lincoln. They found Abe flat on his back on a cellar-door, reading a newspaper. Greene introduced the two, and thus the acquaintance began between the future War-Governor of Illinois and the future President.

LINCOLN UPSETS HIS BREAD AND MILK.

On this same occasion, says Mr. Greene, Lincoln accepted an invitation to go home and take dinner with him and Yates. While they were at the table, Lincoln, in his awkwardness, managed to upset his bowl of bread and milk. Mr. Greene well recollects ''the confusion with which the accident covered Mr. Lincoln, which Mrs. Greene, the hostess, who was always attached to the ungainly backwoodsman, tried to relieve as best she could by declaring it was her fault in setting the bowl at the wrong place on the table.''

A STORY-TELLER BY NATURE.

Lincoln was from boyhood an adept at expedients for avoiding any unpleasant predicament, and ''one of his modes of getting rid of troublesome friends, as well as troublesome enemies, was by telling a story. He began these tactics early in life, and he grew to be wonderfully adept in them. If a man broached a subject which he did not wish to discuss, he told a story which changed the direction of the conversation. If he was called upon to answer a question, he answered it by telling a story. He had a story for everything; something had occurred at some place where he used to live that illustrated every possible phase of every possible subject with which he might have connection." He acquired the habit of story-telling naturally, as we learn from the following statement: "At home, with his step-mother and the children, he was the most agreeable fellow in the world. He was always ready to do everything for everybody. When he was not doing some special act of kindness, he told stories or 'cracked jokes.' He was as full of his yarns in Indiana as ever he was in Illinois. Dennis Hanks was a clever hand at the same business, and so was old Tom Lincoln."

"HONEST ABE."

It was while Lincoln was salesman for Offutt that he acquired the *sobriquet* of "Honest Abe." Says Mr. Arnold: "Of many incidents illustrating his integrity, one or two may be mentioned. One evening he found his cash overran a little, and he discovered that in making change for his last customer, an old woman who had come in a little before sundown, he had made a mistake, not having given her quite enough. Although the amount was small, a few cents, he took the money, immediately walked to her house, and corrected the error. At another time, on his arrival at the store in the morning, he found on the scales a weight which he remembered having used just before closing, but which was not the one he had intended to use. He had sold a parcel of tea, and in the hurry had placed the wrong weight on the scales, so that the purchaser had a few ounces less of tea than had been paid for. He immediately sent the quantity required to make up the deficiency. These and many similar incidents are told, exhibiting his scrupulous honesty in the most trifling matters; and for these the people gave him the name which clung to him through life.''

The natural integrity of Lincoln's character is brought out in a conversation he once held with a New Salem friend, Mr. William McNeeley, who says: "Lincoln said he did not believe in total depravity, and, although it was not popular to believe it, it was easier to do right than wrong; that the first thought was, what was right? and the second, what was wrong? Therefore it was easier to do right than wrong, and easier to take care of it, as it would take care of itself. It took an effort to do wrong, and a still greater effort to take care of it; but do right, and it would take care of itself. Then you had nothing to do but to go ahead and do right, and nothing to trouble you. I was acquainted with him a long time, and I never knew him to do a wrong act.'' Another of his early friends says: "He possessed the judicial quality of mind in a degree so eminent, and it was so universally recognized, that he never could attend a horse-race without being importuned to act as a judge, or witness a bet without assuming the responsibility of a stakeholder.'' "In the spring or summer of 1832,'' says Henry McHenry, "I had a horse-race with George Warburton. I got Lincoln, who was there, to be a judge of the race, much against his will, and after hard persuasion. Lincoln decided correctly; and the other judge said, 'Lincoln is the fairest man I ever had to deal with; if Lincoln is in this county when I die, I want him to be my administrator, for he is the only man I ever met with who was wholly and unselfishly honest.''

CHAPTER V.

A TURN IN AFFAIRS.——THE BLACK HAWK WAR.——SCENE IN THE WAR PIC-
TURED BY MR. LINCOLN.——A REMARKABLE MILITARY MANŒUVRE.——GET-
TING THE COMPANY THROUGH A GATE.——LINCOLN PROTECTING AN IN-
DIAN.——THE POET BRYANT MEETS CAPTAIN LINCOLN.——LINCOLN AND
STUART.——LINCOLN AS A PRIVATE SOLDIER.——A MEETING OF NOTABLE
MEN.——WRESTLING-MATCHES IN CAMP.——LINCOLN'S MILITARY RECORD.
——NOMINATED FOR THE LEGISLATURE.——TRIES STUMP SPEAKING.——
QUEER EXPERIENCES.——LINCOLN AS A MERCHANT.——THE DEBATING CLUB.
——POSTMASTER AT NEW SALEM.——"ANYTHING HERE FOR ME?"——LIN-
COLN'S WAY OF KEEPING TRUST FUNDS.

THE spring of 1832 brought a new turn in Lincoln's career. Mr. Offutt's trading enterprises ended disastrously.
"The store was shut up, the mill was closed, and Lincoln
was out of business. The year had been one of great advances in many respects. He had made new and valuable
acquaintances, read many books, mastered the grammar of
his own tongue, won multitudes of friends, and become ready
for a step still further in advance. Those who could appreciate brains respected him, and those whose highest ideas of a
man related to his muscles were devoted to him. Every one
trusted him. He was judge, arbitrator, referee, umpire
authority in all disputes, games, and matches of man-flesh
and horse-flesh; a pacificator in all quarrels; everybody's
friend; the best natured, the most sensible, the best informed,
the most modest and unassuming, the kindest, gentlest, roughest, strongest, best young fellow in all New Salem and the
region round about."

THE BLACK HAWK WAR.

At the moment when Lincoln found himself adrift once
more, Illinois was filled with excitement over the Black
Hawk war. The center of alarm was in the Rock River
Valley, in the northern part of the State, which had formerly
been the home of the Sac tribe of Indians. Discontented

with their life on the reservation west of the Mississippi, to which they had been removed, the Sacs, with several other tribes, resolved to recover their old hunting-grounds. The warlike chief, Black Hawk, was at the head of the revolt, and his march toward the Rock river was signalized by a number of massacres. Governor Reynolds, of Illinois, issued a proclamation calling for volunteers to aid the regular troops in the emergency. Lincoln was one of the first to answer the call, the brave "Clary Grove boys" also coming promptly to the rescue. "The volunteers gathered," writes Mr. Arnold, "at Rushville, in Schuyler county, at which place they were to be organized, and elected officers. Lincoln was a candidate for the place of captain, and in opposition to him was one William Kirkpatrick. The mode of election was novel. By agreement, each candidate walked off to some distance, and took position by himself; the men were then to form, and those who voted for Kirkpatrick to range on a line with their candidate. When the lines were formed, Lincoln's was three times as long as that of Kirkpatrick, and so Lincoln was declared elected. Speaking of this affair when President, he said that he was more gratified with this his first success than with any other election of his life. Neither Lincoln nor his company was in any engagement during the campaign, but there was plenty of hardships and fatigue, and some incidents occurred to illustrate his courage and power over men."

SCENE IN THE BLACK HAWK WAR, AS PICTURED BY MR. LINCOLN.

Many years afterward,—in fact, while Lincoln was President,—he referred to those early scenes in a way that illustrates his wonderful memory and his power of recalling the minutest incidents of his past life. Meeting an old Illinois friend, he naturally fell to talking of Illinois, and related several stories of his early life in that region. Particularly, he remembered his share in the Black Hawk war, in which he was a captain.

He referred to his part of the campaign lightly, and said that he saw but very little fighting. But he remembered coming on a camp of white scouts one morning just as the sun was rising. The Indians had surprised the camp, and had killed and scalped every man. "I remember just how those men looked," said Lincoln, "as we rode up the little hill where their camp was. The red light of the morning sun was streaming upon them as they lay, heads toward us, on the ground, and every man had a round red spot on the top of his head, about as big as a dollar, where the redskins had taken his scalp. It was frightful, but it was grotesque, and the red sunlight seemed to paint everything all over." Lincoln paused, as if recalling the vivid picture, and added, somewhat irrelevantly, "I remember that one man had buckskin breeches on."

A REMARKABLE MILITARY MANŒUVRE.—GETTING A COMPANY THROUGH A GATE.

Mr. Lincoln also told a good story of his first experience in drilling raw troops during the Black Hawk war. He was crossing a field with a front of twenty men, when he came to a gate through which it was necessary to pass. In describing the incident, he said: "I could not, for the life of me, remember the proper word of command for getting my company *endwise*, so that it could pass through the gate; so, as we came near the gate, I shouted, 'Halt! this company is dismissed for two minutes, when it will fall in again on the other side of the gate.'" The manœuvre was successfully executed.

LINCOLN PROTECTING AN INDIAN.

During this campaign, an incident occurred which well serves to show Lincoln's keen sense of justice, his great common sense, and his resoluteness when aroused. One day there came to the camp an old Indian, footsore and hungry. He was provided with a letter of safe-conduct from General Cass; but there was a feeling of great irritation against the Indians,

SCENE IN THE BLACK HAWK WAR.—CAPTAIN LINCOLN PROTECTING AN
INDIAN CAPTIVE.

and the men objected strongly to receiving him. They pronounced him a spy and his passport a forgery, and were rushing upon the defenseless Indian to kill him, when the tall figure of their captain, Lincoln, suddenly appeared between them and their victim. His men had never seen him so aroused, and they cowed before him. "Men," said he, "this must not be done! He must not be killed by us!" His voice and manner produced an effect on the mob; they paused, listened, and fell back, then sullenly obeyed him, although there were still some murmurs of disappointed rage. At length one man, probably thinking he spoke for the crowd, cried out: "This is cowardly on your part, Lincoln!" Lincoln only gazed with lofty contempt on the men who would have murdered one unarmed Indian, but who quailed before his single hand. "If any man thinks I am a coward," said he, "let him test it." "Lincoln," was the reply, "you are larger and heavier than any of us." "That you can guard against," responded the captain. "Choose your weapons!" The insubordination ended, and the word "coward" was never associated with Lincoln's name again. He afterward said that at this time he felt that his life and character were both at stake, and would probably have been lost had he not at the supreme moment forgotten the officer and asserted the man. His men could hardly have been called soldiers; they were merely armed citizens, with a military organization in name only. Had he ordered them under arrest he would have created a serious mutiny; and to have tried and punished them would have been impossible.

THE POET BRYANT MEETS CAPTAIN LINCOLN.

William Cullen Bryant, the distinguished American poet, made a journey to Illinois in 1832, to visit his brothers—one of whom, Mr. John H. Bryant, is still living (1886) at Princeton, Illinois. While crossing the prairies the poet encountered a company of raw Illinois volunteers, who were going forward to take part in the Black Hawk Indian war. "They were led by a tall, awkward, uncouth lad, whose appearance particularly attracted Mr. Bryant's attention, and whose conversation delighted him by its raciness and originality, garnished as it probably was by not a few rough frontier jokes. He learned, many years afterward, from a person who had been one of the troop, that this captain of theirs was named Abraham Lincoln.''

LINCOLN AND STUART.

It was while Lincoln was a captain that he met for the

MAJOR JOHN T. STUART.

first time Major John T. Stuart, afterwards his law-partner, a gentleman who was destined to have an important influence upon his life. Stuart was already a lawyer by profession, and commanded one of the Sangamon county companies. He was soon afterwards elected major of a spy battalion, formed from some of these companies. He had the best opportunities to observe the merits of Captain Lincoln, and testifies that Lincoln was exceedingly popular among the soldiers, in consequence of his excellent care of the men in his command, his never-failing good nature, and his ability to tell more stories and better ones than any man in the service. He was popular also among these hardy men on account of his great physical strength. For several years after the Black Hawk war, Mr. Lincoln retained his military title, and was usually addressed as "Captain Lincoln." But this in time was discontinued. Stuart's title of "Major," on the contrary, adhered to him through life; he was best known as "Major Stuart" down to the time of his death, which occurred early in the winter of 1886.

LINCOLN AS A PRIVATE SOLDIER.

The time for which Captain Lincoln's company enlisted soon ran by, but, the trouble with the Indians not being ended, Governor Reynolds called for a second body of volunteers. Lincoln again responded, and was enrolled as a private in the independent company commanded by Elijah Iles of Springfield. A note of this occurrence, made in 1868, by Captain Iles, contains the following statement: "The term of Governor Reynolds' first call being about to expire, he made a second call, and the first was disbanded. I was elected a captain of one of the companies. I had as members of my company, General James D. Henry, John T. Stuart, and A. Lincoln, and we were mustered into service on the 29th of May, 1832, at the mouth of Fox river, now Ottawa, by Lieutenant Robert Anderson, Assistant Inspector General in the United States Army. We reported to Colonel Zachary Taylor, at Dixon's Ferry (on Rock river). Mr. Lincoln remained with the company to the close of the war."

A MEETING OF NOTABLE MEN.

While Mr. Lincoln was a member of Captain Iles' company, there met one day, in camp on Rock river, near the site of Dixon, Lieutenant Colonel Zachary Taylor, Lieutenant Jefferson Davis, Lieutenant Robert Anderson, and Private Abraham Lincoln.   Lincoln and Anderson did not meet again till some time in 1861, after Major Anderson had evacuated Fort Sumter.   He then visited Washington, and called at the White House to pay his respects to the President.   After having expressed his thanks to Anderson for his conduct in South Carolina, Mr. Lincoln said: "Major, do you remember ever meeting me before?"   "No, Mr. President, I have no recollection of ever having had the pleasure before."   "My memory is better than yours," said Mr. Lincoln.   "You mustered me into the service of the United States, in 1832, at Dixon's Ferry, in the Black Hawk war."

WRESTLING-MATCHES IN CAMP.

Wrestling was an every-day amusement in Illinois in those days, and was a favorite diversion of the soldiers of the Black Hawk war.   Lincoln had, it is said, only one superior in the whole army.   His old friend and military comrade, W. G. Greene, relates that one day, while lying in camp near Rock Island, "the boys got up a wrestling match, and pitted Lincoln against a famous athlete and wrestler by the name of Dow Thompson, from Union county, Illinois.   We Sangamon county boys believed Mr. Lincoln could throw any one, and the Union county boys knew no one could throw Thompson; so we staked all our slick and well-worn quarters and empty bottles on the wrestle.   The first fall was *clearly* in Thompson's favor; the second fall was *rather* in Thompson's favor, but Lincoln's backers claimed that it was what in those days was called a 'dog-fall.'   Thompson's backers claimed the stakes, while we demurred; and it really looked for some time as though there would be at least a hundred fights as the result.   Mr. Lincoln, after getting up and brushing the dust and dirt off his jeans pants, said: 'Boys, give up your bets; if he has not thrown me fairly, he could.'   Every bet was at once surrendered, and peace and order were restored in a minute. During the Rebellion, in 1864, I had occasion to see Mr. Lincoln in his office at Washington, and after having recalled many of our early recollections, he said: 'Bill, what ever became of our old antagonist, Thompson, that big curly-headed fellow who threw me at Rock Island?' I replied I did not know, and wondered why he asked. He playfully remarked that if he knew where he was living he would give him a post-office, by way of showing him that he bore him no ill-will.''

LINCOLN'S MILITARY RECORD.

Mr. Lincoln displayed the same courage and fidelity in performing the duties of a soldier that had marked his conduct in all other relations of life. Father Dixon, the guide, who was attached to Captain Iles' company of mounted rangers, remarks that in their marches, when scouts were sent forward to examine thickets and ravines where the enemy might be lurking, it often became necessary for many of the men to dismount and attend to their riding-gear. When Lincoln was detailed for such service, his "saddle was always in order." During the contest between General Lewis Cass and General Zachary Taylor for the Presidency, in the year 1848, Mr. Lincoln, in the course of a speech in Congress, referred to his services in the Black Hawk war with characteristic humor. "By the way, Mr. Speaker," said he, "did you know I am a military hero? Yes, sir; in the days of the Black Hawk war I fought, bled, and came away. Speaking of General Cass' career reminds me of my own. I was not at Stillman's defeat, but I was about as near it as Cass was to Hull's surrender; and, like him, I saw the place very soon afterwards. It is quite certain I did not break my sword, for I had none to break; but I bent my musket pretty badly on one occasion. If Cass broke his sword, the idea is he broke it in desperation. I bent my musket by accident. If General Cass went in advance of me in picking whortleberries, I guess I surpassed him in charges upon the wild onions. If he saw any live fighting Indians, it was more than I did; but I had a good many bloody struggles with the musquitoes, and, although I never fainted from loss of blood, I can truly say I was often very hungry. Mr. Speaker, if I should ever conclude to doff whatever our Democratic friends may suppose there is of black cockade federalism about me, and thereupon they shall take me up as their candidate for the Presidency, I protest they shall not make fun of me as they have of General Cass, by attempting to write me into a military hero.''

NOMINATED FOR THE LEGISLATURE.—TRIES STUMP SPEAKING.—QUEER EXPERIENCES.

Lincoln's popularity among his comrades in the field was so great that at the close of his military service, which had lasted three months, he was nominated as a candidate for the State Legislature. "His first appearance on the stump, in the course of the canvass, was at Pappsville, about eleven miles west of Springfield, upon the occasion of a public sale. The sale over, speech-making was about to begin, when Mr. Lincoln observed strong symptoms of inattention in his audience, who had taken that particular moment to engage in a general fight. Lincoln saw that one of his friends was suffering more than he liked, and, stepping into the crowd, he shouldered them sternly away from his man, until he met a fellow who refused to fall back; him he seized by the nape of the neck and the seat of his breeches, and tossed him 'ten or twelve feet easily.' After this episode—as characteristic of him as of the times—he mounted the platform, and delivered, with awkward modesty, the following speech: 'Gentlemen and Fellow-Citizens, I presume you all know who I am. I am humble Abraham Lincoln. I have been solicited by my friends to become a candidate for the Legislature. My politics are short and sweet, like the old woman's dance. I am in favor of a national bank. I am in favor of the internal-improvement system and a high protective tariff. These are my sentiments and political principles. If elected, I shall be thankful; if not, it will be all the same.'" His friend, Mr. A. Y. Ellis, who was with him during a part of this campaign, says: "He wore a mixed-jeans coat, claw-hammer style, short in the sleeves, and bobtail—in fact, it was so short in the tail he could not sit on it—flax and tow linen pantaloons, and a straw hat. I think he wore a vest, but do not remember how it looked. He wore pot-metal boots. I accompanied him on one of his electioneering trips to Island Grove; and he made a speech which pleased his party friends very well indeed, though some of the Jackson men tried to make sport of it. He told several anecdotes in his speech, and applied them, as I thought, very well."

The election took place in August; and though Lincoln was defeated, he received 277 votes of the 284 cast in his precincts. He was so little known outside of New Salem that the chances of election were hopelessly against him, yet the extraordinary evidence of favor shown by the vote of his fellow-townsmen was a flattering success in the midst of defeat. It is perhaps to the history of this election that the following anecdote, told by Mr. Ellis, belongs: "I remember once seeing Mr. Lincoln out of temper and laughing at the same time. It was at New Salem. The boys were having a jollification after an election. They had a large fire made of shavings and hempstalks; and some of the boys made a bet with a fellow that I shall call 'Ike' that he couldn't run his little bob-tail pony through the fire. Ike took the bet, and trotted his pony back about one hundred yards to 'give him a good start,' as he said. The boys all formed a line on either side to make way for Ike and his pony. Presently Ike came, full tilt, with his hat off; and just as he reached the blazing fire, Ike raised in his saddle for the jump straight ahead; but the pony was not of the same mind, so he flew the track, and pitched poor Ike into the devouring element. Mr. Lincoln saw it, and ran to his assistance, saying: 'You have carried this thing far enough!' I could see he was mad, though he could not help laughing himself. The poor fellow was considerably scorched about the head and face. Jack Armstrong took him to the doctor, who shaved his head to fix him up, and put salve on the burn. I think Mr. Lincoln was a little mad at Armstrong, and Jack himself was very sorry for it. Jack gave Ike next morning a dram, his breakfast. and a seal-skin cap, and sent him home."

LINCOLN AS A MERCHANT.

Lincoln was once more without occupation, and, as Dr. Holland declares, "seriously took into consideration the project of learning the blacksmith's trade. He was without means, and felt the immediate necessity of undertaking some business that would give him bread. It was while he was entertaining this project that an event occurred, which, in his undetermined state of mind, seemed to open a way to success in another quarter." The particulars of the event referred to are given by one closely concerned therein, Mr. W. G. Greene. "A man named Reuben Radford," says Mr. Greene, "was the keeper of a small store in the village of New Salem. A friend told him to look out for the 'Clary Grove boys,' or they would smash him up. He said he was not afraid. He was a great big fellow. But his friend said, 'They don't come alone. If one can't whip you, two or three can, and they'll do it.' One day he left his store in charge of his brother, with injunctions that if the 'Clary Grove boys' came, not to let them have more than two drinks. All the stores in those days kept liquor to sell, and had a corner for drinking. The store was nicely fitted up, and had many things in glass jars nicely labeled. The Clary Grove boys came, and took two drinks. The clerk refused them any more, as politely as he could. Then they went behind the counter and helped themselves. They got roaring drunk, and went to work smashing everything in the store. The fragments on the floor were an inch deep. They left, and went off on their horses, whooping and yelling. Coming across the herds of cattle, they took off the bells from their necks and fastened them to the tails of the leaders and chased them over the country yelling like mad. Radford heard them, and, mounting, rode in hot haste to the store. "I had been sent that morning with a grist to Lincoln's mill. It was at the dam, and I had to pass the store. I saw Radford ride up. His horse was in a lather of foam. He dismounted, and looked in on the wreck through the open door. He was aghast at the spectacle, and said, 'I'll sell out this thing to the next man that comes along!' I rode up, and looking through the window that had been smashed, said: 'I'll give you four hundred dollars for it.' 'Done!' said he. I said, 'But I have no money. I must have time.' 'How much?' 'Six months.' 'Agreed.' He drew up a note for $400 at six months, and I signed it. I began to think I was stuck. The boys came in, among them Lincoln. 'Cheer up, Billy,' said he. 'It's a good thing. We'll take an inventory.' 'No more inventories for me,' said I, not knowing what he meant. He explained that we should take an account of stock to see what was left. We found it amounted to about $1,200. Lincoln and Berry consulted over it, and offered me $250 for my bargain. I accepted, stipulating that they should assume my notes. Berry was a wild fellow, a gambler. He had a fine horse and splendid saddle and bridle. He turned over the horse as part pay. Lincoln let Berry run the store, and it soon ran out. I had to pay the note. Lincoln said he would pay it some day. We used to talk about it as the 'National debt.' Finally he paid it, with interest."

THE DEBATING CLUB.

Mr. Lincoln's ambition to fit himself for public speaking has been demonstrated in a number of anecdotes in the preceding narrative. Even at this early date the settlers in New Salem were infected with the national desire to take part in the general march of intellectual improvements, and to aid in their object they had established a club entitled the New

Salem Literary Society. Before this association the studious Lincoln was invited to speak. Mr. R. B. Rutledge, the brother of Anne Rutledge, says of the event: "About the year 1832 or 1833, Mr. Lincoln made his first effort at public speaking. A debating club, of which James Rutledge was president, was organized, and held regular meetings. As Lincoln arose to speak, his tall form towered above the little assembly. Both hands were thrust down deep in the pockets of his pantaloons. A perceptible smile at once lit up the faces of the audience, for all anticipated the relation of some humorous story. But he opened up the discussion in splendid style, to the infinite astonishment of his friends. As he warmed with his subject, his hands would forsake his pockets and would enforce his ideas by awkward gestures, but would very soon seek their easy resting-places. He pursued the question with reason and argument so pithy and forcible that all were amazed. The president, after the meeting, remarked to his wife that there was more in Abe's head than wit and fun; that he was already a fine speaker; that all he lacked was culture to enable him to reach the high destiny which he knew was in store for him."

POSTMASTER AT NEW SALEM.

On the 7th of May, 1833, Mr. Lincoln was appointed postmaster at New Salem by President Jackson. The duties of the position were light, there being only a weekly mail, and the remuneration was correspondingly small. "The office was too insignificant to be considered politically, and it was given to the young man because everybody liked him, and because he was the only man willing to take it who could make out the returns. He was exceedingly pleased with the appointment, because it gave him a chance to read every newspaper that was taken in the vicinity. He had never been able to get half the newspapers he wanted, and the office gave him the prospect of a constant feast. Not wishing to be tied to the office, as it yielded him no revenue that would reward him for the confinement, he made a post-office of his hat. Whenever he went out, the letters were placed in his hat. When an anxious looker for a letter found the post-master, he had found his office; and the public officer, taking off his hat, looked over his mail wherever the public might find him. He kept the office until it was discontinued, or removed to Petersburg."

"ANYTHING HERE FOR ME?"

The incumbent of every public office is subject to annoy-ances, as Mr. Lincoln learned while dealing out letters to the few correspondents dwelling at New Salem. An anecdote in illustration is furnished by Mr. Hill: "One Elmore Johnson, an ignorant but ostentatious, proud man, used to go to Lin-coln's post-office every day—sometimes three or four times a day, if in town—and inquire: 'Anything here for me?' This bored Lincoln, yet it amused him. Lincoln fixed a plan— wrote a letter to Johnson as coming from a negress in Ken-tucky, saying many funny things about opossums, dances, corn-shuckings, etc.: 'John's! come and see me; and old master won't kick you out of the kitchen any more!' Elmore took the letter; opened it; couldn't read a word; pretended to read it; went away; got some friends to read it; they read it correctly; he thought the reader was fooling him, and went to others with the same result. At last he said he would get Lincoln to read it, and presented it to Lincoln. It was almost too much for Lincoln, but he read it. The man never asked afterwards, 'Anything here for me?'"

LINCOLN'S WAY OF KEEPING TRUST FUNDS.

A balance due the government remained in the hands of Mr. Lincoln at the discontinuance of the office. Time passed on, and he had removed to Springfield and was practicing law, having his place of business in Dr. Henry's office. Mean-while his struggle with poverty was unabated, and he had often been obliged to borrow money from his friends to purchase the barest necessities.   It was at this juncture that the agent of the United States called for a settlement of his post-office accounts. The interview took place in the presence of Dr. Henry, who thus describes it: "I did not believe he had the money on hand to meet the draft, and I was about to call him aside and loan him the money, when he asked the agent to be seated a moment, while he went over to his trunk at his boarding-house, and returned with an old blue sock with a quantity of silver and copper coin tied up in it.   Untying the sock, he poured the contents on the table and proceeded to count the coin, which consisted of such silver and copper pieces as the country people were then in the habit of using in paying postage.   On counting it up, there was found the exact amount of the draft to a cent, and in the identical coin which had been received.   He never used, under any circumstances, trust funds."

CHAPTER VI.

LINCOLN STUDIES LAW. ——LAWYER, SURVEYOR, AND STOREKEEPER.——FISHING
AND QUOTING POETRY.——ELECTED TO THE LEGISLATURE.——BEGINNING
SLOWLY AS A LEGISLATOR.——PERSONAL CHARACTERISTICS AT THIS PERIOD.
——THE ROMANCE OF LINCOLN'S LIFE.——ANNE RUTLEDGE.——THE CLOSE
OF YOUTH.——NEW SALEM REVISITED.——A DESERTED VILLAGE.

Mr. Lincoln began studying law sometime in 1832, using
an old copy of "Blackstone's Commentaries" which he had
bought at auction in Springfield. This book was soon mastered, and then the young man looked about him for more.
His friend, John T. Stuart, had a considerable law library for
those days, and to him Lincoln applied in his extremity. The
library was placed at his disposal, and thenceforth he was engrossed in the acquisition of its contents. But the books were
in Springfield, where their owner resided; and New Salem
was some fourteen miles distant. This proved no obstacle in
the way of Lincoln, who made nothing of the walk back and
forth in the pursuit of his purpose. Mr. Stuart's partner, Mr.
H. C. Dummer, took note of the youth in his frequent visits
to the office, and declares: "He was an uncouth looking lad;
did not say much, but what he did say he said straight and
sharp." "He used to read law," says Henry McHenry, "in
1832 or 1833, barefooted, seated in the shade of a tree, and
would grind around with the shade, just opposite Berry's grocery store, and a few feet south of the door. He occasionally
varied the attitude by lying flat on his back, and putting his
feet up the tree," a situation which might have been unfavorable to mental application in the case of a man with shorter
extremities. "The first time I ever saw Abe with a law-book
in his hand," says Squire Godbey, "he was sitting astride Jake
Bates' woodpile in New Salem. Says I, 'Abe, what are you
studying?' 'Law,' says Abe. 'Good God Almighty!' responded I." It was too much for Godbey; he could not sup-

"WHAT ARE YOU STUDYING, ABE?"   "LAW."   "GOOD GOD ALMIGHTY!"

press the exclamation of surprise at seeing such a figure acquiring learning in such an odd situation. Mr. Arnold states that Lincoln made a practice of reading in his walks between Springfield and New Salem; and so intense was his application, and so absorbed was he in his study, that he would pass his best friends without observing them, and some people said that Lincoln was going crazy with hard study. He very soon began to make a practical application of his knowledge. He bought an old form-book, and began to draw up contracts, deeds, leases, mortgages, and all sorts of legal instruments for his neighbors. He also began to exercise his forensic ability in trying small cases before justices of the peace and juries, and he soon acquired a local reputation as a speaker, which gave him considerable practice. But he was able in this way to earn scarcely money enough for his maintenance.

LAWYER, SURVEYOR, AND STOREKEEPER.

To add to his means, he again took up the study of surveying, and soon became, like Washington, a skillful and accurate surveyor. John Calhoun, an intelligent and courteous gentleman, was at that time surveyor of the county of Sangamon. He became interested in Lincoln, and appointed him his deputy. His work was so accurate, and the settlers had such confidence in him, that he was much sought after, to survey, fix, and mark the boundaries of farms, and to plot and lay off the town of Petersburg. His accuracy must have been attained with some difficulty; for the old settlers who survive say that when he began to survey, his chain was a grape-vine. He did not speculate in the land he surveyed. Had he done so, the rapid advance in the value of real estate would have made it easy for him to make good investments. But he was not in the least like one of his appointees when President—a surveyor-general of a western territory, who bought up much of the best land, and to whom the President said: "I am told, sir, you are *monarch of all you survey.*"

An old friend of Mr. Lincoln, Mr. Ellis, says of this period (1833): "I kept a store at New Salem, and boarded at the same log-tavern where Lincoln was. Lincoln, being engaged in no particular business, merely endeavoring to make a lawyer, a surveyor, and a politician of himself, used to assist me in the store on busy days; but he always disliked to wait on the ladies; he preferred trading with the men and boys, as he used to say. I also remember that he used to sleep on the counter, when they had too much company at the tavern. I well remember how he was dressed; he wore flax and tow linen pantaloons—I thought about five inches too short in the legs,—and frequently he had but one suspender; no vest or coat. He wore a calico shirt, such as he had in the Black Hawk war; coarse brogans, tan color; blue yarn socks, and straw hat, without a band. Mr. Lincoln was in those days very shy of ladies. On one occasion, while we boarded at this tavern, there came a family, containing an old lady and her son and three stylish daughters, from the State of Virginia, and stopped there for two or three weeks; and during their stay I do not remember Mr. Lincoln eating once at the same table where they did."

FISHING AND QUOTING POETRY.

"There lived at New Salem at this time," continues Mr. Ellis, "a festive gentleman named Kelso, a school-teacher, a merchant, or a vagabond, according to the run of his somewhat variable luck. When other people got drunk at New Salem, it was the usual custom to tussle and fight, and trample each other's toes, and pull each other's noses; but when Kelso got drunk he astonished the rustic community with copious quotations from Robert Burns and William Shakespeare—authors but little known to fame among the literary men of New Salem. Besides Shakespeare and Burns, Mr. Kelso was likewise very fond of fishing, and could catch his game 'when no other man could get a bite.' Mr. Lincoln hated fishing with all his heart. But it is the testimony of the country-side, from Petersburg to Island Grove, that Kelso 'drew Lincoln after him by his talk;' that they became exceedingly intimate; that they loitered away whole days together along the banks of the quiet streams; that Lincoln learned to love inordinately our 'divine William' and 'Scotia's Bard,' whom his friend mouthed in his cups, or expounded more soberly in his intervals of fixing bait and dropping line. Finally, he and Kelso boarded at the same place; and with another 'merchant,' named Sincho, of tastes congenial and wits as keen as Kelso's, they were 'always found together, battling and arguing.'"

ELECTED TO THE LEGISLATURE.

The nomination of Abraham Lincoln for the State Legislature, on his return from the Black Hawk war, was premature. The people of New Salem had voted for him almost to a man; but his acquaintance had not then extended far enough into the district round about to insure his election. In the campaign of 1834 the choice of a candidate fell again upon him, and this time there was a favorable prospect of success. Mr. Lincoln entered into the contest with intense earnestness, using every legitimate means to secure victory. Mr. Herndon relates in his reminiscences: "He (Lincoln) came to my house, near Island Grove, during harvest. There were some thirty men in the field. He got his dinner, and went out in the field where the men were at work. I gave him an introduction, and the boys said they could not vote for a man unless he could 'make a hand.' 'Well, boys,' said he, if that is all, I am sure of your votes.' He took hold of the cradle, and led the way all the round, with perfect ease. The boys were satisfied, and I don't think he lost a vote in the crowd. The next day there was speaking at Berlin. He went from my house with Dr. Barnett, the man that had asked me who this man Lincoln was. I told him that he was a candidate for the Legislature. He laughed, and said, 'Can't the party raise better material than that?' I said, 'Go, to-morrow, and hear all, before you pronounce judgment.' When he came back, I said: 'Doctor, what say you now?' 'Why, sir,' said he, 'he is a perfect *take-in*; he knows more than all of them put together.' "

BEGINNING SLOWLY AS A LEGISLATOR.

The result of the election was that Mr. Lincoln was chosen to represent the Sangamon district. When the Legislature convened at the opening session, he was in his place in the lower house; but he bore himself quietly in his new position. He had much to learn in his novel situation as one of the law-makers of the State, and as a co-worker with an assembly comprising the most talented and prominent men gathered from all parts of Illinois. He was keenly watchful of the pro-ceedings of the house, weighing every measure, as we may be-lieve, with scrutinizing sagacity, but, except in the announce-ment of his vote, his voice was seldom heard. At the pre-vious session, Mr. G. S. Hubbard, afterwards a well-known citizen of Chicago, had exerted himself to procure an act for the construction of the Illinois and Michigan Canal. His ef-fort was defeated, but he continued, as a lobbyist, to push the measure during several winters, until it was finally adopted. Mr. Lincoln lent him efficient aid in the accomplishment of his object. "Indeed," remarks Mr. Hubbard, "I very much doubt if the bill could have passed as easily as it did without his valuable help."

PERSONAL CHARACTERISTICS AT THIS PERIOD.

"We were thrown much together," continues Mr. Hub-bard, "our intimacy increasing. I never had a friend to whom I was more warmly attached. His character was al-most faultless. Possessing a warm and generous heart, genial, affable, honest, courteous to his opponents, persevering, indus-trious in research; never losing sight of the principal point under discussion; aptly illustrating by his stories, always brought into good effect; free from political trickery or denunciation of the private character of his opponents; in debate firm and collected; 'with charity towards all, with malice towards none,' he won the confidence of the public, even of his political opponents.''

General U. F. Linder, a noted lawyer of Illinois, who first met Lincoln at this period, says he impressed him as ''a very modest and retiring man. He had not then been admitted to the bar, although he had some celebrity, having been a captain in the Black Hawk campaign, and had just finished a term in the Illinois Legislature; but he won no special fame at that session. If Lincoln at this time felt the 'divine afflatus' of greatness stir within him, I have never heard of it. It was rather common then to suppose that there was no presidential timber growing in the Northwest; yet we doubtless had at that time the stuff out of which to make half a dozen Presidents.''

THE ROMANCE OF LINCOLN'S LIFE.—HIS LOVE FOR ANNE RUTLEDGE.

Among the reminiscences of Lincoln's boyhood and youth, there is no hint of tender relations with any individual of the opposite sex, until he met Anne Rutledge. The romance which connects her name with his had a brief existence, but it is believed by many that its memory threw a melancholy shadow over his whole life. The father of Anne, James Rutledge, was a descendant of the eminent Rutledge family of North Carolina. His daughter Anne was about nineteen years old when Lincoln was thrown into her company, shortly after the episode of the Black Hawk war. She is described by those who knew her as ''a winsome maiden, with a blonde complexion, golden hair, cherry-red lips, and a bonny blue eye.'' The heart of Lincoln was captivated by her sweet looks and gentle manners, and though she had other admirers —one, indeed, to whom, if the story be true, she had plighted her girlish affections—she accepted the love of this last ardent suitor. They were betrothed, and the marriage was to take place as soon as Lincoln should finish his law studies. But in August, 1835, the grass was growing over the mound where she lay buried. An old neighbor who saw Lincoln immediately after his parting interview with the dying girl, says there were "signs of the most terrible distress in his face and conduct." After Anne's death "his grief became frantic; he lost all self-control, even the consciousness of identity, and every friend he had in New Salem pronounced him insane, mad, crazy. 'He was watched with especial vigilance,' as William Greene tells us, 'during storms, fogs, damp, gloomy weather, for fear of an accident.' At such times he raved piteously, declaring, among other wild expressions of his woe, 'I can never be reconciled to have the snow, rains, and storms beating upon her grave!' About three-quarters of a mile below New Salem, at the foot of the main bluff, and in a hollow between two lateral bluffs, stood the house of Bowlin Greene, built of logs and weather-boarded. Thither the friends of Lincoln, who feared a total loss of reason, determined to transport him, partly for the benefit of a mere change of scene, and partly to keep him within constant reach of his near and noble friend, Bowlin Greene. During this period of his darkened and wavering intellect, when 'accidents' were momentarily expected, it was discovered that Bowlin Greene possessed a power to persuade and guide him proportioned to the affection that had subsisted between them in former and better times. Bowlin Greene came for him, but Lincoln was cunning and obstinate; it required the most artful practices of a general conspiracy of all his friends to 'disarm his suspicions,' and induce him to go and stay with his most anxious and devoted friend. But at last they succeeded; and Lincoln remained down under the bluff for two or three weeks, the object of undisguised solicitude and of the strictest surveillance. At the end of that time his mind seemed to be restored, and it was thought safe to let him go back to his old haunts,—to the study of law, to the writing of legal papers for his neighbors, to pettifogging before the justice of the peace, and perhaps to a little surveying. But Mr. Lincoln was never precisely the same man again. At the time of his release, he was thin, haggard, and careworn, like one risen from the verge of the grave. He had always been subject to fits of great mental depression, but after this they were more frequent and alarming. It was then that he began to repeat, with a feeling which seemed to inspire every listener with awe, and to carry him to the fresh grave of Anne at every one of his solemn periods, the lines entitled, 'Immortality;' or, 'Why Should the Spirit of Mortal be Proud?' None heard him but knew that he selected these wonderfully impressive lines to celebrate a grief which lay with continual heaviness on his heart, but to which he could not with becoming delicacy directly allude. He muttered them as he rambled through the woods, or walked by the roaring Sangamon. He was heard to murmur them to himself as he slipped into the village at night-fall, after a long walk of six miles, and an evening visit to the Concord graveyard; and he would suddenly break out with them in little social assemblies after noticeable periods of silent gloom. They came unbidden to his lips, while the air of affliction in face and gesture, the moving tones and touching modulations of his voice, made it evident that every syllable of the recitation was meant to commemorate the mournful fate of Anne.''

Nearly thirty years after Anne Rutledge was buried, Mr. Lincoln said, in talking with a boyhood friend: "I have loved the name of Rutledge to this day. * * I loved the woman dearly. She was a handsome girl; would have made a good, loving wife; was natural, quite intellectual, and highly educated. I did honestly and truly love the girl, and think often, often of her now.'' "The love and death of this girl,'' said Mr. Herndon, "shattered Lincoln's purposes and tendencies. He threw off his infinite sorrow only by leaping wildly into the political arena.'' "He needed,'' said another, "whip and spur to save him from despair.''

THE CLOSE OF YOUTH.

The period of Abraham Lincoln's boyhood and youth had closed when he stood by the grave of Anne Rutledge. He had long been a man in stature; he was now a man in years; yet the rough path he had been forced to travel had made his progress toward maturity painfully slow. In spite of his low birth, of his dire poverty, of the rudeness and illiteracy of his associates, of the absence of refinement in his surroundings, of his scanty means of education, of his homely figure and awkward manners, of his coarse fare and shabby dress, he dared to believe there was an exalted career in store for him. He hewed out the foundations for it with indomitable spirit. It was to be grounded on manly virtues. It seems as though the boy felt the consecration of a high destiny from the very dawn of his intelligence, and it set him apart, secure amid the temptations and safe from the vices that corrupt many men. In the rough garb of the backwoodsman he preserved the instincts of a gentleman. He was the companion of bullies and boors; he shared their work and their sports; but he never stooped to their vulgarity; he very seldom drank with them, and they never heard him speak an oath. He could throw the stoutest in a wrestling match; and was ready, when brought to it, to whip any insolent braggart who made a cruel use of his strength. He never flinched from hardship or danger, yet his heart was as soft and tender as a woman's. The great gentle giant had a feeling of sympathy for every living creature. He was not ashamed to rock a cradle, or carry a pail of water or an armful of wood to spare a tired woman's arms. Though destitute of worldly goods, he was rich in friends. All the people of his acquaintance knew they could count on his doing the right thing so far as he was able every time. Hence they trusted and loved him; and the title of "Honest Abe," which he bore through life, was a seal of knighthood rarer and prouder than any king or queen could confer with the sword. Abraham Lincoln was one of nature's noblemen. He showed himself a hero in every circumstance of his boyhood and youth. The elements of greatness were visible even then. The boy who was true to duty, patient in privation, modest in merit, kind to every form of distress, determined to rise by wresting opportunities from the grudging hand of fate, was sure to make a man distinguished among his fellows ; a man noted among great men in the world, as the boy had been among his neighbors in the wilds of Spencer county and New Salem.

NEW SALEM RE-VISITED.—A DESERTED VILLAGE.

The site of the town where Lincoln spent the last three years of the period delineated in this portion of his biography, is now a desolate waste. A gentleman who visited the spot during the summer of 1885, thus describes the mournful scene : "From the hill where I sit under the shade of three trees whose branches make one, I look out over the Sangamon river and its banks covered apparently with primeval forests. Around are fields overgrown with weeds and stunted oaks. It was a town of ten or twelve years only ; it began in 1824, and ended in 1836. Yet in that time it had a history which the world will not let die ; not so long as it venerates the memory of the noble liberator and martyr President, Abraham Lincoln. I came here with a few of the old settlers. We drove up from Petersburg about two miles, passing on the way the site of the old mill run by Lincoln, and the remains of the old dam at Sangamon Falls, on which his flatboat lodged when floating down from Sangamon town on the way to New Orleans. After much debate as to the mode of reaching the old site, we entered an old field through a gate, and driving up a hill showing a wheel-track through tall weeds, we rode over the streets of the old town. The weeds were high as the horses' backs. Judge Tice, one of our party, stood up in his buggy, and surveying the landscape, pointed out a number of old familiar places. There was Cameron's boarding house, where Lincoln boarded when he kept store for

Ruins of Salem Hotel Lincoln's Boarding House

Sangamon Falls

Grocery sold by W.G. Greene to Abe Lincoln Salem. Ill.

SCENES ABOUT NEW SALEM, ILLINOIS.—LINCOLN'S BOARDING PLACE,
GROCERY, AND MILL.

Denton Offutt. Near it was George Warburton's store. Beyond was Sam Hill's. Over there to the south was the Baptist church, and the cemetery alongside. Mr. Greene pointed out the site of Mr. Rutledge's house. 'There,' said he, 'Anne Rutledge lived. Lincoln was engaged to her. Her death almost broke his heart. He told me once that he didn't want to live.' He 'couldn't bear the thought that the rain was falling on her grave and she sleeping in the cold ground.' We had to watch him to keep him from harming himself. Right here was Denton Offutt's store, where Lincoln and I were clerks together.' Mr. Greene had not been here for forty years, yet recognized the spot. A small depression showed a former cellar. Out of it grew three trees about fifty feet high, with boughs interlaced, making one in their outline. There was the locust thorn, with leaves like a fine fringe, an elm, and a cotton-wood. The elm and cotton-wood grew out of the same stump, as if forming one tree. The dark leaves of the elm and bright broad leaves of the sycamore were intermingled, as from one trunk. At one time there were three stores here, and a church, serving as a school-house. Now all is desolate. Petersburg, started by George Warburton and Peter Sukins, took the wind out of its sails. Then all disappeared, and only a few holes are left to show where the houses and stores once were. A scheme is on foot to revive the memory of Old Salem, and have a park laid out embracing the old site. It would be an attraction to tourists, and to those who wish to see from what humble beginnings and under what circumstances greatness could spring."

LINCOLN AT THE AGE OF FIFTY.

From an original photograph in possession of Hon. E. M. Haines.
(See note on opposite page.)

134

PART II.

LINCOLN as LAWYER and POLITICIAN.

CHAPTER I.

BEGINNING A NEW CAREER.——POLITICAL EXPERIENCES.——LINCOLN AND THE LIGHTNING-ROD MAN.——ABE AS AN ARISTOCRAT.——REPLY TO DR. EARLY. ——A MANLY LETTER.——THE "LONG NINE."——LINCOLN ON HIS WAY TO THE CAPITAL.——LINCOLN'S AMBITION IN 1836.——FIRST MEETING WITH DOUGLAS.——REMOVAL OF THE ILLINOIS CAPITAL.——TWO UGLY MEN.—— "FOOTING IT" HOME.——ONE OF LINCOLN'S EARLY SPEECHES.——PRO-SLAVERY SENTIMENT IN ILLINOIS——CONTEST WITH GENERAL EWING.—— LINCOLN LAYS OUT A TOWN.——THE TITLE "HONEST ABE."

ABRAHAM LINCOLN'S career as a lawyer covered a period of a quarter of a century, beginning about 1834 or '35, and ending with his election to the Presidency, in November, 1860. When he began his professional life he was an obscure and unpromising youth of twenty-five, with but little learning and fewer accomplishments, and without the advantages of social influence or wealthy friends. Step by step, with patient industry and unflinching determination, he climbed the ladder of professional advancement, until he stood among the foremost

The admirable portrait of Lincoln on the opposite page is from a negative made in October, 1859, by S. M. Fassett, of Chicago. A letter to Mr. Fassett from the late D. B. Cooke, of Chicago, written just after Mr. Lincoln's death, in 1865, says: "S. M. FASSETT, ESQ., *Dear Sir:*—Little thought we in October, 1859, when, at my solicitation, Abraham Lincoln visited with me your gallery, for the purpose of sitting for his photograph, what a value five years would give to the picture! Mrs. Lincoln pronounced this the best likeness she had ever seen of her husband. It shows him as he was, previous to his first nomination, and just as his old friends remember him. Consequently no recent picture can be so valuable to many; and the public ought to be truly grateful that you have preserved the negative with such care. There are so many caricatures of Mr. Lincoln in circulation that a reliable portrait is invaluable, and should adorn every house in the land."

135

lawyers of the West. He had, indeed, won a national reputation; and when he laid aside his law books, a mature man
of fifty, it was to enter upon the great honors and responsibilities of the Presidency of the American Republic.

POLITICAL EXPERIENCES.

Mr. Lincoln was devoted to his profession, and his success
in it was earned by hard and constant application. But his
natural taste for politics led him to take a full share in the
activities of political life. He had already served a term in
the Illinois Legislature (1834-35); and so well satisfied were
his constituents that they renominated him for the succeeding
term. In the canvass which followed he greatly distinguished himself as a stump-speaker; showing, by his tact and
ability, by the skill and ingenuity with which he met his opponents in debate, by his shrewdness in attack and readiness
in retort, how much he had profited by the training of the
previous years.

LINCOLN AND THE LIGHTNING-ROD MAN.

An occasion for the especial display of his oratorical powers occurred early in the campaign, at Springfield, where a
public discussion was to be held between the opposing candidates. An interesting version of this incident is given by Mr.
Arnold: "There lived at this time in the most pretentious
house in Springfield a prominent citizen named George Forquer. He had been long in public life, had been a leading
Whig—the party to which Lincoln belonged—but had lately
gone over to the Democrats, and received from the Democratic administration an appointment to the lucrative post of
Register of the Land Office at Springfield. Upon his handsome new house he had lately placed a lightning-rod, the first
one ever put up in Sangamon county. As Lincoln was riding into town, with his friends, they passed the fine house
of Forquer, and observed the novelty of the lightning-rod,
discussing the manner in which it protected the house from

being struck by lightning. There were seven Whig and seven Democratic candidates for the lower branch of the Legislature, and after several had spoken, it fell to Lincoln to close the discussion. He did it with great ability. Forquer, though not a candidate, then asked to be heard for the Democrats, in reply to Lincoln. He was a good speaker, and well-known throughout the county. His special task that day was to attack and ridicule the young man from Salem. Turning to Lincoln, who stood within a few feet of him, he said: 'This young man must be taken down, and I am truly sorry that the task devolves upon me.' He then proceeded, in a very overbearing way, and with an assumption of great superiority, to attack Lincoln and his speech. Lincoln stood calm, but his flashing eye and pale cheek showed his indignation. As soon as Forquer had closed, he took the stand, and first answered his opponent's arguments fully and triumphantly. So impressive were his words and manner that a hearer believes that he can remember to this day, and repeat, some of the expressions. Among other things, he said: 'The gentleman commenced his speech by saying that this *young* man —alluding to me—must be taken down. I am not so young in years as I am in the tricks and trades of a politician; but,' said he, pointing to Forquer, 'live long or die young, I would rather die now, than, like the gentleman, change my politics for a three thousand dollar office, and then feel obliged to erect a lightning-rod over my house to protect a guilty conscience from the vengeance of an offended God!'

"It is difficult to-day," says Mr. Arnold, "to appreciate the effect on the old settlers, of this figure. This lightning-rod was the first which most of those present had ever seen. They had slept all their lives in their cabins in conscious security. Here was a man who seemed, to these simple-minded people, to be afraid to sleep in his own house without special and extraordinary protection from Almighty God. These old settlers thought nothing but the consciousness of guilt, the stings of a guilty conscience, could account for such timidity. Forquer and his lightning-rod were talked over in every settlement from Sangamon to the Illinois and the Wabash. Whenever he rose to speak thereafter, they said: 'There is the man who dare not sleep in his own house without a lightning-rod to keep off the vengeance of the Almighty.'"

ABE AS AN ARISTOCRAT.

A most amusing incident of the same campaign, and one which illustrates Lincoln's love of a practical joke, is as follows: "Among the Democrats stumping the county at this time was one Dick Taylor, a most pompous person, who was always arrayed in the richest attire—ruffled shirts, seals, etc., besides a rich and embroidered vest. Notwithstanding this, he made great pretentions of being one of the 'hard-handed yeomanry,' and ridiculed with much sarcasm the 'rag barons' and 'manufacturing lords' of the Whig party. One day, when he was particularly aggravating in a speech of this kind, Abe decided on a little sport, and, sidling up to Taylor, suddenly threw open the latter's coat, showing to the astonished spectators a glittering mass of ruffled shirt, gold watch, and glittering jewels. The crowd shouted uproariously. Lincoln said: 'While he (Colonel Taylor) was making these charges against the Whigs over the country, riding in fine carriages, wearing ruffled shirts, kid gloves, massive gold watch-chains with large gold seals, and flourishing a heavy gold-headed cane, he (Lincoln) was a poor boy, hired on a flatboat at eight dollars a month, and had only one pair of breeches to his name, and they were buckskin,— and if you know the nature of buckskin, when wet and dried by the sun, it will shrink,—and mine kept shrinking until they left several inches of my legs bare between the tops of my socks and the lower part of my breeches; and, whilst I was growing taller, they were becoming shorter, and so much tighter that they left a blue streak around my legs that can be seen to this day. If you call this aristocracy, I plead guilty to the charge.' "

LINCOLN'S REPLY TO DR. EARLY.

"The Saturday evening preceding the election," says Mr. Lamon, "the candidates were addressing the people in the Court House at Springfield. Dr. Early, one of the candidates on the Democratic side, made some charge, which Mr. N. W. Edwards, one of the candidates on the Whig side, deemed untrue. Edwards climbed on a table, so as to be seen by Early and by every one in the house, and at the top of his voice told Early that the charge was false. The excitement that followed was intense,—so much so, that fighting men thought that a duel must settle the difficulty. Mr. Lincoln, by the programme, followed Early. He took up the subject in dispute, and handled it fairly, and with such ability that every one was astonished and pleased. So that difficulty ended there. Then, for the first time, developed by the excitement of the occasion, he spoke in that tenor intonation of voice that ultimately settled down into that clear, shrill monotone style of speaking that enabled his audience, however large, to hear distinctly the lowest sound of his voice." Mr. Arnold says that Lincoln's reply to Dr. Early was "often spoken of as exhibiting wonderful ability, and a crushing power of sarcasm and ridicule. When he began he was embarrassed, spoke slowly, and with some hesitation and difficulty, but soon becoming warm, and excited by his subject, he forgot himself entirely, and went on with argument and wit, anecdote and ridicule, until his opponent was completely crushed. Old settlers of Sangamon county, who heard this reply, speak of his personal transformation as wonderful. When Lincoln began, they say, he seemed awkward, homely, unprepossessing. As he went on, and became excited, his figure rose to its full height, and became commanding and majestic. His plain face was illuminated and glowed with expression. His dreamy eye flashed with inspiration, and his whole person,

his voice, his gestures, were full of the magnetism of powerful feeling, of conscious strength and true eloquence.''

A MANLY LETTER.

The inflexible honesty and the fine sense of honor which
lay at the foundation of Abraham Lincoln's character, are
nobly exhibited in the following letter, which needs no comment by way of explanation :

"NEW SALEM, June 21, 1836.

"DEAR COLONEL:—I am told that during my absence last week, you
passed through this place, and stated publicly that you were in possession of a fact or facts which, if known to the public, would entirely destroy the prospects of N. W. Edwards and myself at the ensuing
election ; but that, through favor to us, you would forbear to divulge
them. No one has needed favors more than I, and, generally, few have
been less unwilling to accept them ; but in this case favor to me would be
injustice to the public, and therefore I must beg your pardon for declin-
ing it. That I once had the confidence of the people of Sangamon county is
sufficiently evident ; and if I have since done anything, either by design
or misadventure, which, if known, would subject me to a forfeiture of
that confidence, he that knows of that thing and conceals it, is a traitor
to his country's interest.

"I find myself wholly unable to form any conjecture of what fact or
facts, real or supposed, you spoke. But my opinion of your veracity
will not permit me for a moment to doubt that you, at least, believed what
you said. I am flattered with the personal regard you manifested for
me ; but I do hope that on more mature reflection you will view the
public interest as a paramount consideration, and therefore determine to
let the worst come.

"I assure you that the candid statement of facts on your part, however
low it may sink me, shall never break the ties of personal friendship between us.

"I wish an answer to this, and you are at liberty to publish both, if
you choose.   Very respectfully,
  "*Col. Robert Allen.*   A. LINCOLN.''

THE ''LONG NINE.''

Sangamon county sent nine delegates to the Legislature
convened in 1836—two to the Senate and seven to the Lower
House. They happened to be men of remarkable stature,

each one measuring six feet or more in height, and very naturally were nick-named the "Long Nine." Lincoln overtopped all the rest, and as a consequence was called the "Sangamon Chief." Associated with Lincoln in this notable company, were Ninian W. Edwards, a son of Governor Edwards; A. G. Herndon, Robert L. Wilson, Dan Stone, and John Calhoun.

LINCOLN ON HIS WAY TO THE CAPITAL.

Judge J. D. Caton, one of the early lawyers of Illinois, afterwards Chief Justice of the State, and an intimate friend of Lincoln, gives the following interesting account of their first meeting: "I first met Mr. Lincoln about the last of November, 1835, when on my way to Vandalia to join the Supreme Court, which there met the first Monday in December, at the same time as the meeting of the Legislature. There were a great many people and all sorts of vehicles on the road from Springfield to Vandalia. The roads were very bad, and most of the passengers got out and walked a considerable portion of the distance. It seemed almost like the movement of a little army. While walking thus along the side of the road, I met Mr. Lincoln for the first time, and in the course of a two day's journey we became quite well acquainted. If he had been admitted to the bar at that time, he had not become known as a lawyer out of his own immediate circuit. He was going to Vandalia as a member of the Legislature. He was one of the 'Long Nine,' as it was called, from Sangamon county, who, by their successful maneuvering and united efforts, succeeded in getting the seat of government moved from Vandalia to Springfield. During my stay of a few weeks in Vandalia I frequently met Mr. Lincoln. He was a very pleasant companion; but as we walked along the road, on the occasion referred to, talking about indifferent subjects, nothing impressed me with any idea of his future greatness."

LINCOLN'S AMBITION IN 1836.

When Lincoln took his seat in the first session of the new Legislature at Vandalia, he was full of new projects. His real public service was now about to begin, and, having spent his time in the previous Legislature mainly as an observer and listener, he was determined during this session to identify himself conspicuously with the "liberal" legislation, dreaming of a fame far different from that he actually obtained as an anti-slavery leader. As he remarked to his friend Speed, he hoped to obtain the great distinction of being called "the De Witt Clinton of Illinois."

FIRST MEETING WITH DOUGLAS.

It was at a special session of this Legislature that Lincoln first saw Stephen A. Douglas, whom he describes as "the *least* man" he ever saw. Douglas had come into the State, from Vermont, only the previous year; but, having studied law for several months, considered himself eminently qualified to be State's attorney for the district in which he lived, and was now come to Vandalia for that purpose. General Linder says of Lincoln at this time: "I here had an opportunity of measuring the intellectual stature of Abraham Lincoln better than any I had previously possessed. He was then about twenty-seven years old—my own age. Douglas was four years our junior; consequently he could not have been over twenty-three years old. Yet he was a very ready and expert debater, even at that early period of his life. He and Lincoln were very frequently pitted against each other, being of different politics. They both commanded marked attention and respect from the House."

REMOVAL OF THE ILLINOIS CAPITAL.

A notable measure effected by the "Long Nine" during this session of the Legislature was the removal of the State Capital from Vandalia to Springfield. It was accomplished by dint of shrewd and persistent management, in which Mr. Lincoln was a leading spirit. Mr. Wilson says: "When our bill, to all appearance, was dead beyond resuscitation, and our friends could see no hope, Lincoln never for a moment despaired but collecting his colleagues in his room for consultation, his practical common-sense, his thorough knowledge of human nature, made him an overmatch for his compeers, and for any man I have ever known."

TWO UGLY MEN.

A member of the State Legislature of 1836 and 1837 was Mr. Archie Williams, a prominent lawyer, of whom General Linder says: "He was over six feet high, and as angular and ungainly in his form as Mr. Lincoln himself; and for homeliness of face and feature, surpassed Mr. Lincoln. I think I never saw but one man uglier than Archie, and that was Patrick H. Darbey, of Kentucky. * * * Archie Williams sat near Mr. Lincoln in the southeast corner of the old State House in Vandalia, on his left, and I remember one day a friend of mine asking me 'Who in——those two ugly men were.' Archie and Mr. Lincoln were great friends. I recollect Mr. Lincoln asking me on one occassion if I didn't think Archie Williams was one of the strongest-minded and clearest-headed men in Illinois. I don't know what reply I made at the time, but I know Mr. Lincoln said that he thought him the strongest-minded and clearest-headed man he ever saw."

"FOOTING IT" HOME.

It is asserted that Lincoln borrowed two hundred dollars from his friend Coleman Smoot, to pay his travelling expenses at the time of his first attendance at the State Legislature, and that he rode from New Salem to Vandalia and back in the regular stage-coach. Other biographers declare that he walked the hundred miles between the two towns, both going and coming, in 1834 and 1836. A gentleman in Menard county remembers meeting him and a detachment of the "Long Nine" on their way home at the close of the second session.

They were all mounted, he says, except Lincoln, who had thus far kept up with them on foot. If he had money, he was keeping it for more important purposes than that of saving leg-weariness and leather. The weather was raw, and Lincoln's clothing was none of the warmest. Complaining of being cold, one of his companions told the future President that it was no wonder he was cold—"there was so much of him on the ground." None of the party appreciated this homely joke at the expense of his feet more thoroughly than Lincoln himself.

ONE OF LINCOLN'S EARLY SPEECHES.

Mr. Lincoln's reputation as an orator was gradually extending beyond the circle of his friends and constituents. He was gaining notice as a ready and forcible speaker, with shrewd and sensible ideas, which he expressed with striking originality and independence. He was invited to address the Young Men's Lyceum at Springfield, January 27, 1837, and accordingly read before them a carefully prepared paper on "The Perpetuation of Our Political Institutions." The essay gave such satisfaction to the society that a request was made for its publication, and it appeared subsequently in the Springfield Weekly Journal. The address was crude and strained in style, as the discourses of untrained writers when attempting difficult subjects are apt to be; but the feeling pervading it was fervent and honest, and its patriotic sentiment and sage reflection gave promise of the author's future success in efforts of the kind. A few paragraphs culled from this paper, some of them containing remarkable prophetic passages, will indicate the stage of intellectual development which Lincoln had obtained at the age of twenty-seven:

"In the great journal of things happening under the sun, we, the American people, find our account running under date of the nineteenth century of the Christian era. We find ourselves in the peaceful possession of the fairest portion of the earth, as regards extent of territory, fertility of soil, and salubrity of climate. We find ourselves under the government of a system of political institutions conducing more essentially to the ends of civil and religious liberty than any of which the history of former times tells us. We, when mounting the stage of existence, found ourselves the legal inheritors of these fundamental blessings. We toiled not in the acquisition or establishment of them; they are a legacy bequeathed us by a once hardy, brave and patriotic, but now lamented and departed race of ancestors. Theirs was the task (and nobly they performed it) to possess themselves, and, through themselves, us, of this goodly land, and to uprear upon its hills and valleys a political edifice of liberty and equal rights; 'tis ours only to transmit these—the former unprofaned by the foot of an invader, the latter undecayed by the lapse of time and untorn by usurpation—to the latest generation that fate shall permit the world to know. This task, gratitude to our fathers, justice to ourselves, duty to posterity, all imperatively require us faithfully to perform.

"How, then, shall we perform it? At what point shall we expect the approach of danger? Shall we expect some transatlantic military giant to step the ocean and crush us at a blow? Never! All the armies of Europe, Asia and Africa combined, with all the treasure of the earth (our own excepted) in their military chest, with a Bonaparte for a commander, could not, by force, take a drink from the Ohio, or make a track on the Blue Ridge, in a trial of a thousand years! At what point, then, is the approach of danger to be expected? I answer, if it ever reach us, *it must spring up amongst ourselves.* It cannot come from abroad. If destruction be our lot, we must ourselves be its author and finisher. As a nation of free men, we must live through all time, or die by suicide. I hope I am not over-wary; but, if I am not, there is even now something of ill-omen amongst us. I mean the increasing disregard for law which pervades the country, the growing disposition to substitute the wild and furious passions in lieu of the sober judgment of the courts, and the worse than savage mobs for the executive ministers of justice. This disposition is awfully fearful in any community; and that it now exists in ours, though grating to our feelings to admit it, it would be a violation of truth and an insult to our intelligence to deny. Accounts of outrages committed by mobs form the every-day news of the times. They have pervaded the country from New England to Louisiana; they are neither peculiar to the eternal snows of the former, nor the burning sun of the latter. They are not the creature of climate; neither are they confined to the slaveholding or non-slaveholding States. Alike they spring up among the pleasure-hunting masters of Southern slaves and the order-loving citizens of the land of steady habits. Whatever their course may be, it is common to the whole country. Here, then, is one point at which danger may be expected. The question recurs, How shall we fortify against it? The answer is simple. Let every American, every lover of liberty, every well-wisher to his posterity, swear by the blood of the Revolution, never to violate in the least particular the laws of the country, and never to tolerate their violation by others. As the patriots of 'seventy-six' did to the support of the Declaration of Independence, so to the support of the Constitution and the Laws, let every American pledge his life, his property, and his sacred honor ; let every man remember that to violate the law is to trample on the blood of his father, and to tear the charter of his own and his children's liberty. Let reverence for the laws be breathed by every American mother to the lisping babe that prattles on her lap. Let it be taught in schools, in seminaries, and in colleges. Let it be written in primers, spelling-books, and in almanacs. Let it be preached from the pulpit, proclaimed in legislative halls, and enforced in courts of justice. And, in short, let it become the political religion of the nation.''

PRO-SLAVERY SENTIMENT IN ILLINOIS.

During the years of Lincoln's service in the Legislature of Illinois, the Democratic party was strongly dominant throughout the State. The feeling on the subject of slavery was decidedly in sympathy with the South. A large percentage of the settlers in the southern and middle portions of Illinois were from the States in which slave labor was sustained, and although the determination not to permit the institution to obtain a foothold in the new commonwealth was general, the people were opposed to any action which should affect its condition where it was already established. During the sessions of 1836-'37, resolutions of an extreme pro-slavery character were carried through the Legislature by the Democratic party. The aim of the measure was to prevent the Abolitionists from obtaining a foothold in the State. Mr. Lincoln could not conscientiously support the resolutions, nor hold his peace concerning them. He did not shrink from the issue, but at the hazard of losing his political popularity and the gratifying prospects that were opening before him, he drew up a protest against the unjust enactment and had it entered upon the Journal of the House. Only one of the hundred Representatives in the House at this time had the courage to sign it with him. The presentation of this document was one of the many honest acts of Mr. Lincoln's course. The protest was as follows:

"March 3, 1837.

"The following protest was presented to the House, which was read, and ordered to be spread on the journals, to-wit:—

"Resolutions upon the subject of domestic slavery having passed both branches of the General Assembly at its present session, the undersigned hereby protest against the passage of the same.

"They believe that the institution of slavery is founded on both injustice and bad policy; but that the promulgation of abolition doctrines tends rather to increase than abate its evils.

"They believe that the Congress of the United States has no power, under the Constitution, to interfere with the institution of slavery in the different States.

"They believe that the Congress of the United States has the power, under the Constitution, to abolish slavery in the District of Columbia, but that the power ought not to be exercised, unless at the request of the people of the District.

"The difference between these opinions and those contained in the said resolutions, is their reason for entering this protest.

"(Signed) "DAN STONE,

"A. LINCOLN,

"Representatives from the County of Sangamon."

CONTEST WITH GENERAL EWING.

The great financial panic which swept over the country in 1837, rendered expedient an extra session of the Législature, which was called together in July. General Lee D. Ewing had been elected to this session from Fayette county, for the express purpose of repealing the law removing the capital from Vandalia to Springfield. "General Ewing was," says Mr. Linder, "a man of considerable notoriety, popularity, and talents. He had been a member of Congress from Illinois, and had filled various State offices in his time. He was a man of elegant manners, great personal courage, and would grace either the *salons* of fashion or the Senate chamber at Washington. The Legislature opened its special session (I was there as a spectator), and General Ewing sounded the tocsin of war. He said that 'the arrogance of Springfield, its presumption in claiming the seat of government, was not to be endured; that the law had been passed by chicanery and trickery; that the Springfield delegation had sold out to the internal improvement men, and had promised their support to every measure that would gain them a vote to the law removing the seat of government.' He said many other things, cutting and sarcastic. Lincoln was chosen by his colleagues as their champion, to reply to Ewing; and I want to say here that this was the first time that I began to conceive a very high opinion of the talents and personal courage of Abraham Lincoln. He retorted upon Ewing with great severity, denouncing his insinuations imputing corruption to him and his colleagues, and paying back with usury all that Ewing had said, when everybody thought and believed that he was digging his own grave; for it was known that Ewing would not quietly pocket any insinuations that would degrade him personally. I recollect his reply to Lincoln well. After addressing the Speaker, he turned to the Sangamon delegation, who all sat in the same portion of the house, and said: 'Gentlemen, have you no other champion than this coarse and vulgar fellow to bring into the lists against me? Do you suppose that I will condescend to break a lance with your low and obscure colleague?' We were all very much alarmed for fear there would be a personal conflict between Ewing and Lincoln. It was confidently believed that a challenge must pass between them; but friends on both sides took it in hand, and it was settled without anything serious growing out of it."

LINCOLN LAYS OUT A TOWN.—THE TITLE "HONEST ABE."

In January, 1836, an old friend of Mr. Lincoln's, Mr. John Bennett, took up his residence in the little village of Petersburg, just north of Salem. "My earliest acquaintance with Mr. Lincoln," he says, "commenced in February of that year, on his return from Vandalia, where he had spent the winter as a member of the Legislature from Sangamon county. Mr. Lincoln spent most of the month of March in Petersburg, finishing up the survey and planning of the town he had commenced the year before. I was a great deal in his company, and formed a high estimate of his worth and social qualities, which was strengthened by many years of subsequent social intercourse and business transactions, finding him always strictly honest; in fact, he was universally spoken of in this region as 'Honest Abe.' After Menard county was formed out of a portion of Sangamon county, and the county seat established at Petersburg, Mr. Lincoln was a regular attendant at the courts, and as I was then keeping a hotel, he was one of my regular customers, where he met many of his old cronies of his early days at Salem, and they uniformly spent the most of the nights in telling stories, or spinning long yarns, of which Mr. Lincoln was particularly fond."

CHAPTER II.

ANOTHER REMOVAL.——NEW SALEM TO SPRINGFIELD.——HOW IT HAPPENED.
——"SPEED, I'M MOVED!"——"STUART & LINCOLN, ATTORNEYS AT LAW."
——PROPOSES TO BECOME A CARPENTER.——"RIDING THE CIRCUIT."——
INCIDENTS OF A TRIP ROUND THE CIRCUIT.——WAITING FOR "UNCLE ABE."
——A PEN PICTURE OF LINCOLN.——LINCOLN AND THE YOUNG BIRDS.——
RESCUING A PIG.——DEFENDING FUGITIVE SLAVES.——LOVE OF JUSTICE.——
"TALKING AGAINST TIME."——AN "EVASIVE" ARGUMENT.——THE STORY OF
JOHNNIE KONGAPOD.——DAN VOORHEES "NIPPED IN THE BUD."——A QUICK
RETORT.——TWO GALLONS OF WHISKY FOR "MEDICINE."——A JOKE ON
HIMSELF.——AN INVETERATE STORY-TELLER.——DELAYING COURT TO HEAR
A STORY.

THE removal of Mr. Lincoln to Springfield, where his active life as a lawyer began, occurred in April, 1837. The event was closely connected with the removal of the State capital from Vandalia to Springfield, the law for which was passed at the legislative session of 1836-'37. As has been stated, Lincoln was a member of that Legislature, and was active in procuring the passage of the bill. The citizens of Springfield were very anxious for the removal of the capital to their town, and many of them were present at the session when the measure was up for discussion. They had thus become acquainted with Mr. Lincoln, and were favorably impressed as to his abilities and character, and pleased with his efforts in the matter in which they were so greatly interested.

HOW IT HAPPENED.

Among the gentlemen referred to was Mr. Wm. Butler, afterward State Treasurer of Illinois, and an old resident of Springfield. He has given a very clear and interesting account of the circumstances which led to Mr. Lincoln's removal to that place. In those days, says Mr. Butler, the journey to Vandalia was usually made on horseback. The members of the Legislature from Sangamon and Morgan counties returned home together, accompanied by those citizens of Springfield who had been in attendance. On their way home they stayed all night at a tavern at a place called Macoupin's Point, which was the last place of stopping over-night on a journey. At this place, during the evening, the company became very merry over the success of the selection of Springfield as the State Capital. It was noticed that Mr. Lincoln did not join in the merriment; on the contrary, there was rather a marked sadness in his appearance. On retiring to bed—several beds being in one room, as was usual in that day of limited accommodations—some one of the company spoke to Mr. Lincoln of his depression, and asked why he did not join in the merriment of the others. He answered that, unlike most others present, he had no interest in the subject of their rejoicing; that he had been struggling for some time for a start in the world, with rather poor success; that he was in debt, and the amount he had remaining of his pay as a member, which he was taking home, would all be needed to pay a debt he owed, and would leave him nothing; that he had no pecuniary interests in Springfield, and had no interests anywhere that were to be favorably affected by the location of the capital at that place; therefore, it was a matter which in no way concerned him personally, and that his mind was running upon what his course of life should be in the future. Thereupon Mr. Butler asked him what he would do if he had sufficient means furnished him. He answered that he would pursue the profession of the law. Mr. Butler says that it was thereupon arranged by those present, comprising many who were largely interested in Springfield, that Mr. Lincoln should come over from New Salem to Springfield, and settle there and pursue the practice of law; and Mr. Butler asked him to come to his house and make it his home as long as he chose.

"SPEED, I'M MOVED!"

Lincoln's first interview, after his arrival in Springfield, was with Mr. Joshua F. Speed, with whom he already had a slight acquaintance, and who details the circumstances of their meeting. "He had ridden into town," says Mr. Speed, "on a borrowed horse, with no earthly property save a pair of saddle-bags containing a few clothes. I was a merchant at Spring-field, and kept a large country store, embracing dry goods, groceries, hardware, books, medicines, bed-clothes, mattresses, in fact everything that the country needed. Lincoln came into the store with his saddle-bags on his arm, and said he wanted to buy the furniture for a single bed. The mattresses,

JOSHUA F. SPEED.

blankets, sheets, coverlid and pillow, according to the figures made by me, would cost seventeen dollars. He said that was perhaps cheap enough, but small as the sum was, he was un-able to pay it. But if I would credit him till Christmas, and his experiment as a lawyer was a success, he would pay then, saying, in the saddest tone, 'If I fail in this, I do not know that

I can ever pay you.' As I looked up at him I thought then, and think now, that I never saw a sadder face. I said to him, 'You seem to be so much pained at contracting so small a debt, I think I can suggest a plan by which you can avoid the debt and at the same time attain your end. I have a large room with a double bed up-stairs, which you are very welcome to share with me.' 'Where is your room?' said he. 'Up-stairs,' said I, pointing to a pair of winding stairs which led from the store to my room. He took his saddle-bags on his arm, went up stairs, set them down on the floor, and came down with the most changed countenance. Beaming with pleasure, he exclaimed, 'Well, Speed, I'm moved!' Lincoln was then twenty-seven years old: a lawyer without a client, with no money, all his earthly wealth consisting of the clothes he wore and the contents of his saddle-bags.''

Mr. Lincoln shared the room of Mr. Speed during his early residence in Springfield, taking his meals with his companion at the house of Mr. William Butler, with whom he boarded for five years.

PROPOSES TO BECOME A CARPENTER.

An old settler of Illinois, named Page Eaton, says: "I knew Lincoln when he first came to Springfield. He was an awkward but hard-working young man. Everybody said he would never make a good lawyer, because he was too honest. He came to my shop one day, after he had been here five or six months, and said he had a notion to quit studying law and learn carpentering. He thought there was more need of carpenters out here than lawyers.''

"STUART & LINCOLN, ATTORNEYS AT LAW."

Soon after Lincoln's settlement in Springfield, he formed a law partnership with Major John T. Stuart, whom he had known for some years, and who already had a good position at the bar. This partnership began, according to the statement of Major Stuart, April 27, 1837. It continued just four

years, when it was dissolved, and Mr. Lincoln and Judge Steph-
en T. Logan became partners.   This latter partnership continued until September 20, 1843 ; when the firm of "Lincoln &
Herndon" was formed, and continued to the time of Mr. Lincoln's death.

RIDING THE CIRCUIT.

When Lincoln began the practice of law, it was the custom in Illinois to "ride the circuit," a proceeding of which the

HON. STEPHEN T. LOGAN, LINCOLN'S LAW PARTNER, 1841-'43.

older communities of the East know nothing.   The State of
Illinois, for instance, is divided into a number of districts, each
composed of a number of counties, of which a single judge,
appointed or elected, as the case may be, for that purpose,
makes the circuit, holding courts at each county seat.   Rail-

roads being scarce, the earlier circuit judges made their trips from county to county on horseback or in a gig; and the prominent lawyers living within the limits of the circuit made the tour of the circuit with the judge. It is said that when Mr. Lincoln first began to "ride the circuit," he was too poor to own a horse or vehicle, and was compelled to borrow from his friends. But in due time he became the proprietor of a horse, which he fed and groomed himself, and to which he was very much attached. On this animal he would set out from home, to be gone for weeks together, with no baggage but a pair of saddle-bags containing a change of linen, and an old cotton umbrella to shelter him from sun or rain. When he got a little more of this world's goods, he set up a one-horse buggy, a very sorry and shabby-looking affair, which he generally used when the weather promised to be bad. But the lawyers were always glad to see him, and the landlords hailed his coming with pleasure; yet he was one of those peculiar, gentle, uncomplaining men whom those servants of the public who keep "hotels" would generally put off with the most indifferent accommodations. It was a very significant remark of a lawyer, thoroughly acquainted with his habits and disposition, that "Lincoln was never seated next the landlord at a crowded table, and never got a chicken-liver or the best cut from the roast." Lincoln once remarked to Mr. Gillespie that he never felt his own unworthiness so much as when in the presence of a hotel clerk or waiter. If rooms were scarce, and one, two, three or four gentlemen were required to lodge together, in order to accommodate some surly man who "stood upon his rights," Lincoln was sure to be one of the unfortunates. Yet he loved the life, and never went home without reluctance.

INCIDENTS OF A TRIP ROUND THE CIRCUIT.

In describing the many experiences of the lawyers who travelled the circuits at this period, Mr. Arnold says: "The State was settled with a hardy, fearless and honest, but very

litigious, population. The court house was sometimes framed
and boarded, but more frequently of logs. The judge sat
upon a raised platform, behind a rough board, sometimes
covered with green baize, for a table on which to write his
notes. A small table stood on the floor in front for the clerk;
and another larger table stood in front of the clerk in the center of the room, around which in rude chairs the lawyers were
grouped, too often with their feet on top of it. Rough benches were placed there for the jury, parties to the suit, witnesses and bystanders. The court rooms were nearly always crowded, for here were rehearsed and acted the dramas,
the tragedies, and the comedies of real life. The court house
has always been a very attractive place to the people of the
frontier. It supplied the place of theatres, lecture and concert
rooms, and other places of interest and amusement in the
older settlements and towns. The leading lawyers and judges
were the star actors, and had each his partisans. Hence crowds
attended the courts to see the judges, to hear the lawyers contend, with argument and law and wit, for success, victory
and fame. The merits and ability of the leading advocates,
their success or discomfiture in examining or cross-examining
a witness, the ability of this or that one to obtain a verdict,
were canvassed at every cabin-raising, bee, or horse-race, and
at every log house and school in the county. Thus the lawyers were stimulated to the utmost exertion of their powers,
not only by controversy and desire of success, but by the consciousness that their efforts were watched with eagerness by
friends, clients, partisans, or rivals. From one to another of
these rude court houses the gentlemen of the bar passed, following the judge around his circuits from county to county,
travelling generally on horseback, with saddle-bags, brushes,
an extra shirt or two, and perhaps two or three law books.
Sometimes two or three lawyers would unite and travel in a
buggy, and the poorer and younger ones not seldom walked.
But a horse was not an unusual fee; and in those days, when

horse thieves, as clients, were but too common, it was not long before a young man of ability found himself well mounted. There was great freedom in social intercourse. Manners were rude, but genial, kind and friendly. Each was always ready to assist his fellows, and selfishness was not tolerated. The relations between the bench and bar were familiar, free and easy; and flashes of wit, humor and repartee were constantly exchanged. Such was the life upon which Lincoln now entered; and there gathered with him, around those pine tables of the frontier court house, a very remarkable combination of men; men who would have been leaders of the bar at Boston or New York, Philadelphia or Washington; men who would have made their mark in Westminster Hall, or upon any English circuit. At the capital were John T. Stuart, Stephen T. Logan, Edward D. Baker, Ninian W. Edwards, Josiah Lamborn, attorney-general, and many others. Among the leading lawyers from other parts of the State, who practiced in the Supreme and Federal Courts at the capital, were Stephen A. Douglas; Lyman Trumbull, for many years chairman of the judiciary committee of the United States Senate; O. H. Browning, Senator and member of the Cabinet at Washington; William H. Bissell, Member of Congress, and Governor of the State; David Davis, justice of the Supreme Court, Senator and Vice-President of the United States; Justin Butterfield, of Chicago; and many others, almost or quite equally distinguished. This 'circuit riding' involved all sorts of adventures. Hard fare at miserable country taverns, sleeping on the floor, and fording streams, were every-day occurrences. All such occurrences were met with good humor, and often turned into sources of frolic and fun. In fording swollen streams, Lincoln was frequently sent forward as a scout or pioneer. His extremely long legs enabled him, by taking off his boots and stockings, and by rolling up or otherwise disposing of his trousers, to test the depth of the stream, find the most shallow water, and thus to pilot the party through the current without wetting his garments.''

WAITING FOR "UNCLE ABE."

A gentleman now living in San Francisco gives the following graphic and interesting reminiscences of this period of Lincoln's life: "A number of years ago, the writer of this lived in one of the judical circuits of Illinois in which Abraham Lincoln had an extensive though not very lucrative practice. The terms of the court were held quarterly, and usually lasted about two weeks. The occasions were always seasons of great importance and much gayety in the little town that had the honor of being the county seat. Distinguished members of the bar from surrounding and even from distant counties, ex-judges and ex-Members of Congress, attended, and were personally and many of them popularly known to almost every adult, male and female, of the limited population. They came in by stages and on horseback. Among them, the one above all whose arrival was looked forward to with the most pleasurable anticipations, and whose possible absence—although he never was absent—was feared with the liveliest emotions of anxiety, was 'Uncle Abe,' as he was lovingly called by us all. Sometimes he might happen to be a day or two late; and then, as the Bloomington stage came in at sundown, the bench and bar, jurors and citizens, would gather in crowds at the hotel where he always put up, to give him a welcome if he should happily arrive, and to experience the keenest feelings of disappointment if he should not. If he arrived, as he alighted and stretched out both his long arms to shake hands with those nearest to him and with those who approached, his homely face handsome in its broad and sunshiny smile, his voice touching in its kindly and cheerful accents, every one in his presence felt lighter in heart and became joyous. He brought light with him. He loved his fellow-men with all the strength of his great nature, and those who came in contact with him could not help reciprocating the love. His tenderness of the feelings of others was of sensitiveness in the extreme."

PEN-PICTURE OF LINCOLN.

An old friend describes Mr. Lincoln as being at this time "very plain in his costume, as well as rather uncourtly in his address and general appearance. His clothing was of home Kentucky jean, and the first impression made by his tall, lank figure upon those who saw him was not specially prepossessing. He had not outgrown his hard backwoods experience, and showed no inclination to disguise or to cast behind him the honest and manly though unpolished characteristics of his earlier days. Never was a man further removed from all snobbish affectation. As little was there, also, of the demagogue art of assuming an uncouthness or rusticity of manner and outward habit, with the mistaken notion of thus securing particular favor as 'one of the masses.' He chose to appear then, as in all his later life, precisely what he was. His deportment was unassuming, though without any awkwardness of reserve."

Mr. Crane, an old settler of Tazewell county, says he used to see Mr. Lincoln when passing through Washington, in that county, on his way to attend court at Metamora; and he remembers him as "dressed in a homespun coat that came below his knees and was out at both elbows."

LINCOLN AND THE YOUNG BIRDS.

Lincoln's tenderness of heart was displayed in his treatment of animals, toward which he was often performing unusual acts of kindness. On one occasion, as Mr. Speed relates, Lincoln and the other members of the Springfield bar had been attending court at Christiansburg, and Speed was riding with them towards Springfield. There was quite a party of these lawyers, riding two by two along a country lane. Lincoln and John J. Hardin brought up the rear of the cavalcade. "We had passed through a thicket of wild plum and crab-apple trees," says Mr. Speed, "and stopped to water our horses. Hardin came up alone. 'Where is

LINCOLN RESTORING THE YOUNG BIRDS TO THEIR NEST.—AN INCIDENT OF
"CIRCUIT RIDING" IN ILLINOIS.

Lincoln?' we inquired. 'Oh,' replied he, 'when I saw him last, he had caught two young birds, which the wind had blown out of their nests, and he was hunting the nest to put them back.' In a short time Lincoln came up, having found the nest and placed the young birds in it. The party laughed at him; but he said: 'I could not have slept if I had not restored those little birds to their mother.'"

RESCUING A PIG.

Again, as Dr. Holland narrates, "Lincoln was one day riding by a deep slough, in which, to his exceeding pain, he saw a pig struggling, and with such faint efforts that it was evident that he could not extricate himself from the mud. Mr. Lincoln looked at the pig and the mud which enveloped him, and then looked at some new clothes in which he had but a short time before enveloped himself. Deciding against the claims of the pig, he rode on; but he could not get rid of the vision of the poor brute, and at last, after riding two miles, he turned back, determined to rescue the animal at the expense of his new clothes. Arrived at the spot, he tied his horse, and coolly went to work to build of old rails a passage to the bottom of the hole. Descending on these rails, he seized the pig and dragged him out, but not without serious damage to the clothes he wore. Washing his hands in the nearest brook, and wiping them on the grass, he mounted his gig and rode along. He then fell to examining the motive that sent him back to the release of the pig. At the first thought it seemed to be pure benevolence; but at length he came to the conclusion that it was selfishness, for he certainly went to the pig's relief in order (as he said to the friend to whom he related the incident,) to 'take a pain out of his own mind.'"

DEFENDING FUGITIVE SLAVES.

Instances showing the integrity, candor, unselfishness and humanity of Mr. Lincoln's conduct before the bar, could be multiplied indefinitely. The following have been collected by

Dr. Holland: "The lawyers of Springfield, particularly those who had political aspirations, were afraid to undertake the defense of any one who had been engaged in helping off fugitives slaves. It was a very unpopular business in those days and in that locality; and few felt that they could afford to engage in it. One who needed such aid went to Edward D. Baker, and was refused, distinctly and frankly, on the ground that, as a political man, he could not afford it. The man applied to an ardent anti-slavery friend for advice. He spoke of Mr. Lincoln, and said, 'He's not afraid of an unpopular case. When I go for a lawyer to defend an arrested fugitive slave, other lawyers will refuse me; but if Mr. Lincoln is at home, he will always take my case.' "

LINCOLN'S LOVE OF JUSTICE.

In another case, Mr. Lincoln was conducting a suit against a railroad company. "Judgment having been given in his favor, and the court being about to allow the amount claimed by him, deducting a proved and allowed offset, he rose and stated that his opponents had not proved all that was justly due them in offset; and he proceeded to state and allow a further sum against his client, which the court allowed in its judgment. His desire for the establishment of exact justice always overcame his own selfish love of victory, as well as his partiality for his clients' feelings and interests. To a poor client he was quite as apt to give money as to take it from him. He never encouraged the spirit of litigation. Henry McHenry, one of his old clients, says that he went to Mr. Lincoln with a case to prosecute, and that Mr. Lincoln refused to have anything to do with it, because he was not strictly in the right. 'You can give the other party a great deal of trouble,' said the lawyer, 'and perhaps beat him; but you had better let the suit alone.'

"An old woman of seventy-five years, the widow of a revolutionary pensioner, came tottering into his law office one day, and, taking a seat, told him that a certain pension agent had charged her the exorbitant fee of two hundred dollars for collecting her pension. Mr. Lincoln was satisfied by her representations that she had been swindled, and finding that she was not a resident of the town, and that she was poor, gave her money, and set about the work of procuring restitution. He immediately entered suit against the agent to recover a portion of his ill-gotten money. The suit was entirely successful; and Mr. Lincoln's address to the jury before which the case was tried is remembered to have been peculiarly touching in its allusions to the poverty of the widow, and the patriotism of the husband she had sacrificed to secure the nation's independence. He had the gratification of paying back to her a hundred dollars, and sending her home rejoicing."

"TALKING AGAINST TIME."

Judge Gillespie tells a good story, to the effect that Lincoln and General U. P. Linder were once defending a man who was being tried on a criminal charge before Judge David Davis, who said at dinner-time that the case must be disposed of that night. Lincoln suggested that the best thing they could do would be to run Benedict, the prosecuting attorney, as far into the night as possible, in hopes that he might, in his rage, commit some indiscretion that would help their case. Lincoln began, but to save his life he could not speak one hour, and the laboring oar fell into Linder's hands; 'but,' said Lincoln, 'he was equal to the occasion. He spoke most interestingly three mortal hours, about everything in the world. He discussed Benedict from head to foot, and put in about three-quarters of an hour on the subject of Benedict's whiskers.' Lincoln said he never envied a man so much as he did Linder on that occasian. He thought he was inimitable in his capacity to talk interestingly about everything and nothing, by the hour.

AN "EVASIVE" ARGUMENT.

But if Mr. Lincoln had not General Linder's art of "talking against time," his wit often suggested some readier method of gaining advantage in a case. On one occasion, a suit was on trial in the Circuit Court of Sangamon county, in which Lincoln was attorney for the plaintiff, and Mr. James C. Conkling, then a young man just entering practice, was attorney for the defendant. It was a jury trial, and Mr. Lincoln waived the opening argument to the jury, leaving Mr. Conkling to sum up his case for the defense. The latter spoke at considerable length, in a sort of sophomoric style, laboring under the impression that unless he made an extraordinary exertion to influence the jury, he would be quite eclipsed by Mr. Lincoln in his closing speech. But he was completely taken back by the unlooked for light manner in which Mr. Lincoln treated the case in his closing. Mr. Lincoln proceeded to reply; but in doing so, he talked on without making the slightest reference to the case on hearing, or to the argument of Mr. Conkling.

THE STORY OF JOHNNIE KONGAPOD.

Mr. Lincoln's summing-up to the jury, in the case above referred to, was to the following effect: "Gentlemen of the jury: In early days there lived in this vicinity, over on the Sangamon river, an old Indian of the Kickapoo tribe, by the name of Johnnie Kongapod, who had been taken in charge by some good missionaries, converted to Christianity, and educated to such extent that he could read and write. He took a great fancy to poetry, and became somewhat of a poet himself. His desire was that after his death there should be placed at the head of his grave an epitaph, which he prepared himself, in rhyme, in the following words:

'Here lies poor Johnnie Kongapod;
Have mercy on him, gracious God,
As he would do if he were God
And you were Johnnie Kongapod.' "

Of course all this had no reference to the case, nor did Mr. Lincoln intend it should have any. It was merely his way of ridiculing the eloquence of his opponent. The verdict of the jury was for the plaintiff, as Mr. Lincoln expected it would be; and this was the reason of his treating the case as he did.

DAN VOORHEES "NIPPED IN THE BUD."

A story somewhat similar to the above was told by the late Judge John Pearson, shortly before his death. In the February term, 1850, of the Circuit Court of Vermilion county, Illinois, a case was being tried, in which a young lady had brought suit for $10,000 against a recreant lover, who had married another girl. The amount sued for was thought to be an enormous sum in those days, and the ablest talent to be found was brought into requisition by both sides. Hon. Richard Thompson and Daniel W. Voorhees were associated with O. L. Davis for the fair plaintiff. H. W. Beckwith, Ward Lamon, and Abraham Lincoln were for the defendant. The little town of Danville was crowded with people from far and near, who had come to hear the big speeches. The evidence brought out in the trial was in every way against the defendant, and the sympathy of the public was, naturally enough, with the young lady plaintiff. Lincoln and his associate counsel plainly saw the hopelessness of their cause; and they wisely concluded to let their side of the case stand upon its merits, without even a plea of extenuating circumstances. Voorhees was young, ambitious, and anxious to display his oratory. He arranged with his colleagues at the beginning for a speech; and he spent several hours in his room at the old McCormack House in the preparation of an oratorical avalanche. It became generally known that Dan was going to out-do himself; and the expectation of the community was at its highest tension. The little old court house was crowded. The ladies were out in full force. Voorhees came in a little late, glowing with the excitement of the moment. It had been arranged that Davis was to open, Lincoln was to follow, and Voorhees should come next. Mr. Davis made a clear statement of the case, recited the character of the evidence, and closed with a plain, logical argument. Then Mr. Lincóln arose, and stood in silence for a moment, looking at the jury. He deliberately re-arranged some of the books and papers on the table before him, as though "making a good ready," as he used to say; and began in a spirited but deliberate way, saying: "Your Honor, the evidence in this case is all in, and doubtless all concerned comprehend its fullest import, without the aid of further argument. Therefore, we will rest our case here." This move, of course, cut off all future discussion. Voorhees, with his load of pyrotechnics, was shut out. An ominous silence followed Mr. Lincoln's remark. Then Voorhees arose, white with rage, and entered a protest against the tactics of the defense. All the others were disappointed, but amused, and the only consolation that Voorhees got out of this affair was a verdict for the full amount claimed by his client. But he never forgave Lincoln for thus "nipping" his great speech "in the bud."

TWO GALLONS OF WHISKY FOR "MEDICINE."

During the early part of Mr. Lincoln's career as a lawyer, he had quite a practice in and around Tazewell county, Illinois. Many anecdotes and stories are still current there, and among them is the following, which was told by a descendant of one of the parties referred to in the story: An old settler of the place, a Mr. A., kept a general supply store, and among other things sold liquor, always for "medicinal" purposes, there being a local ordinance against selling it as a beverage. One of Mr. A.'s neighbors, a Mr. X., a pious but somewhat meddlesome man, had Mr. A. arrested on the charge of selling ardent spirits in defiance of the statute referred to. Mr. Lincoln was retained as the counsel of the defendant, and on learning the character of the complainant he concluded that he could make things decidedly warm for that gentleman. Accordingly, on the day of the trial, among many other witnesses the worthy Mr. X. and his hired man (a German) were summoned. Mr. X. was closely questioned as to whether he was a patron of Mr. A.'s, and whether he himself had ever purchased liquor from him. He admitted that he had, at one time, "sent for a very little, by his hired man, Hans; but it was *only for medicine.*" On getting this admission from his witness, Mr. Lincoln dismissed him, and the German was called to the stand. "Hans," said Mr. Lincoln, "is it true that you have bought liquor from Mr. A. for your employer?" "Oh, yaw!" was the hearty response. "Well, Hans, will you please tell the court when you last bought any, and about how much?" "Aboudt doo veeks ago I vent down to dot vellow's schtore, undt I puys me doo gallons of der fery pest vhiskey vot he vas got; dot shentlemans, Mr. X., said he vas sick." "Thank you, Hans," said Mr. Lincoln, "that is all very good. Now, will you tell us where Mr. X. keeps his jug?" "In der zellar," was the reply. Lincoln sent for the jug and also for a two-gallon pail, and in the presence of the judge and a breathless audience, he drew the cork, and emptied the contents of the jug—about a quart of whisky—into the pail. "There," said he, with a droll expression on his face and a twinkle in his eye, "are the remains of two gallons of liquor used by a *sick man* in less than two weeks! It seems to me the medicine must have been taken in pretty good doses." Of course this killed Mr. X.'s case, and he at once withdrew his charge and paid the costs, with a most crestfallen air.

A QUICK RETORT.

Mr. Wickizer gives a story which illustrates the off-hand readiness of Mr. Lincoln's wit: "In the court at Bloomington, Mr. Lincoln was engaged in a case of no great importance; but the attorney on the other side, Mr. S., a young lawyer of fine abilities, was always very sensitive about being beaten, and in this case manifested unusual zeal and interest. The case lasted until late at night, when it was finally submitted to the jury. Mr. S. spent a sleepless night in anxiety, and early next morning learned, to his great chagrin, that he had lost the case. Mr. Lincoln met him at the court house, and asked him what had become of his case. With lugubrious countenance and melancholy tone, Mr. S. said, 'It's gone to hell!' 'Oh, well!'' replied Lincoln, 'then you'll see it again!' ''

A JOKE ON HIMSELF.

Mr. Lincoln was always ready to join in a laugh at his own expense, and used to tell the following story with intense enjoyment: ''In the days when I used to be 'on the circuit,' I was accosted in the cars by a stranger, who said, 'Excuse me sir, but I have an article in my possession which belongs to you.' 'How is that?' I asked, considerably astonished. The stranger took a jack-knife from his pocket. 'This knife,' said he, 'was placed in my hands some years ago, with the injunction that I was to keep it until I found a man uglier than myself. I have carried it from that time to this. Allow me to say, sir, that I think you are fairly entitled to the property.' ''

AN INVETERATE STORY-TELLER.

Mr. Gillespie says of Mr. Lincoln's passion for story-telling: ''As a boon companion, Mr. Lincoln, although he never drank liquor or used tobacco in any form, was without a rival. No one would ever think of 'putting in' when he was talking. He could illustrate any subject, it seemed to me, with an appropriate and amusing anecdote. He did not tell stories merely for the sake of telling them, but rather by way of illustration of something that had happened or been said. There seemed to be no end to his fund of stories.'' Mr. Lamon states, ''Mr. Lincoln frequently said that he lived by his humor, and would have died without it. His manner of telling a story was irresistibly comical, the fun of it dancing in his eyes and playing over every feature. His face changed in an instant; the hard lines faded out of it, and the mirth seemed to diffuse itself all over him, like a spontaneous tickle. You could see it coming long before he opened his mouth, and he began to enjoy the 'point' before his eager auditors could catch the faintest glimpse of it. Telling and hearing ridiculous stories was one of his ruling passions."

DELAYING COURT TO HEAR A STORY.

An illustration of his great fondness for story-telling is given by Judge Sibley, of Quincy, Illinois, who knew Lincoln when practicing law at Springfield. One day a party of lawyers were sitting in the law library of the court house at Springfield, awaiting the opening of court, and telling stories to fill the time, when Judge Breese, of the Supreme bench,— one of the most distinguished of American jurists, and a man of great personal dignity,—passed through the room where the lawyers were sitting, on his way to open court. Lincoln, seeing him, called out in his hearty way, "Hold on, Breese! Don't open court yet! Here's Bob Blackwell just going to tell a new story!" The judge passed on without replying, evidently regarding it as beneath the dignity of the Supreme Court to delay proceedings for the sake of a story.

CHAPTER III.

AGAIN IN THE LEGISLATURE.——LINCOLN BRINGS DOWN THE HOUSE.——TAKES
A HAND IN NATIONAL POLITICS.——A "LOG CABIN" REMINISCENCE.——
SOME MEMORABLE POLITICAL ENCOUNTERS.——A TILT WITH DOUGLAS.——
LINCOLN FACING A MOB.——HIS PHYSICAL COURAGE.——MEETS MARTIN
VAN BUREN.——COURTSHIP AND MARRIAGE.——A PAINFUL EPISODE.——
DESCRIPTION OF THE WEDDING BY ONE WHO WAS PRESENT.——LINCOLN
AS A DUELLIST.——THE AFFAIR WITH GENERAL SHIELDS.——AN EYE-WIT-
NESS' ACCOUNT OF THE DUEL.

IN 1838 Mr. Lincoln was again a candidate for the State
Legislature.   Mr. Wilson, one of his colleagues from Sangamon county, states that "a question of the division of the
county was one of the local issues.   Mr. Lincoln and myself,
among others, residing in the portion of the county sought to
be organized into a new county, and opposing the division,
it became necessary that I should make a special canvass
through the northwest part of the county, then known as
Sand Ridge.   I made the canvass; Mr. Lincoln accompanied
me, and being personally acquainted with every one, we
called at nearly every house.   At that time it was the universal custom to keep some whisky in the house, for private use
and to treat friends.   The subject was always mentioned as a
matter of politeness, but with the usual remark to Mr. Lincoln, 'We know you never drink, but maybe your friend
would like to take a little.'   I never saw Mr. Lincoln drink.
He often told me he never drank; had no desire for drink,
nor for the companionship of drinking men."

The result of this canvass was that Lincoln was elected to
the Legislature for the session of 1838-39.   The next year
(1840) he was again elected; and this ended his legislative
service.   In these sessions he was as active and prominent in
the house as he had been in the earlier times (1834, '35, '36,
'37), when a member from New Salem.

LINCOLN BRINGS DOWN THE HOUSE.

Lincoln's faculty for getting the better of an adversary by an apt illustration or anecdote was seldom better shown than by an incident which occurred during his last term in the Legislature. Hon. James C. Conkling has given the following graphic description of the scene. He says: "A gentleman who had formerly been Attorney-General of the State, was also a member. Presuming upon his age, experience and former official position, he thought it incumbent upon himself to oppose Mr. Lincoln, who was then one of the acknowledged leaders of his party. He at length attracted the attention of Mr. Lincoln, who replied to his remarks, and then told one of his humorous anecdotes, and making a personal application to his opponent, which placed the latter in such a ridiculous attitude that it convulsed the whole house. All business was at once suspended. In vain the speaker rapped with his gavel. Members of all parties, without distinction, were compelled to laugh. They not only laughed, but they screamed and yelled; they thumped upon the floor with their canes; they clapped their hands; they threw up their hats; they shouted and twisted themselves into all sorts of contortions, until their sides ached and the tears rolled down their cheeks. One paroxysm passed away, but was speedily succeeded by another, and again they laughed and screamed and yelled. Another lull occurred, and still another paroxysm; until they seemed to be perfectly exhausted. The ambition of Mr. Lincoln's opponent was abundantly gratified, and for the remainder of the session he lapsed into profound obscurity."

TAKES A HAND IN NATIONAL POLITICS.

Mr. Lincoln's eight years of legislative service had given him considerable reputation in politics, and he had become the acknowledged leader of the Whig party in Illinois. In the exciting Presidential campaign of 1840, known as the "Log Cabin" campaign, he took a very active part. He had been nominated as Presidential Elector on the Harrison ticket, and stumped a large portion of the State.

A "LOG-CABIN" REMINISCENCE.

A peculiarly interesting reminiscence of Lincoln's appearance on one occasion during the "Log Cabin" campaign is furnished by Mr. G. W. Harris, who says: "In the fall of the year 1840, there came into the log school-house, in a village in Southern Illinois, where I, a lad, was a pupil, a tall, awkward, and plain-looking young man, dressed in a full suit of 'blue jean.' Approaching the master, he gave his name, and, apologizing for the intrusion, said, 'I am told you have a copy of Byron's Works. I would like to borrow it for a few hours.' The book was produced and loaned to him. With thanks and a 'Good-day' to the teacher, and a smile such as I have never seen on any other man's face, and a look that took in all of us lads and lassies, the stranger passed out of the room. This was during a Presidential canvass; and Isaac Walker, a candidate for Democratic Elector, and Abraham Lincoln, a candidate for Whig Elector, were by appointment to discuss political matters in the afternoon of that day. I asked for, and got, a half-holiday. I had given no thought to the matter until the appearance of Lincoln (for he it was) in the school-room; but something in the man had aroused, not only in me, but others of the scholars, a strong desire to see him again and to hear him speak. Isaac Walker, in his younger days, had been a resident of the village. Lincoln was aware of this, and shrewdly suspected that Walker in his remarks would allude to the circumstance; and Lincoln, having the opening speech, determined to 'take the wind out of his sails.' He did so; how effectually, it is hardly necessary for me to say. He had borrowed Byron's works, to read the opening lines of 'Lara':

> "He, the unhoped but unforgotten lord,
> The long self-exiled chieftain is restored;
> There be bright faces in the busy hall,
> Bowls on the board, and banners on the wall.

He comes at last, in sudden loneliness,
And whence they know not, why they need not guess ;
They more might marvel when the greetings o'er,
Not that he came, but came not long before."

SOME MEMORABLE POLITICAL ENCOUNTERS.

During this period Mr. Lincoln continued to enjoy the hospitality of Mr. Speed, who says : "After he made his home with me, on every winter's night at my store, by a big wood fire, no matter how inclement the weather, eight or ten choice spirits assembled, without distinction of party. It was a sort of social club without organization. They came there because they were sure to find Lincoln. His habit was to engage in conversation upon any and all subjects except politics. But one evening a political argument sprang up between Lincoln and Douglas, which for a time ran high. Douglas sprang to his feet and said : 'Gentlemen, this is no place to talk politics ; we will discuss the questions publicly with you.'" A few days after, the Whigs held a meeting, and challenged the Democrats to a joint debate. The challenge was accepted, and Douglas, Lamborn, Calhoun and Jesse Thomas were deputed by the Democrats to meet Logan, Baker, Browning and Lincoln on the part of the Whigs. The intellectual encounter between these noted champions is still described by those who witnessed it as "The great debate." It took place in the Second Presbyterian church at Springfield, and lasted eight nights, each speaker occupying a night in turn. When Mr. Lincoln's turn came the audience had thinned out, but, for all that, his speech was by many persons considered the best one of the series. Mr. Speed says : "Mr. Lincoln delivered this speech without manuscript or notes. He had a wonderful faculty in that way. He might be writing an important document, be interrupted in the midst of a sentence, turn his attention to other matters entirely foreign to the subject on which he was engaged, and then take up his pen and begin where he left off without reading the previous part of the sentence. He could grasp, exhaust, and quit any subject with more facility than any man I have ever seen or heard of." The subjoined paragraphs from the speech above referred to show the impassioned feeling which Lincoln poured forth that night:

"Many free countries have lost their liberty, and ours may lose hers; but if she shall, be it my proudest plume, not that I was the last to desert, but that I never deserted her. I know that the great volcano at Washington, aroused and directed by the evil spirit that reigns there, is belching forth the lava of political corruption in a current broad and deep, which is sweeping with frightful velocity over the whole length and breadth of the land, bidding fair to leave unscathed no green spot or living thing; while on its bosom are riding, like demons on the waves of hell, the imps of the Evil Spirit, and fiendishly torturing and taunting all those who dare resist its destroying course with the hopelessness of their effort; and knowing this, I cannot deny that all may be swept away. Broken by it, I too may be; bow to it, I never will. The probability that we may fall in the struggle ought not to deter us from the support of a cause which we deem to be just. It shall not deter me. If I ever feel the soul within me elevate and expand to those dimensions not wholly unworthy of its Almighty architect, it is when I contemplate the cause of my country deserted by all the world beside, and I, standing up boldly and alone, hurling defiance at her victorious oppressors. And here, without contemplating consequences, before high Heaven and in the face of the whole world, I swear eternal fidelity to the just cause, as I deem it, of the land of my life, my liberty, and my love. And who that thinks with me will not fearlessly adopt the oath I take? Let none falter who thinks he is right, and we may succeed. But if, after all, we shall fail, be it so. We shall have the proud consolation of saying to our conscience and to the departed shade of our country's freedom, that the cause approved by our judgments and adored by our hearts in disaster, in chains, in torture, and in death, we never failed in defending."

A TILT WITH DOUGLAS.

In this canvass Lincoln came again into collision with Douglas, the adversary whom he had met two years before and with whom he was to sustain an almost life-long political conflict. During a fierce discussion in the Harrison campaign, Lincoln made some charge against Van Buren, which Douglas promptly denied. Lincoln proceeded to prove his statement by reading from a 'Life of Van Buren' a letter from Van Buren; whereupon Douglas became very angry, snatched up the book, and, tossing it into the crowd, remarked, '*Damn such a book!*'"

LINCOLN FACING A MOB.

It was during this canvass that Lincoln protected Edward D. Baker from a mob which threatened to drag him off the stand. "Baker was speaking in a large room," says Mr. Arnold, "rented and used for the court sessions, and Lincoln's office was in an apartment over the court room, and communicating with it by a trap-door. Lincoln was in his office listening to Baker through the open trap-door, when Baker, becoming excited, abused the Democrats, many of whom were present. A cry was raised, 'Pull him off the stand!' The instant Lincoln heard the cry, knowing a general fight was imminent, his athletic form was seen descending from above through the opening of the trap-door, and, springing to the side of Baker, and waving his hand for silence, he said with dignity: 'Gentlemen, let us not disgrace the age and country in which we live. This is a land where freedom of speech is guaranteed. Baker has a right to speak. I am here to protect him, and no man shall take him from this stand if I can prevent it.' Quiet was restored, and Baker finished his speech without further interruption."

A similar occurrence, happening about the same period, is detailed by General Linder: "On a later occasion, when Colonel Baker and myself were both battling together in the Whig cause, at a convention held in Springfield, I made a speech at the State House, which I think now, looking back at it from this point, was the very best I ever made in my life; and while I was addressing the vast assembly, some ruffian in the galleries flung at me a gross personal insult, accompanied with a threat. Lincoln and Colonel Baker, who were both present, and were warm personal and political friends of mine, anticipating that I might be attacked when I left the State House, came upon the stand a little before I concluded my speech and took their station on each side of me; and when I was through, and after my audience had greeted me with three hearty cheers, each took one of my arms, and Lincoln said to me: 'Linder, Baker and I are apprehensive that you may be attacked by some of those ruffians who insulted you from the galleries, and we have come up to escort you to your hotel. We both think we can do a little fighting, so we want you to walk between us until we get you to your hotel. Your quarrel is our quarrel, and that of the great Whig party of this nation; and your speech upon this occasion is the greatest one that has been made by any of us, for which we wish to honor, love and defend you.' This I consider no ordinary compliment, coming from Mr. Lincoln, for he was no flatterer, nor disposed to bestow praise where it was undeserved. Colonel Baker heartily concurred in all he said, and between those two glorious men I left the stand, and we marched out of the State House through our friends, who trooped after us, evidently anticipating what Lincoln and Baker had suggested to me, accompanying us to my hotel; and receiving three more hearty cheers from the multitude, I made my bow and retired to my room.''

HIS PHYSICAL COURAGE.

That Lincoln had an abundance of physical courage, and was well able to defend himself when necessity demanded, is clear from the incidents just given. Mr. Herndon, his intimate friend, adds his testimony on this point. As Lincoln was grand in his good nature, says Mr. Herndon, so he was grand in his rage. "Once I saw him incensed at a judge for giving an unfair decision. It was a terrible spectacle. At another time I saw two men come to blows in his presence; he picked them up separately and tossed them apart like a couple of kittens. He was the strongest man I ever knew, and has been known to lift a man of his own weight and throw him over a worm fence. Once, in Springfield, the Irish voters meditated taking possession of the polls. News came down the street that they would permit nobody to vote but those of their own party. Mr. Lincoln seized an axe-handle from a hardware store, and went alone to open a way to the ballot-box. His appearance intimidated them, and we had neither threats nor collisions all that day. He was never sick during the whole of our long acquaintance ; being a man of slow circulation, and of most regular habits, capable of subsisting upon a morsel. He was wiry and enduring beyond the best of our Western men.''

LINCOLN MEETS MARTIN VAN BUREN.

In June, 1842, ex-President Van Buren was journeying through Illinois, with a company of friends. When near Springfield they were delayed by bad roads, and were compelled to spend the night at Rochester, some miles out. The accommodations at this place were very poor, and a few of the ex-President's Springfield friends proposed to go out to meet him and try to aid in entertaining him. Knowing Lincoln's ability as a talker and story-teller, they begged him to go with them and aid in making their guest at the country inn pass the evening as pleasantly as possible. Lincoln, with his usual good nature, went with them, and entertained the party for hours with graphic descriptions of Western life, anecdotes and witty stories. Judge Peck, who was of the party, and a warm friend of the ex-President, says that Lincoln was at his best, and declares, ''I never passed a more joyous night.'' There was a constant succession of brilliant anecdotes and funny stories, accompanied by loud laughter in which Van Buren bore his full share. ''He also,'' says the Judge, ''gave us incidents and anecdotes of Elisha Williams, and other leading members of the New York bar, and going back to the days of Hamilton and Burr. Altogether there was a right merry time ; and Mr. Van Buren said the only drawback upon his enjoyment was that his sides were sore from laughing at Lincoln's stories for a week thereafter.''

LINCOLN'S COURTSHIP AND MARRIAGE.

Miss Mary Todd, daughter of Hon. Robert T. Todd, of Lexington, Kentucky, came to Springfield in 1839, to live with her sister, Mrs. Ninian W. Edwards. "She was young," says Mr. Lamon, "just twenty-one,—her family was of the best, and her connections in Illinois among the most refined and distinguished people. Her mother having died when she

MRS. ABRAHAM LINCOLN.

was a little girl, she had been educated under the care of a French lady. She was gifted with rare talents, had a keen sense of the ridiculous, a ready insight into the weaknesses of individual character, and a most fiery and ungovernable temper. Her tongue and her pen were equally sharp. High-bred, proud, brilliant, witty, and with a will that bent every one else to her purpose, she took Mr. Lincoln captive. He was a rising politician, fresh from the people, and possessed of great power among them; Miss Todd was of aristocratic and distinguished family, able to lead through the awful portals of 'good society' whomsoever they chose to countenance. It was thought that a union between them could not fail of numerous benefits to both parties. Mr. Edwards thought so; Mrs. Edwards thought so; and it was not long before Mary Todd herself thought so. She was very ambitious, and even before she left Kentucky announced her belief that she was destined to be the wife of some future President. For a while she was courted by Douglas as well as by Lincoln. Being asked which of them she intended to have, she answered, 'the one that has the best chance of being President.' She decided in favor of Lincoln; and, in the opinion of some of her husband's friends, aided to no small extent in the fulfillment of the prophecy which the bestowal of her hand implied." Mrs. Edwards, Miss Todd's sister, relates that "Mr. Lincoln was charmed with Mary's wit, and fascinated with her quick sagacity, her will, her nature and culture. I have happened in the room," she says, "where they were sitting, often and often, and Mary led the conversation. Lincoln would listen, and gaze on her as if drawn by some superior power,—irresistibly so; he listened, but seldom said a word."

A PAINFUL EPISODE.

Preparations were made for the marriage between Mr. Lincoln and Miss Todd; but they were interrupted by a painful occurrence—a sudden breaking out of a fit of melancholy, or temporary insanity, such as had afflicted Mr. Lincoln on a former occasion. This event has been made the subject of no little gossip, into which it is not now necessary or desirable to go, further than to mention that at about this time Mr. Lincoln seems to have formed a strong attachment for Miss Matilda Edwards, a sister of Ninian W. Edwards; and that the engagement with Miss Todd was for a time broken off. In consequence of these complications, Mr. Lincoln's health was seriously affected. He suffered from melancholy, which was so profound "his friends were alarmed for his life." His intimate companion, Mr. Speed, endeavored to rescue him from the terrible depression, urging that he would die unless he rallied. Lincoln replied, "I am not afraid to die, and would be more than willing. But I have an irrepressible desire to live till I can be assured that the world is a little better for my having been in it."

Mr. Herndon gives as his opinion that Mr. Lincoln's insanity grew out of a most extraordinary complication of feelings—aversion to the marriage proposed, a counter-attachment to Miss Edwards, and a revival of his tenderness for the memory of Anne Rutledge. At all events, his derangement was nearly, if not quite, complete. "We had to remove razors from his room," says Mr. Speed, "take away all knives, and other dangerous things. It was terrible." Mr. Speed determined to do for him what Bowlin Greene had done on a similar occasion at New Salem. Having sold out his store on the first of January, 1841, he took Mr. Lincoln with him to his home in Kentucky, and kept him there during most of the Summer and Fall, or until he seemed sufficiently restored to be given his liberty again, when he was brought back to Springfield. His health was soon regained, and on the 4th of November, 1842, the marriage between him and Miss Todd was celebrated.

DESCRIPTION OF THE WEDDING BY ONE WHO WAS PRESENT.

A highly interesting account of the affair is furnished by Judge J. H. Matheny, of Springfield, an intimate friend of Mr. Lincoln, who, at his request, was present at the ceremony: "Marriages in Springfield," says Judge Matheny, "up to the time of Mr. Lincoln's wedding, had been rather commonplace affairs. His was about the first, if not the very first, ever performed with all the requirements of the Episcopalian ceremony. A large number of his friends had gath-

THE LINCOLN HOMESTEAD AT SPRINGFIELD.

ered, and among them was Thomas C. Browne, one of the Justices of the Supreme Court. Judge Browne was in truth an old-timer. He had been on the bench from the very beginning,—was a quaint, rough, curious character. He was standing close beside Mr. Lincoln. Old Parson Dressar, with canonical robes on, in an exceedingly solemn and impressive manner, was performing the beautiful Episcopal ceremony. He handed the ring to Mr. Lincoln, who placed it upon the bride's finger, repeating the formula, 'With this ring I thee endow, with all my goods and chattel lands and tenements.' This struck the old Judge as nonsense, and he cried out loud enough to be heard by everybody, 'Good gracious, Lincoln, the statute fixes all that!'' The unexpected interruption, and its utter absurdity, completely upset the old parson, who had a keen sense of the ridiculous, and it was some minutes before he could proceed.''

After the marriage Mr. Lincoln secured pleasant rooms for himself and wife at the ''Globe Tavern,'' at a cost of four dollars a week. In 1844 he purchased of the Rev. Nathan Dressar the plain dwelling which was his home for the ensuing seventeen years, and which he left to enter the White House in 1861.

LINCOLN AS A DUELLIST.—THE AFFAIR WITH GENERAL
SHIELDS.

A serio-comic incident occurred in Mr. Lincoln's career in 1842. Mr. Arnold says of it: ''About this time there was living at Springfield, James Shields (afterwards a distinguished General and U. S. Senator), a gallant, hot-headed bachelor, from Tyrone county, Ireland. Like most of his countrymen, he was an ardent Democrat, and he was also a great beau in society. He had been so fortunate as to be elected Auditor of the State. Miss Todd, full of spirit, very gay, and a little wild and mischievous, published in the 'Sangamon Journal,' under the name of 'Aunt Rebecca; or, The Lost Townships,' some amusing satirical papers, ridiculing the susceptible and sensitive Irishman. Indeed, Shields was so sensitive he could not bear ridicule, and would much rather die than be laughed at. On seeing the papers, he went at once to Mr. Francis, the editor, and furiously demanded the name of the author, declaring that unless the name of the writer was given he would hold the editor personally responsible. Francis was a large, broad man, and Shields was very thin and slim, and the editor realized that with his great bulk it would be very unsafe for him to stand in front of Shields' pistol. He had plenty of stomach, but none for such a fight. He was a warm personal and political friend of Lincoln ; and knowing the relations between him and Miss Todd, in this dilemma he disclosed the facts to Lincoln, and asked his advice and counsel. He was not willing to expose the lady's name, and yet was extremely reluctant himself to meet the fiery Irishman on the field. Lincoln at once told Francis to tell Shields to regard him as the author. The Tazewell Circuit Court, at which he had several cases of importance to try, being in session, Lincoln departed for Tremont, the county seat. As soon as Francis had notified Shields that Lincoln was the author of the papers, Shields and his second, General Whitesides, started in hot pursuit of Lincoln. Hearing of this, Dr. Merryman and Lincoln's old friend Butler started also for Tremont, 'to prevent,' as Merryman said, 'any advantage being taken of Lincoln, either as to his honor or his life.' They passed the belligerent Shields and Whitesides in the night, and arrived at Tremont in advance. They told Lincoln what was coming, and he replied that he was altogether opposed to duelling, and would do anything to avoid it that would not degrade him in the estimation of himself and of his friends ; but if a fight were the only alternative of such degradation, he would fight." Mr. Lincoln's second, Merryman, advised him to select broadswords as the weapons ; and Merryman, being a splendid swordsman, trained Lincoln himself, so that it was almost certain that Shields would get the worst of it.   They decided on a neck of land near the confluence of the Mississippi and Missouri rivers, at Alton, Illinois, as the duelling-grounds.   They had arrived at Alton, and the preparations were all made, when, says Gen. Linder, "John J. Hardin, hearing of the contemplated duel, determined to prevent it, and hastened to Alton with all imaginable celerity, where he fell in with the belligerent parties, and, aided by some other friends of both Lincoln and Shields, succeeded in effecting a reconciliation.   After this affair between Lincoln and Shields, I met Lincoln at the Danville court, and in a walk we took together, seeing him make passes with a stick, such as are made in the broadsword exercise, I was induced to ask him why he had selected that weapon with which to fight Shields.   He promptly answered, in that sharp, ear-splitting voice of his, 'To tell you the truth, Linder, I did not want to kill Shields, and felt sure I could disarm him, having had about a month to learn the broadsword exercise; and furthermore, I didn't want the darned fellow to kill me, which I rather think he would have done if we had selected pistols.' "

AN EYE-WITNESS' ACCOUNT OF LINCOLN'S DUEL.

Major J. M. Lucas, late U. S. Consul at Tunstall, England, and a pioneer citizen of Illinois, was perfectly familiar with all the circumstances of the Lincoln-Shields "unpleasantness," and, in fact, was an eye-witness of the duel which took place—or, rather, which did not take place—at Alton, across the Mississippi river, in 1842.   The details of that now almost forgotten "affair of honor" are still present to his mind. The idea of Abraham Lincoln going to the field armed with a broadsword, to fight a duel, seems to those who knew him in his later days so inconsistent with his pacific character that many have doubted the authenticity of the story.   But it verily did occur, says Major Lucas, who rode down to the spot, and was there when the affair was amicably adjusted.

The challenge of Shields arose out of a quizzical newspaper article which was written by Miss Mary Todd—afterwards Mrs. Lincoln. This gave such offense to General Shields that he went to the editor and demanded to know who the writer was. The editor of the paper was in a quandary, and meeting Lincoln on the street asked him what he had better do. "Oh," said Lincoln, "just tell Shields that it was me." The editor did so, and Shields sent a challenge to Lincoln, who had just gone to Tazewell county to attend to a lawsuit. Lincoln accepted the challenge, and the weapons selected were broadswords, which 'Uncle Abe' knew well how to handle, having been thoroughly drilled in their use by Major Duncan, a brother-in-law of Major Lucas. The field selected for the combat was near Alton, and thither the combatants proceeded. But the affair got wind and reached the ears of General Hardin, who immediately started after the party, reaching the scene just as the preliminaries were being arranged. He interposed, saying, "This is all nonsense," and succeeded in putting a stop to the whole proceeding. Major Lucas says he saddled a horse and got to the field about the same time Lincoln did. He had no doubt Lincoln meant to fight. Said the Major, "Lincoln was no coward, and he would unquestionably have held his own against his antagonist, for he was a powerful man in those days, and was quite well skilled in the use of the broad-sword. He said to me after the affair was all over, 'I could have split him in two.'"

CHAPTER IV.

POLITICS ON A LARGER SCALE.——CONGRESSIONAL ASPIRATIONS.——NEW LAW-
PARTNERSHIP.——THE CAMPAIGN OF 1844.——VISIT TO HENRY CLAY.——
ELECTED TO CONGRESS.——CONGRESSIONAL LIFE.——LINCOLN'S REPUTA-
TION IN CONGRESS.——FIRST SPEECH IN CONGRESS.——"GETTING THE
HANG" OF THE HOUSE.——THE WAR ON MEXICO.——LINCOLN'S COURSE IN
REGARD TO THE MEXICAN WAR.——NOTABLE SPEECH IN CONGRESS.——RID-
ICULE OF GENERAL CASS.——BILL FOR THE ABOLITION OF SLAVERY.——
WHIG CONVENTION OF 1848, AT PHILADELPHIA.——ADVICE TO YOUNG POL-
ITICIANS.——"OLD ABE."——A POLITICAL DISAPPOINTMENT.——LINCOLN'S
APPEARANCE AS AN OFFICE-SEEKER IN WASHINGTON.——"A DIVINITY THAT
SHAPES OUR ENDS."

In the spring of 1843 Mr. Lincoln was among the nomi-
nees proposed to represent the Sangamon district in Congress;
but Mr. Edward D. Baker carried the delegation, and was
elected. In writing to his friend Speed, Mr. Lincoln treated
the circumstance with his usual merry humor. "We had,"
he says, "a meeting of the Whigs of the county here last
Monday to appoint delegates to a district convention; and
Baker beat me, and got the delegation instructed to go for
him. The meeting, in spite of my attempt to decline it, appointed me one of the delegates; so that, in getting Baker the
nomination, I shall be 'fixed' a good deal like a fellow who is
made groomsman to the man who 'cut him out,' and is marry-
ing his own girl."

A NEW LAW-PARTNERSHIP.

On the 20th of September, 1843, the partnership was dissolved between Lincoln and Judge Logan; and the same day
a new association was formed with William H. Herndon, a
relative of one of Lincoln's former friends of Clary Grove.
It is said that in spite of their close friendship, Mr. Herndon
could not understand it, when Lincoln one day darted up the
office stairs and said, "Herndon, should you like to be my
partner?" "Don't laugh at me, Mr. Lincoln," was the response. Persistent repetition of the question could hardly gain

a hearing; but at last Mr. Herndon said: "Mr. Lincoln, you know I am too young, and I have no standing and no money; but if you are in earnest, there is nothing in this world that would make me so happy." Nothing more was said till the papers were brought to Herndon to sign.

THE CAMPAIGN OF 1844.—A VISIT TO THE OLD INDIANA HOME.

The "Life of Henry Clay," which Lincoln read in his

HON. WILLIAM H. HERNDON, LINCOLN'S LAW PARTNER AFTER 1843.

boyhood, had filled him with enthusiasm for the great Whig leader, and when the latter was nominated for the Presidency, in 1844, there was no more earnest adherent of his cause than the "Sangamon Chief," as Lincoln was now called. Lincoln canvassed Illinois and a part of Indiana during the campaign, meeting the chief Democratic speakers, and especially

Douglas, in debate. Among the places visited at this time
was Gentryville, the little town only a mile or two from Lincoln's old home. A curious and ludicrous adventure which
marked his visit here is related by Mr. Lamon. "While he
was in the midst of his speech at Gentryville, his old friend,
Nat Grigsby, entered the room. Lincoln recognized him on
the instant, and, stopping short in his remarks, cried out,
'There's Nat!' Without the slightest regard for the proprieties of the occasion, he suspended his address totally, and,
striding from the platform, began scrambling through the audience and over the benches toward the modest Nat, who stood
near the door. When he reached him, Lincoln shook his
hand cordially; and after felicitating himself sufficiently upon
the happy meeting, he returned to the platform and finished
his speech. When that was over, Lincoln could not make up
his mind to part with Nat, but insisted that they must sleep
together. Accordingly they wended their way toward Colonel
Jones's, where that fine old Jackson Democrat received his
distinguished clerk with all the honors he could show him.
Nat says that in the night 'a cat began mewing, scratching,
and making a fuss generally.' Lincoln got up, took the cat
in his hands, and stroking its back gently and kindly, made it
sparkle for Nat's amusement. He then gently put it out of
the door, and, returning to bed, commenced telling stories and
talking over old times."

A VISIT TO HENRY CLAY.

Mr. Lincoln had not, at this time, heard the "silvery-
tongued orator" of Kentucky; but two years later the opportunity was afforded and eagerly embraced. It is possible, as
Dr. Holland remarks, that he "needed the influence of this
visit to restore a healthy tone to his feelings, and to teach him
that the person whom his imagination had transformed into a
demigod was only a man, possessing the full measure of
weaknesses common to men. In 1846 Mr. Lincoln learned

that Mr. Clay had agreed to deliver a speech at Lexington, Kentucky, in favor of gradual emancipation. He had never seen the great Kentuckian, and this event seemed to give him an excuse for breaking away from his business and satisfying his curiosity to look his demigod in the face and hear the music of his eloquence. He accordingly went to Lexington, and arrived there in time to attend the meeting. On returning to his home from this visit, he did not attempt to disguise his disappointment. The speech itself was written and read. It lacked entirely the fire which Mr. Lincoln had anticipated, and was not eloquent at all. At the close of the meeting, Mr. Lincoln secured an introduction to the great orator, and as Mr. Clay knew what a friend to him Mr. Lincoln had been, he invited his admirer and partisan to Ashland. No invitation could have delighted Mr. Lincoln more; but the result of his private intercourse with Mr. Clay was no more satisfactory than that which followed the speech. Those who have known both men will not wonder at this, for two men could hardly be more unlike in their motives and manners than the two thus brought together. One was a proud man; the other was a humble man. One was princely in his bearing; the other was lowly. One was distant and dignified; the other was as simple and teachable as a child. One received the deference of men as his due; the other received it with an uncomfortable sense of his unworthiness. A friend of Mr. Lincoln, who had a long conversation with him after his return from Ashland, found that his old enthusiasm was gone. Mr. Lincoln said that though Mr. Clay was polished in his manners, and very hospitable, he betrayed a consciousness of superiority that none could mistake."

ELECTED TO CONGRESS.

For two years after the Presidential contest between Clay and Polk, Mr. Lincoln devoted himself assiduously to his law practice. But in 1846 he was again active in the strife for a seat in the National Congress. His chief opponent among the Whig candidates was his old friend John J. Hardin, who soon withdrew from the contest, leaving Mr. Lincoln alone in the field. The candidate on the Democratic ticket was Peter Cartwright, the famous Methodist preacher. It was supposed, from his great popularity as a pulpit orator, that Mr. Cartwright would run far ahead of his ticket; but instead of this, Mr. Lincoln received a majority of 1,511 in his district, which in 1844 had given Clay a majority of only 914, and in 1848 allowed the Whig candidate for Congress to be defeated by 106.

CONGRESSIONAL LIFE.

Mr. Lincoln took his seat in the 30th Congress, in December, 1847, the only Whig member from Illinois. Among the notable members of this Congress were ex-President John Quincy Adams; Andrew Johnson, elected Vice-President with Lincoln on his second election; A. H. Stephens, afterwards Vice-President of the Confederacy; besides Toombs, Rhett, Cobb, and others who afterwards became leaders of the Rebellion. In the Senate were Daniel Webster, Simon Cameron, Lewis Cass, Mason, Hunter, John C. Calhoun, and Jefferson Davis.

LINCOLN'S REPUTATION IN CONGRESS.

Mr. Lincoln entered Congress as the Illinois leader of the Whig party. He was reputed to be an able and effective speaker. In speaking of the impression he made upon his associates, the Hon. Robert C. Winthrop says: "I recall vividly the impressions I then formed, both of his ability and amiability. We were old Whigs together, and agreed entirely upon all questions of public interest. I could not always concur in the policy of the party which made him President, but I never lost my personal regard for him. For shrewdness and sagacity, and keen practical sense, he has had no superior in our day or generation."

Alexander H. Stephens, writing seventeen years after

Lincoln's death, and recalling their service together in Congress, says: "I knew Mr. Lincoln well and intimately. We were both ardent supporters of General Taylor for President in 1848. Mr. Lincoln, Toombs, Preston, myself, and others, formed the first Congressional Taylor Club, known as 'The Young Indians,' and organized the Taylor movement, which resulted in his nomination. Mr. Lincoln was careless as to his manners and awkward in his speech, but possessed a very strong, clear, vigorous mind. He always attracted and riveted the attention of the House when he spoke. His manner of speech as well as of thought was original. He had no model. He was a man of strong convictions, and what Carlyle would have called an *earnest* man. He abounded in anecdote. He illustrated everything he was talking about by an anecdote, always exceedingly apt and pointed; and socially he always kept his company in a roar of laughter."

FIRST SPEECH IN CONGRESS.—"GETTING THE HANG" OF THE HOUSE.

Alluding to his first speech in Congress—on some post-office question of no special interest—Mr. Lincoln wrote to his friend Herndon that his principal object was to "get the hang of the House;" and adds that he "found speaking here and elsewhere about the same thing. I was about as badly scared, and no more, than when I spoke in court."

THE WAR ON MEXICO.

During his term of service in the House, Mr. Lincoln was zealous in the performance of his duties, and alert to seize every opportunity to strike a blow for his party and acquit himself to the satisfaction of his constituents. In January, 1848, he made a telling speech in support of the "Spot Resolutions," in which his antagonism to the course of the Administration in regard to the war on Mexico was uncompromisingly announced. These resolutions were offered for the purpose of getting from President Polk a statement of facts re-

garding the beginning of the war; and in his speech he warned
the President not to try to "escape scrutiny by fixing the public gaze upon the exceeding brightness of military glory—that
attractive rainbow that rises in showers of blood, that serpent's
eye that charms but to destroy." In writing, a few days
after the delivery of this speech, to Mr. Herndon, Lincoln said: "I will stake my life that if you had been in my
place you would have voted just as I did. Would you have
voted what you felt and knew to be a lie? I know you would
not. Would you have gone out of the House—skulked the
vote? I expect not. If you had skulked one vote, you would
have had to skulk many more before the end of the session.
Richardson's resolutions, introduced before I made any move or
gave any vote upon the subject, make a direct question of the
justice of the war; so that no man can be silent if he would.
You are compelled to speak; and your only alternative is to
tell the *truth* or tell a *lie*. I cannot doubt which you would
do."

LINCOLN'S COURSE REGARDING THE MEXICAN WAR, AS EX-PLAINED BY HIMSELF.

Mr. Lincoln's position regarding the Mexican war has
been generally approved by the moral sense of the country;
but it gave his political enemies an opportunity, which they
were not slow to improve, for trying to make political capital
out of it, and using it to create a prejudice against Mr. Lincoln. Mr. Douglas, particularly, never missed an opportunity
of referring to it; and in the great joint debate in 1858 he
spoke of Lincoln's having "distinguished himself in Congress
by his opposition to the Mexican war, taking the side of the
common enemy against his own country." No better refuta-
tion of these oft-repeated charges could be made than that
given by Mr. Lincoln on this occasion. "The Judge charges
me," he said, "with having, while in Congress, opposed our
soldiers who were fighting in the Mexican war. I will tell

you what he can prove by referring to the record. You remember I was an old Whig; and whenever the Democratic party tried to get me to vote that *the war had been righteously begun* by the President, I would not do it. But whenever they asked for any money or land-warrants, or anything to pay the soldiers, I gave *the same vote that Judge Douglas did*. Such is the truth, and the Judge has a right to make all he can out of it."

A NOTABLE SPEECH IN CONGRESS.

The most ambitious utterance of Mr. Lincoln during this term in Congress was that of July 27, 1848, when he took for his subject the very comprehensive one of "the Presidency and General Politics." It was a piece of sound and forcible argumentation, relieved by strong and effective imagery and quiet humor. A considerable portion of it was occupied with an exposure of the weaknesses of General Cass, the candidate opposed to General Taylor, whom he ridiculed with all the wit at his command. An extract from this speech has already been quoted in the account of the Black Hawk war. Another passage, equally telling, relates to the vacillating action of General Cass on the Wilmot Proviso. After citing a number of facts in reference to the case, Mr. Lincoln says: "These extracts show that in 1846 General Cass was for the Proviso *at once*; that in March, 1847, he was still for it, *but not just then;* and that in December, 1847, he was *against it* altogether. This is a true index to the whole man. When the question was raised in 1846, he was in a blustering hurry to take ground for it. He sought to be in advance, and to avoid the uninteresting position of a mere follower; but soon he began to see glimpses of the great Democratic ox-gad waving in his face, and to hear indistinctly a voice saying, 'Back! Back, sir! Back a little!' He shakes his head, and bats his eyes, and blunders back to his position of March, 1847; but still the gad waves, and the voice grows more distinct, and sharper still, 'Back, sir! Back, I say! Further back!' and back he goes to the position of December, 1847; at which the gad is still, and the voice soothingly says, 'So! Stand still at that!'"

RIDICULE OF GENERAL CASS.

Again, after extended comment on the extra charges of General Cass upon the Treasury for military services, he continued, in a still more sarcastic vein: "But I have introduced General Cass' accounts here, chiefly to show the wonderful physical capacities of the man. They show that he not only did the labor of several men *at the same time*, but that he often did it *at several places* many hundred miles apart, *at the same time*. And at eating, too, his capacities are shown to be quite as wonderful. From October, 1821, to May, 1822, he ate ten rations a day in Michigan, ten rations a day here in Washington, and near five dollars' worth a day besides, partly on the road between the two places. And then, there is an important discovery in his example—the art of being paid for what one eats, instead of having to pay for it. Hereafter, if any nice young man shall owe a bill which he cannot pay in any other way, he can just board it out. Mr. Speaker, we have all heard of the animal standing in doubt between two stacks of hay, and starving to death; the like of that would never happen to General Cass. Place the stacks a thousand miles apart, he would stand stock-still, midway between them, and eat them *both at once;* and the green grass along the line would be apt to suffer some too, at the same time. By all means, make him President, gentlemen. He will feed you bounteously—if—if—there is any left after he shall have helped himself."

A BILL FOR THE ABOLITION OF SLAVERY.

Lincoln's most important act in the Congress of 1848-9 was the introduction of a bill for the gradual abolition of slavery in the District of Columbia. But the state of feeling on the subject of emancipation was so feverish at the time, that the bill could not even be got before the House.

THE WHIG CONVENTION OF 1848, AT PHILADELPHIA.

The Whig National Convention met at Philadelphia the first of June, to nominate a candidate for the Presidency. Mr. Lincoln attended the Convention as a delegate from Illinois. During the campaign of 1848 he labored earnestly for the election of General Taylor, speaking in New York and New England as well as in Illinois and the West.

ADVICE TO YOUNG POLITICIANS.

Once again in Washington, his correspondence was resumed with Mr. Herndon, and, endeavoring to incite the latter to political ambition, he offered some good advice:—
"Nothing could afford me more satisfaction than to learn that you and others of my young friends at home were doing battle in the contest, endearing themselves to the people, and taking a stand far above any I have ever been able to reach in their admiration. I cannot conceive that other old men feel differently. Of course, I cannot demonstrate what I say; but I was young once, and I am sure I was never ungenerously thrust back. The way for a young man to rise is to improve himself in every way he can, never suspecting that anybody wishes to hinder him. Allow me to assure you that suspicion and jealousy never did help any man in any situation. There may sometimes be ungenerous attempts to keep a young man down; and they will succeed, too, if he allows his mind to be diverted from its true channel, to brood over the attempted injury. Cast about, and see if this feeling has not injured every person you have ever known to fall into it. Now, in what I have said I am sure·you will suspect nothing but sincere friendship. I would save you from a fatal error. You have been a laborious, studious young man. You are far better informed on almost all subjects than I have ever been. You cannot fail in any laudable object, unless you allow your mind to be improperly directed. I have some the advantage of you in the world's experience, merely by being older; and it is this that induces me to advise."

"OLD ABE."

It will be observed that Mr. Lincoln speaks of himself in this letter as an "old man." This had been a habit with him for years; and yet at this date he was under forty. He was already beginning to be known as "Old Abe." Hon. E. B. Washburne states that he remembers hearing him thus called, in Chicago, in July, 1847. "One afternoon," says Mr. Washburne, "several of us sat on the sidewalk under the balcony in front of the Sherman House, and among the number was the accomplished scholar and unrivalled orator, Lisle Smith, who suddenly interrupted the conversation by exclaiming, 'There is Lincoln on the other side of the street! *Just look at old Abe!*' And from that time we all called him 'Old Abe.' No one who saw him can forget his personal appearance at that time. Tall, angular, and awkward, he had on a short-waisted, thin, swallow-tail coat, a short vest of the same material, thin pantaloons scarcely coming down to his ankles, a straw hat, and a pair of brogans, with woollen socks."

A POLITICAL DISAPPOINTMENT.

During the summer following the expiration of Mr. Lincoln's term in Congress (March 4, 1849), he made a strong effort to secure the position of Commissioner of the General Land Office, but without success. The place was given to Justin Butterfield of Chicago. It was a severe disappointment to Mr. Lincoln.

MR. LINCOLN'S APPEARANCE AS AN OFFICE-SEEKER IN WASHINGTON.

Major Wilcox, who, at the period referred to, lived in McDonough county, Illinois, and in early days was a Whig politician, visited Washington to aid Mr. Lincoln in seeking this appointment, and has furnished a graphic account of the circumstances and of Mr. Lincoln's appearance at the National Capital in the novel capacity of an office-seeker. Major Wilcox says that in June, 1849, he went to Washington and had an interview with the newly-inaugurated President, General Taylor, regarding Mr. Lincoln's appointment to the desired office. The interview was but partially satisfactory, the President remarking that he was favorable to Mr. Lincoln, but that Mr. Butterfield was very strongly urged for the place, and the chances of appointment were in his favor. Mr. Lincoln had arranged to be in Washington at a time specified, after Major Wilcox should have got settled and had sufficient opportunity to look the ground over. Major Wilcox says that he went to the railroad depot to meet Mr. Lincoln at the train. It was in the afternoon, towards night; the day had been quite warm, and the road was dry and dusty. He found Mr. Lincoln just emerging from the depot. He had on a thin suit of summer clothes, his coat being a linen duster, much soiled; and his whole appearance was decidedly shabby. He carried in his hand an old-fashioned carpet-sack, which added to the oddity of his appearance. Major Wilcox says if it had been anybody else he would have been rather shy of being seen in his company, from the awkward and unseemly appearance he presented. Mr. Lincoln immediately began to talk about his chances for the appointment; whereupon Major Wilcox related to him everything that had transpired, and what President Taylor had said to him. They proceeded at once to Major Wilcox's room, where they sat down to look over the situation. Mr. Lincoln took from his pocket a paper he had prepared in the case, which comprised eleven reasons why he should be appointed Commissioner of the General Land Office. Amongst other things, Mr. Lincoln presented the fact that he had been a member of Congress from Illinois two years; that his location was in the West, where the government lands were; that he was a native of the West, and had been reared under Western influences. He gave reasons why the appointment should be given to Illinois, and particularly to the southern part of the State. Major Wilcox says that he was forcibly struck by the clear, convincing and methodical statement of Mr. Lincoln, as contained in these eleven reasons why he should have the appointment. But it was given to Mr. Butterfield.

A DIVINITY THAT SHAPES OUR ENDS.

After Mr. Lincoln became President, a Member of Congress asked for an appointment in the army in behalf of a son of the same Justin Butterfield. When the application was presented, the President paused, and after a moment's silence, said: "Mr. Justin Butterfield once obtained an appointment I very much wanted, and in which my friends believed I could have been useful, and to which they thought I was fairly entitled; and I hardly ever felt so bad at any failure in my life. But I am glad of an opportunity of doing a service to his son." And he made an order for his commission. In lieu of the desired office, General Taylor offered Mr. Lincoln the post of Governor, and afterwards of Secretary, of Oregon Territory; but these offers he declined. In after years, a friend remarked to him, alluding to the event: "How fortunate that you declined! If you had gone to Oregon, you might have come back as Senator, but you would never have been President." "Yes, you are probably right," said he; and then, with a musing, dreamy look, he added: "I have all my life been a fatalist. What is to be, will be; or, rather, I have found all my life, as Hamlet says,—

> 'There's a divinity that shapes our ends,
> Rough-hew them how we will.' "

CHAPTER V

RETIRING somewhat reluctantly from Washington life, which he seems to have liked very much, Mr. Lincoln returned to Springfield in 1849, and resumed the practice of the law. He declined an advantageous offer of a law-partnership at Chicago, made him by Judge Goodrich, giving as a reason that if he went to Chicago he would have to sit down and study hard, and this would kill him; that he would rather go around the circuit than to sit down and die in Chicago. So he settled down once more at Springfield.

LINCOLN'S PERSONAL APPEARANCE.

A gentleman who knew Lincoln intimately in Springfield has given the following capital description of him: "He stands six feet four inches high in his stockings. His frame is not muscular, but gaunt and wiry; his arms are long, but not disproportionately so for a person of his height; his lower limbs are not disproportioned to his body. In walking, his gait, though firm, is never brisk. He steps slowly and deliberately, almost always with his head inclined forward and his hands clasped behind his back. In matters of dress he is by no means precise. Always clean, he is never fashionable; he is careless, but not slovenly. In manner he is remarkably cordial, and, at the same time, simple. His politeness is always sincere, but never elaborate and oppressive. A warm shake of the hand, and a warmer smile of recognition, are his methods of greeting his friends. At rest, his features, though those of a man of mark, are not such as belong to a handsome man; but when his fine dark gray eyes are lighted up by any emotion, and his features begin their play, he would be chosen from among a crowd as one who had in him not only the kindly sentiments which women love, but the heavier metal of which full-grown men and Presidents are made. His hair is black, and, though thin, is wiry. His head sits well on his shoulders, but beyond that it defies description. It nearer resembles that of Clay than that of Webster; but it is unlike either. It is very large, and, phrenologically, well proportioned, betokening power in all its developments. A slightly Roman nose, a wide-cut mouth, and a dark complexion, with the appearance of having been weather-beaten, complete the description.''

GLIMPSES OF HOME-LIFE.

Of Mr. Lincoln's life at this period, another writer says: ''He lived simply, comfortably, and respectably, with neither expensive tastes nor habits. His wants were few and simple. He occupied a small, unostentatious house in Springfield, and was in the habit of entertaining, in a very simple way, his friends and his brethren of the bar, during the terms of the court and the sessions of the Legislature. Mrs. Lincoln often entertained small numbers of friends at dinner, and somewhat larger numbers at evening parties. In his modest and simple home, everything was orderly and refined, and there was always, on the part of both Mr. and Mrs. Lincoln, a cordial and hearty Western welcome which put every guest perfectly at ease. Yet it was the wit and humor, anecdote, and unrivalled conversation of the host, which formed the chief attraction, and made a dinner at Lincoln's cottage an event to be remembered. Lincoln's income from his profession was now from $2,000 to $3,000 per annum. His property consisted of his house and lot in Springfield, a lot in the town of Lincoln, which had been given to him, and 160 acres of wild land in Iowa, which he had received for his services in the Black Hawk war. He owned a few law and miscellaneous books. All his property may have been of the value of $10,000 or $12.000.''

LINCOLN'S FAMILY.

Mr. Lincoln was at this time the father of two sons: Robert Todd, born on the 1st day of August, 1843; and Edward Baker, on the 10th of March, 1846. In a letter to his friend Speed, dated October 22 of the latter year, Mr. Lincoln writes: ''We have another boy, born the 10th of March. He is very much such a child as Bob was at his age, rather of a *longer* order. Bob is 'short and low,' and I expect he always will be. He talks very plainly, almost as plainly as anybody. He is quite smart enough. I sometimes fear he is one of the little *rare-ripe* sort, that are smarter at about five than ever after. He has a great deal of that sort of mischief that is the offspring of much animal spirits. Since I began this letter, a messenger came to tell me Bob was lost; but by the time I reached the house his mother had found him, and had him whipped; and by now, very likely, he is run away again.''

December 21, 1850, a third son, William Wallace, was born to him; and on April 4, 1853, a fourth and last child, named Thomas.

LINCOLN'S ABSENT-MINDEDNESS.

''A young man bred in Springfield,'' says Dr. Holland, ''speaks of a vision that has clung to his memory very vividly, of Mr. Lincoln as he appeared in those days. His way to school led by the lawyer's door. On almost any fair summer morning, he would find Mr. Lincoln on the sidewalk, in front of his house, drawing a child backward and forward in a child's gig. Without hat or coat, and wearing a pair of rough shoes, his hands behind him holding to the tongue of the gig, and his tall form bent forward to accommodate himself to the service, he paced up and down the walk, forgetful of everything around him, and intent only on some subject that absorbed his mind.   The young man says he remembers wondering, in his boyish way, how so rough and plain a man should happen to live in so respectable a house.   The habit of mental absorption or 'absent-mindedness,' as it is called, was common with him always, but particularly during the formative periods of his life.   The New Salem people, it will be remembered, thought him crazy, because he passed his best friends in the street without seeing them.   At the table, in his own family, he often sat down without knowing or realizing where he was, and ate his food mechanically.   When he 'came to himself,' it was a trick with him to break the silence by the quotation of some verse of poetry from a favorite author.   It relieved the awkwardness of the situation, served as a 'blind' to the thoughts which had possessed him, and started conversation in a channel that led as far as possible from the subject that he had set aside."

A LITTLE GIRL'S OPINION OF LINCOLN.

Mr. Lincoln was a lover of children, and easily won their confidence.   Once a little girl, who had been told that Mr. Lincoln was a very homely man, was taken by her father to call upon him at his house.   Mr. Lincoln took her upon his knee and chatted with her a moment in his merry way, when she turned to her father and exclaimed: "O, pa! He isn't ugly at all; he's beautiful!"

A PAINFUL SUBJECT.

Mr. Lamon has written with great freedom of the sorrow that brooded over Lincoln's home.   Some knowledge of the blight which this cast upon his life is necessary for a right interpretation of the gloomy moods which constantly oppressed him, and which left their indelible impress on his face and character.   Mr. Lamon states unreservedly that Mr. Lincoln's marriage was an unhappy one.   The circumstances preceding

his union with Miss Todd have been related. Mr. Lamon
says: "He was conscientious and honorable and just. There
was but one way of repairing the injury he had done Miss
Todd, and he adopted it. They were married; but they understood each other, and suffered the inevitable consequences.
But such troubles seldom fail to find a tongue; and it is not
strange that in this case neighbors and friends, and ultimately
the whole country, came to know the state of things in that
house. Mr. Lincoln scarcely attempted to conceal it, but
talked of it with little or no reserve to his wife's relatives as
well as to his own friends. Yet the gentleness and patience
with which he bore this affliction from day to day, and from
year to year, was enough to move the shade of Socrates. It
touched his acquaintances deeply, and they gave it the widest
publicity." Mrs. Colonel Chapman, daughter of Dennis
Hanks, and a relative of Mr. Lincoln, made him a long visit
previous to her marriage. "You ask me," says she, "how Mr.
Lincoln acted at home. I can say, and that truly, he was all
that a husband, father and neighbor should be, kind and affectionate to his wife and child ('Bob' being the only one
they had when I was with them), and very pleasant to all
around him. Never did I hear him utter an unkind word."

A MAN OF SORROWS.

It seems impossible to arrive at all the causes of Mr. Lincoln's melancholy disposition. He was, according to his
most intimate friends, totally unlike other people, and was, in
fact, a "mystery." But whatever the history or the cause—
whether physical reasons, the absence of domestic concord, a
series of painful recollections of his mother, of early sorrows
and hardships, of Anne Rutledge and fruitless hopes, or all
these combined,—Mr. Lincoln was a terribly sad and gloomy
man. "I do not think that he knew what happiness was for
twenty years," says Mr. Herndon. " '*Terrible*' is the word
which all his friends used to describe him in the black mood.
'It was terrible! It was terrible!' said one to another."

Judge Davis believes that Mr. Lincoln's hilarity was mainly simulated, and that "his stories and jokes were intended to whistle off sadness." "The groundwork of his social nature was sad," says Judge Scott; "but for the fact that he studiously cultivated the humorous, it would have been very sad indeed. His mirth to me always seemed to be put on, and did not properly belong there. Like a plant produced in the hot-bed, it had an unnatural and luxuriant growth." Mr. Herndon, Lincoln's law-partner and intimate friend, describes him at this period as a "thin, tall, wiry, sinewy, grizzly, raw-boned man, looking 'woe-struck.' His countenance was haggard and careworn, exhibiting all the marks of deep and protracted suffering. Every feature of the man—the hollow eyes, with the dark rings beneath; the long, sallow, cadaverous face, intersected by those peculiar deep lines; his whole air; his walk; his long silent reveries, broken at long intervals by sudden and startling exclamations, as if to confound an observer who might suspect the nature of his thoughts,—showed he was a man of sorrows, not sorrows of to-day or yesterday, but long-treasured and deep, bearing with him a continual sense of weariness and pain. He was a plain, homely, sad, weary-looking man, to whom one's heart warmed involuntarily, because he seemed at once miserable and kind."

FAMILIAR APPEARANCE IN THE STREETS OF SPRINGFIELD.

Mr. Page Eaton, an old resident of Springfield, says: "Mr. Lincoln always did his own marketing, even after he was elected President, and before he went to Washington. I used to see him at the butcher's or the baker's every morning, with his basket on his arm. He was kind and sociable, and would always speak to every one. He was so kind, so child-like, that I don't believe there was one in the city who didn't love him as a father or brother." "On a winter's morning," says Mr. Lamon, "he could be seen wending his way to the market, with a basket on his arm and a little boy at his side, whose small feet rattled and pattered over the ice-bound pavement, attempting to make up by the number of his short steps for the long strides of his father. The little fellow jerked at the bony hand which held his, and prattled and questioned, begged and grew petulant, in a vain effort to make his father talk to him. But the latter was probably unconscious of the other's existence, and stalked on, absorbed in his own reflections. He wore on such occasions an old gray shawl, rolled into a coil, and wrapped like a rope around his neck. The rest of his clothes were in keeping. 'He did not walk cunningly,—Indian-like,—but cautiously and firmly.' His tread was even and strong. He was a little pigeon-toed; and this, with another peculiarity, made his walk very singular. He set his whole foot flat on the ground, and in turn lifted it all at once,—not resting momentarily upon the toe as the foot rose, nor upon the heel as it fell. He never wore his shoes out at the heel and the toe, as most men do, more than at the middle of the sole. Yet his gait was not altogether awkward, and there was manifest physical power in his step. As he moved along thus, silent and abstracted, his thoughts dimly reflected in his sharp face, men turned to look after him as an object of sympathy as well as curiosity. His melancholy, in the words of Mr. Herndon, 'dripped from him as he walked.' If, however, he met a friend in the street, and was roused by a loud, hearty 'Good-morning, Lincoln!' he would grasp the friend's hand with one or both of his own, and, with his usual expression of 'Howdy! howdy!' would detain him to hear a story; something reminded him of it; it happened in Indiana, and it must be told, for it was wonderfully pertinent. It was not at home that he most enjoyed seeing company. He preferred to meet his friends abroad,—on a street-corner, in an office, at the court house, or sitting on nail-kegs in a country store." Mrs. Lincoln experienced great difficulty in securing the punctual attendance of her husband at the family meals. Dr. Bateman has repeatedly seen two of the boys pulling with all their might at his coat-tails, and a third pushing in front, while *paterfamilias* stood upon the street cordially shaking the hand of an old acquaintance.

A GAME OF CHESS INTERRUPTED.

On one occasion Mr. Lincoln was engaged in a game of chess with Judge Treat, when the irrepressible Tad entered the office to bring his father home to supper. As Mr. Lincoln did not obey the summons, Tad attempted one or two offensive movements against the chess-board, but was warded off by the long outstretched arm of his father. When a cessation of hostilities occurred, Mr. Lincoln, intent upon the game, fell off his guard. It was not long, however, before the table suddenly *bucked*, sending the chess-board and pieces to the floor. Judge Treat was naturally vexed, and strongly urged the infliction of summary punishment upon the miscreant. But Mr. Lincoln only said, as he calmly took his hat to go home: "Considering the position of your pieces, Judge, at the time of the upheaval, I think you had no reason to complain." The Judge, however, has always said that he never could forgive Lincoln for not chastising that urchin.

SCENES IN THE LAW-OFFICE.

After his breakfast-hour, says Mr. Lamon, he would appear at his office, and go about the labors of the day with all his might, displaying prodigious industry and capacity for continuous application, although he never was a fast worker. Sometimes it happened that he came without his breakfast; and then he would have in his hands a piece of cheese, or bologna sausage, and a few crackers, bought by the way. At such times he did not speak to his partner or his friends, if any happened to be present; the tears, perhaps, struggling into his eyes, while his pride was struggling to keep them back. Mr. Herndon knew the whole story at a glance; there was no speech between them; but neither wished the visitors at the office to witness the scene; and therefore Mr. Lincoln retired to the back office, while Mr. Herndon locked the front one and walked away with the key in his pocket. In an hour or more the latter would return, and perhaps find Mr. Lincoln calm and collected; otherwise he went out again, and waited until he was so. Then the office was opened, and everything went on as usual.

FOREBODINGS OF A "GREAT OR MISERABLE END."

"His mind was filled with gloomy forebodings and strong apprehensions of impending evil, mingled with extravagant visions of personal grandeur and power. He never doubted for a moment that he was formed for some 'great or miserable end.' He talked about it frequently and sometimes calmly. Mr. Herndon remembers many of these conversations in their office at Springfield, and in their rides around the circuit. Mr. Lincoln said the impression had grown in him 'all his life;' but Mr. Herndon thinks it was about 1840 that it took the character of a 'religious conviction.' He had then suffered much, and, considering his opportunities, achieved great things. He was already a leader among men, and a most brilliant career had been promised him by the prophetic enthusiasm of many friends. Thus encouraged and stimulated, and feeling himself growing gradually stronger and stronger in the estimation of 'the plain people,' whose voice was more potent than all the Warwicks, his ambition painted the rainbow of glory in the sky, while his morbid melancholy supplied the clouds that were to overcast and obliterate it with the wrath and ruin of the tempest. To him it was fate, and there was no escape or defense. The presentiment never deserted him; it was as clear, as perfect, as certain, as any image conveyed by the senses. He had now entertained it so long, that it was as much a part of his nature as the consciousness of identity. All doubts had faded away, and he submitted humbly to a power which he could neither comprehend nor resist. He was to fall,—fall from a lofty place, and in the performance of a great work.''

AN EVENING WITH LINCOLN.

On one occasion Mr. Lincoln visited Chicago as counsel in a case in the U. S. District Court. The Hon. N. B. Judd, an intimate friend of Mr. Lincoln, was also engaged upon the case, and took Mr. Lincoln home with him as a guest. The following pleasant account of this visit is given by Mrs. Judd in Oldroyd's Memorial Album: ''Mr. Judd had invited Mr. Lincoln to spend the evening at our pleasant home on the shore of Lake Michigan. After tea, and until quite late, we sat on the broad piazza, looking out upon as lovely a scene as that which has made the Bay of Naples so celebrated. A number of vessels were availing themselves of a fine breeze to leave the harbor, and the lake was studded with many a white sail. I remember that a flock of sea-gulls were flying along the beach, and dipping their beaks and white-lined wings in the foam that capped the short waves as they fell upon the shore. Whilst we sat there the great white moon appeared on the rim of the eastern horizon, and slowly crept above the water, throwing a perfect flood of silver light upon the dancing waves. The stars shone with the soft light of a midsummer night, and the breaking of the low waves upon the shore, repeating the old rhythm of the song which they have sung for ages, added the charm of pleasant sound to the beauty of the night. Mr. Lincoln, whose home was far inland from the great lakes, seemed greatly impressed with the wondrous beauty of the scene, and carried by its impressiveness away from all thought of the jars and turmoil of earth. In that mild, pleasant voice, attuned to harmony with his surroundings, and which was his wont when his soul was stirred by aught that was lovely or beautiful, Mr. Lincoln began to speak of the mystery which for ages enshrouded and shut out those distant worlds above us from our own; of the poetry and beauty which was seen and felt by seers of old when they contemplated Orion and Arcturus as they wheeled, seemingly around the earth, in their nightly course; of the discoveries since the invention of the telescope, which had thrown a flood of light and knowledge on what before was incomprehensible and mysterious; of the wonderful computations of scientists who had measured the miles of seemingly endless space which separated the planets in our solar system from our central sun, and our sun from other suns, which were now gemming the heavens above us with their resplendent beauty. He speculated on the possibilities of knowledge which an increased power of the lens would give in the years to come; and then the wonderful discoveries of late centuries, as proving that beings endowed with such capacities as men must be immortal, and created for some high and noble end by Him who had spoken those numberless worlds into existence, and made man a little lower than the angels that he might comprehend the glories and wonders of His creation. When the night air became too chilling to remain longer on the piazza, we went into the parlor, and, seated on the sofa, his long limbs stretching across the carpet, and his arms folded behind him, Mr. Lincoln went on to speak of other discoveries, and also of the inventions which had been made during the long cycles of time lying between the present and those early days when the sons of Adam began to make use of material things about them, and invent instruments of various kinds in brass and gold and silver. He gave us a short but succinct account of all the inventions referred to in the Old Testament, from the time when Adam walked in the garden of Eden until the Bible record ended, 600 B. C. I said, 'Mr. Lincoln, I did not know you were such a Bible student.' He replied: 'I must be honest, Mrs. Judd, and tell you just how I come to know so much about these early inventions.' He then went on to say that, discussing with some friend the relative age of the discovery and use of the precious metals, he went to the Bible to satisfy himself, and became so interested in his researches that he made memoranda of the different discoveries and inventions; that soon after he was invited to lecture before some literary society, I think in Bloomington; that the interest he had felt in the study convinced him that the subject would interest others, and he therefore prepared and delivered his lecture on the 'Age of Different Inventions,' and 'of course,' he added, 'I could not after that forget the order or time of such discoveries and inventions.'"

LINCOLN'S TENDERNESS TO HIS RELATIVES.

In all the years since he had left his father's humble house, Abraham Lincoln had preserved an affectionate interest in the welfare of its various members. He paid them visits whenever he could find opportunity, and never failed to extend his aid and sympathy whenever needed. He had risen to success in his profession, was widely known throughout his section, and, though still a poor man, had good prospects and considerable influence; yet he ever retained a considerate regard and remembrance for the poor and obscure relatives he had left plodding in the humble ways of life. He never assumed the slightest superiority to them. Whenever, upon his circuit, he found time, he always visited them. Countless times he was known to leave his companions at the village hotel, after a hard day's work in the court room, and spend the evening with these old friends and companions of his humbler days. On one occasion, when urged not to go, he replied, "Why, Aunt's heart would be broken if I should leave town without calling upon her;" yet he was obliged to walk several miles to make the call. As his fortunes improved, he often sent money and presents to his father and step-mother, bought land for them, and tried in every way to make them comfortable and happy. The father was gratified at these marks of affection, and felt great pride in the rising prosperity of his son. "Mr. Lincoln," Mr. Herndon says, "for years supported, or helped to support, his aged father and mother; it is to his honor that he dearly loved his step-mother, and it is equally true that she idolized her step-son. He purchased a piece of property in Coles county as a home for his father and mother, and had it deeded in trust for their use and benefit. This was true and genuine comfort and material aid. It was not all gush, sympathy, and tears on paper; it was real, solid, genuine comfort and support, such as we can live upon.''

DEATH OF LINCOLN'S FATHER.

In 1851 his father died, at the age of seventy-three. The following letter, written a few days before this event, reveals the affectionate solicitude of the son:

"SPRINGFIELD, Jan. 12, 1851.

"DEAR BROTHER:—On the day before yesterday I received a letter from Harriet, written at Greenup. She says she has just returned from your house, and that father is very low, and will hardly recover. She also says that you have written me two letters, and that, although you do not expect me to come now, you wonder that I do not write. I received both your letters; and although I have not answered them, it is not because I have forgotten them, or not been interested about them, but because it appeared to me I could write nothing which could do any good. You already know I desire that neither father nor mother shall be in want of any comfort, either in health or sickness, while they live; and I feel sure you have not failed to use my name, if necessary, to procure a doctor or anything else for father in his present sickness. My business is such that I could hardly leave home now, if it were not, as it is, that my wife is sick a-bed. I sincerely hope father may yet recover his health; but, at all events, tell him to remember to call upon and confide in our great and good and merciful Maker, who will not turn away from him in any extremity. He notes the fall of a sparrow, and numbers the hairs of our heads; and He will not forget the dying man who puts his trust in Him. Say to him, that, if we could meet now, it is doubtful whether it would not be more painful than pleasant; but that, if it be his lot to go now, he will soon have a joyous meeting with loved ones gone before, and where the rest of us, through the help of God, hope ere long to join them.

"Write me again when you receive this.

"Affectionately,   A. LINCOLN.''

A SENSIBLE ADVISER.

The step-brother, John Johnson, to whom the foregoing letter is addressed, was a source of considerable anxiety to Mr. Lincoln. It was with him that their parents resided, and frequent were his appeals to Mr. Lincoln to extricate him from some pecuniary strait into which he had fallen through his confirmed thriftlessness and improvidence. "John Johnson was," says Mr. Herndon, "an indolent and shiftless man, one who was 'born tired.' Yet he was clever, generous and hospitable." The following communications afford a hint of Mr. Lincoln's perplexing relations with this member of his father's family:

"DEAR JOHNSON:—Your request for eighty dollars I do not think it best to comply with now. At the various times when I have helped you a little, you have said to me, 'We can get along very well now;' but in a very short time I find you in the same difficulty again. Now, this can only happen by some defect in your conduct. What that defect is, I think I know. You are not lazy, and still you are an idler. I doubt whether, since I saw you, you have done a good whole day's work in any one day. You do not very much dislike to work, and still you do not work much, merely because it does not seem to you that you could get much for it. This habit of uselessly wasting time is the whole difficulty; and it is vastly important to you, and still more so to your children, that you should break the habit. It is more important to them, because they have longer to live, and can keep out of an idle habit before they are in it easier than they can get out after they are in. You are now in need of some money; and what I propose is that you shall go to work, 'tooth and nail,' for somebody who will give you money for it. Let father and your boys take charge of things at home, prepare for a crop, and make the crop, and you go to work for the best money-wages, or in discharge of any debt you owe, that you can get; and, to secure you a fair reward for your labor, I now promise you, that, for every dollar you will, between this and the first of next May, get for your own labor, either in money or as your own indebtedness, I will then give you one other dollar. By this, if you hire yourself at ten dollars a month, from me you will get ten more, making twenty dollars a month for your work. In this I do not mean you shall go off to St. Louis, or the lead-mines, or the gold-mines in California; but I mean for you to go at it, for the best wages you can get, close to home, in Coles county. Now, if you will do this you will soon be out of debt, and, what is better, you will have a habit that will keep you from getting in debt again. But if I should now clear you out of debt, next year you would be in just as deep as ever. You say you would almost give your place in heaven for $70 or $80. Then you value your place in heaven very cheap; for I am sure you can, with the offer I make, get the seventy or eighty dollars for four or five months' work. You say, if I will furnish you the money, you will deed me the land, and if you don't pay the money back, you will deliver possession. Nonsense! If you can't now live with the land, how will you then live without it? You have always been kind to me, and I do not mean to be unkind to you. On the contrary, if you will but follow my advice, you will find it worth more than eighty times eighty dollars to you.

"Affectionately your brother,   A. LINCOLN."

CARE OF HIS STEP-MOTHER.

Lincoln's affectionate care for the step-mother who had loved and cared for him so tenderly in his boyhood, continued unabated so long as.she lived. "He could not bear," says Mr. Speed, "to have anything said by any one against her." In the following letters his consideration for her welfare and his regard for the children of his step-brother are very apparent.

"SHELBYVILLE, Nov. 4, 1851.

"DEAR BROTHER:—When I came into Charleston, day before yesterday, I learned that you are anxious to sell the land where you live, and move to Missouri. I have been thinking of this ever since, and cannot but think such a notion is utterly foolish. What can you do in Missouri better than here? Is the land any richer? Can you there, any more than here, raise corn and wheat and oats without work? Will any body there, any more than here, do your work for you? If you intend to go to work, there is no better place than right where you are; if you do not intend to go to work, you can not get along any where. Squirming and crawling about from place to place can do no good. You have raised no crop this year; and what you really want is to sell the land, get the money and spend it. Part with the land you have, and, my life upon it, you will never after own a spot big enough to bury you in. Half of what you will get for the land you will spend in moving to Missouri, and the other half you will eat and drink and wear out, and no foot of land will be bought. Now, I feel it is my duty to have no hand in such a piece of foolery. I feel that it is so even on your own account, and particularly on mother's account. The eastern forty acres I intend to keep for mother while she lives; if you will not cultivate it, it will rent for enough to support her; at least, it will rent for something. Her dower in the other two forties she can let you have, and no thanks to me. Now, do not misunderstand this letter. I do not write it in any unkindness. I write it in order, if possible, to get you to face the truth, which truth is, you are destitute because you have idled away all your time. Your thousand pretences for not getting along better are all nonsense. They deceive nobody but yourself. *Go to work* is the only cure for your case. A word to mother. Chapman tells me he wants you to go and live with him. If I were you, I would try it awhile. If you get tired of it (as I think you will not), you can return to your own home. Chapman feels very kindly to you; and I have no doubt he will make your situation very pleasant.

"Sincerely your son,   A. LINCOLN."

"SHELBYVILLE, Nov. 9, 1851.

"DEAR BROTHER:—When I wrote you before, I had not received your letter. I still think as I did; but if the land can be sold so that I get $300 to put at interest for mother, I will not object, if she does not. But before I will make a deed, the money must be had, or secured beyond all doubt, at ten per cent. As to Abram, I do not want him on my own account; but I understand he wants to live with me, so that he can go to school, and get a fair start in the world, which I very much wish him to have. When I reach home, if I can make it convenient I will take him, provided there is no mistake between us as to the object and terms of my taking him.

"In haste, as ever,   A. LINCOLN."

AN INTERVIEW WITH SARAH LINCOLN.

In speaking of Lincoln's regard for his step-mother, it is interesting also to learn her opinion of him. A gentleman, visiting the old lady after her son's death, says: "She is eighty-four years old and quite feeble. She is a plain, unsophisticated old lady, with a frank, open countenance, a warm heart, full of kindness toward others, and in many respects very much like the President. Abraham was evidently her idol; she speaks of him still as her 'good boy,' and with much feeling said, 'He was always a good boy, and willing to do just what I wanted. He and his step-brother never quarreled but once, and that, you know, is a great deal for step-brothers. I didn't want him elected President. I knowed they would kill him.'" She died in April, 1869, and was buried by the side of her husband, Thomas Lincoln.

CHAPTER VI.

LINCOLN'S LAW PRACTICE.——APPEARANCE IN COURT.——REMINISCENCES OF A LAW-STUDENT IN LINCOLN'S OFFICE.——AN "OFFICE COPY" OF BYRON. ——NOVEL WAY OF KEEPING PARTNERSHIP ACCOUNTS.——CHARGES FOR LEGAL SERVICES.——TRIAL OF BILL ARMSTRONG.——KINDNESS TOWARD UNFORTUNATE CLIENTS.—— REFUSING TO DEFEND A GUILTY MAN.—— WANTED TO WASH HIS HANDS.——COULDN'T TAKE PAY FOR DOING HIS DUTY.——"BETTER MAKE SIX HUNDRED DOLLARS SOME OTHER WAY."—— "A SMALL CROP OF FIGHT FOR AN ACRE OF GROUND."——FIXING A "PLUG FOR HIS GALLOWS."——"TAKING UP TACKLING" BEFORE A JURY.——A MAN "WHO HADN'T SENSE ENOUGH TO PUT ON HIS SHIRT."——LINCOLN AS A HORSE-TRADER.——SOME STRIKING OPINIONS OF LINCOLN AS A LAWYER.

THE ten years following the close of Lincoln's Congressional service, in 1849, were given to the uninterrupted practice of the law, to which he devoted himself laboriously and successfully, though not with great pecuniary gains. His legal fees were regarded by his brethren at the bar as "ridiculously small." His practice had extended to the Supreme Court of his State and to the United States District and Circuit Courts, and he was occasionally retained for cases in other States. With greater love of money and less sympathy for his fellows, he might easily have acquired a fortune from his business.

APPEARANCE IN COURT.

An unusually interesting and vivid description of Mr. Lincoln's personal appearance and manner in the trial of a case is furnished by one who was a witness of the scenes which he so admirably describes. The writer says: "While living in Danville, Illinois, in 1854, I saw Abraham Lincoln for the first time. The occasion of Mr. Lincoln's visit was as prosecutor of a slander suit brought by Dr. Fithian against a wealthy farmer, whose wife died under the doctor's hands. The defense was represented by Edward A. Hannegan, of Indiana, ex-United States Senator and afterward Minister to Berlin, an able and eloquent man; and O. B. Ficklin, who,

after Douglas and Lincoln, was considered the best lawyer in
Illinois. Mr. Lincoln had all he could do to maintain himself
against his two formidable adversaries, but he was equal to the
occasion. The trial lasted three or four days, the examination
of witnesses consuming most of the time. In this part of the
work Mr. Lincoln displayed remarkable tact. He did not
badger the witnesses, or attempt to confuse them. His questions were plain and practical, and elicited answers that had a
direct bearing upon the case. He did nothing for effect, and
made no attempt to dazzle the jury or captivate the audience.
When he arose to speak he was confronted by an audience
that was too numerous for all to find seats in the court room.
He was attired in a fine broadcloth suit, silk hat, and polished
boots. His neck was encircled by an old-fashioned silk choker.
He perspired freely, and used a red silk handkerchief to remove the perspiration. His clothes fitted him, and he was
as genteel-looking as any man in the audience. The slouchy
appearance which he is said to have presented later in life was
conspicuously absent. As he stood before the vast audience,
towering above every person around him, he was the center
of attraction. I can never forget how he looked, as he cast
his eyes over the crowd before beginning his argument. His
face was long and sallow; high cheek bones; large, deep-set
eyes, of a greyish-brown color, shaded by heavy eyebrows;
high but not broad forehead; large, well-formed head, covered with an abundance of coarse black hair, worn rather
long, through which he frequently passed his fingers; arms
and legs of unusual length; head inclined slightly forward,
which made him appear stoop-shouldered. His features betrayed neither excitement nor anxiety; they were calm and
fixed; in short, his appearance was that of a man who felt
the responsibility of his position, and was determined to acquit himself to the best of his ability. I do not remember
the points of his speech; but his manner was so peculiar, so
different from that of other orators whom I have heard, that

I can never forget it. He spoke for almost two hours, entirely without notes, and with an eloquence that I have never heard surpassed. He was all life, all motion; every muscle and fibre of his body seemed brought into requisition. His voice was clear, distinct, and well modulated. Every word was clean-cut and exactly suited to its place. At times he would stoop over until his hands almost swept the floor. Then he would straighten himself up, fold his arms across his breast, and take a few steps forward or back. This movement completed, he would fling his arms above his head, or thrust them beneath his coat-tails, elevating or depressing his voice to suit the attitude assumed and the sentiment expressed. Arms and legs were continually in motion. It seemed impossible for him to stand still. In the midst of the most impassioned or pathetic portions of his speech, he would extend his long arms toward the judge or jury, and shake his bony fingers with an effect that is indescribable. He held his audience to the last; and when he sat down, there was a murmur of applause, which the judge with difficulty prevented from swelling to a roar. The argument must have been as able as the manner of the speaker was attractive, for the verdict was in favor of his client.

"When he had retired to his hotel after the trial, and while conversing with a number of gentlemen who had called to pay their respects to him, Mr. Lincoln was informed that an old colored woman, who had known him years before in Kentucky, wished to see him. She was too feeble to come to him, and desired him to go to her. Ascertaining where she lived, Mr. Lincoln started at once, accompanied by a boy who acted as pilot. He found the woman in a wretched hovel in the outskirts of the town, sick and destitute. He remembered her very well, as she had belonged to the owner of the farm upon which Mr. Lincoln was born. He gave her money to supply her immediate wants, promised her that he would see she did not suffer for the necessaries of life, and when he returned to town hunted up a physician and engaged him to give the old woman all the medical attention that her case demanded.''

REMINISCENCES OF A LAW-STUDENT IN LINCOLN'S OFFICE AT SPRINGFIELD.

Mr. G. W. Harris, whose first meeting with Mr. Lincoln in a log school-house has been previously described (page 172), subsequently became a clerk in Lincoln's law-office at Springfield, and furnishes some excellent reminiscences of that interesting period. "A crack-brained attorney who lived in Springfield, supported mainly, as I understood, by the other lawyers of the place, became indebted, in the sum of two dollars and fifty cents, to a wealthy citizen of the county, a recent comer. The creditor, failing, after repeated efforts, to collect the amount due him, came to Mr. Lincoln and asked him to bring suit. Mr. Lincoln explained the man's condition and circumstances, and advised his client to let the matter rest; but the creditor's temper was up, and he insisted on having suit brought. Again Mr. Lincoln urged him to let the matter drop, adding, 'You can make nothing out of him, and it will cost you a good deal more than the debt to bring suit.' The creditor was still determined to have his way, and threatened to seek some other attorney who would be more willing to take charge of the matter than Mr. Lincoln appeared to be. Mr. Lincoln then said, 'Well, if you are determined that suit shall be brought, I will bring it; but my charge will be ten dollars.' The money was paid him, and peremptory orders were given that the suit be brought that day. After the client's departure, Mr. Lincoln went out of the office, returning in about an hour with an amused look on his face. I asked what pleased him, and he replied, 'I brought suit against ——, and then hunted him up, told him what I had done, handed him half of the ten dollars, and we went over to the squire's office. He confessed judgment and paid the bill.' Mr.

Lincoln added that he didn't see any other way to make things satisfactory for his client as well as the rest of the parties.

"Mr. Lincoln was not an abolitionist in those early days; but he was a growing man, and those who were the closest to him knew which way his steps were leading him. It was said that when the Whig party died, Mr. Lincoln 'was at sea,' not knowing whither to go. I never believed it. His clear perception of the right, his honesty of character, and his kindness of heart, left no doubt in the minds of those knowing him where he would be found when the time for action came. Recognizing fully, as he did, that this government could not exist half-slave and half-free, but must become all one or the other, it was impossible for him to do otherwise than attach himself to the Republican party.

"Mr. Lincoln had a heart that was more a woman's than a man's—filled to overflowing with sympathy for those in trouble, and ever ready to relieve them by any means in his power. He was ever thoughtful of others' comforts, even to the forgetting of himself. Even in those early days his face wore a sad look when at rest—a look that made you feel that you would like to take from him a part of his burden. One who knew him then, and had since known his career, would be inclined to think that he already felt premonitions of the heavy burdens that his broad shoulders were to bear, and the sorrows that his kind heart would have to endure.

"Mr. Lincoln was fond of playing chess and checkers, and usually acted cautiously upon the defensive until the game had reached a stage where aggressive movements were clearly justified. He was also somewhat fond of ten-pins, and occasionally indulged in a game. Whatever may have been his tastes in his younger days, at this period of his life he took no interest in fishing-rod or gun. He was indifferent to dress, careless almost to a fault of his personal appearance. The same indifference extended to money. So long as his wants were supplied—and they were few and simple—he seemed to have no further use for money, except in the giving or the lending of it, with no expectation or desire for its return, to those whom he thought needed it more than he. Debt he abhorred, and under no circumstances would he incur it. He was abstemious in every respect. I have heard him say that he 'did not know the taste of liquor. At the table he preferred plain food, and a very little satisfied him.

"Under no circumstances would he, as an attorney, take a case he knew to be wrong. Every possible means was used to get at the truth, before he would undertake a case. More cases, by his advice, were settled without trial, than he carried into the courts; and that, too, without charge. When, on one occasion, I suggested that he ought to make a charge in such cases, he laughingly answered, 'They wouldn't want to pay me; they don't think I have earned a fee unless I take the case into court and make a speech or two.' When trivial cases were brought to him, such as would most probably be carried no farther than a magistrate's office, and he could not induce a settlement without trial, he would generally refer them to some young attorney, for whom he would speak a good word at the same time. He was ever kind and courteous to these young beginners when he was the opposing counsel. He had a happy knack of setting them at their ease, and encouraging them. The consequence was, he was the favorite of all who came in contact with him. When his heart was in a case he was a powerful advocate. I have heard more than one attorney say that it was little use to expect a favorable verdict in any case where Lincoln was opposing counsel, as his simple statements of the facts had more weight with the jury than those of the witnesses.

"As a student (if such a term could be applied to Mr. Lincoln) one who did not know him might have called him indolent. He would pick up a book and run rapidly over the pages, pausing here and there. At the end of an hour— never, as I remember, more than two or three hours—he would close the book, stretch himself out on the office lounge, and with hands under his head, and eyes shut, he would digest the mental food he had just taken.

"Alexander Campbell, the founder of a religious sect, once delivered a lecture in Springfield. Mr. Lincoln was in the audience. At the close of the lecture, he, with many others, was introduced to the speaker. Upon Lincoln's return to the office he remarked to me, with evident pleasure, that he had just been introduced to and shaken the hand of a man whose name would go honorably down to posterity. He little thought how much more enduring would be his own name and fame. He was always quick to see talent in others, but failed to appreciate himself.

"In the spring of 1846, war between the United States and Mexico broke out. Mr. Lincoln was opposed to the war. He looked upon it as unnecessary and unjust. Volunteers were called for. John J. Hardin, who lost his life in that war, and Edward D. Baker, who was killed at Ball's Bluff during our Civil War,—both Whigs,—were engaged in raising regiments. Meetings were held and speeches made. At one of them, after Baker and others had spoken, Lincoln, who was in the audience, was called for, and the call was repeated, until at last he ascended the platform. He thanked the audience for the compliment paid him in the wish they had expressed to hear him talk, and said he would gladly make them a speech if he had anything to say. But he was not going into the war; and as he was not going himself, he did not feel like telling others to go. He would simply leave it to each individual to do as he thought his duty called for. After a few more remarks, and a story 'with a nib to it,' he bowed himself off the platform.

"About a year after this, Mr. Lincoln was seeking to be nominated as a candidate for Congress. Finding the writing of letters (at his dictation) to influential men in the different counties and even precincts of the district somewhat burdensome, I suggested printing circulars. He objected, on the ground that a printed letter would not have the same effect that a written one would; the latter had the appearance of personality; it was more flattering to the receiver, and would more certainly gain his assistance, or at least his good-will. In discussing the probabilities of his nomination, I remarked that there was so much unfairness if not downright trickery used, that it appeared to me almost useless to seek a nomination without resort to similar means. His reply was: 'I want to be nominated; I would like to go to Congress; but if I cannot do so by fair means, I prefer to stay at home.' He was nominated, and in the following fall was elected by a majority over three times as large as the district had ever before given.

"Mr. Lincoln, like many others in their callow days, scribbled verses; and so far as I was capable of judging, their quality was above the average. It was accidentally that I learned this. In arranging the books and papers in the office, I found two or three quires of letter-paper stitched together in book form, and nearly filled with poetical effusions in Mr. Lincoln's handwriting, and evidently original. I looked through them somewhat hurriedly, and when Mr. Lincoln came in, showed him the manuscript, asking him if it was his. His response was, 'Where did you find it?' and rolling it up put it in his coat-tail pocket; and I saw it no more. Afterwards, in speaking of the matter to Mr. Lincoln's partner, he said, 'I believe he has at times scribbled some verses; but he is, I think, somewhat unwilling to have it known.'"

AN "OFFICE COPY" OF BYRON.

Lincoln's love of poetry is further shown by the following incident, related by a gentleman who visited the old law-office of Lincoln & Herndon, at Springfield. He says: "I took up carelessly, as I stood thinking, a handsome octavo volume on the business table. It opened so persistently at one place, as I played with it, that I looked to see what it was, and found that somebody had thoroughly thumbed the pages of 'Don Juan.' I knew Mr. Herndon was not a man to dwell on it, and it darted through my mind that perhaps it had been a favorite with Mr. Lincoln. 'Did Mr. Lincoln ever read this book?' I said, hurriedly. 'That book!' said Herndon, looking up from his writing, with the utmost innocence, and taking it out of my hand. 'Oh, yes; he read it often. It is the office copy.'" Mr. Lincoln was so fond of the book that he kept it ready to his hand.

KEEPING PARTNERSHIP ACCOUNTS.

Major John T. Stuart, Lincoln's first law-partner, says of him that his accounts were correctly kept, but in a manner peculiar to himself. Soon after their law-partnership was formed, Mr. Stuart was elected to Congress, thereafter spending much of his time in Washington. Mr. Lincoln conducted the business of the firm in his absence. When Mr. Stuart reached home, at the close of the first session of Congress, Mr. Lincoln proceeded to give him an account of the earnings of the office during his absence. The charges for fees and entry of receipts of money were not in an account book, but stowed away in a drawer in Lincoln's desk, among the papers in each case. He proceeded to lay the papers before Mr. Stuart, taking up each case by itself. The account would run in this way:

Fees charged in this case.............................. $
Amount collected.. .... $
Stuart's half.. $

The half belonging to Mr. Stuart would invariably accompany the papers in the case, and it was produced and paid over on the spot.

LINCOLN'S CHARGES FOR LEGAL SERVICES.

Mr. Lincoln had the reputation of being very moderate in his charges. He was never grasping, and seemed incapable of believing that his services could be worth much to any one.

Isaac Hawley, a citizen of Springfield, and long a prosperous merchant at that place, who became acquainted with Mr. Lincoln in his early manhood, relates an instance showing Mr. Lincoln's estimate of fees for his professional sevices. Mr. Hawley says that a suit in an action of ejectment for a pieee of land in Brown county, in the "military tract," was commenced against him in the United States Court at Chicago. Mr. Lincoln happening in his store one day, he informed him of the matter, knowing that he was going to Chicago to attend the next term of the United States Court, and asked him if he would give the suit attention. Mr. Lincoln took the case in charge. After a term or two had passed, Mr. Lincoln having asked some attorney residing in Chicago to look after the case during term time, in his absence, the latter presently got the case dismissed from the docket. Although the case never came to trial, yet it appears that it must have received considerable attention from Mr. Lincoln, first and last. Meeting Mr. Lincoln a considerable time thereafter, Mr. Hawley asked him how his case was getting along at the United States Court at Chicago. Mr. Lincoln replied that the client would hear nothing more about it; that a lawyer, a friend of his in Chicago, who had looked after the case in his absence, had got it dismissed from the docket, and the matter was at an end. Mr. Hawley thought it was time to inquire of Mr. Lincoln about his charges, which he supposed, from what he knew of lawyers' fees, would be about fifty dollars. In answer to his inquiry, Mr. Lincoln said: "Well, Isaac, I think I will charge you about ten dollars; I think that would be about right." Mr. Hawley responded that he certainly thought it was very reasonable.

THE TRIAL OF BILL ARMSTRONG.

One of the most famous cases in which Mr. Lincoln engaged was that of William D. Armstrong, son of Jack and Hannah Armstrong of New Salem, the child whom Mr. Lincon had rocked in the cradle while Mrs. Armstrong attended to other household duties. Jack Armstrong, it will be remembered, was an early friend of Lincoln's, whom he had conquered in a wrestling-match on his first arrival in New Salem. He and his wife had from that time treated the youth with the utmost kindness, giving him a home when he was out of work, and showing him every kindness it was in their power to offer. Lincoln never forgot his debt of gratitude to them; and when Hannah, now a widow, wrote to him of the peril her boy was in, and besought him to help them in their extremity, he replied promptly that he would do what he could. The circumstances were these: "In the summer of 1857, at a camp-meeting in Mason county, one Metzgar was most brutally murdered. The affray took place about half a mile from the place of worship, near some wagons loaded with liquor and provisions. Two men, James H. Norris and William D. Armstrong, were indicted for the crime. Norris was tried in Mason county, convicted of manslaughter, and sentenced to the penitentiary for a term of eight years. The popular feeling being very high against Armstrong in Mason county, he took a change of venue to Cass county, and was there tried (at Beardstown) in the spring of 1858. Hitherto Armstrong had had the services of two able counsellors; but now their efforts were supplemented by those of a most determined and zealous volunteer. The case was so clear against the accused that defense seemed almost useless. The strongest evidence was that of a man who swore that at eleven o'clock at night he saw Armstrong strike the deceased on the head; that the moon was shining brightly, and was nearly full; and that its position in the sky was just about that of the sun at ten o'clock in the morning, and by it he saw Armstrong give the mortal blow." This was fatal, unless the effect could be broken by contradiction or impeachment. Lincoln quietly looked up an almanac, and found that at the time this witness declared the moon to have been shining with full light, there was no moon at all. Mr. Lincoln made the closing argument. "At first," says Mr. Walker, one of the counsel associated with him, "he spoke very slowly and carefully, reviewed the testimony, and pointed out its contradictions, discrepancies and impossibilities. When he had thus prepared the way, he called for the almanac, and showed that at the hour at which the principal witness swore he had seen, by the light of the full moon, the mortal blow given, *there was no moon*. The last fifteen minutes of his speech was as eloquent as I ever heard; and such were the power and earnestness with which he spoke to that jury, that all sat as if entranced, and, when he was through, found relief in a gush of tears." Said one of the prosecutors: "He took the jury by storm. There were tears in Mr. Lincoln's eyes while he spoke, but they were genuine. His sympathies were fully enlisted in favor of the young man, and his terrible sincerity could not help but arouse the same passion in the jury. I have said a hundred times that it was Lincoln's speech that saved that man from the gallows." "Armstrong was not cleared by any want of testimony against him, but by the irresistible appeal of Mr. Lincoln in his favor," says Mr. Shaw, one of the associates in the prosecution. His mother, who sat near during Mr. Lincoln's appeal, says: "He told the stories about our first acquaintance, and what I did for him, and how I did it. Lincoln said to me, 'Hannah, your son will be cleared before sundown.' He and the other lawyers addressed the jury, and closed the case. I went down to Thompson's pasture. Stator came to me and told me that my son was cleared and a free man. I went up to the court house; the jury shook hands with me, so did the court, so did Lincoln. We were all affected, and tears streamed down Lincoln's eyes. He then remarked to me, 'Hannah, what did I tell you? I pray to God that William may be a good boy hereafter; that this lesson may prove in the end a good lesson to him and to all.' After the trial was over, Lincoln came down to where I was in Beardstown. I asked him what he charged me; told him I was poor. He said, 'Why, Hannah, I shan't charge you a cent—never. Anything I can do for you I will do willingly and without charges.' He wrote to me about some land which some men were trying to get from me, and said, 'Hannah, they can't get your land. Let them try it in the Circuit Court, and then you appeal it; bring it to the Supreme Court, and Herndon and I will attend to it for nothing.'"

KINDNESS TO UNFORTUNATE CLIENTS.

Lincoln regarded himself not only as the legal adviser of unfortunate people, but as their friend and protector; and he would never press them for pay for his services. A client named Cogdal was unfortunate in business, and gave Mr. Lincoln a note in payment of legal fees. Soon afterwards he met with an accident by which he lost a hand. Meeting Mr. Lincoln some time after, on the steps of the State House, the kind lawyer asked him how he was getting along. "Badly enough," replied Mr. Cogdal; "I am both broken up in business and crippled." Then he added, "I have been thinking about that note of yours." Mr. Lincoln, who had probably known all about Mr. Cogdal's troubles, and had prepared himself for the meeting, took out his pocket-book, and saying, with a laugh, "Well you needn't think any more about it," handed him the note. Mr. Cogdal protesting, Mr. Lincoln said, "Even if you had the money, I would not take it," and hurried away.

REFUSING TO DEFEND A GUILTY MAN.

Mr. G. L. Austin thus describes an incident of Lincoln's career at the bar: "Mr. Lincoln was once associated with Mr. Leonard Swett in defending a man accused of murder. He listened to the testimony which witness after witness gave against his client, until his honest heart could stand it no longer; then, turning to his associate, he said: 'Swett, the man is guilty; you defend him; I can't.' Swett did defend him, and the man was acquitted. When proffered his share of the large fee, Lincoln most emphatically declined it, on the ground that 'all of it belonged to Mr. Swett, whose ardor and eloquence saved a guilty man from justice.' "

WANTED TO WASH HIS HANDS.

At a term of court in Logan county, a man named Hoblit had brought suit against a man named Farmer. The suit had been appealed from a justice of the peace, and Lincoln knew nothing of it until he was retained by Hoblit to try the case in the Circuit Court. G. A. Gridley, then of Bloomington, appeared for the defendant. Judge Treat, afterwards on the United States bench, was the presiding judge at the trial. Lincoln's client went upon the witness stand and testified to the account he had against the defendant, gave the amount due after allowing all credits and set-offs, and swore positively that it had not been paid. The attorney for the defendant simply produced a receipt in full, signed by Hoblit prior to the beginning of the case. Hoblit had to admit the signing of the receipt, but told Lincoln he "supposed the cuss had lost it." Lincoln at once arose and left the court room. The Judge told the parties to proceed with the case; and Lincoln not appearing, Judge Treat directed a bailiff to go to the hotel and call him. The bailiff ran across the street to the hotel, and found Lincoln sitting in the office with his feet on the stove, apparently in a deep study, when he interrupted him with: "Mr. Lincoln, the Judge wants you." "Oh, does he?" replied Mr. Lincoln. "Well, you go back and tell the Judge I cannot come. Tell him I have to *wash my hands.*" The bailiff returned with the message, and Lincoln's client suffered a non-suit. It was Lincoln's way of saying he wanted nothing more to do with such a case.

COULDN'T TAKE PAY FOR DOING HIS DUTY.

Mr. Lincoln would never advise clients into unwise or unjust lawsuits. He would always sacrifice his own interests, and refuse a retainer, rather than be a party to a case which did not command the approval of his sense of justice. He was once waited upon by a lady, who held a real-estate claim which she desired to have him prosecute, putting into his hands, with the necessary papers, a check for two hundred and fifty dollars as a retaining fee. Mr. Lincoln said he would look the case over, and asked her to call again the next day. Upon presenting herself, Mr. Lincoln told her that he had gone through the papers very carefully, and was obliged to tell her frankly that there was "not a peg" to hang her claim upon, and he could not conscientiously advise her to bring an action. The lady was satisfied, and, thanking him, rose to go. "Wait," said Mr. Lincoln, fumbling in his vest pocket; "here is the check you left with me." "But, Mr. Lincoln," returned the lady, "I think you have earned that." "No, no," he responded, handing it back to her; "that would not be right. I can't take pay for doing my duty."

"BETTER MAKE SIX HUNDRED DOLLARS SOME OTHER WAY."

To a client who had carefully stated his case, to which Mr. Lincoln had listened with the closest attention, he said: "Yes, there is no reasonable doubt that I can gain your case for you. I can set a whole neighborhood at loggerheads; I can distress a widowed mother and her six fatherless children, and thereby get for you six hundred dollars, which rightfully belongs, it appears to me, as much to the woman and her children as it does to you. You must remember that some things that are *legally* right are not *morally* right. I shall not take your case, but will give you a little advice, for which I will charge you nothing. You seem to be a sprightly, energetic man. I would advise you to try your hand at *making six hundred dollars some other way.*"

"A SMALL CROP OF FIGHT FOR AN ACRE OF GROUND."

Senator McDonald states that he saw a jury trial in Illinois, at which Lincoln defended an old man charged with assault and battery. No blood had been spilled, but there was malice in the prosecution, and the chief witness was eager to make the most of it. On cross-examination, Lincoln "gave him rope" and drew him out; asked him how long the fight lasted, and how much ground it covered. The witness thought the fight must have lasted half an hour, and covered an acre of ground. Lincoln called his attention to the fact that nobody was hurt, and then, with an inimitable air, asked him if he didn't think it was *"a mighty small crop for an acre of ground."* The jury rejected the case with contempt, as beneath their dignity.

FIXING A "PLUG" FOR HIS "GALLUS."

Many of the stories told of Lincoln at the bar are extremely ridiculous, and represent him in anything but a dignified light. But they are a part of the character of the man, and should be given wherever there is reason to suppose they are genuine. Besides, they are usually full of a humor that is irresistible. Such an incident is given by the Hon. Lawrence Weldon, Lincoln's old friend and legal associate in Illinois. "I can see him now," says Judge Weldon, "through the decaying memories of thirty years, standing in the corner of the old court room, and as I approached him with a paper I did not understand, he said: 'Wait until I fix this plug for my "gallus," and I will pitch into that like a dog at a root.' While speaking, he was busily engaged in trying to connect his suspender with his trousers by making a 'plug' perform the function of a button. Mr. Lincoln liked old-fashioned words, and never failed to use them if they could be sustained as proper. He was probably taught to say 'gallows,' and he never adopted the modern word 'suspender.'"

"TAKING UP TACKLING" BEFORE A JURY.

The Hon. Jesse O. Norton, of Will county, for many years Judge of the Circuit Court, relates that Mr. Lincoln, having rendered the Illinois Central Railroad some valuable services, for which at this day a fee of ten thousand dollars would be considered moderate, charged the company five thousand dollars. The company refused to pay; whereupon Mr. Lincoln brought suit for the amount. The case was tried in the Circuit Court where Judge Norton was presiding. Mr. Lincoln conducted the case in person for himself. It was in the summer time, and the day was exceedingly warm. Mr. Lincoln was dressed in a linen suit, consisting of a pair of pantaloons hanging loosely upon him, and an ill-fitting somewhat soiled coat; he wore neither vest nor cravat. The jury was impanelled, and he proceeded to state his case. He said: "Gentlemen of the Jury: This case is brought by myself against the Illinois Central Railroad Company, to recover the sum of five thousand dollars for services which I rendered them as a lawyer; and although the charge is reasonable, as I think, they have refused to pay it. Therefore, I have been compelled to bring this suit." At this moment, happening to look down upon himself, he discovered that his pantaloons were drawing rather heavily upon his suspenders; and stopping his speech to the jury, he remarked, "Well, I may as well take up my tackling a hitch or two," and thereupon proceeded to readjust his suspenders through the buckles, rendering his apparel more fitted to his person. Then he continued his remarks to the jury, as if nothing had happened.

A MAN WHO "HADN'T SENSE ENOUGH TO PUT ON HIS SHIRT."

On a certain occasion Mr. Lincoln appeared at the trial of a case in which his friend Judge Logan was his opponent. It was a suit between two farmers who had had a disagreement over a horse-trade. On the day of the trial, Mr. Logan, having bought a new shirt, open in the back, with a huge standing collar, dressed himself in extreme haste, and put on the shirt with the *bosom at the back*, a linen coat concealing the blunder. He dazed the jury with his knowledge of "horse points;" and as the day was sultry, took off his coat and "summed up" in his shirt-sleeves.   Lincoln, sitting behind him, took in the situation, and when his turn came, remarked to the jury: "Gentlemen, Mr. Logan has been trying for over an hour to make you believe he knows more about a horse than these honest old farmers who are witnesses.   He has quoted largely from his 'horse doctor,' and now, gentlemen, I submit to you," (here he lifted Logan out of his chair, and turned him with his back to the jury and the crowd, at the same time flapping up the enormous standing collar) "what dependence can you place in his horse knowledge, when he *has not sense enough to put on his shirt?*"   The roars of laughter that greeted this exhibition, and the verdict that Lincoln got soon after, gave Logan a permanent prejudice against bosom shirts.

LINCOLN AS A HORSE-TRADER.

The preceding incident leads to another, in which Mr. Lincoln himself figures as a horse-trader.   The scene is a very humorous one; and, as usual in an encounter of wit, Mr. Lincoln came out ahead.   He and a certain Judge once got to bantering one another about trading horses; and it was agreed that the next morning at nine o'clock they should make a trade, the horses to be unseen up to that hour,—and no backing out, under a forfeit of twenty-five dollars.   At the hour appointed, the Judge came up, leading the sorriest looking specimen of a nag ever seen in those parts.   In a few minutes Mr. Lincoln was seen approaching with a *wooden saw-horse* upon his shoulders.   Great were the shouts and the laughter of the crowd; and these increased, when Mr. Lincoln, surveying the Judge's animal, set down his saw-horse, and exclaimed: "Well, Judge, this is the first time I ever *got the worst of it* in a horse-trade!"

SOME STRIKING OPINIONS OF LINCOLN AS A LAWYER.

Among the great number of opinions of Lincoln's rank as a lawyer, expressed by his professional brethren, a few may

"WELL, JUDGE, THIS IS THE FIRST TIME I EVER GOT THE WORST OF IT IN A HORSE-TRADE."

properly be given in closing this chapter, which has been devoted chiefly to Mr. Lincoln's professional career. First, we may quote the brief but emphatic words of the distinguished jurist, Judge Sidney Breese, Chief Justice of Illinois, who said: "For my single self, I have for a quarter of a century regarded Mr. Lincoln as the finest lawyer I ever knew, and of a professional bearing so high-toned and honorable, as justly, and without derogating from the claims of others, entitling him to be presented to the profession as a model well worthy of the closest imitation."

Another distinguished Chief Justice, Hon. John D. Caton, says: "In 1840 or 1841, I met Mr. Lincoln, and was for the first time associated with him in a professional way. We attended the Circuit Court at Pontiac, Judge Treat presiding, where we were both engaged in the defense of a man by the name of Lavinia. That was the first and only time I was associated with him at the bar. He practiced in a circuit that was beyond the one in which I practiced, and consequently we were not brought together much in the practice of the law. He stood well at the bar from the beginning. I was a younger man, but an older lawyer. He was not admitted to the bar till after I was. I was not closely connected with him. Indeed, I did not meet him often, professionally, until I went on the bench in 1842; and he was then in full practice before the Supreme Court, and continued to practice there regularly at every term until he was elected President. Mr. Lincoln understood the relations of things, and hence his deductions were rarely wrong from any given state of facts. So he applied the principles of law to the transactions of men with great clearness and precision. He was a close reasoner. He reasoned by analogy, and enforced his views by apt illustration. His mode of speaking was generally of a plain and unimpassioned character, and yet he was the author of some of the most beautiful and eloquent passages in our language, which, if collected, would form a valuable contribution to

American literature. The most punctilious honor ever marked his professional and private life."

The Hon. Thomas Drummond, for many years Judge of the United States District Court at Chicago, said: "It is not necessary to claim for Mr. Lincoln attributes or qualities which he did not possess. He had enough to entitle him to the love and respect and esteem of all who knew him. He was not skilled in the learning of the schools, and his knowledge of the law was acquired almost entirely by his own unaided study and by the practice of his profession. Nature gave him great clearness and acuteness of intellect and a vast fund of common-sense, and, as a consequence of these, much sagacity in judging of the motives and springs of human conduct. With a voice by no means pleasing, and, indeed, when excited, in its shrill tones sometimes almost disagreeable; without any of the personal graces of the orator; without much in the outward man indicating superiority of intellect; without great quickness of perception,—still, his mind was so vigorous, his comprehensions so exact and clear, and his judgments so sure, that he easily mastered the intricacies of his profession, and became one of the ablest reasoners and most impressive speakers at our bar. With a probity of character known to all; with an intuitive insight into the human heart; with a clearness of statement which was itself an argument; with an uncommon power and facility of illustration, often, it is true, of a plain and homely kind, and with that sincerity and earnestness of manner to carry conviction, he was perhaps one of the most successful jury lawyers we have ever had in the State. He always tried a case fairly and honestly. He never intentionally misrepresented the testimony of a witness nor the arguments of an opponent. He met both squarely, and if he could not explain the one or answer the other, substantially admitted it. He never misstated the law according to his own intelligent view of it. Such was the transparent candor and integrity of his nature that he could not well or strongly argue a side or a cause that he thought wrong. Of course, he felt it his duty to say what could be said, and to leave the decision to others; but there could be seen in such cases the inward struggle in his own mind. In trying a cause he might occasionally dwell too long or give too much importance to an inconsiderable point; but this was the exception, and generally he went straight to the citadel of a cause or a question, and struck home there, knowing if that were won the outwork would necessarily fall. He could hardly be called very learned in his profession, and yet he rarely tried a cause without fully understanding the law applicable to it. I have no hesitation in saying he was one of the ablest lawyers I have ever known. If he was forcible before the jury, he was equally so with the court. He detected, with unerring sagacity, the marked points of his opponents' arguments, and pressed his own views with overwhelming force. His efforts were quite unequal, and it may have been that he would not on some occasions strike one as at all remarkable; but let him be thoroughly aroused, let him feel that he was right and that some great principle was involved in his case, and he would come out with an earnestness of conviction, a power of argument, and a wealth of illustration, that I have never seen surpassed. *   *   *   * Simple in his habits, without pretensions of any kind, and distrustful of himself, he was willing to yield precedence and place to others, when he ought to have claimed them for himself; and he rarely, if ever, sought office except at the urgent solicitations of his friends. In substantiation of this, I may be permitted to relate an incident which now occurs to me. Prior to his nomination for the Presidency, and, indeed, when his name was first mentioned in connection with that high office, I broached the subject upon the occasion of meeting him here. His response was, 'I hope they will select some abler man than myself.' "

Mr. C. S. Parks, a lawyer associated with Mr. Lincoln for some years, furnishes the following testimony concerning his more prominent qualities: "I have often said that, for a man who was for a quarter of a century both a lawyer and a politician, he was the most *honest* man I ever knew. He was not only morally honest, but intellectually so. He could not reason falsely; if he attempted it, he failed. In politics he

JUDGE DAVID DAVIS.

would never try to mislead. At the bar, when he thought he was wrong, he was the weakest lawyer I ever saw."

Hon. David Davis, afterwards Associate Justice U. S. Supreme Court and U. S. Senator, presided over the Eighth Judicial Circuit of Illinois during the remaining years of Mr. Lincoln's practice at the bar. He was united to Lincoln in close bonds of friendship, and year after year travelled with him over the circuit, put up with him at the same hotels, and often occupied with him the same room. "This simple life," says Judge Davis, "Mr. Lincoln loved, preferring it to the practice of the law in the city. In all the elements that constitute the great lawyer, he had few equals. He seized the strong points of a cause, and presented them with clearness and great compactness. He read law-books but little, except when the cause in hand made it necessary; yet he was unusually self-reliant, depending on his own resources, and rarely consulting his brother lawyers, either on the management of his case or the legal questions involved. He was the fairest and most accommodating of practitioners, granting all favors which he could do consistently with his duty to his client, and rarely availing himself of an unwary oversight of his adversary. He hated wrong and oppression everywhere, and many a man, whose fraudulent conduct was undergoing review in a court of justice, has withered under his terrific indignation and rebuke."

Mr. Speed says: "As a lawyer, after his first year, he was acknowledge among the best in the State. His analytical powers were marvellous. He always resolved every question into its primary elements, and gave up every point on his own side that did not seem to be invulnerable. One would think, to hear him present his case in the court, he was giving his case away. He would concede point after point to his adversary. But he always reserved a point upon which he claimed a decision in his favor, and his concessions magnified the strength of his claim. He rarely failed in gaining his cases in court."

The special characteristics of Mr. Lincoln's practice at the bar are thus ably summed up: "He did not make a specialty of criminal cases, but was engaged frequently in them. He could not be called a great lawyer, measured by the extent of his acquirement of legal knowledge; he was not an ency-clopædia of cases; but in the text-books of the profession and in the clear perception of legal principles, with natural capacity to apply them, he had great ability. He was not a case lawyer, but a lawyer who dealt in the deep philosophy of the law. He always knew the cases which might be quoted as absolute authority, but beyond that he contented himself in the application and discussion of general principles. In the trial of a case he moved cautiously, and never examined or cross-examined a witness to the detriment of his side. If the witness told the truth, he was safe from his attacks; but woe betide the unlucky and dishonest individual who suppressed the truth, or colored it against Mr. Lincoln's side. His speeches to the jury were very effective specimens of forensic oratory. He talked the vocabulary of the people, and the jury understood every point he made and every thought he uttered. I never saw him when I thought he was trying to make an effort for the sake of mere display; but his imagination was simple and pure in the richest gems of true eloquence. He constructed short sentences of small words, and never wearied the mind of the jury by mazes of elaboration.''

CHAPTER VII.

LINCOLN AND SLAVERY.——VIEWS EXPRESSED BY HIM IN 1850.——HIS MIND MADE UP.——THE HOUR AND THE MAN.——LINCOLN AND THE KANSAS STRUGGLE.——CROSSING SWORDS WITH DOUGLAS.——A NOTABLE SPEECH BY LINCOLN.——"HARK! FROM THE TOMBS A DOLEFUL SOUND!"——ADVICE TO KANSAS BELLIGERENTS.——HONOR IN POLITICS.——ANECDOTE OF LINCOLN AND YATES.——CONTEST FOR THE U. S. SENATE IN 1855.——LINCOLN'S DEFEAT.——SKETCH BY A MEMBER OF THE LEGISLATURE OF '55.

At the death of Henry Clay, in June, 1852, Mr. Lincoln was invited to deliver a eulogy on his life and character before the citizens of Springfield. He complied with the request on the 16th of July. In the same season he made a speech before the "Scott Club" of Springfield, in reply to the addresses with which Mr. Douglas opened his extended campaign of that summer at Richmond, Virginia. With these exceptions, Mr. Lincoln took but little part in politics until the passage of the "Nebraska bill" in 1854. The enactment of this measure by Congress impelled him to take a firmer stand upon the question of slavery than he had ever assumed before. He had been opposed to the institution, from sentiment, since the days of his boyhood; but henceforth he determined to fight it from principle. Mr. Herndon states that Lincoln became an anti-slavery man during his visit to New Orleans in 1831, when he was deeply affected by the horrors of the traffic in human beings. On one occasion, he saw a slave, a beautiful mulatto girl, sold at auction. She was felt over, pinched, trotted around to show bidders she was sound, etc. Lincoln walked away from the sad and inhuman scene with a deep feeling of unsmotherable hate. He said to John Hanks, *"By God! if I ever get a chance to hit that institution, I'll hit it hard, John!"* Again, in the summer of 1841, he was painfully impressed by a scene witnessed during his journey home from Kentucky, described in a letter written at the time to the sister of his friend Speed, in which he says: "A fine example was presented on board the boat for contemplating the effect of condition upon human happiness. A man had purchased twelve negroes in different parts of Kentucky, and was taking them to a farm in the South. They were chained six and six together; a small iron clevis was around the left wrist of each, and this was fastened to the main chain by a shorter one, at a convenient distance from the others, so that the negroes were strung together like so many fish upon a trot-line. In this condition they were being separated forever from the scenes of their childhood, their friends, their fathers and mothers, brothers and sisters, and many of them from their wives and children, and going into perpetual slavery.''

VIEWS EXPRESSED BY LINCOLN IN 1850.

Judge Gillespie records a conversation which he had with Lincoln in 1850, on the slavery question, remarking, by way of introduction, that the subject of slavery was the only one on which he (Lincoln) would become excited. ''I recollect meeting him once at Shelbyville,'' says Judge Gillespie, ''when he remarked that something must be done, or slavery would overrun the whole country. He said there were about six hundred thousand non-slaveholding whites in Kentucky to about thirty-three thousand slaveholders; that in the convention then recently held it was expected that the delegates would represent these classes about in proportion to their respective numbers; but when the convention assembled, there was not a single representative of the non-slaveholding class; every one was in the interest of the slaveholders; 'and,' said he, 'the thing is spreading like wildfire over the country. In a few years we will be ready to accept the institution in Illinois, and the whole country will adopt it.' I asked him to what he attributed the change that was going on in public opinion. He said he had put that question to a Kentuckian shortly before, who answered by saying, 'You might have any amount of land, money in your pocket, or bank-stock, and, while travelling around, nobody would be any wiser; but if you had a darkey trudging at your heels, everybody would see him, and know that you owned a slave. It is the most glittering and ostentatious way of displaying property in the world ; 'and now,' says he, 'if a young man goes courting, the only inquiry is, how many negroes he or she owns.' The love for slave property was swallowing up every other mercenary possession. Its owership betokened, not only the possession of wealth, but indicated the gentleman of leisure, who was above and scorned labor. These things Mr. Lincoln regarded as highly seductive to the thoughtless and giddy-headed young men who looked upon work as vulgar and ungentlemanly. Mr. Lincoln was really excited, and said, with great earnestness, that this spirit ought to be met, and, if possible, checked ; that slavery was a great and crying injustice, an enormous national crime, and we could not expect to escape punishment for it. I asked him how he would proceed in his efforts to check the spread of slavery. He confessed he did not see his way clearly. I think he made up his mind from that time that he would oppose slavery actively. I know that Mr. Lincoln always contended that no man had any right, other than what mere brute force gave him, to hold a slave. He used to say it was singular that the courts would hold that a man never lost his right to his property that had been stolen from him, but that he instantly *lost his right to himself* if he was stolen. Mr. Lincoln always contended that the cheapest way of getting rid of slavery was for the nation to buy the slaves and set them free.''

HIS MIND MADE UP.

While in Congress, Mr. Lincoln had declared himself plainly as opposed to slavery ; and in public speeches, not less than private conversations, he had not hesitated to express his convictions on the subject. In 1850 he said to Major Stuart: ''The time will soon come when we must all be Democrats or Abolitionists. When that time comes *my mind* is made up. The 'slavery question' cannot be compromised.''

THE HOUR AND THE MAN.

The hour had now struck in which Mr. Lincoln was to espouse with his whole heart and soul that cause for which finally he was to lay down his life. In the language of Mr. Arnold, "He had bided his time. He had waited until the harvest was ripe. With unerring sagacity he realized that the day for the triumph of freedom was at hand. He entered upon the conflict with the deepest conviction that the perpetuity of the republic required the extinction of slavery. So, adopting as his motto, 'A house divided against itself cannot stand,' he girded himself for the contest. He sought to take with him, bodily, the old Whig party of Illinois into the new organization called the Republican party. He was to build and consolidate the heterogeneous mass which composed the new party. The years from 1854 to 1860 were, on his part, years of constant, active and unwearied effort. He was now to become the recognized leader of the anti-slavery party in the Northwest, and in all the Valley of the Mississippi. His position in the State of Illinois was central and commanding. He who could lead the Republican party of that State and the surrounding States would be pretty sure to lead that party in the Union. Lincoln was a practical statesman, never attempting the impossible, but seeking to do the best thing practicable under surrounding circumstances. If he was sagacious in selecting the time, he was also skillful in the single issue he made. He took his stand with the fathers of the republic, against the extension of slavery. He knew that prohibition in the territories would result in no more slave states and no slave territory. And now, when the repeal of the Missouri Compromise shattered all parties into fragments, and he came forward to build up the Free Soil party, he threw into the conflict all his strength and vigor, and devoted his life to the struggle. From this time Lincoln was to guide the whirlwind and direct the storm. He realized that the conflict was unavoidable and inevitable. The conviction of his duty was deep and sincere. Hence he pleaded the cause of liberty with an energy, ability, and power, which rapidly gained for him a national reputation. Conscious of the greatness of his cause, inspired by a genuine love of liberty, and animated and made strong by the moral sublimity of the conflict, he solemnly announced his determination to speak for freedom and against slavery until, in his own words, wherever the Federal Government has power, 'the sun shall shine, the rain shall fall, and the wind shall blow upon no man who goes forth to unrequited toil.'"

LINCOLN AND THE KANSAS STRUGGLE.

The absorbing topic in 1855 was the contest in Kansas, which proved the battle-ground for the settlement of the question of introducing slavery into the territories north of the line established by the "Missouri Compromise." Mr. Lincoln's views on the subject are defined in a notable letter to Mr. Speed, who had become a resident of Kentucky. The following extracts show the character of the letter:

SPRINGFIELD, AUGUST 24, 1855.

DEAR SPEED:—You know what a poor correspondent I am. Ever since I received your very agreeable letter of the twenty-second of May, I have been intending to write you in answer to it. You suggest that in political action now, you and I would differ. You know I dislike slavery, and you fully admit the abstract wrong of it. So far, there is no cause of difference. But you say that sooner than yield your legal right to the slave, especially at the bidding of those who are not themselves interested, you would see the Union dissolved. I am not aware that any one is bidding you yield that right—very certainly I am not. I leave the matter entirely to yourself. I also acknowledge your rights and my obligations under the Constitution, in regard to your slaves. I confess I hate to see the poor creatures hunted down, and caught, and carried back to their stripes and unrequited toil; but I bite my lip and keep quiet. In 1841 you and I had together a tedious low-water trip on a steamboat from Louisville to St. Louis. You may remember, as I well do, that from Louisville to the mouth of the Ohio, there were on board ten or a dozen slaves, shackled together with irons. That sight was a continual torment to me; and I see something like it every time I touch the Ohio, or any other slave border. It is not fair for you to assume that I have no interest in a thing which has, and continually exercises, the power of making me miserable. You ought rather to appreciate how much the great body of the people of the North do crucify their feelings, in order to maintain their loyalty to the Constitution and the Union.

"I do oppose the extension of slavery, because my judgment and feelings so prompt me; and I am under no obligations to the contrary. If, for this, you and I must differ, differ we must. You say, if you were President you would send an army and hang the leaders of the Missouri outrages upon the Kansas elections; still, if Kansas fairly votes herself a slave State, she must be admitted, or the Union must be dissolved. But how if she votes herself a slave State unfairly—that is, by the very means for which you would hang men? Must she still be admitted, or the Union dissolved? That will be the phase of the question when it first becomes a practical one. In your assumption that there may be a fair decision of the slavery question in Kansas, I plainly see you and I would differ about the Nebraska law. I look upon that enactment not as a law, but a violence from the beginning. It was conceived in violence, passed in violence, is maintained in violence, and is being executed in violence. I say it was conceived in violence, because the destruction of the Missouri Compromise under the Constitution was nothing less than violence. It was passed in violence, because it could not have passed at all but for the votes of many members in violent disregard of the known will of their constituents. It is maintained in violence, because the elections since clearly demand its repeal; and the demand is openly disregarded. * * That Kansas will form a slave constitution, and with it will ask to be admitted into the Union, I take to be already a settled question, and so settled by the very means you so pointedly condemn. By every principle of law ever held by any court, North or South, every negro taken to Kansas is free; yet, in utter disregard of this—in the spirit of violence merely—that beautiful Legislature gravely passes a law to hang any man who shall venture to inform a negro of his legal rights. This is the substance and real object of the law. If, like Haman, they should hang upon the gallows of their own building, I shall not be among the mourners for their fate. In my humble sphere I shall advocate the restoration of the Missouri Compromise so long as Kansas remains a Territory; and, when, by all these foul means, it seeks to come into the Union as a slave State, I shall oppose it. * * You inquire where I now stand. That is a disputed point. I think I am a Whig; but others say there are no Whigs, and that I am an Abolitionist. When I was in Washington I voted for the Wilmot Proviso as good as forty times, and I never heard of any attempt to unwhig me for that. I now do no more than oppose the extension of slavery. I am not a Know-Nothing—that is certain. How could I be? How can any one who abhors the oppression of the negroes, be in favor of degrading classes of white people? Our progress in degeneracy appears to me to be pretty rapid. As a nation we began by declaring that 'all men are created equal.' We now practically read it 'all men are created equal, except negroes.' When the Know-Nothings get control, it will read, 'all men are created equal, except negroes and foreigners and Catholics.' When it comes to that, I should prefer emigrating to some other country where they make no pretence of loving liberty—to Russia for instance, where despotism can be taken pure, and without the base alloy of hypocrisy.

"Your friend forever,   A. LINCOLN."

CROSSING SWORDS WITH DOUGLAS.

Mr. Lincoln was soon accorded an opportunity to cross swords again with Douglas, the antagonist against whom he had before put forth his strength. As Mr. Arnold narrates the incident,—"When, late in September, 1854, Douglas, after the passage of the Kansas and Nebraska bill, returned to Illinois, he was received with a storm of indignation which would have crushed a man of less power and will. A bold and courageous leader, conscious of his personal power over his party, he bravely met the storm and sought to allay it. In October, 1854, the State Fair being then in session at Springfield, and there being a great crowd of people from all parts of the State, Douglas went there and made an elaborate and able speech in defense of the repeal. Mr. Lincoln was called upon by all the opponents of this repeal to reply, and he did so with a power which he never surpassed and which he had never before equalled. All other issues which had divided the people were as chaff, and were scattered to the winds by the intense agitation which arose on the question of extending slavery, not merely into free territory, but into territory which had been declared free by solemn compact. Douglas had a hard and difficult task in attempting to defend his action in the repeal of this compact. But he spoke with his usual great ability. He had lately come from the discussions of the Senate Chamber, where he had carried the measure against the utmost efforts of Chase, Seward, Sumner, and others, and he was somewhat arrogant and overbearing. Lincoln was present and listened to the speech, and at its close it was announced that he would on the following day reply. This reply occupied more than three hours in delivery, and during all that time Lincoln held the vast crowd in the deepest attention.''

Mr. Herndon said, in his report of the event: ''This anti-Nebraska speech of Mr. Lincoln was the profoundest, in our opinion, that he made in his whole life. He felt burning upon his soul the truths which he uttered, and all present felt that he was true to his own soul. His feelings once or twice swelled within, and came near stifling utterance. He quivered with emotion. The whole house was as still as death. He attacked the Nebraska bill with unusual warmth and energy; and all felt that a man of strength was its enemy, and that he intended to blast it, if he could, by strong and manly efforts. He was most successful, and the house approved the glorious triumph of truth by loud and continued huzzas. Women waved their white handkerchiefs in token of woman's silent but heartfelt assent. Douglas felt the sting; and he frequently interrupted Mr. Lincoln. His friends felt that he was crushed by Lincoln's powerful argument, which was manly and logical, and filled with illustrations from nature around us. The Nebraska Bill was shivered, and, like a tree of the forest, was torn and rent asunder by hot bolts of truth. At the conclusion of this speech, every man, woman and child felt that it was unanswerable.''

In depicting the same incident, Mr. Lamon says: ''Mr. Douglas rose to reply. He was excited, angry, imperious in his tone and manner, and his voice was loud and shrill. Shaking his forefinger at the Democratic malcontents with furious energy, and declaiming rather than debating, he occupied to little purpose the brief interval remaining until the adjournment for supper. Then, promising to resume his address in the evening, he went his way; and that audience 'saw him no more.' Evening came, but not the orator. Many fine speeches were made upon the one absorbing topic. But it is no shame to any one of these, that their really impressive speeches were but slightly appreciated, nor long remembered, beside Mr. Lincoln's splendid and enduring performance,—enduring in the memory of his auditors, although preserved upon no written or printed page.''

A NOTABLE SPEECH BY LINCOLN.

A few days after this encounter, Mr. Douglas spoke in Peoria, and was followed by Mr. Lincoln with the same crushing arguments which had served him at the State Fair, and with the same triumphant effect. Mr. Douglas frankly acknowledged his defeat, and in a private interview requested Mr. Lincoln to unite in an agreement with him that neither should speak again during that campaign. Mr. Lincoln agreed to the proposition; and although both orators were advertised to speak at Lacon the succeeding day, and met the appointment in apparent good faith, Mr. Douglas pleaded hoarseness as an excuse for breaking his engagement; whereat Mr. Lincoln declared he could not take advantage of the disability of his opponent. Mr. Douglas did speak at Princeton later in the season, but Mr. Lincoln held scrupulously to the terms of his compact. His speech at Peoria was written out by him and published after its delivery. As specimens of its urging eloquence, we quote the following passages:

"Argue as you will, and as long as you will, this is the naked front and aspect of the measure; and in this aspect it could not but produce agitation. Slavery is founded in the selfishness of man's nature; opposition to it, in his love of justice. These principles are an eternal antagonism; and when brought into collision so fiercely as slavery extension brings them, shocks, throes and convulsions must ceaselessly follow. Repeal the Missouri Compromise; repeal all compromises; repeal the Declaration of Independence; repeal all past history,—you still cannot repeal human nature. It still will be the abundance of man's heart, that slavery extension is wrong; and, out of the abundance of his heart, his mouth will continue to speak. * * When Mr. Pettit, in connection with his support of the Nebraska bill, called the Declaration of Independence, 'a self-evident lie,' he only did what consistency and candor require all other Nebraska men to do. Of the forty-odd Nebraska Senators who sat present and heard him, no one rebuked him. * * * If this had been said among Marion's men, Southerners though they were, what would have become of the man who said it? If this had been said to the men who captured Andre, the man who said it would probably have been hung sooner than Andre was. If it had been said in old Independence Hall seventy-eight years ago, the very doorkeeper would have throttled the man, and thrust him into the street. * * Thus we see the plain, unmistakable spirit of that early age towards slavery was hostility to the principle, and toleration only by necessity. But now it is to be transformed into a 'sacred right.' Nebraska brings it forth, places it on the high road to extension and perpetuity, and with a pat on its back says to it: 'Go, and God speed you.' Henceforth it is to be the chief jewel of the nation, the very figure-head of the ship of state. Little by little, but steadily as man's march to the grave, we have been giving the old for the new faith. Nearly eighty years ago we began by declaring that all men are created equal; but now from that beginning we have run down to that other declaration, 'that for *some* men to enslave others is a sacred right of self-government.' * * In our greedy chase to make profit of the negro, let us beware lest we cancel and tear to pieces even the white man's charter of freedom. * * * * * If all earthly power were given me, I should not know what to do as to the existing institution. My first impulse would be to free all the slaves, and send them to Liberia—to their own native land. But, if they were all landed there in a day, they would all perish in the next ten days; and there are not surplus shipping and surplus money enough to carry them there in many times ten days. What then? Free them all, and keep them among us as underlings? Is it quite certain that this betters their condition? I think I would not hold one in slavery at any rate; yet the point is not clear enough for me to denounce people upon. What next? Free them, and make them politically and socially our equals? My own feelings will not admit of this; and, if mine would, we well know that those of the great mass of white people will not. A universal feeling, whether well or ill founded, cannot be safely disregarded. We cannot then make them equals. It does seem to me that systems of gradual emancipation might be adopted; but, for their tardiness in this, I will not undertake to judge our brethren of the South. * *

"Our Republican robe is soiled,—trailed in the dust. Let us re-purify it. Let us turn and wash it white, in the spirit, if not the blood, of the Revolution. Let us turn slavery from its claims of 'moral right,' back upon its existing legal rights and its arguments of 'necessity.'

Let us return it to the position our fathers gave it, and there let it rest in peace. Let us re-adopt the Declaration of Independence, and with it the practices and policy which harmonize with it. Let North and South,—let all Americans,—let all lovers of liberty everywhere,—join in the great and good work. If we do this, we shall not only have saved the Union, but we shall have so saved it as to make and to keep it for ever worthy of the saving. We shall have so saved it that the succeeding millions of free and happy people, the world over, shall rise up and call us blessed to the latest generations.''

"HARK! FROM THE TOMBS A DOLEFUL SOUND."

It was in one of these speeches that Mr. Lincoln's power of repartee was admirably illustrated by a most laughable retort made by him to Douglas. Mr. Ralph E. Hoyt, who was present, says: "In the course of his speech, Mr. Douglas had said, 'The Whigs are all dead.' For some time before speaking, Lincoln sat on the platform with only his homely face visible to the audience above the high desk before him. On being introduced, he arose from his chair and proceeded to straighten himself up. For a few seconds I wondered when and where his head would cease its ascent; but at last it did stop, and 'Honest Old Abe' stood before us. He commenced, 'Fellow-citizens: My friend, Mr. Douglas, made the startling announcement to-day that the Whigs are all dead. If this be so, fellow-citizens, you will now experience the novelty of hearing a speech from a dead man; and I suppose you might properly say, in the language of the old hymn:

'Hark! from the tombs a doleful sound!'

This set the audience fairly wild with delight, and at once brought them into full confidence with the speaker."

ADVICE TO KANSAS BELLIGERENTS.

About this time a party of Abolitionists in Illinois had become so excited over the Kansas struggle that they were determined to go to the aid of the Free-State men. As soon as Mr. Lincoln learned of this project, he opposed it strongly. When they spoke to him of "Liberty, Justice, and God's higher law," he replied:

"Friends, you are in the minority,—in a sad minority; and you can't hope to succeed, reasoning from all human experience. You would rebel against the Government, and redden your hands in the blood of your countrymen. If you have the majority, as some of you say you have, you can succeed with the ballot, throwing away the bullet. You can peaceably, then, redeem the Government and preserve the liberties of mankind, through your votes and voice and moral influence. *Let there be peace.* In a democracy, where the majority rule by the ballot through the forms of law, these physical rebellions and bloody resistances are radically wrong, unconstitutional, and are treason. Better bear the ills you have than fly to those you know not of. Our own Declaration of Independence says that governments long established should not be resisted for trivial causes. Revolutionize through the ballot-box, and restore the Government once more to the affection and hearts of men, by making it express, as it was intended to do, the highest spirit of justice and liberty. Your attempt, if there be such, to resist the laws of Kansas by force, will be criminal and wicked; and all your feeble attempts will be follies, and end in bringing sorrow on your heads, and ruin the cause you would freely die to preserve."

No doubt was felt of Mr. Lincoln's sympathies; and, indeed, he is known to have contributed money to the Free-State cause. But it is noticeable that he showed the same coolness, wisdom, moderation, love of law and order, in this exciting episode, that so strongly characterized his conduct in the stormier period of the Civil War, and without which it is doubtful if he would have been able to save the nation.

HONOR IN POLITICS.—ANECDOTE OF LINCOLN AND YATES.

The following reminiscence is furnished by Paul Selby, Esq., of Springfield, Ill.: "While Abraham Lincoln had the reputation of being inspired by an almost unbounded ambition, it was of that generous quality which characterized his other attributes, and often led him, voluntarily, to restrain its gratification in deference to the conflicting aspirations of his friends. All remember his magnanimity towards Edward D. Baker, when the latter was elected to Congress from the Springfield District in 1844, and the frankness with which he informed Baker of his own desire to be a candidate in

1846; when, for the only time in his life, he was elected to
that body. In 1852, Richard Yates, of Jacksonville, then
recognized as one of the rising young orators and statesmen
of the West, was elected to Congress for the second time
from the Springfield District. It was during the term following this election that the Kansas-Nebraska issue was precipitated upon the country by Senator Douglas, in the introduction of his bill for the repeal of the Missouri Compromise.
Yates, in obedience to his impulses, which were always on
the side of freedom, took strong ground against the measure,
—notwithstanding the fact that a majority of his constituents,
though originally Whigs, were strongly conservative, as was
generally the case with people who were largely of Kentucky
and Tennessee origin. In 1854, the Whig party, which had
been divided on the Kansas-Nebraska question, began to
manifest symptoms of disintegration; while the Republican
party, though not yet known by that name, began to take
form. At this time I was publishing a paper at Jacksonville,
Yates's home; and although from the date of my connection
with it, in 1852, it had not been a political paper, the introduction of a new issue soon led me to take decided ground on
the side of free territory. Lincoln at once sprang into prominence as one of the boldest, most vigorous and eloquent opponents of Mr. Douglas's measure, which was construed as a
scheme to secure the admission of slavery into all the new
territories of the United States. At that time his election to a
seat in Congress would probably have been very grateful to
his ambition, as well as acceptable in a pecuniary point of
view; and his prominence and ability had already attracted
the eyes of the whole State towards him in a special degree.
Having occasion to visit Springfield one day while the subject
of the selection of a candidate was under consideration among
the opponents of the Kansas-Nebraska bill, I encountered
Mr. Lincoln on the street between the railroad depot and the
public square. As we walked along, the subject of the choice

of a candidate for Congress to succeed Yates came up, when I stated that many of the old-line Whigs and anti-Nebraska men in the western part of the district were looking to him as an available leader. While he seemed gratified by the compliment, he said: 'No; Yates has been a true and faithful Representative, and should be returned.' Yates was re-nominated, and although he ran ahead of his ticket, yet so far had the disorganization of the Whig party then progressed, and so strong a foothold had the pro-slavery sentiment obtained in the district, that he was defeated by Maj. Thomas L. Harris, of Petersburg, whom he had defeated when he first entered the field as a candidate four years before. While it is scarcely probable that Lincoln, if he had been a candidate, could have changed the result, yet the prize was one which he would then have considered worth contending for; and if the nomination could have been tendered him without doing injustice to his friend, he would undoubtedly have cheerfully accepted it and thrown all the earnestness and ability which he possessed into the contest. This instance only illustrates a feature of his character which has so often been recognized and commented upon—his generosity towards those among his political friends who might be regarded as occupying the position of rivals.''

CONTEST FOR THE UNITED STATES SENATE IN 1855.—LINCOLN'S DEFEAT.

In November, 1854, Mr. Lincoln was elected a representative in the State Legislature. But he did not serve. He had been announced as a candidate from Springfield, by Mr. William Jayne, during his absence; and much persuasion was needed to induce him to accept the nomination. "I went to see him," says Jayne, "in order to get his consent to run. This was at his house. He was then the saddest man I ever saw,—the gloomiest. He walked up and down the floor, almost crying; and to all my persuasions to let his name stand in the paper, he said, 'No, I can't. You don't know all. I say you don't begin to know one-half; and that's enough.'''

His name, however, was allowed to stand, and he was elected by about 600 majority. But Mr. Lincoln was extremely desirous of succeeding General James Shields, whose term in the United States Senate expired the following March. The Senate Chamber had long been the goal of his ambition. He summed up his feelings in a letter to Hon. N. B. Judd, some years after, saying, "I would rather have a full term in the United States Senate than the Presidency." He therefore resigned his seat in the Legislature,—the fact that the majority in both houses was opposed to the Nebraska bill allowing him to do so without injury to his party. But the act was futile. When the Legislature met, in February, 1855, to make choice of a Senator, a clique of anti-Nebraska Democrats held out so firmly against the nomination of Lincoln that there was danger of the Whigs leaving their candidate altogether. In this dilemma Mr. Lincoln was consulted. As Mr. Lamon describes the incident, "He said, unhesitatingly, 'You ought to drop me and go for Trumbull; that is the only way you can defeat Matteson.' Judge Logan came up about that time, and insisted on running Lincoln still; but the latter said, 'If you do, you will lose both Trumbull and myself; and I think the cause, in this case, is to be preferred to men.' We adopted his suggestion, and took up Trumbull and elected him, although it grieved us to the heart to give up Mr. Lincoln. This, I think, shows that Mr. Lincoln was capable of sinking himself for the cause in which he was engaged. It was with great bitterness of spirit that the Whigs accepted this hard alternative. Many of them accused the little squad of anti-Nebraska Democrats of ungenerous and selfish motives. One of them, Mr. Waters, of McDonough county, was especially indignant, and utterly refused to vote for Mr. Trumbull at all. On the last ballot he threw away his ballot on Mr. Williams."

Mr. Parks, a member of the Legislature and one of Lincoln's intimate friends, said, "Mr. Lincoln was very much disappointed, for I think that at that time it was the height of his ambition to get into the United States Senate. He manifested, however, no bitterness towards Mr. Judd or the other anti-Nebraska Democrats by whom politically he was beaten, but evidently thought their motives were right. He told me several times, afterwards, that the election of Trumbull was the best thing that could have happened."

SKETCH BY A MEMBER OF THE LEGISLATURE OF 1855.

Hon. Elijah M. Haines, ex-Speaker of the Illinois Legislature, a resident of the State for over half a century, and one of Mr. Lincoln's early friends, was a member of the Legislature during the Senatorial struggle just referred to, and was familiar with all its incidents. The following interesting sketch is furnished by him: "Abraham Lincoln had been elected a member of the House on the Fusion ticket, with Judge Stephen T. Logan, for the district composed of Sangamon county; but it being settled that the Fusion party—which was an anti-Douglas combination, including Whigs, Free-Soilers, Know-Nothings, etc.—would have a majority of the two houses on ballot, Mr. Lincoln was induced to become a candidate for United States Senator, for the support of that party. He therefore did not qualify as a member. Although Mr. Lincoln never acquired the reputation of being an office-seeker, yet it happened frequently that his name would be mentioned in connection with some important position. He became, quite early in life, one of the prominent leaders of the Whig party of the State, and for a long time, in connection with a few devoted associates, led the forlorn hope of that party. During a period of about twenty years there was seldom but one Whig member in the Illinois delegation of Congressmen. The Sangamon district, in which Mr. Lincoln lived, was always sure to elect a Whig member when the party was united; but it contained quite a number of aspiring Whig orators, and there was a kind of understanding between them that no one who attained the position of Representative in Congress should hold it longer than one term; that he would then give way for the next favorite. Mr. Lincoln had held the position once, and its return to him was far in the future.

"The Fusion triumph in the Legislature was considered by the Whig element as a success, in which they acknowledged

HON. ELIJAH M. HAINES.

great obligation to Mr. Lincoln. That element in the Fusion party therefore urged his claims as the successor of General Shields. His old associate and tried friend in the Whig cause, Judge Logan, became the champion of his interests in the House of Representatives. I was present and saw something of Mr. Lincoln during the early part of the session, before the vote for Senator was taken. He was around among the members much of the time. His manner was agreeable and unasssuming; he was not forward in pressing his case upon the attention of members, yet, before the interview would come to a close, some allusion to the Senatorship would generally occur, when he would respond in some such way as this: 'Gentlemen, that is rather a delicate subject for me to talk upon; but I must confess that I would be glad of your support for the office, if you shall conclude that I am the proper person for it.' When he had finished, he would generally take occasion to withdraw before any discussion on the subject arose.

"The joint convention of the two houses for the election of Senator occurred February 8th. The candidates put in nomination before the joint convention were as follows: Mr. Graham nominated James Shields; Senator Palmer nominated Lyman Trumbull; Mr. Dunlap nominated Archibald Williams; Mr. Gray nominated J. A. Matteson; Mr. Richmond nominated Wm. B. Ogden; Senator Gillespie nominated Cyrus Edwards; Mr. Arnold nominated William Kellogg; and Mr. Logan nominated Abraham Lincoln. Fifty-one votes was the number necessary to a choice; the whole number of members elected in the two Houses being 100. The first ballot resulted as follows: Lincoln, 45; Shields, 41; Trumbull, 5; Koerner, 2; Ogden, 2; Matteson, 1,— two members being absent. The balloting continued with varied results. When the ninth ballot was about to proceed, Mr. Lincoln, being present, stepped forward,—or, as Mr. Richmond expresses it, leaned forward from his position in the lobby,—and requested the committee to withdraw his name. Judge Logan objected, insisting that Mr. Lincoln was being betrayed. Mr. Lincoln received his highest vote on the first ballot.   He continued losing on each succeeding ballot.   The ninth ballot being taken, still further loss was shown on his vote.   On the announcement of the result of this ballot, Judge Logan, whose fidelity to his friend was worthy of the highest praise, consented reluctantly that at the next ballot the name of Mr. Lincoln might be dropped; but still he objected to having it formally withdrawn.   The tenth ballot being taken, Judge Trumbull received fifty-one votes, and was declared elected.   The dropping of Mr. Lincoln's name did not necessarily imply that the vote given for him would go over to Judge Trumbull; the result, therefore, was a general surprise.   On the previous ballot Judge Trumbull had received only thirty-five votes.   When Mr. Lincoln's name was taken out of the contest, the fear on the part of Judge Trumbull's friends was that this vote might divide and ultimately go to some other one of the candidates on the Fusion side.   But Mr. Richmond, the chairman of the committee, immediately insisted on giving the united vote of the opposition for Judge Trumbull.   In this he was very earnest, and the influence he exerted no doubt had much to do with the result."

CHAPTER VIII.

BIRTH OF THE REPUBLICAN PARTY.——LINCOLN ONE OF ITS FATHERS.——THE
BLOOMINGTON CONVENTION.——LINCOLN'S GREAT SPEECH.——A RATIFICA-
TION MEETING OF THREE.——THE FIRST NATIONAL REPUBLICAN CONVEN-
TION.——NOMINATION OF FREMONT AND DAYTON.——LINCOLN IN THE CAM-
PAIGN OF 1856.——ON THE STUMP IN OGLE COUNTY.——"A DANGEROUS
MAN!"——VIEWS ON THE POLITICS OF THE FUTURE.——FIRST VISIT TO CIN-
CINNATI.——FIRST MEETING WITH EDWIN M. STANTON.——STANTON'S FIRST
IMPRESSIONS OF LINCOLN.——HE REGARDS HIM AS A "GIRAFFE."——A
VISIT TO NICHOLAS LONGWORTH OF CINCINNATI.——SEEING THE CITY.

THE year 1856 saw the dissolution of the old Whig party.
It had become too narrow and restricted to answer the needs
of the hour. A new platform was demanded, that would admit the great principles and issues growing out of the slavery
agitation. A convention of the Whig leaders throughout the
country met at Pittsburg, Pennsylvania, on the 22d of February, 1856, to consider the necessity of a new organization. A
little later, Mr. Herndon, in the office of Mr. Lincoln, called
a convention at Bloomington, Illinois, "summoning together
all those who wished to see the government conducted on the
principles of Washington and Jefferson." The call was
signed by the most prominent Abolitionists of Illinois, with
the name of A. LINCOLN at the head. The morning after its
publication, Major Stuart entered Mr. Herndon's office in a
state of extreme excitement, and, as the latter relates, demanded: "'Sir, did Mr. Lincoln sign that Abolition call
which is published this morning?' I answered, 'Mr. Lincoln did not sign that call.' 'Did Lincoln authorize you to
sign it?' 'No, he never authorized me to sign it.' 'Then
do you know that you have ruined Mr. Lincoln?' 'I did not
know that I had ruined Mr. Lincoln; did not intend to do so;
thought he was a made man by it; that the time had come
when conservatism was a crime and a blunder.' 'You, then,
take the responsibility of your acts, do you?' 'I do, most
emphatically.' However, I instantly sat down and wrote to
Mr. Lincoln, who was then in Pekin or Tremont,—possibly

at court. He received my letter, and instantly replied, either by letter or telegraph—most likely by letter—that he adopted, *in toto*, what I had done, and promised to meet the radicals—Lovejoy and such like men—among us." Mr. Herndon adds: "Never did a man change as Lincoln did from that hour. No sooner had he planted himself right on the slavery question than his whole soul seemed burning. *He blossomed right out.* Then, too, other spiritual things grew more real to him."

Mr. Herndon had been an Abolitionist from birth. It was an inheritance with him; but Lincoln's conversion was a gradual process, stimulated and confirmed by the influence of his companion. "From 1854 to 1860," says Mr. Herndon, "I kept putting into Lincoln's hands the speeches and sermons of Theodore Parker, Wendell Phillips, and Henry Ward Beecher. I took 'The Anti-slavery Standard' for years before 1856, 'The Chicago Tribune,' and 'The New York Tribune;' kept them in my office; kept them purposely on my table, and would read to Lincoln the good, sharp and solid things well put. Lincoln was a natural anti-slavery man, as I think, and yet he needed watching,—needed hope, faith, energy; and I think I *warmed him.*"

It is stated that "when Herndon was very young—probably before Mr. Lincoln made his first protest in the Legislature of the State in behalf of liberty—Lincoln once said to him: 'I cannot see what makes your convictions so decided as regards the future of slavery. What tells you the thing must be rooted out?' 'I feel it in my bones,' was Herndon's emphatic answer. 'This continent is not broad enough to endure the contest between freedom and slavery!' It was almost in these very words that Mr. Lincoln afterwards opened the great contest between Douglas and himself. From this time forward he submitted all public questions to what he called 'the test of Bill Herndon's *bone philosophy;*' and their arguments were close and protracted."

Long before Mr. Herndon published the call for the Bloomington convention, he had said to a deputation of men from Chicago, in answer to the inquiry whether Mr. Lincoln could be trusted for freedom: "Can you trust yourselves? If you can, you can trust Lincoln forever."

THE BLOOMINGTON CONVENTION.—LINCOLN'S GREAT SPEECH.

The Convention met at Bloomington, May 29, 1856; "and it was there," says Mr. Herndon, in one of his lectures, "that Lincoln was baptized, and joined our church. He made a speech to us. I have heard or read all of Mr. Lincoln's great speeches; and I give it as my opinion that the Bloomington speech was the grand effort of his life. Heretofore, and up to this moment, he had simply argued the slavery question on grounds of policy,—on what are called the *statesman's* grounds,—never reaching the question of the radical and eternal right. Now he was newly baptized and freshly born; he had the fervor of a new convert; the smothered flame broke out; enthusiasm unusual to him blazed up; his eyes were aglow with inspiration; he felt justice; his heart was alive to the right; his sympathies burst forth; and he stood before the throne of the eternal Right, in presence of his God, and then and there unburdened his penitential and fired soul. This speech was fresh, new, genuine, odd, original; filled with fervor not unmixed with a divine enthusiasm; his head breathing out through his tender heart its truths, its sense of right, and its feeling of the good and for the good. This speech was full of fire and energy and force; it was logic; it was pathos; it was enthusiasm; it was justice, equity, truth, right, and good, set ablaze by the divine fires of a soul maddened by wrong; it was hard, heavy, knotty, gnarly, edged, and heated. I attempted for about fifteen minutes, as was usual with me then, to take notes; but at the end of that time I threw pen and paper to the dogs, and lived only in the inspiration of the hour. If Mr. Lincoln was six feet four inches high usually, *at Bloomington he was seven feet*, and inspired at that. From that day to the day of his death, he stood firm on the right. He felt his great cross, had his great idea, nursed it, kept it, taught it to others, and in his fidelity bore witness of it to his death, and finally sealed it with his precious blood.''

The committee on resolutions, at the convention, found themselves, after hours of discussion, unable to agree; and at last they sent for Lincoln. He suggested that all could unite on the principles of the Declaration of Independence and hostility to the extension of slavery. "Let us," said he, "in building our new party, make our corner-stone the Declaration of Independence; let us build on this rock, and the gates of hell shall not prevail against us." The problem was mastered, and the convention adopted the following:

"*Resolved*, That we hold, in accordance with the opinions and practices of all the great statesmen of all parties for the first sixty years of the administration of the government, that, under the Constitution, Congress possesses full power to prohibit slavery in the territories; and that while we will maintain all constitutional rights of the South, we also hold that justice, humanity, the principles of freedom, as expressed in our Declaration of Independence and our National Constitution, and the purity and perpetuity of our government, require that that power should be exerted to prevent the extension of slavery into territories heretofore free.''

The Bloomington Convention concluded its work by choosing delegates to the National Republican Convention to be held at Philadelphia the following month, for the nomination of candidates for the Presidency and Vice-presidency of the United States. And thus was organized the Republican party in Illinois, which revolutionized the State and elected Lincoln to the Presidency. Lincoln's speech to this convention has rarely been equalled. "Never," says one of the delegates, "was an audience more completely electrified by human eloquence. Again and again, during the delivery, the audience sprang to their feet, and by long continued cheers, expressed how deeply the speaker had aroused them.''

A RATIFICATION MEETING OF THREE.

The people of Bloomington seem to have had but little sympathy with this convention. A few days later Herndon and Lincoln tried to hold a ratification meeting; but only three persons were present—Lincoln, Herndon, and John Pain. "When Lincoln came into the court room where the meeting was to be held," says Herndon, "there was an expression of sadness and amusement on his face. He walked to the stand, mounted it in a kind of mockery—mirth and sadness all combined—and said, 'Gentlemen, this meeting is larger than I thought it would be. I knew that Herndon and myself would come, but I did not know that any one else would be here; and yet another has come,—you, John Pain. These are sad times, and seem out of joint. All seems dead, dead, dead; but the age is not yet dead; it liveth as sure as our Maker liveth. Under all this seeming want of life and motion, the world does move nevertheless. Be hopeful. And now let us adjourn and appeal to the people.'"

THE FIRST NATIONAL REPUBLICAN CONVENTION.—NOMINATION OF FREMONT AND DAYTON.

The National Convention of the Republican party met at Philadelphia, in June, 1856, and adopted a declaration of principles substantially based upon those of the Bloomington convention. John C. Fremont was nominated as candidate for President. Among the names presented for Vice-president was that of Abraham Lincoln. He received, however, but 110 votes, against 259 for Mr. Dayton, and 180 scattered; and Mr. Dayton was unanimously declared the nominee.

When the news reached Mr. Lincoln, in Illinois, that he had received 110 votes, some of the lawyers in the court house insisted that it must have been their Lincoln; but he said, "No, it could not be; it must have been the great Lincoln of Massachusetts!" He was then in one of his melancholy moods, full of depression and despondency.

LINCOLN IN THE CAMPAIGN OF 1856.

In the stirring presidential campaign of 1856, Mr. Lincoln was particularly active, and rendered most efficient service to the Republican party. He spoke constantly, discussing the great question of "slavery in the territories" in a manner at once original and masterly. Among the reminiscences of Lincoln in this campaign are those of Hon. William Bross, formerly Lieutenant-Governor of Illinois, and one of the best known journalists and politicians of the West. "I first met Mr. Lincoln, to know him," says Gov. Bross, "at Vandalia, the old capital of the State, in October, 1856. There was to be a political meeting in front of the old State House, in the center of the square, at 2 o'clock. Soon after that hour the sonorous voice of Dr. Curdy rang through the town: 'O, yes! O, yes! All ye who want to hear public speaking, draw near!' The crowd at once began to gather from all sides of the square. The Doctor then introduced the first speaker, and he proceeded to make the best presentation he could of the principles of the then newly formed Republican party, and the reasons why Fremont, 'the gallant path-finder of the West,' should be elected President. About the time the first speaker closed his remarks, Hon. Ebenezer Peck and Abraham Lincoln arrived and took the stand; and both made able and effective speeches. After that, Lincoln and I frequently met during the canvass, and often afterwards I spoke with him from the same platform. The probable result of an election was often canvassed, and a noticeable fact was that in most cases he would mark the probable result below, rather than above, the actual majority."

ON THE STUMP IN OGLE COUNTY.—"A DANGEROUS MAN!"

Some additional reminiscences of Lincoln's appearance and efforts in this campaign are given by Mr. Noah Brooks, the well-known journalist and author, who at that time lived in Northern Illinois, and attended many of the great Republican mass-meetings. "At one of these great assemblies in

Ogle county,'' says Mr. Brooks, "to which the country people came on horseback, in farm wagons, or afoot, from far and near, there were several speakers of local celebrity. Dr. Egan, of Chicago, famous for his racy stories, was one ; and Joe Knox, of Bureau county, a stump speaker of renown, was another attraction. Several other orators were 'on the bills' for this long-advertised 'Fremont and Dayton rally,' among them being a Springfield lawyer, who had won some reputation as a shrewd, close reasoner, and a capital speaker on the stump. This was Abraham Lincoln, popularly known as 'Honest Abe Lincoln.' In those days he was not so famous in our part of the State as the two speakers whom I have named. Possibly he was not so popular among the masses of the people ; but his ready wit, his unfailing good humor, and the candor which gave him his character for honesty, won for him the admiration and respect of all who heard him. I remember once meeting a choleric old Democrat striding away from an open-air meeting where Lincoln was speaking, striking the earth with his cane as he stumped along, and exclaiming, 'He's a dangerous man, sir ! a d——d dangerous man ! He makes you *believe* what he says, in spite of yourself !' It was Lincoln's manner. He admitted away his whole case, apparently,—and yet, as his political opponents complained, he usually carried conviction with him. As he reasoned with his audience, he bent his long form over the railing of the platform, stooping lower and lower as he pursued his argument, until, having reached his point, he clinched it, usually with a question, and then suddenly sprang upright, reminding one of the springing open of a jack-knife blade. At the Ogle county meeting to which I refer, Lincoln led off, the raciest speakers being reserved for the latter part of the political entertainment. I am bound to say that Lincoln did not awaken the boisterous applause which some of those who followed him did, but his speech made a more lasting impression. It was talked about for weeks afterward in the neighborhood, and it probably changed many votes; for that was the time when Free-soil votes were being made in Northern Illinois.''

LINCOLN'S VIEWS ON THE POLITICS OF THE FUTURE.

Mr. Brooks had made Mr. Lincoln's acquaintance early in the day referred to; and after Lincoln had spoken, and while some of the other orators were entertaining the audience, the two drew a little off from the crowd and fell into a discussion over the political situation and prospects. "We crawled under the pendulous branches of a tree," says Mr. Brooks, "and Lincoln, lying flat on the ground, with his chin in his hands, talked on, rather gloomily as to the present, but absolutely confident as to the future. I was dismayed to find that he did not believe it possible that Fremont could be elected. As if half pitying my youthful ignorance, but admiring my enthusiasm, he said, 'Don't be discouraged, if we don't carry the day this year. We can't do it, that's certain. We can't carry Pennsylvania; those old Whigs down there are too strong for us. But we shall, sooner or later, elect our President. I feel confident of that.' 'Do you think we shall elect a Free-soil President in 1860?' I asked. 'Well, I don't know. Everything depends on the course of the Democracy. There's a big anti-slavery element in the Democratic party, and if we could get hold of that we might possibly elect our man in 1860. But it's doubtful, very doubtful. Perhaps we shall be able to fetch it by 1864; perhaps not. As I said before, the Free-soil party is bound to win in the long run. It may not be in my day; but it will be in yours, I do really believe.' " The defeat of Fremont soon verified Lincoln's prediction on that score.

LINCOLN'S FIRST VISIT TO CINCINNATI.

Among Mr. Lincoln's law cases was one connected with the patent of the McCormick Reaper, and in the summer of

1857 he visited Cincinnati to argue the case before Judge Mc-Lean of the U. S. Circuit Court. It was a case of great importance, involving the foundation patent of the machine which was destined to revolutionize the harvesting of grain. Reverdy Johnson was on one side of the case, and E. M. Stanton and George Harding on the other. It became necessary, in addition, to have a lawyer who was a resident of Illinois; and inquiry was made of Hon. E. B. Washburne, then in Congress, as to whether he knew a suitable man. The latter replied that "there was a man named Lincoln at Springfield, who had considerable reputation in the State." Lincoln was secured, and came on to Cincinnati with a brief. Stanton and Harding saw "a tall, dark, uncouth man, who did not strike them as of any account, and, indeed, they gave him hardly any chance."

An interesting account of this visit, and the various incidents connected with it, has been prepared by the Hon. W. M. Dickson of Cincinnati. "Mr. Lincoln came to the city a few days before the argument took place, and remained during his stay at the house of a friend. The case was one of large importance pecuniarily, and in the law questions involved. Reverdy Johnson represented the plaintiff. Mr. Lincoln had prepared himself with the greatest care; his ambition was up to speak in the case, and to measure swords with the renowned lawyer from Baltimore. It was understood between his client and himself before his coming, that Mr. Harding, of Philadelphia, was to be associated with him in the case, and was to make the 'mechanical argument.'

FIRST MEETING WITH EDWIN M. STANTON.

"Mr. Lincoln was a little surprised and annoyed," continues Mr. Dickson, "after reaching Cincinnati, to learn that his client had also associated with him Mr. Edwin M. Stanton, of Pittsburgh, and a lawyer of our own bar; the reason assigned being that the importance of the case required a man of the experience and power of Mr. Stanton to meet Mr. Johnson. The Cincinnati lawyer was appointed 'for his local influence.' These reasons did not remove the slight conveyed in the employment, without consultation with him, of this additional counsel. He keenly felt it, but acquiesced. The trial of the case came on; the counsel for defense met each morning for consultation. On one of these occasions, one of the counsel moved that only two of them should speak in the case. This motion was also acquiesced in. It had always been understood that Mr. Harding was to speak to explain the mechanism of the reapers. So this motion excluded either Mr. Lincoln or Mr. Stanton,—which? By the custom of the bar, as between counsel of equal standing, and in the absence of any action of the client, the original counsel speaks. By this rule Mr. Lincoln had precedence. Mr. Stanton suggested to Mr. Lincoln to make the speech. Mr. Lincoln answered, 'No; you speak.' Mr. Stanton replied, 'I will,' and taking up his hat, said he would go and make preparation. Mr. Lincoln acquiesced in this, but was deeply grieved and mortified; he took but little more interest in the case, though remaining until the conclusion of the trial. He seemed to be greatly depressed, and gave evidence of that tendency to melancholy which so marked his character. His parting on leaving the city cannot be forgotten. Cordially shaking the hand of his hostess, he said: "You have made my stay here most agreeable, and I am a thousand times obliged to you; but in reply to your request for me to come again, I must say to you I never expect to be in Cincinnati again. I have nothing against the city, but things have so happened here as to make it undesirable for me ever to return.' Thus untowardly met for the first time, Mr. Lincoln and Mr. Stanton. Little did either then suspect that they were to meet again on a larger theatre, to become the chief actors in a great historical epoch."

STANTON'S FIRST IMPRESSION OF LINCOLN.—HE REGARDS HIM AS A GIRAFFE.

If Mr. Lincoln was "surprised and annoyed" at the treatment he received from Mr. Stanton, the latter was no less surprised, and a good deal more disgusted, on seeing Mr. Lincoln and learning of his connection with the case. He made no secret of his contempt for the "long, lank creature from Illinois," as he afterwards described him, "wearing a dirty linen duster for a coat, on the back of which the perspiration had splotched wide stains that resembled a dirty map of the continent." He blurted out his wrath and indignation to his associate counsel, declaring that if "that giraffe" was permitted to appear in the case, he would throw up his brief and leave it. Mr. Lincoln keenly felt the affront, but his great nature forgave it so entirely that, recognizing the singular abilities of Mr. Stanton beneath his brusque exterior, he afterwards, for the public good, appointed him to a seat in his Cabinet.

A VISIT TO NICHOLAS LONGWORTH OF CINCINNATI.—SEEING THE CITY.

Mr. Dickson says that while Mr. Lincoln was in the city he visited, among other places of interest, the grounds and conservatories of the late Nicholas Longworth, then living. "The meeting of these remarkable men is worthy of passing note. Nor can it be given without allusion to their dress and bearing. Mr. Lincoln entered the open yard, with towering form and ungainly gait, dressed in plain clothing cut too small. His hands and feet seemed to be growing out of their environment, conspicuously seen from their uncommon size. Mr. Longworth happened at the time to be near the entrance, engaged in weeding the shrubbery by the walk. His alert eye quickly observed the coming of a person of unusual appearance. He rose and confronted him. 'Will a stranger be permitted to walk through your grounds and conservatories?' inquired Mr. Lincoln. 'Y–e–s,' haltingly, half unconsciously, was the reply, so fixed was the gaze of Mr. Longworth. As they stood thus face to face, the contrast was striking. So short in stature was the one that he seemed scarcely to reach the elbow of the other. If the dress of Mr. Lincoln seemed too small for him, the other seemed lost in the baggy bulkiness of his costume; the overflowing sleeves concealed the hands, and the extremities of the pantaloons were piled in heavy folds upon the open ears of the untied shoes. His survey of Mr. Lincoln was searching; beginning with the feet, he slowly raised his head, closely observing, until his upturned face met the eye of Mr. Lincoln. Thus for a moment gazed at each other in mutual and mute astonishment the millionaire pioneer and the now forever famous President. Mr. Lincoln passed on; nor did Mr. Longworth ever become aware that he had seen Mr. Lincoln. The grounds and conservatories were viewed and admired. And so afterward the suburbs of the city—Walnut Hills, Mount Auburn and Spring Grove Cemetery. Mr. Lincoln lingered long in the grounds of Mr. Hoffner, in the study of the statuary. He sought to find out whom the statues represented, and was much worried when he found himself unable to name correctly a single one. A day was given to the county and city courts. An entire morning was spent in the Superior Court, then presided over by Bellamy Storer, eccentric and versatile, in the maturity of his extraordinary powers. His manner of conducting the business of that room, miscellaneous, demurrers, motions, submitted docket, etc., was unique. To mingle in the same hour the gravity of the judge and the jest of the clown was a feat only he could perform without loss of dignity, personal or judicial. On this morning the Judge was in his happiest vein, in exuberant spirits, keeping the bar 'in a roar,' assisted much in this by the lively humor of poor Bob McCook. Mr. Lincoln greatly enjoyed this morning, and was loth to depart. He said to the gentleman accompanying him: 'I wish we had that judge in Illinois. I think he would share with me the fatherhood of the legal jokes of the Illinois bar. As it is now, they put them all on me, while I am not the author of one-half of them.' Mr. Lincoln remained in Cincinnati about a week, moving freely around. Yet not twenty men in the city knew him personally, or knew he was here; not a hundred would have known who he was had his name been given to them. He came with the fond hope of making fame in a forensic contest with Reverdy Johnson. He was pushed aside, humiliated and mortified. He attached to the innocent city the displeasure that filled his bosom, and shook its dust from his feet.''

CHAPTER IX.

THE year 1858 was memorable in the career of Lincoln and memorable in the political history of this country. It was distinguished by the joint discussions between the two great political leaders of Illinois, which rank among the ablest forensic debates that have taken place since the foundation of our republic. On April 21st the Democratic Convention of Illinois met at Springfield and announced Stephen A. Douglas, then United States Senator, as its choice for another term. June 16th the Republican Convention met at the same place and declared unanimously that "Abraham Lincoln is our first and only choice for United States Senator to fill the vacancy about to be created by the expiration of Mr. Douglas's term of office."

For a number of days previous to the meeting of the Republican Convention, Mr. Lincoln had been engaged in preparing a speech for the occasion. It was composed after his usual method—the separate thoughts jotted down as they came to him, on scraps of paper at hand at the moment, which, when the essay was concluded, were copied on large sheets of paper, in a plain, legible handwriting. This was the speech which afterwards came to be so celebrated as

THE "HOUSE–DIVIDED–AGAINST–ITSELF" SPEECH.

On the evening of June 16, Mr. Lincoln went to his office, accompanied by his friend Herndon, and having locked the door proceeded to read his speech. Slowly and distinctly he read the first paragraph, and then turned to Herndon with, "What do you think of that?" Mr. Herndon was startled at its boldness. "I think," said he, "it is all true; but is it entirely politic to read or speak it as it is written?" "That makes no difference," said Mr. Lincoln. "That expression is a truth of all human experience,—'a house divided against itself cannot stand;' and 'he that runs may read.' The proposition is indisputably true, and has been true for more than six thousand years; and I will deliver it as written. I want to use some universally known figure, expressed in simple language, that may strike home to the minds of men, in order to rouse them to the peril of the times. I would rather be defeated with this expression in the speech, and have it held up and discussed before the people, than to be victorious without it." Mr. Herndon was convinced by Mr. Lincoln's language, and advised him to deliver the speech just as it was written. Mr. Lincoln was satisfied, but thought it would be prudent to consult a few other friends in the matter, and about a dozen were called in. "After seating them at the round table," says John Armstrong, one of the number, "he read that clause or section of his speech which reads, 'a house divided against itself cannot stand,' etc. He read it slowly and cautiously, so as to let each man fully understand it. After he had finished the reading, he asked the opinions of his friends as to the wisdom or policy of it. Every man among them condemned the speech in substance and spirit, especially that section quoted above, as unwise and impolitic, if not untrue. They unanimously declared that the whole speech was too far in advance of the times. Herndon sat still while they were giving their respective opinions of its unwisdom and impolicy; then he sprang to his feet and said, 'Lincoln, deliver it *just as it reads.* If it is in advance of the times, let us—you and I, if no one else—lift the people to the level of this speech now, and higher hereafter. The speech is true, wise, and politic, and will succeed now or in the future. Nay, it will aid you, if it will not make you President of the United States.' Mr. Lincoln sat still a moment, rose from his chair, walked backwards and forwards in the hall, stopped, and said: 'Friends, I have thought about this matter a great deal, have weighed the questions well from all corners, and am thoroughly convinced the time has come when it should be uttered; and if it be that I must go down because of this speech, then let me go down linked to truth,—die in the advocacy of what is right and just. This nation cannot live on injustice; 'a house divided against itself cannot stand,' I say again and again.' This was spoken with emotion,—the effects of his love of truth, and sorrow from the disagreement of his friends with himself.''

AN INSPIRED ORATION.

On the evening of the 17th this speech was delivered to an immense audience in the hall of the House of Representatives at Springfield. "The hall and lobbies and galleries were even more densely crowded and packed than at any time during the day," says the official report; and as Mr. Lincoln "approached the speaker's stand, he was greeted with shouts and hurrahs, and prolonged cheers." The prophetic sentences which dropped first from the lips of Mr. Lincoln, as he addressed the throng before him, were freighted with a solemn import which even he could not have wholly divined. The seers of old were not more inspired than he who now, out of the irresistible conviction of his heart, said to his surprised and unbelieving listeners:

"If we could first know where we are and whither we are tending, we could then better judge what to do and how to do it. We are now far on in the fifth year since a policy was initiated with the avowed object and confident promise of putting an end to slavery agitation. Under the operation of that policy, that agitation has not only not ceased, but has constantly augmented. In my opinion it will not cease until a crisis shall have been reached and passed. 'A house divided against itself cannot stand.' I believe this Government cannot endure permanently, half slave and half free. I do not expect the Union to be dissolved—I do not expect the house to fall—but I do expect it will cease to be divided. It will become all one thing or all the other. Either the opponents of slavery will arrest the further spread of it, and place it where the public mind shall rest in the belief that it is in course of ultimate extinction, or its advocates will push it forward till it shall become alike lawful in all the States—old as well as new—North as well as South.''

Mr. Jeriah Bonham, an old citizen of Illinois, relates that he was present as a delegate at the Springfield Convention of June, 1858, which nominated Mr. Lincoln for Senator, and heard the famous speech on the evening of that day. He says: "The speech was prepared with unusual care, every paragraph and sentence carefully weighed. The firm bedrock of his principles, the issues of the campaign on which he proposed to stand and fight his battles, were all well considered, and his arguments incontrovertible. In that memorable speech culminated all the grand thoughts he had ever uttered, embodying divinity, statesmanship, law, and morals, and even fraught with prophecy. As he advanced in this argument, he towered to his full height, forgetting himself entirely as he grew warm in his work. Men and women who heard that speech well remember the wonderful transformation wrought in Mr. Lincoln's appearance. The plain, homely man towered up majestically; his face lit as with angelic light; the long, bent, angular figure, like the strong oak of the forest, stood erect, and his eyes flashed with the fire of inspiration.''

The speech was strong, calm, and earnest throughout, the deliberate and grave utterance of a man who had risen above the aims and the ways of a mere office-seeker, and was fulfilling the mission of a patriot and a teacher of the people.

ALARMING HIS FRIENDS.

The party was not prepared to endorse Mr. Lincoln's restriction of the coming struggle to the single issue of the slavery question. His friends dreaded the result of his uncompromising frankness, while politicians quite generally condemned it. Even so staunch a friend as Leonard Swett, whose devotion to Mr. Lincoln never wavered throughout his whole career, shared these apprehensions. Says Mr. Swett: "The first ten lines of that speech defeated him. The sentiment of the 'house divided against itself' seemed wholly inappropriate. It was a speech made at the commencement of a campaign, and apparently made for the campaign. Viewing it in this light alone, nothing could have been more unfortunate or in-

HON. LEONARD SWETT.

appropriate. It was saying first the wrong thing; yet he saw that it was an abstract truth, and standing by the speech would ultimately find him in the right place. I was inclined at the time to believe these words were hastily and inconsiderately uttered; but subsequent facts have convinced me they were deliberate and had been matured.''

A few days after the delivery of this speech, a gentleman named Dr. Long called on Mr. Lincoln, and gave him a foretaste of the remarks he was to hear during the next few months. ''Well, Lincoln,'' said he, ''that foolish speech of yours will kill you,—will defeat you in this contest, and probably for all offices for all time to come. I am sorry, sorry, very sorry. I wish it was wiped out of existence. Don't you wish so too?'' Laying down the pen with which he had been writing, and slowly raising his head and adjusting his spectacles, Lincoln replied: ''Well, doctor, if I had to draw a pen across and erase my whole life from existence, and I had one poor gift or choice left as to which I should save from the wreck, *I should choose that speech*, and leave it to the world unerased.''

THE CHALLENGE TO A JOINT DISCUSSION.

Mr. Douglas made his first speech in the campaign, at Chicago, on the 9th of July, 1858. Mr. Lincoln was present, and on the next evening spoke in reply from the same place— the balcony of the Tremont House. A week later Mr. Douglas spoke at Bloomington, with Mr. Lincoln again in the audience. The notion of a joint discussion seems to have originated with Mr. Lincoln, who, on the 24th of July, addressed the following note to Mr. Douglas:

'HON. S. A. DOUGLAS—My Dear Sir:—Will it be agreeable to you to make an arrangement for you and myself to divide time, and address the same audiences during the present canvass? Mr. Judd, who will hand you this, is authorized to receive your answer, and, if agreeable to you, to enter into the terms of such arrangement.

''Your obedient servant,   A. LINCOLN.''

The result of this proposition was an agreement that there should be a joint discussion in each of the seven Congressional districts in which they had not both already been heard. The places and dates chosen for the debates were as follows: Ottawa, August 21 ; Freeport, August 27 ; Jonesborough, September 15 ; Charleston, September 18 ; Galesburg, October 7 ; Quincy, October 13 ; and Alton, October 15. It was further decided that the opening speech on each occasion should occupy one hour; the reply, one hour and a half; the close, half an hour; and that Mr. Douglas should have the first and last voice in four of the seven meetings.

THE CHAMPIONS CONTRASTED.

Of the champions who were thus to enter the lists in a decisive trial of forensic strength and skill, Mr. Speed says: "They were the respective leaders of their parties in the State. They were as opposite in character as they were unlike in their persons. Lincoln was long and ungainly; Douglas, short and compact. Douglas, in all elections, was the moving spirit in the conduct and management of an election. He was not content without a blind submission to himself. He could not tolerate opposition to his will within his party organization. He held the reins and controlled the movement of the Democratic chariot. With a large State majority, with many able and ambitious men in it, he stepped to the front in his youth and held his place till his death. Mr. Lincoln, on the other hand, shrank from any controversy with his friends. His party being in a minority in the State, he was forced to the front, because his friends thought he was the only man with whom they could win. In a canvass, his friends had to do all the management. He knew nothing of how to reach the people, except by addressing their reason. If the situation had been reversed—Lincoln representing the majority and Douglas the minority—I think it most likely Lincoln would never have had the place. He had no heart for a fight with friends."

The Hon. James G. Blaine gives a masterly description and analysis of the comparative powers of the two illustrious debaters. Douglas, says Mr. Blaine, "was everywhere known as a debater of singular skill. His mind was fertile in resources. He was a master of logic. No man perceived more quickly than he the strength or the weakness of an argument, and no one excelled him in the use of sophistry and fallacy. Where he could not elucidate a point to his own advantage, he would fatally becloud it for his opponent. In that peculiar style of debate which, in its intensity, resembles a physical combat, he had no equal. He spoke with extraordinary readiness. There was no halting in his phrase. He used good English, terse, vigorous, pointed. He disregarded the adornments of rhetoric,—rarely used a simile. He was utterly destitute of humor, and had slight appreciation of wit. He never cited historical precedents, except from the domain of American politics. Inside that field his knowledge was comprehensive, minute, critical. Beyond it his learning was limited. He was not a reader. His recreations were not in literature. In the whole range of his voluminous speaking, it would be difficult to find either a line of poetry or a classical allusion. But he was by nature an orator, and by long practice a debater. He could lead a crowd almost irresistibly to his own conclusions. He could, if he wished, incite a mob to desperate deeds. He was, in short, an able, audacious, almost unconquerable opponent in public discussion. It would have been impossible to find any man of the same type able to meet him before the people of Illinois. Whoever attempted it would probably have been destroyed in the first encounter. But the man who was chosen to meet him, who challenged him to the combat, was radically different in every phase of character. Scarcely could two men be more unlike, in mental and moral constitution, than Abraham Lincoln and Stephen A. Douglas. Mr. Lincoln was calm and philosophic. He loved the truth for the truth's sake. He would not argue from a false premise, or be deceived himself or deceive others by a false conclusion. He had pondered deeply on the issues which aroused him to action. He had given anxious thought to the problems of free government, and to the destiny of the

Republic. He had for himself marked out a path of duty, and he walked it fearlessly. His mental processes were slower but more profound than those of Douglas. He did not seek to say merely the thing which was best for that day's debate, but the thing which would stand the test of time and square itself with eternal justice. He wished nothing to appear white unless it was white. His logic was severe and faultless. He did not resort to fallacy, and could detect it in his opponent and expose it with merciless directness. He had an abounding sense of humor, and always employed it in illustration of his argument,—but never for the mere sake of provoking merriment. In this respect he had the wonderful aptness of Franklin. He often taught a great truth with the felicitous brevity of an Æsop fable. His words did not flow in an impetuous torrent, as did those of Douglas; but they were always well chosen, deliberate and conclusive.''

Mr. Arnold, in the course of an extended comparison, says: ''At the time of these discussions, both Lincoln and Douglas were in the full maturity of their powers. Douglas was forty-five and Lincoln forty-nine years of age. Physically and mentally, they were as unlike as possible. Douglas was short, not much more than five feet high, with a large head, massive brain, broad shoulders, a wide, deep chest, and features strongly marked. He impressed every one, at first sight, as a strong, sturdy, resolute, fearless man. Lincoln's herculean stature has already been described. A stranger who listened to him for five minutes would say: 'This is a kind, genial, sincere, genuine man; a man you can trust, plain, straightforward, honest and true.' If this stranger were to hear him make a speech, he would be impressed with his clear good sense, by his wit and humor, by his general intelligence, and by the simple, homely, but pure and accurate language he used. In his long residence at Washington, Douglas had acquired the bearing and manners of a perfect gentleman and a man of the world. But he was always a fascinating and attractive man, and always and everywhere personally popular. He had been, for years, carefully and thoroughly trained on the stump, in Congress, and in the Senate, to meet in debate the ablest speakers in the State and Nation. For years he had been accustomed to meet, on the floor of the capital, the leaders of the old Whig and Free-soil parties. Among them were Webster and Seward, Fessenden and Crittenden, Chase, Trumbull, Hale and others of nearly equal eminence; and his enthusiastic friends insisted that never, either in single conflict or when receiving the assault of the senatorial leaders of a whole party, had he been discomfited. His style was bold, vigorous and aggressive; at times even defiant. He was ready, fluent, fertile in resources, familiar with national and party history, severe in denunciation, and he handled with skill nearly all the weapons of debate. His iron will and restless energy, together with great personal magnetism, made him the idol of his friends and party. His long, brilliant and almost universally successful career, gave him perfect confidence in himself, and at times he was arrogant and overbearing. Lincoln was also a thoroughly trained speaker. He had met successfully, year after year, at the bar and on the stump, the ablest men of Illinois and the Northwest, including Lamborn, Stephen T. Logan, John Calhoun, and many others. He had contended, in generous emulation, with Hardin, Baker, Logan and Browning; and had very often met Douglas, a conflict with whom he always courted rather than shunned. His speeches, as we read them to-day, show a more familiar knowledge of the slavery question than those of any other statesman of our country. This is especially true of the Peoria speech and the Cooper Institute speech. Lincoln was powerful in argument, always seizing the strong points, and demonstrating his propositions with a clearness and logic approaching the certainty of mathematics. He had, in wit and humor, a great advantage over Douglas. Then he had the better temper; he was always good humored, while

Douglas, when hard pressed, was sometimes irritable. Douglas, perhaps, carried away the more popular applause. Lincoln made the deeper and more lasting impression. Douglas did not disdain an immediate *ad captandum* triumph; while Lincoln aimed at permanent conviction. Sometimes, when Lincoln's friends urged him to raise a storm of applause, which he could always do by his happy illustrations and amusing stories, he refused, saying, 'The occasion is too serious; the issues are too grave. I do not seek applause, or to amuse the people, but to *convince* them.' It was observed in the canvass that while Douglas was greeted with the loudest cheers, when Lincoln closed the people seemed serious and thoughtful, and could be heard all through the crowd, gravely and anxiously discussing the subjects on which he had been speaking."

WHAT THEY THOUGHT OF EACH OTHER.

Soon after the arrangements for the debate had been made, Senator Douglas visited Alton, Illinois. A delegation of prominent Democrats there paid their respects to him, and during the conversation one of them congratulated Douglas on the easy task he would have in defeating Lincoln; at the same time expressing surprise at the champion whom he had selected. Douglas replied: "Gentlemen, you do not know Mr. Lincoln. I have known him long and well, and I know that I shall have anything but an easy task. I assure you I *would rather meet any other man in the country* in this joint debate *than Abraham Lincoln.*" This was Douglas's mature opinion of the man of whom, years before, he had said, in his characteristic way: "Of all the d——d Whig rascals about Springfield, Abe Lincoln is the ablest and honestest." On another occasion, Douglas said: "I have known Lincoln for nearly twenty-five years. There were many points of sympathy between us when we first got acquainted. We were both comparatively boys, and both struggling with poverty in a strange land. I was a school-teacher in the town of

Winchester, and he a flourishing grocery-keeper in the town of Salem. He was more successful in his occupation than I was in mine, and hence more fortunate in the world's goods. Lincoln is one of those peculiar men who perform with admirable skill everything they undertake. I made as good a school-teacher as I could, and when a cabinet-maker I made as good bedsteads and tables as I could—although my old boss says that I succeeded better with *bureaus* and *secretaries* than with anything else. But I believe that Lincoln was always more successful in business than I, for his business enabled him to get into the Legislature. I met him there, however, and had a sympathy with him, because of the up-hill struggle we both had had in life. He was then just as good at telling an anecdote as now. He could beat any of the boys in wrestling or running a foot-race, in pitching quoits or pitching a copper; and the dignity and impartiality with which he presided at a horse-race or fist-fight excited the admiration and won the praise of everybody that was present. I sympathized with him because he was struggling with difficulties, and so was I. Mr. Lincoln served with me in the Legislature of 1836, when we both retired, and he subsided, or became submerged, and was lost sight of as a public man for some years. In 1846, when Wilmot introduced his celebrated proviso, and the Abolition tornado swept over the country, Lincoln again turned up as a Member of Congress from the Sangamon district. I was then in the Senate of the United States, and was glad to welcome my old friend.''

Mr. Lincoln, in a speech delivered two years before the joint debate, had said of Senator Douglas: ''Twenty-two years ago, Judge Douglas and I first became acquainted; we were both young then,—he a trifle younger than I. Even then, we were both ambitious,—I perhaps quite as much as he. With me, the race of ambition has been a failure—a flat failure; with him, it has been one of splendid success. His name fills the nation, and is not unknown even in foreign lands. I affect no contempt for the high eminence he has reached; so reached that the oppressed of my species might have shared with me in the elevation, I would rather stand on that eminence than wear the richest crown that ever pressed a monarch's brow."

A few days before the first discussion was to take place, Lincoln, who had become conscious that some of his party friends distrusted his ability to meet successfully a man who, as the Democrats declared and believed, had never had his equal on the stump, met an old friend from Vermilion county, and, shaking hands, inquired the news. His friend replied, "All looks well; our friends are wide awake, but they are looking forward with some anxiety to these approaching joint discussions with Douglas." A shade passed over Lincoln's face, a sad expression came and instantly passed, and then a blaze of light flashed from his eyes, and with his lips compressed, and with a manner peculiar to him, half serious and half jocular, he said: "My friend, sit down a minute, and I will tell you a story. You and I, as we have travelled the circuit together attending court, have often seen two men about to fight. One of them, the big or the little giant, as the case may be, is noisy and boastful; he jumps high in the air, strikes his feet together, smites his fists, brags about what he is going to do, and tries hard to '*skeer*' the other man. The other man says not a word; his arms are at his side, his fists are clenched, his teeth set, his head settled firmly on his shoulders; he saves his breath and strength for the struggle. *This man will whip*, as sure as the fight comes off. Good-bye, and remember what I say."

The spirit and purpose with which Mr. Lincoln went into the contest are shown also in the following words: "I shall not ask any favors at all. Judge Douglas asks me if I wish to push this matter to the point of personal difficulty. I tell him *No!* He did not make a mistake, in one of his early speeches, when he called me an 'amiable' man, though perhaps he did when he called me an 'intelligent' man. I again tell him *No!* I very much prefer, when this canvass shall be over, however it may result, that we at least part without any bitter recollections of personal difficulties.''

LINCOLN AND DOUGLAS ON THE STUMP.

The speeches in these joint discussions were entirely extemporaneous, yet were reprinted in all the prominent papers in the West, and found eager readers throughout the country. The voice and manner, which add so much to the effect of a speaker, could not be reproduced on the printed page; nor could full justice be done, in a hasty transcript, to the beauty and fitness of the language employed. Still, the impressions of the moment, as well as the later and cooler analyses, have agreed in pronouncing these debates among the most able and interesting on record. The scenes connected with the different meetings were intensely exciting. Vast throngs were invariably in attendance, while a whole nation was watching the result. ''At Freeport,'' says an observer, ''Mr. Douglas appeared in an elegant barouche drawn by four white horses, and was received with great applause. But when Mr. Lincoln came up, in a 'prairie schooner,'—an old-fashioned canvas-covered pioneer wagon,—the enthusiasm of the vast throng was unbounded.''

At Charleston Mr. Lincoln opened and closed the debate. It was the fourth discussion, and there was no more doubt of his ability to sustain the conflict. According to Mr. Arnold, ''Douglas's reply to Lincoln was mainly a defense. Lincoln's close was intensely interesting and dramatic. His logic and arguments were crushing, and Douglas's evasions were exposed, with a power and clearness that left him utterly discomfited. Republicans saw it, Democrats realized it, and a sort of panic seized them, and ran through the crowd of upturned faces. Douglas realized his defeat, and, as Lincoln's blows fell fast and heavy, he lost his temper. He could not keep his seat; he rose and walked rapidly up and down the

SCENE IN THE GREAT LINCOLN AND DOUGLAS DEBATE.—"SIT DOWN, LINCOLN!
SIT DOWN! YOUR TIME IS UP!"

platform, behind Lincoln, holding his watch in his hand, and obviously impatient for the call of '*time*.' A spectator says: 'He was greatly agitated, his long grizzled hair waving in the wind, like the shaggy locks of an enraged lion.' It was while Douglas was thus exhibiting to the crowd his eager desire to stop Lincoln, that the latter, holding the audience entranced by his eloquence, was striking his heaviest blows. The instant the second-hand of his watch reached the point at which Lincoln's time was up, Douglas, holding up the watch, called out: 'Sit down, Lincoln, sit down! Your time is up!' Turning to Douglas, Lincoln said calmly: 'I will. I *will* quit. I believe my time *is* up.' 'Yes,' said a man on the platform, 'Douglas has had enough; it is time you let up on him.'"

SLAVERY THE LEADING ISSUE.

The institution of slavery was the topic around which circled all the arguments in these joint discussions. It was the great topic of the hour; the important point of division between the Republican and Democratic parties. Mr. Lincoln's exposition of the subject was profound, logical, and exhaustive. At the meeting in Quincy his argument was strikingly luminous and convincing. In closing the debate, he said:

"I wish to return to Judge Douglas my profound thanks for his public annunciation here to-day, to be put on record, that his system of policy in regard to the institution of slavery contemplates that it shall last *forever*. We are getting a little nearer the true issue of this controversy, and I am profoundly grateful for this one sentence. Judge Douglas asks you, 'Why cannot the institution of slavery, or rather, why cannot the nation, part slave and part free, continue as our fathers made it forever?' In the first place, I insist that our fathers *did not* make this nation half slave and half free, or part slave and part free. I insist that they found the institution of slavery existing here. They did not make it so, but they left it so, because they knew of no way to get rid of it at that time. When Judge Douglas undertakes to say that, as a matter of choice, the fathers of the Government made this nation part slave and part free, he assumes what is historically *a falsehood*. More than that; when the fathers of the Government cut off the source of slavery by the abolition of the slave-trade, and adopted a system of restricting it from the new Territories where it had not existed, I maintain that they placed it where they understood, and all sensible men understood, it was in the course of ultimate extinction; and when Judge Douglas asks me why it cannot continue as our fathers made it, I ask him why he and his friends could not let it remain as our friends made it? It is precisely all I ask of him in relation to the institution of slavery, that it shall be placed upon the basis that our fathers placed it upon. Mr. Brooks, of South Carolina, once said, and truly said, that when this Government was established, no one expected the institution of slavery to last until this day; and that the men who formed this Government were wiser and better than the men of these days; but the men of these days had experience which the fathers had not, and that experience had taught them the invention of the cotton-gin, and this had made the perpetuation of the institution of slavery a necessity in this country. Judge Douglas could not let it stand upon the basis on which our fathers placed it, but removed it, and put it upon the cotton-gin basis. It is a question, therefore, for him and his friends to answer—why they could not let it remain where the fathers of the Government originally placed it?''

He said to a friend during the canvass:

"Sometimes, in the excitement of speaking, I seem to see the end of slavery. I feel that the time is soon coming when the sun shall shine, the rain fall, on no man who shall go forth to unrequited toil.   *   *   How this will come, when it will come, by whom it will come, I cannot tell;— but that time will surely come.''

Again, at the first encounter at Alton, he said:

"On this subject of treating slavery as a wrong, and limiting its spread, let me say a word. Has anything ever threatened the existence of this Union save and except this very institution of slavery? What is it that we hold most dear among us? Our own liberty and prosperity. What has ever threatened our liberty and prosperity, save and except this institution of slavery? If this is true, how do you propose to improve the condition of things by enlarging slavery?—by spreading it out and making it bigger? You may have a wen or cancer upon your person, and not be able to cut it out lest you bleed to death; but surely, it is no way to cure it, to ingraft it and spread it over your whole body—that is no proper way of treating what you regard a wrong. You see, this peaceful way of dealing with it as a wrong—restricting the spread of it, and not allowing it to go into new countries where it has not already existed—that is the peaceful way, the old-fashioned way, the way in which the fathers themselves set us the example. Is slavery wrong? That is the real issue. That is the issue that will continue in this country when these poor tongues of Judge Douglas and myself shall be silent. It is the eternal struggle between these two principles—right and wrong—throughout the world. They are two principles that have stood face to face from the beginning of time; and will ever continue to struggle. The one is the common right of humanity, and the other the divine right of kings. It is the same principle, in whatever shape it develops itself. It is the same spirit that says: 'You work, and toil, and earn bread, and I'll eat it.' No matter in what shape it comes, whether from the mouth of a king who seeks to bestride the people of his own nation and live by the fruit of their labor, or from one race of men as an apology for enslaving another race, it is the same tyrannical principle."

On still another occasion he used these memorable words:

"My declarations upon this subject of negro slavery may be misrepresented, but cannot be misunderstood. I have said that I do not understand the Declaration to mean that all men were created equal in all respects. They are not our equal in color; but I suppose that it does mean to declare that all men are created equal in some respects; they are equal in their right to 'life, liberty, and the pursuit of happiness.' Certainly the negro is not our equal in color, perhaps not in many other respects; still, *in the right to put into his mouth the bread that his own hands have earned, he is the equal of every other man, white or black.*"

SCENES AND ANECDOTES OF THE GREAT DEBATE.

It is not in the scope of this narrative to print extended quotations from the speeches made in this memorable contest, but rather to give such reminiscences and anecdotes, and description by eye-witnesses, as will best serve to bring the scenes and actors vividly to mind. Fortunately, many such eye-witnesses are yet living, and from them some most entertaining personal accounts have been obtained. Among these is an impressive

PEN-PICTURE OF LINCOLN ON THE STUMP,

which is admirably sketched by the Rev. Dr. George C. Noyes, of Chicago. "Mr. Lincoln in repose was a very different man in personal appearance from Mr. Lincoln on the platform or on the stump, when his whole nature was roused by his masterful interest in the subject of his discourse. In the former case he was, as he has often been described, a man of awkward and ungainly appearance, and exceedingly homely countenance. In the latter case, he was a man of magnificent presence and remarkably impressive manner. The writer retains to this day a very vivid impression of his appearance in both these characters, and both on the same day. It was in Jacksonville, in the summer of 1858, and during the great contest with Mr. Douglas, when the prize contended for was a seat in the United States Senate. The day was warm; the streets were dusty, and filled with great crowds of people. When Mr. Lincoln arrived on the train from Springfield, he was met by an immense procession of people on horseback, in carriages, in wagons and vehicles of every description, and on foot, who escorted him through the principal streets to his hotel. The enthusiasm of the multitude was great; but Mr. Lincoln's extremely homely face wore an expression of sadness. He rode in a carriage near the head of the procession, looking dust-begrimed and worn and weary; and though he frequently lifted his hat in recognition of the cheers of the crowds lining the streets, I saw no smile on his face, and he seemed to take no pleasure in the demonstrations of enthusiasm which his presence called forth. His clothes were very ill-fitting, and his long arms and hands protruded far through his coat sleeves, giving him a peculiarly uncouth appearance. Though I had often seen him before, and had heard him in court—always with delight in his clearness and cogency of statement, his illuminating humor, and his conspicuous fairness and candor—yet I had never before seen him when he appeared so homely; and I thought him about the ugliest man I had ever seen. There was nothing in his looks or manner that was prepossessing. Such he appeared as he rode in the procession on the forenoon of that warm summer day. His appearance was not different in the afternoon of that day, when, in the public square, he first stood before the great multitude who had assembled there to hear him. His powers were aroused gradually as he went on with his speech. There was much play of humor. 'Judge Douglas has,' he said, 'one great advantage of me in this contest. When he stands before his admiring friends, who gather in great numbers to hear him, they can easily see, with half an eye, all kinds of *fat offices* sprouting out of his fat and jocund face, and, indeed, from every part of his plump and well-rounded body. His appearance is therefore irresistibly attractive. His friends expect him to be President, and they expect their reward. But when I stand before the people, not the sharpest vision is able to detect in my lean and lank person, or in my sunken and hollow cheeks, *the faintest sign or promise* of an office. I am not a candidate for the Presidency, and hence there is no beauty in me that men should desire me.' The crowd were convulsed with laughter at this sally. As the speech went on, the speaker, though often impressing his points with apposite and laughter-provoking stories, grew more and more earnest. He showed that the government was founded in the interest of freedom, not slavery. He traced the steady aggressions of the slave power step by step, until he came to declare and to dwell upon the fact of the irrepressible conflict between the two. Then, as he went on to show, with wonderful eloquence of speech and of manner, that the country must and would ultimately become, not all slave, but all free, he was transfigured before his audience. His homely countenance fairly glowed with the splendor of his prophetic speech; and his body, no longer awkward and ungainly, but mastered and swayed by his thought, became an obedient and graceful instrument of eloquent expression. The whole man seemed to speak. He seemed like some grand Hebrew prophet, whose face was glorified by the bright visions of a better day which he saw and declared. His eloquence was not merely that of clear and luminous statement, felicitous illustration, or excited yet restrained feeling; it was the eloquence also of *thought*. With something of the imaginative, he united rare dialectic power. He felt the truth before he proved it; but when once it was felt by him, then his logical power came into remarkably effective play. Step by step he led his hearers onward, till at last he placed them on the summit whence they could see all the landscape of his subject in harmonious and connected order. Of these two contrasted pictures of Mr. Lincoln, it is only the last which shows him as he was in his real and essential greatness. And not this fully; for it was in his character that he was greatest. He was not merely a thinker, but a thinker for man, directing his thought to the ends of justice, freedom, and humanity. If he desired and sought high position, it was only that he might thus better serve the cause of freedom to which he was devoted. From the time when he withdrew, in a spirit of magnanimity that was never appreciated, in favor of a rival candidate for the United States Senate, it was evident that the *cause* was more to him than any personal advantage or advancement."

Another graphic description of Mr. Lincoln's appearance and manner on the stump is given by Mr. Jeriah Bonham, whose account of the famous "House-divided-against-itself" speech has found a place in this narrative. "When Mr. Lincoln took the stand," says Mr. Bonham, "he did not, on rising, show his full height, but stood in a stooping posture, his long-tailed coat hanging loosely around his body, and descending over an ill-fitting pair of pantaloons that covered his not very symmetrical legs. He began his speech in a rather diffident manner, seeming for awhile at a loss for words; his voice was irregular, even a little tremulous, as he began his argument. As he proceeded he seemed to gain more confidence, his form straightened up, his face brightened, his language became free and animated. Soon he had drawn the attention of the crowd by two or three well-told stories that illustrated his argument; and then he became eloquent, carrying his audience at will, as tumultuous applause greeted every telling point he made."

HUMORS OF THE CAMPAIGN.

Among the party that attended Mr. Lincoln in the Senatorial campaign was the Hon. Andrew Shuman, afterwards Lieutenant-Governor of Illinois, and one of the veteran journalists of Chicago. Mr. Shuman was detailed to report the joint debates for his paper, the Chicago Evening Journal; and he accompanied Mr. Lincoln through nearly all of the campaign, travelling with him by night—sometimes occupying the same room, and when in crowded quarters, the same bed. He thus saw much of Mr. Lincoln, and had the best of opportunities for studying his character; not only hearing all his public speeches, but having long conversations with him in private, and listening to the stories, anecdotes, and gay or grave discourse, by which the journeys and the frequent "waits" were enlivened. The group consisted of several gentlemen, including Norman B. Judd, of Chicago, afterwards a member of Congress; Robert R. Hitt, who was Lincoln's shorthand reporter, now member of Congress from Illinois; Mr. Villard, the late President of the Northern Pacific Railroad, who was then a newspaper correspondent; Mr. Shuman; and at various times, other politicians and journalists. Of this party, Mr. Lincoln was always the leading spirit in conversation. He would tell stories himself, and draw out stories from others; and his laugh, though not the loudest, was always the heartiest. Then he would pass to soberer themes, and discuss them with a tinge of that melancholy, which, however he might be surrounded, never seemed far distant from him. At night, stopping at the country tavern or at some friend's house, the evenings would be spent in discussion and story-telling, or perhaps in a humorous review of the events of the day; and after retiring, Mr. Lincoln would entertain his companion, often far into the night, discoursing on a great variety of subjects, politics, literature, views of human life and character, or the prominent men and measures then before the country.

"TOO MANY OF US IN THIS BED."

One incident of the many that Mr. Shuman relates indicates both the simplicity and the humor of Mr. Lincoln. Coming from the southern portion of the State on a belated train one afternoon, the party missed their connection with a train on a cross-road in Central Illinois, and were obliged to seek shelter for the night at the small town at which they had expected to make a change of trains. The best public house in the town was a "country tavern," a small wooden structure kept by a Hoosier. As soon as it became evident that they would have to remain in that town all night, Mr. Shuman at once hastened to this tavern, where, after explaining the circumstances, he engaged the only unoccupied room in the house for Mr. Lincoln, who, after days and nights of campaigning, was glad enough of the prospect of enjoying one good night's rest. After supper Mr. Lincoln sat in the public room of the tavern,—which had only one public room in it,—for an hour, talking familiarly with the loungers of the town. Every man present, Mr. Lincoln excepted, smoked or chewed tobacco, and occasionally "indulged" at the bar. It was a rough crowd of a dozen or more, and Mr. Lincoln was the chief talker, and soon became the center of a circle, amusing his listeners with anecdotes and edifying them with his views and statements on current questions of politics and subjects of common interest. Suddenly he arose and requested the landlord to show him to his bed. It was only eight o'clock, and the remark was made that he was retiring very early. "Yes," he replied, "I have a hard day's work before me to-morrow, and want to load up with all the sleep I can get." Before going to his room, he inquired of Mr. Shuman where *he* was going to sleep. "No matter," was the reply; "I can sleep in a chair or anywhere; don't mind me." But Mr. Lincoln insisted that, he having "preempted" the only unoccupied room and bed in the house, Mr. Shuman must share both of them with him; and his friend finally, though reluctantly, consented. Armed with a greasy candle-stick, on which there was a half-burnt tallow candle and a dirty pair of snuffers, the landlord piloted the two to their room. The rooms of a "country-tavern" in those days and in that region were never remarkable either for their luxurious furnishing or their tidiness. This particular room was very plain and simple; it could scarcely have been more so. A rough bedstead, with a few simple bed-clothes upon it, stood in one corner; a rickety old lounge stood on one side; a rag-carpet, the worse for long wear and much tear, covered the center of the floor. This inventory embraced the entire furniture of the room, with the exception of a small stand, made of rough pine, for the accommodation of the candle-stick. But, as he often remarked during his travels, Mr. Lincoln "wasn't at all particular." The two friends hurried into bed; and here is Mr. Shuman's account of the experiences that followed: "I went to sleep right off; but after an hour or so I was awakened by Mr. Lincoln getting up, striking a match and lighting the candle. 'What's the matter, Mr. Lincoln?' I asked. 'I can't get asleep,' he replied, 'and am going to explore a little. The fact is, Shuman, there are *too many of us* in this bed.' Not understanding what he meant, I proposed to go down stairs and sleep in a chair, leaving him alone to get the rest he so much needed. 'Oh, no,' he said, 'I don't mean you. I'll show you what I mean.' Thereupon, with a sudden jerk, he lifted the bed-clothes from the foot of the bed, and pointed to a dozen or two of fleeing bed-bugs. 'See there! those fellows have been feeding upon my shins for the past hour, and I can't stand it any longer.' For the first time since I had known him, Mr. Lincoln exhibited considerable impatience, and something like anger. He left the bed in disgust, and threw himself upon the rickety old lounge at the other side of the room, declaring his purpose to lie there the remainder of the night, with nothing but his apology for a pillow between him and the rough plank which constituted the seat of the lounge. I couldn't permit that, of course; so I took most of the clothing off the bed and tucked it under and around him, making him as comfortable as possible. The light was extinguished, and I rejoined my multitudinous companions in the bed, who, apparently not being fond of young blood, kept their distance. I was just falling off into sleep, when I heard the old lounge creaking. It was evident that its occupant was not getting the sleep he sought for. He turned from one side to the other several times; he gave an occasional kick; finally he groaned. 'Can't you get asleep there, either?' I inquired. 'Not a bit of it,—there's no sleep for me here.' He arose, and so did I. We again lighted the candle, and with it examined 'the lounge. It fairly swarmed with bed-bugs! To make a long and painful story short, it was finally agreed between us that Mr. Lincoln should make a bed for himself on the rag-carpet in the center of the floor, he vigorously protesting at first against taking the 'lion's share' of the bed-clothes; but I insisted, and carried my point. We doubled up the straw-mattress and the carpet on the floor, and Mr. Lincoln, lying down, wadded up his pillow into a bunch under his head, and after I had tucked a quilt and a blanket around him and wished him 'better luck this time,' we resumed our efforts to sleep. It was now eleven o'clock; and in order to take the train it was necessary for us to be up for breakfast at six o'clock. Mr. Lincoln declared, when making his hasty toilet by the sickly light of our tallow candle, next morning, that he never in all his life had a sounder or a more restful sleep than that which followed his 'battle with the bed-bugs.' The last time I ever saw Abraham Lincoln to speak with him, the late Norman B. Judd and several others being present, he narrated this little adventure of ours in that old country tavern.''

LINCOLN SOOTHING AN ANGRY CROWD.

One day, continues Gov. Shuman, Mr. Lincoln had been announced to speak in a town in the extreme southern part of

Illinois, in the very heart of "Egypt," where there was a strong pro-slavery sentiment; and it was feared there might be trouble, as Lincoln's anti-slavery tendencies were well known. To make matters worse, a party of Kentuckians and Missourians had come over to attend the meeting, and it was noised about that they would not allow Lincoln to speak. He heard of it, and both he and his friends were somewhat apprehensive of trouble. The place of the meeting was a grove in the edge of the town, the speakers occupying an improvised stand. The meeting was a large one, and it had every appearance of a Southern crowd. It was customary in those times for the men in that section of the country to carry pistols and ugly-looking knives strapped to their persons, on public occasions. It was a semi-barbarous community, and their hatred of the "Abolitionists," as they called all anti-slavery men, was as intense as was their love of bad whiskey. Mr. Lincoln privately told his friends, who in that locality were very few in number, that "if only they will give me a fair chance to say a few opening words, I'll fix them all right." Before mounting the speaker's stand, occupying a position on the ground, he was introduced to many of the crowd and shook their hands in the usual Western way. Getting a small company of the rough-looking fellows around him, he opened on them. "Fellow-citizens of Southern Illinois,—fellow-citizens of the State of Kentucky,—fellow-citizens of Missouri," he said, in a tone more of conversation than of oratory, looking them "straight in the eye," "I am told that there are some of you here present who would like to make trouble for me. I don't understand why they should. I am a plain, common man, like the rest of you; and why should not I have as good a right to speak my sentiments as the rest of you? Why, good friends, I am one of you; I am not an interloper here! I was born in Kentucky, raised in Illinois, just like the most of you, and worked my way right along by hard scratching. I know the people of Kentucky, and I know the people of Southern Illinois, and I think I know the Missourians. I am one of them, and therefore ought to know them, and they ought to know me better, and if they did know 'me better they would know that I am not disposed to make them trouble; then why should they, or any one of them, want to make trouble for me? Don't do any such foolish thing, fellow-citizens. Let us be friends, and treat each other like friends. I am one of the humblest and most peaceable men in the world,—would wrong no man, would interfere with no man's rights; and all I ask is that, having something to say, you will give me a decent hearing. And, being Illinoisans, Kentuckians, and Missourians,—brave and gallant people,—I feel sure that you will do that. And now let us reason together, like the honest fellows we are." Having uttered these words, his face the very picture of good-nature, and his voice full of sympathetic earnestness, he mounted the speaker's stand and proceeded to make one of the most impressive speeches against the further extension of slavery that he ever made in his life. He was listened to attentively; was applauded when he indulged in flashes of humor, and once or twice his eloquent passages were lustily cheered. His little opening remarks had calmed the threatening storm, had conquered his enemies, and he had smooth sailing. From that day to the time of his death, Abraham Lincoln held a warm place in the respect of very many of those rough and rude "Egyptians," and he had no warmer supporters for the Presidency, or while he was President, than they were.

"HITT! HITT! WHERE'S HITT!"

The Hon. Robert R. Hitt, Representative in Congress from Illinois, furnishes a good story of Mr. Lincoln's off-hand manner while on the stump. Mr. Hitt was Lincoln's stenographic reporter in the debates with Douglas, and had his regular place on the platform or speaker's stand. One afternoon a meeting was held in a grove, and Mr. Lincoln was to open. A great crowd had gathered, and all were eager to hear the famous debater. Mr. Lincoln arose, advanced to the front of the platform, surveyed his audience, and was about to begin, when suddenly he paused, looked around him and behind him, then, searching the audience on every side, he began shouting, "Hitt! Hitt!" The audience had never heard of Hitt, and were puzzled to know who was hit, or what to make of this strange opening. But Lincoln continued calling, "Hitt! Hitt! Where's Hitt?" until some one discovered Mr. Hitt leisurely approaching in a buggy, whereupon Mr. Lincoln sang out, "Here, Hitt! we're waiting for you!" and then coolly went on with his speech, which proved a powerful and effective one, notwithstanding its strange opening. "Where's Hitt?" became almost as much of a by-word as the famous question, "Who in——is Polk?"

"OLD ABE" WITH ALPACA COAT AND GRIP-SACK.

Mr. Leonard Volk, the sculptor who afterwards made an excellent bust of Mr. Lincoln, says: "My first meeting with Abraham Lincoln was in 1858, when the celebrated Senatorial contest opened between him and Stephen A. Douglas. I was invited by the latter to accompany him and his party by a special train to Springfield, to which train was attached a platform-car having on board a cannon, which made considerable noise on the journey. At Bloomington we all stopped over night, as Douglas had a speech to make there in the evening. The party went to the Landon House—the only hotel, I believe, in the place at that time. While we were sitting in the hotel office after supper, Mr. Lincoln entered, carrying an old carpet-bag in his hand, and wearing a weather-beaten silk hat—too large, apparently, for his head,—a long, loosely fitting frock-coat, of black alpaca, and vest and trowsers of the same material. He walked up to the counter, and, saluting the clerk pleasantly, passed the bag over to him, and inquired if he was too late for supper. The clerk replied that supper was over, but perhaps enough could be 'scraped up' for him. 'All right,' said Mr. Lincoln; 'I don't want much.' Meanwhile, he said, he would wash the dust off. He was certainly very dusty; it was the month of June, and quite warm. While he was so engaged, several old friends, who had learned of his arrival, rushed in to see him, some of them shouting, 'How are you, Old Abe?' Mr. Lincoln grasped them by the hand in his cordial manner, with the broadest and pleasantest smile on his rugged face. This was the first good view I had of the 'coming man.' The next day we all stopped at the town of Lincoln, where short speeches were made by the contestants, and dinner was served at the hotel; after which, as Mr. Lincoln came out on the plank-walk in front, I was formally presented to him. He saluted me with his natural cordiality, grasping my hand in both his large hands with a vice-like grip, and looking down into my face with his beaming, dark, full eyes, said: 'How do you do? I am glad to meet you. I have read of you in the papers. You are making a statue of Judge Douglas for Governor Matteson's new house." 'Yes, sir,' I answered; 'and sometime when you are in Chicago, and can spare the time, I would like to have you sit to me for a bust.' 'Yes, I will, Mr. Volk; I shall be glad to, the first opportunity I have.' All were soon on board the long train, crowded with people, going to hear the speeches at Springfield. The train stopped on the track, near Edwards's Grove, in the northern outskirts of the town, where staging was erected and a vast crowd waited under the shade of the trees. On leaving the train, most of the passengers climbed over the fences and crossed the stubble-field, taking a short-cut to the grove,—among them Mr. Lincoln, who stalked forward alone, taking immense strides, the before-mentioned carpet-bag and an umbrella in his hands, and his coat skirts flying in the breeze. I managed to keep pretty close in the rear of the tall, gaunt figure, with the head craned forward, apparently much over the balance, like the Leaning Tower of Pisa, that was moving something like a hurricane across that rough stubble-field."

SOME SHARP REJOINDERS.

The contest between Lincoln and Douglas seemed to be, as expressed by Dr. Newton Bateman, "one between sharpness and greatness. Mr. Lincoln seemed a man strongly possessed by a belief to which he was earnestly striving to win the people over; while the aim of Mr. Douglas seemed rather to be simply to defeat Mr. Lincoln." Yet, though Mr. Lincoln was usually earnest and considerate of his opponent, he could, when occasion required, bring his powers of humor and sarcasm into play in the most effective manner. A few pointed illustrations may be given. In his speech at Galesburg, Douglas sneeringly informed the citizens that "Honest Abe" had been a liquor-seller. Lincoln met this with the candid admission that once in early life he had, under the pressure of poverty, accepted and for a few months held a position in a store where it was necessary for him to retail liquor. "But the difference between Judge Douglas and myself is just this," he added, "that while I was *behind* the bar, he was *in front* of it." On another occasion, Mr. Douglas, who had the first speech, remarked that in early life, his father, who he said was an excellent cooper by trade, apprenticed him to learn the cabinet business. This was too good for Lincoln to let pass; so when his turn came to reply, he said: "I had uuderstood before that Mr. Douglas had been bound out to learn the cabinet-making business, which is all well enough, but I was not aware until now that his father was a cooper. I have no doubt, however, that he was one, for," (here Lincoln gently bowed toward Douglas), "he has made one of the best *whiskey-casks* I have ever seen." As Douglas was a short, heavy-set man, and occasionally imbibed, the joke was heartily enjoyed by all.

"SIT DOWN, MR. DOUGLAS!"

At the close of the joint discussion at Alton, Mr. Douglas led off with a speech an hour long, in which he showed no little irritability. The campaign was evidently wearing on him. Mr. Lincoln, on the contrary, was in capital spirits. "He sat taking in the speech of Douglas with seeming immobility," says Mr. Jeriah Bonham, who was present, "and when it was ended, he rose to reply. As in the opening of all his speeches, he spoke slowly, did not rise to his full height, leaning forward in a stooping posture at first, his person showing all the angularities of limb and face. For the first five or ten minutes he was both awkward and diffident, as in almost monotonous tones he began to untangle the meshes of Douglas's sophistry. Proceeding, he gained confidence gradually; his voice rang out strong and clear; his tall form towered to its full height; his face grew radiant with impassioned feeling, as he poured forth an outburst of crushing argument and inspiring eloquence. The people became wild with enthusiasm, but his voice rang loud above their cheers. Frequently in his speech he would turn toward Douglas, and say with emphasis, 'You *know* these things are so, Mr. Douglas!' or 'You know these things are *not* so, Mr. Douglas!' At one time he bent his long body over his adversary, pouring in his arguments so sharply, that Douglas, chafing under the attack, rose to explain; but Lincoln would not allow it. 'Sit down, Mr. Douglas!' said he, peremptorily. 'I did not interrupt you, and you shall not interrupt me. You will have opportunity to reply to me—if you can—in your closing speech.'"

"ABE'S MORE'N A MATCH FOR ANY MAN."

Captain T. W. S. Kidd, of Springfield, Illinois, relates an incident of this period, illustrating Lincoln's readiness at repartee. The exciting campaign between Lincoln and Douglas was the all-absorbing topic at Springfield. There was then in that town a droll character of local celebrity, who bore the alliterative title of Jim Jackson Jones. His occupation was that of a stock-shipper. He was addicted to periodical sprees, and when under the influence of liquor he would challenge every passer-by with his humorous raillery. One day, "Jim," in a very hilarious mood, was standing on the court-house steps, surrounded by an idle crowd who were laughing at his half-drunken sallies of rough wit. Lincoln passed up the steps, and was hailed by Jim with, "Hello, Abe! Douglas is a little too much for ye, aint he? Now take the advice of a friend, and keep away from Steve Douglas, if you want to save your reputation as a debater." The rude crowd roared with laughter, and Lincoln also laughed; then, assuming a serious air, and looking severely at Jim, he said: "Jones, don't you know you are violating the law every day?" "Why, no, Abe. What am I doin' contrary to law?" rejoined Jim, with much surprise. "Sir, don't you know there is a law against opening *rum-holes*" (pointing to Jones's mouth), "without a license?" Not waiting for further reply, Lincoln passed into the court-house. The jolly crowd saw the point, and sent up a cheer that fairly dazed poor Jones. He was afterwards heard to declare that "Abe Lincoln is more'n a match for any man." .

WORDS OF SOBERNESS.

Beneath all the lighter humors of the campaign, the prevailing tone of Mr. Lincoln's thought was deeply serious and reflective. Toward the close, when indications pointed to his defeat for the Senate, he seemed somewhat depressed, and occasionally his old habitual melancholy would steal over him and impart to his words a touching pathos. It was on such an occasion, in one of the smaller cities of Illinois, when Douglas, having the first speech, made an unusually brilliant effort. He carried the crowd with him; and when Lincoln rose to reply, it was evident that he felt his disadvantage—felt, too, that do what he would, final defeat was probable. He made a good speech, but not one of his best. Concluding his argument, he stopped and stood silent for a moment, looking around upon the throng of half-indifferent, half-friendly faces before him, with those deep-sunken weary eyes that always seemed full of unshed tears. Folding his hands, as if they too

were tired of the hopeless fight, he said, in his peculiar monotone: "My friends, it makes little difference, very little difference, whether Judge Douglas or myself is elected to the
United States Senate; but the great issue which we have submitted to you to-day is far above and beyond any personal
interests or the political fortunes of any man. And, my
friends, that issue will live, and breathe, and burn, when the
poor, feeble, stammering tongues of Judge Douglas and myself are silent in the grave." The crowd swayed as if smitten
by a mighty wind. The simple words, and the manner in
which they were spoken, touched every heart to the core.

CLOSE OF THE CONFLICT.

Mr. Lincoln spoke in all about fifty times during the campaign. At its close, says Mr. Arnold, "both Douglas and
Lincoln visited Chicago. Douglas was so hoarse that he
could hardly articulate, and it was painful to hear him attempt
to speak. Lincoln's voice was clear and vigorous, and he
really seemed in better tone than usual. His dark complexion
was bronzed by the prairie sun and winds; his eye was clear,
his step firm, and he looked like a trained athlete, ready to
enter, rather than one who had closed, a conflict."

Of the speeches in this campaign, Mr. Henry J. Raymond
has pronounced the following well-considered opinion: "While
Mr. Douglas fully sustained his previous reputation, and justified the estimate his friends had placed upon his abilities, he
labored under the comparative disadvantage of being much
better known to the country at large than was his antagonist.
During his long public career, people had become partially
accustomed to his manner of presenting arguments and enforcing them. The novelty and freshness of Mr. Lincoln's addresses, on the other hand, the homeliness and force of his illustrations, their wonderful pertinence, his exhaustless humor, his
confidence in his own resources, engendered by his firm belief
in the justice of the cause he so ably advocated, never once

rising, however, to the point of arrogance or superciliousness, fastened upon him the eyes of the people everywhere, friends and opponents alike. It was not strange that more than once, during the course of the unparalleled excitement which marked this canvass, Mr. Douglas should have been thrown off his guard by the singular self-possession displayed by his antagonist, and by the imperturbable firmness with which he maintained and defended a position once taken. The unassuming confidence which marked Mr. Lincoln's conduct was early imparted to his supporters, and each succeeding encounter added largely to the number of his friends, until they began to indulge the hope that a triumph might be secured in spite of the adverse circumstances under which the struggle was commenced.''

Samuel Bowles, editor of the Springfield (Mass.) Republican, said that Lincoln ''handled Douglas as he would an eel—by main strength. Sometimes, perhaps, he handled him so strongly that he *slipped through his fingers.*''

''In this canvass,'' says Mr. Lamon, ''Mr. Lincoln earned a reputation as a popular debater second to that of no man in America—certainly not second to that of his famous antagonist. He kept his temper; he was not prone to personalities; he was fair, frank and manly; and, if the contest had shown nothing else, it would have shown at least that 'Old Abe' could behave like a gentleman under very trying circumstances. His marked success in these discussions was probably no surprise to the people of the Springfield district, who knew him as well as, or better than, they did Mr. Douglas. But in the greater part of the State, and throughout the Union, the series of brilliant victories successively won by an obscure man over an orator of such wide experience and renown was received with exclamations of astonishment alike by listeners and readers.''

Caleb Cushing, the distinguished Massachusetts lawyer, was one of those acute minds whose attention was attracted to

Mr. Lincoln by his debates with Douglas. Mr. Cushing said that these debates showed Lincoln to be the superior of Douglas "in every vital element of power;" and added that "the world does not yet know how much of a man Lincoln really is." The latter statement is scarcely less true, twenty years after Lincoln's death.

CHAPTER X.

LINCOLN DEFEATED FOR THE SENATE.——DEPRESSION AND NEGLECT.——LIN-
COLN AS A LECTURER.——ON THE STUMP IN OHIO.—A SPEECH TO KEN-
TUCKIANS.——SECOND VISIT TO CINCINNATI.——A SHORT TRIP TO KANSAS.
——LINCOLN IN NEW YORK CITY.——THE FAMOUS COOPER INSTITUTE
SPEECH.——A STRONG AND FAVORABLE IMPRESSION.——VISITS NEW ENG-
LAND.——SECRET OF LINCOLN'S SUCCESS AS AN ORATOR.——BACK TO
SPRINGFIELD.——DISPOSING OF A CAMPAIGN SLANDER.——LINCOLN'S AC-
COUNT OF HIS VISIT TO A FIVE POINTS SUNDAY SCHOOL.

ON the 2d of November, 1858, the State election was held in Illinois. The result showed that Mr. Lincoln had, by his hard efforts, won a victory for his cause and for his party, but not for himself. The Republican State ticket was elected by a majority of about 4,000 votes; but in the Legislature a number of members held over from the election of two years before, and the Republican gains, though considerable, were not quite sufficient to overcome this adverse element. When the Legislature met, Mr. Douglas was re-elected to the Senate, by a small majority. It is said that Mr. Lincoln was deeply grieved by his defeat. When some one inquired of him how he felt over the result, he answered that he felt "like the boy that stubbed his toe,—'it hurt too bad to laugh, and he was too big to cry!'"

A few days after his return to Springfield, there was pressed on the attention of the defeated candidate a matter which must have been peculiarly unwelcome at the time, but which was accepted with habitual fortitude. The following letter tells it all:

"SPRINGFIELD, Nov. 16, 1858.

"HON. N. B. JUDD—*My Dear Sir:*—Yours of the 15th is just received. I wrote you the same day. As to the pecuniary matter, I am willing to pay according to my ability, but I am the poorest hand living to get others to pay. I have been on expense so long, without earning anything, that I am absolutely without money now for even household expenses. Still, if you can put in two hundred and fifty dollars for me towards discharging the debt of the committee, I will allow it when you and I settle the private matter between us. This, with what I have already paid with an outstanding note of mine, will exceed my subscription of five hundred dollars. This, too, is exclusive of my ordinary expenses during the campaign, all of which, being added to my loss of time and business, bears pretty heavily upon one no better off than I am. But as I had the post of honor, it is not for me to be over-nice.

"You are feeling badly. *And this, too, shall pass away;* never fear.

"Yours as ever,   A. LINCOLN."

DEPRESSION AND NEGLECT.

Hon. E. M. Haines, who was a member of the Legislature of 1858-9, and a supporter of Mr. Lincoln for the Senate, states that Mr. Lincoln seemed greatly depressed by his defeat, and that his friends were also somewhat disheartened regarding his future prospects, and neglected him to some extent. "Some time after the Senatorial election," says Mr. Haines, "Governor Bissell gave a reception at his house, which I attended with my wife. After we had paid our respects to the Governor and Mrs. Bissell, we passed on to an adjoining room, where there was quite a throng of people, all engaged in conversation. In the midst was Mr. Lincoln, standing in about the center of the room, entirely alone, with his usual sad countenance, and apparently unnoticed by anyone. I said to my wife, 'Here is Mr. Lincoln; he looks as if he had lost all his friends; come and have an introduction to him, and cheer him up.' Mr. Lincoln received us very cordially, and we entered into a general conversation, apparently unnoticed, and attracting no attention from others as they passed and repassed around us. Dancing was going on in the adjacent rooms, and Mr. Lincoln invited my wife to join him in the dancing, which she did, and he apparently took much pleasure in the recreation. My wife afterwards related to me much that Mr. Lincoln said in their conversation during the evening. His despondency became much dispelled after they became engaged in conversation; indeed, she said that he seemed to be putting forth an effort to get out of the gloomy condition which had come upon him from the result of his Senatorial canvass. He had occasion during their conversation to refer to his age, remarking incidentally that he was almost fifty years old; whereupon, as if suddenly reflecting that his age was a good part of a man's life, and as if unwilling to relinquish his hold upon the future, he suddenly braced himself up, and said: 'But, Mrs. Haines, I feel that I am good for another fifty years yet.'"

LINCOLN AS A LECTURER.

During the winter of 1858-9, following the Senatorial debate, Mr. Lincoln was occupied with his private affairs. The love of public speaking had become so strong with him that he prepared a lecture and delivered it to the public at several places during the winter. It was somewhat humorous in character, but was not much of a success, and he soon declined further invitations to deliver it. To one correspondent he wrote, in March, 1859: "Your note, inviting me to deliver a lecture in Galesburg, is received. I regret to say that I cannot do so now. I must stick to the courts for awhile. I read a sort of a lecture to three different audiences during the last month and this; but I did so under circumstances which made it a waste of no time whatever."

ON THE STUMP IN OHIO.—A SPEECH TO KENTUCKIANS.

The following autumn, Senator Douglas visited Ohio and made speeches for the Democratic party. From the Republican ranks there arose a cry for Lincoln. He promptly answered it, and spoke with marked effect. At Cincinnati he addressed himself especially to Kentuckians, and said, in a strain which is now seen to be prophetic:

"I should not wonder if there were some Kentuckians in this audience; we are close to Kentucky; but whether that be so or not, we are on elevated ground, and by speaking distinctly I should not wonder if some of the Kentuckians would hear me on the other side of the river. For that purpose I propose to address a portion of what I have to say to

the Kentuckians. I say, then, in the first place, to the Kentuckians, that
I am what they call, as I understand it, a 'Black Republican.' I think
slavery is wrong, morally and politically. I desire that it should be no
further spread in these United States, and I should not object if it should
gradually terminate in the whole Union. While I say this for myself, I
say to you, Kentuckians, that I understand you differ radically with me
upon this proposition; that you believe slavery is a good thing; that
slavery is right; that it ought to be extended and perpetuated in this
Union. Now, there being this broad difference between us, I do not pretend, in addressing myself to you, Kentuckians, to attempt proselyting
you; that would be a vain effort. I will tell you, so far as I am authorized to speak for the opposition, what we mean to do with you. We mean
to treat you, as nearly as we possibly can, as Washington, Jefferson, and
Madison treated you. We mean to leave you alone, and in no way to
interfere with your institution; to abide by all and every compromise
of the Constitution, and, in a word, coming back to the original proposition, to treat you, so far as degenerated men (if we have degenerated)
may, according to the examples of those noble fathers—Washington,
Jefferson and Madison. We mean to remember that you are as good as
we; that there is no difference between us, other than the difference of
circumstances. We mean to recognize and bear in mind always, that you
have as good hearts in your bosoms as other people, or as we claim to
have, and treat you accordingly. We mean to marry your girls, when
we have a chance—the white ones, I mean—and I have the honor to inform you that I once did have a chance in that way. I have told you what
we mean to do. I want to know now what you mean to do. I often hear
it intimated that you mean to divide the Union whenever a Republican,
or anything like it, is elected President of the United States. (A voice—
'That is so.') 'That is so,' one of them says; I wonder if he is a Kentuckian? (A voice—'He is a Douglas man.') Well, then, I want to
know what you are going to do with your half of it? Are you going to
split the Ohio down through, and push your half off a piece? Or are
you going to keep it right alongside of us outrageous fellows? Or are
you going to build up a wall some way between your country and ours,
by which that movable property of yours can't come over here any more,
to the danger of your losing it? Do you think you can better yourselves
on that subject by leaving us here under no obligation whatever to return
those specimens of your movable property that come hither? You have
divided the Union because we would not do right with you, as you think,
upon that subject; when we cease to be under obligations to do anything
for you, how much better off do you think you will be? Will you make
war upon us and kill us all? Why, gentlemen, I think you are as gallant

and as brave men as live ; that you can fight as bravely in a good cause, man for man, as any other people living ; that you have shown yourselves capable of this upon various occasions ; but man for man, you are not better than we are, and there are not so many of you as there are of us. You will never make much of a hand at whipping us. If we were fewer in numbers than you, I think that you could whip us ; if we were equal, it would likely be a drawn battle ; but being inferior in numbers, you will make nothing by attempting to master us.''

LINCOLN'S SECOND VISIT TO CINCINNATI.

The Hon. W. M. Dickson, whose interesting account of Mr. Lincoln's first visit to Cincinnati, and the disappointments attending it, has already been given in this narrative, says of this second visit: "He returned to the city, with a fame wide as the continent, with the laurels of the Douglas contest on his brow, and the Presidency in his grasp. He returned, greeted with the thunder of cannon, the strains of martial music, and the joyous plaudits of thousands of citizens thronging the streets. He addressed a vast concourse on Fifth Street Market; was entertained in princely style at the Burnet House; and there received with courtesy the foremost citizens, come to greet this rising star. The manner of the man was changed. The free conversation of unrestraint had given place to the vague phrase of the wary politician; the repose of ease to the agitation of unaccustomed elevation. With high hope and happy heart, Mr. Lincoln left Cincinnati after a three days' sojourn. But a perverse fortune attended him and Cincinnati in their intercourse. Nine months after Mr. Lincoln left us, after he had been nominated for the Presidency, when he was tranquilly waiting in his cottage home at Springfield the verdict of the people, his last visit to Cincinnati and the good things he had had at the Burnet House were rudely brought to his memory by a bill presented to him from its proprietors. Before leaving the hotel he had applied to the clerk for his bill, and was told that it was paid, or words to that effect. This the committee had directed, but had afterwards neglected its payment; and the proprietors shrewdly surmised that a letter to the nominee for the Presidency would bring the money. The only significance in this incident is in the letter it brought from Mr. Lincoln, revealing his indignation at the seeming imputation against his honor, and his greater indignation at one item of the bill. 'As to wines, liquors and cigars, we had none—absolutely none. These last may have been in 'Room 15 by order of committee; but I do not recollect them at all.' "

A SHORT TRIP TO KANSAS.

Mr. Lincoln visited Kansas in December, 1859, and addressed the people upon the political questions then before the country. At Leavenworth, Atchison, Elwood, and other places, he was met by vast assemblages, who were charmed and convinced by his fresh and reassuring utterances. His journeys were complete ovations, and he returned to Illinois, leaving a host of new friends behind him.

LINCOLN IN NEW YORK CITY.

The stirring events of Mr. Lincoln's life had made him tolerably well-known throughout the West; and his fame had extended also to the East, where he seems already to have been looked upon as a rising man. Says President Tuttle: "I had observed his controversy with Mr. Douglas in Illinois with great interest. In some respects it was undoubtedly the ablest debate of its kind that has occurred in this country. Mr. Douglas was regarded as the finest debater in the American Senate. At least, so his friends thought. He had a national reputation as a political debater and leader. Mr. Lincoln, up to that time, was not much known outside of his own State. The keenness of his speeches in those famous mass-meetings before which Mr. Douglas and himself discussed the issues of the day, at once lifted him into a national reputation"

In February, 1860, Mr. Lincoln went to Brooklyn, for the purpose of delivering a lecture in Mr. Beecher's church.

The invitation had been received some time previously, and gave him very great pleasure. He prepared himself thoroughly; indeed, it is said that no effort of his life cost him so much labor as this. In the Plymouth congregation of Brooklyn there was an association of young men which was successful in getting an annual course of six lectures of the highest order. This association discerned in Mr. Lincoln a man worthy of a place in its course, and invited him to give such a lecture. The politicians of New York also desired him to make a speech in that city, in order to determine whether he would be the man to present to the Presidential convention in case Mr. Seward could not be nominated. Mr. Lincoln informed these gentlemen of his engagement, but said he would speak in New York if the Brooklyn club gave its consent. That club agreed to this arrangement; and thus it was decided that Lincoln's speech should be delivered in New York City, instead of Brooklyn, as had been first intended. Mr. R. C. McCormick, who was a member of the committee in charge of the arrangements, says: "When Mr. Lincoln came to New York City, there was some confusion in the arrangements. He had at first been invited to appear in Brooklyn, but upon deliberation his friends thought it best that he should be heard in New York. Reaching the Astor House on Saturday, February 25th, he was surprised to find by announcement, in the public prints, that he was to speak at the Cooper Institute. He said he must review his address if it was to be delivered in New York. What he had prepared for Mr. Beecher's church-folks might not be altogether appropriate to a miscellaneous political audience. Saturday was spent in a review of the speech, and on Sunday morning he went to Plymouth church, where apparently he greatly enjoyed the service. On Monday morning I waited upon him with several of the Young Men's Republican Union, into whose hands the preparations for the meeting at the Cooper Institute had chiefly fallen. We found him in a suit of black, much wrinkled

from its careless packing in a small valise. He received us
cordially, apologizing for the awkward and uncomfortable appearance he made in his new suit, and expressing himself surprised at being in New York. His form and manner were
indeed very odd, and we thought him the most unprepossessing
public man we had ever met. I spoke to him of the manuscript of his forthcoming address, and suggested to him that it
should be given to the press at his earliest convenience, in order that it might be published in full on the morning following its delivery. He appeared in much doubt as to whether
any of the papers would care to print it; and it was only
when I accompanied a reporter to his room and made a request for it, that he began to think his words were to be of interest to the metropolitan public. He seemed wholly ignorant
of the custom of supplying slips to the different journals from
the office first putting the address in type, and was charmingly
innocent of the machinery so generally used, even by some of
our most popular orators, to give success and *eclat* to their
public efforts. The address was written upon blue foolscap,
all in his own hand, and with few interlineations. I was bold
enough to read portions of it, and had no doubt that its delivery would create a marked sensation throughout the country. Mr. Lincoln referred frequently to Mr. Douglas, but always in a generous and kindly manner. It was difficult to
regard them as antagonists. Many stories of the famous Illinois debates were told us, and in a very short time his frank
and sparkling conversation won our hearts and made his
plain face pleasant to us all. During the day it was suggested
that the orator should be taken up Broadway and shown the
city, of which he knew but little—stating, I think, that he had
been here but once before. At one place he met an Illinois
acquaintance of former years, to whom he said, in his dry,
good-natured way: 'Well, B., how have you fared since you
left Illinois?' To which B. replied, 'I have made a hundred
thousand dollars, and lost all. How is it with you, Mr. Lin-

coln?' 'Oh, very well,' said Mr. Lincoln. 'I have the cottage at Springfield, and about eight thousand dollars in money. If they make me Vice-president with Seward, as some say they will, I hope I shall be able to increase it to twenty thousand; and that is as much as any man ought to want.' We visited a photographic establishment upon the corner of Broadway and Bleeker streets, where he sat for his picture, the first taken in New York. At the gallery he met and was introduced to Hon. George Bancroft, and had a brief conversation with that gentleman, who welcomed him to New York. The contrast in the appearance of the men was most striking; the one courtly and precise in his every word and gesture, with the air of a trans-Atlantic statesman; the other bluff and awkward, his very utterance an apology for his ignorance of metropolitan manners and customs. 'I am on my way to Massachusetts,' said he to Mr. Bancroft, 'where I have a son at school, who, if report be true, already knows much more than his father.'"

THE FAMOUS COOPER INSTITUTE SPEECH.

On the evening of February 27th, a large and brilliant audience gathered at Cooper Institute, to hear the famous Western orator—the man who had dared, like Marmion,

"To beard the lion in his den,
The Douglas in his hall."

The scene was one never to be forgotten by those who witnessed it. Upon the platform sat many of the prominent men of the Republican party, and in the body of the hall were many ladies. The meeting was presided over by the illustrious poet, William Cullen Bryant, of whom Mr. Lincoln afterward said, "It was worth a journey to the East merely to see such a man." The orator of the evening was introduced by Mr. Bryant with some very complimentary allusions, especially to his controversy with Mr. Douglas. "When Mr. Lincoln came on the platform and was introduced by Mr. Bryant," says one who was present, "he seemed a giant in contrast

with him.   His first sentence was delivered in a peculiarly
high-keyed voice, and disappointed us.   In a short time the
sharp points of his address began to come, and he had not
been speaking for half an hour before his audience seemed
wild with enthusiasm.''   Another account says: ''Mr. Lincoln began his address in a low, monotonous tone, but as he
advanced, his quaint but clear voice rang out boldly and distinctly enough for all to hear.   His manner was, to a New
York audience, a very strange one, but it was captivating.   He
held the vast meeting spell-bound, and as one by one his oddly
expressed but trenchant and convincing arguments confirmed
the soundness of his political conclusions, the house broke out
in wild and prolonged enthusiasm.   I think I never saw an
audience more thoroughly carried away by an orator.''   This
speech was full of trenchant passages, which called forth tumultuous applause.   The following is a specimen:

''I defy any one to show that any living man in the whole world ever
did, prior to the beginning of the present century, (and I might almost
say prior to the beginning of the last half of the present century), declare that, in his understanding, any proper division of local from Federal
authority, or any part of the Constitution, forbade the Federal Government to control slavery in the Federal territories.   To those who now
so declare, I give not only our fathers who framed the government
under which we live, but with them all other living men within the century in which it was framed, among whom to search, and they shall not
be able to find the evidence of a single man agreeing with them.''

Referring to the South, and the growing political discon-
tent in that quarter, he said:

''Let all who believe that our fathers understood this question just as
well as, and even better than, we do now, speak as they spoke, and act as
they acted upon it.   This is all Republicans ask—all Republicans desire
—in relation to slavery.   As those fathers marked it, so let it be again
marked, as an evil not to be extended, but to be tolerated and protected
only because of, and so far as, its actual presence among us makes that
toleration and protection a necessity.   Let all the guaranties those fathers
gave it be, not grudgingly, but fully and fairly maintained.''

His counsel to the young Republican party was timely and
full of wisdom:

"A few words now to Republicans: It is exceedingly desirable that all parts of this great Confederacy shall be at peace, and in harmony one with another. Let us Republicans do our part to have it so. Even though much provoked, let us do nothing through passion and ill-temper. Even though the Southern people will not so much as listen to us, let us calmly consider their demands, and yield to them, if, in our deliberate view of our duty, we possibly can."

The address closed with the following memorable words :

"Wrong as we think slavery is, we can yet afford to let it alone where it is, because that much is due to the necessity arising from its actual presence in the nation; but can we, while our votes will prevent it, allow it to spread into the National Territories, and to overrun us here in these free States? If our sense of duty forbids this, then let us stand by our duty, fearlessly and effectively. Let us be diverted by none of those sophistical contrivances wherewith we are so industriously plied and belabored—contrivances such as groping for some middle ground between the right and the wrong, vain as the search for a man who should be neither a living man nor a dead man,—such as a policy of 'don't care' on a question about which all true men do care,—such as Union appeals, beseeching true Union men to yield to Disunionists, reversing the divine rule, and calling not the sinners but the righteous to repentance,—such as invocations of Washington, imploring men to unsay what Washington said and undo what Washington did. Neither let us be slandered from our duty by false accusations against us, nor frightened from it by menaces of destruction to the Government, nor of dungeons to ourselves. Let us have faith that right makes might; and in that faith, let us, to the end, dare do our duty, as we understand it."

A STRONG AND FAVORABLE IMPRESSION.

The Cooper Institute speech made a profound impression upon the public. All who saw and heard Mr. Lincoln felt the influence of his strange but powerful personality; and acute minds recognized in the unsophisticated Western lawyer a new force in American politics. This speech made Mr. Lincoln known throughout the country, and undoubtedly did more than anything else to secure him the nomination for the Presidency. Aside from its extensive republication in the newspapers, various editions of it appeared in pamphlet form, one of the best of which was issued by Messrs. C. C. Nott and Cephas Brainard, who appended to their edition an estimate of the speech that is well worth reprintig here: "No one who has not actually attempted to verify its details can understand the patient research and historical labor which it embodies. The history of our earlier politics is scattered through numerous journals, statutes, pamphlets, and letters; and these are defective in completeness and accuracy of statement, and in indexes and tables of contents. Neither can any one who has not travelled over this precise ground appreciate the accuracy of every trivial detail, or the self-denying impartiality with which Mr. Lincoln has turned from the testimony of 'the fathers' on the general question of slavery to present the single question which he discusses. From the first line to the last, from his premises to his conclusion, he travels with a swift, unerring directness which no logician ever excelled,—an argument complete and full, without the affectation of learning, and without the stiffness which usually accompanies dates and details. A single easy, simple sentence of plain Anglo-Saxon words contains a chapter of history that, in some instances, has taken days of labor to verify, and must have cost the author months of investigation to acquire; and though the public should justly estimate the labor bestowed on the facts which are stated, they cannot estimate the greater labor involved on those which are omitted—how many pages have been read—how many works examined—what numerous statutes, resolutions, speeches, letters, and biographies have been looked through. Commencing with this address as a political pamphlet, the reader will leave it as an historical work—brief, complete, profound, impartial, truthful,—which will survive the time and the occasion that called it forth, and be esteemed hereafter no less for its intrinsic worth than for its unpretending modesty."

A VISIT TO NEW ENGLAND.

Mr. Lincoln's oldest son, Robert, was at this time a student in Harvard University, at Cambridge, Mass.; and, chiefly to visit him, Mr. Lincoln made a brief trip to New England. While there, he spoke at Concord and Manchester, in New Hampshire; at Woonsocket, in Rhode Island; and at Hartford, New Haven, Norwich, Meriden, and Bridgeport, in Connecticut. These speeches were heard with delight by large audiences at every point, and received lavish encomiums from the press. At Manchester, "The Mirror," a neutral paper, published the following remarks on Lincoln's style of oratory: "He spoke an hour and a half, with great fairness, great apparent candor, and with wonderful interest. He did not abuse the South, the administration, or the Democrats, nor indulge in any personalities, with the exception of a few hits at 'Douglas's notions.' He is far from prepossessing in personal appearance, and his voice is disagreeable; and yet he wins attention and good-will from the start. He indulges in no flowers of rhetoric, no eloquent passages. He is not a wit, a humorist, or a clown; yet so fine a vein of pleasantry and good-nature pervades what he says, gliding over a deep current of poetical arguments, that he keeps his hearers in a smiling mood, with their mouths open ready to swallow all he says. His sense of the ludicrous is very keen; and an exhibition of that is the clincher of all his arguments,—not the ludicrous acts of persons, but ludicrous ideas. Hence he is never offensive, and steals away willingly into his train of belief persons who were opposed to him. For the first half-hour his opponents would agree with every word he uttered; and from that point he began to lead them off little by little, until it seemed as if he had got them all into his fold."

THE SECRET OF LINCOLN'S SUCCESS AS AN ORATOR.

The Rev. John P. Gulliver, of Norwich, Connecticut, has given a most interesting reminiscence of Mr. Lincoln's speech in that city while on his tour through New England. On the morning following the speech, he met Mr. Lincoln on a train of cars, and entered into conversation with him. In speaking of his speech, Mr. Gulliver remarked to Mr. Lincoln that he thought it the most remarkable one he ever heard. "Are you sincere in what you say?" inquired Mr. Lincoln. "I mean every word of it," replied the minister; "indeed, sir, I learned more of the art of public speaking last evening than I could from a whole course of lectures on rhetoric." Then Mr. Lincoln informed him of a "most extraordinary circumstance" that had occurred at New Haven a few days previous. A professor of rhetoric in Yale College, he had been told, came to hear him, took notes of his speech, and gave a lecture on it to his class the following day, and, not satisfied with that, followed him to Meriden the next evening, and heard him again for the same purpose. All this seemed to Mr. Lincoln to be "very extraordinary." He had been sufficiently astonished by his success at the West, but he had no expectation of any marked success at the East, particularly among literary and learned men. "Now," said Mr. Lincoln, "I should like very much to know what it is in my speech which you thought so remarkable, and which interested my friend the professor so much?" Mr. Gulliver's answer was: "The clearness of your statements, the unanswerable style of your reasoning, and especially your illustrations, which were romance and pathos and fun and logic all welded together." After Mr. Gulliver had fully satisfied his curiosity by a further exposition of the politician's peculiar power, Mr. Lincoln said: "I am much obliged to you for this. I have been wishing for a long time to find some one who would make this analysis for me. It throws light on a subject which has been dark to me. I can understand very readily how such a power as you have ascribed to me will account for the effect which seems to be produced by my speeches. I hope you have not been too flattering in your estimate. Certainly I have had a most wonderful success for a man of my limited education." Then Mr. Gulliver inquired into the processes by which he had acquired his education, and was rewarded with many interesting details. When they were about to part, the minister said: "Mr. Lincoln, may I say one thing to you before we separate?" "Certainly; anything you please," was the response. "You have just spoken," said Mr. Gulliver, "of the tendency of political life in Washington to debase the moral convictions of our representatives there, by the admixture of considerations of mere political expediency. You have become, by the controversy with Mr. Douglas, one of our leaders in this great struggle with slavery, which is undoubtedly the struggle of the nation and the age. What I would like to say is this, and I say it with a full heart: Be true to your principles, and we will be true to you, and God will be true to us all." Mr. Lincoln, touched by the earnestness of his interlocutor, took his hand in both his own, and, with his face full of sympathetic light, exclaimed: "I say *amen* to that! *amen to that!*"

BACK TO SPRINGFIELD.—DISPOSING OF A CAMPAIGN SLANDER.

After the New England tour, Mr. Lincoln returned to his home in Springfield. As often happens, those least appreciative of his success were his own neighbors; and certain reflections gained vogue concerning his motives in visiting the East. It was charged that he had been mercenary, and had "sold himself for a price" for his political speeches. Something of this sort having been brought to Mr. Lincoln's notice, he disposed of the matter in the following manly and characteristic letter:

"SPRINGFIELD, APRIL 6, 1860.

"C. F. MCNEILL, ESQ.—*Dear Sir:*—Reaching home yesterday, I found yours of the 23d March, enclosing a slip from the 'Middleport Press.' It is not true that I ever charged anything for a political speech in my life; but this much is true: Last October I was requested by letter to deliver some sort of speech in Mr. Beecher's church in Brooklyn, $200 being offered in the first letter. I wrote that I could do it in February, provided they would take a political speech if I could find time to get up no other. They agreed; and subsequently I informed them the speech would have to be a political one. When I reached New York, I learned for the first that the place was changed to 'Cooper Institute.' I made the speech, and left for New England, where I have a son at school, neither asking for pay nor having any offered me. Three days after, a check for $200 was sent to me at N. H., and I took it, and did not know it was wrong. My understanding now is—though I knew nothing of it at the time—that they did charge for admittance at the Cooper Institute, and that they took in more than twice $200. I have made this explanation to you as a friend; but I wish no explanation made to our enemies. What they want is a squabble and a fuss; and that they can have if we explain; and they cannot have it if we don't. When I returned through New York from New England, I was told by the gentleman who sent me the check, that a drunken vagabond in the club, having learned something about the $200, made the exhibition out of which the 'Herald' manufactured the article quoted by the 'Press' of your town. My judgment is, and therefore my request is, that you give no denial, and no explanations.

"Thanking you for your kind interest in the matter, I remain,

Yours truly, A. LINCOLN."

LINCOLN'S ACCOUNT OF HIS VISIT TO A FIVE POINTS SUNDAY SCHOOL.

It appears that on the Sunday which Mr. Lincoln spent in New York City, he visited a Sunday School in the notorious region called Five Points, and there made a short address to the scholars. After his return to Springfield, one of his neighbors, hearing of this, thought it would be a good subject for bantering Mr. Lincoln about, and accordingly visited him for that purpose. This neighbor was generally known as "Jim," just as Lincoln was called "Abe." The following account of Jim's visit, furnished by Mr. Edward Eggleston, shows that he did not derive as much fun from the "bantering" as he had expected: "He started for 'Old Abe's' office; but bursting open the door impulsively, found a stranger in conversation with Mr. Lincoln. He turned to retrace his steps, when Lincoln called out, 'Jim! What do you want?' 'Nothing.' 'Yes, you do; come back.' After some entreaty 'Jim' approached Mr. Lincoln, and remarked, with a twinkle in his eye, 'Well, Abe, I see you have been making a speech to Sunday School children. What's the matter?' 'Sit down,

Jim, and I'll tell you all about it.' And with that Lincoln put his feet on the stove, and began: 'When Sunday morning came, I didn't know exactly what to do. Washburne asked me where I was going. I told him I had nowhere to go; and he proposed to take me down to the Five Points Sunday School, to show me something worth seeing. I was very much interested by what I saw. Presently, Mr. Pease came up and spoke to Mr. Washburne, who introduced me. Mr. Pease wanted us to speak. Washburne spoke, and then I was urged to speak. I told them I did not know anything about talking to Sunday Schools, but Mr. Pease said many of the children were friendless and homeless, and that a few words would do them good. Washburne said I must talk. And so I rose to speak; but I tell you, Jim, I didn't know what to say. I remembered that Mr. Pease said that they were homeless and friendless, and I thought of the time when I had been pinched by terrible poverty. And so I told them that I had been poor; that I remembered when my toes stuck out through my broken shoes in winter; when my arms were out at the elbows; when I shivered with the cold. And I told them there was only one rule. That was, always do the very best you can. I told them that I had always tried to do the very best I could; and that, if they would follow that rule, they would get along somehow. That was about what I said. And when I got through, Mr. Pease said it was just the thing they needed. And when the school was dismissed, all the teachers came up and shook hands with me, and thanked me for it; although I did not know that I was saying anything of any account. But the next morning I saw my remarks noticed in the papers.' Just here Mr. L. put his hand in his pocket, and remarked that he had never heard anything that touched him as had the songs which those children sang. With that he drew forth a little book, remarking that they had given him one of the books from which they sang. He began to read a piece with all the earnestness of his great, earnest soul. In the middle of the second verse his friend 'Jim' felt a choking in his throat and a tickling in his nose. At the beginning of the third verse he saw that the stranger was weeping, and his own tears fell fast. Turning toward Lincoln, who was reading straight on, he saw the great blinding tears in his eyes, so that he could not possibly see the pages. He was repeating that little song from memory. How often he had read it, or how long its sweet and simple accents continued to reverberate through his soul, no one can know.''

CHAPTER XI.

IN the latter part of the year 1859, after Mr. Lincoln had gained national prominence through the events narrated in the last chapter, some of his friends began to consider the expediency of bringing him forward as a candidate for the Presidency in 1860. The Republican party had been in the minority, and the necessity was universally felt of nominating a man who would not render himself objectionable by advocating extreme or unpopular measures. The subject was mentioned to Mr. Lincoln, but he seems not to have taken it very seriously. He said that there were distinguished men in the party who were more worthy of the nomination, and whose public services entitled them to it. Towards the Spring of 1860, Mr. Lincoln consented to a conference on the subject with some of his more intimate friends. The meeting took place in a committee-room in the State House. Mr. Bushnell, Mr. Hatch (the Secretary of State), Mr. Judd (Chairman of the Republican State Central Committee), Mr. Peck, and Mr. Grimshaw were present. They were unanimous in opinion as to the expediency and propriety of making him a candidate. But, says Mr. Lamon, "Mr. Lincoln, with his characteristic modesty, doubted whether he could get the nomination, even if he wished it, and asked until the next morning to answer us.   *   *   *   The next day he authorized us to consider him, and work for him, if we pleased, as a candidate for the Presidency.''

It is evident that, while Mr. Lincoln had no serious expectation of receiving the nomination for the Presidency, yet, having consented to become a candidate, he was by no means indifferent on the subject.   The following confidential letter to his friend, N. B. Judd, shows his feelings at this time:

"SPRINGFIELD, ILL., FEBRUARY 9, 1860.

"HON. N. B. JUDD—*Dear Sir:*—I am not in a position where it would hurt much for me not to be nominated on the national ticket; but I am where it would hurt some for me not to get the Illinois delegates.   What I expected when I wrote the letter to Messrs. Dole and others is now happening.   Your discomfited assailants are more bitter against me, and they will, for revenge upon me, lay to the Bates egg in the South and the Seward egg in the North, and go far towards squeezing me out in the middle with nothing.   Can you not help me a little in this matter in your end of the vineyard.   (I mean this to be private).

"Yours as ever,   A. LINCOLN."

It would seem that the original intention of Mr. Lincoln's friends had been to bring him out as a candidate for the Vice-Presidency.   Hon. E. M. Haines relates that as early as the spring of 1859, before the adjournment of the Legislature, of which he was a member, some of the Republican members discussed the feasibility of urging Mr. Lincoln's name for the Vice-Presidency.   Mr. Lincoln appears not to have taken very strongly to the suggestion.   "I recollect," says Mr. Haines, "that one day Mr. Lincoln came to my desk in the House of Representatives, to make some inquiry regarding another member; and during the conversation, I remarked to him that I did not know as we would be able to make him President, but perhaps we could do the next best thing, and make him Vice-President.   He brightened up somewhat, and answered by a story which I do not clearly recall, but the application of which was, that he scarcely considered himself a big enough man for President, while the Vice-Presidency, for which he apparently had no great liking, was scarcely big enough office for one who had aspired to a U. S. Senatorship.''

THE ILLINOIS REPUBLICAN CONVENTION OF 1860.—A "SEND OFF" FOR LINCOLN.

On the 9th and 10th of May, 1860, the Republicans of Illinois met in convention at Decatur. Mr. Lincoln was present, although, says Mr. Lamon, ''he is said to have been there as a mere 'spectator.' He had no special interest in the proceedings, and appears to have had no notion that any business relating to him was to be transacted that day. It was a very large and spirited body, comprising an immense number of delegates, among whom were the most brilliant as well as the shrewdest men in the party. It was evident that something of more than usual importance was expected to transpire. A few moments after the convention organized, 'Old Abe' was seen squatting, or sitting on his heels, just within the door of the Wigwam. ' Governor Oglesby rose and said, amid increasing silence, 'I am informed that a distinguished citizen of Illinois, and one whom Illinois will ever delight to honor, is present ; and I wish to move that this body invite him to a seat on the stand.' Here the Governor paused, as if to tease and dally, and work curiosity up to the highest point ; but at length he shouted the magic name, *'Abraham Lincoln!'* Not a shout but a roar of applause, long and deep, shook every board and joist of the building. The motion was seconded and passed. A rush was made for the hero who sat on his heels. He was seized and jerked to his feet. An effort was made to 'jam him through the crowd' to his place of honor on the stage ; but the crowd was too dense, and it failed. Then he was 'boosted'—lifted up bodily—and lay for a few seconds sprawling, and kicking, upon the heads and shoulders of the great throng. In this manner he was gradually pushed toward the stand, and finally reached it, doubtless to his great relief, 'in the arms of some half-dozen gentlemen,' who set him down in full view of his clamorous admirers. 'The cheering was like the roar of the sea. Hats were thrown up by the Chicago delegation, as if hats were no longer useful.' Mr. Lincoln rose, bowed, smiled, blushed, and thanked the assembly as well as he could in the midst of such a tumult. A gentleman who saw it all says, 'I then thought him one of the most diffident and worst-plagued men I ever saw.' At another stage of the proceedings, Governor Oglesby rose again with another provoking and mysterious speech. 'There was,' he said, 'an old Democrat outside who had something he wished to present to the convention.' 'Receive it!' 'Receive it!' cried some. 'What is it?' 'What is it?' screamed some of the lower Egyptians, who had an idea the old Democrat might want to blow them up with an infernal machine. But the party for Oglesby and the old Democrat was the stronger, and carried the vote with a tremendous hurrah. The door opened; and a fine, robust old fellow, with an open countenance and bronzed cheeks, marched into the midst of the assemblage, bearing on his shoulder 'two small triangular heart rails,' surmounted by a banner with this inscription: '*Two rails from a lot made by Abraham Lincoln and John Hanks, in the Sangamon Bottom, in the year 1830.*' The sturdy bearer was old John Hanks himself, enjoying the great field-day of his life. He was met with wild and tumultuous cheers, prolonged through several minutes; and it was observed that the Chicago and Central-Illinois men sent up the loudest and longest. The whole scene was for a time simply tempestuous and bewildering. But it ended at last; and now the whole body, those in the secret and those out of it, clamored like men beside themselves for a speech from Mr. Lincoln, who in the meantime 'blushed,' but seemed to shake with inward laughter. In response to the repeated appeals, he rose and said: 'Gentlemen, I suppose you want to know something about those things' (pointing to old John and the rails). 'Well, the truth is, John Hanks and I did make rails in the Sangamon Bottom. I don't know whether we made those rails or not ; the fact is, I don't think they are a credit to the makers' (laughing as he spoke). 'But I do know this : I made rails then, and I think I could make better ones than these now.' By this time the innocent Egyptians began to open their eyes ; they saw plainly enough, now, the admirable Presidential scheme unfolded to their view. The result of it all was a resolution declaring that 'Abraham Lincoln is the first choice of the Republican party of Illinois for the Presidency, and instructing the delegates to the Chicago Convention to use all honorable means to secure his nomination, and to cast the vote of the State as a unit for him.' The crowd at Decatur, delegates and private citizens, who took part in these proceedings, was estimated at five thousand. Neither the numbers nor the enthusiasm was a pleasant sight to the divided and demoralized Democrats. They disliked to hear so much about 'honest Old Abe,' 'the rail-splitter,' 'the flatboatman,' 'the pioneer.' These cries had an ominous sound in their ears. Leaving Decatur on the cars, an old man out of Egypt, devoted to the great principles of Democracy, and excessively annoyed by the demonstrations in progress, approached Mr. Lincoln and said, 'So you're Abe Lincoln?' 'That's my name, sir,' answered Mr. Lincoln. 'They say you're a self-made man,' said the Democrat. 'Well, yes,' said Mr. Lincoln, 'what there is of me is self-made.' 'Well, all I've got to say,' observed the old man after a careful survey of the statesman before him, 'is, that it was a d—n bad job.' "

In regard to the introduction of Mr. Lincoln to the people as a "rail-splitter," Dr. J. G. Holland remarks : "The country took Mr. Lincoln at the estimate of his friends ; and those friends thrust him before the country as a man whose grand achievement was the splitting of many rails. It took years for the country to learn that Mr. Lincoln was not a boor. It took years for them to unlearn what an unwise and boyish introduction of a great man to the public had taught them. It took years for them to comprehend the fact that in Mr. Lincoln the country had the wisest, truest, gentlest, noblest, most sagacious President who had occupied the chair of state since Washington retired from it. At this very period he said to Judge Drummond, of Chicago, who had remarked to him that people were talking of him for the Presidency: 'It seems as if they ought to find somebody who knows more than I do.' The rails, and that which they symbolized, were what troubled him, and, in his own judgment, detracted from his qualifications for the high office."

Ex-Governor Bross, of Illinois, relates meeting Lincoln soon after the close of the Decatur Convention. He says: "When leaving the Republican Convention at Decatur, in May, 1860, I found Mr. Lincoln sitting on a trunk, alone, at the end of the hall, with his head bowed down, and leaning it upon his hand. 'I'm not very well,' said he. 'I hope you will soon be better,' said I; 'you should be getting your acceptance speech ready, for your friends will be sure to nominate you for President at the Chicago Convention.' 'Well,' said he, in his quiet, modest way, 'It looks a little that way, but you know how little reliance can be placed on such things.' "

SITTING FOR A PORTRAIT.—INTERESTING REMINISCENCES BY AN ARTIST.

Among the various portraits of Mr. Lincoln is the celebrated life-mask, taken by the distinguished sculptor, Leonard W. Volk. It was made in April, 1860,—just before the Republican Convention which nominated Mr. Lincoln for the Presidency,—and is one of the last of those showing him without a beard. Mr. Volk has given some exceedingly interesting particulars of his experiences with Mr. Lincoln on the occasion referred to. "One morning," he says, "I noticed in the paper that Abraham Lincoln was in town—retained as one of the counsel in a 'Sand-bar' trial, in which the Michigan Central Railroad was either plaintiff or defendant. I at once decided to remind him of his promise to sit to me, made two years before. I found him in the United States District Court room (in a building known at the time as the 'Larmon Block'), his feet on the edge of the table, one of his fingers thrust into his mouth, and his long dark hair standing out at every imaginable angle, apparently uncombed for a week. He was surrounded by a group of lawyers, such as James F. Joy, Isaac N. Arnold, Thomas Hoyne, and others. Mr. Arnold obtained his attention in my behalf, when he instantly arose and met me outside the rail, recognizing me at once with his usual grip of both hands. He remembered his promise, and said, in answer to my question, that he expected to be detained by the case for a week. He added: 'I shall be glad to give you the sittings. When shall I come, and how long will you need me each time?' Just after breakfast, every morning, would, he said, suit him the best, and he could remain till court opened, at ten o'clock. I answered that I would be ready for him the next morning (Thursday). 'Very well, Mr. Volk, I will be there, and I'll go to a barber and have my hair cut before I come.' I requested him not to let the barber cut it too short, and said I would rather he would leave it as it was ; but to this he would not consent. Then, all of a sudden, he ran his fingers through his hair, and said : 'No, I cannot come to-morrow, as I have an engagement with Mr. W—— to go to Evanston, to-morrow and attend an entertainment; but I'd rather come and sit to you for the bust than go there and meet a lot of college professors and others, all strangers to me. And I will be obliged if you will go to Mr. W——'s office now, and get me released from the engagement. I will wait here till you come back.' So off I posted ; but Mr. W—— would not release him, because, he said, it would be a great disappointment to the people he had invited. Mr. Lincoln looked quite sorry when I reported to him the failure of my mission. 'Well,' he said, 'I suppose I must go, but I will come to you Friday morning.' He was there promptly—indeed, he never failed to be on time. My studio was in the fifth story of the Portland Block, and there were no elevators in those days, and I soon learned to distinguish his step on the stairs, and am sure he frequently came up two, if not three, steps at a stride. When he sat down the first time in that hard, wooden, low-armed chair which I still possess, and which has been occupied by Douglas, Seward, and Generals Grant and Dix, he said: 'Mr. Volk, I have never sat before to sculptor or painter—only for daguerreotypes and photographs. What shall I do?' I told him I would only take the measurements of his head and shoulders that time, and next morning, Saturday, I would make a cast of his face, which would save him a number of sittings. He stood up against the wall, and I made a mark above his head, and then measured up to it from the floor and said: 'You are just twelve inches taller than Judge Douglas; that is, just six feet four inches.'

"Before commencing the cast next morning, and knowing Mr. Lincoln's fondness for a story, I told him one in order to remove what I thought an apprehensive expression—as though he feared the operation might be dangerous. He sat naturally in the chair when I made the cast, and saw every move I made in a mirror opposite, as I put the plaster on without interference with his eyesight or his free breathing through the nostrils. It was about an hour before the mould was ready to be removed, and being all in one piece, with both ears perfectly taken, it clung pretty hard, as the cheek-bones were higher than the jaws at the lobe of the ear. He bent his head low, and worked it off without breaking or injury; it hurt a little, as a few hairs of the tender temples pulled out with the plaster and made his eyes water.

"He entered my studio on Sunday morning, remarking that a friend at the hotel (Tremont House) had invited him to go to church, 'but,' said Mr. Lincoln, 'I thought I'd rather come and sit for the bust. The fact is,' he continued, 'I don't like to hear cut–and–dried sermons. No—when I hear a man preach, I like to see him act *as if he were fighting bees!*' And he extended his long arms, at the same time suiting the action to the words. He gave me on this day a long sitting of more than four hours, and when it was concluded, went to our family apartment, on the corner of the building across the corridor from the studio, to look at a collection of photographs which I had made in 1855-6-7, in Rome and Florence. While sitting in the rocking-chair, he took my little son on his lap and spoke kindly to him, asking his name, age, etc. I held the photographs up and explained them to him, but I noticed a growing weariness, and his eyelids closed occasionally as if he were sleepy, or were thinking of something besides Grecian and Roman statuary and architecture. Finally he said: 'These things must be very interesting to you, Mr. Volk; but the truth is, I don't know much of history, and all I do know of it I have learned from law books.'

"The sittings were continued daily till the Thursday following; and during their continuance he would talk almost unceasingly, telling some of the funniest and most laughable of stories, but he talked little of politics or religion during these sittings. He said, 'I am bored nearly every time I sit down to a public dining-table by some one pitching into me on politics.' Upon one occasion he spoke most enthusiastically of his profound admiration of Henry Clay, saying that he 'almost worshiped him.' I remember that he paid a high compliment to the late General William A. Richardson, and said: 'I regard him as one of the truest men that ever lived; he sticks to Judge Douglas through thick and thin—never deserted him and never will. I admire such a man! By the by, Mr. Volk, he is now in town, and stopping at the Tremont. May I bring him with me to-morrow to see the bust?' Accordingly, he brought him and two other old friends, ex-Lieut.-Gov. McMurtry, of Illinois, and Ebenezer Peck, all of whom looked a moment at the clay model, saying it was 'just like him!' Then they began to tell stories and rehearse reminiscences, one after another. I can imagine I now hear their hearty laughs, just as I can see, as if photographed, the tall figure of Lincoln striding across that stubble field.

"Many people, presumably political aspirants with an eye to future prospects, besieged my door for interviews, but I made it a rule to keep it locked, and I think Mr. Lincoln appreciated the precaution. The last sitting was given Thursday morning, and I noticed that Mr. Lincoln was in something of a hurry. I had finished the head, but desired to represent his breast and brawny shoulders as nature presented them; so he stripped off his coat, waistcoat, shirt, cravat and collar, threw them on a chair, pulled his undershirt down a short distance, tying the sleeves behind him, and stood up without a murmur for an hour or so. I then said I had done, and was a thousand times obliged to him for his promptness and patience, and offered to assist him to redress, but he said, 'No, I can do it better alone.' I kept at my work without looking toward him, wishing to catch the form as accurately as possible while it was fresh in my memory. Mr. Lincoln left hurriedly, saying he had an engagement; and with a cordial 'Good-bye! I will see you again soon,' passed out. A few minutes after, I recognized his steps rapidly returning. The door opened and in he came, exclaiming: 'Hello, Mr. Volk! I got down on the sidewalk, and found I had forgotten to put on my undershirt, and thought it wouldn't do to go through the streets this way.' Sure enough, there were the sleeves of that garment dangling below the skirts of his broadcloth frock-coat! I went at once to his assistance, and helped to undress and redress him all right, and out he went, with a hearty laugh at the absurdity of the thing."

THE CHICAGO CONVENTION.

On the 16th of May, 1860, the National Republican Convention met at Chicago. The "Wigwam," an immense building erected for the purpose of holding the convention, was filled with an excited throng numbering fully 12,000. The leading candidates were, besides Lincoln: William H. Seward, of New York; Salmon P. Chase, of Ohio; Simon Cameron, of Pennsylvania; and Edward Bates, of Missouri. From the first, however, the real contest was between Lincoln and Seward. Seward was the acknowledged leader of the Republican party, New York's ex-Governor, and now its most

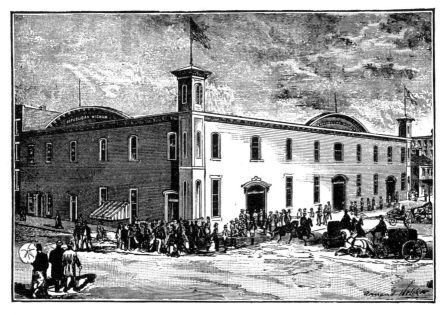

THE OLD CHICAGO WIGWAM.—THE BUILDING IN WHICH LINCOLN WAS NOM-INATED FOR THE PRESIDENCY, MAY 18TH, 1860.

distinguished Senator; hence his position had been far more conspicuous than that of Lincoln. It was expected that Seward would be nominated by acclamation; but his supporters were doomed to a heavy disappointment. Lincoln, on the other hand, had come into prominence mainly as the competitor of Douglas in 1858. His Cooper Institute speech, delivered three months before the convention met, had done much for him in the East; and the homely title of "Honest

Old Abe'' had extended throughout all the free States. Unlike Seward, he had no enemies, and was the second choice of those delegates of whom he was not the first.

TURNING THE TABLES.

Soon after the opening of the convention, Lincoln's friends saw that there was an organized body of men in the crowd who cheered vociferously whenever Seward's name was mentioned. "At a meeting of the Illinois delegation at the Tremont," says Mr. Arnold, "on the evening of the first day, at which Judd, Davis, Cook, and others were present, it was decided that on the second day Illinois and the West should be heard. There was then living in Chicago a man whose voice could drown the roar of Lake Michigan in its wildest fury; nay, it was said that his shout could be heard on a calm day, across that lake. Cook, of Ottawa, knew another man living on the Illinois River, a Dr. Ames, who had never found his equal in his ability to shout and hurra. He was, however, a Democrat. Cook telegraphed to him to come to Chicago by the first train. These two men, with stentorian voices, met some of the Illinois delegation at the Tremont House, and were instructed to organize each a body of men to cheer and shout, which they speedily did, out of the crowds which were in attendance from the Northwest. They were placed on opposite sides of the Wigwam, and instructed that when they saw Cook take out his white handkerchief, they were to cheer, and not to cease until he returned it to his pocket. Cook was conspicuous on the platform, and, at the first utterance of the name of Lincoln, simultaneously with the wave of Cook's handkerchief, there went up such a cheer, such a shout as had never before been heard, and which startled the friends of Seward as the cry of 'Marmion' on Flodden Field 'startled the Scottish foe.' The New Yorkers tried to follow when the name of Seward was spoken, but, beaten at their own game, their voices were instantly and absolutely drowned by cheers for Lincoln. This was kept up until Lincoln was nominated, amidst a storm of applause never before equalled.''

LINCOLN NOMINATED.

On the first ballot, Mr. Seward received 173½ votes; Mr. Lincoln, 102; Mr. Cameron, 50½; Mr. Chase, 49; Mr. Bates, 48; Mr. Dayton, 14; Mr. McLean, 12; Mr. Collamer, 10; and six were scattered. On the second ballot, Mr. Seward had 184½ votes, and Mr. Lincoln 181. "It was clear," says Mr. Lamon, "that the nomination lay between Mr. Seward and Mr. Lincoln, and the latter was receiving great accessions of strength. The third ballot came, and Mr. Lincoln ran rapidly up to 231½ votes; 233 being the number required to nominate. Hundreds of persons were keeping the count; and it was well known, without any announcement, that Mr. Lincoln lacked but a vote and a half to make him the nominee. At this juncture, Mr. Cartter of Ohio rose, and changed four votes from Mr. Chase to Mr. Lincoln. He was nominated. The Wigwam shook to its foundation with the roaring cheers. The multitude in the streets answered the multitude within, and in a moment more all the holiday artillery of Chicago helped to swell the grand acclamation. After a time, the business of the convention proceeded amid great excitement. All the votes that had heretofore been cast against Mr. Lincoln were cast for him before this ballot concluded; and, upon motion, the nomination was made unanimous. The convention then adjourned for dinner, and in the afternoon finished its work by the nomination of Hannibal Hamlin, of Maine, for Vice-President.''

SKETCH OF THE CONVENTION BY AN EYE-WITNESS.

Mr. F. B. Carpenter, who was present on the occasion of Lincoln's nomination, furnishes the following graphic sketch: "The scene surpassed description. Men had been stationed upon the roof of the Wigwam to communicate the result of the different ballots to the thousands outside, far outnumbering the packed crowd inside.   To these men one of the secretaries shouted : 'Fire the salute ! Abe Lincoln is nominated !' Then, as the cheering inside died away, the roar began on the outside, and swelled up from the excited masses like the noise of many waters.   This the insiders heard, and to it they replied.   Thus deep called to deep with such a frenzy of sympathetic enthusiasm that even the thundering salute of cannon was unheard by many on the platform.   When the excitement had partly subsided, Mr. Evarts arose, and, in appropriate words, expressed his grief that Seward had not been nominated.   He then moved that the nomination of Abraham Lincoln be made unanimous.   John A. Andrew, of Massachusetts, and Carl Schurz, of Wisconsin, seconded the motion, and it was carried.   Then the enthusiasm of the multitude burst out anew. A large banner, prepared by the Pennsylvania delegation, was conspicuously displayed, bearing the inscription, 'Pennsylvania good for twenty thousand majority for the people's candidate, Abe Lincoln.'   Delegates tore up the sticks and boards bearing the names of their several States, and waved them aloft over their heads.   A brawny man jumped upon the platform, and, pulling his coat-sleeves up to his elbows, shouted : 'I can't stop !   Three times three more cheers for our next President, Abe Lincoln !'   A full-length portrait of the candidate was produced upon the platform.   Mr. Greeley telegraphed to the N. Y. Tribune : 'There was never another such scene in America.'   Chicago went wild.   One hundred guns were fired from the top of the Tremont House.   Friday night the city was in a blaze of glory.   Bonfires, processions, torchlights, fire-works, illuminations and salutes, 'filled the air with noise and the eye with beauty.'   'Honest Old Abe' was the utterance of every man in the streets.   The Illinois delegation, before it separated, 'resolved' that the millenium had come.''

Dr. Holland says : ''Decorated and illuminated rails were displayed around the newspaper offices.   All the bars and drinking halls were crowded with men who were either worn out with excitement or mad with delight. From Chicago the news spread over the country, and the cannon's throat responded to the click of the telegraph from Maine to the Mississippi. The outgoing trains that night found bonfires blazing at every village, and excited crowds assembled to cheer the retiring delegates, most of whom were either too weak or too hoarse to respond."

LINCOLN HEARING THE NEWS.

"In the little city of Springfield," adds Dr. Holland, "in the heart of Illinois, two hundred miles from where these exciting events were in progress, sat Abraham Lincoln, in close and constant telegraphic communication with his friends in Chicago. He was apprised of the results of every ballot, and, with his home friends, sat in the Journal office receiving and commenting upon the dispatches. It was one of the decisive moments of his life—a moment on which hung his fate as a public man—his place in history. He fully appreciated the momentous results of the convention to himself and the nation, and foresaw the nature of the great struggle which his nomination and election would inaugurate. A moment, and he knew that he would either become the central man of a nation, or a cast-off politician whose ambition for the nation's highest honors would be forever blasted. At last, in the midst of intense and painful excitement, a messenger from the telegraph office entered with the decisive dispatch in his hand. Without handing it to any one, he took his way solemnly to the side of Mr. Lincoln, and said: "The convention has made a nomination, and Mr. Seward is——the second man on the list." Then he jumped upon the editorial table and shouted, "Gentlemen, I propose three cheers for Abraham Lincoln, the next President of the United States!" and the call was boisterously responded to. He then handed the dispatch to Mr. Lincoln, who read in silence, and then aloud, its contents. * * As soon as the news reached Springfield, the citizens, who

had a personal affection for Mr. Lincoln which amounted almost to idolatry, responded with a hundred guns, and during
the afternoon thronged his house to tender their congratulations and express their joy.   In the evening the State House
was thrown open, and a most enthusiastic meeting held by
the Republicans.   At the close, they marched in a body to
the Lincoln mansion, and called for the nominee.   Mr. Lincoln appeared, and after a brief, modest, and hearty speech,
invited as many as could get into the house to enter ; the crowd
responding that after the fourth of March they would give
him a larger house.   The people did not retire until a late
hour, and then moved off reluctantly, leaving the excited
household to their rest.''

On the day of the nomination, Mr. Lamon states, ''About
nine o'clock in the morning, Mr. Lincoln came to the office
of Lincoln & Herndon.   Mr. Zane was there conversing with
a student.   'Well, boys,' said Mr. Lincoln, 'what do you
know?'   'Mr. Rosette,' answered Zane, 'who came from
Chicago this morning, thinks your chances for the nomination
are good.'   Mr. Lincoln wished to know what Mr. Rosette's
opinion was founded upon ; and, while Zane was explaining,
Mr. Baker entered with a telegram, which said the names of
the candidates for nomination had been announced, and that
Mr. Lincoln's had been received with more applause than
any other.   Mr. Lincoln lay down on a sofa to rest.   Soon
after Mr. Brown entered, and Mr. Lincoln said to him, 'Well,
Brown, do you know anything?'   Brown did not know much,
and so Mr. Lincoln, secretly nervous and impatient, rose and
exclaimed, 'Let's go to the telegraph office.'   After waiting
some time at the office, the result of the first ballot came over
the wire.   It was apparent to all present that Mr. Lincoln
thought it very favorable.   He believed that if Mr. Seward
failed to get the nomination, or to 'come very near it,' on the
first ballot, he would fail altogether.   Presently the news of
the second ballot arrived, and Mr. Lincoln showed by his

manner that he considered the contest no longer doubtful. He then went over to the office of 'The Journal,' where other friends were awaiting decisive intelligence. The local editor of that paper, Mr. Zane, and others, remained behind to receive the expected dispatch. In due time it came ; the operator was intensely excited ; at first he threw down his pencil, but, seizing it again, wrote off the news that threw Springfield into a frenzy of delight. The local editor picked it up and rushed to 'The Journal' office. Upon entering the room, he called for three cheers for the next President. They were given, and then the dispatch was read. Mr. Lincoln seemed to be calm, but a close observer could detect in his countenance the indications of deep emotion. In the meantime cheers for Lincoln swelled up from the streets, and began to be heard throughout the town. Some one remarked, 'Mr. Lincoln, I suppose now we will soon have a book containing your life.' 'There is not much,' he replied, 'in my past life about which to write a book, as it seems to me.' Having received the hearty congratulations of the company in the office, he descended to the street, where he was immediately surrounded by 'Irish American citizens ;' and, so long as he was willing to receive it, there was great hand-shaking and felicitating. 'Gentlemen,' said he, with a happy twinkle in his eye, 'you had better come up and shake my hand while you can ; honors elevate some men, you know.' But he soon bethought him of a person who was of more importance to him than all this crowd. Looking towards his house, he said, 'Well, gentlemen, there is a little woman at our house who is probably more interested in this dispatch than I am ; and, if you will excuse me, I will take it up and let her see it.''

THE SCENE AT SPRINGFIELD.—ANOTHER VERSION.

Mr. Lincoln was fond of out-door sports, and was an enthusiast in the then popular game of hand-ball. It afforded him recreation and exercise after office labor and mental toil.

There is a story current that he was engaged in this vigorous pastime when the dispatch was handed him announcing his nomination to the Presidency. That story is not true. Mr. Lincoln was keenly alive to what was transpiring that day, and was fully posted. It was impossible that a man with such a temperament as his could appear indifferent to a matter of such great moment. It would argue an apathy in regard to passing events not at all characteristic of Mr. Lincoln. "That day," says Col. Wickersham, "Lincoln wore a look of deep concern, and was abstracted in his manner. He had been in the telegraph office awaiting dispatches, and had patiently endured the suspense until the convention had begun to take a ballot. He went to the store of Mr. C. M. Smith— Lincoln's brother-in-law—and while standing in the door, in conversation with friends about what had already transpired in the convention, a prolonged yell was heard coming down the stairway from the telegraph office. This was taken up by men upon the streets, until it was carried all over town. A messenger, in incoherent and breathless haste, told Lincoln the news as he handed him a dispatch. Within a minute a hundred persons had gathered about him, wanting to know the particulars, and endeavoring to shake hands with him. He strove to get out of the crowd, and as he moved off he remarked to those near him: 'Well, there is a little woman who will be interested in this news, and I will go home and tell her,' and he hurried on, with the crowd following and cheering."

A VISIT TO LINCOLN AT HIS HOME.

Mr. Volk, the artist, relates that on the day of Lincoln's nomination he was travelling to Springfield, and at Bloomington learned the result of the Chicago Convention. "At three or four o'clock," says Mr. Volk, "we reached Springfield. The afternoon was lovely—bright and sunny, neither too warm nor too cool; the grass, trees, and the hosts of blooming roses, so profuse in Springfield, appeared to be vying with the ringing bells and waving flags. As soon as I had brushed off the dust and registered at the old Chenery House, I went straight to Mr. Lincoln's unpretentious little two-story house. He saw me from his door or window coming down the street, and as I entered the gate, he was on the platform in front of the door, and quite alone. His face looked radiant. I exclaimed: 'I am the first man from Chicago, I believe, who has the honor of congratulating you on your nomination for President.' Then those two great hands took both of mine with a grasp never to be forgotten. And while shaking, I said: 'Now that you will doubtless be the next President of the United States, I want to make a statue of you, and shall do my best to do you justice.' Said he, 'I don't doubt it, for I have come to the conclusion that you are an honest man,' and with that greeting I thought my hands were in a fair way of being crushed. I was invited into the parlor, and soon Mrs. Lincoln entered, holding a rose-bouquet in her hand, which she presented to me after the introduction; and in return I gave her a cabinet-size bust of her husband, which I had modeled from the large one, and happened to have with me. Before leaving the house, it was arranged that Mr. Lincoln would give Saturday forenoon to obtaining full-length photographs to serve me for the proposed statue. On Saturday evening, the committee appointed by the convention to notify Mr. Lincoln formally of his nomination, headed by Mr. Ashmun, of Massachusetts, reached Springfield by special train, bearing a large number of people, two or three hundred of whom carried rails on their shoulders, marching in military style from the train to the old State House Hall of Representatives, where they stacked them like muskets. The evening was beautiful and clear, and the entire population was astir. The bells pealed, flags waved, and cannon thundered forth the triumphant nomination of Springfield's favorite and distinguished citizen. The bonfires blazed brightly, and especially in front of that prim-looking white house on Eighth street. The committee and the vast crowd following it passed in at the front door, and made their exit through the kitchen door in the rear, Mr. Lincoln giving them all a hearty shake of the hand as they passed him in the parlor. After it was all over and the crowd dispersed, late in the evening, I took a stroll and passed the house. A few small boys only were in the street, trying to keep up a little blaze among the dying embers of the bonfire. One of them cried out: 'Here, *Bill Lincoln*—here's a stick.' Another chimed in: 'I've got a good one, Bill'—a picket he had slyly knocked from a door-yard fence. By previous appointment, I was to cast Mr. Lincoln's hands on the Sunday following this memorable Saturday, at nine A. M. I found him ready, but he looked more grave and serious than he had appeared on the previous days. I wished him to hold something in his right hand, and he looked for a piece of pasteboard, but could find none. I told him a round stick would do as well as anything. Thereupon he went to the wood-shed, and I heard the saw go, and he soon returned to the dining-room (where I did the work), whittling off the end of a piece of broom-handle. I remarked to him that he need not whittle off the edges. 'Oh, well,' said he, 'I thought I would like to have it nice.' When I had successfully cast the mould of the right hand, I began the left, pausing a few moments to hear Mr. Lincoln tell me about a scar on the thumb. 'You have heard that they call me a rail-splitter, and you saw them carrying rails in the procession Saturday evening; well, it is true that I did split rails, and one day, while I was sharpening a wedge on a log, the axe glanced and nearly took my thumb off, and there is the scar, you see.' The right hand appeared swollen as compared with the left, on account of excessive hand-shaking the evening before; this difference is distinctly shown in the cast. That Sunday evening I returned to Chicago with the moulds of his hands, three photographic negatives of him, the identical black alpaca campaign suit of 1858, and a pair of Lynn newly-made pegged boots. The clothes were all burned up in the great Chicago fire. The casts of the face and hands I saved by taking them with me to Rome, and they have crossed the sea four times. The last time I saw Mr. Lincoln was in January, 1861, at his house in Springfield. His little parlor was full of friends and politicians. He introduced me to them all, and remarked to me aside that, since he had sat to me for his bust, he had lost forty pounds in weight. This was easily perceptible, for the lines of his jaws were very sharply defined through the short beard which he was allowing to grow. Then he turned to the company, and announced in a general way that I had made a bust of him before his nomination, and that he was then giving daily sittings at the St. Nicholas Hotel, to another sculptor; that he had sat to him for a week or more, but could not see the likeness, though he might yet bring it out. 'But,' continued Mr. Lincoln, 'in two or three days after Mr. Volk commenced my bust, there was the animal himself!' And this was about the last, if not the last, remark I ever heard him utter, except the good-bye and his good wishes for my success.''

AN INVITATION TO SUPPER.

Dr. Newton Bateman, for many years the personal friend of Mr. Lincoln, was selected by his fellow-townsmen to introduce to Mr. Lincoln the deputation of distinguished politicians —many of them Eastern men who had never seen Mr. Lincoln —sent to Springfield to apprise him informally of his nomination. Mr. Lincoln received them, in his simple way, in the plain parlor of the little wooden house on Eighth street. Mr. Lincoln was, as always, perfectly unconstrained and simple, and surprised and charmed those who now saw him for the first time, by his genial humor and artless eloquence. In the midst of the congratulations Tad came into the room, and putting his hand to his mouth and his mouth to his father's ear, said in a boy's whisper: "Ma says, come to supper." All heard the announcement, and Mr. Lincoln, perceiving this, said: "You have heard, gentlemen, the announcement concerning the interesting state of things in the dining room. It will never do for me, if elected, to make this young man a member of my cabinet, for it is plain he cannot be trusted with secrets of state."

RECEIVING THE COMMITTEE OF THE CONVENTION.

Saturday, May 19, the committee of the Chicago Convention arrived at Springfield to notify Mr. Lincoln of his nomination. The Hon. George Ashmun, as chairman of the committee, delivered the formal address, to which Mr. Lincoln listened with dignity, but with an air of profound sadness, as though the trials in store for him had already "cast their shadows before." In response to the address, Mr. Lincoln said:

"MR. CHAIRMAN AND GENTLEMEN OF THE COMMITTEE:—I tender to you, and through you to the Republican National Convention, and all the people represented in it, my profoundest thanks for the high honor done me, which you now formally announce. Deeply and even painfully sensible of the great responsibility which is inseparable from this high honor —a responsibility which I could almost wish had fallen upon some one of the far more eminent men and experienced statesmen whose distinguished names were before the convention—I shall, by your leave, consider more fully the resolutions of the convention, denominated the platform, and, without unnecessary and unreasonable delay, respond to you, Mr. Chairman, in writing, not doubting that the platform will be found satisfactory, and the nomination gratefully accepted. And now I will not longer defer the pleasure of taking you, and each of you, by the hand."

Mr. Speed relates an incident which immediately followed: "Tall Judge Kelly, of Pennsylvania, who was one of the committee, and who is himself a great many feet high, had meanwhile been eyeing Mr. Lincoln's lofty form with a mixture of admiration and very likely jealousy; this had not escaped Mr. Lincoln, and as he shook hands with the Judge he inquired, 'What is your height?' 'Six feet three; what is yours, Mr. Lincoln?' 'Six feet four.' 'Then,' said the Judge, 'Pennsylvania bows to Illinois. My dear sir, for years my heart has been aching for a President that I could *look up to*, and I've found him at last in the land where we thought there were none but *little* giants.' "

A letter was then handed Mr. Lincoln containing the official notice, accompanied by the resolutions of the convention. To this he replied, a few days later, as follows:

"SPRINGFIELD, ILLINOIS, MAY 23, 1860.

"SIR—I accept the nomination tendered to me by the convention over which you presided, of which I am formally apprised in a letter of yourself and others acting as a Committee of the Convention for that purpose. The declaration of principles and sentiments which accompanies your letter meets my approval, and it shall be my care not to violate it, or disregard it in any part. Imploring the assistance of Divine Providence,. and with due regard to the views and feelings of all who were represented in the convention, to the rights of all the States and Territories and people of the nation, to the inviolability of the Constitution, and the perpetual union, harmony and prosperity of all, I am most happy to co-operate for the practical success of the principles declared by the convention."

NOMINATION OF DOUGLAS.—THE CAMPAIGN OF 1860.

In June Mr. Douglas was nominated for the Presidency by the Democratic Convention, which met at Baltimore on the 18th. Mr. Douglas made a personal canvass, speaking in most of the States, North and South, and exerting all the powers of which he was master to win success. The campaign, as Mr. Arnold states, "has had no parallel. The enthusiasm of the people was like a great conflagration, like a prairie fire before a wild tornado. A little more than twenty years had passed since Owen Lovejoy, brother of Elijah Lovejoy, on the bank of the Mississippi, kneeling on the turf not then green over the grave of the brother who had been killed for his fidelity to freedom, had sworn eternal war against slavery. From that time on, he and his associate Abolitionists had gone forth preaching their crusade against oppression, with hearts of fire and tongues of lightning; and now the consummation was to be realized of a President elected on the distinct ground of opposition to the extension of slavery. For years the hatred of that institution had been growing and gathering force. Whittier, Bryant, Lowell, Longfellow, and others, had written the lyrics of liberty; the graphic pen of Mrs. Stowe, in 'Uncle Tom's Cabin,' had painted the cruelties of the overseer and the slaveholder; but the acts of slaveholders themselves did more to promote the growth of anti-slavery than all other causes. The persecutions of Abolitionists in the South; the harshness and cruelty attending the execution of the fugitive slave laws; the brutality of Brooks in knocking down, on the floor of the Senate, Charles Sumner, for words spoken in debate; these and many other outrages had fired the hearts of the people of the free States against this barbarous institution. Beecher, Phillips, Channing, Sumner, and Seward, with their eloquence; Chase, with his logic; Lincoln, with his appeals to the principles of the Declaration of Independence, and to the opinions of the founders of the republic, his clear statements, his apt illustrations, and, above all, his wise moderation,—all had swelled the voice of the people, which found expression through the ballot-box, and which declared that slavery should go no further.''

VARIOUS CAMPAIGN REMINISCENCES.

Among the various reminiscences of the memorable Presidential campaign of 1860, some of peculiar interest are furnished by Dr. Newton Bateman, the President of Knox College, Illinois. Dr. Bateman had known Mr. Lincoln since 1842; and from the year 1858, when Dr. Bateman was elected State Superintendent of Public Instruction in Illinois, to the close of Mr. Lincoln's residence in Springfield in 1861, they saw each other daily. The testimony of so intimate an acquaintance, and one so well qualified to judge the character and abilities of men, is of unusual value; and it is worth noting that Dr. Bateman remarks that, while he was always an admirer of Mr. Lincoln, yet the greatness of the man grows upon him as the years pass by. In his professional and public work, says Dr. Bateman, Mr. Lincoln not only proved himself equal to every emergency and to every successive task, but made, from the outset, the impression upon the mind of those who knew him of being in possession of great reserve force. Perhaps the secret of this lies in part in the fact that he was accustomed to ponder deeply upon the ultimate principles of government and society, and strove to base his discussions upon the firm ground of ethical truth. Says Dr. Bateman, "He was the saddest man I ever knew."

DR. NEWTON BATEMAN.

It was a necessity of his nature to be much alone; and he said that all his serious work—by which he meant the process of getting down to the bed-rock of first principles—must be done in solitude. Upon one occasion he called Dr. Bateman to him, and spent more than two hours in earnest conversation upon the most serious themes. At the close, Dr. Bateman said: "I did not know, Mr. Lincoln, that it was your habit to think so deeply upon this class of subjects." "Didn't you?" said Mr. Lincoln. "I can almost say that I think of *nothing else.*"

"THE BIG SCHOOLMASTER OF ILLINOIS."

During the Presidential campaign of 1860, Mr. Lincoln's reception-room in the State House adjoined the office of Dr. Bateman, who was then State Superintendent of Public Instruction. Between the two rooms there was an inner door, which, at Mr. Lincoln's special request, was generally left open, for the sake of a better circulation of air; and through this door the large deputations that frequently waited upon the Presidential candidate, sometimes overflowed into Dr. Bateman's office. So it came about that Dr. Bateman was eye-witness or ear-witness to a great many interesting scenes and conversations, some mirthful, some touching, some solemn. When Mr. Lincoln desired to consult Dr. Bateman, or introduce him to some friend, as he did almost daily, he often called out to him in such terms as these: "I say, you Big Schoolmaster, just come here, won't you?"—an invitation to which the person addressed always responded with alacrity. It is necessary to mention that the adjective "Big" was intended to have a double reference,—directly to Dr. Bateman's official position, and ironically to his physical stature, which, judged by Mr. Lincoln's standards, would doubtless appear inconsiderable. Mr. Lincoln sometimes introduced the good Doctor to some rural acquaintance in the following terms: "This is my little friend, the Big Schoolmaster of Illinois."

THE OLD LADY AND THE PAIR OF STOCKINGS.

All classes of people, says Dr. Bateman, Senator and ploughman, distinguished foreigners and Southerners, were received by Mr. Lincoln and dealt with in such unaffected sincerity and with such genial self-control, that all went away charmed and disarmed of prejudice. No matter what visitor he had, if some humble friend of his early years was announced, Mr. Lincoln would go himself to the door, lead in his old friend by the hand, seat him, and talk merrily of old times. Upon one occasion, when Mr. Boutwell, of Massachusetts, and other

THE OLD LADY PRESENTING LINCOLN A PAIR OF STOCKINGS.

persons of distinction were present, there entered an old lady from the country, her tanned face peering out from the interior of a huge sun-bonnet. Her errand was to present to "Mr. Linkin" a pair of stockings of her own make, a yard long. Kind tears came to his eyes as she spoke to him, and then, holding the stockings one in each hand, dangling wide apart for general inspection, he assured her that he should take them with him to Washington, where (and here his eyes twinkled) he was sure he should be unable to *find any like them*. The amusement of the company was not at all diminished by Mr. Boutwell's remark, that the lady had evidently made a very correct estimate of Mr. Lincoln's *latitude and longitude*.

LINCOLN AND THE TALL SOUTHERNER.

One day there entered Mr. Lincoln's room a tall Southerner, a Colonel Somebody from Mississippi, whose eye's hard glitter spoke supercilious distrust and whose stiff bearing betokened suppressed hostility. It was beautiful, says Dr. Bateman, to see the cold flash of the Southerner's dark eye yield to a warmer glow, and the haughty constraint melt into frank good-nature, under the influence of Mr. Lincoln's words of simple earnestness and unaffected cordiality. They got so far in half an hour that Mr. Lincoln could say, in his hearty way: "Colonel, how tall are you?" "Well, taller than you, Mr. Lincoln," replied the Mississippian. "You are mistaken there," retorted Mr. Lincoln. "Dr. Bateman, will you measure us?" "You will have to permit me to stand on a chair for that," responded the Doctor. So a big book was adjusted above the head of each, and pencil marks made at the respective points of contact with the white wall. Mr. Lincoln's atitude, as thus indicated, was a quarter-inch above that of the Colonel. "I knew it," said Mr. Lincoln. "They raise tall men down in Mississippi, but you go home and tell your folks that *Old Abe tops you a little*." The Colonel went away much mollified and impressed. "My God!" said he to Dr. Bateman, as he went out. "There's going to be war; but could my people know what I have learned within the last hour, there need be no war."

THE VOTE OF THE SPRINGFIELD CLERGYMEN.

During the Presidential campaign, the vote of the city of Springfield was canvassed house by house. There were at that time twenty-three clergymen residing in the city (not all pastors). All but three of these signified their intention to vote *against* Mr. Lincoln. This fact seemed to grieve him somewhat. Soon after, in conversing upon the subject with Dr. Bateman, he said, as if thinking aloud: "These gentlemen know that Judge Douglas does not care a cent whether slavery in the territories is voted up or voted down, for he has repeatedly told them so. They know that I *do* care." Then, drawing from a breast pocket a well-thumbed copy of the New Testament, he added, after a pause, tapping upon the book with his bony finger: "I do not so understand this book."

"MY NAME IS LINCOLN."

A New York gentleman thus describes a meeting with Mr. Lincoln at Springfield, soon after the nomination: "I was in Chicago when Mr. L. was nominated, and being curious to see the man every one was going wild over, I went to Springfield. I called at his office, but he was not in. Then I went to his residence, and learned that he had a room in the Capitol Building, and that I would find him there. Arrived at the room, I rapped at the door. It was opened by a tall, spare man, plain of face. I told him that I had come to see Mr. Lincoln. Inquiring my name, he took me by the arm and introduced me to some half-dozen persons who were in the room, and then remarked, '*My name is Lincoln.*' In ten minutes I felt as if I had known him all my life. He had the most wonderful faculty I have ever seen in a man to make one feel at ease. I left him, feeling that he was an extraordinary man, and that I should vote for him, and influence all I could to do the same.''

A GRACEFUL LETTER TO THE POET BRYANT.

The poet Bryant was conspicuous among the prominent Eastern men who favored Mr. Lincoln's nomination in 1860 for the Presidency. He had introduced Mr. Lincoln to the people of New York, at the Cooper Institute meeting of the previous winter, and was a firm believer in the Western politician. After the convention Mr. Bryant wrote Mr. Lincoln a most friendly and timely letter, full of good feeling and of wise advice. Especially did he warn Mr. Lincoln to be cautious in committing himself to any specific policy, or making pledges or engagements of any kind. Mr. Bryant's letter contained much political wisdom, and was written in that scholarly style for which he was distinguished. But it could not surpass the simple dignity and grace of Mr. Lincoln's reply:

"SPRINGFIELD, ILL., JUNE 28, 1860.

"Please accept my thanks for the honor done me by your kind letter of the 16th. I appreciate the danger against which you would guard me; nor am I wanting in the *purpose* to avoid it. I thank you for the additional strength your words give me to maintain that purpose.

Your friend and servant, A. LINCOLN."

"LOOKING UP HARD SPOTS."

Mr. A. J. Grover relates that about this time he met Mr. Lincoln, and had a memorable conversation with him on the Fugitive Slave Law. Mr. Lincoln detested this law, but argued that, until it was declared unconstitutional, it must be obeyed. This was a short time after the rescue of a fugitive slave at Ottawa, Ill., by John Hossack, James Stout, Major Campbell, and others, after Judge John D. Caton, acting as United States Commissioner, had given his decision remanding him to the custody of his alleged owner; and the rescuers were either in prison or out on bail, awaiting their trials.

Says Mr. Grover: "When Mr. Lincoln had finished his argument I said, 'Constitutional or not, I will never obey the Fugitive Slave Law. I would have done as Hossack and Stout and Campbell did at Ottawa. I will never catch and return slaves in obedience to any law or constitution. I do not believe a man's liberty can be taken from him constitutionally without a trial by jury. I believe the law to be not only unconstitutional, but most inhuman.' 'Oh,' said Mr. Lincoln, and I shall never forget his earnestness as he emphasized it by striking his hand on his knee, 'it is ungodly! it is ungodly! no doubt it is ungodly! but it is the law of the land, and we must obey it as we find it.' I said: 'Mr. Lincoln, how often have you sworn to support the Constitution? We propose to elect you President. How would you look taking an oath to support what you declare is an ungodly Constitution, and asking God to help you?' He felt the force of the question, and, inclining his head forward and running his fingers through his hair several times, seemed lost in reflection; then he placed his hand upon my knee and said, very earnestly: 'Grover, it's no use to be always *looking up these hard spots*!'"

In the terrible years then almost upon him, Mr. Lincoln found many such "hard spots," without taking the trouble to "look them up."

"LINCOLN'S OUTCOME."

One day a dinner party was given Mr. Lincoln, at which a dozen gentlemen were present. "The host on this occasion," says Rev. Dr. Noyes, one of the guests, "was a physician of high professional and personal character, and a splendid specimen of a man physically—tall, erect, well-proportioned. 'Mr. Lincoln,' said the host, in the hearing of his guests, as all arose from the dinner table, 'I must be a taller man than you are.' 'Oh, no, Doctor,' was the quick reply, 'there is not so much *outcome* to you as there is to me.' Whereupon, suiting the action to the word, Mr. Lincoln straightened up his long, crooked body, when it appeared that he was fully two inches taller than his challenger. These words, taken in another sense than that intended when they were spoken, are prophetic of the final verdict of history upon the character and work of Lincoln. Great as was that character, and grand as was his work, in the judgment of his contemporaries, yet there will be an *outcome* to his fame. To future generations, he will appear greater than he does to the present."

CHAPTER XII.

THE ELECTION OF 1860.——LINCOLN CHOSEN PRESIDENT.——A DELUGE OF VIS-
ITORS AT SPRINGFIELD.-——VARIOUS IMPRESSIONS OF THE PRESIDENT-ELECT.
——SOME QUEER CALLERS.——THE TWO TALL "SUCKERS."——A PROPHETIC
DINNER.——"A WHISTLE FROM A PIG'S TAIL."——TALKS ABOUT THE CABI-
NET.——LOOKING OVER THE SITUATION WITH HIS FRIENDS.——AN IMPAR-
TIAL DISTRIBUTION OF OFFICES.——THURLOW WEED'S VISIT TO SPRING-
FIELD.——URGING SIMON CAMERON FOR THE CABINET.——THE SERIOUS
ASPECT OF NATIONAL AFFAIRS.——THE SOUTH IN REBELLION.——TREASON
AT THE CAPITAL.——LINCOLN'S FAREWELL VISIT TO HIS MOTHER.——THE
OLD SIGN: "LINCOLN & HERNDON."——THE LAST DAY AT SPRINGFIELD.

THE Presidential campaign of 1860, with its excitements
and struggles, its "Wide-awake" clubs and boisterous enthusiasm throughout the North, and its bitter and threatening
character throughout the South, was at last ended; and on
the 6th of November, Abraham Lincoln was elected President
of the United States. The popular vote was as follows:
Lincoln, 1,866,452; Douglas, 1,375,157; Breckenridge,
847,953; Bell, 590,631. Of the electoral votes, Mr. Lincoln
had 180; Breckenridge, 72; Bell, 39; and Douglas, 12.

A DELUGE OF VISITORS AT SPRINGFIELD.

The election was no sooner decided than Mr. Lincoln
was beset with visitors from all parts of the country, who came
to gratify curiosity or to solicit personal favors of the incoming
President. The throng became at last so great, and interfered so much with the comfort of Mr. Lincoln's home, that
the Executive Chamber in the State House was set apart as
his reception room. Here "he met the millionaire and the
menial, the priest and the politician, men, women, and children, old friends and new friends, those who called for love
and those who sought for office. From morning until night
this was his occupation; and he performed it with conscientious care and the most unwearying patience."

VARIOUS IMPRESSIONS OF THE PRESIDENT-ELECT.

Among the visitors to the home of the President-elect was Mr. McCormick, whose account of his meeting with Mr. Lincoln in New York City has already been quoted in these pages. "In January, 1861," says Mr. McCormick, "at the instance of various friends in New York, who wished a position in the cabinet for a prominent Kentuckian, I went to Springfield, armed with documents for his consideration. I remained there a week or more, and was at the Lincoln cottage daily; indeed, I must say in passing, that I felt more at home there than at the barren hotel, and was the more free in my visits from the kind consideration of Mrs. Lincoln, who joined her husband in the suggestion that hotel life was at best comfortless, and that while at Springfield I should escape it as much as possible by tarrying with them, at the same time regretting that their house was not large enough for the entertainment of all their friends. Of the numerous formal and informal interviews had at Springfield, I remember all with the sincerest pleasure. I never found the man upon whom the great responsibilities of a nation—upon the verge of civil commotion—had been placed, impatient or ill-humored. The roughest and most tedious visitors were made welcome and happy in his presence; the poor commanded as much of his time as the rich. His recognition of old friends and companions in rough life, whom many, elevated as he had been, would have found it convenient to forget, was especially hearty. His correspondence was already immense, and the town was alive with cabinet-makers and office-seekers, but he met all with a calm temper."

Mr. Donn Piatt, the well-known writer, relates that he had met Mr. Lincoln during the Presidential campaign, and had been invited to visit Springfield. He did so, and was asked to supper at Mr. Lincoln's house. "It was a plain, comfortable structure," says Mr. Piatt, "and the supper was mainly of cake, pies, and chickens, the last evidently killed in the morning, to be eaten, as best they might, that evening. After the supper, we sat far into the night, talking over the situation. Mr. Lincoln was the homeliest man I ever saw. His body seemed to me a huge skeleton in clothes. Tall as he was, his hands and feet looked out of proportion, so long and clumsy were they. Every movement was awkward in the extreme. He sat with one leg thrown over the other, and the pendent foot swung almost to the floor. And all the while two little boys, his sons, clambered over those legs, patted his cheeks, pulled his nose, and poked their fingers in his eyes, without causing reprimand or even notice. He had a face that defied artistic skill to soften or idealize. It was capable of few expressions, but those were extremely striking. When in repose, his face was dull, heavy, and repellent. It brightened like a lit lantern when animated. His dull eyes would fairly sparkle with fun, or express as kindly a look as I ever saw, when moved by some matter of human interest.''

A writer previously quoted, Mr. Jeriah Bonham, describes a visit that he paid Mr. Lincoln at his room in the State House, where he ''found him quite alone, except that two of his children, one of whom was 'Tad,' were with him. The door was open. We walked in, and were at once recognized and seated,—the two boys still continuing their play about the room. 'Tad' was spinning his top ; and Mr. Lincoln, as we entered, had just finished adjusting the string for him so as to give the top the greatest degree of force. He remarked that he was 'having a little fun with the boys.' ''

The Hon. George W. Julian visited Mr. Lincoln at his home, in January. He says: ''I had a curiosity to see the famous 'rail-splitter,' as he was then familiarly called, and as a member-elect of the Thirty-seventh Congress I desired to form some acquaintance with the man who was to play so conspicuous a part in the impending national crisis. On meeting him I found him far better looking than the campaign pictures had represented. His face, when lighted up in conversation, was not unhandsome, and the kindly and winning tones of his voice pleaded for him, like the smile which played about his rugged features. He was full of anecdote and humor, and readily found his way to the hearts of those who enjoyed a welcome to his fireside. His face, however, was sometimes marked by that touching expression of sadness which became so generally noticeable in the following years. On the subject of slavery I was gratified to find him less reserved and more emphatic than I expected. I was much pleased with our first Republican Executive, and I returned home more fully inspired than ever with the purpose to sustain him to the utmost in facing the duties of his great office."

SOME QUEER CALLERS.—THE TWO TALL "SUCKERS."

Among the callers one day, says Mr. Lamon, were two tall, ungainly fellows, "Suckers," as they were called, who entered the room while Mr. Lincoln was engaged in conversation with a friend. They lingered bashfully near the door, and Mr. Lincoln, noticing their embarrassment, rose and said good-naturedly: "How do you do, my good fellows? What can I do for you? Will you sit down?" The spokesman of the pair, the shorter of the two, declined to sit, and explained the object of the call thus: he had had a talk about the relative height of Mr. Lincoln and his companion, and had asserted his belief that they were of exactly the same height. He had come in to verify his judgment. Mr. Lincoln smiled, went and got his cane, and, placing the end of it upon the wall, said, "Here, young man, come under here!" The young man came under the cane, as Mr. Lincoln held it, and when it was perfectly adjusted to his height, Mr. Lincoln said: "Now come out and hold up the cane." This he did, while Mr. Lincoln stepped under. Rubbing his head back and forth to see that it worked easily under the measurement, he stepped out, and declared to the sagacious fellow who was curiously looking on, that he had guessed with remarkable accuracy—that he and the young man were exactly of the same height. Then he shook hands with them and sent them on their way.

A PROPHETIC DINNER.

The two visitors just referred to had hardly disappeared, when, continues Mr. Lamon, an old and modestly dressed woman made her appearance. She knew Mr. Lincoln, but Mr. Lincoln did not at first recognize her. Then she undertook to recall to his memory certain incidents connected with his rides upon the circuit—especially his dining at her house upon the road at different times. Then he remembered her and her home. Having fixed her own place in his recollection, she tried to recall to him a certain scanty dinner of bread and milk that he once ate at her house. He could not remember it—on the contrary, he only remembered that he had always fared well at her house. "Well," said she, "one day you came along after we had got through dinner, and we had eaten up everything, and I could give you nothing but a bowl of bread and milk; and you ate it; and when you got up you said it was *good enough for the President of the United States.*" The good old woman, remembering the remark, had come in from the country, making a journey of eight or ten miles, to relate to Mr. Lincoln this incident, which in her mind had doubtless taken the form of prophecy. Mr. Lincoln placed the honest creature at her ease, chatted with her of old times, and dismissed her in the most happy and complacent frame of mind.

"A WHISTLE FROM A PIG'S TAIL."

"About the last of January, 1861," says Hon. E. M. Haines, "Mr. Lincoln vacated his house, and went with his wife and family to board at the Chenery House, in Springfield. The Legislature, of which I was a member, still being in session, I happened in one evening, at the Chenery House, to make a call on some friends, whom I found in the parlor. Mr. Lincoln and his wife were sitting in the parlor, amongst others. We shortly engaged in a general conversation. Mr. Lincoln's little boy, who I think is the one they called 'Tad,' was in the room, when a lady present, with whom I was acquainted, called the boy to her and said to me, 'This boy has something that I wish to show you.' The article was handed to me, and I saw that it was a whistle made, as was remarked, *from a pig's tail*. The lady said, 'You know this is something that it has been said could not be done.' Mr. Lincoln remarked that it was sent to him after his election, to show that the thing *could* be done. Rough as this joke was, Mr. Lincoln, as well as Mrs. Lincoln, took it in the utmost good humor. My recollection is that the whistle came from some one in the Southern States."

LOOKING OVER THE SITUATION WITH HIS FRIENDS.

Among the judicious friends of Mr. Lincoln, who gave him timely counsel at this important epoch of his life, was Judge John D. Caton, who, though a Democrat, saw plainly the tendency of political affairs, and was anxious for the preservation of the Union. "I met him in Springfield," writes Judge Caton, "and we had a conference in the law-library. I told him it was plain that he had a war on his hands; that there was a determination on the part of the South to secede from the Union, and that there would be throughout the North an equal determination to maintain the Union. I advised him that it would require all his energies, and that of all of his friends, in the conduct of the struggle which was certainly coming. I told him that my advice would be not to act hastily, but to let the people of the South commit themselves as palpably as possible. In other words, to allow them apparently to drive him to the wall before he resorted to the war power; for the reason that such a course would convince those in the North who might sympathize with the South that he had no other course to pursue. I advised him that he should not bring on the war by precipitate action, but let the

Southerners commence it; forbear as long as forbearance could be tolerated, in order to unite the North the more effectually to support his hands in the struggle that was certain to come, and also to convince those in the South who were opposed to the rebellion that the war was not forced upon them by the North; that by such a course the great body of the people of the North, of all parties, would come to his support, and that he would be given a cordial and earnest support. I further advised him that in the heat of the struggle which must ensue, there would be strong temptations sometimes to overstep the recognized law, and this might be necessary in emergencies, but that it should be done only from absolute necessity; and especially the shedding of blood should be avoided, except in actual battle. Mr. Lincoln listened intently, and replied that he foresaw that the struggle was inevitable, but that it would be his desire and his effort to unite the people in support of the Government and for the maintenance of the Union; that he was aware that no single party could sustain him successfully, and that he must rely upon the great masses of the people of all parties, and he would try to pursue such a course as would secure their support. He thanked me for my suggestions, and seemed to approve of them. The interview continued perhaps an hour."

TALKS ABOUT THE CABINET.—AN IMPARTIAL DISTRIBUTION OF OFFICES.

Judge Davis, a most intimate and confidential friend of Mr. Lincoln, states that the latter was firmly determined to appoint "Democrats and Republicans alike to office." Mr. Lamon corroborates the statement, pointedly remarking: "He felt that his strength lay in conciliation at the outset; that was his ruling conviction during all those months of preparation for the great task before him. It showed itself, not only in the appointments which he sought to make, but in those which he did make. Harboring no jealousies, entertaining no fears concerning his personal interests in the future, he called around him the most powerful of his late rivals—Seward, Chase, Bates,—and unhesitatingly gave into their hands powers which most Presidents would have shrunk from committing to their equals, and much more to their superiors in the conduct of public affairs." In a noted instance where the most powerful influence was brought to bear upon Mr. Lincoln to induce him to make what he regarded as an unworthy appointment, he exclaimed: "All that I am in the world,— the Presidency and all else,—I owe to the opinion of me which the people express when they call me 'Honest Old Abe.' Now, what would they think of their *honest* Abe, if he should make such an appointment as the one proposed?"

Hon. Leonard Swett, who knew Mr. Lincoln from 1848 to the time of his death, and had "travelled the circuit" with him in Illinois, relates that soon after the election he and Judge Davis advised Mr. Lincoln to consult Thurlow Weed regarding the formation of the Cabinet and on political affairs generally. "Mr. Lincoln asked me," says Mr. Swett, "to write Mr. Weed and invite him to a conference at Mr. Lincoln's house in Springfield. I did so, and the result was that Judge Davis, Thurlow Weed and myself spent a whole day with him in discussing the men and measures of his administration. At that meeting, which took place in less than a month after Mr. Lincoln's election, or about December 1, 1860, Mr. Lincoln became convinced that war was imminent between the North and South. Mr. Weed was a very astute man, and had a wonderful knowledge of what was going on. He told Mr. Lincoln of preparations being made in the Southern States that could mean nothing less than war. It was a serious time with all of us, of course, but Mr. Lincoln took it with the imperturbability that always distinguished him."

THURLOW WEED'S VISIT TO SPRINGFIELD.

The account given by Thurlow Weed, the veteran New York editor and journalist, of his visit to Mr. Lincoln on this occasion, is of peculiar interest. Mr. Weed remained in

Springfield two or three days in close consultation with the President-elect, the formation of the new Cabinet being the subject principally discussed. After expressing gratification at his election, and an apprehension of the dangers which threatened the incoming administration, says Mr. Weed, in his au-

tobiography, "Mr. Lincoln remarked, smiling, 'that he supposed I had had some experience in cabinet-making; that he had a job on hand, and as he had never learned that trade he was disposed to avail himself of the suggestions of friends.'

Taking up his figure, I replied, 'that though never a boss cabinet-maker, I had, as a journeyman, been occasionally consulted about State Cabinets; and that, although President Taylor once talked with me about re-forming his Cabinet, I had never been concerned in, or presumed to meddle with, the formation of an original Federal Cabinet, and that he was the first President-elect I had ever seen.' The question thus opened became the subject of conversation, at intervals, during that and the following day. I say at intervals, because many hours were consumed in talking of the public men connected with former administrations, interspersed, illustrated and seasoned pleasantly with Mr. Lincoln's stories, anecdotes, etc. And here I feel called upon to vindicate Mr. Lincoln, as far as my opportunities and observation go, from the frequent imputation of telling indelicate and ribald stories. I saw much of him during his whole Presidential term, with familiar friends and alone, when he talked without restraint; but I never heard him use a profane or indecent word, or tell a story that might not be repeated in the presence of ladies.

"Mr. Lincoln observed that 'the making of a Cabinet, now that he had it to do, was by no means as easy as he had supposed; that he had, even before the result of the election was known, assuming the probability of success, fixed upon the two leading members of his Cabinet, but that in looking about for suitable men to fill the other departments, he had been much embarrassed, partly from his want of acquaintance with the prominent men of the day, and partly, he believed, that while the population of the country had immensely increased, *really great men were scarcer than they used to be.*' He then inquired whether I had any suggestions of a general character, affecting the selection of a Cabinet, to make. * * * As the conversation progressed, Mr. Lincoln remarked that he intended to invite Governor Seward to take the State and Governor Chase the Treasury Department, remarking that, aside from their long experience in public affairs and their eminent fitness, they were prominently before the people and the convention as competitors for the Presidency, each having higher claims than his own for the place which he was to occupy. On naming Hon. Gideon Welles as the gentleman he thought of as the representative of New England in the Cabinet, I remarked that I thought he could find several New England gentlemen whose selection for a place in his Cabinet would be more acceptable to the people of New England. 'But,' said Mr. Lincoln, 'we must remember that the Republican party is constituted of two elements, and that we must have men of Democratic as well as of Whig antecedents in the Cabinet.' Then Mr. Lincoln remarked that Judge Blair had been suggested. I inquired, '*What* Judge Blair?' and was answered, 'Judge Montgomery Blair.' 'Has he been suggested by any one except his father, Francis P. Blair, Sr.?' 'Your question,' said Mr. Lincoln, 'reminds me of a story;' and he proceeded, with infinite humor, to tell a story which I would repeat, if I did not fear that its spirit and effect would be lost. 'But,' said Mr. L., 'to be serious, what do you think of Judge Blair?' I said that I had no personal acquaintance with that gentleman, but that I had been accustomed to regard him as anything but an agreeable political bedfellow, and that I hoped he would not punish himself and others by taking a man into his Cabinet who would keep it constantly in hot water. 'Then you think,' said Mr. L., 'that Judge Blair, like farmer Tabor's brindle ox, should be unyoked in the yard?' I finally remarked that if we were legislating on the question, I should move to strike out the name of Montgomery Blair, and insert that of William Cost Johnson. Mr. Lincoln laughingly replied, 'Davis has been posting you up on this question. He came from Maryland and has got Cost Johnson on the brain. Maryland must, I think, be like New Hampshire, a good State to move from.' And then he told a story of a witness in a neighboring county, who on being asked his age replied, 'Sixty.' Being satisfied that he was much older, the Judge repeated the question, and on receiving the same answer, admonished the witness, saying that the court knew him to be much older than sixty. 'Oh,' said the witness, 'you're thinking about the fifteen years that I lived down on the Eastern shore of Maryland; that was so much *lost time* and *don't count.*' This story, I perceived, was thrown in to give the conversation a new direction. * * * General Cameron's name was next introduced; and upon the peculiarities and characteristics of Pennsylvania statesmen, we had a long conversation. * * * I now renewed my suggestion about having the slave States represented in the Cabinet. 'But,' said Mr. Lincoln, 'you object to Judge Blair because he represents nobody, he has no following; and because his appointment would be obnoxious to the Union men of Maryland; and that, as I believe, while he can look into Maryland, he actually resides in the District of Columbia. Very well,' said Mr. Lincoln, 'I will now give you the name of a gentleman who not only resides in a slave State, but who is emphatically a representative man. What objection have you to Edward Bates, of Missouri?' 'None—not a shadow or a shade of an objection. That is a selection, as Mr. Webster might have said, 'eminently fit to be made.'

"It was now settled that Governor Seward was to be Secretary of State, Governor Chase Secretary of the Treasury, and Mr. Bates the Attorney-General. I was satisfied that Mr. Lincoln intended to give Mr. Welles one of the other places in the Cabinet, that he was strongly inclined to give another place to Mr. Blair, and that his mind was not quite clear in regard to General Cameron. Only one place, therefore, remained open, and that, it was understood, was to be given to Indiana; but whether it was to be Caleb B. Smith, or Colonel Lane, was undetermined. I inquired whether, in the shape which the question was taking, it was just or wise to concede so many seats in his Cabinet to the Democratic element in the Republican party. He replied that, as a Whig, he thought he could afford to be liberal to a section of the Republican party without whose votes he could not have been elected. I admitted the justice and wisdom of this, adding that in arranging and adjusting questions of place and patronage in our State, we had acted in that spirit; but that I doubted both the justice and the wisdom, in inaugurating his administration, of giving to a minority of the Republican party a majority in his Cabinet. I added that the National Convention indicated unmistakably the sentiment of its constituency by nominating for President a candidate with Whig antecedents, while its nominee for Vice-President had been for many years a Democratic Representative in Congress. 'But,' said Mr. Lincoln, 'why do you assume that we are giving that section of our party a majority in the Cabinet?' I replied that if Messrs. Chase, Cameron, Welles and Blair should be designated, the Cabinet would stand four to three. 'You seem to forget that *I expect to be there;* and *counting me as one,* you see how nicely the Cabinet would be balanced and ballasted. Besides,' said Mr. Lincoln, 'in talking of General Cameron, you admitted that his political status was unexceptionable. I suppose we could say of General Cameron without offense, that he is not Democratic enough to hurt him. I remember that people used to say, without disturbing my self-respect, that I was not lawyer enough to hurt me.' I admitted that I had no political objection to General Cameron, who, I was quite sure, would forget whether applicants for appointment had been Whig or Democrat. I then renewed the suggestion relating to North Carolina or Tennessee, earnestly pressing its importance. Messrs. Davis and Swett united with me in these views. Mr. Lincoln met us with strong counterviews, the force of which we were constrained to admit. 'If,' said Mr. Lincoln, 'contrary to our hopes, North Carolina and Tennessee should secede, could their men remain in the Cabinet? Or, if they remained, of what use would they be to the Government?' We, however, continued to press our point, until Mr. Lincoln yielded so far as to say that he would write a letter to the Hon. John A. Gilmore, then member of Congress from North Carolina, briefly stating his views of the duty of the Government in reference to important questions then pending, and inviting him, if those views met his approval, to accept a seat in the Cabinet. 'Now,' said Mr. Lincoln, 'if Mr. Gilmore should come in, some one else must stay out, and that other somebody must be either Judge Blair or Mr. Bates.' Messrs. Davis, Swett, and myself exclaimed against dropping Mr. Bates; and so Mr. Lincoln left us to infer that if Mr. Gilmore came in, Mr. Blair would be excluded.

"In this way, the conversation being alternately earnest and playful, two days passed very pleasantly. I wish it were possible to give, in Mr. Lincoln's amusing but quaint manner, the many stories, anecdotes and witticisms with which he interlarded and enlivened what with almost any of his predecessors in the high office of President would have been a grave, dry consultation. The great merit of Mr. Lincoln's stories, like Captain Bunsby's opinion, 'lays in the application on it.' They always and exactly suited the occasion and the object, and none to which I ever listened were far-fetched or pointless. I will attempt, however, to repeat one of them. If I have an especial fondness for any particular luxury, it manifests itself in a remarkable way when properly made December sausages are placed before me. While at breakfast, Judge Davis, noticing that, after having been bountifully served with sausage, Oliver Twist like, I wanted some more, said, 'You seem fond of our Illinois sausages.' To which I responded affirmatively, adding that I thought the article might be relied on where pork was cheaper than dogs. 'That,' said Mr. Lincoln, 'reminds me of what occurred down at Joliet, where a popular grocer supplied all the villagers with sausages. One Saturday evening, when his grocery was filled with customers, for whom he and his boys were busily engaged in weighing sausages, a neighbor with whom he had had a violent quarrel that day, came into the grocery, made his way up to the counter, holding two enormous dead cats by the tail, which he deliberately threw on to the counter, saying, 'This makes seven to-day. I'll call around Monday, and get my money for them.'

"In the course of our conversations, Mr. Lincoln remarked that it was particularly pleasant to him to reflect that he was coming into office unembarrassed by promises. He owed, he supposed, his exemption from importunities to the circumstance that his name as a candidate was but a short time before the people, and that only a few sanguine friends anticipated the possibility of his nomination. 'I have not,' said he, 'promised an office to any man, nor have I, but in a single instance, mentally committed myself to an appointment.'

"A year or two after this visit, President Lincoln, while talking with me about the peculiarities of his Cabinet, said that immediately after his election, thinking that the Vice-president, from his high character and long experience, was entitled to a voice in the Cabinet, the selection of the New England man was conceded to him, and that Mr. Hamlin named 'Father Welles.'

"It is proper to add that Mr. Lincoln made me the bearer of his letter to Mr. Gilmore, with which I repaired to Washington. It being an open letter, Mr. G., after reading it attentively, entered into a frank conversation with me upon the question which was exciting profound interest and anxiety in and out of Congress. He said that he entirely approved of the views of Mr. Lincoln on that question, and that he was gratified with the confidence reposed in him ; but that before replying to it, he deemed it proper to confer with members of Congress from Southern States who, like himself, were opposed to secession. Soon afterward the 'Border State Proposition' was rejected by the House of Representatives. Under these circumstances, hopeless of keeping North Carolina in the Union, Mr. Gilmore declined the offer of a seat in the Cabinet.''

URGING SIMON CAMERON FOR THE CABINET.

"A few days after the opening of the legislative session in January, 1861," says Hon. E. M. Haines, "a plain, portly, smooth-faced elderly gentleman, of medium height, called upon me, and introduced himself as Isaac Newton, of Philadelphia. He belonged to the sect of Quakers, or Friends, who were formerly quite numerous in Pennsylvania. He said that he had called upon me to solicit my influence in a matter of considerable importance, which was, that he desired to secure the appointment by Mr. Lincoln of Simon Cameron, of Pennsylvania, as Secretary of the Treasury. Cameron had been a candidate at the convention at Chicago, at which Mr. Lincoln was nominated, and at which he had the support of the Pennsylvania delegation; but he withdrew as a candidate, transferring the support of his friends to Mr. Lincoln. This it was supposed would be favorably considered by Mr. Lincoln, in the claims of Mr. Cameron for this position. When Mr. Cameron was first announced as a candidate for President from Pennsylvania, Mr. Lincoln's name had not been much mentioned, and he was scarcely considered as available, or as having any chances for the nomination; but there was quite a strong move in the North, especially in Pennsylvania, for Cameron for President and Lincoln for Vice-president. I had identified myself with this movement; but as Mr. Lincoln became more prominent, before the country, as a candidate for President, I classed myself among his friends, but was ranked among the friends of Mr. Cameron, and as favorable to the movement for transferring his strength to Mr. Lincoln. These circumstances, and the fact that I was a member of the Legislature, were probably the reasons why Mr. Newton called on me to join him in urging the claims of Mr. Cameron for the position mentioned. At that time I knew nothing of Mr. Cameron save what had been presented by his friends. This having been favorable, and having been in the move to nominate him for President, I responded to the request of Mr. Newton, and assured him that I would add what little influence I could to obtain favorable consideration of his case with Mr. Lincoln. Soon thereafter, I met Mr. Lincoln in the street, on the north side of the State House square, and presented the matter to him. We stepped around the corner of the adjacent building, to talk it over. He was quite cordial and frank, and treated what I had to say with much consideration. He said that Mr. Cameron was being mentioned and strongly urged by the people of Pennsylvania; and he remarked that it was a singular fact, that whilst everybody in Pennsylvania seemed to be in favor of Mr. Cameron, everybody *out* of Pennsylvania seemed opposed to him. This was about the substance of our interview; and of course he could not properly give, neither could I expect, any positive assurance from him as to what would be his course in the premises.''

THE SERIOUS ASPECT OF NATIONAL AFFAIRS.

During the months intervening between his election and his departure for Washington, Mr. Lincoln maintained a keen though quiet watchfulness of the threatening aspect of affairs at the National Capital, and throughout the South. He was careful not to commit himself by needless utterances; but in all his demeanor, as a friend said, he displayed all the firmness and determination, without the temper, of Jackson. In December, 1860, he wrote the following letters to his intimate friend, Hon. E. B. Wasburne, then a member of Congress from Illinois:

"SPRINGFIELD, ILL., Dec. 13, 1860.

"HON. E. B. WASHBURNE—*My Dear Sir:* Your long letter received. Prevent, as far as possible, any of our friends from demoralizing themselves and our cause by entertaining propositions for compromise of any sort on the slavery extension. There is no possible compromise upon it, but which puts us under again, and leaves us all our work to do over again. Whether it be a Missouri line, or Eli Thayer's Popular Sovereignty, it is all the same. Let either be done, and immediately filibustering and extending slavery recommences. On that point hold firm, as with a chain of steel.   Yours as ever,   A. LINCOLN.''

"SPRINGFIELD, ILL., Dec. 21, 1860.
"HON. E. B. WASHBURNE—*My Dear Sir:*   Last night I received your letter, giving an account of your interview with General Scott, and for which I thank you. Please present my respects to the General, and tell him confidentially, I shall be obliged to him to be as well prepared as he can to either *hold*, or retake, the forts, as the case may require, at and after the inauguration.   Yours as ever,   A. LINCOLN.''

THE SOUTH IN REBELLION.

The Southern States, led on by South Carolina, which formally severed its connection with the Union November 17, 1860, were preparing to dissolve their alliance with the Free States. Mississippi passed the ordinance of secession January 9, 1861; Florida followed on the 10th; Alabama, on the 11th; Georgia, on the 19th; Louisiana, on the 25th; and Texas, on the 1st day of February.

TREASON AT THE CAPITAL.

Meanwhile, treason had full liberty to accomplish its nefarious work at the capital of the United States. Traitors in the Cabinet and in Congress conspired to deplete the resources of the Government, leaving it helpless to contest the assumptions of the confederacy arising in the South. The treasury was deliberately bankrupted; the ships of the navy were banished to distant ports; the Northern arsenals were rifled to furnish arms for the rebels in the seceded States; the fortified places on the Southern coast were delivered into the hands of the enemy, with the exception of Fort Sumter, which was gallantly held by Major Robert Anderson. While this system of bold and unscrupulous treachery was carried out by men in the highest places of trust, the chief Executive of the nation remained a passive spectator of the portentous scene. The South was in open rebellion, and the North was powerless to interfere. The weeks prior to the inauguration of the new administration dragged slowly along, each day adding fresh cause for anxiety and alarm.

LINCOLN'S FAREWELL VISIT TO HIS MOTHER.

Early in February, Mr. Lincoln made a parting visit to his relatives in Coles county, to whom, in this hour of grave trial, his heart turned with fresh yearning. He spent a night at Charleston, where his cousin, Dennis Hanks, and Mrs. Colonel Chapman, a daughter of Dennis, resided. "The people crowded by hundreds to see him; and he was serenaded by 'both the string and brass bands of the town, but declined making a speech.'" The following morning he passed on to Farmington, to the home of his step-mother, who was living with her daughter, Mrs. Moore. Mr. Lamon relates that "the meeting between him and the old lady was of a most affectionate and tender character. She fondled him as her own 'Abe,' and he her as his own mother. It was soon arranged that she should return with him to Charleston, so that they might enjoy by the way the unrestricted and uninterrupted intercourse which they both desired above all things, but which they were not likely to have where the people could get at him. Then Mr. Lincoln and Colonel Chapman drove to the house of John Hall, who lived on the old 'Lincoln farm,' where Abe split the celebrated rails and fenced in the little clearing in 1830. Thence they went to the spot where old Tom Lincoln was buried. The grave was unmarked and utterly neglected. Mr. Lincoln said he wanted to 'have it enclosed, and a suitable tombstone erected.' He told Colonel Chapman to go to a marble-dealer, ascertain the cost of the work proposed, and write him in full. He would then send Dennis Hanks the money and inscription for the stone, and Dennis would do the rest." "We then returned," says Col. Chapman, "to Farmington, where we found a large crowd of citizens—nearly all old acquaintances—waiting to see him.

His reception was very enthusiastic, and appeared to gratify him very much. After taking dinner at his step-sister's (Mrs. Moore's), he returned to Charleston, his step-mother coming with us. Our conversation during the trip was mostly concerning family affairs. Mr. Lincoln spoke to me on the way down to Farmington of his step-mother in the most affectionate manner; said she had been his best friend in the world, and that no son could love a mother more than he loved her. He also told me of the condition of his father's family at the time he married his step-mother, and of the change she made in the family, and of the encouragement he (Abe) received from her. * * * He spoke of his father, and related some amusing incidents of the old man; of the bull-dog's biting the old man on his return from New Orleans; of the old man's escape, when a boy, from an Indian who was shot by his uncle Mordecai. He spoke of his uncle Mordecai as being a man of very great natural gifts, and spoke of his step-brother, John Johnson, who had died a short time previous, in the most affectionate manner. Arriving at Charleston on our return from Farmington, we proceeded to my residence. Again the house was crowded by persons wishing to see him. The crowd finally became so great that he authorized me to announce that he would hold a public reception at the Town Hall that evening at seven o'clock; but that, until then, he wished to be left with relations and friends. After supper he proceeded to the Town Hall, where large numbers from the town and surrounding country, irrespective of party, called to see him. He left this place Wednesday morning at four o'clock, to return to Springfield. * * * Mr. Lincoln appeared to enjoy his visit here remarkably well. His reception by his old acquaintances appeared to be very gratifying to him. They all appeared so glad to see him, irrespective of party, and all appeared so anxious that his administration might be a success, and that he might have a pleasant and honorable career as President."

"LINCOLN & HERNDON."—THE OLD SIGN.

A characteristic anecdote of Mr. Lincoln, showing his enduring friendship and love of old associations, is told among those relating to his last days at Springfield. When he was about to leave for Washington, he went to the dingy little law office which had sheltered his saddest hours. He sat down on the couch, and said to his law-partner, Herndon, "Billy, you and I have been together more than twenty years, and have never 'passed a word.' Will you let my name stay on the old sign till I come back from Washington?" The tears started to Mr. Herndon's eyes. He put out his hand. "Mr. Lincoln," said he, "I will never have any other partner while you live;" and to the day of the assassination, all the doings of the firm were in the name of "Lincoln & Herndon."

THE LAST DAY AT SPRINGFIELD.

Governor Bross, of Illinois, relates that he was with Mr. Lincoln at Springfield on the day before he left for Washington. "We were walking slowly to his home from some place where we had met, and the condition and prospects of the country, and his vast responsibility in assuming the high position of President, were the subjects of his thoughts. These were discussed with a breadth and anxiety full of that pathos peculiar to Mr. Lincoln in his thoughtful moods. He seemed to have a thorough prescience of the dangers through which his administration was to pass. No President had ever had before him such vast and far-reaching responsibilities. He regarded war—long, bitter, and dreadful—as almost sure to come. He distinctly and reverently placed his hopes for the result in the strength and guidance of Him on whom Washington relied in the darkest hours of the Revolution. He would take the place to which Providence and his countrymen had called him, and do the best he could for the integrity and the welfare of the Republic. For himself, he scarcely expected ever again to see his home in Springfield."

CHAPTER XIII.

OFF FOR THE CAPITAL.——FAREWELL SPEECH AT SPRINGFIELD.——THE JOUR-
NEY TO WASHINGTON.——SPEECHES ALONG THE ROUTE.——A HAND-SHAKING
EPISODE.——AT CINCINNATI.——AN UNCOMFORTABLE RIDE.——A HITHERTO
UNPUBLISHED SPEECH BY MR. LINCOLN.——AT CLEVELAND.——PERSONAL
IMPRESSIONS OF MR. AND MRS. LINCOLN.——THE LITTLE GIRL WHO ADVISED
MR. LINCOLN TO RAISE A BEARD.——IN NEW YORK CITY.——PERILS OF THE
JOURNEY.——THE PLOT TO ASSASSINATE MR. LINCOLN IN BALTIMORE.——A
CHANGE OF PROGRAMME.——ARRIVAL AT THE CAPITAL.——THE DANGERS
AT BALTIMORE NOT IMAGINARY.

ON the morning of the 11th of February, 1861, Mr. Lincoln left his home in Springfield for the scene where he was to spend the most anxious, toilsome, and painful years of his life. An elaborate programme had been prepared for his journey to Washington, which was to conduct him through the principal cities of Indiana, Ohio, New York, New Jersey, and Pennsylvania, and consume much of the time intervening before the 4th of March. Special trains, preceded by pilot-engines, were prepared for his accommodation. He was accompanied at his departure by his wife and three sons, and a party of friends, including Governor Yates, ex-Governor Moore, Dr. W. M. Wallace (his brother-in-law), N. B. Judd, O. H. Browning, Ward H. Lamon, David Davis, Col. E. E. Ellsworth, and John M. Hay and J. G. Nicolay, afterwards his private secretaries. Mr. Lamon, describing the incidents of his leave-taking, says: "It was a gloomy day; heavy clouds floated overhead, and a cold rain was falling. Long before eight o'clock, a great mass of people had collected at the station of the Great Western Railway to witness the event of the day. At precisely five minutes before eight, Mr. Lincoln, preceded by Mr. Wood, emerged from a private room in the depot building, and passed slowly to the car, the people falling back respectfully on either side, and as many as possible shaking his hands. Having finally reached the train, he ascended the rear platform, and, facing about to the throng which had closed around him, drew himself up to his full height, removed his hat, and stood for several seconds in profound silence. His eye roved sadly over that sea of upturned faces; and he thought he read in them again the sympathy and friendship which he had often tried, and which he never needed more

LEAVING SPRINGFIELD FOR WASHINGTON.—LINCOLN'S FAREWELL TO HIS FRIENDS.

than he did then. There was an unusual quiver in his lip, and a still more unusual tear on his shrivelled cheek. His solemn manner, his long silence, were as full of melancholy eloquence as any words he could have uttered. What did he think of? Of the mighty changes which had lifted him from the lowest to the highest estate on earth? Of the weary road which had brought him to this lofty summit? Of his poor mother lying beneath the tangled underbrush in a distant forest? Of that other grave in the quiet Concord cemetery? Whatever the particular character of his thoughts, it is evident that they were retrospective and painful. To those who were anxiously waiting to catch words upon which the fate of the nation might hang, it seemed long until he had mastered his feelings sufficiently to speak. At length he began, in a husky tone of voice, and slowly and impressively delivered his farewell to his neighbors. Imitating his example, many in the crowd stood with heads uncovered in the fast-falling rain.''

FAREWELL SPEECH AT SPRINGFIELD.

"*My Friends:*—No one, not in my position, can realize the sadness I feel at this parting. To this people I owe all that I am. Here I have lived more than a quarter of a century. Here my children were born, and here one of them lies buried. I know not how soon I shall see you again. I go to assume a task more difficult than that which has devolved upon any other man since the days of Washington. He never would have succeeded except for the aid of Divine Providence, upon which he at all times relied. I feel that I cannot succeed without the same Divine blessing which sustained him; and on the same Almighty Being I place my reliance for support. And I hope you, my friends, will all pray that I may receive that Divine assistance, without which I cannot succeed, but with which success is certain. Again, I bid you an affectionate farewell.''

Abraham Lincoln spoke none but true and sincere words, and none more true and heartfelt ever fell from his lips than these, so laden with pathos, with humility, with a craving for the sympathy of his friends and the people, and for help above and beyond all earthly power and love.

THE JOURNEY TO WASHINGTON.—SPEECHES ALONG THE ROUTE.

The route chosen for the journey to Washington was a somewhat circuitous one, traversing the States of Indiana, Ohio, New York, New Jersey and Pennsylvania, and passing through Maryland to the District of Columbia. It seems to have been the desire of Mr. Lincoln to meet personally the people of the great Northern States, upon whose devotion and loyalty he prophetically felt he must depend for the salvation of the Republic. Everywhere he met the warmest and most generous greetings from the throngs assembled at the railway stations in the various cities through which he passed. At Indianapolis, where the first important halt was made, cannon announced the arrival of the party, and a royal welcome was accorded the distinguished traveller. In this, as in the other cities at which he stopped, Mr. Lincoln made a brief address to the people. On each occasion his remarks were well considered and temperate. His manner was serious, his expressions thoughtful and feeling. He entreated the people to be calm and patient; to stand by the principles of liberty inwrought into the fabric of the Constitution; to have faith in the strength and reality of the Government, and faith in his purpose to discharge his duties honestly and impartially. He referred continually to his trust in the Almighty Ruler of the Universe, to guide the nation safely out of its present peril and perplexity. "I judge," he said at Columbus, "that all we want is time and patience, and a reliance in that God who has never forsaken His people." Again, he said: "Let the people on both sides keep their self-possession, and just as other clouds have cleared away in due time, so will this; and this great nation shall continue to prosper as heretofore." And, alluding more definitely to his purposes for the future, he declared: "I shall do all that may be in my power to promote a peaceful settlement of all our difficulties. The man does not live who is more devoted to peace than I am—none who would do more to preserve it. But it may be *necessary to put the foot down firmly.*"

A HAND-SHAKING EPISODE.

At the conclusion of Mr. Lincoln's speech at Columbus, a tremendous crowd surged forward to shake his hand. It was something fearful. Says Dr. Holland: "Every man in the crowd was anxious to wrench the hand of Abraham Lincoln.

He finally gave both hands to the work, with great good nature. To quote one of the reports of the occasion: 'People plunged at his arms with frantic enthusiasm, and all the infinite variety of shakes, from the wild and irrepressible pump-handle movement to the dead grip, was executed upon the devoted *dexter* and *sinister* of the President. Some glanced at his face as they grasped his hand; others invoked the blessings of heaven upon him; others affectionately gave him their last gasping assurance of devotion; others, bewildered and furious, with hats crushed over their eyes, seized his hands in a convulsive grasp, and passed on as if they had not the remotest idea who, what, or where they were.' The President at last escaped, and took refuge in the Governor's residence, although he held a levee at the State House in the evening, where, in a more quiet way, he met many prominent citizens.''

AT CINCINNATI.—AN UNCOMFORTABLE RIDE.—A HITHERTO UNPUBLISHED SPEECH BY MR. LINCOLN.

At Cincinnati, where Mr. Lincoln had had so unfavorable an experience a few years before, a magnificent ovation greeted him. The scene is freshly described by one who witnessed it—Hon. William Henry Smith, at that time a resident of Cincinnati. "It was on the 13th of February," writes Mr. Smith, "that Mr. Lincoln reached the Queen City. The day was mild for mid-winter, but the sky was overcast with clouds, emblematic of the gloom that filled the hearts of the unnumbered thousands who thronged the streets and covered the house-tops. Mr. Lincoln rode in an open carriage, standing erect with uncovered head, and steadying himself by holding on to a board fastened to the front part of the vehicle. A more uncomfortable ride than this, over the bouldered streets of Cincinnati, cannot well be imagined. Perhaps a journey over the broken roads of Eastern Russia, in a tarantass, would secure to the traveller as great a degree of discomfort. Mr. Lincoln bore it with characteristic patience. His face was very sad, but he seemed to take a deep interest in everything.

"It was not without due consideration that the President-elect touched on the border of a slave State on his way to the capital. In his speech in reply to the Mayor of Cincinnati, recognizing the fact that among his auditors were thousands of Kentuckians, he addressed them directly, calling them 'Friends,' 'Brethren.' He reminded them that, when speaking in Fifth Street Market square in 1859, he had promised that when the Republicans came into power they would treat the Southern or slave-holding people as Washington, Jefferson, and Madison treated them; to interfere with their institutions in no way; to abide by all and every compromise of the Constitution, and 'to recognize and bear in mind always that you have as good hearts in your bosoms as other people, or as we claim to have, and treat you accordingly.' Then, to emphasize this, he said—in a passage omitted by Mr. Raymond and all other biographers of Lincoln—

'And now, fellow-citizens of Ohio, have you who agree in political sentiment with him who now addresses you, ever entertained other sentiments towards our brethren of Kentucky than those I have expressed to you. [*Loud and repeated cries of 'No!' 'No!'*] If not, then why shall we not, as heretofore, be recognized and acknowledged as brethren again, living in peace and harmony, one with another? [*Cries of 'We will!'*] I take your response as the most reliable evidence that it may be so, along with other evidence, trusting to the good sense of the American people, on all sides of all rivers in America, under the Providence of God, who has never deserted us, that we shall again be brethren, forgetting all parties—ignoring all parties.'

"This statesmanlike expression of conservative opinion alarmed some of the Republicans, who feared that the new President might sell out his party; and steps were taken, later in the day, to remind him of certain principles deemed fundamental by those who had been attracted to the party of Freedom. The sequel will show how this was done, and how successfully Mr. Lincoln met the unexpected attack.

"In the evening, in company with R. H. Stephenson and Edward F. Noyes (afterwards the gallant General), I called at Mr. Lincoln's rooms at the Burnet House to pay my respects. Of those who were present, I recall Richard Smith, Judge Dickson, Flamen Ball (partner of Mr. Chase), Frederick Hassaurek, and Enoch T. Carson, well known Republicans, afterwards conspicuous in the work of saving the Union. Mr. Lincoln had put off the melancholy mood that appeared to control him during the day, and was entertaining those present with genial, even lively, conversation. The pleasant entertainment was interrupted by the announcement that a delegation of German workingmen were about to serenade Mr. Lincoln. Proceeding to the balcony, there were seen the faces of nearly two thousand of the substantial German citizens who had voted for Mr. Lincoln because they believed him to be a stout champion of free labor and free homesteads. The remarks of their spokesman, Frederick Oberkleine, set forth in clear terms what they expected. He said: 'We, the German free workingmen of Cincinnati, avail ourselves of this opportunity to assure you, our chosen Chief Magistrate, of our sincere and heartfelt regard. You earned our votes as the champion of Free Labor and Free Homesteads. Our vanquished opponents have, in recent times, made frequent use of the terms "Workingmen" and "Workingmen's Meetings," in order to create an impression that the mass of workingmen were *in favor of compromises between the interests of free labor and slave labor, by which the victory just won would be turned into a defeat.* This is a despicable device of dishonest men. *We spurn such compromises. We firmly adhere to the principles which directed our votes in your favor. We trust that you, the self-reliant because self-made man, will uphold the Constitution and the laws against secret treachery and avowed treason.* If to this end you should be in need of men, the German free workingmen, with others, will rise as one man at your call, ready to risk their lives in the effort to maintain the victory already won by freedom over slavery.'

"This was bringing the rugged issue boldly to the front, and challenging the President-elect to meet the issue, or risk the loss of the support of an important section of his own party. Oberkleine spoke with great effect, but the remarks were hardly his own. Some abler man had put into his mouth these significant words. Mr. Lincoln replied, very deliberately, but without hesitation, as follows:

"MR. CHAIRMAN:—I thank you, and those you represent, for the compliment paid me by the tender of this address. In so far as there is an allusion to our present national difficulty, and the suggestion of the views of the gentlemen who present this address, I beg you will excuse me from entering particularly upon it. I deem it due to myself and the whole country, in the present extraordinary condition of the country and of public opinion, that I should wait and see the last development of public opinion before I give my views or express myself at the time of the inauguration. I hope at that time to be false to nothing you have been taught to expect of me. [*Cheers.*]

"I agree with you, Mr. Chairman, and with the address of your constituents, in the declaration that workingmen are the basis of all governments. That remark is due to them more than to any other class, for the reason that there are more of them than of any other class. And as your address is presented to me not only on behalf of workingmen, but especially of Germans, I may say a word as to classes. I hold that the value of life is to improve one's condition. Whatever is calculated to advance the condition of the honest, struggling laboring man, so far as my judgment will enable me to judge of a correct thing, I am for that thing.

"An allusion has been made to the Homestead Law. I think it worthy of consideration, and that the wild lands of the country should be distributed so that every man should have the means and opportunity of benefitting his condition. [*Cheers.*] I have said that I do not desire to enter into details, nor will I.

"In regard to Germans and foreigners, I esteem foreigners no better than other people—nor any worse. [*Laughter and cheers.*] They are all of the great family of men, and if there is one shackle upon any of them, it would be far better to lift the load from them than to pile additional loads upon them. [*Cheers.*] And inasmuch as the continent of America is comparatively a new country, and the other countries of the world are old countries, there is more room here, comparatively speaking, than there is elsewhere; and if they can better their condition by leaving their old homes, there is nothing in my heart to forbid them coming, and I bid them all God speed. [*Cheers.*] Again, gentlemen, thanking you for your address, I bid you good-night.'

"If any one had expected to trap Mr. Lincoln into imprudent utterances, or the indulgence of the rhetoric of a demagogue, this admirable reply showed how completely they were disappointed. The preservation of this speech is due to my accidental presence. The visitation of the Germans was not on the programme, and none of the representatives of the press charged with the duty of reporting the events of the day were present. On observing this, I took short-hand notes on the envelope of an old letter loaned me for the occasion by Mr. Stephenson, and afterwards wrote them out. The words of Mr. Lincoln, exactly as spoken, are given above."

AT CLEVELAND.—PERSONAL IMPRESSIONS OF MR. AND MRS.
LINCOLN.

At Cleveland the party remained over for a day, and Mr. Lincoln was greeted with the usual friendly enthusiasm. An immense crowd met him at the depot, and he was escorted to the Weddell House, where a reception was given him in the evening. The Hon. A. G. Riddle, then a resident of Cleveland, and a newly-elected member of the Congress which was to share with Mr. Lincoln the burdens and responsibilities of the Civil War, was present on that occasion, and furnishes some interesting personal recollections of it. "I saw Abraham Lincoln for the first time," writes Mr. Riddle, "at the Weddell House that evening. He stood on the landing-place at the top of a broad stairway, and the crowd approached him from below. This gave him an exaggerated advantage of his six feet four inches of length. The shapelessness of the lathy form, the shock of coarse black hair surmounting the large head, the retreating forehead—these were not apparent where we stood. My heart sprang up to him—the coming man. Of the thousand times I afterward saw him, the first view remains the most distinct impression; and never again to me was he more imposing. As we approached him, some one whispered of me to him; for he took my hand in both his for an instant, and we wheeled into the already crowded rooms. His manner was strongly Western; his speech and pronunciation Southwestern. Wholly without self-consciousness with men, he was constrained and ill at ease, surrounded, as he several times was, by well-dressed ladies. One incident of the evening was a trial. Ab McElrath was in the crowd,—a handsome giant, an Apollo in youth, of about Mr. Lincoln's height. What brought it about, I do not know; but I saw them standing back to back, in a contest of altitude,—Mr. Lincoln and Ab McElrath—the President-elect, the chosen, the nation's leader in the thick-coming darkness, and the tavern-keeper and fox-hunter. The crowd applauded.

"Mr. Lincoln presented me to the gentlemen of his party— Mr. Browning, Mr. Judd, and Mr. Lamon, I remember, as I later became very well acquainted with them; also the rough-looking Colonel Sumner of the army. Mr. Lincoln invited me to accompany him, for at least a day, on his eastward journey. I joined him the next morning at the station. The vivacity of the night before had utterly vanished, and the rudely-sculptured, cliffy face struck me as one of the saddest I had ever seen. The eyes, especially, had a depth of melancholy which I had never seen in eyes before. Some things he wished to know from me, especially regarding Mr. Chase, whom, among others, he had called to Springfield. He asked me no direct questions, but I very soon found myself speaking freely to him, and was able to explain some not well-known features of Ohio politics—and much to his satisfaction, as he let me see. There was then some talk of Mr. Seward, and more of Senator Cameron. All three had been his rivals at Chicago, and were, as I then thought, in his mind as possible Cabinet ministers. Of course, no word was said by him of such an idea in reference to either. Presently he conducted me to Mrs. Lincoln, whom I had not before seen. Presenting me, he returned to the gentlemen of the party, and I saw little more of him, save he once returned to us, before I left the train. Mrs. Lincoln impressed me very favorably, as a woman of spirit, intelligence, and decided opinions, which she put very clearly. Our conversation was mainly of her husband. I remarked that all the likenesses I had ever seen of him did him injustice. This evidently pleased her. I suggested that a full beard from the underlip down (his face was shaven), would relieve and help him very much. This interested her, and we discussed it and the character of his face quite fully. The impression I then formed of this most unfortunate lady was only deepened by the pleasant acquaintance she permitted, down to the time of the national calamity, which unsettled her mind, as I always thought."

THE LITTLE GIRL WHO ADVISED MR. LINCOLN TO RAISE A BEARD.

In the journey through the State of New York, the train was delayed for a short time at a place called Westfield; and Mr. Lincoln was, as usual, called out by the crowd and asked for a speech. In his remarks he alluded humorously to the fact that soon after his election he had received a letter from a little girl in that very town, in which she said that she had seen his picture and thought he would be a better looking man if he would let his beard grow. Then stroking his face, he added, dryly, "I intend to follow her advice." He then said if his little correspondent were present, he would like very much to speak with her. She came forward, and was very pleasantly greeted by Mr. Lincoln.

IN NEW YORK CITY.

Dr. S. Irenæus Prime gives the following description of the New York visit and speech: "The country was at that moment in the first throes of the great rebellion. Millions of hearts were beating anxiously in view of the advent to power of this untried man. Had he been called of God to the throne of power at such a time as this, to be the leader and deliverer of the people? As the carriage in which he sat passed slowly by me on the Fifth avenue, he was looking weary, sad, feeble, and faint. My disappointment was excessive; so great, indeed, as to be almost overwhelming. He did not look to me to be the man for the hour. The next day I was with him and others in the Governor's room in the City Hall, when the Mayor of the city made to Mr. Lincoln an official address. Of this speech I will say nothing; but the reply by Mr. Lincoln was so modest, firm, patriotic, and pertinent, that my fears of the day before began to subside, and I saw in this new man a promise of great things to come. It was not boldness nor dash, nor high-sounding pledges; nor did he, in office, with the mighty armies of a roused nation at his command, ever assume to be more than he promised in that little upper chamber in New York, on his journey to the seat of Government, to take the helm of the ship of state then tossing in the storm.''

PERILS OF THE JOURNEY.—THE PLOT TO ASSASSINATE MR. LINCOLN IN BALTIMORE.

Before the end of the journey was reached, strong fears prevailed in the minds of Mr. Lincoln's friends that an attempt would be made to assassinate him before he should reach Washington. Every precaution was taken to thwart such endeavor; although Mr. Lincoln himself was disturbed by no thought of danger. He had done, he contemplated doing, no wrong, no injustice to any citizen of the United States; why, then, should there be a desire to strike him down? Thus he reasoned; and he was free from any dread of personal peril. But the officials of the railroads over which he was to pass, and his friends in Washington, felt that there was cause for apprehension. It was believed by them that a plot existed for making away with Mr. Lincoln while passing through Baltimore, a city in the heart of a slave State, and rife with the spirit of rebellion. Detectives had been employed to discover the facts in the matter, and their reports served to confirm the most alarming conjectures. A messenger was despatched from Washington to intercept the Presidential party and warn Mr. Lincoln of the impending danger. Dr. Holland states that "the detective and Mr. Lincoln reached Philadelphia nearly at the same time, and there the former submitted to a few of the President's friends the information he had secured. An interview between Mr. Lincoln and the detective was immediately arranged, which took place in the apartments of the former at the Continental Hotel. Mr. Lincoln having heard the officer's statement in detail, then informed him that he had promised to raise the American flag on Independence Hall the following morning —the morning of the anniversary of Washington's birthday— and that he had accepted an invitation to a reception by the Pennsylvania Legislature in the afternoon of the same day. 'Both of these engagements I will keep,' said Mr. Lincoln, *'if it costs me my life.'* For the rest, he authorized the detective to make such arrangements as he thought proper for his safe conduct to Washington."

A CHANGE OF PROGRAMME.

In the meantime, continues Dr. Holland, General Scott and Senator Seward, both of whom were in Washington, learned from independent sources that Mr. Lincoln's life was in danger, and concurred in sending Mr. Frederick W. Seward to Philadelphia, to urge upon him the necessity of proceeding immediately to Washington in a quiet way. The messenger arrived late on Thursday night, after Mr. Lincoln had retired, and requested an audience. Mr. Lincoln's fears had already been aroused, and he was cautious, of course, in the matter of receiving a stranger. But satisfied that the messenger was indeed the son of Mr. Seward, he gave him audience. Nothing needed to be done but to inform him of the plan entered into with the detective, by which the President was to arrive in

Washington early on Saturday morning, in advance of his family and party.

On the morning of the 22d, Mr. Lincoln, as he had promised, attended the flag-raising at Independence Hall in Philadelphia, the historic building in which had been adopted the Declaration of Independence. The occasion was a memorable one, and Mr. Lincoln's address eloquent and impressive. "All the political sentiments I entertain," said he, "have been drawn from the sentiments which were given to the world from this hall." He spoke calmly but firmly of his resolve to stand by the principles of the immortal Declaration and of the Constitution of his country; and, as though conscious of the dangers of his position, he added solemnly: "I have said nothing but what I am willing to live by, *and, if it be the pleasure of Almighty God, to die by.*"

From Philadelphia Mr. Lincoln went immediately to Harrisburg, and attended the reception given him by the Pennsylvania Legislature, in the afternoon of the same day. Then, leaving his hotel in the evening, attended only by Mr. Lamon and the detective (Mr. Allan Pinkerton), he was driven to the depot, where he took the regular train for Washington.

ARRIVAL AT THE CAPITAL.

The train passed through Baltimore in the night, and early the next morning (February 23) reached the capital. Mr. Washburne, who had been notified to be at the depot on the arrival of the train, says: "I planted myself behind one of the great pillars in the old Washington and Baltimore depot, where I could see and not be observed. Presently, the train came rumbling in on time. When it came to a stop I watched with fear and trembling to see the passengers descend. I saw every car emptied, and there was no Mr. Lincoln. I was well-nigh in despair, and when about to leave I saw slowly emerge from the last sleeping-car three persons. I could not mistake the long, lank form of Mr. Lincoln, and my heart bounded with joy and gratitude. He had on a soft low-crowned hat, a muffler around his neck, and a short bob-tailed overcoat. Any one who knew him at that time could not have failed to recognize him at once; but I must confess he looked more like a well-to-do farmer from one of the back towns of Jo Daviess county, coming to Washington to see the city, take out his land warrant and get the patent for his farm, than the President of the United States. The only persons that accompanied Mr. Lincoln were Pinkerton, the well-known detective, recently deceased, and Ward H. Lamon. When they were fairly on the platform, and a short distance from the car, I stepped forward and accosted the President: 'How are you, Lincoln?' At this unexpected and rather familiar salutation the gentlemen were apparently somewhat startled; but Mr. Lincoln, who had recognized me, relieved them at once by remarking in his peculiar voice: 'This is only Washburne!' Then we all exchanged congratulations, and walked out to the front of the depot, where I had a carriage in waiting. Entering the carriage (all four of us), we drove rapidly to Willard's Hotel, entering on Fourteenth street, before it was fairly daylight.''

THE DANGERS AT BALTIMORE NOT IMAGINARY.

General Stone, who was in command at Washington at that time, states that both General Scott and himself "considered it almost a certainty that Mr. Lincoln could not pass through Baltimore alive on the day fixed," and adds: "I recommended that Mr. Lincoln should be officially warned; and suggested that it would be best that he should take the train that evening from Philadelphia, and so reach Washington early the next day. Gen. Scott directed me to see Mr. Seward, to whom he wrote a few lines, which he handed me. I did not succeed in finding Mr. Seward until past noon. I handed him the General's note. He listened attentively to what I said, and asked me to write down my information and suggestions. Then, taking the paper I had written, he hastily left. The note I wrote was what Mr. Frederick Seward carried to Mr. Lincoln in Philadelphia. Mr. Lincoln has stated that it was *this note* which induced him to change his journey as he did. *The stories of disguises are all nonsense.* Mr. Lincoln merely took the sleeping-car in the night train.''

There is little doubt that the fears of Mr. Lincoln's friends, regarding his passage through Baltimore, were well grounded ; and that, but for the timely warnings and precautions, the assassination of April, 1865, might have taken place in February, 1861. Who can contemplate that dreadful probability without a shudder, in the light of subsequent history?

PART III.

LINCOLN AS PRESIDENT.

CHAPTER. I.

FIRST DAYS IN WASHINGTON.——MEETING PUBLIC MEN AND DISCUSSING PUBLIC AFFAIRS.——"I'LL TRY TO STEER HER THROUGH."——SPEECH TO THE MAYOR AND COUNCIL.——A "CLOSE CALL" FOR THE INAUGURAL MESSAGE.——THE INAUGURATION.——THE SCENE DESCRIBED.——THE INAUGURAL ADDRESS. ——A NEW ERA BEGUN.——LINCOLN IN THE WHITE HOUSE.——THE FIRST CABINET.——THE PRESIDENT AND THE OFFICE-SEEKERS.——SOUTHERN PREJUDICE AGAINST MR. LINCOLN.——GENERAL SHERMAN WORRIED, BUT MR. LINCOLN THINKS "WE'LL MANAGE TO KEEP HOUSE."——THE PRESIDENT'S RECEPTION ROOM.——IMPRESSIONS OF THE NEW PRESIDENT.—— GUARDING THE WHITE HOUSE.

THE week following Mr. Lincoln's arrival in Washington, and preceding his inauguration, was one of incessant activity for him. From almost the first moment of his arrival in the capital he was constantly engrossed, either in preparations for his inauguration and the official responsibilities which would immediately follow that event, or in receiving the distinguished callers who hastened to meet him, and in discussing with them the grave aspect of political affairs. Without rest or opportunity to survey the field that lay before him, or any preparations, save such as the resources of his own strong character might afford him, he was plunged instantly into the great political maelstrom in which he was to remain for four long years, and whose wild vortex might well have bewildered an eye less sure, a will less resolute, and a brain less cool than his.

MEETING PUBLIC MEN AND DISCUSSING PUBLIC AFFAIRS.

"Mr. Lincoln's headquarters," says Congressman Riddle of Ohio, "were at Willard's Hotel and the few days before the inauguration were a continuous reception in the broad corridor of the second floor, near the stairway. I remember a notable morning, when I there presented a half-dozen gentlemen. Soon after, the majestic General Scott, in full dress, sword, plumes, and bullion, came to pay his respects to the incoming President. The scene was impressive. By the unknown law that ruled his spirits, Mr. Lincoln was at his best, complete master of himself, of all who came within the magic of his presence. Never was he happier, speaking most of the time, flashing with anecdote and story. That time now seems as remote as things of a hundred years ago. The war antiquated all that went before. The Washington, the men, the spirit of that now ancient time, have faded, past all power to recall and reproduce them to the present apprehension. The real Washington was as essentially Southern as Richmond or Baltimore. 'Lincoln and his vandals,' fresh from the North and West, were thronging the wide, squat, unattractive city, from which the bolder and braver rebel element had not yet departed.''

Dr. George B. Loring, of Massachusetts, who was one of the first to meet Mr. Lincoln after his arrival in Washington, says: ''I saw him on his arrival, and when he made his first appearance in a public place. I was standing in the upper hall of Willard's Hotel, conversing with a friend and listening to the confused talk of the crowded drawing-room adjoining. As we stood there, a tall and awkward form appeared above the stairs, especially conspicuous, as it came into view, for a new and stylish hat. It was evidently President Lincoln, whom neither of us had seen before; and as soon as his presence was known, the hall was thronged from the drawing-rooms. He seemed somewhat startled by the crowd, did not remove his hat, wended his way somewhat rapidly and with mere passing recognition, and took shelter in his room. There was a manifest attempt on his part to brace himself up to the occasion, and an evident consciousness that his situation was by no means usual with incoming Presidents. When he had reached his room and the crowd had dispersed, my friend and myself, who had opposed his election, called upon him to pay our respects. He received us with great cordiality, spoke freely of the difficulties by which he was surrounded, and referred to the support he had received in Massachusetts with evident satisfaction. 'I like your man Banks,' said he, 'and have tried to find a place for him in my Cabinet, but I am afraid I shall not quite fetch it.' He bore the marks of anxiety in his countenance, which, in its expression of patience, determination, resolve, and deep innate modesty, was extremely touching."

"I'LL TRY TO STEER HER THROUGH."

General John A. Logan relates that on the morning of President Lincoln's arrival in Washington (February 23), he called upon him at Willard's Hotel, in company with Mr. Lovejoy, of Illinois; and that both gentlemen urged the necessity of a firm and vigorous policy. The President listened to the end, then said, very seriously but cheerfully, "As the country has placed me at the helm of the ship, *I'll try to steer her through.*"

SPEECH TO THE MAYOR AND COUNCIL.

On the 27th of February, the Mayor and Common Council of Washington waited upon Mr. Lincoln, and extended to him a formal welcome to the city. In his brief reply Mr. Lincoln expressed the kindly and conciliatory sentiments with which he regarded the citizens of the District of Columbia and of the South:

"I think very much of the ill-feeling that has existed, and still exists, between the people in the sections from which I came and the people here, is dependent upon a misunderstanding of one another. I therefore avail myself of this opportunity to assure you, Mr. Mayor, and all the gentlemen present, that I have not now, and never have had, any other than as kindly feelings towards you as the people of my own section. I have not now, and never have had, any disposition to treat you in any respect otherwise than as my own neighbors. I have not now any purpose to withhold from you any of the benefits of the Constitution, under any circumstances, that I would not feel myself constrained to withhold from my own neighbors; and I hope, in a word, that when we shall become better acquainted—and I say it with great confidence—we shall like each other the more. I have reached this city of Washington under circumstances considerably differing from those under which any other man has ever reached it. I hope that, if things shall go along as prosperously as I believe we all desire they may, I may have it in my power to remove something of this misunderstanding; that I may be enabled to convince you, and the people of your section of the country, that we regard you as in all things our equals, and in all things entitled to the same respect and the same treatment that we claim for ourselves; that we are in no wise disposed, if it were in our power, to oppress you, to deprive you of any of your rights under the Constitution of the United States, or even narrowly to split hairs with you in regard to these rights, but are determined to give you, as far as lies in our hands, all your rights under the Constitution—not grudgingly, but fully and fairly. I hope that, by thus dealing with you, we shall become better acquainted, and be better friends.''

A ''CLOSE CALL'' FOR THE INAUGURAL MESSAGE.

Mr. Lincoln had prepared his inaugural message with great care before leaving Springfield, and placed it in a ''gripsack'' for transportation to Washington. An odd incident, by which the message came near being lost on the journey, was afterwards related by Mr. Lincoln to a friend. ''When we reached Harrisburg,'' said Mr. Lincoln, ''and had washed up, I asked Bob where the message was, and was taken aback by his confession that, in the excitement caused by the enthusiastic reception, he believed he had let a waiter have the gripsack. My heart went up into my mouth, and I started down stairs, where I was told that if a waiter had taken the gripsack, I should probably find it in the baggage room. Going there I saw a large pile of gripsacks and other baggage, and thought that I discovered mine. My key fitted it, but on opening there was nothing inside but a few paper collars and a flask of whiskey. A few moments afterward I came across my gripsack, with the document in it all right.''

LINCOLN'S INAUGURATION.

In describing the ceremonies attending the installation of Mr. Lincoln into the highest office in the gift of the Republic, Dr. Holland says: "The morning of the fourth of March broke beautifully clear, and it found General Scott and the Washington police in readiness for the day. The friends of Mr. Lincoln had gathered in from far and near, determined that he should be inaugurated. In the hearts of the surging crowds there was anxiety; but outside, all looked as usual on such occasions, with the single exception of an extraordinary display of soldiers. The public buildings, the schools, and most of the places of business, were closed during the day, and the stars and stripes were floating from every flag-staff. There was a great desire to hear Mr. Lincoln's inaugural; and, at an early hour, Pennsylvania Avenue was full of people, wending their way to the east front of the Capitol, from which it was to be delivered. At five minutes before twelve o'clock, Vice-president Breckenridge and Senator Foote escorted Mr. Hamlin, the Vice-president-elect, into the Senate Chamber, and gave him a seat at the left of the chair. At twelve o'clock, Mr. Breckenridge announced the Senate adjourned without day, and then conducted Mr. Hamlin to the seat he had vacated. At this moment, the foreign diplomats, of whom there was a very large and brilliant representation, entered the chamber, and took the seats assigned to them. At a quarter before one o'clock, the Judges of the Supreme Court entered, with the venerable Chief Justice Taney at their head, each exchanging salutes with the new Vice-president, as they took their seats. At a quarter past one o'clock, an unusual stir and excitement announced the coming of the most important personage of the occasion. It was a relief to many to know that he was safely within the building; and those who were assembled in the hall regarded with the profoundest interest the entrance of President Buchanan and the President-elect—the outgoing and the incoming man. A procession was then formed which passed to the platform erected for the ceremonies of the occasion, in the following order: Marshal of the District of Columbia, Judges of the Supreme Court and Sergeant-at-Arms, Senate Committee of Arrangements, President of the United States and President-elect, Vice-president, Clerk of the Senate, Senators, Diplomatic Corps, heads of Departments, Governors of States, and such others as were in the chamber.   On arriving at the platform, Senator Baker, of Oregon, one of Mr. Lincoln's old friends and political rivals in Illinois, introduced Mr. Lincoln to the assembly.   There was not a very hearty welcome given to the President as he stepped forward to read his inaugural.   His enemies were too many, and his friends too much in fear of exasperating them. The representative of American loyalty carried his burden alone.   The inaugural was listened to with profound attention, every passage being vociferously cheered which contained any allusion to the Union ; and none listening more carefully than Mr. Buchanan and Judge Taney, the latter of whom, with much agitation, administered the oath of office to Mr. Lincoln when his address was ended.''

THE SCENE DESCRIBED.

An eye-witness of the impressive scene has described its principal incidents in the following graphic paragraphs: ''Near noon I found myself a member of the motley crowd gathered around the side entrance to Willard's Hotel.   Soon an open barouche drove up, and the only occupant stepped out.   A large, heavy, awkward-moving man, far advanced in years, short and thin gray hair, full face, plentifully seamed and wrinkled, head curiously inclined to the left shoulder, a low-crowned, broad-brimmed silk hat, an immense white cravat like a poultice, thrusting the old-fashioned standing collar up to the ears, dressed in black throughout, with swallow-tail coat not of the newest style.   It was President Buchanan, calling to take his successor to the Capitol.   In a few minutes he reappeared, with Mr. Lincoln on his arm; the two took seats side by side, and the carriage rolled away, followed by a rather disorderly and certainly not very imposing procession. I had ample time to walk to the Capitol, and no difficulty in securing a place where everything could be seen and heard to the best advantage. The attendance at the inauguration was, they told me, unusually small; many being kept away by anticipated disturbance, as it had been rumored—truly, too— that General Scott himself was fearful of an outbreak, and had made all possible military preparations to meet the emergency. A square platform had been built out from the steps to the eastern portico, with benches for distinguished spectators on three sides. Douglas, the only one I recognized, sat at the extreme end of the seat on the right of the narrow passage leading from the steps. There was no delay, and the gaunt form of the President-elect was soon visible, slowly making his way to the front. To me, at least, he was completely metamorphosed—partly by his own fault, and partly through the efforts of injudicious friends and ambitious tailors. He was raising (to gratify a very young lady, it is said,) a crop of whiskers, of the blacking-brush variety, coarse, stiff and ungraceful; and in so doing spoiled, or at least seriously impaired, a face which, though never handsome, had, in its original state, a peculiar power and pathos. On the present occasion the whiskers were reinforced by brand-new clothes from top to toe; black dress coat, instead of the usual frock; black cloth or satin vest, black pantaloons, and a glossy hat evidently just out of the box. To cap the climax of novelty, he carried a huge ebony cane, with a gold head the size of an egg. In these, to him, strange habiliments, he looked so miserably uncomfortable that I could not help pitying him. Reaching the platform, his discomfort was visibly increased by not knowing what to do with hat and cane; and so he stood there, the target for ten thousand eyes, holding cane in one hand and hat in the other, the very picture of helpless embarrassment. After some hesitation, he pushed the cane into a corner of the railing, but could not find a place for the hat, except on the floor, where I could see he did not like to risk it. Douglas, who fully took in the situation, came to the rescue of his old friend and rival, and held the precious hat until the owner needed it again; a service which, if predicted two years before, would probably have astonished him. The oath of office was administered by Chief Justice Taney, whose black robes, attenuated figure and cadaverous countenance reminded me of a galvanized corpse. Then the President came forward, and read his inaugural address in a clear and distinct voice. It was attentively listened to by all, but the closest listener was Douglas, who leaned forward as if to catch every word, nodding his head emphatically at those passages which most pleased him. There was some applause, not very much nor very enthusiastic. I must not forget to mention the presence of a Mephistopheles in the person of Senator Wigfall, of Texas, who stood with folded arms leaning against the doorway of the Capital looking, down upon the crowd and the ceremony with a contemptuous air, which sufficiently indicated his opinion of the whole performance. To him, the Southern Confederacy was already an accomplished fact. He lived to see it the saddest of fictions.''

"Under the shadow of the great Eastern Portico of the Capitol at Washington,'' says General John A. Logan, "with the retiring President and Cabinet, the Supreme Court Justices, the Foreign Diplomatic Corps, and hundreds of Senators, Representatives, and other distinguished persons, filling the great platform on either side and behind them—Abraham Lincoln stood bareheaded before full thirty thousand people, upon whose uplifted faces the unveiled glory of the mild Spring sun now shone—stood reverently before that far greater and mightier Presence termed by himself, 'My rightful masters, the American People'—and pleaded in a manly, earnest and affectionate strain with 'such as were dissatisfied' to listen to the 'better angels' of their nature. 'Temperate, reasonable, kindly persuasive'—it seems strange that Mr. Lincoln's inaugural address did not disarm at least the personal resentment of the South toward him, and sufficiently strengthen Union-loving people there against the red-hot Secessionists, to put the 'breaks' down on rebellion."

THE INAUGURAL ADDRESS.

The inaugural address was devoted exclusively to the great and absorbing topic of the hour—the attempt of the Southern States to withdraw from the Union and erect an independent republic. The calm, firm, moderate, judicious spirit which pervaded Mr. Lincoln's address is apparent in the following quotations, which contain some of its best passages:

"*Fellow-Citizens of the United States:*—In compliance with a custom as old as the Government itself, I appear before you to address you briefly, and to take in your presence the oath prescribed by the Constitution of the United States to be taken by the President 'before he enters on the execution of his office.' * * * Apprehension seems to exist among the people of the Southern States, that by the accession of a Republican Administration their property and their peace and personal security are to be endangered. There has never been any reasonable cause for such apprehension Indeed, the most ample evidence to the contrary has all the while existed and been open to their inspection. It is found in nearly all the published speeches of him who now addresses you. I do but quote from one of those speeches when I declare that 'I have no purpose, directly or indirectly, to interfere with the institution of slavery in the States where it exists. I believe I have no lawful right to do so, and I have no inclination to do so.' Those who nominated and elected me, did so with full knowledge that I had made this and many similar declarations, and had never recanted them. * * * * I now reiterate these sentiments; and, in doing so, I only press upon the public attention the most conclusive evidence of which the case is susceptible, that the property, peace, and security of no section are to be in anywise endangered by the now incoming Administration. I add, too, that all the protection which, consistently with the Constitution and the laws, can be given, will be cheerfully given to all the States, when lawfully demanded, for whatever cause—as cheerfully to one section as to another. * * * * * * I hold that, in contemplation of universal law, and of the Constitution, *the Union of these States is perpetual.* Perpetuity is implied, if not expressed, in the fundamental law of all National Governments. It is safe to assert that no Government proper ever had a provision in its organic law for its own termination. Continue to execute all the express provisions of our National Constitution, and the Union will endure forever. * * * I, therefore, consider that, in view of the Constitution and the laws, the Union is unbroken, and to the extent of my ability I shall take care, as the Constitution itself expressly enjoins upon me, that the laws of the Union be faithfully executed in all. the States. Doing this I deem to be only a simple duty on my part; and I shall perform it, so far as practicable, unless my rightful masters, the American people, shall withhold the requisite means, or, in some authoritative manner, direct the contrary. I trust this will not be regarded as a menace, but only as the declared purpose of the Union that it will constitutionally defend and maintain itself. In doing this, there need be no bloodshed or violence; and there shall be none, unless it be forced upon the national authority. The power confided to me will be used to hold, occupy, and possess the property and places belonging to the Government, and to collect the duties and imposts; but beyond what may be but necessary for these objects, there will be no invasion, no using of force against or among the people anywhere. * * * * * * Physically speaking, we cannot separate. We cannot remove our respective sections from each other, nor build an impassable wall between them. A husband and wife may be divorced, and go out of the presence and beyond the reach of each other; but the different parts of our country cannot do this. They cannot but remain face to face; and intercourse, either amicable or hostile, must continue between them. It is impossible, then, to make that intercourse more advantageous or more satisfactory after separation than before. Can aliens make treaties easier than friends can make law? Can treaties be more faithfully enforced between aliens than laws can among friends? Suppose you go to war, you cannot fight always; and when, after much loss on both sides and no gain on either, you cease fighting, the identical old questions, as to terms of intercourse, are again upon you. * * * This country, with its institutions, belongs to the people who inhabit it. Whenever they shall grow weary of the existing Government, they can exercise their constitutional right of amending it, or their revolutionary right to dismember or overthrow it. I cannot be ignorant of the fact that many worthy and patriotic citizens are desirous of having the National Constitution amended. While I make no recommendation of amendments, I fully recognize the rightful authority of the people over the whole subject, to be exercised in either of the modes prescribed in the instrument itself; and I should, under existing circumstances, favor rather than oppose a fair opportunity being afforded the people to act upon it. * * * * The Chief Magistrate derives all his authority from the people, and they have conferred none upon him to fix terms for the separation of the States. The people themselves can do this also, if they choose; but the Executive, as such, has nothing to do with it. His duty is to administer the present Government as it came to his hands, and to transmit it, unimpaired by him, to his successor. * * * * * By the frame of the Government under which we live, the same people have wisely given their public servants but little power for mischief; and have, with equal wisdom, provided for the return of that little to their own hands at very short intervals. While the people retain their virtue and vigilance, no administration, by any extreme of wickedness or folly, can very seriously injure the Government in the short space of four years.

"My countrymen, one and all, think calmly and well upon this whole subject. Nothing valuable can be lost by taking time. If there be an object to hurry any of you in hot haste to a step which you would never take deliberately, that object will be frustrated by taking time; but no good can be frustrated by it. Such of you as are now dissatisfied still have the old Constitution unimpaired, and, on the sensitive point, the laws of your own framing under it; while the new administration will have no immediate power, if it would, to change either. If it were admitted that you who are dissatisfied hold the right side in the dispute, there still is no single good reason for precipitate action. Intelligence, patriotism, Christianity, and a firm reliance on Him who has never yet forsaken this favored land, are still competent to adjust, in the best way, all our present difficulty.

"In your hands, my dissatisfied fellow-countrymen, and not in mine, is the momentous issue of civil war. The Government will not assail you. You can have no conflict without being yourselves the aggressors. You have no oath registered in heaven to destroy the Government; while I shall have the most solemn one to 'preserve, protect and defend' it.

"I am loth to close. We are not enemies, but friends. We must not be enemies. Though passion may have strained, it must not break, our bonds of affection. The mystic chords of memory, stretching from every battlefield and patriot grave to every living heart and hearthstone all over this broad land, will yet swell the chorus of the Union, when again touched, as surely they will be, by the better angels of our nature."

A NEW ERA BEGUN.

At the close of the address, which was delivered with the utmost earnestness and solemnity, Mr. Lincoln, "with reverent look and impressive emphasis, repeated the oath to preserve, protect and defend the Constitution of his country. Douglas, who knew from his personal familiarity with the conspirators, better than Lincoln, the dangers that surrounded and were before him, who knew the conspirators and their plots, with patriotic magnanimity then grasped the hand of the President, gracefully extended his congratulations, and the assurance that in the dark future he would stand by him, and give to him his utmost aid in upholding the Constitution and enforcing the laws of his country."

"At the inauguration," says Congressman Riddle, "I stood within a yard of Mr. Lincoln when he pronounced his famous address. How full of life and power it then was, with the unction of his utterance! Surely, we thought, the South, which rejected the concessions of Congress, would accept him. How dry and quaint, yet ingenious, much of that inaugural appears to me now, when the life and soul seems to have gone out of it! A sad thing—a spectre of the day—will forever haunt my memory: Poor old President Buchanan, short, stout, pale, white-haired, yet bearing himself resolutely throughout, linked by the arm to the new President, into whom from himself was passing the qualifying unction of the Constitution, jostled hither and thither, as already out of men's sight, yet bravely maintaining the shadow of dignity and place. How glad he must have been to take leave of his successor at the White House, when all was ended!"

LINCOLN IN THE WHITE HOUSE.

The formalities of the inauguration concluded, Mr. Lincoln passed back through the Senate Chamber, and, again escorted by Mr. Buchanan, was conducted to the White House, where the cares and vicissitudes of his position immediately descended upon him.

"Strange indeed," says General Logan, "must have been the thoughts that crowded through the brain and oppressed the heart of Abraham Lincoln that night—his first at the White House. The City of Washington swarmed with rebels and rebel sympathizers, and all the departments of Government were honeycombed with treason and shadowed with treachery and espionage. Every step proposed or contemplated by the Government would be known to the so-called Government of the Confederate States almost as soon as thought of. All means to thwart and delay the carrying out of the Government's purposes that the excuses of routine and red tape admitted of would be used by the traitors within the camp to aid the traitors without.

"No one knew all this better than Mr. Lincoln. With no army, no navy, not even a revenue cutter left—with forts and arsenals, ammunition and arms in possession of the rebels, with no money in the National Treasury, and the National credit blasted—the position must, even to his hopeful nature, have seemed at this time desperate. To be sure, despite threats, neither few nor secret, which had been made, that he should not live to be inaugurated, he had passed the first critical point—he had taken the inaugural oath, and was now duly installed in the White House. That was something, of course, to be profoundly thankful for. But the matter regarded by him of larger moment—the safety of the Union—how about that?

"How the great, and just, and kindly brain, in the dim shadows of that awful first night at the White House, must have searched up and down and along the labyrinths of history and 'corridors of time' everywhere in the past, for any analogy or excuse for the madness of this secession movement —and searched in vain. Surely, surely, thus ran his thoughts, when the brave, and gallant, and generous people of that section came to read his message of peace and good will, they must see the suicidal folly of their course! Surely their hearts must be touched and the mists of prejudice dissolved, so that reason would resume her sway, and reconciliation follow! A

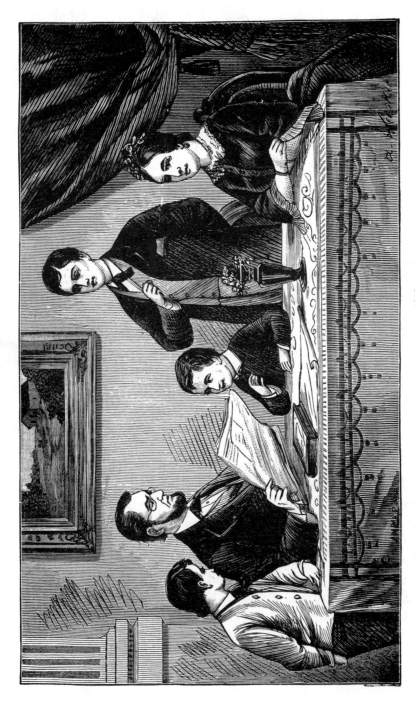

THE LINCOLN FAMILY AT HOME IN THE WHITE HOUSE IN 1861.—THE PRESIDENT AND MRS. LINCOLN, ROBERT, TAD AND WILLIE.

little more time for reflection would yet make all things right. The young men of the South, fired by the Southern leaders' false appeals, must soon return to reason. The prairie fire is terrible while it sweeps along, but it soon burns out. When the young men face the emblem of their Nation's glory— the flag of the land of their birth—*then* will come the reaction, and their false leaders will be hurled from place and power, and might will again be right. Yea, when it comes to firing on the old, old flag, they will not, cannot do it! Between the compromise within their reach, and such sacrilege as this, they cannot waver long.

"So, doubtless, all the long night, whether waking or sleeping, the mind of this true-hearted son of the West throbbed with the mighty weight of the problem entrusted to him for solution and the vast responsibilities which he had just assumed toward his fellow men, his Nation and his God. And when, at last, the long lean frame was thrown upon the couch, and 'tired nature's sweet restorer' held him briefly in her arms, the smile of hopefulness on the wan cheek told that, despite all the terrible difficulties of the situation, the sleeper was sustained by a strong and cheerful belief in the Providence of God, the patriotism of the people, and the efficacy of his inaugural peace-offering to the South."

THE FIRST CABINET.

The President's first official act was the announcement of his Cabinet, which was composed of the following persons: William H. Seward, Secretary of State; Simon Cameron, Secretary of War; Salmon P. Chase, Secretary of the Treasury; Gideon Welles, Secretary of the Navy; Caleb B. Smith, Secretary of the Interior; Montgomery Blair, Postmaster General; and Edward Bates, Attorney General. Mr. Lincoln had selected these counsellers with grave deliberation. In reply to the remonstrances urged, for political reasons, against the appointment of one or two of them, he had said: "Gentlemen, the times are too grave and perilous for ambitious schemes and personal rivalries. I need the aid of all of these men. They enjoy the confidence of their several States and sections, and they will strengthen the administration."

On another occasion he remarked: "It will require the utmost skill, influence, and sagacity of all of us, to save the country; let us forget ourselves, and join hands like brothers to save the Republic. If we succeed, there will be glory enough for all."

THE PRESIDENT AND THE OFFICE-SEEKERS.

The first weeks of Mr. Lincoln's residence in the Executive Mansion were occupied with the arduous work of selecting loyal and capable men for the responsible positions in the Government service. The departments at Washington were filled with traitors, who used the means and influence pertaining to their places in aid of the rebellious States. It was of vital importance that these faithless officials should be removed at the earliest moment, and their positions filled with men of tried integrity. Mr. Lincoln desired to appoint for the purpose stanch, competent, and trustworthy citizens, regardless of party distinctions. But the labor involved in this onerous duty was enormous and exhausting. There was a multitude of vacant places, there were difficult questions to be considered in a majority of cases, and there was a host of applicants and their friends to be satisfied. Mr. Charles A. Dana relates a circumstance which hints at the troubles encountered by Mr. Lincoln in this province of his Presidential duties. "The first time I saw Mr. Lincoln," says Mr. Dana, "was shortly after his inauguration. He had appointed Mr. Seward to be his Secretary of State, and some of the Republican leaders of New York, who had been instrumental in preventing Mr. Seward's nomination to the Presidency and in securing that of Mr. Lincoln, had begun to fear that they would be left out in the cold in the distribution of the offices. Accordingly several of them determined to go to Washington, and I was asked to go with them. We all went up to the

White House together, except Mr. Stanton, who stayed away because he was himself an applicant for office. Mr. Lincoln received us in the large room upstairs in the east wing of the White House, where the President had his working office, and stood up while General Wadsworth, who was our principal spokesman, and Mr. Opdyke, stated what was desired. After the interview was begun, a big Indianian, who was a messenger in attendance in the White House, came into the room and said to the President: 'She wants you.' 'Yes, yes,' said Mr. Lincoln, without stirring. Soon afterward the messenger returned again, exclaiming, 'I say she wants you.' The President was evidently annoyed, but, instead of going out after the messenger, he remarked to us: 'One side shall not gobble up everything. Make out a list of the places and men you want, and I will endeavor to apply the rule of give and take.' General Wadsworth answered: 'Our party will not be able to remain in Washington, but we will leave such a list with Mr. Carroll, and whatever he agrees to will be agreeable to us.' Mr. Lincoln continued, 'Let Mr. Carroll come in to-morrow, and we will see what can be done.'"

SOUTHERN PREJUDICE AGAINST MR. LINCOLN.

Mr. Lincoln was regarded with violent animosity by all persons in sympathy with the peculiar prejudices of the slave States. The inhabitants of the District of Columbia looked upon him with especial dislike. He was to them an odious embodiment of the abhorred principles of Abolitionism. As an illustration of this bitter feeling, Mr. Arnold narrates the folowing anecdote: "A distinguished South Carolina lady—one of the Howards—the widow of a Northern scholar, called upon him out of curiosity. She was very proud and aristocratic, and was curious to see a man who had been represented to her as a monster, a mixture of the ape and the tiger. She was shown into the room where were Mr. Lincoln, and Senators Seward, Hale, Chase, and other prominent members of Congress. As Mr. Seward, whom she knew, presented her to the President, she hissed in his ear: 'I am a South Carolinian.' Instantly reading her character, he turned and addressed her with the greatest courtesy, and dignified and gentlemanly politeness. After listening a few moments, astonished to find him so different from what he had been described to her, she said: 'Why, Mr. Lincoln, you look, act, and speak like a kind, good-hearted, generous man.' 'And did you expect to meet a savage?' said he. 'Certainly I did, or even something worse,' replied she. 'I am glad I have met you,' she continued, 'and now the best way to preserve peace, is for you to go to Charleston, and show the people what you are, and tell them you have no intention of injuring them.' Returning home, she found a party of secessionists, and on entering the room she exclaimed: 'I have seen him! I have seen him!' 'Who?' they inquired. 'That terrible monster, Lincoln, and I found him a gentleman, and I am going to his first levee after his inauguration.' At his first reception, this tall daughter of South Carolina, dressing herself in black velvet, with two long white plumes in her hair, repaired to the White House. She was nearly six feet high, with black eyes, and black hair, and, in her velvet and white feathers, she was a very striking and majestic figure. As she approached, the President recognized her immediately. 'Here I am again,' said she, 'that South Carolinian.' 'I am glad to see you,' replied he, 'and I assure you that the first object of my heart is to preserve peace, and I wish that not only you but every son and daughter of South Carolina were here, that I might tell them so.' Mr. Cameron, Secretary of War, came up, and after some remarks, he said: 'South Carolina (which had already seceded), South Carolina is the prodigal son.' 'Ah! Mr. Secretary,' said she, 'if South Carolina is the prodigal son, Uncle Sam, our father, ought to divide the inheritance, and let her go; but they say you are going to make war upon us, is it so?' 'Oh! come back,' said he, 'tell South Carolina to come back now, and we will kill the fatted calf.' ''

GENERAL SHERMAN WORRIED, BUT MR. LINCOLN THINKS "WE'LL MANAGE TO KEEP HOUSE."

"One day," says General Sherman, "my brother, Senator Sherman, took me with him to see Mr. Lincoln. We found the room full of people, and Mr. Lincoln sat at the end of a table, talking with three or four gentlemen, who soon left. John walked up, shook hands, and took a chair near him, holding in his hand some papers referring to minor appointments in the State of Ohio, which formed the subject of conversation. Mr. Lincoln took the papers, said he would refer them to the proper heads of departments, and would be glad to make the appointments asked for, if not already promised. John then turned to me, and said, 'Mr. President, this is my brother, Colonel Sherman, who is just up from Louisiana; he may give you some information you want.' 'Ah!' said Mr. Lincoln, 'how are they getting along down there?' I said, 'They think they are getting along swimmingly—they are preparing for war.' 'Oh, well!' said he, 'I guess we'll manage to keep house.' I was silenced, said no more to him, and we soon left. I was sadly disappointed, and remember that I broke out on John, cursing the politicians generally, saying, 'You have got things in a —— of a fix, and you may get them out as best you can,' adding that the country was sleeping on a volcano that might burst forth at any minute, but that I was going to St. Louis, to take care of my family, and would have no more to do with it. John begged me to be more patient, but I said I would not; that I had no time to wait, that I was off for St. Louis; and off I went."

THE PRESIDENT'S RECEPTION ROOM.

The apartment which Mr. Lincoln used as an office in which to transact daily business and to receive informal visits, was on the second floor of the White House. Its simple equipments are thus described by Mr. Arnold: "It was about twenty-five by forty feet in size. In the center, on the west, was a large white marble fire-place, with big old-fashioned brass andirons, and a large and high brass fender. A wood fire was burning in cool weather. The large windows opened on the beautiful lawn to the south, with a view of the unfinished Washington Monument, the Smithsonian Institute, the Potomac, Alexandria, and down the river towards Mt. Vernon. Across the Potomac were Arlington Heights, and Arlington House, late the residence of Robert E. Lee. On the hills around, during nearly all of his administration, were the white tents of soldiers, and field fortifications and camps, and in every direction could be seen the brilliant colors of the national flag. The furniture of this room consisted of a large oak table covered with cloth, extending north and south, and it was around this table that the Cabinet sat when it held its meetings. Near the end of the table, and between the windows, was another table, on the west side of which the President sat in a large arm chair, and at this table he wrote. A tall desk with pigeon-holes for papers stood against the south wall. The only books usually found in this room were the Bible, the United States Statutes, and a copy of Shakespeare. There were a few chairs, and two plain hair-covered sofas. There were two or three map frames, from which hung military maps on which the position and movements of the armies were traced. There was an old and discolored engraving of General Jackson on the mantel, and a later photograph of John Bright. Doors opened into this room from the room of the Secretary, and from the outside hall running east and west across the House. A bell cord within reach of his hand extended to the Secretary's office. A messenger stood at the door opening from the hall, who took in the cards and names of visitors. Here, in this plain room, Mr. Lincoln spent most of his time while President. Here he received every one, from the Chief Justice and Lieutenant-General to the private soldier and humblest citizen. Custom had fixed certain rules of precedence, and the order in which officials should be received. Members of the Cabinet and the high officers of the army and navy were generally promptly admitted. Senators and members of Congress were received in the order of their arrival. Sometimes there would be a crowd of Senators and members of Congress waiting their turn. While thus waiting, the loud, ringing laugh of Mr. Lincoln—in which he would be joined by those *inside*, but which was rather provoking to those *outside*—would be heard by the waiting and impatient crowd. Here, day after day, often from early morning to late at night, Lincoln sat, listened, talked, and decided. He was patient, just, considerate, and hopeful. The people came to him as to a father. He saw every one, and many wasted his precious time. Governors, Senators, Congressmen, officers, clergymen, bankers, merchants— all classes approached him with familiarity. This incessant labor, the study of the great problems he had to decide, the worry of constant importunity, the quarrels of officers of the army, the care, anxiety, and responsibility of his position, wore upon his vigorous frame.''

Mr. Ben. Perley Poore states that ''the White House, while Mr. Lincoln occupied it, was a fertile field for news, which he was always ready to give those correspondents in whom he had confidence, but the surveillance of the press—first by Secretary Seward, and then by Secretary Stanton—was as annoying as it was inefficient. * * * Often when Mr. Lincoln was engaged, correspondents would send in their cards, bearing requests for some desired item of news, or for the verification of some rumor. He would either come out and give the coveted information, or he would write it on the back of the card, and send it to the owner. He wrote a legible hand, slowly and laboriously perfecting his sentences before he placed them on paper. The long epistles that he wrote to his generals he copied himself, not wishing any one else to see them, and these copies were kept in pigeon-holes for reference. * * * * Mr. Lincoln used to wear at the White House in the morning, and after dinner, a long-skirted faded dressing-gown, belted around his waist, and slippers. His favorite attitude when listening—and he was a good listener—was to lean forward, and clasp his left knee with both hands, as if fondling it, and his face would then wear a sad, wearied look. But when the time came for him to give an opinion on what he had heard, or to tell a story which something said 're-minded him of,' his face would lighten up with its homely, rugged smile, and he would run his fingers through his bristly black hair, which would stand out in every direction like that of an electric experiment doll.''

IMPRESSIONS OF THE NEW PRESIDENT.

John G. Nicolay, afterward Lincoln's private secretary, says: ''The people beheld in the new President a man six feet four inches in height, a stature which of itself would be hailed in any assemblage as one of the outward signs of leadership; joined to this was a spare but muscular frame, and large and strongly marked features corresponding to his unusual stature. Quiet in demeanor, but erect in bearing, his face even in repose was not unattractive; and when lit up by his open, genial smile, or illuminated in the utterance of a strong or stirring thought, his countenance was positively handsome. His voice, pitched in rather a high key, but of great clearness and penetration, made his public remarks audible to a wide circle of listeners.''

Henry Champion Deming says of Lincoln's appearance at this time: ''Conceive a tall and giant figure, more than six feet in height, not only unencumbered with superfluous flesh, but reduced to the minimum working standard of cord and sinew and muscle, strong and indurated by exposure and toil, with legs and arms long and attenuated, but not disproportionately to the long and attenuated trunk; in posture and carriage not ungraceful, but with the grace of unstudied and careless ease, rather than of cultivated airs and high-bred pretensions. His dress is uniformly of black throughout, and would attract but little attention in a well-dressed circle, if it hung less loosely upon him, and the ample white shirt collar was not turned over his cravat in Western style. The face that surmounts this figure is half Roman and half Indian,

bronzed by climate, furrowed by life struggles, seamed with humor; the head is massive and covered with dark, thick and unmanageable hair; the brow is wide and well developed, the nose large and fleshy, the lips full, cheeks thin and drawn down in strong, corded lines, which, but for the wiry whiskers, would disclose the machinery which moves the broad jaw. The eyes are dark gray, sunk in deep sockets, but bright, soft and beautiful in expression, and sometimes lost and half abstracted, as if their glance was reversed and turned inward, or as if the soul which lighted them was far away. The teeth are white and regular, and it is only when a smile, radiant, captivating and winning as was ever given to mortal, transfigures the plain countenance, that you begin to realize that it is not impossible for artists to admire and women to love it.

"As the world has rung with ridicule of the ungainliness of his manners, I may be permitted to say, that without any pretensions to superfine polish, they were frank, cordial and dignified, without rudeness, without offense, and without any violation of the proprieties and etiquettes of his high position. To borrow one of his own conversational phrases, he didn't brag on deportment. * * * He stood and moved and bowed without affectation, and without obtrusive awkwardness, pretty much as nature prompted, and as if he regarded *carriage* about as bad a criterion as *color*, of the genuine nobility of soul."

The Hon. Aaron F. Perry of Cincinnati, writes: "I never saw Mr. Lincoln but once. It was when they were putting sand-bags in front of the Treasury Building, and regiments of volunteers were beginning to reach Washington, at the opening of the war. The introduction was informal, as he was passing to a Cabinet meeting. An ungainly person, with a clear, happy eye, as genial and sympathetic as a woman's. That *eye* is my personal experience with Abraham Lincoln."

General E. D. Keyes well says: "If ever there was a diamond in the rough, or good fruit enclosed in shabby husk, it was Abraham Lincoln. A correspondent described him as 'tall, gaunt, and as awkward and shuffling in his gait as Horace Greeley.' A stranger, on seeing Mr. Lincoln, would have concurred in that description, and would have found in his unreserved conversations with all approachers a strain of indescribable jocular freedom. I doubt if any man or woman could have had an interview of five minutes' duration with 'Old Abe,' as he was called, upon any subject, without hearing him relate an anecdote to illustrate it.''

The poet Bryant wrote, in a letter to his friend Dr. H. N. Powers: ''I saw the President, and had a long conversation with him on the affairs of the country, in which I expressed myself plainly and without reserve. He bore it well, and I must say that I left him with a perfect conviction of the excellence of his intentions and the singleness of his purpose.''

Private Secretary Hay thus writes of Mr. Lincoln's character and disposition: ''All agree that the most marked characteristic of Mr. Lincoln's manners was his simplicity and artlessness; this immediately impressed itself upon the observation of those who met him for the first time, and each successive interview deepened the impression. People seemed delighted to find in the ruler of the nation freedom from pomposity and affectation, mingled with a certain simple dignity which never forsook him. Though oppressed with the weight of responsibility resting upon him as President of the United States, he shrank from assuming any of the honors, or even the titles, of the position. After years of intimate acquaintance with Mr. Lincoln, the writer cannot now recall a single instance in which he spoke of himself as President, or used that title for himself, except when acting in an official capacity. He always spoke of his position and office vaguely, as, 'this place,' 'here,' or other modest phrase. Once, speaking of the room in the Capitol used by the Presidents of the United States during the close of a session of Congress, he said, 'That room, you know, that they call'—dropping his voice and hesitating— 'the President's room.' To an intimate friend who addressed him always by his own proper title, he said, 'Now call me Lincoln, and I'll promise not to tell of the breach of etiquette

—if you won't—and I shall have a resting-spell from 'Mister President.' With all his simplicity and unacquaintance with courtly manners, his native dignity never forsook him in the presence of critical polished strangers ; but mixed with his angularities and *bonhomie* was something which spoke the fine fibre of the man ; and, while his sovereign disregard of courtly conventionalities was somewhat ludicrous, his native sweetness and straightforwardness of manner served to disarm criticism and impress the visitor that he was before a man pure, self-poised, collected, and strong in unconscious strength. Of him an accomplished foreigner, whose knowledge of the courts was more perfect than that of the English language, said, 'He seems to me one grand *gentilhomme* in disguise.' " Mr. Hay adds that Mr. Lincoln's simplicity of manner "was marked in his total lack of consideration of what was due his exalted station. He had an almost morbid dread of what he called 'a scene'—that is, a demonstration of applause, such as always greeted his appearance in public. The first sign of a cheer sobered him ; he appeared sad and oppressed, suspended conversation, and looked out into vacancy ; and when it was over, resumed the conversation just where it was interrupted, with an obvious feeling of relief. * * Speaking of an early acquaintance, who was an applicant for an office which he thought him hardly qualified to fill, the President said, 'Well, now, I never thought M——had any more than average ability, when we were young men together ; really I did not.' [A pause.] 'But, then, I suppose he thought just the same about me ; he had reason to, and—here I am !' ' "

Another observer, who knew him well, furnishes amusing evidence of the same tenor : "Mr. Lincoln's habits at the White House were as simple as they were at his old home in Illinois. * * * Friends cautioned him against exposing himself so openly in the midst of enemies ; but he never heeded them. He frequently walked the streets at night, entirely unprotected ; and he felt any check upon his free movements as a great annoyance.

He delighted to see his familiar Western friends; and he gave them, always, a cordial welcome. He met them on the old footing, and fell at once into the accustomed habits of talk and story-telling. An old acquaintance, with his wife, visited Washington. Mr. and Mrs. Lincoln proposed to these friends a ride in the Presidential carriage. It should be stated, in advance, that the two men had probably never seen each other with gloves on in their lives, unless when they were used as protection from the cold. The question of each—Mr. Lincoln at the White House, and his friend at the hotel—was, whether he should wear gloves. Of course, the ladies urged gloves; but Mr. Lincoln only put his in his pocket, to be used or not, according to circumstances. When the Presidential party arrived at the hotel, to take in their friends, they found the gentleman, overcome by his wife's persuasions, very handsomely gloved. The moment he took his seat, he began to draw off the clinging kids, while Mr. Lincoln began to draw his on. 'No! no! no!' protested his friend, tugging at his gloves. 'It is none of my doings; put up your gloves, Mr. Lincoln.' So the two old friends were on even and easy terms, and had their ride after their old fashion.''

Mr. Carl Schurz says: "In the White House, as in his simple home in Springfield, Illinois, Mr. Lincoln was the same plain, unaffected, and unpretentious citizen. He won the admiration and affection of even the most punctilious of the foreign diplomats by the tenderness of his nature and the touching simplicity of his demeanor. * * * He was, in mind and heart, the very highest type of development of a plain man. He was a natural born leader of men, and the qualities that made him a leader were of the plain, common-sense type. * * * Lincoln had one great advantage over all the chief statesmen of his day. He had a thorough knowledge of the plain people. He knew their habits, their modes of thought, and their unfailing sense of justice and right. He relied upon the popular feeling, in great measure, for his guidance.''

Mrs. Harriet Beecher Stowe has said of the qualities which Mr. Lincoln exhibited in the White House: "Lincoln is a strong man, but his strength is of a peculiar kind; it is not aggressive so much as passive; and among passive things, it is like the strength not so much of a stone buttress as of a wire cable. It is strength swaying to every influence, yielding on this side and on that, to popular needs, yet tenaciously and inflexibly bound to carry its great end. * * * Slow and careful in coming to resolutions, willing to talk with every person who has anything to show on any side of a disputed subject, long in weighing and pondering, attached to constitutional limits and time-honored landmarks, Lincoln certainly was the *safest* leader a nation could have at a time when the *habeas corpus* must be suspended, and all the constitutional and minor rights of citizens be thrown into the hands of their military leader. A reckless, bold, theorizing, dashing man of genius might have wrecked our Constitution, and ended us in a splendid military despotism."

GUARDING THE WHITE HOUSE.

The fear lest the virulent enemies of the administration should attempt to assassinate Mr. Lincoln was so wide-spread that military measures were enforced to protect him from secret assault. Gen. Charles P. Stone, to whom the duty was entrusted of establishing the necessary precautions, has furnished a brief report on the subject. "From the first," says General Stone, "I took, under the orders of the General-in-chief, especial care in guarding the Executive Mansion; without, however, doing it so ostentatiously as to attract public attention. It was not considered advisable that it should appear that the President of the United States was, for his personal safety, obliged to surround himself by armed guards. Mr. Lincoln was not consulted in the matter. But Captain Todd, formerly an officer of the regular army, who was, I believe, the brother-in-law of Mr. Lincoln, was then residing in the Presidential Mansion, and with him I was daily and nightly in communication, in order that, in case of danger, one person in the President's household should know where to find the main body of the guard, to the officer commanding which Captain Todd was each night introduced. Double sentries were placed in the shrubbery all around the mansion, and the main body of the guard was posted in a vacant basement-room, from which a stair-case led to the upper floors. A person entering by the main gate and walking up to the front door of the Executive Mansion during the night could see no sign of a guard; but from the moment any one entered the grounds by any entrance, he was under the view of at least two riflemen standing silent in the shrubbery, and any suspicious movement on his part would have caused his immediate arrest; and inside, the call of Captain Todd would have been promptly answered by armed men. The precautions were taken before Fort Sumter was fired on, as well as afterward. One night, near midnight, I entered the grounds for the purpose of inspecting the guard, and was surprised to see a bright light in the East room. As I entered the basement, I heard a loud noise, as of many voices talking loudly, mingled with the ringing of arms, coming from the great reception room. On questioning the commander of the guard, I learned that many gentlemen had entered the house at a late hour, but they had come in boldly; no objection had been made from within, but on the contrary Captain Todd had told him all was right. I ascended the interior staircase and entered the East room, where I found more than fifty men, among whom were Hon. Cassius M. Clay and General Lane. All were armed with muskets, which they were generally examining, and it was the ringing of many rammers in the musket barrels which had caused the noise I had heard. Mr. Clay informed me that he and a large number of political friends, *deeming it very improper that the President's person should in such times be unguarded*, had formed a voluntary guard which would remain there every night and see to it that Mr. Lincoln was well protected. I applauded the good spirit exhibited, but did not, however, cease the posting of the outside guards, nor the nightly inspections myself as before, until the time came when others than myself became responsible for the safety of the President.''

It is stated that Mr. Lincoln ''had an almost morbid dislike to an escort, or guard, and daily exposed himself to the deadly aim of an assassin. One morning, passing by the White House at an early hour, the writer saw the President standing at the gateway, looking anxiously down the street, and in reply to a salutation, he said, 'Good morning, good morning! I am looking for a newsboy; when you get to that corner I wish you would start one up this way.' * * * In reply to the remonstrances of friends, who were afraid of his constant exposure to danger, he had but one answer: 'If they kill me, the next man will be just as bad for them; and in a country like this, where our habits are simple, and must be, assassination is always possible, and will come, if they are determined upon it.' A cavalry guard was once placed at the gates of the White House for a while, and he said, privately, that 'he worried until he got rid of it.' While the President's family were at their summer-house, near Washington, he rode into town of a morning, or out at night, attended by a mounted escort; but if he returned to town for a while after dark, he rode in unguarded, and often alone, in his open carriage. On more than one occasion, the writer has gone through the streets of Washington at a late hour of the night with the President, without escort, or even the company of a servant, walking all the way, going and returning. Considering the many open and secret threats to take his life, it is not surprising that Mr. Lincoln had many thoughts about his coming to a sudden and violent end. He once said that he felt the force of the expression, 'To take one's life in his hand;' but that he would not like to face death suddenly. He said that he thought himself a great coward physically, and was sure that he would make a poor soldier, for, unless there was something inspiriting in the excitement of a battle, he was sure that he would drop his gun and run, at the first symptom of danger. That was said sportively, and he added, 'Moral cowardice is something which I think I never had.'"

Mr. Lincoln once remarked to Col. Halpine: "It would never do for a President to have guards with drawn sabres at his door, as if he fancied he were, or were trying to be, or were assuming to be, an emperor."

CHAPTER II.

CIVIL WAR.——UPRISING OF THE NATION.——THE PRESIDENT'S FIRST CALL FOR
TROOPS.——RESPONSE OF THE LOYAL NORTH.——THE RIOTS IN BALTIMORE.
——ATTITUDE OF STEPHEN A. DOUGLAS.——HIS LOYALTY.——HIS DEATH.
——BLOCKADE OF SOUTHERN PORTS.——ADDITIONAL WAR MEASURES.——
MR. LINCOLN DEFINES THE POLICY OF THE GOVERNMENT. ——HIS CONCILIA-
TORY COURSE.——DESIRE TO SAVE KENTUCKY.——THE PRESIDENT'S FIRST
MESSAGE TO CONGRESS.——GATHERING OF TROOPS IN WASHINGTON.——RE-
VIEWS AND PARADES.——THE DISASTER AT BULL RUN.——MR. LINCOLN
SUMS IT UP.——THE PRESIDENT VISITS THE ARMY.——TALKS TO THE SOL-
DIERS.——GOOD ADVICE TO AN ANGRY OFFICER.——A PECULIAR CABINET
MEETING.——DARK DAYS FOR MR. LINCOLN.——A "BLACK MOOD" IN THE
WHITE HOUSE.——"NOT A BED OF ROSES."——LINCOLN'S UNFALTERING
COURAGE.——RELIEF IN STORY-TELLING.——"NOT TAKING OATS NOW."——
A PRETTY GOOD LAND TITLE.——MEASURING BACKS WITH CHARLES SUM-
NER.——GEN. SCOTT "UNABLE AS A POLITICIAN."——A GOOD DRAWING-
PLASTER.——THE "POINTS" OF A HORSE.——"DON'T CROSS A RIVER BEFORE
YOU GET TO IT."——A GOOD BRIDGE-BUILDER.——A SICK LOT OF OFFICE-
SEEKERS.——DIDN'T KNOW ILLINOIS WAS IN KENTUCKY.——GETTING RID OF
BORES.

THE attack upon Fort Sumter, April 12, 1861, was the
signal that a civil war in the United States had actually begun. Mr. Lincoln had thus far maintained a conciliatory
policy toward the States in rebellion, hoping to the last that
good sense and reason, prevailing over rash and violent impulses, would induce them to resume their allegiance to the
Government. Their resort to arms decided the course of the
administration; and on the 15th of April—forty-two days after
his accession to the Presidency—Mr. Lincoln issued a proclamation asking for the immediate enlistment of 75,000 volunteers, and summoning Congress to convene in an extra session on the 4th of July. The call was sent forth in the following form:

PROCLAMATION.

By the President of the United States.

"WHEREAS, the laws of the United States have been for some time past
and now are opposed, and the execution thereof obstructed, in the States

of South Carolina, Georgia, Alabama, Florida, Mississippi, Louisiana and Texas, by combinations too powerful to be suppressed by the ordinary course of judicial proceedings, or by the powers vested in the marshals by law; now, therefore, I, ABRAHAM LINCOLN, President of the United States, in virtue of the power in me vested by the Constitution and the laws, have thought fit to call forth, and hereby do call forth, the militia of the several States of the Union, to the aggregate number of seventy-five thousand, in order to suppress said combinations, and to cause the laws to be duly executed.

"The details of this object will be immediately communicated to the State authorities through the War Department. I appeal to all loyal citizens to favor, facilitate, and aid this effort to maintain the honor, the integrity and existence of our National Union, and the perpetuity of popular government, and to redress wrongs already long enough endured. I deem it proper to say that the first service assigned to the forces hereby called forth will probably be to repossess the forts, places and property which have been seized from the Union; and in every event the utmost care will be observed, consistently with the objects aforesaid, to avoid any devastation, any destruction of, or interference with, property, or any disturbance of peaceful citizens of any part of the country; and I hereby command the persons composing the combinations aforesaid to disperse and retire peaceably to their respective abodes, within twenty days from this date.

"Deeming that the present condition of public affairs presents an extraordinary occasion, I do hereby, in virtue of the power in me vested by the Constitution, convene both houses of Congress. The Senators and Representatives are, therefore, summoned to assemble at their respective chambers, at twelve o'clock, noon, on Thursday, the fourth day of July next, then and there to consider and determine such measures as, in their wisdom, the public safety and interest may seem to demand.

"In witness whereof, I have hereunto set my hand, and caused the seal of the United States to be affixed.

"Done at the City of Washington, this fifteenth day of April, in the year of our Lord one thousand eight hundred and sixty-one, and of the independence of the United States the eighty-fifth.

"*By the President:*   ABRAHAM LINCOLN.

"WILLIAM H. SEWARD, Secretary of State."

RESPONSE OF THE LOYAL NORTH.

"The issue of this proclamation," says Mr. Raymond, "created the most intense enthusiasm throughout the country.

Scarcely a voice was raised in any of the Northern States against this measure, which was seen to be one of absolute necessity and of self-defence on the part of the Government. Every Northern State responded promptly to the President's demand, and from private persons, as well as by the Legislatures, men, arms, and money were offered in unstinted profusion and with the most zealous alacrity, in support of the Government. Massachusetts was first in the field ; and on the first day after the issue of the proclamation, her Sixth regiment, completely equipped, started from Boston for the National Capital. Two more regiments were also made ready, and took their departure within forty-eight hours."

THE RIOTS IN BALTIMORE.

The Sixth Massachusetts regiment, on its way to Washington, on the 19th of April was attacked by a mob in Baltimore, carrying a secession flag, and several of its members were killed or severely wounded. "This inflamed to a still higher point the excitement which already pervaded the country. The whole Northern section of the Union felt outraged that troops should be assailed and murdered on their way to protect the Capital of the Nation. In Maryland, where the secession party was strong, there was also great excitement, and the Governor of the State and the Mayor of Baltimore united in urging, for prudential reasons, that no more troops should be brought through that city." In answer to the remonstrances of Governor Hicks and a committee of secessionists from Maryland, who presented their petition in person, Mr. Lincoln, intent on avoiding every cause of offense, replied : "For the future, troops must be brought here ; but I make no point of bringing them through Baltimore. Without any military knowledge myself, of course I must leave details to General Scott. He hastily said this morning, in the presence of these gentlemen, 'March them around Baltimore, and not through it.' I sincerely hope the General, on fuller reflection, will consider this practical and proper, and that you will not object to it. By this, a collision of the people of Baltimore with the troops will be avoided, unless they go out of their way to seek it. I hope you will exert your influence to prevent this. Now and ever, I shall do all in my power for peace, consistently with the maintenance of the Government.''

ATTITUDE OF STEPHEN A. DOUGLAS.—HIS LOYALTY.—HIS DEATH.

Instantly on the announcement that the North and South were arming for a deadly contest, the great leader of the Democracy, and the life-long political opponent of Mr. Lincoln, declared his purpose to stand by the Government. "One of the most encouraging incidents of this opening chapter of the war," says Dr. Holland, "was a visit of Mr. Douglas to Mr. Lincoln, in which the former gave to the latter the assurance of his sympathy and support in the war for the preservation of the Union. It is to be remembered that Mr. Douglas was an ambitious man, that he was a strong party man, that he had battled for power with all the persistence of a strong and determined nature, and that he was a sadly disappointed man. The person with whom he had had his hardest fights occupied the chair to which he had for many years aspired. On Sunday, the fourteenth of April, all Washington was alive with excitement under the effect of the news of the fall of Sumter. Secessionists could not conceal their joy, and the loyal were equally sad and indignant. Churches were forsaken, and the opening of the war was the only topic of thought and conversation. Under these circumstances, Hon. George Ashmun, of Massachusetts, who was personally on the most friendly terms with Mr. Lincoln and Mr. Douglas, called on the latter in the evening, to obtain from him some public declaration that should help the Government in its extremity. He found the Senator surrounded by political friends, who were soon dismissed; and then, for an hour, the two men discussed the relations of Mr. Douglas to the administration.

The first impulse of the Senator was against Mr. Ashmun's wishes, who desired him to go to the President at once, and tell him he would sustain him in all the needful measures which the exigency demanded. His reply was: 'Mr. Lincoln has dealt hardly with me, in removing some of my friends from office, and I don't know as he wants my advice or aid.' Mr. Ashmun remarked that he had probably followed Democratic precedents in making removals, but that the present question was above party, and that it was now in the power of Mr. Douglas to render such a service to his country as would not only give him a title to its lasting gratitude, but would show that in the hour of his country's need he could trample all party considerations and resentments under feet. At this juncture Mrs. Douglas came in, and gave the whole weight of her affectionate influence in the direction in which Mr. Ashmun was endeavoring to lead him. He could not withstand the influence of his friend, his wife, and that better nature to which they appealed. He gave up all his enmity, all his resentment, cast every unworthy sentiment and selfish feeling behind him, and cordially declared his willingness to go to Mr. Lincoln, and offer him his earnest and hearty support. It was nearly dark when the two gentlemen started for the President's house. Mr. Lincoln was alone; and on learning their errand, gave them a most cordial welcome. For once, the life-long antagonists were united in heart and purpose. Mr. Lincoln took up the proclamation, calling for 75,000 troops, which he had determined to issue the next day, and read it. When he had finished, Mr. Douglas rose from his chair and said: 'Mr. President, I cordially concur in every word of that document, except that instead of the call for 75,000 men I would make it 200,000. You do not know the dishonest purposes of these men as well as I do.' Then he asked the President and Mr. Ashmun to look at a map of the United States which hung at one end of the room. On this he pointed out, in detail, the principal strategic points which should be at once strengthened for the coming contest. Among the more prominent of these were Fortress Monroe, Washington, Harper's Ferry, and Cairo. He then enlarged upon the firm, warlike course which should be pursued, while Mr. Lincoln listened with earnest interest, and the two old foes parted that night thorough friends, perfectly united in a patriotic purpose. After leaving the President, Mr. Ashmun said to Mr. Douglas: 'You have done justice to your own reputation and to the President; and the country must know it. The proclamation will go by telegraph all over the country in the morning, and the account of this interview must go with it. I shall send it either in my own language or yours. I prefer that you should give your own version.' Mr. Douglas said he would write it; and so the dispatch went with the message wherever the telegraph could carry it, confirming the wavering of his own party, and helping to raise the tide of loyal feeling among all parties and classes to its flood." The dispatch was as follows:

"April 15th, 1861, Senator Douglas called on the President, and had an interesting conversation on the present condition of the country. The substance of it was, on the part of Mr. Douglas, that while he was unalterably opposed to the administration in all its political issues, he was prepared to fully sustain the President in the exercise of all his Constitutional functions, to preserve the Union, maintain the Government, and defend the Federal Capital. A firm policy and prompt action was necessary. The Capital was in danger, and must be defended at all hazards, and at any expense of men and money. He spoke of the present and future without any reference to the past."

Faithful to his pledge to support the Union, Mr. Douglas set out immediately upon a tour through the Northwest, to strengthen, by his words and presence, the spirit of loyalty among the people. He made a series of eloquent speeches on his journey to Chicago, where he arrived worn and spent with the fatigue and excitement of his undertaking. It was the last and most noble service of his life. Illness ensued, and after a few weeks of suffering, he passed away, June 3d, at the age

of forty-eight.   His death was an irreparable loss, mourned
by the President and the nation.

BLOCKADE OF SOUTHERN PORTS.

The President's call for troops was succeeded, on the 19th
of April, by a proclamation declaring, in the following terms,
a blockade of Southern ports:

"*Whereas*, An insurrection against the Government of the United
States has broken out in the States of South Carolina, Georgia, Alabama,
Florida, Mississippi, Louisiana, and Texas, and the laws of the United
States for the collection of the revenue can not be efficiently executed
therein, conformably to that provision of the Constitution which requires
duties to be uniform throughout the United States:

"*And whereas*, A combination of persons, engaged in such insurrection, have threatened to grant pretended letters of marque to authorize
the bearers thereof to commit assaults on the lives, vessels, and property
of good citizens of the country lawfully engaged in commerce on the high
seas, and in waters of the United States:

"*And whereas*, An Executive Proclamation has already been issued,
requiring the persons engaged in these disorderly proceedings to desist
therefrom, calling out a militia force for the purpose of repressing the
same, and convening Congress in extraordinary session to deliberate and
determine thereon:

"Now, therefore, I, ABRAHAM LINCOLN, President of the United States,
with a view to the same purposes before mentioned, and to the protection
of the public peace, and the lives and property of quiet and orderly citizens pursuing their lawful occupations, until Congress shall have assembled and deliberated on the said unlawful proceedings, or until the same
shall have ceased, have further deemed it advisable to set on foot a blockade of the ports within the States aforesaid, in pursuance of the laws of
the United States, and of the laws of nations in such cases provided.
For this purpose a competent force will be posted so as to prevent entrance and exit of vessels from the ports aforesaid.   If, therefore, with
a view to violate such blockade, a vessel shall approach or shall attempt to leave any of the said ports, she shall be duly warned by the
commander of one of the blockading vessels, who shall indorse on her
register the fact and date of such warning; and if the same vessel shall
again attempt to enter or leave the blockaded port, she will be captured
and sent to the nearest convenient port, for such proceedings against her
and her cargo, as prize, as may be deemed advisable.

"And I hereby proclaim and declare, that if any person, under the
pretended authority of said States, or under any other pretense, shall

molest a vessel of the United States, or the persons or cargo on board of her, such person will be held amenable to the laws of the United States for the prevention and punishment of piracy.

 "*By the President:*   ABRAHAM LINCOLN.
  WILLIAM H. SEWARD, Secretary of State."
"*Washington, April 19, 1861.*"

ADDITIONAL WAR MEASURES.

On the 27th of April the President issued a proclamation by which the blockade of rebel ports was extended to the ports of North Carolina and Virgina. It was followed, on the 3d of May, by a proclamation calling into the service of the United States forty-two thousand and thirty-four volunteers for three years, and ordering an addition of twenty-two thousand one hundred and fourteen officers and men to the regular army, and eighteen thousand seamen to the navy. And on the 16th, by another proclamation, the President directed the commander of the United States forces in Florida to "permit no person to exercise any office or authority upon the islands of Key West, Tortugas, and Santa Rosa, which may be inconsistent with the laws and Constitution of the United States; authorizing him, at the same time, if he shall find it necessary, to suspend the writ of *habeas corpus*, and to remove from the vicinity of the United States fortresses all dangerous and suspected persons."

MR. LINCOLN DEFINES THE POLICY OF THE GOVERNMENT.

The Virginia Convention which passed the ordinance of secession, having appointed a committee to wait upon the President and "respectfully ask him to communicate to this Convention the policy which the Federal Executive intends to pursue in regard to the Confederate States," Mr. Lincoln, in reply, thus clearly outlined the policy and purposes of the Government:

"In answer I have to say, that having, at the beginning of my official term, expressed my intended policy as plainly as I was able, it is with deep regret and mortification I now learn there is great and injurious uncertainty in the public mind as to what that policy is, and what course I intend to pursue. Not having as yet seen occasion to change, it is now my purpose to pursue the course marked out in the Inaugural Address. I commend a careful consideration of the whole document as the best expression I can give to my purposes. As I then and therein said, I now repeat: 'The power confided in me will be used to hold, occupy, and possess property and places belonging to the Government, and to collect the duties and imposts; but beyond what is necessary for these objects there will be no invasion, no using of force against or among the people anywhere.' By the words 'property and places belonging to the Government,' I chiefly allude to the military posts and property which were in possession of the Government when it came into my hands. But if, as now appears to be true, in pursuit of a purpose to drive the United States authority from these places, an unprovoked assault has been made upon Fort Sumter, I shall hold myself at liberty to repossess, if I can, like places which had been seized before the Government was devolved upon me; and in any event I shall, to the best of my ability, repel force by force. In case it proves true that Fort Sumter has been assaulted, as is reported, I shall, perhaps, cause the United States mails to be withdrawn from all the States which claim to have seceded, believing that the commencement of actual war against the Government justifies and possibly demands it. I scarcely need to say that I consider the military posts and property situated within the States which claim to have seceded, as yet belonging to the Government of the United States as much as they did before the supposed secession. Whatever else I may do for the purpose, I shall not attempt to collect the duties and imposts by any armed invasion of any part of the country; not meaning by this, however, that I may not land a force deemed necessary to relieve a fort upon the border of the country. From the fact that I have quoted a part of the Inaugural Address, it must not be inferred that I repudiate any other part, the whole of which I reaffirm, except so far as what I now say of the mails may be regarded as a modification.

(Signed)   ABRAHAM LINCOLN.''

THE PRESIDENT'S CONCILIATORY COURSE.—HIS DESIRE TO SAVE KENTUCKY.

In the early period of Mr. Lincoln's administration, he was hopeful that many serious phases of the threatened trouble might be averted, and that the better judgment of the citizens of the South might prevail. But he was very decided and determined as to what his duty was and what his action would be, if the secessionists and disunionists pressed their case. He said: "The disunionists did not want me to take the oath of office. I have taken it, and I intend to administer the office for the benefit of the people, in accordance with the Constitution and the law." He was especially anxious that Kentucky should not be plunged into a rebellious war, as he saw that State would be of the utmost importance to the Union cause. Soon after the bombardment of Fort Sumter, a conference was held between the President and a number of prominent Kentuckians then in Washington, at which Mr. Lincoln expressed himself in the most earnest words. "Kentucky," he declared, "must not be precipitated into secession. She is the key to the situation. With her faithful to the Union, the discord in the other States will come to an end. She is now in the hands of those who do not represent the people. The sentiment of her State officials must be counteracted. We must arouse the young men of the State to action for the Union. We must know what men in Kentucky have the confidence of the people and who can be relied on for good judgment, that may be brought to the support of the Government at once." He paid a high tribute to the patriotism of the Southern men who had stood up against secession. "But," said he, "they are, as a rule, beyond the meridian of life, and their counsel and example do not operate quickly, if at all, on the excitable nature of young men, who become inflamed by the preparations for war, and who, in such a war as this will be, if it goes on, are apt to go in on the side that gives the first opportunity. The young men must not be permitted to drift away from us. I know that the men who voted against me in Kentucky will not permit this Government to be swept away by any such issue as that framed by the disunionists. We need only to organize against Governor Magoffin's followers to beat them."

As Mr. Markland relates, in his reminiscences of the period: "Immediately a campaign for the Union was begun in Kentucky. The State could not be dragooned into open secession, therefore the neutrality policy was adopted. That policy was more rigidly observed by Mr. Lincoln than it was by his opponents, but he was not misled by it. On the contrary, he knew its treachery and prepared for it. Lieutenant William Nelson, of the United States Navy, a native of the State of Kentucky, was detailed for a special service, a service requiring intelligence, courage, and an accurate knowledge of men. Judge Joseph Holt made eloquent appeals for the Union through the columns of the press and from the forum, as did the Speeds, the Goodloes, and many others of prominence. Rousseau, Jacobs, Poundbaker, and others, stood guard in the Legislature, and by their eloquence stayed the tide of disunion there. Camps for recruiting for the Union were formed on the north bank of the Ohio River. Cairo, Illinois, was occupied by Union troops. The neutrality doctrine of Kentucky was fast approaching the end of its usefulness to the Confederates. It had been violated by them in the establishment of Camps Boone and Trousdale, on the Southern border. Generals Pillow and Polk occupied Hickman and Columbus respectively. General Grant and his Union troops at once occupied Paducah, Ky., and the headquarters of the Department of the Ohio were, about the same time, removed from Cincinnati, to Central Kentucky. The special service of Lieutenant (afterwards Major General) William Nelson had been prudently and faithfully performed, and the arms and munitions of war with which he had been entrusted were in the hands of Union men in the very centre of the State. The labors of Judge Holt, the Speeds, the Goodloes, Cassius M. Clay, and their followers, had brought forth fruit for the Union. The patriotic men in the Legislature had done their work well. The men in the camps on the north side of the Ohio river moved over into Kentucky, and the invasion of Confederates which was to sweep Kentucky into secession was at an end. Kentucky was saved to the Union by the wise counsel and pacific policy of Abraham Lincoln.''

THE PRESIDENT'S FIRST MESSAGE TO CONGRESS.

A special session of Congress convened on the 4th of July, in obedience to the summons of the President in his proclamation of April 15th. The following day the message of the Executive rehearsed to the joint Houses the circumstances which had rendered their assembling necessary. It portrayed, in clear and succinct words, the situation of affairs, the aggressive acts of the States aiming to destroy the Federal Union, and the measures adopted by the administration to frustrate their attempts. The assailants of the Government, it announced, "have forced upon the country the distinct issue, 'immediate dissolution or blood.' And this issue embraces more than the fate of these United States. It presents to the whole family of man the question, whether a constitutional Republic or Democracy—a Government of the people by the same people—can or cannot maintain its territorial integrity against its own domestic foes. It presents the question, whether discontented individuals, too few in numbers to control administration according to organic law in any case, can always, upon the pretences made in this case, or on any other pretences, or arbitrarily, without any pretence, break up their Government, and thus practically put an end to free government upon the earth. It forces us to ask, 'Is there, in all Republics, this inherent and fatal weakness? Must a Government, of necessity, be too strong for the liberties of its own people, or too weak to maintain its own existence?'" It requested of Congress "the legal means for making this contest a short and decisive one; that you place at the control of the Government, for the work, at least four hundred thousand men and $400,000,000. That number of men is about one-tenth of those of proper ages within the regions where, apparently, all are willing to engage; and the sum is less than a twenty-third part of the money value owned by the men who seem ready to devote the whole. A debt of $600,000,000 now is a less sum per head than was the debt of our Revolution when we came out of that struggle; and the money value in the country now bears even a greater proportion to what it was then, than does the population. Surely each man has as strong a motive now to preserve our liberties as each had then to establish them. * * * The evidence reaching us from the country leaves no doubt that the material for the work is abundant, and that it needs only the hand of legislation to give it legal sanction, and the hand of the Executive to give it practical shape and efficiency. One of the greatest perplexities of the Government is to avoid receiving troops faster than it can provide for them. In a word, the people will save their Government, if the Government itself will do its part only indifferently well." It dwelt upon the encouraging facts "that the free institutions we enjoy have developed the powers and improved the condition of our whole people beyond any example in the world. Of this we now have a striking and an impressive illustration. So large an army as the Government has now on foot was never before known without a soldier in it but who had taken his place there of his own free choice. But more than this; there are many single regiments whose members, one and another, possess full practical knowledge of all the arts, sciences, professions, and whatever else, whether useful or elegant, is known in the world; and there is scarcely one from which there could not be selected a President, a Cabinet, a Congress, and perhaps a court, abundantly competent to administer the Government itself." Finally, and eloquently, the message demonstrated the significance of the war in its effect upon the liberties and prayers of all mankind. The President wrote:

"This is essentially a people's contest. On the side of the Union it is a struggle for maintaining in the world that form and substance of government whose leading object is to elevate the condition of men; to lift artificial weights from all shoulders; to clear the paths of laudable pursuits for all; to afford all an unfettered start and a fair chance in the race of life. Yielding to partial and temporary departures, from necessity, this is the leading object of the Government for whose existence we contend. I am most happy to believe that the plain people understand and appreciate this. It is worthy of note, that while in this the Government's hour of trial, large numbers of those in the army and navy who have been favored with the offices have resigned and proved false to the hand which had pampered them, not one common soldier or common sailor is known to have deserted his flag. Great honor is due to those officers who remained true, despite the example of their treacherous associates; but the greatest honor, and most important fact of all, is the unanimous firmness of the common soldiers and common sailors. To the last man, so far as known, they have successfully resisted the traitorous efforts of those whose commands but an hour before they obeyed as absolute law. This is the patriotic instinct of plain people. They understand, without an argument, that the destroying the Government which was made by Washington means no good to them. Our popular Government has often been called an experiment. Two points in it our people have already settled—the successful establishing and the successful administering of it. One still remains—its successful maintenance against a formidable internal attempt to overthrow it. It is now for them to demonstrate to the world that those who can fairly carry an election can also suppress a rebellion; that ballots are the rightful and peaceful successors of bullets; and that when ballots have fairly and constitutionally decided, there can be no successful appeal back to bullets; that there can be no successful appeal, except to ballots themselves, at succeeding elections. Such will be a great lesson of peace; teaching men that what they cannot take by an election, neither can they take by a war; teaching all the folly of being the beginners of a war."

GATHERING OF TROOPS IN WASHINGTON.—REVIEWS AND PARADES.

Through the early summer of 1861, Washington was alive with the preparations for a military movement against the enemy in Virginia. Troops from the North were constantly arriving, and as rapidly as possible were assigned to different organizations and drilled in the art of war. Mr. Lincoln was incessantly engaged in urging forward these active preparations. He was in daily conference with the officers of the army and of the War Department, and was present at innumerable reviews and parades of the soldiers.

The 4th of July was memorable for a grand review of all the New York troops in and about the city. It was a brilliant and impressive scene. Says a spectator, Hon. A. G. Riddle: "As they swept past—twenty-five thousand boys in blue—their muskets flashing, bands playing, and banners waving, I stood near a distinguished group surrounding the President, and noted his countenance as he turned to the massive moving column. All about him were excited, confident, exultant. He stood silent, pale, profoundly sad, as though his prophetic soul saw what was to follow. He seemed to be gazing beyond the splendid pageant before him, upon things hidden from other eyes. Was there presaged to him a vision of that grander review of our victorious armies at the close of the war, which he was not to see?"

THE DISASTER AT BULL RUN.—MR. LINCOLN SUMS IT UP.

A few days later all the troops in Washington crossed the Long Bridge and marched, gallant and exultant, straight toward the enemy in Virginia. The advance of our army resulted, on the 21st of July, in the shameful disaster at Bull Run. The North was filled with surprise and dismay, and even the stoutest hearts were burdened with anxiety for the future. Mr. Lincoln at first shared somewhat in the general depression, but his elastic spirits quickly rallied from the shock. Three or four days after the battle, some gentlemen who had been on the field called upon him. He inquired very minutely regarding all the circumstances of the affair, and after listening with the utmost attention, said, with a touch of humor: "So it's your notion that we *whipped the rebels*, and then *ran away from them!*"

THE PRESIDENT VISITS THE ARMY.—TALKS TO THE SOLDIERS.

A few days after the battle of Bull Run, Mr. Lincoln made a personal visit to the army in Virginia. General Sherman, at that time connected with the army of the Potomac, says: "I was near the river-bank, looking at a block-house which had been built for the defense of the aqueduct, when I saw a carriage coming by the road that crossed the Potomac river at

Georgetown by a ferry. I thought I recognized in the carriage the person of President Lincoln. I hurried across a bend, so as to stand by the roadside as the carriage passed. I was in uniform, with a sword on, and was recognized by Mr.

Lincoln and Mr. Seward, who rode side by side in an open hack. I inquired if they were going to my camp, and Mr. Lincoln said: 'Yes; we heard that you had got over the big scare, and we thought we would come over and see the boys.' The roads had been much changed and were rough. I asked if I might give directions to his coachman; he promptly invited me to jump in, and to tell the coachman which way to drive. Intending to begin on the right and follow round to the left, I turned the driver into a side-road which led up a very steep hill, and, seeing a soldier, called to him and sent him up hurriedly, to announce to the Colonel that the President was coming. As we slowly ascended the hill, I discovered that Mr. Lincoln was full of feeling, and wanted to encourage our men. I asked if he intended to speak to them, and he said he would like to. I asked him then to please discourage all cheering, noise, or any sort of confusion; that we had had enough of it before Bull Run to ruin any set of men, and that what we needed were cool, thoughtful, hard-fighting soldiers—no more hurrahing, no more humbug. He took my remarks in the most perfect good-nature. Before we had reached the first camp, I heard the drum beating the 'assembly,' saw the men running for their tents, and in a few minutes the regiment was in line, arms presented, and then brought to an order and 'parade rest.' Mr. Lincoln stood up in the carriage, and made one of the neatest, best, and most feeling addresses I ever listened to, referring to our late disaster at Bull Run, the high duties that still devolved on us, and the brighter days yet to come. At one or two points the soldiers began to cheer, but he promptly checked them, saying: 'Don't cheer, boys. I confess I rather like it myself, but Colonel Sherman here says that it is not military; and I guess we had better defer to his opinion.' In winding up, he explained that, as President, he was commander-in-chief; that he was resolved that the soldiers should have everything that the law allowed; and he called on one and all to appeal to him personally in case they were wronged. The effect of this speech was excellent. We passed along in the same manner to all the camps of my brigade; and Mr. Lincoln complimented me highly for the order, cleanliness, and discipline that he observed. Indeed, he and Mr. Seward, both assured me that it was the first bright moment that they had experienced since the battle."

GOOD ADVICE TO AN ANGRY OFFICER.

"In the crowd at Fort Corcoran," continues General Sherman, "I saw an officer with whom I had had a little difficulty that morning. His face was pale, and lips compressed. I foresaw a scene, but sat on the front seat of the carriage as quiet as a lamb. This officer forced his way through the crowd to the carriage, and said: 'Mr. President, I have a cause of grievance. This morning I went to speak to Colonel Sherman, and he threatened to shoot me.' Mr. Lincoln, who was still standing, said, 'Threatened to *shoot you?*' 'Yes, sir, he threatened to shoot me.' Mr. Lincoln looked at him, then at me; and stooping his tall, spare form toward the officer, said to him in a loud stage-whisper, easily heard for some yards around: 'Well, if I were you, and he threatened to shoot, *I would not trust him*, for *I believe he would do it.*' The officer turned about and disappeared, and the men laughed at him. Soon the carriage drove on, and, as we descended the hill, I explained the facts to the President, who answered, 'Of course I didn't know anything about it, but I thought you knew your own business best.' I thanked him for his confidence, and assured him that what he had done would go far to enable me to maintain good discipline; and it did."

A PECULIAR CABINET MEETING.

"The first time I ever saw Abraham Lincoln," says Rev. Robert Collyer, "was in McVicker's Theatre, Chicago, in the winter of 1859-60, when I was greatly impressed by the signs of power, and a deep brooding touched with sadness, in his face; and I whispered to a friend, 'Who is that man over there?' and he answered, 'That's Abe Lincoln.' I saw him again in the summer of 1861, on the steps of the White House, answering very simply and kindly to the marks of respect some soldiers had come to pay him, who stood in deep ranks on the grass, that had been top-dressed with compost enough to cover the whole District of Columbia, as the chairman of the committee that had to pass the account told me. And once, curiously, I saw *only his feet*. It was in the summer of the first Bull Run, when some say that *we* ran, and some say that *they* ran. And all was quiet on the Potomac; but the nation was stamping and champing the bit. And passing the White House one day, I saw three pairs of feet on the sill of an open window; and pausing for a moment, a good-natured fellow said, '*That's the Cabinet a sittin'*, and *them big feet's old Abe's.*' So, lecturing in Boston not long after, I said, like a fool as I was, 'That's about all they are good for in Washington, to point their feet out o' window and talk, but go nowhere and do nothing.' When, indeed, the good President's heart was even then breaking with anxiety and trouble."

DARK DAYS FOR MR. LINCOLN.

The days following the Bull Run disaster were full of depression and discouragement, but Mr. Lincoln bore up bravely. He began to feel the terrible realities of his position, and saw himself brought face to face with the most awful responsibilities that ever rested upon human shoulders. A disrupted Union, the downfall of the great American Republic, so long predicted by envious critics of our institutions, seemed about to be accomplished. At the best, the Union could be saved only by the shedding of seas of priceless blood and the expenditure of untold treasures. And *he* must act, control, choose, and direct the measures of the Government and the movements of its vast armies. And what if all should fail?

What if the resources of the Government should prove inadequate, and its enemies too powerful to be subdued by force? No wonder he was appalled and well-nigh overwhelmed by the dark prospect before him.

A "BLACK MOOD" IN THE WHITE HOUSE.

"One day," says Mr. Riddle, "I called at the White House to present a distinguished stranger, who had important matters to bring to Mr. Lincoln's notice. It was evening —cold, rainy, and cheerless. The Executive Mansion was gloomy and silent. At Mr. Lincoln's door we were told by the attendant to enter. We found the room quite dark, and seemingly vacant. I advanced a step or two, to determine if any one were present, and was arrested by a strange apparition, at first not distinguishable : the long, seemingly lifeless, limbs of a man, as if thrown upon a chair and left to sprawl in unseemly disorder. A step further, and the fallen head disclosed the features of the President. I turned back ; a word from my companion reached the drooping figure, and a sepulchral voice bade us advance. We came upon a man, in some respects the most remarkable of any time, in the hour of his prostration and weakness—in the depths of that depression to which his inherited melancholy at times reduced him, now perhaps coming to overwhelm him as he thought of the calamities of his country."

NOT "A BED OF ROSES."

An old and intimate friend from Springfield, who visited Mr. Lincoln at this period, found the door of his office at the White House locked ; but going through a private room and through a side entrance, he found the President lying on a sofa, evidently greatly disturbed and much excited, manifestly displeased with the outlook. Jumping up from his reclining position, he advanced, saying : "You know better than any man living that from my boyhood up my ambition was to be President. I am President of one part of this divided country at least ; but look at me ! I wish I had never been born !

I've a white elephant on my hands, one hard to manage. With a fire in my front and rear, having to contend with the jealousies of the military commanders, and not receiving that cordial co-operation and support from Congress that could reasonably be expected with an active and formidable enemy in the field threatening the very life-blood of the Government, my position is anything but a bed of roses.''

LINCOLN'S UNFALTERING COURAGE.

But in the darkest hours of the nation's peril, Mr. Lincoln never faltered. Anxious and careworn, his heart bleeding with grief for the losses of our brave soldiers, and harassed by the grave duties constantly demanding his attention, he had but one purpose: to go on unfalteringly and unhesitatingly in his course, until the supremacy of the Government was restored in every portion of its territory. Whatever he suffered or feared, no gloomy forebodings or weak repinings came from him.

RELIEF IN STORY-TELLING.

Mr. Lincoln had, however, one important resource in his dark hours, an ever-ready relief for his overcharged emotions. It was his love of story-telling. The habit had been formed in his early years, and now it was his unfailing solace. Hon. Hugh McCullough, afterward Secretary of the Treasury, relates that about a week after the battle of Bull Run he called at the White House, in company with a few friends, and was amazed, when, referring to something which had been said by one of the company about the battle which was so disastrous to the Union forces, the President remarked, in his usual quiet manner: "That reminds me of a story," which he told in a manner so humorous as almost to lead his listeners to believe that he was free from care and apprehension. Mr. McCullough could not then understand how the President could feel like telling a story, when Washington was in danger of being captured, and the whole North was dismayed. He learned his mistake afterwards, however, and perceived that his estimate of Lincoln before his election was well grounded, and that he possessed even higher qualities than he had been given credit for; that he was "a man of sound judgment, great singleness and tenacity of purpose, and extraordinary sagacity; that story-telling was to him a safety-valve, and that he indulged in it, not only for the pleasure it afforded him, but for a temporary relief from oppressing cares; that the habit had been so cultivated that he could make a story illustrate a sentiment and give point to an argument. Many of his stories were as apt and instructive as the best of Æsop's fables."

"NOT TAKING OATS NOW."

The Hon. T. J. Coffey, who was a law-officer of the Government under Mr. Lincoln, relates a story concerning the U. S. Marshals and their eagerness to get hold of a fund of money that had been appropriated by Congress for their relief in certain suits pending against them. They had previously been petitioning the Government to defend them in these suits; but as soon as they heard of the appropriation, they changed their tactics and clamored for the money. "They remind me," said Mr. Lincoln, when the matter had been brought to his attention, "of the man in Illinois whose cabin was burned down, and, according to the kindly custom of early days in the West, his neighbors all contributed something to start him again. In his case they had been so liberal that he soon found himself better off than before the fire, and he got proud. One day a neighbor brought him a bag of oats, but the fellow refused it with scorn. 'No,' said he, 'I'm *not taking oats now*. I take nothing but money.'"

A PRETTY GOOD LAND TITLE.

Hon. Lawrence Weldon relates that on one occasion he called upon the President to inquire the probable outcome of a conflict between the civil and military authorities, for the possession of a quantity of cotton in a certain insurrectionary district. As soon as the inquiry had been made, Mr. Lincoln's face began lighting up, and he said: "What has become of our old friend Bob Lewis, of DeWitt county? Do you remember a story that Bob used to tell us about his going to Missouri to look up some Mormon lands that belonged to his father? You know that when Robert became of age he found among the papers of his father a number of warrants and patents for lands in Northeast Missouri, and he concluded the best thing he could do was to go to Missouri and investigate the condition of things. It being before the days of railroads, he started on horseback, with a pair of old-fashioned saddlebags. When he arrived where he supposed his land was situated, he stopped, hitched his horse, and went into a cabin standing close by the roadside. He found the proprietor, a lean, lank, leathery looking man, engaged in the pioneer business of making bullets preparatory to a hunt. Mr. Lewis observed, on entering, a rifle suspended in a couple of buck horns above the fire. He said to the man: 'I am looking up some lands that I think belong to my father,' and inquired of the man in what section he lived. Without having ascertained the section, Mr. Lewis proceeded to exhibit his title papers in evidence, and, having established a good title, as he thought, said to the man: 'Now, that is my title. What is yours?' The pioneer, who had by this time become somewhat interested in the proceedings, pointed his long finger toward the rifle. Said he: 'Young man, do you see that gun?' Mr. Lewis frankly admitted that he did. 'Well,' said he, 'that is my title, and if you don't get out of here pretty d—d quick, you will feel the force of it.' Mr. Lewis very hurriedly put his title papers in his saddle-bags, mounted his pony and galloped down the road, and, as Bob says, the old pioneer snapped his gun twice at him before he could turn the corner. Lewis said that he had never been back to disturb that man's title since. 'Now,' said Mr. Lincoln, 'the military authorities have the same title against the civil authorities that closed out Bob's Mormon title in Missouri.' " Judge Weldon says that, after this anecdote, he understood what would be the policy of the Government in

HON. CHARLES SUMNER.

the matter referred to as well as though a proclamation had been issued.

MEASURING BACKS WITH CHARLES SUMNER.

It is related that Charles Sumner, who was a tall man, and proud of his height, once worried the President about

some perplexing matter, when Mr. Lincoln sought to change
the subject by abruptly challenging Sumner to measure backs.
"Sumner," said Mr. Lincoln, "declined to stand up with me,
back to back, to see which was the tallest man, and made a
fine speech about this being the time for uniting our fronts
against the enemy, and not our backs. But I guess he was
afraid to measure, though he is a good piece of a man. I
have never had much to do with Bishops where I live, but, do
you know, Sumner is *my idea of a Bishop*."

GENERAL SCOTT "UNABLE AS A POLITICIAN."

A good story of President Lincoln and General Scott is
reported by Major-General Keyes, who at the beginning of the
war was on the staff of General Scott, then commander-in-
chief of the armies of the United States. "I was sent," says
General Keyes, "by my chief to the President with a message
that referred to a military subject, and led to a discussion.
Finding that Mr. Lincoln's observations were beginning to
tangle my arguments, I said: 'That is the opinion of General Scott, and you know, Mr. President, he is a very able
military man.' 'Well,' said the President, 'if he is as *able*
a military man as he is *un*able as a politician, I give up.'
This was said with an expression of the eye, which he turned
on me, that was peculiar to him, and which signified a great
deal. The astounding force of Mr. Lincoln's observation
was not at all diminished by the fact that I had long suspected
that my chief lacked something which is necessary to make
a successful politician."

A GOOD DRAWING-PLASTER.

Among the numerous delegations which thronged Washington in the early part of the war, was one from New York,
which urged very strenuously the sending of a fleet to the
southern cities—Charleston, Mobile and Savannah—with the
object of drawing off the rebel army from Washington. Mr.
Lincoln said the object reminded him of the case of a girl in

New Salem, who was greatly troubled with a "singing" in her head. Various remedies were suggested by the neighbors, but nothing seemed to afford any relief. At last a man came along—"a common-sense sort of man," said he, inclining his head towards the gentlemen complimentarily—"who was asked to prescribe for the difficulty. After due inquiry and examination, he said the cure was very simple. 'What is it?' was the question. 'Make a plaster of *psalm-tunes*, and apply to her feet, and draw the singing *down*,' was the rejoinder."

THE "POINTS" OF A HORSE.

A gentleman once called upon the President in reference to a newly invented gun, concerning which a committee had been appointed to make a report. The report was sent for, and when it came in was found to be of the most voluminous description. Mr. Lincoln glanced at it, and said: "I should want a new lease of life to read this through!" Throwing it down upon the table, he added: "Why can't a committee of this kind occasionally exhibit a grain of common-sense? If I send a man to buy a horse for me, I expect him to tell me his *points*—not how many *hairs* there are in his tail."

"DON'T CROSS A RIVER BEFORE YOU GET TO IT."

One of Mr. Lincoln's Springfield neighbors, a clergyman, visiting Washington early in the administration, asked the President what was to be his policy on the slavery question. "Well," said he, "I will answer by telling you a story. You know Father B., the old Methodist preacher? and you know Fox river and its freshets? Well, once in the presence of Father B., a young itinerant was worrying about Fox river, and expressing fears that he should be prevented from fulfilling some of his appointments by a freshet in the river. Father B. checked him in his gravest manner. Said he: 'My young brother, I have made it a rule of my life not to cross Fox river till I get to it!' And," added Mr. Lincoln,

"I am not going to worry myself over the slavery question till I get to it."

A GOOD BRIDGE-BUILDER.

"Mr. Lincoln had his joke and his 'little story' over the disruption of the Democracy. He once knew, he said, a sound churchman, of the name of Brown, who was the member of a very sober and pious committee, having in charge the erection of a bridge over a dangerous and rapid river. Several architects failed, and at last Brown said he had a friend named Jones who had built several bridges, and could undoubtedly build that one. So Mr. Jones was called in. 'Can you build this bridge?' inquired the committee. 'Yes,' replied Jones, 'or any other. I could build a bridge to h—l, if necessary.' The committee were shocked, and Brown felt called upon to defend his friend. 'I know Jones so well,' said he, 'and he is so honest a man, and so good an architect, that if he states soberly and positively that he can build a bridge to—to—the infernal regions, why, I believe it; but I feel bound to say that I have my doubts about the abutment on the other side.' 'So,' said Mr. Lincoln, 'when politicians told me that the northern and southern wings of the Democracy could be harmonized, why, I believed them, of course; but I always had my *doubts about the abutment on the other side.*"

A SICK LOT OF OFFICE-SEEKERS.

A delegation once called on Mr. Lincoln to ask the appointment of a gentleman as commissioner to the Sandwich Islands. They presented their case as earnestly as possible, and, besides his fitness for the place, they urged that he was in bad health and a residence in that balmy climate would be of great benefit to him. The President closed the interview with the good-humored remark: "Gentlemen, I am sorry to say that there are eight other applicants for that place, and they are all sicker than your man."

GETTING RID OF BORES.

Mr. Lincoln's tact in ridding himself of importunate suppliants is illustrated in the following: "Joshua Bell, of Kentucky, was sent, at the head of a delegation from the Kentucky Legislature, to represent certain facts to Mr. Lincoln and secure some desired action from the Executive. The committee was admitted to the White House, where Bell, who was an able man and strong speaker, made a powerful representation of his case. At its close, Lincoln got up and came among the Kentuckians. He began to talk with one and the other about old Kentucky friends. Then he linked arms with Bell, and walked back and forth with him for an hour, chatting and talking, and especially telling funny stories. Finally, other visitors pressed for his attention, and the Kentuckians withdrew and started for home. They got as far as Cincinnati before it occurred to Bell that they had not secured a single expression from Lincoln concerning the object of their visit."

DIDN'T KNOW ILLINOIS WAS IN KENTUCKY.

General Rousseau, a Union officer who distinguished himself at the battle of Shiloh, furnishes a good story which is a neat specimen of Mr. Lincoln's powers of sarcasm. It was early in the war, at the time of the border-state troubles which occupied so much of Lincoln's attention. A State Senator from Paducah, Ky., John M. Johnson by name, who had made himself notorious as a secessionist, wrote to Mr. Lincoln, in May, 1861, a very solemn and emphatic protest, in the name of the sovereign State of Kentucky, against the occupation and fortification of Cairo, on the Illinois side of the Ohio river. Mr. Lincoln replied in a letter written in his own peculiar vein, apologizing for the movement, promising it should not be done again, and declaring that if he had suspected that Cairo, Illinois, *was in Dr. Johnson's Kentucky senatorial district*, he would have thought twice before sending troops there.

CHAPTER III.

LINCOLN'S WISE STATESMANSHIP.——THE MASON AND SLIDELL AFFAIR.——
COMPLICATIONS WITH ENGLAND.——LINCOLN'S "LITTLE STORY" ON THE
TRENT AFFAIR.——THE BUILDING OF THE MONITOR.——LINCOLN'S PART IN
THE ENTERPRISE.——THE PRESIDENT'S FIRST ANNUAL MESSAGE.——DISCUS-
SION OF THE LABOR QUESTION.——A PRESIDENT'S RECEPTION IN WAR TIME.
——A GREAT AFFLICTION.——DEATH OF WILLIE LINCOLN.——SOME CHAP-
TERS FROM THE SECRET SERVICE.——A MORNING CALL ON THE PRESIDENT.
——"DARKEY ARITHMETIC."——GOLDWIN SMITH'S OPINION OF LINCOLN.
——MR. LINCOLN AND "FATHER GIDDINGS."——STANDING BY OLD FRIENDS.

IN November, 1861, occurred one of the most important and perilous episodes of the war; one whose full significance was not understood, except by a few cool heads, until long afterwards. Two influential Southern politicians, Mason and Slidell, had been sent by the Confederate Government as Commissioners to Great Britain and France, to try and secure the recognition of the Confederacy; and while on board the British steamer "Trent," they were taken prisoners by the U. S. steamer "San Jacinto," and brought to Washington. Great Britain loudly protested against what she regarded as an unwarrantable seizure of passengers under the British flag, and for a time excitement ran high, and war with England seemed almost inevitable. Fortunately for our country, the controversy was amicably settled by the surrender of the prisoners, without any sacrifice of the dignity of the Government of the United States. As happily stated by Mr. Hosea Biglow:

> "We gave the critters back, John,
> Cos Abraham thought 'twas right;
> It wa'nt your bullyin' clack, John,
> Provokin' us to fight."

The statesmanship displayed by our Government through-out this difficult affair was of the highest order. The credit of it has usually been given to Mr. Seward, the able Secretary of State, by whom the correspondence and negotiations were conducted. No man could have managed these details better; yet the course that was so happily determined on was undoubtedly due to the good sense and shrewd wisdom of the President. He not only dictated the policy to be followed by Mr. Seward in his dispatches to the American Minister in London, but the more important documents were revised and extensively altered by Mr. Lincoln's own hand. Recent writers declare that his management of the Trent affair would alone suffice to establish his reputation as the ablest diplomatist of the war. Coming, as it did, at a time when Mr. Lincoln was overwhelmed with the burden of home affairs, it showed the surprising resources of his character. The readiness and ability with which he met this perilous emergency, in a field in which he had had absolutely no experience or preparation, was equalled only by his cool courage and his self-reliance in following a course radically opposed to the prevailing public sentiment, to the views of Congress, and to the advice of his own Cabinet. The Secretary of the Navy hastened to approve officially the act of Captain Wilkes, and Secretary Stanton "cheered and applauded" it. Even Mr. Seward, cautious and conservative diplomat as he was, "opposed any concession or surrender of the prisoners." But Mr. Lincoln said significantly, *"one war at a time."* Events have long since afforded the most ample approval of his course in this important matter. He avoided a foreign war, while at the same time gaining a substantial diplomatic victory over Great Britain.

An excellent description of the circumstances of the Trent affair is given by Mr. B. J. Lossing, the distinguished author and historian, who was in Washington when the events occurred. "The act of Captain Wilkes, commander of the 'San Jacinto,'" says Mr. Lossing, "was universally applauded by all loyal Americans, and the land was filled with rejoicings because two of the most mischievous men among the enemies of the Government were in custody. For the moment, men did not stop to consider the law or the expediency involved in the act.   Public honors were tendered to Captain Wilkes, and resolutions of thanks were passed by public bodies.   The Secretary of the Navy wrote him a congratulatory letter on the 'great public services' he had rendered in 'capturing the rebel emissaries, Mason and Slidell,' and assured him that his conduct had 'the emphatic approval of the department.'   The House of Representatives tendered him their thanks for the service he had done.   But there was one thoughtful man in the nation, in whom was vested the tremendous executive power of the Republic at that time, and whose vision was constantly endeavoring to explore the mysteries of the near future, who had indulged calmer and wiser thoughts than most men at that critical moment, because his feelings were kept in subjection to his judgment by a sense of heavy responsibility. That man was Abraham Lincoln.   The writer was in the office of the Secretary of War when the telegraphic dispatch announcing the capture of Mason and Slidell was brought in and read.   He can never forget the scene that ensued.   Led by Secretary Stanton, who was followed by Governor Andrew of Massachusetts, and others who were present, cheer after cheer was heartily given by the company.   A little later, the writer, accompanied by the late Elisha Whittlesey, then the venerable First Comptroller of the Treasury, was favored with a brief interview with the President, when the clear judgment of that far-seeing and sagacious statesman uttered through his lips the words which formed the suggestion of, and the keynote to, the judicious action of the Secretary of State afterwards.   'I fear the traitors will prove to be white elephants,' said Mr. Lincoln.   'We must stick to American principles concerning the rights of neutrals,' he continued.   'We fought Great Britain for insisting, by theory and practice, on the right to do just what Captain Wilkes has just done.   If Great Britain shall now protest against the act and demand their release, we must give them up, apologize for the act as a violation of our doctrines, and thus *forever bind her over to keep the peace in relation to neutrals,* and so acknowledge that she has been wrong for sixty years.' Great Britain did protest and make the demand, also made preparations for war against the United States at the same moment. On the same day that Lord John Russell sent the protest and demand to Lord Lyons, the British Minister at Washington, Secretary Seward forwarded a dispatch to Minister Adams in London, informing him that this Government disclaimed the act of Captain Wilkes, and giving assurance that it was ready to make a satisfactory arrangement of all difficulties arising out of the unauthorized act. These dispatches passed each other in midocean. The Government, in opposition to popular sentiment, decided at once to restore Mason and Slidell to the protection of the British flag. It was soon afterwards done, war between the two nations was averted, and, in the language of President Lincoln, the British Government was 'forever bound to keep the peace in relation to neutrals.' The wise statesmanship exhibited at that critical time was originated by Abraham Lincoln."

LINCOLN'S "LITTLE STORY" ON THE TRENT AFFAIR.

Mr. Lincoln once confessed that the Trent affair, occurring, as it did, at a very critical period of the war, had given him great uneasiness. When asked whether it was not a great trial to surrender the two captured Commissioners, he said: "Yes, that was a pretty bitter pill to swallow, but I contented myself with believing that England's triumph in the matter would be short-lived, and that after ending our war successfully we should be so powerful that we could call England to account for all the embarrassments she had inflicted upon us. I felt a good deal like the sick man in Illinois who was told he probably hadn't many days longer to live, and he ought to make peace with any enemies he might have. He said the man he hated worst of all was a fellow named Brown, in the next village, and he guessed he had better commence on him first. So Brown was sent for, and when he came the sick man began to say, in a voice as meek as Moses', that he **wanted** to die at peace with all his fellow-creatures, and hoped he and **Brown** could now shake hands and bury all their enmity. The scene was becoming altogether too pathetic for Brown, who had to get out his handkerchief and wipe the gathering tears from his eyes. It wasn't long before he melted and gave his hand to his neighbor, and they had a regular love-feast. After a parting that would have softened the heart of a grindstone, Brown had about reached the room door, when the sick man rose up on his elbow and said, 'But, see here, Brown, if I *should* happen to get well, mind *that old grudge stands!*' So I thought if this nation should happen to get well, we might want that old grudge against England to stand."

THE BUILDING OF THE MONITOR.—MR. LINCOLN'S PART IN THE ENTERPRISE.

In the Autumn of 1861 was originated the plan of a new naval vessel, which became the Monitor—the same formidable little craft that saved the Federal Navy and beat back the Merrimac ram at Hampton Roads, March 9, 1862, and revolutionized naval architecture throughout the world. The interesting story of the project and Mr. Lincoln's relation to it is thus told: "The invention belongs to Captain John Ericsson, a man of marvelous ability and most fertile brain; but the creation of the Monitor belongs to two distinguished iron-masters of the State of New York, viz.: the Hon. John F. Winslow and his partner in business, the Hon. John A. Griswold. These two gentlemen were in Washington in the Autumn of 1861, in the adjustment of some claims against the Government for iron plating, furnished by them for the war-ship Galena. There, through Mr. C. S. Bushnell, the agent of Captain Ericsson, they learned that the plans and specifications for a naval machine, or a floating iron battery, presented by Captain Ericsson, found no favor with the special board appointed by Congress in 1861, to examine and report upon the subject of iron-clad ships of war. Ericsson and his agent, Mr. Bushnell, were thoroughly disheartened and demoralized at this failure to interest the Government in their plans. The papers were placed in the hands of Messrs. Winslow and Griswold, with the earnest request that they would examine them, and, if they thought well of them, use their influence with the Government for their favorable consideration. Mr. Winslow carefully read the papers and became satisfied that Ericsson's plan was both feasible and desirable. After conference with his friend and partner, Mr. Griswold, it was determined to take the whole matter to President Lincoln. Accordingly, an interview was arranged with Mr. Lincoln, to whom the plans of Captain Ericsson were presented, with all the unction and enthusiasm of an honest and mastering conviction, by Mr. Winslow and Mr. Griswold, who had now become thoroughly interested in the undertaking. The President listened with attention and growing interest. When they were done, Mr. Lincoln said, 'Gentlemen, why do you bring this matter to me? why not take it to the Department having these things in charge?' 'It has been taken already to the Department, and there met with a repulse, and we come now to you with it, Mr. President, to secure your influence. We are here not simply as business men, but as lovers of our country, and we believe most thoroughly that here is something upon which we can enter that will be of vast benefit to the Republic,' was the answer. Mr. Lincoln was roused by the terrible earnestness of Mr. Winslow and his friend Griswold, and said, in his inimitable manner, 'Well, I don't know much about ships, though I once contrived a canal-boat, the model of which is down in the Patent Office, the great merit of which was that it could run where there was no water. But I think there is something in this plan of Ericsson's. I'll tell you what I will do. I will meet you to-morrow at ten oclock, at the office of Commodore Smith, and we will talk it all over.'' The next morning the meeting took place according to the appointment. Mr. Lincoln was present. The Secretary of the Navy, with many of the influential men of the Navy Department, were also there. The office where they met was rude in all its belongings. Mr. Lincoln sat upon a rough box. Mr. Winslow, without any knowledge of naval affairs other than that which general reading would give, entered upon his task with considerable trepidation, but his whole heart was in it, and his showing was so earnest, practical, and patriotic, that a profound impression was made. 'Well,' said Mr. Lincoln, after Mr. Winslow had finished, 'well, Commodore Smith, what do you think of it?' The Commodore made some general and non-committal reply, whereupon the President, rising from the box, added: 'Well, I think there is something in it, as the girl said when she put her foot in the stocking. Good morning, gentlemen,' and went out. From this interview grew a Government contract with Messrs. Winslow and Griswold for the construction of the Monitor, the vessel to be placed in the hands of the Government within one hundred days, at a cost of $275,000. The work was pushed with all diligence, till the 30th of January, 1862, when the ship was launched at Greenpoint, one hundred and one days from the execution of the contract by all the parties thereto, thus making the work, probably, the most expeditious of any recorded in the annals of mechanical engineering.''

THE PRESIDENT'S FIRST ANNUAL MESSAGE.—DISCUSSION OF THE LABOR QUESTION.

At the assembling of Congress in December, 1861, Mr. Lincoln presented his first Annual Message. Among its most noteworthy passages was that which touched upon the relations between labor and capital—a subject so prominent in our later day. It was alluded to in its connection with the evident tendency of the Southern Confederacy to discriminate in its legislation in favor of the monied class and against the laboring people.

"In my present position," the President said, "I could scarcely be justified were I to omit raising a warning voice against this approach of returning despotism. It is not needed nor fitting here, that a general argument should be made in favor of popular institutions; but there is one point, with its connections, not so hackneyed as most others, to which I ask a brief attention. It is the effort to place *capital* on an equal footing with, if not above, *labor*, in the structure of government. It is assumed that labor is available only in connection with capital; that nobody labors unless somebody else, owning capital, somehow, by the use of it, induces him to labor. This assumed, it is next considered whether it is best that capital shall *hire* laborers, and thus induce them to work by their own consent, or *buy* them, and drive them to it without their consent. Having proceeded so far, it is naturally concluded that all laborers are either hired laborers or what we call slaves. And further, it is assumed that whoever is once a hired laborer is fixed in that condition for life. Now, there is no such relation between capital and labor as assumed; nor is there any such thing as a free man being fixed for life in the condition of a hired laborer. Both these assumptions are false, and all inferences from them are groundless. Labor is prior to and independent of capital. Capital is only the fruit of labor, and could never have existed if labor had not first existed. Labor is the superior of capital, and deserves much the higher consideration. Capital has its rights, which are as worthy of protection as any other rights. Nor is it denied that there is, and probably always will be, a relation between labor and capital, producing mutual benefits. The error is in assuming that the whole labor of community exists within that relation. A few men own capital, and those few avoid labor themselves, and, with their capital, hire or buy another few to labor for them. A large majority belong to neither class—neither work for others, nor have others working for them. In most of the Southern States, a majority of the whole people of all colors are neither slaves nor masters; while in the North, a large majority are neither hirers nor hired. Men, with their families—wives, sons, and daughters—work for themselves, on their farms, in their houses, and in their shops, taking the whole product to themselves, and asking no favors of capital, on the one hand, nor of hired laborers or slaves on the other. It is not forgotten that a considerable number of persons mingle their own labor with capital—that is, they labor with their own hands, and also buy or hire others to labor for them; but this is only a mixed, not a distinct class. No principle stated is disturbed by the existence of this mixed class. Again, as has already been said, there is not, of necessity, any such thing as the free hired laborer being fixed to that condition for life. Many independent men everywhere in these States, a few years back in their lives, were hired laborers. The prudent, penniless beginner in the world labors for wages awhile, saves a surplus with which to buy tools or land for himself; then labors on his own account another while, and at length hires another new beginner to help him. This is the just and generous and prosperous system, which opens the way to all, gives hope to all, and consequent energy and progress and improvement of condition to all. No men living are more worthy to be trusted than those who toil up from poverty—none less inclined to take, or touch, aught which they have not honestly earned. Let them beware of surrendering a political power which they already possess, and which, if surrendered, will surely be used to close the door of advancement against such as they, and to fix new disabilities and burdens upon them till all of liberty shall be lost.

"The struggle *of* to-day is not altogether *for* to-day—it is for a vast future also. With a reliance on Providence, all the more firm and earnest, let us proceed in the great task which events have devolved upon us."

A PRESIDENT'S RECEPTION IN WAR TIME.

The reception given at the White House on New Year's day, 1862, was a brilliant and memorable affair. It was attended by distinguished army officers, prominent men from civil life, and the leading ladies of Washington society. "Army uniforms preponderated over black dress coats, and the young Germans of Blenker's division were gorgeously arrayed in tunics embroidered with gold on the collars and cuffs, sword-belts of gold lace, high boots, and jingling spurs." It was such a scene as that before the battle of Waterloo, when the

> ———" capital had gathered then
> Her beauty and her chivalry, and bright
> The lamps shone o'er fair women and brave men;
> A thousand hearts beat happily; and when
> Music arose, with its voluptuous swell,
> Soft eyes looked love to eyes that spake again,
> And all went merry as a marriage bell."

How many of these brave men were destined never to see another New Year's day; and how many of those soft eyes would soon be dimmed with tears! Something of this feeling must have come over the sad soul of Lincoln. An eye-witness says that he "looked careworn and thoughtful, if not anxious, yet he had a pleasant word for all."

A GREAT AFFLICTION.—DEATH OF WILLIE LINCOLN.

Early in 1862 an event occurred that added to the sorrow that seemed to enshroud the life of Mr. Lincoln. It was the death of his son Willie, a bright and promising boy, to whom his father was devotedly attached. "This," says Dr. Holland, "was a new burden; and the visitation which, in his firm faith in Providence, he regarded as providential, was also inexplicable. Why should he, with so many burdens upon him, and with such necessity for solace in his home and his affections, be brought into so tender a trial? It was to him a trial of faith, indeed. A Christian lady of Massachusetts, who was officiating as nurse in one of the hospitals, came in to attend the sick children. She reports that Mr. Lincoln watched with her about the bedside of the sick ones, and that he often walked the room, saying sadly: 'This is the hardest trial of my life; why is it? Why is it?' In the course of conversations with her, he questioned her concerning her situation. She told him she was a widow, and that her husband and two children were in heaven; and added that she saw the hand of God in it all, and that she had never loved Him so much before as she had since her affliction. 'How is that brought about?' inquired Mr. Lincoln. 'Simply by trusting in God, and feeling that He does all things well,' she replied. 'Did you submit fully under the first loss?' he asked. 'No,' she answered, 'not wholly; but, as blow came upon blow, and all were taken, I could and did submit, and was very happy.' He responded: 'I am glad to hear you say that. Your experience will help me to bear my afflictions.' On being assured that many Christians were praying for him on the morning of the funeral, he wiped away the tears that sprang in his eyes, and said: 'I am glad to hear that. I want them to pray for me. I need their prayers.' As he was going out to the burial, the good lady expressed her sympathy with him. He thanked her gently, and said: 'I will try to go to God with my sorrows.' A few days afterward, she asked him if he could trust God. He replied: 'I think I can, and I will try. I wish I had that childlike faith you speak of, and I trust He will give it to me.' And then he spoke of his mother, whom so many years before he had committed to the dust among the wilds of Indiana. In this hour of his great trial, the memory of her who had held him upon her bosom, and soothed his childish griefs, came back to him with tenderest recollections. 'I remember her prayers,' said he, 'and they have always followed me. They have clung to me all my life.' ''

SOME CHAPTERS FROM THE SECRET SERVICE.

An interesting passage in the secret history of the war at this period is narrated by one of the chief actors, Mr. A. M. Ross, a distinguished ornithologist who has enriched the natural history of America by a mass of valuable notes on the birds of Canada. A few months after the inauguration of President Lincoln, Mr. Ross received a letter from the Hon. Charles Sumner, requesting him to come to Washington at his earliest convenience. "The day after my arrival in Washington," says Mr. Ross, "I was introduced to the President. Mr. Lincoln received me very cordially, and invited me to dine with him. After dinner, Mr. Lincoln led me to a window, distant from the rest of the party, and said: 'Mr. Sumner sent for you at my request; we need a confidential person in Canada to look after our interests, and keep us posted as to the schemes of the Confederates in Canada. You have been strongly recommended to me for the position. Your mission shall be as confidential as you please; no one here but your friend Mr. Sumner and myself shall have any knowledge of your position. Think it over to-night, and if you can accept the mission come up and see me at nine o'clock to-morrow morning.' When I took my leave of him, he said, 'I hope you will decide to serve us.' The position thus offered was one not suited to my tastes, but, as Mr. Lincoln appeared very desirous that I should accept it, I concluded to lay aside my prejudices and accept the responsibilities of the mission. I was also persuaded to this conclusion by the wishes of my friend, Mr. Sumner.

"At nine o'clock next morning, I waited upon the President, and announced my decision. He grasped my hand in a hearty manner, and said: 'Thank you, thank you; I am glad of it. You must help us to circumvent the machinations of the rebel agents in Canada. There is no doubt they will use your country as a communicating link with Europe, and also with their friends in New York. It is quite possible, also, that they may make Canada a base to harrass and annoy our people along the frontier.'

"After a lengthy conversation relative to private matters connected with my mission, I rose to leave, when he said: 'I will walk down to Willard's with you; the hotel is on my way to the Capitol, where I have an engagement at noon.' Before we reached the hotel, a man came up to the President and thrust a letter into his hand, at the same time applying for some office in Wisconsin. I saw that the President was offended at the rudeness, for he passed the letter back without looking at it, saying: 'No, sir! I am not going to open shop here.' This was said in a most emphatic manner, but accompanied by a comical gesture which caused the rejected applicant to smile. As we continued our walk, the President spoke of the annoyances incident to his position, saying: 'These office-seekers are a curse to the country; no sooner was my election certain, than I became the prey of hundreds of hungry, persistent applicants for office, whose highest ambition is to feed at the Government crib.' When he bid me good-bye, he said: 'Let me hear from you once a week at least.' As he turned to leave me a young army officer stopped him and made some request, to which the President replied with a good deal of humor: 'No, I can't do that; I must not interfere; they would scratch my eyes out, if I did. You must go to the proper department.'

"Some time later," says Mr. Ross, "I again visited Washington. On my arrival there (about midnight) I went direct to the Executive Mansion, and sent my card to the President, who had retired. In a few minutes the porter returned and requested me to accompany him to the President's office, where, in a short time, Mr. Lincoln would join me. The room into which I was ushered was the same in which I had spent several hours with the President on the occasion of my first interview with him. Scattered about the floor, and lying open on the table, were several military maps and documents, indicating recent use. In a few minutes the President came in and welcomed me in a most friendly manner; I expressed my regret at disturbing him at such an hour. He replied in a good humored manner, saying: 'No, no! You did right; you may waken me up whenever you please. I have slept with one eye open ever since I came to Washington; I never close both, except when an office-seeker is looking for me.' I then laid before the President the 'rebel mail.' He carefully examined the address of each letter, making occasional remarks. At length he found one addressed to Franklin Pierce, ex-President of the United States, then residing in New Hampshire, and another to ex-Attorney-General Cushing, a resident of Massachusetts. He appeared much surprised, and remarked, with a sigh, but without the slightest tone of asperity: 'I will have these letters inclosed in official envelopes, and sent to these parties.' When he had finished examining the addresses, he tied up all those addressed to private individuals, saying: 'I won't bother with them; but these look like official letters; I guess I'll go through them now.' He then opened them, and read their contents, slowly and carefully. While he was thus occupied, I had an excellent opportunity of studying this extraordinary man. A marked change had taken place in his countenance since my first interview with him. He looked much older, and bore traces of having passed through months of painful anxiety and trouble. There was a sad, serious look in his eyes that spoke louder than words of the disappointments, trials and discouragements he had encountered since the war began. The wrinkles about the eyes and forehead were deeper; the lips were firmer, but indicative of kindness and forbearance. The great struggle had brought out the hidden riches of his noble nature, and developed virtues and capacities which surprised his oldest and most intimate friends. He was simple, but astute; he possessed the rare faculty of seeing things just as they are; he was a just, charitable and honest man.

"Having finished reading the letters, I rose to go, saying that I would go to Willard's, and have a rest. 'No, no,' said the President, 'it is now three o'clock, you shall stay with me while you are in town; I'll find you a bed;' and leading the way, he took me into a bedroom, saying: 'Take a good sleep; you shall not be disturbed.' Bidding me 'good-night,' he left the room to go back and pore over the rebel letters until daylight, as he afterwards told me. I did not awake from my sleep until eleven o'clock in the forenoon, soon after which Mr. Lincoln came into my room, and laughingly said: 'When you are ready, I'll pilot you down to breakfast,' which he did, and seating himself at the table near me, expressed his fears that trouble was brewing on the New Brunswick border; that he had gathered further information on that point from the correspondence, which convinced him that such was the case. He was here interrupted by a servant, who handed him a card, upon reading which he arose, saying: 'The Secretary of War has received important tidings; I must leave you for the present; come to my room after breakfast, and we'll talk over this New Brunswick affair.

"On entering his room, I found him busily engaged in writing; at the same time repeating in a low voice the words of a poem, which I remembered reading many years before. When he stopped writing I asked him who was the author of that poem. He replied: 'I do not know. I have written the verses down from memory, at the request of a lady who is much pleased with them.' He passed the sheet, on which he had written the verses, to me, saying: 'Have you ever read them?' I replied that I had, many years previously, and that I should be pleased to have a copy of them in his handwriting, when he had time and an inclination for such work. He said, 'Well, you may keep that copy, if you wish.' "

A MORNING CALL ON THE PRESIDENT.

Hon. Wm. D. Kelly, a Member of Congress from Pennsylvania, relates that about the time of the Peninsular campaign he called at the White House one morning, and while waiting to see the President, "Senator Wilson, of Massachussetts, entered the chamber, having with him four Englishmen of ripe years and dignified bearing. The President had evidently had an early appointment, and had not completed his toilet. He was in slippers, and his pantaloons, when he crossed one knee over the other, disclosed the fact that he wore heavy blue woollen stockings.

"It was an agreeable surprise to learn that the chief of the visiting party was Professor Goldwin Smith, one of the firmest of our British friends. As the President rose to greet them, he was the very impersonation of easy dignity, notwithstanding the negligence of his costume; and, with a tact that never deserted him, he opened the conversation with an inquiry as to the health of his friend, John Bright, whom he said he regarded as a friend of our country and of freedom everywhere. The visitors having been seated, the magnitude of recent battles was referred to by Professor Smith as preliminary to the question whether the enormous losses which were so frequently occurring would not so reduce the industrial resources of the North as to seriously affect the prosperity of individual citizens and consequently the revenue of the country. He justified the question by proceeding to recite the number killed, wounded, and missing, reported after some of the great battles recently fought.

"DARKEY ARITHMETIC."

"There were two of Mr. Lincoln's devoted friends who lived in dread of his little stories. Neither of them was gifted with humor, and both could understand his propositions, which were always distinct and clean cut, without such familiar illustrations as those in which he so often indulged; and they were chagrined whenever they were compelled to hear him resort to them in the presence of distinguished strangers. They were Senator Wilson and Mr. Stanton, Secretary of War; and, as Professor Smith closed his arithmetical statement, the time came for the Massachusetts Senator to bite his lips; for the President, crossing his legs in such a manner as to show that his blue stockings were long as well as thick, said that in settling such matters as that, we must resort to 'darkey arithmetic.' 'To darkey arithmetic!' exclaimed the dignified representative of the learning and higher thought of Great Britain and her American Dominion. 'I did not know, Mr. President, that you have two systems of arithmetic.' 'Oh, yes,' said the President; 'I will illustrate that point by a little story: Two young contrabands, as we have learned to call them, are said to have been seated together, when one said to the other: 'Jim, do you know 'rithmetic?' Jim answered: 'No; what is 'rithmetic?' 'Well,' said the other, 'it's when you add up things. When you have one and one, and you put dem togedder, dey makes two. And when you subtracts things, when if you have two things and you takes one away, only one remains.' 'Is dat 'rithmetic?' 'Yah.' 'Well, 'taint true, den. It's no good!' Here a dispute arose, when Jim said: 'Now, you 'spose three pigeons sit on that fence, and somebody shoot one of dem; do 'tother two stay dar? I guess not! dey flies away quickern odder feller falls.' And, Professor, trifling as the story seems, it illustrates the arithmetic you must use in estimating the actual losses resulting from our great battles. The statements you have referred to give the killed, wounded and missing at the first roll-call after the battle, which always exhibits a greatly exaggerated total, especially in the column of missing."

GOLDWIN SMITH'S OPINION OF LINCOLN.

The distinguished author and statesman referred to in the above anecdote, Prof. Goldwin Smith, of Canada, has admirably summarized his impressions of Mr. Lincoln in a single paragraph: "Such a person as Abraham Lincoln," said he, "is quite unknown to our official circles or to those of Continental nations. Indeed, I think his place in history will be unique. He has not been trained to diplomacy or administrative affairs, and is in all respects one of the people. But how wonderfully he is endowed and equipped for the performance of the duties of the chief executive officer of the United States at this time! The precision and minuteness of his information on all questions to which we referred was a succession of surprises to me."

MR. LINCOLN AND "FATHER GIDDINGS."

Congressman Riddle relates that in the early part of the war he saw Mr. Lincoln almost daily, and became quite familiar with his views and his methods. "He was," says Mr. Riddle, "the most approachable of men. His good nature and pithy sayings, his power of endurance, were exhaustless; and he showed wonderful tact in dealing with men, whose character and purposes he usually recognized at sight. While trying to avoid being detained by them, he seldom offended them. A little story often sufficed a room-full. Seemingly, he had no secrets; he made no enemies, not even of the rejected. The venerable Joshua R. Giddings, whose services, in length of time and value to his country, ranked him with the most deserving who ever sat in the House of Representatives, had greatly offended Mr. Seward at Chicago, and had given Mr. Lincoln no cause for gratitude. He had lost his seat in Congress, and was broken in health and fortune. The Consulate General of Canada had recently been created, with a handsome salary. Mr. Giddings desired the position, but was too old and too proud to ask it. I undertook to present the matter to Mr. Lincoln. He received me very kindly, and spoke in the most appreciative terms of Mr. Giddings's great services, saying that his long habit of aggressive warfare perhaps disqualified him from apprehending the difficulties of the present position. Then he spoke of public affairs: 'What will the South do? What will the Northern Democrats do? At a pinch, what will the Republicans do? There's still a distinction between you abolitionists and the mass of our side. We have not yet won. We have gained a position where we may win. I hope we shall. I wish we had something better to offer Father Giddings. Go to Seward, and he will fix it for you.' I went to Mr. Seward, and secured the appointment of Mr. Giddings, who died in the Consulate in 1864."

STANDING BY OLD FRIENDS.

Fidelity to his old friends was one of the strongest traits in Mr. Lincoln's character. To serve him once unselfishly was to secure a claim upon his grateful memory which time never cancelled. As an illustration of this sincere loyalty, the following narrative is full of interest: George Clark, an eccentric man in humble circumstances, was an early friend of Lincoln, and subsequently removed to Lawrence, Mass. He met Lincoln in Boston during a stumping tour in the East. A few years passed, and Mr. Lincoln was the man of the hour. "Clark," says the writer, "whenever I met him, was talking about him. 'I can have any office I want,' he said, emphatically; 'Abe will look out for me.' I thought him a dreamer, and, like all his acquaintances, doubted his claim. Shortly after, Clark said he was going to have an office, and that in order to get it he must have twelve dollars to pay his fare to Washington. I told him it was a useless undertaking. He laughed at me. 'Abe' wouldn't refuse him anything he asked. He had made up his mind he must have a post-office. I told him that twelve dollars would only pay his fare, and that everything was so high and the hotels so crowded that he couldn't live twenty-four hours in Washington. Again he laughed in my face, and said: 'What do I care for high prices and hotels? Abe'll take care of me. All I want is money enough to get there.' Half in earnest, half in jest, the money was raised, and Clark went to Washington. A reception was taking place at the White House, and a man of his plebeian appearance was not only 'out of place,' but was hustled about in an unceremonious manner and in one way and another deterred from approaching Mr. Lincoln. Clark's patience under the embarrassing situation served him for more than an hour, when hunger and anxiety about a place to 'put up for the night' caused him to lose his discretion and become desperate. Mounting a chair, he sang out, 'Abe! Abe!' Mr. Lincoln instantly recognized the speaker. The passing pageant became to his mind like the unreality of a dream from which he had been suddenly aroused, and in all the brilliant assembly he saw only George Clark, the man who had shared with him the hardships and privations of frontier life in the days of small things. 'Make way for my friend!' exclaimed the President; and the surprised ladies and gentlemen paused in astonishment as Mr. Clark approached Mr. Lincoln, and was received with a cordiality and warmth of greeting that had not been accorded any other guest of the evening. A few minutes later, Mr. Lincoln excused himself from the reception and passed into another room with his old friend, and closed the door. Mr. Lincoln, so Clark repeatedly told his friends, was as familiar and off-hand as in their youth. He leaned against the wall and laughed. He was like an overjoyed boy. 'You don't know,' he said, 'how glad I am to see you. The face of an old friend is like a ray of sunshine through dark and gloomy clouds. I've shook hands till I am tireder than I ever was splitting rails.' He inquired where Clark was stopping, and if he had been to supper; and when Clark told him that he was 'stopping with Abe Lincoln, and hadn't had anything of any account to eat since leaving home,' he ordered the best the White House afforded set before him, while he returned to 'finish up the business he had in hand.' Finally Clark told Mr. Lincoln the object of his visit, and solicited the Lawrence postmastership. Mr. Lincoln laughed at him, and said: 'You ain't quite up enough in education, George, to take that kind of a job. But I've fixed you all snug and right. Take this letter.' The letter was addressed: 'To the Collector of the Port of Boston.' Clark presented himself at the Custom House one morning, and, upon being snubbed by one and another when he inquired for the Collector, remarked that he had a letter from his friend Abraham Lincoln, addressed to the gentleman for whom he had inquired. This opened the doors. The letter said, in substance: 'The bearer is my friend, George Clark. Give him the best position he can fill. If he fails in one place, give him another.' The Collector settled him as watchman on board vessels in the harbor—a berth in which he could sleep as much as he liked—at $1,200 a year.''

CHAPTER IV.

IN January, 1862, Hon. Simon Cameron, Secretary of
War, resigned his position, and Hon. Edwin M. Stanton was
appointed his successor. The change was a most fortunate one
for the country. Mr. Stanton was a man of singular fitness
for the responsible position he assumed, and his patriotic and
energetic services can never be overestimated. He had been
a Democrat, a member of Buchanan's Cabinet, and was, says
Dr. Holland, "the first one in that Cabinet to protest against
the downright treason into which it was drifting. He was a man
of indomitable energy, devoted loyalty, and thorough honesty.
Contractors could not manipulate him, and traitors could not
deceive him. Impulsive, perhaps, but true; willful, it is possible, but placable; impatient, but persistent and efficient,—
he became at once one of the most marked and important
of the members of the Cabinet." Lincoln and Stanton together were emphatically "a strong team."

MR. CAMERON'S VERSION OF HIS RETIREMENT.

Mr. Cameron, who is now (1886) in his eighty-eighth
year, has given, from his home in Harrisburg, Pa., a very interesting account of his personal relations with Mr. Lincoln,
and the causes that led to his retirement from the Cabinet and

the appointment of Mr. Stanton in his place. Mr. Cameron had been the choice of the Pennsylvania delegation for President, at the Chicago Convention in 1860, and it was largely due to him that Mr. Lincoln was nominated.

"After the election," says Mr. Cameron, "I made a trip West at Mr. Lincoln's request. He had, by letter, tendered

me the position of either Secretary of War or Secretary of the Treasury, but when I went to see him he said that he had concluded to make Mr. Seward Secretary of State, and he wanted to give a place to Mr. Chase. 'Salmon P. Chase,' said he, 'is a very ambitious man.' 'Very well,' said I, 'then the War Department is the place for him. We are going to have an armed conflict over your election, and the place for an ambitious man is in the War Department. There he will have lots of room to make a reputation.' These thoughts of mine, that we were to have war, disturbed Mr. Lincoln very much, and he seemed to think I was entirely too certain about it. Finally, when he came to make up his Cabinet, doubtless remembering what I had said about the War Department, he appointed me Secretary of War.

"There has been a great deal of misstatement as to Mr. Stanton's appointment as my successor. Edwin M. Stanton had been my attorney from the time I had gone into the War Department until he took my place. I had hardly made a move in which the legality of any question could arise. I had taken his advice. I believed in the vigorous prosecution of the war from the start, while Mr. Seward believed in dallying and compromising, and Mr. Chase was constantly agitated about the expenditure of money; therefore it was that I was careful to have the advice of an able lawyer. When the question of changing the War Department for the Russian mission came up, Mr. Lincoln said to me: 'Whom shall I appoint in your place?' My prompt response was, 'Edwin M. Stanton.' 'But,' said he, 'I had thought of giving it to Holt.' 'Mr. Lincoln,' said I, 'if I am to retire in the present situation of affairs, it seems but proper that a friend of mine, or at least a man not unfriendly to me, should be appointed in my place. If you give Mr. Stanton the position, you will not only accomplish this object, but please the State of Pennsylvania and get an excellent officer.' 'Very well,' said Mr. Lincoln, 'you go and see him, and if he will accept he shall have the place.'

"I left the White House and started to find Stanton, passing through the Treasury Department on my way. As I passed Mr. Chase's office, I stepped in and told him what had occurred between the President and myself. He said: 'Let's send for Stanton; bring him here and talk it over.' 'Very well,' said I, and a messenger was at once sent. He came immediately, and I told him of the conference between the President and myself. He agreed to accept. We walked to the White House, and the matter was settled.

"One of the troubles in the Cabinet which brought about this change was, that I had recommended in my annual report, in the fall of 1861, that the negroes should be enlisted as soldiers after they left their masters. This advanced step was regarded by most of the Cabinet with alarm. Mr. Lincoln thought it would frighten the border States out of the Union, and Mr. Seward and Mr. Chase thought it would never do at all."

A "LITTLE STORY" ON THE CABINET CHANGE.

Just before the retirement of Mr. Cameron, a number of influential Senators waited upon the President, and represented to him that, inasmuch as the Cabinet had not been chosen with reference to the war, and had more or less lost the confidence of the country, and since the President had decided to select a new war minister, they thought the occasion was opportune to change the whole seven Cabinet ministers. They, therefore, earnestly advised him to make a clean sweep, and select seven new men, and so restore the waning confidence of the country. The President listened with patient courtesy, and when the Senators had concluded, he said, with a characteristic gleam of humor in his eye: "Gentlemen, your request for a change of the whole Cabinet because I have made one change, reminds me of a story I once heard in Illinois of a farmer who was much troubled by skunks. They annoyed his household at night, and his wife insisted that he should take measures to get rid of them. One moonlight night he loaded his old shot-gun and stationed himself in the yard to watch for the intruders, his wife remaining in the house, anxiously awaiting the result. After some time she heard the shotgun go off, and in a few minutes the farmer entered the house. 'What luck had you?' said she. 'I hid myself behind the woodpile,' said the old man, 'with the shot-gun pointed toward the hen-roost, and before long there appeared, not one skunk, but *seven*. I took aim, blazed away, killed one—and he raised such a fearful smell, I concluded it was best to let the other six alone.'" The Senators retired, and nothing more was heard from them about Cabinet reconstruction.

GENERAL GRANT'S OPINION OF LINCOLN AND STANTON.

Of the character and abilities of Secretary Stanton, and the relations between him and the President, General Grant has admirably said: "I had the fullest support of the President and Secretary of War. No General could want better backing; for the President was a man of great wisdom and moderation, the Secretary a man of enormous character and will. Very often where Lincoln would want to say *Yes*, his Secretary would make him say *No;* and more frequently, when the Secretary was driving on in a violent course, the President would check him. United, Lincoln and Stanton made about as perfect a combination as I believe could, by any possibility, govern a great nation in time of war. * * * The two men were the very opposite of each other in almost every particular, except that each possessed great ability. Mr. Lincoln gained influence over men by making them feel that it was a pleasure to serve him. He preferred yielding his own wish to gratify others, rather than to insist upon having his own way. It distressed him to disappoint others. In matters of public duty, however, he had what he wished, but in the least offensive way. Mr. Stanton never questioned his own authority to command, unless resisted. He cared nothing for the feelings of others."

LINCOLN, NOT STANTON, THE RULING POWER.

With all his force of character and somewhat overbearing disposition, Mr. Stanton did not undertake to rule the President—though this has sometimes been asserted. He would frequently overawe and browbeat others, but he was never imperious in dealing with Mr. Lincoln. Mr. Watson, for some time Assistant Secretary of War, and Mr. Whiting, Solicitor of the War Department, have borne positive testimony to this fact. The Hon. George W. Julian, a member of the House Committee on the Conduct of the War, says: "On the 24th day of March, 1862, Secretary Stanton sent for the committee for the purpose of having a confidential conference as to military affairs. He was thoroughly discouraged. He told us the President had gone back to his first love as to General McClellan, and that it was *needless for him* or for us to labor with him." This language clearly shows that Lincoln, not Stanton, was the dominant mind.

"I RECKON YOU'LL HAVE TO DO IT, STANTON."

Whenever it was possible, Mr. Lincoln gave Stanton his own way, and did not oppose him. But there were occasions when, in a phrase used by Mr. Lincoln long before, it was "necessary to *put the foot down firmly.*" Such an occasion is described by Gen. J. B. Fry, Provost Marshal of the United States during the war. An enlistment agent had applied to the President to have certain credits of troops made to his county, and the President promised him it should be done. The agent then went to Secretary Stanton, who flatly refused to allow the credits as described. The agent returned to the President, who reiterated the order, but again without effect. Mr. Lincoln then went in person to Stanton's office. General Fry was called in by Stanton to state the facts in the case. After he concluded, Stanton remarked that Lincoln must see, in view of such facts, that his order could not be executed. What followed is thus related by General Fry: "Lincoln sat upon a sofa, with his legs crossed, and did not say a word until the Secretary's last remark. Then he said, in a somewhat positive tone: 'Mr. Secretary, I reckon you'll have to execute the order.' Stanton replied, with asperity: 'Mr. President, I cannot do it. The order is an improper one, and I cannot execute it.' Lincoln fixed his eye upon Stanton, and in a firm voice and with an accent that clearly showed his determination, he said: 'Mr. Secretary, *it will have to be done.*' Stanton then realized that he was overmatched. He had made a square issue with the President, and had been defeated. Upon an intimation from him, I withdrew, and did not witness his surrender. A few minutes after I reached my office I received instructions from the Secretary to carry out the President's order."

A CALM PRESIDENT AND A FURIOUS SECRETARY.

Vice-president Wheeler relates a characteristic incident of the relations between Lincoln and Stanton. The President had promised Mr. Wheeler an appointment for an old friend as army paymaster, stating that the Secretary of War would instruct the gentleman to report for duty. Hearing nothing further from the matter, Mr. Wheeler at length called upon the Secretary and reminded him of the appointment. Mr. Stanton denied all knowledge of the matter, but stated, in his brusque manner, that the name would be sent in with hundreds of others, to the Senate for its consideration. Mr. Wheeler argued that his friend had been appointed by the commander-in-chief of the Army, and that it was unjust to ask him to wait for the tardy action of the Senate upon the nomination, and that he was entitled to be mustered in at once. But all in vain; the only reply that could be got from the iron Secretary was: "You have my answer; no argument."

Mr. Wheeler went to the chief clerk of the department, and asked for Mr. Lincoln's letter directing the appointment. Receiving it, he proceeded to the White House, although it was after executive hours. "I can see Mr. Lincoln now," says Mr. Wheeler, "as he looked when I entered the room. He wore a long calico dressing-gown, reaching to his heels; his feet were encased in a pair of old-fashioned leathern slippers, such as we used to find in the old-time country hotels, and which had evidently seen much service in Springfield. Above these appeared the home-made blue woollen stockings which he wore at all seasons of the year. He was sitting in a splint rocking-chair, with his legs elevated and stretched across his office table. He greeted me warmly. Apologizing for my intrusion at that unofficial hour, I told him I had called simply to ascertain which was the paramount power in the Government, he or the Secretary of War. Letting down his legs and straightening himself up in his chair, he answered: 'Well, it is generally supposed *I am*. What's the matter?' I then briefly recalled the facts attending Sabin's appointment, when, without comment, he said: 'Give me my letter.' Then, taking his pen, he indorsed upon it:

'Let the within named J. A. Sabin be mustered AT ONCE. It is due to him and to Mr. W., under the circumstances.   A. LINCOLN.' "

Armed with this peremptory order, Mr. Wheeler called on Mr. Stanton the next morning. The Secretary was furious. He charged Mr. Wheeler with interfering with his prerogatives. Mr. Wheeler remarked that he would call the next morning for the order to muster in. He called accordingly, and, handing him the order, in a rage, Stanton said: "I hope I shall never hear of this matter again."

AN UNCOMPLIMENTARY OPINION OF THE PRESIDENT.

It is related by the Hon. George W. Julian, that on a certain occasion a committee of Western men, headed by Mr. Lovejoy, procured from the President an important order looking to the exchange and transfer of Eastern and Western soldiers, with a view to more effective work. "Repairing to the office of the Secretary, Mr. Lovejoy explained the scheme, as he had before done to the President, but was met with a flat refusal. 'But we have the President's order, sir,' said Lovejoy. 'Did Lincoln give you an order of that kind?' said Stanton. 'He did, sir.' 'Then he is a d—d fool,' said the irate Secretary. 'Do you mean to say the President is a d—d fool?' asked Lovejoy, in amazement. 'Yes, sir, if he gave you such an order as that.' The bewildered Illinoisan betook himself at once to the President, and related the result of his conference. 'Did Stanton say I was a d—d fool?' asked Lincoln, at the close of the recital. 'He did, sir, and repeated it.' After a moment's pause, and looking up, the President said: 'If Stanton said I was a d—d fool, then *I must be one*, for he is nearly always right, and generally says what he means. *I will step over and see him.*'"

LINCOLN'S SELF-CONSTITUTED ADVISERS.

Not the least of Mr. Lincoln's trials while he was sustaining the vast responsibilities of the war and the administration, was the daily invasion of a horde of visitors, each intent upon securing some personal favor, or upon helping him in the conduct of affairs by unsought and intrusive advice. One day, when he was alone and busily engaged on an important subject, he was disturbed by the intrusion of three men, who, without apology, proceeded to lay their claim before him. The spokesman of the three informed the President that they were the owners of some torpedo, or other warlike invention, which, if the Government would only adopt it, would soon crush the rebellion. "Now," said the spokesman, "we have been here to see you time and again; you have referred us to the Secretary of War, to the Chief of Ordnance and the General of the army, and they will give us no satisfaction. We have been kept here waiting till money and patience are exhausted, and we now come to demand of you a final reply to our application." Mr. Lincoln listened quietly to this tirade, and at its close the old twinkle came into his eye. "You three gentlemen," said he, "remind me of a story I once heard of a poor little boy out West who had lost his mother. His father wanted to give him a religious education, and so placed him in the family of a clergyman whom he directed to instruct the little fellow carefully in the Scriptures. Every day the boy was required to commit to memory and recite one chapter of the Bible. Things proceeded smoothly until they reached that chapter which details the story of the trials of

Shadrach, Meshach, and Abednego, in the fiery furnace. The boy got on well until he was asked to repeat these three names, but he had forgotten them. His teacher told him he must learn them, and gave him another day to do so. Next day the boy again forgot them. 'Now,' said the teacher, 'you have again failed to remember those names, and you can go no further till you have learned them. I will give you another day on this lesson, and if you don't repeat the names I will punish you.' A third time the boy came to recite, and got down to the stumbling-block, when the clergyman said: 'Now tell me the names of the men in the fiery furnace.' 'Oh,' said the boy, 'here come those three infernal old bores! I wish the devil had them!'" Having received their "final answer," the three patriots retired; and at the Cabinet meeting, which followed directly after, the President, in high good humor, related how he had got rid of his untimely visitors.

THE GOVERNMENT ON A TIGHT-ROPE.

Some gentlemen from the West called at the White House one day, excited and troubled about some of the commissions or omissions of the administration. The President heard them patiently, and then replied: "Gentlemen, suppose all the property you were worth was in gold, and you had put it in the hands of Blondin to carry across the Niagara river on a rope; would you shake the cable, or keep shouting out to him, 'Blondin, stand up a little straighter!—Blondin, stoop a little more—go a little faster—lean a little more to the north—lean a little more to the south?' No! you would hold your breath as well as your tongue, and keep your hands off until he was safe over. The Government is carrying an immense weight. Untold treasures are in their hands. They are doing the very best they can. Don't badger them. Keep silence, and we'll get you safe across."

HOW MANY REBELS THERE WERE.

Mr. Lincoln sometimes had a very effective way of dealing with men who asked troublesome or improper questions. A visitor once asked him how many men the rebels had in the field. The President replied, very seriously, "*Twelve hundred thousand*, according to the best authority." The interrogator blanched in the face, and ejaculated, "Good heavens!" "Yes, sir, twelve hundred thousand—no doubt of it. You see, all of our generals, when they get whipped, say the enemy outnumbered them from three or five to one, and I must believe them. We have four hundred thousand men in the field, and three times four makes twelve. Don't you see it?"

"DIRECT FROM THE ALMIGHTY."

On one occasion an anti-slavery delegation from New York was pressing the adoption of the emancipation policy. During the interview the "chairman," the Rev. Dr. C——, made a characteristic and powerful appeal, largely made up of quotations from the Old Testament Scriptures. Mr. Lincoln received the "bombardment" in silence. As the speaker concluded, he continued for a moment in thought, and then, drawing a long breath, responded : "Well, gentlemen, it is not often one is favored with a delegation *direct* from the Almighty !"

THE NEW YORK MILLIONAIRES WHO WANTED A GUN-BOAT.

In 1862, after the appearance of the rebel ram Merrimac, the President was waited upon by a delegation of New York millionaires, who represented to him that they were very uneasy about the unprotected situation of their city, which was exposed to attack and bombardment by rebel rams ; and requested him to detail a gun-boat to defend the city. The gentlemen were fifty in number, very dignified and respectable in appearance, and stated that they represented in their own right $100,000,000. Of course Mr. Lincoln did not wish to offend these gentlemen, and yet he intended to give them a little lesson. He listened with great attention, and seemed to be much impressed by their presence and their statements. Then

AN UNSATISFACTORY INTERVIEW.—THE NEW YORK MILLIONAIRES WHO WANTED PRESIDENT LINCOLN TO SEND THEM A GUN-BOAT.

he replied, very deliberately: "Gentlemen, I am by the Constitution commander-in-chief of the army and navy of the United States; and, as a matter of law, can order anything done that is practicable to be done. But, as a matter of fact, I am not in command of the gun-boats or ships of war; as a matter of fact, I do not know exactly where they are, but presume they are actively engaged. It is impossible for me, in the present condition of things, to furnish you a gun-boat. The credit of the Government is at a very low ebb; greenbacks are not worth more than forty or fifty cents on the dollar; and in this condition of things, if I was worth half as much as you, gentlemen, are represented to be, and as badly frightened as you seem to be, I *would build a gun-boat and give it to the Government.*" A gentleman who accompanied the delegation says he never saw one hundred millions sink to such insignificant proportions, as the committee recrossed the threshold of the White House, sadder but wiser men.

ANOTHER "ADVISORY COMMITTEE."

Mr. Joshua F. Speed relates that on one occasion, when Kentucky was overrun, Nelson had been beaten in battle near Richmond and lay wounded in Cincinnati, and Ohio, Indiana, and Illinois were alarmed, and Kentucky was aroused, a self-constituted committee of distinguished gentlemen determined to visit and advise with the President as to what would best be done. "I happened," says Mr. Speed, "to be present at the interview. The committee was composed of able and distinguished men. Senator Lane opened for Indiana, Garrett Davis followed for Kentucky, and other gentlemen for Ohio and Illinois. They all had complaints to make of the conduct of the war in the West. Like the expression in the prayer-book, the Government was doing every thing it ought not to do, and leaving undone every thing it ought to do. The President sat on a revolving chair, looking at every one till they were all done. I never saw him exhibit more tact or talent than he did on this occasion. He said, 'Now, gentlemen, I am going to make you a curious kind of a speech. I announce to you that I am not going to do one single thing that any one of you have asked me to do. But it is due to myself and to you that I should give my reasons.' He then, from his seat, answered each man, taking them in the order in which they spoke, never forgetting a point that any one had made. When he was done, he rose from his chair and said, 'Judge List, this reminds me of an anecdote which I heard a son of yours tell in Burlington, Iowa. He was trying to enforce upon his hearers the truth of the old adage that 'three removes are worse than a fire.' As an illustration, he gave an account of a family who started from Western Pennsylvania, pretty well off in this world's goods when they started. But they moved and moved, having less and less every time they moved, till after a while they could carry every thing in one wagon. He said that the chickens of the family got so used to being moved, that whenever they saw the wagon sheets brought out they laid themselves on their backs and crossed their legs, ready to be tied. Now, gentlemen, if I were to be guided by every committee that comes in at that door, I might just as well cross my hands and let you tie me. Nevertheless, I am glad to see you.' "

WHOSE LEG WAS THE LARGEST?

Hon. Daniel W. Gooch, a member of Congress from Massachusetts, who saw much of Mr. Lincoln during the war, says that one day a gentleman from his district asked to be introduced to the President. He took him to the White House, and after the introduction the gentleman entered upon a rather pompous discourse on public affairs, urging the adoption of certain measures, and giving a good deal of advice generally. The President listened patiently to it all, seeming to be much impressed; and at the conclusion thanked the gentleman, and promised to consider what he had said. Then,

turning to Mr. Gooch, who sat near, he slapped him familiarly on the leg, and exclaimed, "Gooch, your leg is a good
deal bigger than mine ! How does your leg happen to be so
thick, and mine so thin?" and so went on, laughing and
joking, until the Massachusetts gentleman retired, greatly
pleased to think he had made so favorable an impression
on the President.

HE FORGAVE HIM.

Among the innumerable nuisances and "cranks" who
called on Mr. Lincoln at the White House, were the many
chaps who sought to win favor by claiming to have been the
first to suggest his nomination as President. One of these
claimants, who was the editor of a weekly paper published in
a little village in Missouri, called one day, and was admitted
to Mr. Lincoln's presence. He at once commenced stating
to Mr. Lincoln that he was the man who first suggested his
name for the Presidency, and pulling from his pocket an old,
worn, defaced copy of his paper, exhibited to the President
an item on the subject. "Do you really think," said Mr.
Lincoln, "that announcement was the occasion of my nomination?" "Certainly," said the editor, "the suggestion was so
opportune that it was at once taken up by other papers, and the
result was your nomination and election." "Ah ! well," said
Mr. Lincoln, with a sigh, and assuming a rather gloomy
countenance, "I am glad to see you and to know this ; but you
will have to excuse me, I am just going to the War Department to see Mr. Stanton." "Well," said the editor, "I will
walk over with you." The President, with that apt good
nature so characteristic of him, took up his hat and said:
"Come along." When they reached the door of the Secretary's office, Mr. Lincoln turned to his companion and said:
"I shall have to see Mr. Stanton alone, and you must excuse
me," and taking him by the hand he continued, "Good-bye.
I hope you will feel perfectly easy about having nominated
me ; don't be troubled about it ; *I forgive you.*"

A PASS TO RICHMOND IN 1862.

One day, in the Spring of 1862, a gentleman from some Northern city entered Mr. Lincoln's private office, and earnestly requested a pass to Richmond. "A pass to Richmond!" exclaimed the President. "Why, my dear sir, if I should give you one it would do you no good. You may think it very strange, but there's a lot of fellows between here and Richmond, who either can't read or are prejudiced against every man who totes a pass from me. I have given McClellan and more than two hundred thousand others passes to Richmond, *and not a single one of 'em has yet gotten there!*"

MAKING SOME ONE RESPONSIBLE.

An incident is narrated by ex-Senator W. S. Wilkinson, of Minnesota, of a member of Congress who called upon the President one day to urge the appointment of a constituent as an Indian Agent. The President took great interest in these appointments, and was anxious that none but good men should fill them. He told the member this, and said, plainly: "I don't know this man that you recommend so highly, and I have no means of finding out, except by inquiring of some one, and I know of no more proper persons to consult in such matters than those whom the people have selected to look after their interests in Congress. Now I will tell you what I will do. If you will sit down at the table, and write out what you have told me about this man, and recommend his appointment, and sign your name to it, I will appoint him, and if your man proves unworthy I will *hold you responsible*." It is needless to add that this ended the efforts of the Congressman.

A BOMBASTIC PROPOSAL SQUELCHED.

Senator Wilkinson further relates that "in the early part of the war there were a great many men who were ready to volunteer advice to the President as to the conduct of the war, and also their services, provided they could be placed in positions of authority or profit. In 1862, after the Indian outbreak in Minnesota and Dakota, an Indian Agent came on to Washington to volunteer his services to put it down. He called on John Covode of Pennsylvania, and Senator Wade of Ohio, and the writer of this, and disclosed his plan. It was for the President to authorize this agent to raise a brigade of cavalry, to be composed of frontiersmen, and commanded by this agent as brigadier-general. The Indian campaigner wanted a separate and independent command, of which he was to have supreme control, not only conducting operations in the field, but also in the purchase of horses and supplies for the brigade. I reluctantly consented to go with the parties above named to Mr. Lincoln, and there I heard the proposition submitted to him. This would-be brigadier said that with such a command as he proposed he could put down the outbreak and restore quiet on the frontier in six weeks; that he could save the lives of hundreds of settlers in the West and the Government millions of dollars; such men as he proposed to enlist in this service were alone competent to perform this important duty; and that his own acquaintance with Indian character and habits would enable him to do more prompt and successful work in this particular field than any one that could be sent there. Mr. Lincoln listened patiently up to this time, but he could stand it no longer. 'Sir,' said he, 'since the war began I have received a great deal of advice from all classes of men, and in the army great promises have been made, and my experience and observation has been that those who promise the most *do the least.*' This ended the interview. Mr. Lincoln was a keen and accurate judge of character, and could detect fraud and imposture as readily as any man I ever knew. He saw through this fellow at once, and that his object was to make money out of this scheme. It was fortunate for the country that such a man was at the head in such a crisis as was upon the country under his administration."

ALL THE GOOD MEN IN JAIL.

Ex-Congressman Rice tells a story of a boy, from one of the country towns of Massachusetts, who had entered a store in Boston, and becoming dazzled by the apparent universal distribution of wealth, without any definite idea of how it was acquired, "fell into the fault of robbing his employer's letters as he took them to and from the post-office, and, having been convicted of the offense, was serving out his sentence in jail. The father of this boy came to Washington to obtain a pardon for his son, and I accompanied him to the White House and introduced him. A petition, signed by a large number of respectable citizens, was presented. The President put on his spectacles and stretched himself at length upon his arm-chair while he deliberately read the document, and then he turned to me and asked if I met a man going down the stairs as I came up. I said that I did. 'Yes,' said the President, 'he was the last person in this room before you came, and his errand was to get a man pardoned out of the penitentiary, and now you have come to get a boy out of jail.' Then, with one of those bursts of humor which were both contagious and irresistible, he said: 'I'll tell you what it is, we must abolish those courts, or they will be the death of us. I thought it bad enough that they put so many men in the penitentaries for me to get out; but if they have now begun on the boys and the jails, and have roped you into the delivery, let's after them! And they deserve the worst fate,' he soon continued, 'because, according to the evidence that comes to me, they pick out the very best men and send them to the penitentiary; and this present petition shows they are playing the same game on the good boys, and sending them all to jail. The man you met on the stairs affirmed that his friend in the penitentiary is a most exemplary citizen, and Massachusetts must be a happy State if her boys out of jail are as virtuous as this one appears to be who is in. Yes; down with the courts, and deliverance to their victims, and then we can have some peace!' During all this time the President was in a most merry mood. Then his face assumed a sad and thoughtful expression, and he proceeded to say that he could quite understand how a boy from simple country life might be overcome by the sight of universal abundance in a large city, and by a full supply of money in the pockets of almost everybody, and be led to commit even such an offense as this one had done, and yet not be justly put into the class of hopeless criminals; and if he could be satisfied that this was a case of that kind, and that the boy would be placed under proper influences and probably saved from a bad career, he would be glad to extend the clemency asked for. The father explained his purpose in that respect, the Congressmen from the State in which he belonged united in the petition, and the boy was pardoned.''

THE STORY OF THE STUTTERING JUSTICE.

Vice-president Wheeler relates that on one occasion he met in Washington an old friend of Mr. Lincoln, Orlando Kellogg, of Illinois, a well-known lawyer, and member of Congress during the same term as Mr. Lincoln's. Together they went to the White House, where a Cabinet meeting was in session, during which, as was well known, it was extremely difficult to obtain access to the President. "Sauntering up carelessly to the door-keeper," says Mr. Wheeler, "with watch chain and large seals dangling from his fob, and with hands in his pockets, Kellogg said: 'Young man, you go in and tell the President that Orlando Kellogg is at the door, and wants to tell him the story of the stuttering justice.' The door-keeper said he did not like to take such a message to the President, as a Cabinet meeting was in session. In his most imperative manner, Kellogg ordered him to go in, or he would regret it. The young man obeyed, and, returning in a moment, said the President directed him to bring Mr. Kellogg in. Some time afterward, Secretary Chase, who was the impersonation of official and personal propriety, described to me, with evident disgust, the scene. On Kellogg's entry,

Mr. Lincoln met him at the door and grasped him warmly by the hand with great delight. 'Gentlemen,' said Mr. Lincoln, addressing his Cabinet, 'this is my old friend, Orlando Kellogg, and he wants to tell us the story of the stuttering justice. Let us lay all business aside, for it is a good story.' And the wheels of the public business stopped, although the clouds of war were lowering, while the humorous Kellogg, with Lincoln convulsed with laughter, furnished them a little lubrication with a 'good story.'"

"THE 'RARE' RANK GOES RIGHT BEHIND THE FRONT."

On a certain occasion in the early part of the war, some military gentlemen were instructed to prepare plans for various operations and present them to the President. General E. D. Keyes, one of the officers referred to, thus describes the interview: "We found the President and Secretary of State waiting to receive us in the Executive Mansion. Mr. Lincoln was sitting behind the table, near the end; his right leg, from the knee to the foot, which was not small, rested on the table, his left leg on a chair, and his hands were clasped over his head. These positions were changed frequently during the conference, and I never saw a man who could scatter his limbs more than he. We sat down, and the places occupied by the four persons were about the corners of a square of eight feet sides. Mr. Lincoln then said: 'There's no time to lose. Let us hear your reports, gentlemen.' Meigs read first. Then I read. Meigs went more into the details of engineering, and I into those of artillery, which was my specialty. When we spoke of scarps, counterscarps, terreplains, barbettes, trench cavaliers, etc., Mr. Seward interrupted, saying: 'Your excellency and I don't understand all those technical military terms.' 'That's so,' said Mr. Lincoln, 'but we understand that the *rare* rank goes right behind the front!' and then he brought both feet to the floor, and clasped his hands between his knees."

Mr. Lincoln once remarked that when he became President, he was "deplorably ignorant" of all marine matters, being only "a prairie lawyer." And, with one of his keenest touches of humor, he added: "But I do think I knew the difference between the bow of a ship and her stern, and I don't believe Secretary Welles did."

CHAPTER V.

MR. LINCOLN'S PERSONAL ATTENTION TO THE MILITARY PROBLEMS OF THE WAR.
——"A BORN STRATEGIST," UNEQUALLED IN MILITARY SAGACITY.——SOME
REMARKABLE PROPHECIES BY MR. LINCOLN.——EFFORTS TO PUSH FORWARD
THE WAR.——DISHEARTENING DELAYS.——"NO ONE SEEMS READY."——
MR. LINCOLN'S WORRY AND PERPLEXITY.—"POOR GENTLEMAN!"——
BRIGHTENING PROSPECTS.——UNION VICTORIES IN NORTH CAROLINA AND
TENNESSEE.——PROCLAMATION BY THE PRESIDENT.——MR. LINCOLN WANTS
TO SEE FOR HIMSELF.——VISITS FORTRESS MONROE.——WITNESSES AN AT-
TACK ON THE REBEL RAM MERRIMAC.——THE CAPTURE OF NORFOLK.——MR.
LINCOLN'S ACCOUNT OF THE AFFAIR.

EARLY in 1862, Mr. Lincoln began giving more of his personal attention to military affairs. He was dissatisfied with the slow progress and small achievements of our armies, and sought to infuse new zeal and energy into the Union commanders. He also began a thorough study of the great military problems pressing for solution ; and seemed resolved to assume the full responsibilities of his position, not only as the civil head of the Government, but as the commander-in-chief of the armies and navies of the United States. In this he was influenced by no desire for personal control of, or interference with, the commanders in the field ; he always preferred to leave them the fullest liberty of action. But he felt that the situation demanded a single head, ready and able to take full responsibility for the most important steps ; and, true to himself and his habits of a lifetime, he neither sought responsibility nor flinched from it.

The leading officers of the Union army were mostly young and inexperienced, and none of them had as yet developed the capacity of a great commander. At the best, it was a process of experiment, to see what generals and what strategic movements were most likely to succeed. And in order to be able to judge correctly of measures and of men, Mr. Lincoln undertook to familiarize himself with the practical details of military affairs. The plain country lawyer, unversed in the art of war, was suddenly transformed into the great civil ruler and military chieftain. "He was already," says Mr. Riddle, "one of the wariest, coolest and most skillful managers of men. *A born strategist*, he was now rapidly mastering the great outline ideas of the art of war."

UNEQUALLED IN MILITARY SAGACITY.

Says a distinguished Union officer, General Keyes: "The elements of selfishness and ferocity, which are not unusual with first-class military chiefs, were wholly foreign to Mr. Lincoln's nature. Nevertheless, *there was not one of his most trusted warlike counsellors in the beginning of the war who equalled him in military sagacity.*" His reliance, in the new duties and perils that confronted him, was upon that simple common-sense, that native power of judgment and discernment, which were intuitive with him. "Military Science," says a distinguished officer, "is *common-sense applied to the affairs of war.*" While Mr. Lincoln made no claim to technical knowledge in this sphere, and preferred to leave details to his subordinates, he yet developed an insight into military problems, and an understanding of practical operations in the field, which enabled him not only to approve or disapprove, but to direct and plan.

A striking proof of Mr. Lincoln's knowledge of military affairs is given by Mr. J. M. Winchell, who thus relates what happened in a personal interview with the President: "I was accompanied by one of Mr. Lincoln's personal friends; and when we entered the well-known reception-room, a very tall, lanky man came quickly forward to meet us. His manner seemed to me the perfection of courtesy. I was struck with the simplicity, kindness, and dignity of his deportment, so different from the clownish manners with which it was then customary to invest him. His face was a pleasant surprise, formed as my expectations had been from the poor photographs then in vogue, and the general belief in his ugliness. I remember thinking how much better-looking he was than I had anticipated, and wondering that any one should consider him ugly. His expression was grave and care-worn, but still enlivened with a cheerfulness that gave me instant hope. After a brief interchange of commonplaces, he entered on a description of the situation, giving the numbers of the contending armies, their movements, and the general strategical purposes which should govern them both. Taking from the wall a large map of the United States, and laying it on the table, he pointed out with his long finger the geographical features of the vicinity, clearly describing the various movements so far as known, reasoning rigidly from step to step, and creating a chain of probabilities too strong for serious dispute. His apparent knowledge of military science, and his familiarity with the special features of the present campaign, were surprising in a man who had been all his life a civilian, engrossed with politics and the practice of the law, and whose attention must necessarily be so much occupied with the perplexing detail of duties incident to his position. It was clear that he made the various campaigns of the war a subject of profound and intelligent study, forming opinions thereon as positive and clear as those he held in regard to civil affairs.''

SOME REMARKABLE PROPHECIES BY MR. LINCOLN.

At a later period of the war, the writer just quoted had opportunity to witness a still more striking instance of Mr. Lincoln's far-seeing military sagacity. He had occasion to call upon the President, and the conversation again drifted into a military channel. "Presently Mr. Lincoln startled us all," says Mr. Winchell, "by declaring that he saw no hope of success for any of the campaigns then being opened. Having gone thus far, and seeing our surprise and perplexity, he seemed animated by a desire to justify his statement. Going to the wall, and again taking down the large map which he had pressed into service on the previous occasion, he proceeded to inform us that there were three important movements being attempted by our forces toward points against which our efforts had previously proved unsuccessful. One of these, he said, was against Richmond, on the same general plan substantially attempted by Burnside; one against Charleston, from the sea, by the combined land and naval forces; and one against Vicksburg, by way of the Yazoo pass and the network of bayous and small streams by which the Mississippi is flanked, and through some of which it was hoped to transfer General Grant's forces to a point from which a successful assault might be made on that great stronghold, which had thus far defied our most determined attacks. 'I cannot see,' remarked Mr. Lincoln, 'how either of these plans can succeed;' and, forthwith throwing aside all reserve, and speaking with as much apparent frankness as though conversing with his confidential advisers, he freely criticised the conduct of the campaigns in question, going into all the details of a military argument, and logically demonstrated in advance that Grant would again be foiled in his strategy against Vicksburg; that Hooker would fail to reach Richmond, and that Du Pont and Hunter would be compelled to retire, baffled, from before Charleston. I do not now remember the reasons he gave for his judgment in regard to the two movements last named, but I recollect well his clear description of the narrow and winding water-courses through which Grant was endeavoring to conduct his gunboats, generally impassable for large craft, either through too high or too low water, and capable of fatal obstruction in the forests which they penetrate, by an enemy intimately acquainted with every feature of the country, and who had proved himself only too well informed of all our movements, and equally active and successful in opposing our progress into his own country. * * * We took our leave soon after, but I was long haunted with the recollection of what I had heard. My admiration for the man and his high moral and intellectual qualities was increased, and my confidence in our military chieftains, never very high previously, was proportionately diminished. As before, the events justified his prediction. Our attacking forces were beaten off from Charleston; the army of the Potomac was hurled back upon the North at Chancellorsville, and Grant and Porter were completely baffled in the ill-judged experiment in the hostile swamps of Mississippi, which they attempted to penetrate through streams too narrow to turn a gunboat in, and surrounded by a restless foe ever ready to exhaust all the means of impediment and destruction. And though Mr. Lincoln's opinions *may* have owed their correctness to accident, yet I could not resist a feeling that he had a strength of brain and soundness of judgment which measurably supplied the want of military training, and which fitted him better to plan campaigns than any of the professional soldiers to whose views he felt himself compelled to yield."

EFFORTS TO PUSH FORWARD THE WAR.—DISHEARTENING DELAYS.—"NO ONE SEEMS READY."

Toward the end of January, 1862, Mr. Lincoln sought to overcome the inertia that seemed settling upon the Union forces, by issuing the "President's General Order, No. 1," directing that on the 22d day of February following, "a general movement of the land and naval forces of the United States" be made against the insurgent forces, and giving warning that "the heads of departments, and especially the Secretaries of War and of the Navy, with all their subordinates, and the General-in-Chief, with all other commanders and subordinates of land and naval forces, will severally be held to their strict and full responsibilities for prompt execution of this order." This order, while it doubtless served to infuse new energy into commanders and officials, did not result in any substantial successes to our arms. The President, worn by his ceaseless activities and anxieties, seems to have been momentarily disheartened at the situation. Admiral Dahlgren, who was in command of the Washington navy-yard in 1862, narrates that one day, at this period, "the President drove down to see the hundred-and-fifty-pounder cannon fired. For the first time, I heard the President speak of the bare possibility of our being two nations—as if alluding to a previous suggestion. He could not see how the two could exist so near each other. He was evidently much worried at our lack of military success, and remarked that '*no one seemed ready.*' "

MR. LINCOLN'S WORRY AND PERPLEXITY.—"POOR GENTLE-MAN !"

It is difficult to portray the worry and perplexity that beset Mr. Lincoln's life, and the incessant demands upon his attention, in his efforts to familiarize himself, as he felt compelled to do, with the practical operations of the war. Admiral Dahlgren, who saw him almost daily, relates that one morning the President sent for him, and said: "Well, Captain, here's a letter about some new powder." He read the letter and showed the sample of powder,—adding that he had burned some of it and it did not seem a good article; there was too much residuum. "Now I'll show you," said he. So he got a small sheet of paper and placed some of the powder on it, then went to the fire, and with the tongs picked up a coal, which he blew, with his spectacles still on his nose; then he clapped the coal to the powder, and after the explosion, remarked: "There is too much left there." There is something humorous, but touching and pathetic as well, in this picture of the President of the United States, with all his enormous cares and responsibilities, engaged in such a petty matter as testing a sample of powder. And yet so great was his anxiety for the success of the armies and navies under his control, that he wished to become personally satisfied as to every detail. He didn't wish to lose battles on account of bad powder.

"At another time," says Admiral Dahlgren, "the President sent for me regarding some new invention. After the agent of the inventor left, the President began on army matters. 'Now,' said he, 'I am to have a sweat of five or six days.' " (Alluding to an impending battle, for the result of which he was very anxious.) Again: "The President sent for me. Some man in trouble about arms. President holding a breech-loader in his hand. This done, he asked me about the iron-clads, and Charleston." And again: "Went to the Department and found the President there. *He looks thin and badly*, and is very nervous. Said they were doing nothing at Charleston, only asking for one iron-clad after another. The canal at Vicksburg was of no account, and he wondered how any sensible man would do it. He feared the favorable state of public expectation would pass away before anything was done. Then he levelled a couple of jokes at the doings at Vicksburg and Charleston." No wonder the sympathetic Dahlgren, witnessing the sufferings of the tortured President, should exclaim: *"Poor gentleman!* How thin and wasted he is!"

BRIGHTENING PROSPECTS.—UNION VICTORIES IN NORTH CAR-
OLINA AND TENNESSEE.

The gloomy outlook in the Spring of 1862 was relieved by the substantial victories of Gen. Burnside in North Carolina and Gen. Grant in Tennessee. The President was cheered and elated by these successes. It is related that Gen. Burnside, visiting Washington at this time, called on the President, and that "the meeting was a grand spectacle. The two stalwart men rushed into each other's arms, and warmly clasped each other for some minutes. When General Burnside was about to leave, the President inquired: 'Is there anything, my dear General, that I can do for you?' 'Yes! yes!' was the quick reply, 'and I am glad you asked me that question. My three brigadiers, you know; everything depended upon them, and they did their duty grandly!—Oh, Mr. President, we owe so much to them! I should so much love, when I go back, to take them their promotions.' 'It shall be done!' was Mr. Lincoln's hearty response, and on the instant the promotions were ordered, and General Burnside had the pleasure of taking back with him to Foster, Reno, and Parke their commissions as Major-Generals.''

PROCLAMATION BY THE PRESIDENT.

Our brightening prospects impelled the President to issue, on the 10th of April, the following proclamation:

"It has pleased Almighty God to vouchsafe signal victories to the land and naval forces engaged in suppressing an internal rebellion, and at the same time to avert from our country the dangers of foreign intervention and invasion. It is therefore recommended to the people of the United States that, at their next weekly assemblages in their accustomed places of public worship which shall occur after the notice of this Proclamation shall have been received, they especially acknowledge and render thanks to our Heavenly Father for these inestimable blessings; that they then and there implore spiritual consolation in behalf of all those who have been brought into affliction by the casualties and calamities of sedition and civil war; and that they reverently invoke the Divine guidance for our national counsels, to the end that they may speedily result in the restoration of peace, harmony, and unity throughout our borders, and hasten the establishment of fraternal relations among all the countries of the earth. ABRAHAM LINCOLN.''

MR. LINCOLN WANTS TO SEE FOR HIMSELF.—A VISIT TO FORTRESS MONROE.

Early in May Mr. Lincoln determined on a personal visit to Fortress Monroe, in order to learn what he could from his own observation of affairs in that region. The trip was a welcome respite from the cares and burdens of official life, and Mr. Lincoln enjoyed it heartily. The Secretary of War (Mr. Stanton) and the Secretary of the Treasury (Mr. Chase) accompanied the President. A most interesting account of the expedition is given by General Viele, who was a member of the party, and had an opportunity to observe Mr. Lincoln closely. "When, on the afternoon of May 4th," says General Viele, "I was requested by the Secretary of War to meet him within an hour at the navy-yard, with the somewhat mysterious caution to speak to no one of my movements, I had no conception whatever of the purpose or intention of the meeting. It was quite dark when I arrived there simultaneously with the Secretary, who led the way to the wharf on the Potomac, to which a steamer was moored that proved to be the revenue cutter, the Miami. We went on board and proceeded at once to the cabin, where, to my surprise, I found the President and Mr. Chase, who had preceded us. The vessel immediately got under way and steamed down the Potomac. * * * After supper the table was cleared, and the remainder of the evening was spent in a general review of the situation, which lasted long into the night. The positions of the different armies in the field, the last reports from their several commanders, the probabilities and possibilities as they appeared to each member of the group, together with many other topics, relevant and irrelevant, were discussed, interspersed with the usual number of anecdotes from the never-failing supply with which the President's mind was stored. It was a most interesting study to see these men relieved for the moment from the surroundings of their onerous official duties. The President, of course, was the center of the group—kind, genial, thoughtful, tender-hearted, magnanimous Abraham Lincoln! It was difficult to know him without knowing him intimately, for he was as guileless and single-hearted as a child; and no man ever knew him intimately who did not recognize and admire his great abilities, both natural and acquired, his large-heartedness and sincerity of purpose. * * * He would sit for hours during the trip, repeating the finest passages of Shakespeare's best plays, page after page of Browning, and whole cantos of Byron. His inexhaustible stock of anecdotes gave to superficial minds the impression that he was not a thoughtful and reflecting man; whereas the fact was directly the reverse. These anecdotes formed no more a part of Mr. Lincoln's mind than a smile forms a part of the face. They came unbidden, and, like a forced smile, were often employed to conceal a depth of anxiety in his own

heart, and to dissipate the care that weighed upon the minds
of his associates. Both Mr. Chase and Mr. Stanton were
under great depression of spirits when we started, and Mr.
Chase remarked, with a good deal of seriousness, that he had
forgotten to write a very important letter before leaving. It
was too late to remedy the omission, and Mr. Lincoln at once
drove the thought of it from his mind by telling him that a
man was sometimes lucky in forgetting to write a letter, for
he seldom knew what it contained until it appeared again
some day to confront him with an indiscreet word or expression; and then he told a humorous story of a sad catastrophe
that happened in a family, which was ascribed to something
that came in a letter—a catastrophe so far beyond the region
of possibility that it set us all laughing, and Mr. Chase lost
his anxious look. That reminded Mr. Stanton of the dilemma
he had been placed in, just before leaving, by the receipt of a
telegram from General Mitchell, who was in Northern Alabama. The telegram was indistinct, and could not be clearly
understood; there was no time for further explanation, and
yet an immediate answer was required; so the Secretary took
the chances and answered back: 'All right; go ahead.'
'Now, Mr. President,' said he, 'if I have made a mistake, I
must countermand my instructions.' 'I suppose you meant,'
said Mr. Lincoln, 'that it was all right if it was good for him,
and all wrong if it was not. That reminds me,' said he, 'of a
story about a horse that was sold at the cross-roads, near
where I once lived. The horse was supposed to be fast, and
quite a number of people were present at the time appointed
for the sale. A small boy was employed to ride the horse
backward and forward to exhibit his points. One of the
would-be buyers followed the boy down the road and asked
him confidentially if the horse had a splint. 'Well, mister,'
said the boy, 'if it's good for him he has got it, but if it isn't
good for him he hasn't.' 'And that's the position,' said the
President, 'you seem to have left General Mitchell in. Well,

Stanton, I guess he'll come out right; but at any rate you can't help him now.'

"The President's berth was on the same side of the cabin with mine, and he suggested that, as I had more room than I required and he had not enough, a movable partition would have been a great convenience ; recommended that Mr. Chase should provide some arrangement of this kind in case we took another such trip. * * * Mr. Lincoln always had a pleasant word to say the last thing at night and the first thing in the morning. He was always the first one to awake, although not the first to rise. The day-time was spent principally upon the quarter-deck, and the President entertained us with numerous anecdotes and incidents of his life, of the most interesting character. Few were aware of the physical strength possessed by Mr. Lincoln. In muscular power he was one in a thousand. One morning, while we were sitting on deck, he saw an ax in a socket on the bulwarks, and taking it up, held it at arm's length at the extremity of the helve with his thumb and forefinger, continuing to hold it there for a number of minutes. The most powerful sailors on board tried in vain to imitate him. Mr. Lincoln said he could do this when he was eighteen years of age, and had never seen a day since that time when he could not.

"Physically, as every one knows, Mr. Lincoln was not a prepossessing man, with scarcely a redeeming feature, save his benignant eye, which was the very symbol of human kindness. 'If I have one vice,' he said to me one morning,— 'and I can call it nothing else,—it is not to be able to say *no!* Thank God,' he continued, 'for not making me a woman, but if he had, I suppose He would have made me just as ugly as He did, and no one would ever have tempted me. It was only the other day, a poor parson, whom I knew some years ago in Joliet, came to the White House with a sad story of his poverty and his large family,—poor parsons seem always to have large families,—and he wanted me to do something for him.   I knew very well that I could do nothing for him, and yet I couldn't bear to tell him so, and so I said I would see what I could do.   The very next day the man came back for the office which he said that I had promised him, —which was not true, but he seemed really to believe it.   Of course there was nothing left for me to do except to get him a place through one of the Secretaries.   But if I had done my duty, I should have said *no* in the beginning.' "

THE PRESIDENT WITNESSES AN ATTACK ON THE REBEL RAM MERRIMAC.

"It was late in the evening," continues Gen. Viele, "when we arrived at Fortress Monroe. * * * Answering the hail of the guard-boats we made a landing, and the Secretary of War immediately dispatched a messenger for General Wool, the commander of the fort; on whose arrival it was decided to consult at once with Admiral Goldsborough, the commander of the fleet, whose flag-ship, the Minnesota, a superb model of naval architecture, lay a short distance off the shore. The result of this conference was a plan to get up an engagement the next day between the Merrimac and the Monitor, so that during the fight, the Vanderbilt, which had been immensely strengthened for the purpose, might put on all steam and run her down. Accordingly, the next morning, the President and party went over to the Rip Raps to see the naval combat. The Merrimac moved out of the mouth of the Elizabeth river, quietly and steadily, just as she had come out only a few weeks before, when she had sunk the Congress and the Cumberland. She wore an air of defiance and determination even at that distance. The Monitor moved up and waited for her. All the other vessels got out of the way to give the Vanderbilt and the Minnesota room to bear down upon the rebel terror in their might, as soon as she should clear the coast line. It was a calm Sabbath morning, and the air was still and tranquil. Suddenly, the stillness was broken by the cannon from the vessels and the great guns from the Rip Raps, that filled the air with sulphurous smoke and a terrific noise that reverberated from the fortress and the opposite shore like thunder. The firing was maintained for several hours, but all to no purpose; the Merrimac moved sullenly back to her position. It was determined that night that on the following day vigorous offensive operations should be undertaken. The whole available naval force was to bombard Sewall's Point, and under cover of the bombardment the available troops from Fortress Monroe were to be landed at that point and march on Norfolk. Accordingly, the next morning, a tremendous cannonading of Sewall's Point took place. The wooden sheds at that place were set on fire and the battery was silenced. The Merrimac, coated with mail and lying low in the water, looked on but took no part. Night came on, and the cannonading ceased. It was so evident that the Merrimac intended to act only on the defensive, and that so long as she remained where she was no troops could be landed in that vicinity, that they were ordered to disembark.

"That night the President, with the Secretary of War and the Secretary of the Treasury, went over on the Miami to the Virginia shore, and by the light of the moon landed on the beach and walked up and down a considerable distance to assure himself that there could be no mistake in the matter. How little the Confederacy dreamed what a visitor it had that night to the 'sacred soil.'"

CAPTURE OF NORFOLK.

The following morning an advance was made upon Norfolk by the route proposed by Gen. Viele. The attempt was successful, and before night Gen. Viele was in command of the captured city. Some time after midnight, as Gen. Viele records, "with a shock that shook the city, and with an ominous sound that could not be mistaken, the magazine of the Merrimac was exploded, the vessel having been cut off from supplies and deserted by the crew; and thus this most formidable engine of destruction, that had so long been a terror, not only to Hampton Roads, but to the Atlantic coast, went to her doom, a tragic and glorious finale to the trip of the Miami.''

MR. LINCOLN'S ACCOUNT OF THE AFFAIR.

Secretary Chase had accompanied the expedition against Norfolk, returning to Fortress Monroe, with Gen. Wool, immediately after the surrender of the city. The scene which ensued on the announcement of the good tidings they brought back to the anxious parties awaiting news of them, was thus described by the President: "Chase and Stanton," said Mr. Lincoln, "had accompanied me to Fortress Monroe. While we were there, an expedition was fitted out for an attack on Norfolk. Chase and Gen. Wool disappeared about the time we began to look for tidings of the result, and after vainly waiting their return till late in the evening, Stanton and I concluded to retire. My room was on the second floor of the Commandant's house, and Stanton's was below. The night was very warm,—the moon shining brightly,—and, too restless to sleep, I sat for some time by the table, reading. Suddenly hearing footsteps, I looked out of the window, and saw two persons approaching, whom I knew by their relative size to be the missing men. They came into the passage, and I heard them rap at Stanton's door and tell him to get up and come up-stairs. A moment afterward they entered my room. 'No time for ceremony, Mr. President,' said Gen. Wool; 'Norfolk is ours!' Stanton here burst in, just out of bed, clad in a long night-gown, which nearly swept the floor, his ear catching, as he crossed the threshold, Wool's last words. Perfectly overjoyed, he rushed at the General, whom he hugged most affectionately, fairly lifting him from the floor in his delight. The scene altogether must have been a comical one, though at the time we were all too greatly excited to take much note of mere appearances.''

CHAPTER VI.

LINCOLN AND M'CLELLAN.——THE PENINSULAR CAMPAIGN OF 1862.——LINCOLN
IMPATIENT WITH M'CLELLAN'S DELAY.——LINCOLN DEFENDS M'CLELLAN
FROM UNJUST CRITICISM.——SOME HARROWING EXPERIENCES.——THE TER-
RIBLE REALITIES OF WAR.——M'CLELLAN RECALLED FROM THE PENINSULA.
——THE DEFEAT OF GENERAL POPE.——A CRITICAL SITUATION.——M'CLEL-
LAN AGAIN IN COMMAND.——LINCOLN TAKES THE RESPONSIBILITY.——AN-
NOUNCES HIS DECISION TO AN ASTONISHED CABINET.——M'CLELLAN'S AC-
COUNT OF HIS REINSTATEMENT.——THE BATTLE OF ANTIETAM.——THE
PRESIDENT VINDICATED.——LINCOLN AGAIN DISSATISFIED WITH M'CLELLAN.
——VISITS THE ARMY IN THE FIELD.——MR. LINCOLN IN THE SADDLE.——
"RIDING DOWN THE LINES" WITH GEN. M'CLELLAN.——CORRESPONDENCE
BETWEEN LINCOLN AND M'CLELLAN.——M'CLELLAN'S FINAL REMOVAL.——
LINCOLN'S SUMMING-UP OF M'CLELLAN.——A "STATIONARY" ENGINEER.——
M'CLELLAN'S "BODY-GUARD."

PRESIDENT LINCOLN'S relations with no other person have been so much discussed as those with General McClellan. Volumes have been written on this one subject, and many heated and intemperate words have been uttered on both sides. Much that has been said, no doubt, has been exaggerated; and it will require time, and careful sifting of all the evidence, to arrive at the exact truth. Whatever defects may have marked Gen. McClellan's qualities as a soldier, he must ever remain one of the most conspicuous figures of the war. He was the first Union commander of whom great things were expected; and when he failed to realize the extravagant expectations of the period when it was believed the war was to be ended within a year, he received equally extravagant condemnation. It is worth remembering that the war was not ended until two and a half years after McClellan's retirement, and until trial after trial had been made, and failure after failure had been met, in the effort to find a successful leader for our armies.

It is not, however, in the province of the present narrative to enter into a consideration of the merits or demerits of Gen. McClellan as a soldier, but only to treat of his personal rela-

tions with President Lincoln. Between the two men, notwithstanding many sharp differences of opinion and of policy,
there seems to have been a feeling of warm personal friendship and sincere respect. Now that both have passed beyond

the reach of earthly praise or blame, we may well honor their
memory and credit them with having done each the best he
could to serve his country.

THE PENINSULAR CAMPAIGN OF 1862.

Gen. McClellan was appointed to the command of the Union armies, upon the retirement of the veteran Gen. Scott, in November, 1861. It was soon after this that President Lincoln began giving close personal attention to the direction of military affairs. He formed a plan of operations against the Confederate army defending Richmond, which, unfortunately, differed entirely from the plan proposed by Gen. McClellan. The President's plan was, in effect, to repeat the Bull Run expedition, by moving against the enemy in Virginia at or near Manassas. Gen. McClellan preferred a removal of the army to the region of the lower Chesapeake, and thence up the Peninsula by the shortest land route to Richmond. (This was a movement, it may be remarked, which was finally carried out, before Richmond fell, in 1865.) The President discussed the relative merits of the two plans, in the following frank and explicit letter to Gen. McClellan:

"EXECUTIVE MANSION, WASHINGTON, D. C., February 3, 1862.

"*Major-General McClellan.*—MY DEAR SIR:—You and I have distinct and different plans for a movement of the Army of the Potomac; yours to be done by the Chesapeake, up the Rappahannock to Urbana, and across to the terminus of the railroad on the York river; mine to move directly to a point on the railroad southwest of Manassas. If you will give me satisfactory answers to the following questions, I shall gladly yield my plan to yours:

"1st. Does your plan involve a greatly larger expenditure of *time* and *money* than mine?

"2d. Wherein is a victory more certain by your plan than mine?

"3d. Wherein is a victory *more valuable* by your plan than mine?

"4th. In fact, would it not be *less* valuable in this, that it would break no great line of the enemy's communication, while mine would?

"5th. In case of a disaster, would not a retreat be more difficult by your plan than mine?

"Yours truly,   ABRAHAM LINCOLN."

To this communication Gen. McClellan made an elaborate reply, discussing the situation very fully, and answering the inquiries apparently to the satisfaction of the President, who consented to the plan submitted by McClellan, and concurred in by a council of his division commanders, by which the base of the Army of the Potomac should be transferred from Washington to the lower Chesapeake. Yet Mr. Lincoln must have had misgivings in the matter, for some weeks later he wrote to Gen. McClellan: "You will do me the justice to remember I always insisted that going down the bay in search of a field, instead of fighting at or near Manassas, was only shifting, and not surmounting, a difficulty; that we would find the same enemy, and the same or equal intrenchments, at either place."

LINCOLN IMPATIENT WITH M'CLELLAN'S DELAY.

After the transfer of the Army of the Potomac to the Peninsula, there was great impatience at the delays in the expected advance on Richmond. The President shared this impatience, and his dispatches to McClellan took an urgent and imperative, though always friendly, tone. April 9 he wrote: "Your dispatches, complaining that you are not properly sustained, while they do not offend me, do pain me very much. I suppose the whole force which has gone forward for you is with you by this time. And, if so, I think it is the precise time for you to *strike a blow*. By delay, the enemy will relatively gain upon you—that is, he will gain faster by fortifications and reinforcements than you can by reinforcements alone. And once more let me tell you, it is indispensable to you that you *strike a blow*. * * I beg to assure you that I have never written to you or spoken to you in greater kindness of feeling than now, nor with a fuller purpose to sustain you, so far as, in my most anxious judgment, I consistently can. But you *must act*."

LINCOLN DEFENDS M'CLELLAN FROM UNJUST CRITICISM.

While Mr. Lincoln was thus imperative toward McClellan, he would not permit him to be unjustly criticised. Considerable ill-feeling having been developed between McClellan and Secretary Stanton, which was made worse by certain meddlesome persons in Washington, the President took occasion, at a public meeting, to express his views in these frank and manly words: "There has been a very wide-spread attempt to have a quarrel between General McClellan and the Secretary of War. Now, I occupy a position that enables me to observe that these two gentlemen are not nearly so deep in the quarrel as some pretending to be their friends. General McClellan's attitude is such that, in the very selfishness of his nature, he cannot but wish to be successful, and I hope he will—and the Secretary of War is in precisely the same situation. If the military commanders in the field cannot be successful, not only the Secretary of War, but myself, for the time being the the master of them both, cannot but be failures. I know General McClellan wishes to be successful, and I know he does not wish it any more than the Secretary of War for him, and both of them together no more than I wish it. Sometimes we have a dispute about how many men General McClellan has had, and those who would disparage him say he has had a very large number, and those who would disparage the Secretary of War insist that General McClellan has had a very small number. The basis for this is, there is always a wide difference, and on this occasion perhaps a wider one than usual, between the grand total on McClellan's rolls and the men actually fit for duty; and those who would disparage him talk of the grand total on paper, and those who would disparage the Secretary of War talk of those at present fit for duty. General McClellan has sometimes asked for things that the Secretary of War did not give him. General McClellan is not to blame for asking what he wanted and needed, and the Secretary of War is not to blame for not giving when he had none to give."

SOME HARROWING EXPERIENCES.—THE TERRIBLE REALITIES OF WAR.

The Summer of 1862 was a sad one for the country, and peculiarly sad for Mr. Lincoln. The Army of the Potomac fought battle after battle, without substantial results; while thousands and thousands of our brave soldiers perished on the field, or filled the hospitals from the fever-swamps of the Chickahominy. The terrible realities of that dreadful Summer, and their effects on Mr. Lincoln, are well shown in the following incident: Colonel Scott, of a New Hampshire regiment, had been ill, and his wife nursed him in the hospital. After his convalescence, he received leave of absence, and started for home; but by a steamboat collision in Hampton Roads, his noble wife was drowned. Col. Scott reached Washington, and learning, a few days later, of the recovery of his wife's body, he requested permission of the Secretary of War to return for it. A great battle was imminent, and the request was denied. Col. Scott thereupon sought the President. It was Saturday evening; and Mr. Lincoln, worn with the cares and anxieties of the week, sat alone in his room, coat thrown off, and seemingly lost in thought, perhaps pondering the issue of the coming battle. Silently he listened to Colonel Scott's sad story; then, with an unusual irritation, which was probably a part of his excessive weariness, he exclaimed: "Am I to have no rest? Is there no hour or spot when or where I may escape this constant call? Why do you follow me here with such business as this? Why do you not go to the War-office, where they have charge of all this matter of papers and transportation?" Col. Scott told of Mr. Stanton's refusal; and the President continued: "Then, probably, you ought not to go down the river. Mr. Stanton knows all about the necessities of the hour; he knows what rules are necessary, and rules are made to be enforced. It would be wrong for me to override his rules and decisions in cases of this kind; it might work disaster to important movements. And then, you ought to remember that I have other duties to attend to—heaven knows, enough for one man!—and I can give no thought to questions of this kind. Why do you come here to appeal to my humanity? Don't you know that we are in the midst of war? That suffering and death press upon all of us? That works of humanity and affection, which we would cheerfully perform in days of peace, are all trampled upon and outlawed by war? That there is no room left for them? There is but one duty now—*to fight.* The only call of humanity now is to conquer peace through unrelenting warfare. War, and war alone, is the duty of all of us. Your wife might have trusted you to the care which the Government has provided for its sick soldiers. At any rate, you must not vex me with your family troubles. Why, every family in the land is crushed with sorrow; but they must not each come to me for help. I have all the burden I can carry. Go to the War Department. Your business belongs there. If they cannot help you, then bear your burden, as we all must, until this war is over. Everything must yield to the paramount duty of finishing the war.''

Colonel Scott withdrew, crushed and overwhelmed. The next morning, as he sat in his hotel pondering upon his troubles, he heard a rap at his door, and opening it, found, to his surprise, the President standing before him. Grasping his hands impulsively and sympathetically, Mr. Lincoln broke out: ''My dear Colonel, I was a brute last night. I have no excuse for my conduct. Indeed, I was weary to the last extent, but I had no right to treat a man with rudeness who had offered his life for his country, much more a man who came to me in great affliction. I have had a regretful night, and come now to beg your forgiveness.'' He added that he had just seen Secretary Stanton, and all the details were arranged for sending the Colonel down the Potomac and recovering the body; then, taking him in his carriage, he drove to the steamer's wharf, where, again pressing his hand, he wished him God-speed on his sad errand.

Such were Mr. Lincoln's harrowing experiences; and thus did his noble and sympathetic nature assert itself over his momentary weakness.

M'CLELLAN RECALLED FROM THE PENINSULA.—DEFEAT OF GENERAL POPE.

In August, 1862, General McClellan was ordered to withdraw his army from the Peninsula. "With a heavy heart," says McClellan, "I relinquished the position gained at the cost of so much time and blood." His troops were sent to join Gen. Pope, who had been placed in command of a considerable force in Virginia, for the purpose of trying the President's favorite plan of an advance on Richmond by way of Manassas. Either from a confusion of orders, or a lack of zeal in executing them, the Union forces failed to co-operate; and Pope's expected victory (Manassas, August 30,) proved a disastrous and humiliating defeat. His army was beaten and driven back on Washington in a rout little less disgraceful than that of Bull Run a year before. This battle came to be known as the "Second Bull Run."

A CRITICAL SITUATION.—M'CLELLAN AGAIN IN COMMAND.

Thus the Autumn of 1862 set in amidst gloom, disorder, and dismay. Our armies in and around the National Capital were on the defensive; while the victorious Lee, following up his successes at Manassas, was invading Maryland and threatening Washington and the North. The President was anxious; the Cabinet and Congress were alarmed. The troops had lost confidence in Gen. Pope, and there was practically no one in chief command. The situation was most critical; but Mr. Lincoln faced it, as he always did, unflinchingly. He took what was at once the wisest and the most unpopular step possible under the circumstances: he placed Gen. McClellan in command of all the troops in and around Washington.

LINCOLN TAKES THE RESPONSIBILITY.—ANNOUNCES HIS DECISION TO AN ASTONISHED CABINET.

Perhaps no act of Mr. Lincoln as President showed more strongly his moral courage and self-reliance than the re-appointment of McClellan. It was, outside the army, the most unpopular thing he could possibly have done. McClellan was bitterly disliked, not only by Secretary Stanton, but by all members of the Cabinet and prominent officials. At the North there was a very common, though unjust and foolish, belief that he was disloyal.

When it was rumored in Washington that McClellan was to be re-instated, every one was thunderstruck. A Cabinet meeting was held on the 2d day of September, at which the President, without asking any one's opinion, announced that he had re-instated McClellan. Regret and surprise were openly expressed. Mr. Stanton, with some excitement, remarked that no such order had issued from the War Department. The President then said, with great calmness: "No, Mr. Secretary, *the order was mine, and I will be responsible for it to the country.*" He added, by way of explanation, that something had to be done, and as there did not appear to be any one else to do it, he took the responsibility on himself. He remarked that McClellan had the confidence of the troops beyond any other officer, and could, under the circumstances, more speedily and effectually reorganize them and put them in fighting trim than any other general. "This is what is now wanted most," said he, "and these were my reasons for placing McClellan in command."

Hon. Gideon Welles, Secretary of the Navy, who was present at the Cabinet meeting referred to, has given the following graphic account of the scene: "Mr. Stanton entered the council room a few moments in advance of Mr. Lincoln, and said, with great excitement, that he had just learned from General Halleck that the President had placed McClellan in command of the forces in Washington. The President soon came in, and in answer to an inquiry from Mr. Chase, confirmed what Stanton had stated. General regret was expressed; and Stanton, with some feeling, remarked that no order to that effect had issued from the War Department. The President, calmly but with some emphasis, said the order was his, and he would be responsible for it to the country. With a retreating and demoralized army tumbling in upon us, and alarm and panic in the community, it was necessary, the President said, that something should be done, but there seemed to be no one to do it. He therefore had directed McClellan, who knew this whole ground, who was the best organizer in the army, whose faculty was to organize and defend, and who would here act upon the defensive, to take this defeated and broken army and reorganize it. In stating what he had done, the President was deliberate, but firm and decisive. His language and manner were kind and affectionate, especially toward two of the members, who were greatly disturbed; but every person present felt that he was truly the chief, and every one knew his decision was as fixed and unalterable as if given out with the imperious command and determined will of Andrew Jackson. A long discussion followed, closing with acquiescence in the decision of the President; but before separating, the Secretary of the Treasury expressed his apprehension that the re-instatement of McClellan would prove a national calamity. In this instance the President, unaided by others, put forth with firmness and determination the executive will—the *one-man* power—against the temporary general sense of the community, as well as of his Cabinet, two of whom, it has been generally supposed, had with him an influence almost as great as the Secretary of State. They had been ready to make issue and resign their places unless McClellan was dismissed; but knowing their opposition, and in spite of it and of the general dissatisfaction in the community, the President had in that perilous moment exalted him to new and important trusts. In an interview with the President on the succeeding Friday, when only he and myself were present, he unburthened his mind freely. * * * He said most of our troubles grew out of military jealousies. Whether changing the plan of operations (discarding McClellan and placing Pope in command) was wise or not, was not now the matter in hand. These things, right or wrong, had been done. If the administration had erred, the country should not have been made to suffer and our brave men cut down and butchered. Pope should have been sustained, but he was not. These personal and professional quarrels came in. Whatever may have been said to the contrary, it could not be denied that the army was with McClellan. The soldiers certainly had not transferred their confidence to Pope. He could, however, do no more good in this quarter. Personal considerations must be sacrificed for the public safety."

GEN. M'CLELLAN'S ACCOUNT OF HIS RE–INSTATEMENT.

It appears from the statement of Gen. McClellan, made shortly before his death, that on the morning of his re-instatement (before the Cabinet meeting just described) the President visited him at his headquarters, near Washington, to ask if he would again assume command. "While at breakfast, at an early hour," says Gen. McClellan, "I received a call from the President, accompanied by General Halleck. The President informed me that Colonel Kelton had returned and represented the condition of affairs as much worse than I had stated to Halleck on the previous day; that there were 30,000 stragglers on the roads; that the army was entirely defeated and falling back to Washington in confusion. He then said that he regarded Washington as lost, and asked me if I would, under the circumstances, consent to accept command of all the forces. Without one moment's hesitation, and without making any conditions whatever, I at once said that I would accept the command, and would stake my life that I would save the city. Both the President and Halleck again asserted that it was impossible to save the city, and I repeated my firm conviction that I could and would save it. They then left, the President verbally placing me in entire command of the city and of the troops falling back upon it from the front."

THE BATTLE OF ANTIETAM.—THE PRESIDENT VINDICATED.

The result of the reappointment of McClellan soon vindicated the step.   He possessed the confidence of the army beyond any other of our generals at that time; and at its head he fought, within two weeks after his reinstatement, the bloody but successful battle of Antietam (Sept. 17, '62), which com-

PRESIDENT LINCOLN'S CONFERENCE WITH GEN. M'CLELLAN, AFTER THE
BATTLE OF ANTIETAM.

pelled Lee to retreat to the southern side of the Potomac, and relieved Washington of any immediate danger from the enemy.

LINCOLN AGAIN DISSATISFIED WITH M'CLELLAN.—VISITS THE
ARMY IN THE FIELD.

After the Antietam campaign, the Army of the Potomac rested awhile from its almost superhuman labors, Gen. Mc-

Clellan considering it necessary to get supplies and reinforcements before resuming active operations. This delay gave rise to no little dissatisfaction in Washington, where it was thought McClellan should have followed up his successes at Antietam by immediately pursuing Lee into Virginia. In this dissatisfaction the President shared to some extent. He made a personal visit to the army for the purpose of satisfying himself of its condition. Of this occasion Gen. McClellan says: "On the first day of October, his Excellency the President honored the Army of the Potomac with a visit, and remained several days, during which he went through the different encampments, reviewed the troops, and went over the battle-field of South Mountain and Antietam. I had the opportunity, during this visit, to describe to him the operations of the army since it left Washington, and gave him my reasons for not following the enemy after he recrossed the Potomac."

MR. LINCOLN IN THE SADDLE.—"RIDING DOWN THE LINES" WITH GEN. M'CLELLAN.

Before the grand review that was to be made by the President, some of McClellan's staff, knowing that the General was a man of great endurance and expertness in the saddle, laughed at the idea of Mr. Lincoln's attempting to keep up with him in the severe ordeal of "riding down the lines." "They rather hinted," says a narrator, "that the General would move rapidly, to test Mr. Lincoln's capacity as a rider. There were those on the field, however, who had seen Mr. Lincoln in the saddle in Illinois; and they were very confident. They knew their man. A splendid black horse, very spirited, was selected for the President to ride. When the time came, Mr. Lincoln walked up to the animal, and the instant he seized the bridle to mount, it was evident to horsemen that he 'knew his business.' He had the animal in hand at once. No sooner was he in the saddle, than the coal-black steed began to prance, and whirl, and dance, as if he was

MR. LINCOLN "RIDING DOWN THE LINES" WITH GEN. M'CLELLAN.

proud of his burden. But the President sat as unconcerned and fixed to the saddle as if he and the horse were one. The test of endurance soon came. McClellan, with his magnificent staff, approached the President, who joined them, and away they dashed to a distant part of the field. The artillery began to thunder, the drums beat, and the bands struck up 'Hail to the Chief,' while the troops cheered. Mr. Lincoln, holding the bridle-rein in one hand, lifted his tall hat from his head, and much of the time held it in the other hand. Grandly did Lincoln receive the salute, appearing as little disturbed by the dashing movements of the proud-spirited animal as if he had passed through such an ordeal with the same creature many times before. Next came a further test of endurance—a long dash over very rough, untravelled ground, with here and there a ditch or a hole to be jumped, or a siding to be passed. But Mr. Lincoln kept well up to McClellan, who made good time. Finally, the 'riding down the lines' was performed, amidst the flaunting of standards, the beating of drums, the loud cheering of the men, and rapid discharges of artillery, startling even the best-trained horses. Lincoln sat easy to the end, when he wheeled his horse into position to witness the vast columns march in review. McClellan was surprised at so remarkable a display of horsemanship.

"Mr. Lincoln was a great lover of the horse, and a skilled rider. His awkwardness of form did not show in the saddle. He always looked well when mounted."

CORRESPONDENCE BETWEEN LINCOLN AND M'CLELLAN.

After the President's return to Washington, he began urging McClellan to resume active operations; desiring him to "cross the Potomac, and give battle to the enemy or drive him south." On the 13th of October he addressed to him the following letter, which is a notable expression of Mr.

Lincoln's views of the military problem as presented at that time :

"EXECUTIVE MANSION, WASHINGTON, October 13, 1862.

"MY DEAR SIR:—You remember my speaking to you of what I called your over-cautiousness. Are you not over-cautious when you assume that you cannot do what the enemy is constantly doing? Should you not claim to be at least his equal in prowess, and act upon the claim?

"As I understand, you telegraphed General Halleck that you cannot subsist your army at Winchester unless the railroad from Harper's Ferry to that point be put in working order. But the enemy does now subsist his army at Winchester, at a distance nearly twice as great from railroad transportation as you would have to do, without the railroad last named. He now wagons from Culpepper Court-House, which is just about twice as far as you would have to do from Harper's Ferry. He is certainly not more than half as well provided with wagons as you are. I certainly should be pleased for you to have the advantage of the railroad from Harper's Ferry to Winchester; but it wastes all the remainder of Autumn to give it to you, and, in fact, ignores the question of *time*, which cannot and must not be ignored.

"Again, one of the standard maxims of war, as you know, is, 'to operate upon the enemy's communications as much as possible, without exposing your own.' You seem to act as if this applies *against* you, but cannot apply in your *favor*. Change positions with the enemy, and think you not he would break your communication with Richmond within the next twenty-four hours? You dread his going into Pennsylvania. But if he does so in full force, he gives up his communications to you absolutely, and you have nothing to do but to follow and ruin him; if he does so with less than full force, fall upon and beat what is left behind all the easier. Exclusive of the water line, you are now nearer Richmond than the enemy is, by the route that you *can* and he *must* take. Why can you not reach there before him, unless you admit that he is more than your equal on the march? His route is the *arc* of a circle, while yours is the *chord*. The roads are as good on yours as on his.

"You know I desired, but did not order, you to cross the Potomac below instead of above the Shenandoah and Blue Ridge. My idea was, that this would at once menace the enemy's communications, which I would seize if he would permit. If he should move northward, I would follow him closely, holding his communications. If he should prevent our seizing his communications, and move toward Richmond, I would press closely to him, fight him if a favorable opportunity should present, and at least try to beat him to Richmond on the inside track. I say 'try,' for if we never try, we shall never succeed. If he make a stand at Winchester, moving neither north nor south, I would fight him there, on the idea that if we cannot beat him when he bears the wastage of coming to us, we never can when we bear the wastage of going to him. This proposition is a simple truth, and is too important to be lost sight of for a moment. In coming to us, he tenders us an advantage which we should not waive. We should not so operate as to merely drive him away. As we must beat him somewhere, or fail finally, we can do it, if at all, easier near to us than far away. If we cannot beat the enemy where he now is, we never can, he again being within the intrenchments of Richmond. Recurring to the idea of going to Richmond on the inside track, the facility of supplying from the side away from the enemy is remarkable, as it were, by the different spokes of a wheel, extending from the hub toward the rim, and this whether you move directly by the chord, or on the inside arc, hugging the Blue Ridge more closely. The chord-line, as you see, carries you by Aldie, Haymarket, and Fredericksburg, and you see how turnpikes, railroads, and finally the Potomac by Aquia Creek, meet you at all points from Washington. The same, only the lines lengthened a little, if you press closer to the Blue Ridge part of the way. The gaps through the Blue Ridge I understand to be about the following distances from Harper's Ferry, to wit: Vestal's, five miles; Gregory's, thirteen; Snicker's, eighteen; Ashby's, twenty-eight; Manassas, thirty-eight; Chester, forty-five; and Thornton's, fifty-three. I should think it preferable to take the route nearest the enemy, disabling him to make an important move without your knowledge, and compelling him to keep his forces together for dread of you. The gaps would enable you to attack if you should wish. For a great part of the way you would be practically between the enemy and both Washington and Richmond, enabling us to spare you the greatest number of troops from here. When, at length, running to Richmond ahead of him enables him to move this way, if he does so, turn and attack him in the rear. But I think he should be engaged long before such point is reached. It is all easy if our troops march as well as the enemy, and it is unmanly to say they cannot do it. This letter is in no sense an order.

Yours truly,   A. LINCOLN."

"Major-Gen. McCLELLAN.

M'CLELLAN'S FINAL REMOVAL.

Subsequent communications from the President to McClellan showed more and more impatience. On the 25th he telegraphed: "I have just read your dispatch about sore-tongue and fatigued horses. Will you pardon me for asking what the horses of your army have done since the battle of Antietam that fatigues anything?" And the next day, after receiving Gen. McClellan's answer to his inquiry, he responded: "Most certainly I intend no injustice to any one, and if I have done any I deeply regret it. To be told, after more than five weeks' total inaction of the army, and during which period we had sent to that army every fresh horse we possibly could, amounting in the whole to 7,918, that the cavalry horses were too much fatigued to move, presented a very cheerless, almost hopeless, prospect for the future, and it may have forced something of impatience into my dispatches. If not recruited and rested then, when could they ever be? *I suppose the river is rising, and I am glad to believe you are crossing.*" But McClellan did not cross; his preparations for a new campaign were not yet complete; and the President, at last losing patience, removed him from command, and put Gen. Burnside in his place, November 5, 1862.

LINCOLN'S SUMMING-UP OF M'CLELLAN.—A "STATIONARY" ENGINEER.—"M'CLELLAN'S BODY-GUARD."

Mr. Lincoln seldom criticised McClellan to others; and when he did, it was in a good-natured, humorous way,—as when he remarked, "If General McClellan does not want to *use* the army for some days, I should like to *borrow it* and see if it cannot be made to do something." At another time, he said: "McClellan's tardiness reminds me of a man in Illinois, whose attorney was not sufficiently aggressive. The client knew a few law phrases, and finally, after waiting until his patience was exhausted by the non-action of his counsel, he sprang to his feet and exclaimed: 'Why don't you go at him with a *fi. fa.*, *a demurrer*, a *capias*, a *surrebutter*, or a *ne exeat*, or something; and not stand there like a *nudum pactum* or a *non est?*'" Perhaps the severest thing of all, was this: "General McClellan is a pleasant and scholarly gentleman. He is an admirable engineer, but he *seems to have a special talent for a stationary engine.*"

Hon. O. M. Hatch, a former Secretary of State of Illinois, relates that a short time before Gen. McClellan's removal he went with President Lincoln to visit the army, near Antietam. They reached Antietam late in the afternoon of a very hot day, and were assigned a special tent for their occupancy during the night. "Early next morning," says Mr. Hatch, "I was awakened by Mr. Lincoln. It was very early—daylight was just lighting the east—the soldiers were all asleep in their tents. Scarce a sound could be heard except the notes of early birds, and the farm-yard voices from distant farms. Lincoln said to me, 'Come, Hatch, I want you to take a walk with me.' His tone was serious and impressive. I arose without a word, and as soon as we were dressed we left the tent together. He led me about the camp, and then we walked upon the surrounding hills overlooking the great city of white tents and sleeping soldiers. Very little was spoken between us, beyond a few words as to the pleasantness of the morning or similar casual observations. Lincoln seemed to be peculiarly serious, and his quiet, abstract way affected me also. It did not seem a time to speak. We walked slowly and quietly, meeting here and there a guard, our thoughts leading us to reflect on that wonderful situation. A nation in peril—the whole world looking at America—a million men in arms—the whole machinery of war engaged throughout the country, while I stood by that kind-hearted, simple-minded man who might be regarded as the Director-General, looking at the beautiful sunrise and the magnificent scene before us. Nothing was to be said, nothing needed to be said. Finally, reaching a commanding point where almost that entire camp could be seen—the men were just beginning their morning duties, and evidences of life and activity were becoming apparent—we involuntarily stopped. The President, waving his hand towards the scene before us, and leaning towards me, said in an almost whispering voice: 'Hatch—Hatch, what is all this?' 'Why, Mr. Lincoln,' said I, 'this is the Army of the Potomac.' He hesitated a moment, and then, straightening up, said in a louder tone: 'No, Hatch, no. This is *General McClellan's body-guard.*' Nothing more was said. We walked to our tent, and the subject was not alluded to again.''

CHAPTER VII.

LINCOLN AND SLAVERY.——PLAN FOR GRADUAL EMANCIPATION.——ANTI-SLA-
VERY LEGISLATION IN 1862.——PRESSURE BROUGHT TO BEAR ON THE EXEC-
UTIVE. ——THE DELEGATION OF QUAKERS.——A VISIT FROM CHICAGO CLER-
GYMEN.——INTERVIEW BETWEEN LINCOLN AND CHANNING.——LINCOLN
AND HORACE GREELEY.——THE PRESIDENT'S ANSWER TO "THE PRAYER OF
TWENTY MILLIONS OF PEOPLE."——CONFERENCE BETWEEN LINCOLN AND
GREELEY.-——EMANCIPATION RESOLVED ON.——THE PRELIMINARY PROCLA-
MATION.——MR. LINCOLN'S ACCOUNT OF IT.——PREPARING FOR THE FINAL
ACT.——HIS MIND WAS "MADE UP."——THE EMANCIPATION PROCLAMA-
TION. ——PARTICULARS OF THE GREAT DOCUMENT.——FATE OF THE ORIGI-
NAL DRAFT.——MR. LINCOLN'S OUTLINE OF HIS COURSE AND VIEWS RE-
GARDING SLAVERY.

THE emancipation of slaves in America—the crowning
act of Mr. Lincoln's eventful career, and the one with which
his fame is most indissolubly linked,—is a subject of supreme
interest in a study of his life and character. For this great
act all his previous life and training had been but a preparation. From the first awakening of his convictions of the
enormity of human slavery, through all his public and private
utterances, may be traced one logical and consistent development of the principles which at last found sublime expression
in the Proclamation of Emancipation. In this, as always, he
was true to his own inner promptings. He would not be hurried, nor worried, nor badgered, into premature and inoper-
ative measures. He bided his time ; and when that time came
the deed was done, unalterably and irrevocably : approved by
the logic of events, and by the enlightened conscience of the
world.

The final Emancipation Proclamation was issued on the
first day of January, 1863. The various official measures
that preceded it may be briefly sketched, together with closely
related incidents. As early as the Fall of 1861, the problem
of the relation of the war to slavery was brought forcibly to
Mr. Lincoln's attention, by the action of Gen. J. C. Fremont, the Union commander in Missouri, who issued an order

declaring the slaves of rebels in his department free. The order was premature and unauthorized, and the President promptly annulled it. Gen. Fremont was thus, in a sense, the pioneer in military emancipation; and he lived to see the policy proposed by him carried into practical operation by all our armies. Mr. Lincoln afterwards said: "I have great respect for General Fremont and his abilities, but the fact is that the pioneer in any movement is not generally the best

man to carry that movement to a successful issue. It was so in old times; Moses began the emancipation of the Jews, but didn't take Israel to the Promised Land after all. He had to make way for Joshua to complete the work. It looks as if the first reformer of a thing has to meet such a hard opposition, and gets so battered and bespattered, that afterward, when people find they have to accept his reform, they will accept it more easily from another man."

Mr. Lincoln favored a policy of gradual emancipation. In a special message to Congress, on the 6th of March, 1862, he proposed such a plan for the abolition of slavery: "In my judgment," he remarked, "gradual, and not sudden, emancipation is better for all." He suggested to Congress the adoption of a joint resolution, declaring "that the United States ought to co-operate with any State which may adopt a gradual abolition of slavery, giving to such State pecuniary aid to compensate for the inconvenience, public and private, produced by such change of system." In conclusion he urged: "In full view of my great responsibility to my God and to my country, I earnestly beg the attention of Congress and the people to this subject."

On the 16th of April, Congress passed a bill abolishing slavery in the District of Columbia—a measure for which Mr. Lincoln had himself introduced a bill while a member of Congress. In confirming the act as President, he remarked privately: "Little did I dream in 1849, when I proposed to abolish slavery at this capital, and could scarcely get a hearing for the proposition, that it would be so soon accomplished."

June 19, Congress enacted a measure prohibiting slavery forever in all present and future territories of the United States. July 17, a law was passed authorizing the employment of negroes as soldiers, and conferring freedom on all who should render military service, and on the families of all such as belonged to rebel owners. Two days later, in a conference appointed by him at the Executive Mansion, the President submitted to the members of Congress from the Border States a written appeal, in which he said:

"Believing that you, in the border States, hold more power for good than any other equal number of members, I feel it a duty which I cannot justifiably waive, to make this appeal to you. * * * I intend no reproach or complaint when I assure you that, in my opinion, if you all had voted for the resolution in the gradual emancipation message of last

March, the war would now be substantially ended. And the plan therein proposed is yet one of the most potent and swift means of ending it. Let the States which are in rebellion see definitely and certainly that in no event will the States you represent ever join their proposed confederacy, and they cannot much longer maintain the contest. * * * If the war continues long, as it must, if the object be not sooner attained, the institution in your States will be extinguished by mere friction and abrasion, by the mere incidents of the war. It will be gone, and you will have nothing valuable in lieu of it. Much of its value is gone already. How much better for you and for your people to take the step which at once shortens the war and secures substantial compensation for that which is sure to be wholly lost in any other event! How much better to thus save the money which else we sink forever in the war! How much better to do it while we can, lest the war ere long render us pecuniarily unable to do it! How much better for you as seller, and the nation as buyer, to sell out and buy out that without which the war could never have been, than to sink both the thing to be sold and the price of it in cutting one another's throats! * * * I do not speak of emancipation *at once*, but of a *decision* to emancipate *gradually*. * * * Upon these considerations I have again begged your attention to the message of March last. Before leaving the capital consider and discuss it among yourselves. You are patriots and statesmen, and as such I pray you consider this proposition, and at the least commend it to the consideration of your States and people. As you would perpetuate popular government for the best people in the world, I beseech you that you do in nowise omit this. Our common country is in great peril, demanding the loftiest views and boldest action to bring a speedy relief. Once relieved, its form of government is saved to the world, its beloved history and cherished memories are vindicated, and its happy future fully assured and rendered inconceivably grand. To you, more than any others, the privilege is given to assure that happiness and swell that grandeur, and to link your own names therewith forever.''

In an interview with Mr. Lovejoy and Mr. Arnold, of Illinois, the day following this conference, Mr. Lincoln exclaimed: ''Oh, how I wish the border States would accept my proposition. Then, you, Lovejoy, and you, Arnold, and all of us, would not have lived in vain! The labor of your life, Lovejoy, would be crowned with success. You would live to see the end of slavery.''

PRESSURE BROUGHT TO BEAR ON THE EXECUTIVE.—THE
DELEGATION OF QUAKERS.

It has been shown again and again, by the words of Mr.
Lincoln and by the testimony of his friends, that he heartily
detested the practice of slavery, and would joyfully have set
every bondman free. But his respect for the laws of the land
surmounted every other consideration, and he waited patiently
until the right hour had struck, before he issued the edict of
emancipation so eagerly demanded by a large class of earnest
and loyal men at the North. Many of these good people,
misunderstanding his views and intentions, were very impatient; and their criticisms and expostulations were a constant
burden to the sorely-tried Executive.

In June of this year (1862) the President was waited on
by a deputation of Quakers, or Friends, fifteen or twenty in
number, who had been charged by the Yearly Meeting of
their association to present a "minute" to the President on
the subject of slavery and the duty of immediate emancipation. The visit of these excellent people was not altogether
timely. Bad news had been received from McClellan's army
on the Peninsula, and Mr. Lincoln was harassed with cares
and anxieties. He, however, gave the deputation a cordial
though brief greeting, as he announced that he was ready to
hear from the Friends. In the reading of the minute, it
appeared that the document took occasion to remind the President that, years before, he had said: "I believe that this
Government cannot permanently endure half slave and half
free," and from this was implied a suggestion of his failure to
perform his duty as he had then seen it. Mr. Lincoln was decidedly displeased with this criticism; and after the document
had been read to the close, he received it from the speaker,
then drawing himself up, he said, with unusual severity of
manner: "It is true that on the 17th of June, 1858, I said:
'I believe that this Government cannot permanently endure
half slave and half free,' but I said it in connection with

other things from which it should not have been separated in an address discussing moral obligations; for this is a case in which the repetition of half a truth, in connection with the remarks just read, produces the effect of a whole falsehood. What I did say was: 'If we could first know where we are, and whither we are tending, we could better judge what to do and how to do it. We are now far into the fifth year since a policy was initiated with the avowed object and confident promise of putting an end to the slavery agitation. Under the operation of that policy that agitation has not only not ceased, but has constantly augmented. In my opinion, it will not cease until a crisis shall have been reached and passed. 'A house divided against itself cannot stand.' I believe that this Government cannot permanently endure half slave and half free. I do not expect the Union to be dissolved—I do not expect the house to fall—but I do expect that it will cease to be divided. It will become all one thing or all the other. Either the opponents of slavery will arrest the further spread of it, and place it where the public mind shall rest in the belief that it is in the course of ultimate extinction, or its advocates will push it forward till it shall become alike lawful in all the States, old as well as new, North as well as South.' Take this statement as a whole, and it does not furnish a text for the homily to which this audience has listened."

As Mr. Lincoln concluded, he was turning away, when another member of the delegation, a woman, requested permission to detain him with a few words. Somewhat impatiently, he said, "I will hear the Friend." Her remarks were a plea for the emancipation of the slaves, urging that he was the appointed minister of the Lord to do the work, and enforcing her argument by many Scriptural citations. At the close, he asked: "Has the Friend finished?" and receiving an affirmative answer, he said: "I have neither time nor disposition to enter into discussion with the Friend, and end this occasion by suggesting for her consideration the question, whether, if it be true that the Lord has appointed me to do the work she has indicated, it is not probable that He would have communicated knowledge of the fact to me as well as to her?''

A VISIT FROM CHICAGO CLERGYMEN.

Something like the same views were expressed by Mr. Lincoln, on another occasion, when, in response to a memorial presented by a delegation representing most of the religious organizations of Chicago, he said, respectfully but pointedly: ''I am approached with the most opposite opinions and advice, and by religious men who are certain they represent the Divine Will. * * * I hope it will not be irreverent in me to say that if it be probable that God would reveal his will to others, on a point so connected with my duty, it might be supposed he would reveal it directly to me. * * * If I can learn his will, I will do it. These, however, are not the days of miracles, and I suppose I am not to expect a direct revelation. I must study the plain physical facts of the case, and learn what appears to be wise and right. * * * Do not misunderstand me because I have mentioned these objections. They indicate the difficulties which have thus far prevented my action in some such way as you desire. I have not decided against a proclamation of emancipation, but hold the matter in advisement. The subject is in my mind by day and by night. Whatever shall appear to be God's will, I will do.''

INTERVIEW BETWEEN CHANNING AND LINCOLN.

About this period the President had a very interesting conversation with William Henry Channing, in which the question of emancipation was frankly discussed. Mr. M. D. Conway, who was present at the interview, says: ''Mr. Channing having begun by expressing his belief that the opportunity of the nation to rid itself of slavery had arrived, Mr. Lincoln asked how he thought they might avail themselves of it. Channing suggested emancipation, with compensation for the slaves. The President said he had for years been in favor of that plan. When the President turned to me, I asked whether we might not look to him as the coming deliverer of the nation from its one great evil? What would not that man achieve for mankind who should free America from slavery? He said: 'Perhaps we may be better able to do something in that direction after a while than we are now.' I said: 'Mr. President, do you believe the masses of the American people would hail you as their deliverer if, at the end of this war, the Union should be surviving and slavery still in it?' 'Yes, if they were to see that slavery was on the down hill.' I ventured to say: 'Our fathers compromised with slavery because they thought it on the down hill; hence war to-day.' The President said: 'I think the country grows in this direction daily, and I am not without hope that something of the desire of you and your friends may be accomplished. When the hour comes for dealing with slavery, *I trust I shall be willing to do my duty, though it costs my life*. And, gentlemen, lives will be lost.' These last words were said with a smile, yet with a sad and weary tone. During the conversation Mr. Lincoln recurred several times to Channing's suggestion of pecuniary compensation for emancipated slaves, and professed profound sympathy with the Southerners who, by no fault of their own, had become socially and commercially bound up with their peculiar institution. Being a Virginian myself, with many dear relatives and beloved companions of my youth in the Confederate ranks, I responded warmly to his kindly sentiments toward the South, albeit feeling more angry than he seemed to be against the institution preying upon the land like a ghoul. I forget whether it was on this occasion or on a subsequent one when I was present that he said, in parting: 'We shall need all the anti-slavery feeling in the country, and more; you can go home and try to bring the people to your views; and you may say anything you like about me, if that will help. Don't spare me !' This was said with some laughter, but still in earnest.''

Horace Greeley

LINCOLN AND HORACE GREELEY.—ANSWER TO ''THE PRAYER OF TWENTY MILLIONS OF PEOPLE.''

One of the severest opponents of President Lincoln's policy regarding slavery was Horace Greeley. He criticised Mr. Lincoln freely in the New York Tribune, of which he was editor, and said many harsh and bitter things of the administration. Mr. Lincoln took the abuse good-naturedly, saying on one occasion: "It reminds me of the big fellow whose little wife was wont to beat him over the head without resistance. When remonstrated with, the man said, 'Let her alone. It don't hurt me, and it does her a power of good.' "

In August, 1862, Mr. Greeley published a letter in the New York Tribune, headed "The prayer of twenty millions of people," in which he urged the President, with extreme emphasis, to delay the act of emancipation no longer. Mr. Lincoln answered the vehement entreaty in the following calm, firm, and terse words:

"EXECUTIVE MANSION, Washington, Friday, Aug. 22, 1862.

"*Hon. Horace Greeley:*—DEAR SIR: I have just read yours of the 19th instant, addressed to myself, through the New York Tribune.

"If there be in it any statements or assumptions of fact, which I may know to be erroneous, I do not now and here controvert them. If there be any inferences which I believe to be falsely drawn, I do not now and here argue against them. If there be perceptible in it an impatient and dictatorial tone, I waive it, in deference to an old friend whose heart I have always supposed to be right.

"As to the policy I 'seem to be pursuing,' as you say, I have not meant to leave any one in doubt. I would save the Union. I would save it in the shortest way under the Constitution. The sooner the national authority can be restored, the nearer the Union will be—the Union as it was. If there be those who would not save the Union unless they could at the same time save slavery, I do not agree with them. If there be those who would not save the Union unless they could at the same time destroy slavery, I do not agree with them. *My paramount object is to save the Union, and not either to save or destroy slavery.* If I could save the Union without freeing any slave, I would do it. And if I could save it by freeing all the slaves, I would do it. And if I could save it by freeing some, and leaving others alone, I would do that.

"What I do about slavery and the colored race, I do because I believe it helps to save the Union; and what I forbear, I forbear because I do not believe it would help to save the Union. I shall do less whenever I believe what I am doing hurts the cause; and shall do more whenever I believe doing more will help the cause. I shall try to correct errors, when shown to be errors; and I shall adopt new views, so fast as they shall appear to be true views.

"I have here stated my purpose, according to my view of official duty, and I intend no modification of my oft-expressed personal wish that all men everywhere could be free.   Yours,   A. LINCOLN."

CONFERENCE BETWEEN LINCOLN AND GREELEY.

Mr. Greeley being dissatisfied with the explanation of Mr. Lincoln, and the Tribune still teeming with complaints and criticisms of his administration, he requested Mr. Greeley to come to Washington and make known in person his complaints, to the end that they might be obviated if possible. The editor of the Tribune came. Mr. Lincoln said: "You complain of me. What have I done, or omitted to do, which has provoked the hostility of the Tribune?" The reply was: "You should issue a proclamation abolishing slavery." Mr. Lincoln answered: "Suppose I do that. There are now twenty thousand of our muskets on the shoulders of Kentuckians, who are bravely fighting our battles. Every one of them will be thrown down or carried over to the rebels." The reply was: "Let them do it. The cause of the Union will be stronger if Kentucky should secede with the rest than it is now." Mr. Lincoln answered: "Oh, I can't think that."

EMANCIPATION RESOLVED ON.

It is evident that all these solicitations and counsellings from outside persons were unnecessary and idle. Mr. Lincoln's far-seeing and practical mind had already grasped, more surely than had his would-be advisers, the ultimate wisdom and justice of the emancipation of the slaves. But he was resolved to do nothing rashly. He would wait till the time was ripe, and then abolish slavery on grounds that would be approved throughout the world; namely, as a necessary step to the preservation of the Union. In the first year of the war he had said to a Southern Unionist, who warned him against meddling with slavery: *"You must not expect me to give up this Government without playing my last card."* This "last card" was undoubtedly emancipation.

When the time came, it was played unhesitatingly and triumphantly.

On the 22d of September, 1862, President Lincoln issued

THE PRELIMINARY PROCLAMATION.

"I, Abraham Lincoln, President of the United States of America, and Commander-in-Chief of the army and navy thereof, do hereby proclaim and declare that hereafter, as heretofore, the war will be prosecuted for the object of practically restoring the constitutional relations between the United States and each of the States and the people thereof, in which States that relation is or may be suspended or disturbed.

"That it is my purpose, upon the next meeting of Congress, to again recommend the adoption of a practical measure tendering pecuniary aid to the free acceptance or rejection of all slave States, so called, the people whereof may not then be in rebellion against the United States, and which States may then have voluntarily adopted, or thereafter may voluntarily adopt, immediate or gradual abolishment of slavery within their respective limits; and that the effort to colonize persons of African descent, with their consent, upon this continent or elsewhere, with the previously obtained consent of the governments existing there, will be continued.

"That on the first day of January, in the year of our Lord one thousand eight hundred and sixty-three, all persons held as slaves within any State or designated part of a State, the people whereof shall then be in rebellion against the United States, shall be then, thenceforward, and forever FREE; and the Executive government of the United States, including the military and naval authority thereof, will recognize and maintain the freedom of such persons, and will do no act or acts to repress such persons, or any of them, in any efforts they may make for their actual freedom.

"That the Executive will, on the first day of January aforesaid, by proclamation, designate the States and parts of States, if any, in which the people thereof respectively shall then be in rebellion against the United States; and the fact that any State, or the people thereof, shall on that day be, in good faith, represented in the Congress of the United States by members chosen thereto at elections wherein a majority of the qualified voters of such State shall have participated, shall, in the absence of strong countervailing testimony, be deemed conclusive evidence that such State, and the people thereof, are not in rebellion against the United States.

"That attention is hereby called to an act of Congress entitled "An act to make an additional article of war," approved March 13, 1862, and which act is in the words and figures following:

"Be it enacted by the Senate and House of Representatives of the United States of America in Congress assembled, That hereafter the following shall be promulgated as an additional article of war, for the government of the army of the United States, and shall be obeyed and observed as such.

"ARTICLE.—All officers or persons in the military or naval service of the United States are prohibited from employing any of the forces under their respective commands for the purpose of returning fugitives from service or labor who may have escaped from any persons to whom such service or labor is claimed to be due, and any officer who shall be found guilty by a court-martial of violating this article shall be dismissed from the service.

"SEC. 2. *And be it further enacted,* That this act shall take effect from and after its passage."

"Also to the ninth and tenth sections of an act entitled, "An act to suppress insurrection, to punish treason and rebellion, to seize and confiscate property of rebels, and for other purposes," approved July 17, 1862, and which sections are in the words and figures following:

"SEC. 9. *And be it further enacted,* That all slaves of persons who shall hereafter be engaged in rebellion against the government of the United States or who shall in any way give aid or comfort thereto, escaping from such persons and taking refuge within the lines of the army; and all slaves captured from such persons or deserted by them, and coming under the control of the government of the United States; and all slaves of such persons found *on* [or] being within any place occupied by rebel forces, and afterwards occupied by the forces of the United States, shall be deemed captives of war, and shall be forever free of their servitude, and not again held as slaves.

"SEC. 10. *And be it further enacted,* That no slave, escaping into any State, Territory, or the District of Columbia, from any other State, shall be delivered up, or in any way impeded or hindered of his liberty, except for crime, or some offense against the laws, unless the person claiming said fugitive shall first make oath that the person to whom the labor or service of such fugitive is alleged to be due is his lawful owner, and has not borne arms against the United States in the present rebellion, nor in any way given aid and comfort thereto; and no person engaged in the military or naval service of the United States shall, under any pretence whatever, assume to decide on the validity of the claim of any person to the service or labor of any other person, or surrender up any such person to the claimant, on pain of being dismissed from the service."

"And I do hereby enjoin upon and order all persons engaged in the military and naval service of the United States to observe, obey, and enforce, within their respective spheres of service, the act and sections above recited.

"And the Executive will in due time recommend that all the citizens of the United States who shall have remained loyal thereto throughout the rebellion, shall (upon the restoration of the constitutional relation between the United States and their respective States and people, if that relation shall have been suspended or disturbed) be compensated for all losses by acts of the United States, including the loss of slaves.

"In witness whereof, I have hereunto set my hand, and caused the seal of the United States to be affixed.

"Done at the city of Washington, this twenty-second day of September, in the year of our Lord, one thousand eight hundred and sixty-two, and of the Independence of the United States the eighty-seventh.

"*By the President:*   ABRAHAM LINCOLN.

WILLIAM H. SEWARD, *Secretary of State.*"

MR. LINCOLN'S ACCOUNT OF THE PROCLAMATION.

A most interesting account of this proclamation, and of the steps that led to it, is given by Mr. F. B. Carpenter, in Mr. Lincoln's own words: "It had," said Mr. Lincoln, "got to be midsummer, 1862. Things had gone on from bad to worse, until I felt that we had reached the end of our rope on the plan of operations we had been pursuing; that we had about played our last card, and must change our tactics or lose the game. I now determined upon the adoption of the emancipation policy; and, without consultation with, or the knowledge of, the Cabinet, I prepared the original draft of the proclamation, and, after much anxious thought, called a Cabinet meeting upon the subject. This was the last of July, or the first part of the month of August, 1862. This Cabinet meeting took place, I think, upon a Saturday. All were present, excepting Mr. Blair, the Postmaster-general, who was absent at the opening of the discussion, but came in subsequently. I said to the Cabinet that I had resolved upon this step, and had called them together, not to ask their advice, but to lay the subject-matter of a proclamation before them; suggestions as to which would be in order, after they had heard it read. Mr. Lovejoy was in error when he informed you that it excited no comment, excepting on the part of Secretary Seward. Various suggestions were offered. Secretary Chase wished the language stronger in reference to the arming of the blacks. Mr. Blair, after he came in, deprecated the policy, on the ground that it would cost the administration the fall elections. Nothing, however, was offered that I had not already fully anticipated and settled in my own mind, until Secretary Seward spoke. He said in substance: 'Mr. President, I approve of the proclamation, but I question the expediency of its issue at this juncture. The depression of the public mind, consequent upon our repeated reverses, is so great that I fear the effect of so important a step. It may be viewed as the last measure of an exhausted government, a cry for help; the government stretching forth its hands to Ethiopia, instead of Ethiopia stretching forth her hands to the government.' His idea,' said the President, 'was that it would be considered our last *shriek* on the retreat.' (This was his precise expression.) 'Now,' continued Mr. Seward, 'while I approve the measure, I suggest, sir, that you postpone its issue until you can give it to the country supported by military success, instead of issuing it, as would be the case now, upon the greatest disasters of the war!'" Mr. Lincoln continued: "The wisdom of the view of the Secretary of State struck me with very great force. It was an aspect of the case that, in all my thought upon the subject, I had entirely overlooked. The result was that I put the draft of the proclamation aside, waiting for a victory. From time to time I added or changed a line, touching it up here and there, anxiously waiting the progress of events. Well, the next news we had was of Pope's disaster at Bull Run. Things looked darker than ever. Finally, came the week of the battle of Antietam. I determined to wait no longer. The news came, I think, on Wednesday, that the advantage was on our side. I was then staying at the Soldiers' Home (three miles out of Washington). Here I finished writing the second draft of the preliminary proclamation; came up on Saturday; called the Cabinet together to hear it; and it was published the following Monday."

At the final meeting of September 20, another interesting incident occurred in connection with Secretary Seward. The President had written the important part of the proclamation in these words: "That on the first day of January, in the year of our Lord one thousand eight hundred and sixty-three, all persons held as slaves within any State or designated part of a State, the people whereof shall then be in rebellion against the United States, shall be then, thenceforward, and forever FREE; and the Executive Government of the United States, including the military and naval authority thereof, will *recognize* the freedom of such persons, and will do no act or acts to repress such persons, or any of them, in any efforts they may make for their actual freedom." "When I finished reading this paragraph," remarked Mr. Lincoln, "Mr. Seward stopped me, and said, 'I think, Mr. President, that you should insert after the word *"recognize,"* *"and maintain."*'" I replied that I had already fully considered the import of that expression in this connection, but I had not introduced it, because it was not my way to promise what I was not entirely *sure* that I could perform, and I was not prepared to say that I thought we were exactly able to maintain this. But Seward insisted that we ought to take this ground, and the words finally went in."

Hon. George S. Boutwell, of Massachusetts, says that Mr. Lincoln stated to him personally: "When Lee came over the river, I made a resolution that if McClellan drove him back I would send the proclamation after him. The battle of Antietam was fought Wednesday, and until Saturday I could not find out whether we had gained a victory or lost a battle. It was then too late to issue the proclamation that day; and the fact is, I fixed it up a little on Sunday, and Monday I let them have it."

PREPARING FOR THE FINAL ACT.—HIS MIND WAS "MADE UP."

In his second annual message to Congress, transmitted to that body in December, 1862, Mr. Lincoln touched, in conclusion, upon the great subject of the emancipation, in these words of deep import:

"I do not forget the gravity which should characterize a paper addressed to the Congress of the nation by the Chief Magistrate of the nation. Nor do I forget that some of you are my seniors, nor that many of you have more experience than I in the conduct of public affairs. Yet I trust that in view of the great responsibility resting upon me, you will perceive no want of respect to yourselves in any undue earnestness I may seem to display. * * * The dogmas of the quiet past are inadequate to the stormy present. The occasion is piled high with difficulty, and we must rise with the occasion. As our case is new, so we must think anew and act anew.

"Fellow citizens, we cannot escape history. We of this Congress and this administration will be remembered in spite of ourselves. No personal significance, or insignificance, can spare one or another of us. The fiery trial through which we pass will light us down, in honor or dishonor, to the latest generation. We say we are for the Union. The world will not forget that we say this. We know how to save the Union. The world knows we do know how to save it. We—even we here—hold the power and bear the responsibility. In giving freedom to the slave we assure freedom to the free—honorable alike in what we give and what we preserve. We shall nobly save, or meanly lose, the last best hope of earth. Other means may succeed, this could not fail. The way is plain, peaceful, generous, just—a way which, if followed, the world will forever applaud, and God must forever bless."

Hon. John Covode relates that a few days before the final issue of the Emancipation Proclamation, he called on the President and found him walking his room in great excitement. Reference being made to the forthcoming proclamation, Mr. Lincoln said with great earnestness: "I have studied that matter well; my mind is made up—it *must be done.* I am driven to it. There is to me no other way out of our troubles. But although my duty is plain, it is in some respects painful, and I trust the people will understand that I act not in anger but in expectation of a greater good."

THE EMANCIPATION PROCLAMATION.

An immense concourse attended the reception at the White House on the first day of 1863, and the President stood hour after hour shaking hands with the endless train of men and women who pressed forward to greet him. The exhausting ceremonial being ended, the proclamation which abrogated, finally and forever, the institution of slavery in the United States, was handed to him for his signature. "Mr. Seward," remarked the President, "I have been shaking hands all day, and my right hand is almost paralyzed. If my name ever gets into history, it will be for this act, and my whole soul is in it. If my hand trembles when I sign the proclamation, those who examine the document hereafter will say I hesitated." Then, resting his arm a moment, he turned to the table, took up the pen, and slowly and firmly wrote, ABRAHAM LINCOLN. He smiled as, handing the paper to Mr. Seward, he said, "That will do." A few hours after, he remarked: "The signature looks a little tremulous, for my hand was tired; but my resolution was firm. I told them in September, if they did not return to their allegiance, I would strike at this pillar of their strength. And now the promise shall be kept, and not one word of it will I ever recall."

The wording of the momentous measure is as follows:

"Whereas, on the 22d day of September, in the year of our Lord one thousand eight hundred and sixty-two, a proclamation was issued by the President of the United States, containing, among other things, the following, to-wit:

"That on the first day of January, in the year of our Lord one thousand eight hundred and sixty-three, all persons held as slaves within any States or designated part of a State, the people whereof shall then be in rebellion against the United States, shall be then, thenceforward and forever free; and the Executive Government of the United States, including the military and naval authority thereof, will recognize and maintain the freedom of such persons, and will do no act or acts to repress such persons, or any of them, in any efforts they may make for their actual freedom.

"That the Executive will, on the first day of January aforesaid, by proclamation, designate the States and parts of States, if any, in which the people thereof respectively shall then be in rebellion against the United States; and the fact that any State, or the people thereof, shall on that day be in good faith represented in the Congress of the United States, by members chosen thereto at elections wherein a majority of the qualified voters of such State shall have participated, shall, in the absence of strong countervailing testimony, be deemed conclusive evidence that such State, and the people thereof, are not then in rebellion against the United States.

"Now, therefore, I, Abraham Lincoln, President of the United States, by virtue of the power in me vested as Commander-in-Chief of the Army and Navy of the United States in time of actual armed rebellion against the authority and Government of the United States, and as a fit and necessary war measure for suppressing said rebellion, do, on this first day of January, in the year of our Lord one thousand eight hundred and sixty-three, and in accordance with my purpose so to do, publicly proclaimed for the full period of one hundred days, from the day first above mentioned, order and designate as the States and parts of States wherein the people thereof respectively are this day in rebellion against the United States, the following, to-wit: Arkansas, Texas, Louisiana (except the parishes of St. Bernard, Plaquemines, Jefferson, St. John, St. Charles, St. James, Ascension, Assumption, Terre Bonne, Lafourche, Ste. Marie, St. Martin, and Orleans, including the city of New Orleans), Mississippi, Alabama, Florida, Georgia, South Carolina, North Carolina, and Virginia (except the forty-eight counties designated as West Virginia, and also the counties of Berkeley, Accomac, Northampton, Elizabeth City, York, Princess Anne, and Norfolk, including the cities of Norfolk and Portsmouth), and which excepted parts are for the present left precisely as if this proclamation were not issued.

"And by virtue of the power and for the purpose aforesaid, I do order and declare that all persons held as slaves within said designated States and parts of States are and henceforward shall be FREE; and that the Executive Government of the United States, including the military and naval authorities thereof, will recognize and maintain the freedom of said persons.

"And I hereby enjoin upon the people so declared to be free to abstain from all violence, unless in necessary self-defense; and I recommend to them that, in all cases when allowed, they labor faithfully for reasonable wages.

"And I further declare and make known that such persons, of suitable condition, will be received into the armed service of the United States to garrison forts, positions, stations, and other places, and to man vessels of all sorts in said service.

"And upon this act, sincerely believed to be an act of justice, warranted by the Constitution, upon military necessity, I invoke the considerate judgment of mankind and the gracious favor of Almighty God.

"In testimony whereof, I have hereunto set my name, and caused the seal of the United States to be affixed.

"Done at the City of Washington, this first day of January, in the year of our Lord one thousand eight hundred and sixty-three, and of the independence of the United States the eighty-seventh.

"*By the President:*   ABRAHAM LINCOLN.
WILLIAM H. SEWARD, Secretary of State."

PARTICULARS OF THE GREAT DOCUMENT.

It is stated that Mr. Lincoln gave the most earnest study to the composition of the Emancipation Proclamation. He realized, as he afterwards said, that the proclamation was the central act of his administration, and the great event of the nineteenth century. When the document was completed, a printed copy of it was placed in the hands of each member of the Cabinet, and criticisms and suggestions were invited. Mr. Chase remarked: "This paper is of the utmost importance, greater than any state paper ever made by this Government.

A paper of so much importance, and involving the liberties of so many people, ought, I think, to make some reference to Deity. I do not observe anything of the kind in it." Mr. Lincoln said: "No, I overlooked it. Some reference to Deity must be inserted. Mr. Chase, won't you make a draft of what you think ought to be inserted?" Mr. Chase promised to do so, and at the next meeting presented the following: "And upon this act, sincerely believed to be an act of justice, warranted by the Constitution, upon military necessity, I invoke the considerate judgment of mankind and the gracious favor of Almighty God." When Mr. Lincoln read the paragraph, Mr. Chase said: "You may not approve it, but I thought this, or something like it, would be appropriate." Lincoln replied: "I do approve it; it cannot be bettered, and I will adopt it in the very words you have written."

To a large concourse of people, who, two days after the proclamation was issued, assembled before the White House, with music, the President said: "What I did, I did after a very full deliberation, and under a heavy and solemn sense of responsibility. I can only trust in God I have made no mistake."

Mr. Ben. Perley Poore makes the interesting statement that "Mr. Lincoln carefully put away the pen which he had used, for Mr. Sumner, who had promised it to his friend, George Livermore, of Cambridge, the author of an interesting work on slavery. It was a steel pen with a wooden handle, the end of which had been gnawed by Mr. Lincoln,—a habit that he had when composing anything that required thought."

FATE OF THE ORIGINAL DRAFT.

In response to a request of the ladies in charge of the Northwestern Fair for the Sanitary Commission, which was held in Chicago in the Autumn of 1863, Mr. Lincoln conveyed to them the original draft of the proclamation; saying, in his note of presentation, "I had some desire to retain the paper; but if it shall contribute to the relief or comfort of the soldiers, that will be better." The document was purchased at the Fair by Mr. Thomas B. Bryan, and given by him to the Chicago Historical Society. It perished in the great fire of October, 1871.

MR. LINCOLN'S OUTLINE OF HIS COURSE AND VIEWS REGARDING SLAVERY.

More than a year after the issue of the Emancipation Proclamation, Mr. Lincoln, in writing to a prominent Kentucky Unionist, gave an admirable outline of his views and course regarding slavery. The statement should have a place in this chapter:

"I am naturally anti-slavery. If slavery is not wrong, nothing is wrong. I cannot remember when I did not so think and feel; and yet I have never understood that the Presidency conferred upon me an unrestricted right to act officially upon this judgment and feeling. It was in the oath I took that I would, to the best of my ability, preserve, protect, and defend the Constitution of the United States. I could not take the office without taking the oath. Nor was it my view that I might take an oath to get power, and break the oath in using the power. I understood, too, that in ordinary civil administration this oath even forbade me to practically indulge my primary abstract judgment on the moral question of slavery. I had publicly declared this many times and in many ways. And I aver that, to this day, I have done no official act in mere deference to my abstract judgment and feeling on slavery. I did understand, however, that my oath to preserve the Constitution to the best of my ability imposed upon me the duty of preserving, by every indispensable means, that Government—that Nation of which that Constitution was the organic law. Was it possible to lose the nation and yet preserve the Constitution? By general law, life *and* limb must be protected; yet often a limb must be amputated to save a life; but a life is never wisely given to save a limb. I felt that measures, otherwise unconstitutional, might become lawful, by becoming indispensable to the preservation of the Constitution, through the preservation of the nation. Right or wrong, I assumed this ground, and now avow it. I could not feel that, to the best of my ability, I had even tried to preserve the Constitution, if, to save slavery, or any minor matter, I should permit the wreck of government, country, and constitution, altogether. When, early in the war, General Fremont attempted military emancipation, I forbade it, because I did not then think it an indispensable necessity. When a little later, General Cameron, then Secretary of War, suggested the arming of the blacks, I objected, because I did not yet think it an indispensable necessity. When, still later, General Hunter attempted military emancipation, I again forbade it, because I did not yet think the indispensable necessity had come. When, in March and May and July, 1862, I made earnest and successive appeals to the border States to favor compensated emancipation, I believed the indispensable necessity for military emancipation and arming the blacks would come, unless averted by that measure. They declined the proposition; and I was, in my best judgment, driven to the alternative of either surrendering the Union, and with it the Constitution, or of laying strong hand upon the colored element. I chose the latter. In choosing it, I hoped for greater gain than loss; but of this I was not entirely confident. More than a year of trial now shows no loss by it in our foreign relations, none in our home popular sentiment, none in our white military force, no loss by it anyhow or anywhere. On the contrary, it shows a gain of quite a hundred and thirty thousand soldiers, seamen, and laborers. These are palpable facts, about which, as facts, there can be no cavilling. We have the men; and we could not have had them without the measure.

"And now let any Union man who complains of the measure, test himself by writing down in one line that he is for subduing the rebellion by force of arms; and in the next, that he is for taking three hundred and thirty thousand men from the Union side, and placing them where they would be but for the measure he condemns. If he cannot face his case so stated, it is only because he cannot face the truth.

"I attempt no compliment to my own sagacity. I claim not to have controlled events, but confess plainly that events have controlled me. Now, at the end of three years' struggle, the nation's condition is not what either party or any man devised or expected. God alone can claim it. Whither it is tending seems plain. If God now wills the removal of a great wrong, and wills also that we of the North, as well as you of the South, shall pay fairly for our complicity in that wrong, impartial history will find therein new causes to attest and revere the justice and goodness of God.

Yours truly,   A. LINCOLN."

CHAPTER VIII.

IN a work which is not intended to cover fully the events of a great historic period, but rather to trace out the life of a single individual connected with that period, much must be included which, although not possessing any historical signifi-cance, cannot be overlooked in a personal study of the subject of the biography. Mr. Lincoln's life as President was not made up of Cabinet meetings, official messages and procla-mations, or reviews of armies. Interspersed with these con-spicuous acts was a multitude of less heroic but scarcely less interesting details, with incidents and experiences humorous or sad, but all, even the most trivial, being true expressions of the life and character of the man whom we are seeking to portray.

SOCIETY AT THE WHITE HOUSE IN 1862–'63.

Society, as now understood at the National Capital, had no existence during the war. At the White House there were the usual President's receptions, which were quite public in character, and were never so largely attended as then. Aside from these democratic gatherings, there was little enough of gaiety. During the winter of 1862–'63, a good deal of clamor was raised over a party given by Mrs. Lincoln, at which, it was asserted, dancing was indulged in; and Mrs. Lincoln was severely censured for what was regarded as inexcusable frivolity. Hon. A. G. Riddle, who was present on the occasion referred to, states positively that there was no dancing. The party was a quiet one, intended only to relieve the rather dull and formal receptions. The President was pained by the rumors that "fashionable balls" were permitted at the White House in war-time; and the party was not repeated.

THE PRESIDENT'S INFORMAL RECEPTIONS.

It was the custom of President Lincoln to open, twice a week, the doors of his office in the Executive Mansion, for the admission of all visitors who might wish to speak with him. These brief interviews, stripped of ceremony, seemed the better to reveal the man in his true character, and to set forth the salient traits that fitted him for his great position and work, and endeared him so greatly to the popular heart. They showed how easily accessible he was to all classes of citizens, how readily he could adapt himself to people of any station or degree, how deep and true his human sympathies were, how quickly and keenly he could discriminate character, and how heartily he detested meanness and all unworthy acts and appliances to compass a selfish or sordid end. On these occasions, as may well be imagined, many curious and memorable incidents occurred. Mr. Lincoln was usually clad "in a black broadcloth suit, nothing in all his dress betokening disregard of conventionality, save, perhaps, his neat cloth slippers, which were doubtless worn for comfort. He was seated beside a plain cloth-covered table, in a commodious arm-chair." As each visitor approached the President, he was greeted with an encouraging nod and smile, and a few moments were cordially given him in which to state the object of the visit; the President listening with the most respectful and patient attention, and deciding each case with the greatest tact, delicacy, and clearness. "His *Yes*," says Mr. Riddle, "was most gracious and satisfactory; his *No*, when reached, was often spoken by the petitioner, and left only a soothed disappointment. He saw the point of a case unerringly. He had a confidence in the homely views and speech of the common people, with whom his heart and sympathies ever were."

A VARIETY OF CALLERS.—THE ONE-LEGGED GERMAN SOLDIER.

Taking advantage of the opportunity, there came one day, says Mr. C. Van Santvoord, "a sturdy, honest-looking German soldier, minus a leg, who hobbled up to the President on crutches. In consideration of his disabled condition, he wanted some situation about Washington, the duties of which he might be able to discharge, and he had come to the President, hoping that he would provide the desired situation for him. On being interrogated as to how he had lost his leg, he answered that it was the effect of a wound received in battle, mentioning the time and the place. 'Let me look at your papers,' said Mr. Lincoln. The man replied that he had none, and that he supposed his word would be sufficient. 'What!' exclaimed the President, 'no papers, no credentials, nothing to show how you lost your leg! How am I to know that you lost it in battle, or did not lose it by a trap after getting into somebody's orchard?' This was spoken with a droll expression, which amused the bystanders, all except the applicant, who, with a very solemn visage, earnestly protested the truth of his statement, muttering something about the reasons for not being able to produce his papers. 'Well, well,' said the President, 'it is dangerous for an army man to be wandering around without papers to show where he belongs and what he is, but I will see what can be done for you.' And taking a blank card from a little pile of similar blanks on the table, he wrote some lines upon it, addressed it, and handing it to the man bade him deliver it to a certain quartermaster, who would attend to his case."

A CHANGE OF HUMOR.

The next to approach the President was a man "apparently sixty years of age, with dress and manner which showed that he was acquainted with the usages of good society, whose whole exterior, indeed, would have impressed people who form opinions from appearances. The object of his visit was to solicit aid in some commission project, for the success of which Mr. Lincoln's favor was regarded as essential. The President heard him patiently, but demurred against being connected with or countenancing the affair, suggesting mildly that the applicant would better set up an office of the kind described, and run it in his own way and at his own risk. The man plead his advanced years and obscurity as a reason for not attempting this, but said if the President would only let him use his name to advertise and recommend the enterprise, he would then, he thought, need nothing more. At this the eyes of the President flashed with sudden indignation, and his whole aspect and manner underwent a portentous change. 'No!' he broke forth, with startling vehemence, springing from his seat under the impulse of his emotion. 'No! I'll have nothing to do with this business, nor with any man who comes to me with such degrading propositions. What! Do you take the President of the United States to be a commission broker? You have come to the wrong place; and for you and every one who comes for such purposes, there is the door!' The man's face blanched as he cowered and slunk away confounded, without uttering a word. The President's wrath subsided as speedily as it had risen."

At another time a Catholic priest called with two ladies. The priest, turning to the President, said: "I should like a private interview." "I do nothing privately," was the answer; "all is public." The priest glanced angrily at the President, and said, rather pompously: "Then we are to have no hearing?" "Certainly you shall be heard; I will listen to you now." "That will not do. I wish to see you alone." "I can only tell you, as I did before, that I do nothing privately," answered the President, coldly. The priest at once arose and left the room, followed by his companions.

"COME UNDER !"

When these visitors had gone, "an immense specimen of a man presented himself. Broad-shouldered, robust, with thews and sinews to match his great height, and with an honest, good-natured countenance—all seemed to mark him as belonging to the hardy yeomanry of the West. He sidled up awkwardly to the President, seeming almost afraid to accost him, but after some hesitation contrived to say, that being on a visit to Washington, he simply wanted, before leaving, to see the President, and have the honor of shaking hands with him. He found a kindly reception, and after some introductory civilities, Mr. Lincoln ran his eye curiously over his huge caller, surveying him from head to foot, and then saying with a humorous look and accent it would be hard to describe, 'I rather think you have a little the advantage of me in height; you are a taller man than I am.' 'I guess not, Mr. President,' replied the visitor, with the self-abnegating air of one who seemed to regard any claim on his part of possessing an *advantage* over the Chief Magistrate as an offense little short of treason; 'the advantage cannot be on my side.' 'Yes, it is,' was the rejoinder; 'I have a pretty good eye for distances, and I think I can't be mistaken in the fact of the advantage being slightly with you. I measure six feet, three and a half inches, in my stockings; and you go, I think, a little beyond that.' The man still demurred, insisting very respectfully that the advantage must lay on the President's side. 'It is very easily tested,' said the President; and rising briskly from his chair, and taking a book from the table, he placed it edgewise against the wall, just higher than his head. Then, turning to his doubting competitor for the nonce, he bade him 'Come under.' This the man did not do at once, pausing, with flushed face and irresolute look, as if uncertain how far

SCENE IN THE PRESIDENT'S OFFICE.—MR. LINCOLN MEASURING HEIGHT
WITH A COUNTRY VISITOR.

he might venture to trust the lion in his playful mood,—his countenance the while wearing a bewildered, half-frightened and yet half-smiling expression that was really comical to see. 'Come under, I say,' repeated the President in a more peremptory tone, and then the visitor slowly complied. 'Now straighten yourself up, and move your head in this way'— suiting the action to the word. This being done, Mr. Lincoln added, 'Now you hold the book, and be sure not to let it slip down a hair-breadth, and I will try.' Planting himself accordingly underneath the book, and moving his head from right to left, it was found that he fell a trifle short of the other measurement. 'There,' said he, 'it is as I told you. I knew I could not be mistaken. I rarely fail in taking a man's true altitude by the eye.' 'Yes, but, Mr. President,' said the man, his courage, amid the merriment of the company, beginning to return, 'you have slippers on, and I boots ; and that makes a difference.' 'Not enough to amount to anything in *this* reckoning,' was the reply. 'You ought at least to be satisfied, my honest friend, with the proof given that you actually *stand higher* to-day than your President.' "

THE SOLDIER'S DAUGHTER.

Another petitioner was a young girl of singular beauty, who besought the President for a pass to go to her father, who was badly wounded in a recent battle. "I cannot let you go down there," said the President sadly. "*How* can I?" he asked, looking up at the sweet face, so earnest and truthful. "I cannot let you go, and I cannot refuse you. What *shall* I do?" "Let me go there," she pleaded, "I am not afraid. God will take care of me." "I don't know—I don't know," he said. "Your faith is beautiful—but I don't know. There is not a woman down there." "I know it," she answered, thoughtfully. "Are you not afraid—not the least afraid?" "No, sir, I am not afraid. I have trusted our Heavenly Father many times before, and He has never forsaken me." "And He never will !" exclaimed the President, springing to his feet. "No, my child, He never will!" And, drawing a chair closer to the fire, he went on: "Come, sit here, until you are quite warm. I will write you a pass. You shall go to your father." Then, as though he felt pained at seeming inquisitive, he stopped suddenly, when just upon the verge of asking something; but the interest he felt in the petitioner prevailed, and he asked if she were fully prepared for her journey. "Yes, sir, I have plenty of money. If money could make the heart glad, I have enough. But I have no mother, and my father is perhaps dying. I cannot stay to get warm,—I can *never* get warm. Good-bye, kind, good President Lincoln! I may never see you again in this world; so shake hands with both of mine." A moment more, and she was gone.

CHARACTERISTIC TRAITS OF LINCOLN.—HIS FIRMNESS AND GOOD SENSE.

Among the many illustrations of the sturdy sense and firmness of Mr. Lincoln's character, the following should be recorded: During the early part of 1863, the Union men in Missouri were divided into two factions, which waged a bitter controversy with each other. General Curtis, commander of the military district comprising Missouri, Kansas, and Arkansas, was at the head of one faction, while Governor Gamble led the other. Their differences were a source of great embarrassment to the Government at Washington, and of harm to the Union cause. The President was in constant receipt of remonstrances and protests from the contesting parties, to one of which he made the following curt reply:

"Your dispatch of to-day is just received. It is very painful to me that you in Missouri cannot, or will not, settle your factional quarrel among yourselves. I have been tormented with it beyond endurance, for months, by both sides. Neither side pays the least respect to my appeals to reason. I am now compelled to take hold of the case.

A. LINCOLN."

The President promptly followed up this warning by removing General Curtis, and appointing in his place General

Schofield, to whom he soon after addressed the following
letter:

"EXECUTIVE MANSION, WASHINGTON; May 27, 1863.

"*General J. M. Schofield.*—DEAR SIR: Having removed General
Curtis and assigned you to the command of the Department of the Missouri, I think it may be of some advantage to me to state to you why I
did it. I did not remove General Curtis because of my full conviction
that he had done wrong by commission or omission. I did it because of
a conviction in my mind that the Union men of Missouri, constituting,
when united, a vast majority of the people, have entered into a pestilent,
factious quarrel, among themselves; General Curtis, perhaps not of
choice, being the head of one faction, and Governor Gamble that of the
other. After months of labor to reconcile the difficulty, it seemed to
grow worse and worse, until I felt it my duty to break it up somehow,
and as I could not remove Governor Gamble, I had to remove General
Curtis. Now that you are in the position, I wish you to undo nothing
merely because General Curtis or Governor Gamble did it, but to exercise
your own judgment, and do right for the public interest. Let your military measures be strong enough to repel the invaders and keep the peace,
and not so strong as to unnecessarily harrass and persecute the people. It
is a difficult *role*, and so much greater will be the honor if you perform it
well. If both factions, or neither, shall abuse you, you will probably be
about right. Beware of being assailed by one and praised by the other.

Yours truly, A. LINCOLN."

HIS TACT IN SETTLING QUARRELS.

Mr. Lincoln, though firm and unyielding when necessity
compelled him to be, was yet by nature a peace-maker, and
was ever anxious that personal differences be adjusted happily. In his efforts to this end, he never failed to show that tact
and shrewdness of which he possessed so large a share. He
would, if necessary, sacrifice his own preferences, in the interests of peace and harmony. A characteristic instance of the
exercise of these traits occurred in connection with the Missouri troubles, just referred to. Gen. Schofield's course in
command of his department proved satisfactory to Mr. Lincoln, and he had been nominated for a Major-General's
commission. He was, however, a somewhat conservative
man, and in spite of his efforts to carry out the President's

injunctions of impartiality, he had given offense to certain Missouri radicals, who now opposed his promotion, and were able to exert sufficient influence in the Senate to prevent the confirmation of his appointment as a Major-General. The Missouri delegation appealed to the more radical Senators, and the nomination was "hung up" for about six weeks. Mr. Lincoln was very anxious that it should be confirmed, and the Missouri Congressmen were equally bent on its defeat. In this dilemma, Mr. Lincoln sent for Senator Zack Chandler, of Michigan, and proposed a compromise. "General Rosecrans," said he, "has a great many friends; he fought the battle of Stone River and won a brilliant victory, and his advocates begin to grumble about his treatment. Now, I will tell you what I have been thinking about. If you will confirm Schofield, I will remove him from the command in Missouri and send him down to Sherman. That will satisfy the radicals. Then I will send Rosecrans to Missouri, and that will please the latter's friends. In this way the whole thing can be harmonized, and our friends hang together like a sausage." As soon as the Senate grasped the plan of the President, there was no longer any opposition to the confirmation of Schofield. He was sent to join Sherman in the South, Rosecrans was appointed to the command in Missouri, and everything worked harmoniously and pleasantly, as the President had predicted and desired.

INTERCEDING FOR A WAR CORRESPONDENT, BANISHED BY GENERAL SHERMAN.

General Sherman's dislike of newspaper correspondents in his army, and the harsh measures which he sometimes adopted, are quite generally known. While he was commanding a division in General Grant's army in the West, a certain newspaper man had given him offense, and was ordered beyond the army lines. The case was taken up by journalists in Washington, and a memorial was prepared, asking the President to set aside the order of General Sherman. Mr. J. M.

Winchell, one of three persons who presented the memorial, says: "Mr. Lincoln evidently considered it a delicate question, and was disposed to give it a careful investigation. He was resolved, I think, to conciliate the press, and equally resolved not to absolutely annul the action of the military authorities. The petition asked that he positively restore to the injured correspondent his lost privileges; while the President, not absolutely refusing at first, endeavored to satisfy us with a recommendation to General Grant to himself remit the sentence. But the committee believed that General Grant would stand stubbornly by the action of General Sherman, unless the President gave his wishes the force of an actual order. The discussion was long and animated. At length, while walking about the room, which he did a good deal, the President exclaimed: 'Well, you want me to make an order setting aside the action of the court. I wish to do what is right, and what you ask; for it seems to me, from all the evidence, that our newspaper friend has been a little too severely dealt with. Still, I am not on the spot to judge of all the circumstances, and General Grant is; and I do not see how I can properly grant your request without being sustained by his consent. But let us see what we can do; I will write something to put our ideas into shape;' and with a pleasant laugh he began at once to search for paper and pen. He was aided in this effort by little 'Tad,' who was present, and toward whom his father frequently manifested the most anxious and considerate affection. He found a piece of paper, with some difficulty, on the table (littered with documents lying in complete disorder), and a very poor pen, with which he at once set to work. The draft which he made was quite satisfactory. It was brief, clear and precise; it stated the case truly, revoked the sentence of the court, and gave the correspondent the privilege of returning to General Grant's headquarters. We were delighted with the document, and of course said so. 'But,' said the President, 'I had better make this conditional on the approval of General Grant. You see it would not seem right for me to send back a correspondent to the General's headquarters in case he knew of any reason why the man should not be there. I will just add a few words; and so he did, making the order close as follows: 'And to remain if General Grant shall give his express assent; and to again leave the department if General Grant shall refuse said assent.' 'There,' he remarked, 'I think that will be about right, and I have no doubt General Grant will assent.' And so he did.''

HIS SHREWD KNOWLEDGE OF MEN.

Secretary Welles remarks that "the President was a much more shrewd and accurate observer of the characteristics of men—better and more correctly formed an estimate of their power and capabilities—than the Secretary of State or most others. Those in the public service he closely scanned, but was deliberate in forming a conclusion adverse to any one he had appointed. In giving or withdrawing confidence he was discriminating and just in his final decision; careful never to wound unnecessarily the sensibilities of any for their infirmities, always ready to praise, but nevertheless firm and resolute in discharging the to him always painful duty of censure, reproof, or dismissal.'' As an instance of this sure judgment of the abilities and characters of men, Mr. Welles gives an anecdote relating to the naval movement under Admiral Du Pont, against Charleston, S. C.: "One day,'' says Mr. Welles, "the President said to me that he had but slight expectation that we should have any great success from Du Pont. 'He, as well as McClellan,' said Mr. Lincoln, 'hesitates—has *the slows*. McClellan always wanted more regiments; Du Pont is everlastingly asking for more gun-boats—more iron-clads. He will do nothing with any. He has intelligence and system, and will maintain a good blockade. You did well in selecting him for that command, but he will never take Sumter or get to Charleston. He is no Farragut, though unquestionably a good routine officer, who obeys orders and in a general way carries out his instructions.' "

Loyalty to his friends was one of the strongest traits in Mr. Lincoln's simple and steadfast nature. It was put to the proof daily during his life in Washington, and withstood every test. Mr. Gurdon S. Hubbard, in a brief but interesting memorial, relates one or two interviews held with the President, in which the simplicity of his character and his fidelity to old friendships appear very conspicuously. Mr. Hubbard's acquaintance with Mr. Lincoln was of long standing. They had first met while the latter was serving in the Legislature of Illinois, in the Winter of 1832–3, and an attachment had immediately sprung up between them. Mr. Hubbard's feeling toward the then young and rising lawyer was imbued with the enthusiasm which Lincoln inspired in all who knew him. "His character was nearly faultless," writes Mr. Hubbard. "Possessing a warm, generous heart, genial, affable, honest, courteous to his opponents, persevering, industrious in research, never losing sight of the principal point under discussion, aptly illustrating by his stories, always brought into good effect; free from political trickery or denunciation of the private character of his opponents; in debate firm and collected, with 'charity toward all, malice toward none,' he won the confidence of the public, even of his political opponents. * * * I called on him in Washington the year of his inauguration, and was alone with him for an hour or more. I found him greatly changed, his countenance bearing an expression of great mental anxiety. The whole topic of our conversation was the war, which affected him deeply. Examining the map hanging on the wall, pointing out the points most strong in the rebel district, he said: 'Douglas and myself have studied this map very closely. I am indebted to him for wise counsel. I have no better adviser, and feel under great obligations to

him.' I left Washington with a feeling that our nation had
not misplaced its confidence in choosing him as its President.
Two years after, I again visited Washington, and went to the
White House to pay my respects. In the ante-room I found
my friend Thomas L. Forrest. About six o'clock the band
from the navy-yard appeared and began to play, when Mr.
Forrest said: 'This is Saturday, when the grounds are open
to the public; the President will present himself on the balcony below; let us join the crowd.' So we adjourned and
filed in with the crowd. The President, with Adjutant-Gen.
Thomas, were seated on the balcony. The crowd was great,
marching compactly past the President, the men raising their
hats in salutation. As my friend and myself passed he said to
me: 'The President seems to notice you—turn toward him.'
'No,' I said, 'I don't care to be recognized.' At that instant
Mr. Lincoln started from his seat, advancing quickly to the
iron railing, and leaning over, beckoning with his long arm,
called: 'Hubbard! Hubbard! come here!' I left the ranks
and ascended the stone steps to the gate of the balcony, which
was locked, General Thomas saying: 'Wait a moment, I
will get the key.' 'Never mind, General,' said Mr. Lincoln,
'Hubbard is used to jumping—he can scale that fence.' I
climbed over, and for about an hour we conversed and watched
the large crowd, the rebel flag being in sight on Arlington
Heights. This was the last time I ever saw his face in life.''

VIEWS OF HIS OWN POSITION.—THE "ATTORNEY FOR THE PEOPLE."

It was noted by those about Mr. Lincoln during his residence at the White House, that he usually avoided speaking of
himself as President, or making any reference to the office
which he held. He used some such roundabout phrase
as "since I came into this place," instead of saying, "since I
became President." The war he usually spoke of as "this
great trouble," and he almost never alluded to the enemy as
"Confederates" or "the Confederate Government," but he

used the word "rebel" in his talk and in his letters. He also had an unconquerable reluctance to appear to lead public opinion, and often spoke of himself as the "attorney for the people." Once, however, when a Senator was urging on him a certain course, which the President was not disposed to pursue, the Senator said, "You say you are the people's attorney. Now, you will admit that this course would be most popular." "But I am not going to let my client manage the case against my judgment," Lincoln replied quickly. "As long as I am attorney for the people I shall manage the case to the best of my ability. They will have a chance to put me out, by and by, if my management is not satisfactory."

"ONLY THE LEAD-HORSE, AND MUST NOT KICK OUT OF THE TRACES."

Some characteristic utterances of Mr. Lincoln, defining his views of his position, were made to his friend Admiral Dahlgren, at the period pending the issue of the emancipation proclamation. Says Admiral Dahlgren: "The President had every disposition to do the thing, but it was evident that others overruled. As he said, he was *only the lead-horse in the team, and must not kick over the traces.*' He remarked that he knew his proclamation 'would not make a single negro free beyond our military reach.'"

HIS DESIRE THAT "THE PEOPLE" SHOULD UNDERSTAND HIM.

In all Mr. Lincoln's writings, even his most important state papers, his chief desire was to make himself clearly understood by the common reader. He had a great aversion to what he called "machine writing," and used the fewest words possible to express his meaning. He never hesitated to employ a homely expression, when it suited his purpose. In his first message the phrase "sugar-coated" occurred; and when it was printed, Mr. Defrees, the Public Printer, being on familiar terms with Mr. Lincoln, ventured an objection to the

phrase,—suggesting that Mr. Lincoln was not now preparing
a campaign document, or delivering a stump speech in Illinois, but constructing an important state paper, that would
go down historically to all coming time; and that, therefore,

he did not consider the phrase, "sugar-coated," as entirely a
becoming and dignified one. "Well, Defrees," said Mr. Lincoln, good-naturedly, "if you think the time will ever come

when the people will not understand what 'sugar-coated' means, I'll alter it; otherwise, I think I'll let it go.''

On the same subject, Mrs. Harriet Beecher Stowe says: ''Our own politicians were somewhat shocked with his state papers at first. 'Why not let *us* make them a little more conventional, and file them to a classical pattern?' 'No,' was his reply, 'I shall write them myself. *The people will understand them.*' 'But this or that form of expression is not elegant, not classical.' '*The people will understand it,*' has been his invariable reply. And whatever may be said of his state papers as compared with the classic standards, it has been a fact that they have always been wonderfully well understood by the people, and that since the time of Washington the state papers of no President have more controlled the popular mind. And one reason for this is, that they have been informal and undiplomatic. They have more resembled a father's talks to his children than a state paper. And they have had that relish and smack of the soil that appeal to the simple human heart and head, which is a greater power in writing than the most artful devices of rhetoric. Lincoln might well say with the apostle, 'But though I be rude in speech, yet not in knowledge, but we have been thoroughly *made manifest among you* in all things.' His rejection of what is called 'fine writing' was as deliberate as St. Paul's, and for the same reason—because he felt that he was speaking on a subject which must be made clear to the lowest intellect, though it should fail to captivate the highest. But we say of Lincoln's writing, that for all true manly purposes there are passages in his state papers that could not be better put; they are absolutely perfect. They are brief, condensed, intense, and with a power of insight and expression which make them worthy to be inscribed in letters of gold.''

HIS PRACTICAL KINDNESS.—GETTING OUT OF BED TO WRITE A PARDON.

Among the innumerable stories of Mr. Lincoln's kindness of heart is one narrated by Vice-president Wheeler, of a young man, a soldier in an Illinois regiment, who had been convicted by military court of sleeping at his post—a grave offense, and punishable with death, to which he had been sentenced. "He was but nineteen years of age, and the only son of a widowed mother. He had suffered greatly with homesickness, and, overpowered at night with cold and watching, sleep overmastered him. He had always been an honest, faithful, temperate soldier. His comrades telegraphed his mother of his fate. She at once went to Lincoln's old friend, Orlando Kellogg, whose kind heart promptly responded to her request, and he left for Washington by the first train. He arrived in that city at midnight. The boy was to be executed on the afternoon of the next day. Kellogg came at once to my boarding-house, knowing that he could not pass the military guard about the White House at that hour. I had the pass of Gen. Heintzelman, then commanding the defences of Washington. This was a necessity to me, as I was often called at every hour of the night to some city hospital to visit the suffering and dying. Dressing myself hastily, I went with Kellogg to the White House, easily passed the guard, and reached the door-keeper, whom I knew well, and briefly telling Kellogg's errand, asked him to take Kellogg to Mr. Lincoln's sleeping-room—which he did. Arousing Mr. Lincoln, Kellogg in a few words made known the emergency. Without stopping to dress, the President went to a near-by room and awakened a messenger. Then sitting down, still in undress, he wrote to the officer commanding at Yorktown to suspend the execution of the boy until further orders. The telegram was sent at once to the War Department, with directions to the messenger to remain until an answer was received. Getting uneasy at the seeming delay, Mr. Lincoln dressed, went to the department and remained until the receipt of his telegram was acknowledged. Then turning to Kellogg, with trembling voice he said: 'Now you just telegraph that mother that her boy is safe, and I will go home and go to bed. I guess we shall all sleep better for this night's work.' The poor boy was pardoned, restored to his company, and a short time afterward was killed while fighting bravely in battle.''

A PLACE FOR A GOOD LITTLE BOY.

Hon. A. H. Rice, of Massachusetts, tells how he and Senator Wilson were once kept waiting by the President, while a little boy of ten or twelve years, who wanted to be appointed page in the House of Representatives, was given an audience. ''The boy soon told his story,'' says Mr. Rice. ''It was, in substance, that he had come to Washington seeking employment as a page in the House of Representatives, and he wished the President to give him such an appointment. To this the President replied that such appointments were not at his disposal, and that application must be made to the Door-keeper of the House at the Capitol. 'But, sir,' said the lad, still undaunted, 'I am a good boy, and have a letter from my mother, and one from the supervisors of my town, and one from my Sunday-school teacher, and they all told me that I could earn enough in one session of Congress to keep my mother and the rest of us comfortable all the remainder of the year.' The President took the lad's papers, and ran his eye over them with that penetrating and absorbing look so familiar to all who knew him, and then took his pen and wrote upon the back of one of them: 'If Captain Goodnow can give a place to this good little boy, I shall be gratified,' and signed it 'A. Lincoln.' The boy's face became radiant with hope, and he walked out of the room with a step as light as though all the angels were whispering their congratulations. Only after the lad had gone did the President seem to realize that a Senator and another person had been for some time waiting to see him.''

A PARDON, WITH A STORY THROWN IN.

General Fisk, attending the reception at the White House, on one occasion saw, waiting in the ante-room, a poor old man from Tennessee. Sitting down beside him, he inquired his errand, and learned that he had been waiting three or four days to get an audience, and that on his seeing Mr. Lincoln probably depended the life of his son, who was under sentence of death for some military offense. General Fisk wrote his case in outline on a card, and sent it in, with a special request that the President would see the man. In a moment the order came; and past Senators, Governors, and Generals, waiting impatiently, the old man went into the President's presence. He showed Mr. Lincoln his papers, and he, on taking them, said he would look into the case and give him the result on the following day. The old man, in an agony of apprehension, looked up into the President's sympathetic face, and exclaimed: "To-morrow may be too late! My son is under sentence of death! The decision ought to be made now!" and the streaming tears told how much he was moved. "Come," said Mr. Lincoln, "wait a bit, and I'll tell you a story;" and then he told the old man General Fisk's story about the swearing mule-driver, as follows: "The General had begun his military life as a Colonel, and, when he raised his regiment in Missouri, he proposed to his men that he should do all the swearing for the regiment. They assented; and for months no instance was known of the viola-tion of the promise. The Colonel had a teamster named John Todd, who, as roads were not always the best, had some difficulty in commanding his temper and his tongue. John happened to be driving a mule-team through a series of mud-holes a little worse than usual, when, unable to restrain him-self any longer, he burst forth into a volley of energetic oaths. The Colonel took notice of the offense, and brought John to account. 'John,' said he, 'didn't you promise to let me do all the swearing of the regiment?' 'Yes, I did, Colonel,' he replied, 'but the fact was, the swearing had to be done *then*, or not at all, and *you weren't there to do it.*' As he told the story, the old man forgot his boy, and both the President and his listener had a hearty laugh together at its conclusion. Then Mr. Lincoln wrote a few words, which the old man read, and in which he found new occasion for tears; but the tears were tears of joy, for the words saved the life of his son.''

A BADLY SCARED PETITIONER.

The President was so tormented by visitors seeking interviews for every sort of frivolous and impertinent matter, that he resorted sometimes, in desperation, to curious and effective inventions to rid himself of the intolerable nuisance. At one time, when he had been quite ill, and therefore less inclined than usual to listen to these bores, one of them had just seated himself for a long interview, when the President's physician happened to enter the room, and Mr. Lincoln said, holding out his hands: "Doctor, what are these blotches?" "That's varioloid, or mild small-pox," said the doctor. "They're all over me. It is contagious, I believe," said Mr. Lincoln. "Very contagious, indeed!" replied the doctor. "Well, I can't stop, Mr. Lincoln; I just called to see how you were," said the visitor. "Oh, don't be in a hurry, sir!" placidly remarked the Executive. "Thank you, sir; I'll call again," replied the visitor, executing a masterly retreat from the White House. "Some people," said the President, looking after him, "said they could not take very well to my proclamation; but now, I am happy to say, I have *something that everybody can take.*"

TELLING A STORY TO RELIEVE BAD NEWS.

A gentleman who, after the dreadful disaster at Fredericksburg, called at the White House with news direct from the front, says that Mr. Lincoln appeared so overwhelmed with grief that he was led to remark: "I heartily wish I might be a welcome messenger of good news instead,—that I could tell you how to conquer or get rid of these rebellious States." Looking up quickly, with a marked change of expression, Lincoln said: "That reminds me of two boys in

Illinois who took a short cut across an orchard, and did not become aware of the presence of a vicious dog until it was too late to reach either fence. One was spry enough to escape the attack by climbing a tree; but the other started around the tree, with the dog in hot pursuit, until by making smaller circles than it was possible for his pursuer to make, he gained sufficiently to grasp the dog's tail, and held with desperate grip until nearly exhausted, when he hailed his companion and called to him to come down. 'What for?' said the boy. 'I want you to help me let this dog go.' If I could only let them go," said the President, in conclusion; "but that is the trouble. I am compelled to hold on to them and make them stay."

A BREAKING HEART BENEATH THE SMILES.

It is related that on the morning after the battle at Fredericksburg, Hon. I. N. Arnold, then a member of Congress from Illinois, called on the President; and to his amazement found him engaged in reading "Artemus Ward." Making no reference to that which occupied the universal thought, he asked Mr. Arnold to sit down while he read to him Artemus' description of his visit to the Shakers. Shocked at this proposition, Mr. Arnold said: "Mr. President, is it possible that with the whole land bowed in sorrow and covered with a pall in the presence of yesterday's fearful reverse, you can indulge in such levity?" Throwing down the book, with the tears streaming down his cheeks, and his huge frame quivering with emotion, Mr. Lincoln answered: "Mr. Arnold, if I could not get momentary respite from the crushing burden I am constantly carrying, my heart would break!"

Hon. J. M. Ashley called on Mr. Lincoln just after news of a fresh disaster to our armies. The President commenced some trifling story, to which the Congressman was in no mood to listen. Rising to his feet, he said: "Mr. President, I did not come here this morning to hear stories; it is too serious a time." The smile instantly faded from Lincoln's face, as he said: "Ashley, sit down! I respect you as an honest, sincere man. You cannot be more anxious than I have been constantly since the beginning of the war; and I say to you now, that were it not for this occasional *vent*, I should die."

LINCOLN'S DEEPLY RELIGIOUS NATURE.

A lady who was a member of the President's household, says that once, while a great battle was in progress, he came into the room where she was, looking very worn and haggard, and saying that he was so anxious that he could not eat. The possibility of defeat depressed him greatly; but the lady told him he must trust, and that he could at least pray. "Yes," said he, and taking up a Bible, he started for his room. Could all the people of the nation have overheard the earnest petition that went up from that inner chamber, says the lady by whom the incident is related, they would have fallen upon their knees with tearful and reverential sympathy.

Alluding to this phase of Mr. Lincoln's character, and to his trials and sufferings, Mrs. H. B. Stowe says: "Among the many accusations which in hours of ill-luck have been thrown upon Mr. Lincoln, it is remarkable that he has never been called self-seeking or selfish. When we were troubled and sat in darkness, and looked doubtfully towards the Presidential chair, it was never that we doubted the good-will of our pilot—only the clearness of his eyesight. But Almighty God has granted to him that clearness of vision which he gives to the true-hearted, and enabled him to set his honest foot in that promised land of freedom which is to be the patrimony of all men, black and white; and from henceforth nations shall rise up to call him blessed. We believe he has never made any religious profession, but we see evidence that in passing through this dreadful national crisis he has been forced by the very anguish of the struggle to look upward, where any rational creature must look for support. No man in this agony has suffered more and deeper, albeit with a dry, weary,

patient pain, that seemed to some like insensibility. 'Which-
ever way it ends,' he said to the writer, 'I have the impression
that *I* sha'n't last long after it's over.' After the dreadful
repulse of Fredericksburg, his heavy eyes and worn and weary
air told how our reverses wore upon him; and yet there
was a never-failing fund of patience at bottom that sometimes
rose to the surface in some droll, quaint saying, or story, that
forced a laugh even from himself. There have been times
with many, of impetuous impatience, when our national ship
seemed to lie water-logged, and we have called aloud for a
deliverer of another fashion,—a brilliant General, a dashing,
fearless statesman, a man who could dare and do, who would
stake all on a die, and win or lose by a brilliant *coup de
main*. It may comfort our minds that since He who ruleth in
the armies of nations set no such man to this work, that perhaps He saw in the man whom He did send some peculiar
fitness and aptitude therefor."

THE CHANGES WROUGHT BY GRIEF.

The care and sorrow which Mr. Lincoln was called upon
to endure in his high position, wrote their melancholy
marks on each feature of his face. He was a changed man.
A pathetic picture of his appearance at this time is given by
his old friend, Noah Brooks, whose description of him as he
appeared tn 1856, on the stump in Ogle county, has already
been given a place in these pages. "I did not see Lincoln again," says Mr. Brooks, "until 1862, when I went to
Washington as a newspaper correspondent from California.
When Lincoln was on the stump, in 1856, his face, though
naturally sallow, had a rosy flush. His eyes were full and
bright, and he was in the fullness of health and vigor. I
shall never forget the shock which my first sight of him gave
me in 1862. I took it for granted that he had forgotten the
young man whom he had met five or six times during the
Fremont and Dayton campaign. He was now President,
and was, like Brutus, 'vexed with many cares.' The change

which a few years had made was simply appalling. His whiskers had grown, and had given additional cadaverousness to his face, as it appeared to me. The light seemed to have gone out of his eyes, which were sunken far under his enormous brows. But there was over his whole face an expression of sadness, and a far-away look in the eyes, which were utterly unlike the Lincoln of other days. I was intensely disappointed. I confess that I was so pained that I could almost have shed tears."

CHAPTER IX.

TRIALS OF THE ADMINISTRATION IN 1863.——HOSTILITY TO WAR MEASURES.
——LACK OF CONFIDENCE AT THE NORTH.——OPPOSITION IN CONGRESS.
——HOW MR. LINCOLN FELT ABOUT THE "FIRE IN THE REAR."——CRITI-
CISMS FROM ABOLITION LEADERS.——VISIT OF "THE BOSTON SET."——
THE ENLISTMENT OF COLORED TROOPS.——INTERVIEW BETWEEN MR. LIN-
COLN AND FREDERICK DOUGLASS.——CHANGES IN MILITARY LEADERS.——
FROM BURNSIDE TO HOOKER.——MR. LINCOLN'S FIRST MEETING WITH
"FIGHTING JOE."——THE PRESIDENT'S SOLICITUDE.——HIS WARNING LET-
TER TO HOOKER.——HIS VISIT TO THE RAPPAHANNOCK.——HOOKER'S
SELF-CONFIDENCE THE "WORST THING ABOUT HIM."——THE DEFEAT AT
CHANCELLORSVILLE.——THE PRESIDENT OVERWHELMED WITH GRIEF.——
"OH, WHAT WILL THE COUNTRY SAY!"——THE FAILURE OF OUR GEN-
ERALS.——"WANTED, A MAN."

IT is impossible, without a close study of the inner history
of the war and of the acts of the administration, to conceive of
the harassing and baffling difficulties which beset the President's course in every direction, and of the jealous, narrow
and bitter opposition which his more important measures provoked. As the struggle advanced, he found in his front a
solid and defiant South, behind him a divided and distrustful
North. What might be called the party of action and of extreme measures developed a sharp hostility to the President.
He would not go fast enough to suit them; they thought him
disposed to compromise. They began by criticising his policy, and his methods of prosecuting the war; from this they
passed rapidly to a criticism of the President himself. Everybody has forgotten now how weak and poor and craven they
found him then. So far had this gone, that early in 1863 we
find Mr. Greeley searching everywhere for a fitting successor
to Mr. Lincoln for the Presidency. There were but few men
in high official station in Washington who at that time un-
qualifiedly sustained him.

OPPOSITION IN CONGRESS.

In the House of Representatives there were but two members who could make themselves heard, who stood actively by

the President. This matter, long since forgotten, should be recalled to show clearly the President's straits, and his action and bearing amidst his difficulties. It should be remembered that party lines, which disappeared at the beginning of the war, were again clearly drawn; and the Democratic wing of Congress, under the leadership of Vallandigham of Ohio, opposed actively many of the necessary measures for the prosecution of the war. The cry had already been raised in Congress, "The South cannot be subjugated;" and every fresh disaster to the national arms was hailed as proof of the assertion.

As an illustration of the state of things in Congress, and as the testimony of an eye-witness, given at the time, we quote a few striking passages from a speech delivered in the House of Representatives, February 28, 1863, on a bill to indemnify the President for certain measures requiring the sanction of Congress. The speaker (Hon. A. G. Riddle, of Ohio) said:

"Whoever has listened to the speeches of gentlemen in opposition to this bill might suppose that the President was the most unscrupulous usurper that ever oppressed a people, and that the majority on this floor were in conspiracy to betray into his hands the last shadow of human rights. * * * The outspoken comments here and elsewhere have at least the merit of boldness; but what shall be said of that muttering, unmanly, yet swelling under-current of complaining criticism, that reflects upon the President, his motives and capacity, so freely and feebly indulged in by men having the public confidence?—whisperings and complainings, and doubtings, and misgivings, and exclamations, and predictions, by men who are never so happy as when they can gloat over the sum of our disasters, which they charge over to the personal account of the President. * * * He is an unimpassioned, cool, shrewd, sagacious, far-seeing man, with a capacity to form his own judgments, and a will to execute them; and he possesses an integrity pure and simple as the white rays of light that play about the Throne. Like all extraordinary men, he is an original, and must stand in his own niche. He has assiduously studied the teachings of this war; has learned its great lesson; and in full time he uttered its great word. He commits errors. Who would have committed fewer? Think of the fierce and hungry demands that incessantly devour him! Remember the repeated instances in our own times when the ablest of our statesmen in that chair, with Cabinets of their choice, and sustained by majorities in Congress, in times of profound peace, have gone down, and their administrations have perished under the bare weight of the government. And then contemplate, if you can, in addition to the burdens that have crushed so many strong men, the fearful responsibilities imposed upon this man. Is it not a marvel, a most living wonder, that he sustains them so well?''

THE ''FIRE IN THE REAR.''—HOW MR. LINCOLN REGARDED IT.

The effect of all this abuse and opposition was exceedingly painful to Mr. Lincoln. He said: ''I have been caused more anxiety, I have *passed more sleepless nights*, on account of the temper and attitude of the Democratic party in the North in regard to the suppression of the rebellion, than by the rebels in the South. I have always had faith that our armies would ultimately and completely triumph; but these enemies in the North cause me a great deal of anxiety and apprehension. Can it be that there can be opposing opinions in the North as to the necessity of putting down this rebellion? How can men hesitate a moment as to the duty of the Government to restore its authority in every part of the country? It is incomprehensible to me that men living in their quiet homes under the protection of laws, in possession of their property, can sympathize with, and give aid and comfort to, those who are doing their utmost to overthrow that Government which makes life and everything they possess valuable.''

CRITICISMS FROM ABOLITION LEADERS.—VISIT OF ''THE BOSTON SET.''

In January, 1863, a party of distinguished gentlemen from Boston visited the capital, in order to confer with the President on the workings of the emancipation policy. They made the visit chiefly at the suggestion of Mr. R. W. Emerson, who, during all the trying years of the war, never lost faith in Mr. Lincoln's honesty and justice. Secretary Stanton made no secret of his opposition to these gentlemen, who were spoken of rather slightingly as "that Boston set." The "Boston set" were uncompromising abolitionists, and nothing would satisfy their desire but immediate and aggressive measures for enforcing the policy of emancipation. As it was the President's instinct to feel his way slowly, in pushing on the great measures rendered necessary in the management of the nation in its perilous crisis, they were naturally dissatisfied with his conservative methods and tendencies. The visitors —including Senator Wilson, Wendell Phillips, Francis W. Bird, Elizur Wright, J. H. Stephenson, George L. Stearns, Oakes Ames, and Moncure D. Conway,—called on the President one Sunday evening, at the White House. "The President met us," says Mr. Conway, "laughing like a boy, saying that in the morning one of his children had come to inform him that the cat had kittens, and now another had just announced that the dog had puppies, and the White House was in a decidedly sensational state. Some of our party looked a little glum at this hilarity; but it was pathetic to see the change in the President's face when he presently resumed his burden of care. We were introduced by Senator Wilson, who began to speak of us severally, when Mr. Lincoln said he knew perfectly who we were, and requested us to be seated. Nothing could be more gracious than his manner, or more simple. The conversation was introduced by Wendell Phillips, who, with all his courtesy, expressed our gratitude and joy at the Proclamation of Emancipation, and asked how it seemed to be working. The President said that he had not expected much from it at first, and consequently had not been disappointed; he had hoped, and still hoped, that something would come of it after awhile. Phillips then alluded to the deadly hostility which the proclamation had naturally excited in pro-slavery quarters, and gently hinted that the Northern people, now generally anti-slavery, were not satisfied that it was being honestly carried out by all of the nation's agents and Generals in the South. 'My own impression, Mr. Phillips,' said the President, 'is that the masses of the country generally are only dissatisfied at our lack of military successes. Defeat and failure in the field make everything seem wrong.' His face was now clouded, and his next words were somewhat bitter: 'Most of us here present have been nearly all our lives working in minorities, and many have got into a habit of being dissatisfied.' Several of those present having deprecated this, the President said: 'At any rate, it has been very rare that an opportunity of "running" this administration has been lost.' To this Mr. Phillips answered, in his sweetest voice: 'If we see this administration earnestly working to free the country from slavery and its rebellion, we will show you how we can "run" it into another four years of power.' The President's good humor was restored by this, and he said: 'Oh, Mr. Phillips, I have ceased to have any personal feeling or expectation in that matter—I do not say I never had any—so abused and borne upon as I have been.' * * * On taking our leave, we expressed to the President our thanks for his kindly reception, and for his attention to statements of which some were naturally not welcome. The President bowed graciously at this, and, after saying he was happy to have met gentlemen known to him by distinguished services, if not personally, and glad to listen to their views, added: 'I must bear this load which the country has intrusted to me as well as I can, and do my best.' "

THE ENLISTMENT OF COLORED TROOPS.—INTERVIEW WITH
FREDERICK DOUGLASS.

In 1863, the Government, following logically the policy of the Emancipation act, began the experiment of introducing colored soldiers into our armies. This caused not only intense anger at the South, but much doubt and dissatisfaction at the North. To discuss some of the practical and difficult questions growing out of this measure, Frederick Douglass, the most distinguished representative of the race which America had so long held in chains, was first presented to Mr. Lincoln. The account of the conference, given by Mr. Douglass, is singularly interesting. He says: "I was never more quickly or more completely put at ease in the presence of a

[From a pen and ink sketch furnished by Mr. Douglass expressly for this work.]

great man than in that of Abraham Lincoln. He was seated, when I entered, in a low arm-chair, with his feet extended on the floor, surrounded by a large number of documents and several busy secretaries. The room bore the marks of business, and the persons in it, the President included, appeared to be much overworked and tired. Long lines of care were already deeply written on Mr. Lincoln's brow, and his strong face, full of earnestness, lighted up as soon as my name was mentioned. As I approached and was introduced to him, he arose and extended his hand, and bade me welcome. I at once felt myself in the presence of an honest man—one whom I could love, honor, and trust without reserve or doubt. Proceeding to tell him who I was and what I was doing, he promptly, but kindly, stopped me, saying: 'I know who you are, Mr. Douglass; Mr. Seward has told me all about you. Sit down; I am glad to see you.' I urged, among other things, the necessity of granting the colored soldiers equal pay and promotion with white soldiers, and retaliation for colored prisoners killed by the enemy. Mr. Lincoln admitted the justice of my demand for equal pay and promotion of colored soldiers, but on the matter of retaliation he differed from me entirely. I shall never forget the benignant expression of his face, the tearful look of his eye, and the quiver in his voice, when he deprecated a resort to retaliatory measures. 'Once begun,' said he, 'I do not know where such a measure would stop.' He said he could not take men out and kill them in cold blood for what was done by others. If he could get hold of the persons who were guilty of killing the colored prisoners in cold blood, the case would be different; but he could not kill the innocent for the guilty. Afterwards we discussed the means most desirable to be employed outside the army to induce the slaves in the rebel States to come within the Federal lines. The increasing opposition to the war, in the North, and the mad cry against it because it was being made an abolition war, alarmed Mr. Lincoln, and made him apprehensive that a peace might be forced upon him which would leave still in slavery all who had not come within our lines. What he wanted was to make his proclamation as effective as possible in the event of such a peace. He said, in a regretful tone, 'The slaves are not coming so rapidly and so numerously to us as I had hoped.' I replied that the slaveholders knew how to keep such things from their slaves, and probably very few knew of his proclamation. 'Well,' he said, 'I want you to set about devising some means of making them acquainted with it, and for bringing them into our lines.' What he said on this day showed a deeper moral conviction against slavery than I had ever seen before in anything spoken or written by him. I listened with the deepest interest and profoundest satisfaction, and, at his suggestion, agreed to undertake the organizing of a band of scouts, composed of colored men, whose business should be, somewhat after the original plan of John Brown, to go into the rebel States, beyond the lines of our armies, and carry the news of emancipation, and urge the slaves to come within our boundaries.

"An incident occurred during this interview which illustrates the character of this great man, though the mention of it may savor a little of vanity on my part. While in conversation with him his Secretary twice announced 'Governor Buckingham of Connecticut,' one of the noblest and most patriotic of the loyal Governors. Mr. Lincoln said, 'Tell Governor Buckingham, to wait, for I want to have a long talk with my friend Frederick Douglass.' This was probably the first time in the history of the Republic when its chief magistrate found occasion or disposition to exercise such an act of impartiality between persons so widely different in their positions and supposed claims upon his attention. From the manner of the Governor, when he was finally admitted, I inferred that he was as well satisfied with what Mr. Lincoln had done, or had omitted to do, as I was."

Mr. Douglass once remarked that Mr. Lincoln was one of the few white men he ever passed an hour with, who failed to remind him in some way, before the interview terminated, that he was a negro. "He always impressed me as a strong, earnest man, having no time or disposition to trifle; grappling with all his might the work he had in hand. The expression of his face was a blending of suffering with patience and fortitude. Men called him homely, and homely he was ; but it was manifestly a human homeliness. His eyes had in them the tenderness of motherhood, and his mouth and other features the highest perfection of a genuine manhood.''

CHANGES IN MILITARY LEADERS.—FROM BURNSIDE TO HOOKER.

The political difficulties that beset President Lincoln in the first half of 1863 were attended by disheartening reverses to our arms. It will be remembered that on the removal of General McClellan from command of the Army of the Potomac, in November, 1862, General Burnside succeeded him. The change cannot be regarded as a fortunate one. General Burnside was an earnest and gallant soldier, but was not equal to the vast responsibilities of his new position. It is said, to his credit, that he was three times offered the command of the Army of the Potomac, and three times he declined. Finally, it was pressed upon him by positive orders, and he could no longer, without insubordination, refuse it. In addressing General Halleck, after his appointment, he said : ''Had I been asked to take it, I should have declined ; but being ordered, I cheerfully obey.'' After his fearful defeat at Fredericksburg (December 13, 1862,) he said : *''The fault was mine.* The entire responsibility of failure must rest on my shoulders.'' By his manly and courageous bearing, and the strong sincerity of his character, he retained the respect and sympathy of the President and of the country. He immediately retired from command of the Army of the Potomac, which, under his brief leadership, had fought the most bloody and disastrous battle in its history.

MR. LINCOLN'S FIRST MEETING WITH ''FIGHTING JOE.''

General Joseph Hooker, the fourth commander of the noble but unfortunate Army of the Potomac, was appointed to that position by President Lincoln, in January, 1863. The two men had met briefly early in the war, when Hooker, then living in California, hastened to Washington to offer his services to the Government; but for some reason General Scott disliked him, and his offer was not accepted. After some

months, Hooker, giving up the idea of getting a command, decided to return to California; but before leaving he called to pay his respects to Mr. Lincoln. He was introduced as "Captain Hooker." The President, being pressed for time, was about to dismiss him with a few civil phrases; when, to his surprise, Hooker began the following speech: "Mr.

President, my friend makes a mistake. I am not 'Captain Hooker,' but was once 'Lieutenant-Colonel Hooker' of the regular army. I was lately a farmer in California, but since the rebellion broke out I have been trying to get into the service, but I find I am not wanted. I am about to return home; but before going, I was anxious to pay my respects to you, and to express my wishes for your personal welfare and success in quelling this rebellion. And I want to say one word more. I was at Bull Run the other day, Mr. President, and it is no vanity in me to say *I am a d—d sight better general than you had on that field.*" This was said, not in the tone of a braggart, but of a man who knew what he was talking about; and, as the President afterward said, he appeared at that moment as if perfectly able to make good his words. Mr. Lincoln seized his hand, making him sit down, and began a social chat. The result was, that Hooker did not return to California, but in a few weeks *Captain* Hooker was *Brigadier-General* Hooker. He served with distinction under McClellan in the Peninsular campaign and at Antietam, and commanded the right wing of the army at Fredericksburg. He had come to be known as "Fighting Joe Hooker," and was generally regarded as one of the most vigorous and efficient Generals of the Union army. Such was the man who, in one of the darkest hours of the Union cause, was selected to lead once more the Army of the Potomac against the enemy.

THE PRESIDENT'S SOLICITUDE.—HIS WARNING LETTER TO HOOKER.

This army, since its defeat at Fredericksburg, had remained disorganized and ineffective. Its new commander was, unlike his predecessor, Burnside, full of ambition and confidence. The President, made cautious by experience, deemed it his duty to accompany the appointment by some timely words of warning; and accordingly he addressed General Hooker the following frank, manly, and judicious letter:

"EXECUTIVE MANSION, WASHINGTON, D. C., January 26, 1863.

"*Major-General Hooker.*—GENERAL:—I have placed you at the head of the Army of the Potomac. Of course I have done this upon what appear to me to be sufficient reasons; and yet I think it best for you to know that there are some things in regard to which I am not satisfied with you. I believe you to be a brave and skillful soldier, which of course I like. I also believe that you do not mix politics with your profession, in which you are right. You have confidence in yourself, which is a valuable if not indispensable quality. You are ambitious, which, within reasonable bounds, does good rather than harm; but I think that, during General Burnside's command of the army, you have taken counsel with your ambition, and thwarted him as much as you could, in which you did a great wrong to the country, and to a most meritorious and honorable brother officer. I have heard, in such a way as to believe it, of your recently saying that both the army and the Government needed a dictator. Of course, it was not for this, but in spite of it, that I have given you the command. Only those generals who gain success can be dictators. What I now ask from you is military success, and I will risk the dictatorship. The Government will support you to the utmost of its ability, which is neither more nor less than it has done and will do for all commanders. I much fear that the spirit which you have aided to infuse into the army, of criticising their commander and withholding confidence from him, will now turn upon you. I shall assist you, as far as I can, to pull it down. Neither you nor Napoleon, if he were alive again, could get any good out of an army while such a spirit prevails in it. And now, beware of rashness. *Beware of rashness;* but with energy and sleepless vigilance, go forward and give us victories.   Yours, very truly,   A. LINCOLN."

In all Mr. Lincoln's writings, there is scarcely anything finer than this letter. In its candor and friendliness, its simplicity and deep wisdom, it is almost perfect in expression; and the President's own deep solicitude for the safety of the army and anxiety for its success, give a pathetic touch to the closing sentences. But all that came of Hooker's confidence and Lincoln's hopes were three months of elaborate preparation, a grand forward movement into Virginia, and then the bloody repulse at Chancellorsville.

MR. LINCOLN'S VISIT TO THE RAPPAHANNOCK.

The solicitude of the President found some relief in a personal inspection of the Army of the Potomac, which was

made in April, and occupied five or six days. He was accompanied by Attorney-General Bates, Mrs. Lincoln, his son
Tad, and by Mr. Noah P. Brooks. The first night out was
spent on the little steamer which conveyed the party to their des-
tination. After all had retired to rest, except the anxious President and one or two others, Mr. Lincoln gave utterance to
his deep-seated apprehensions in the whispered query to his
friend: "How many of our monitors will you wager are at
the bottom of Charleston Harbor?" "I essayed," writes Mr.
Brooks, "to give a cheerful view of the Charleston situation.
But he would not be encouraged. He then went on to say
that he did not believe that an attack by water on Charleston
could ever possibly succeed. He talked a long time about his
'notions,' as he called them; and at General Halleck's headquarters next day, the first inquiries were for 'rebel papers,'
which were usually brought in from the picket lines. These
he examined with great anxiety, hoping that he might find an
item of news from Charleston. And, one day, having looked
all over a Richmond paper several times, without finding a
paragraph, which he had been told was in it, he was mightily
pleased to have it pointed out to him, and said, 'It is plain
that newspapers are made for newspaper men; being only a
layman, it was impossible for me to find that.'"

The out-door life, the constant riding, and the respite from
the monstrous burdens at the capital, appeared to afford mental and physical benefit to the worn President. But in answer
to a remark expressing this conviction, he replied sadly, "I
don't know about 'the rest' as you call it. I suppose it is
good for the body. But the tired part of me is *inside* and out
of reach." "He rode a great deal," says Mr. Brooks, "while
with the army, always preferring the saddle to the elegant ambulance which had been provided for him. He sat his horse
well, but he rode hard, and during his stay I think he regularly used up at least one horse each day. Little Tad invariably followed in his father's train; and mounted on a smaller

horse, accompanied by an orderly, the youngster was a conspicuous figure, as his gray cloak flew in the wind while we hung on the flanks of Hooker and his Generals."

GEN. HOOKER'S SELF-CONFIDENCE.—"THE WORST THING ABOUT HIM."

General Hooker was now planning his great movement on Richmond, and talked freely of the matter with the President. In the course of a conversation, Mr. Lincoln casually remarked: "If you get to Richmond, General." But Hooker interrupted him with—"Excuse me, Mr. President, but there is no 'if' in the case. *I am going straight to Richmond, if I live!*" Later in the day, Lincoln, privately referring to this self-confidence of the General, said to Mr. Brooks, rather mournfully, "It is about the worst thing I have seen since I have been down here."

In further illustration of General Hooker's confidence in himself, Mr. Brooks says: "One night, Hooker and I being alone in his hut, the General standing with his back to the fire-place, alert, handsome, full of courage and confidence, said, laughingly, 'The President says you know about that letter he wrote me on taking command.' I acknowledged that the President had read it to me. The General seemed to think that the advice was well-meant, but unnecessary. Then he added, with that charming assurance which became him so well, 'After I have been to Richmond, I am going to have that letter printed.'"

CHANCELLORSVILLE.—THE PRESIDENT OVERWHELMED WITH GRIEF.—"OH, WHAT WILL THE COUNTRY SAY?"

The first of May, 1863, the Army of the Potomac, under Hooker, met the Army of Northern Virginia, under Lee and Jackson, near Chancellorsville, Virginia. It was here that Jackson performed his most brilliant and successful flank movement around the Union right, ensuring a victory for his side, but losing his own life. After a contest of several days involving the fruitless sacrifice of thousands of gallant soldiers, Hooker's army fell back and recrossed the Rappahannock.

The news of this fresh disaster was an almost stunning shock to President Lincoln. While the battle was in progress, Mr. Noah Brooks relates that, in company with an old friend of Mr. Lincoln's, he was waiting in one of the family

"READ IT—NEWS FROM THE ARMY."

rooms of the White House. "A door opened and Lincoln appeared, holding an open telegram in his hand. The sight of his face and figure was frightful. He seemed stricken with death. Almost tottering to a chair, he sat down, and then I mechanically noticed that his face was of the same color as the wall behind him—not pale, not even sallow, but gray, like ashes. Extending the dispatch to me, he said, with a sort of far-off voice, 'Read it—news from the army.' The telegram was from General Butterfield, I think, then chief of staff to Hooker. It was very brief, simply saying that the Army of the Potomac had 'safely recrossed the Rappahannock' and was now at its old position on the north bank of that stream. The President's friend, Dr. Henry, an old man and somewhat impressionable, burst into tears,—not so much, probably, at the news, as on account of its effect upon Lincoln. The President regarded the old man for an instant with dry eyes, and said: 'What will the country say? Oh, what will the country say?' He seemed hungry for consolation and cheer, and sat a little while talking about the failure. Yet, it did not seem that he was disappointed. He only thought that the country would be.''

THE FAILURE OF OUR GENERALS.—"WANTED, A MAN."

Mr. Lincoln's solicitude regarding the effect at the North of these repeated reverses was not without sufficient cause. Aside from those who were positively opposed to the war, the loyal people were wearying of the useless slaughter, the unavailing struggles, of the gallant soldiers. The feeling of that time is so well expressed in a stirring poem entitled "Wanted, A Man," written by Mr. E. C. Stedman, that we give it here. It has an additional personal interest connected with President Lincoln, in the fact that he was so impressed with the piece that he read it aloud to his assembled Cabinet:

> "Back from the trebly crimsoned field
> Terrible words are thunder-tost;
> Full of the wrath that will not yield,
> Full of revenge for battles lost!
> Hark to their echo, as it crost
> The Capital, making faces wan:
> End this murderous holocaust;
> Abraham Lincoln, give us a MAN!

"Give us a man of God's own mould,
  Born to marshal his fellow-men;
One whose fame is not bought and sold
  At the stroke of a politician's pen;
  Give us the man of thousands ten,
Fit to do as well as to plan;
  Give us a rallying-cry, and then,
Abraham Lincoln, give us a MAN!

"No leader to shirk the boasting foe,
  And to march and countermarch our brave
Till they fall like ghosts in the marshes low,
  And swamp-grass covers each nameless grave;
  Nor another, whose fatal banners wave
Aye in Disaster's shameful van;
  Nor another, to bluster, and lie, and rave,—
Abraham Lincoln, give us a MAN!

"Hearts are mourning in the North,
  While the sister rivers seek the main,
Red with our life-blood flowing forth—
  Who shall gather it up again?
  Though we march to the battle-plain
Firmly as when the strife began,
  Shall all our offerings be in vain?—
Abraham Lincoln, give us a MAN!

"Is there never one in all the land,
  One on whose might the Cause may lean?
Are all the common ones so grand,
  And all the titled ones so mean?
  What if your failure may have been
In trying to make good bread from bran,
  From worthless metal a weapon keen?—
Abraham Lincoln, find us a MAN!

"O, we will follow him to the death,
  Where the foeman's fiercest columns are!
O, we will use our latest breath,
  Cheering for every sacred star!
  His to marshal us high and far;
Ours to battle, as patriots can
  When a Hero leads the Holy War!—
Abraham Lincoln, give us a MAN!"

CHAPTER X.

MIDSUMMER of 1863 brought a turn in the tide of military affairs. It came none too soon for the safety of the nation. The repeated reverses to the Union arms, ending with the shocking disasters at Fredericksburg and Chancellorsville, (although slightly relieved by the bloody success of Stone River,) had seemed to throw the chances of war in favor of the South; and the Union cause was at the crisis of its fate. But now fortune smiled upon the North, and its lost hope and lost ground were regained at Gettysburg and Vicksburg. These great battles are justly regarded as marking the turning-point of the war. It was yet far from finished; there remained nearly two years of desperate fighting, with heroic struggles and terrible sacrifice of life, before the end should come. But from this time the character of the struggle seemed to change. The armies of the South fought, not less desperately, but more on the defensive; and their final overthrow was thenceforth, in all human probability, chiefly a question of time.

LEE'S INVASION OF PENNSYLVANIA.—A THREATENING CRISIS.

Emboldened by his success at Chancellorsville in May, Gen. Lee again assumed the offensive, and recrossed the Potomac river into Maryland. Late in June he invaded Pennsylvania, and occupied a position threatening Philadelphia, Baltimore, and Washington. The situation was most critical. If Lee could once more beat the Army of the Potomac, as he had done so many times, these three great cities, and even New York, would be at his mercy.

CHANGE OF UNION COMMANDERS.—MEADE SUCCEEDS HOOKER.
THE BATTLE OF GETTYSBURG.

Following Lee, the Army of the Potomac, under General Hooker, also recrossed the Potomac, and pursued the enemy, keeping carefully between him and Washington. The occasion was one calling for the best resources of a great military commander; and General Hooker, realizing his unfitness for the responsibility, asked to be relieved of the command. Thus was thrown upon the President the hazardous necessity of changing commanders upon the eve of a great battle. It was a terrible emergency. Even the stout-hearted Stanton was appalled. He afterward stated that when he received the dispatch from Hooker, his heart sank within him, and he was more depressed than at any other moment of the war. "I could not say," said Mr. Stanton, "that any other officer knew General Hooker's plans, or the position, even, of the various divisions of the army. I sent for the President to come to the War Office at once. It was in the evening, but the President soon appeared. I handed him the dispatch. As he read it his face became like lead, and I said, 'What shall be done?' He replied instantly, '*Accept his resignation.*'"

Immediately an order was sent to General George G. Meade, one of the most efficient of the corps commanders of the Army of the Potomac, appointing him to the chief command. He was a quiet, unassuming man, very unlike Gen. Hooker. Three days after assuming command, he led his army against the Southern host, at Gettysburg, where, after a most bloody and memorable battle of three days' duration, was won the first decisive victory in the history of the gallant Army of the Potomac. Lee retired, with disastrous losses, across the Potomac to Virginia; and Washington and the North breathed free again.

MR. LINCOLN'S SOLICITUDE DURING THE FIGHT.

Senator Zach. Chandler, speaking of Mr. Lincoln's terrible anxiety during the progress of the battle of Gettysburg,

said: "I shall never forget the painful anxiety of those few days when the fate of the nation seemed to hang in the balance; nor the restless solicitude of Mr. Lincoln, as he paced up and down the room, reading dispatches, soliloquizing, and often stopping to trace the map which hung on the wall; nor the relief we all felt when the fact was established that victory, though gained at such fearful cost, was indeed on the side of the Union."

AFFAIRS IN THE SOUTHWEST.—THE CAPTURE OF VICKSBURG.

While the eyes of the nation were fastened upon the great drama being enacted near the Capital, events scarcely less important were occurring in the Southwest. The campaign against Vicksburg, the great stronghold on the Mississippi river, had been in active progress, under the personal command of General Grant, for several months. The importance of this strategic point was fully understood by the enemy, and it was defended most stubbornly. At first, Grant's plans proved unsuccessful; the cutting of canals and opening of bayous failed—as President Lincoln had expected and predicted. But these failures only served to develop the unsuspected energy of Grant's character, and the extent of his military resources. He boldly changed his entire plan of operations, abandoned his line of communication, removed his army to a point *below* Vicksburg, and attacked the city in the rear. With dogged persistence he pressed forward, gaining point by point, beating off General Johnston's forces on one side, and driving Pemberton before him into Vicksburg; till finally, by the aid of Admiral Porter's gun-boats on the Mississippi, he had entirely invested the city. Gradually and persistently his lines closed in, pushed forward by assault and siege; until Vicksburg accepted its doom, and on the 4th of July, 1863, the city and garrison surrendered to the victorious Grant.

LINCOLN'S CONGRATULATIONS TO GRANT.

The capture of Vicksburg caused great rejoicing at the North, and gave added zest to the celebration of the national patriotic holiday. President Lincoln, mindful of the "almost inestimable services," as he termed them, of General Grant, and as it was his wont to do in all circumstances, made haste to acknowledge his personal indebtedness to the man who had accomplished a great deed. He addressed to the conqueror of Vicksburg the following letter:

"EXECUTIVE MANSION, WASHINGTON, D. C., July 13, 1863.

"*Major-General Grant:*—MY DEAR GENERAL:—I do not remember that you and I ever met personally. I write this now as a grateful acknowledgement for the almost inestimable service you have done the country. I write to say a word further. When you first reached the vicinity of Vicksburg, I thought you should do what you finally did— march the troops across the neck, run the batteries with the transports, and thus go below; and I never had any faith, except a general hope that you knew better than I, that the Yazoo Pass expedition, and the like, could succeed. When you got below, and took Port Gibson, Grand Gulf, and vicinity, I thought you should go down the river, and join General Banks, and when you turned northward, east of the Big Black, I feared it was a mistake. I now wish to make the personal acknowledgement that you were right and I was wrong. Yours truly,

A. LINCOLN."

THINKS HE WAS RIGHT IN STANDING BY HIM.

An officer who was the first from Grant's army to reach Washington after the surrender of Vicksburg, has recorded the circumstances of his interview with the President: "Mr. Lincoln received me very cordially, and, drawing a chair near to himself and motioning me to be seated, said: 'Now, I want to hear all about Vicksburg.' I gave him all the information I could, though he appeared to be remarkably well posted himself. He put to me a great many questions in detail touching the siege, the losses, the morale of the army, its sanitary condition, the hospital service, and General Grant. Said he: 'I guess I was right in standing by Grant, although there was great pressure made after Pittsburg Landing to have him removed. I thought I saw enough in Grant to convince me that he was one on whom the country could depend. That 'unconditional surrender' message to Buckner at Donelson suited me. It indicated the spirit of the man.'"

BLUFF BEN. WADE'S OPINION.

Before the capture of Vicksburg, the protracted campaign had occasioned wide dissatisfaction with General Grant, and the President had been importuned to remove him. Only a few days before the capitulation of the beleaguered city, Senator Wade, of Ohio—"Bluff Ben Wade," as he was termed —called upon the President and urged Grant's dismissal; to which Mr. Lincoln good-naturedly replied: "Senator, that reminds me of a story." "Yes, yes," rejoined Wade petulantly, "that is the way it is with you, sir, all *story—story!* You are the father of every military blunder that has been made during the war. You are on your road to h—l, sir, with this Government, and you are not a mile off this minute." Mr. Lincoln calmly retorted: "Senator, that is just about the distance from here to the Capitol, is it not?" The exasperated Wade grabbed his hat, and rushed angrily from the White House.

RETURNING CHEERFULNESS.—CONGRATULATIONS TO THE COUNTRY.

The improved condition of public affairs, and the increasing cheerfulness of the President, after the victories at Gettysburg and Vicksburg, are exhibited in a letter written by him, in August, 1863, to friends at Springfield, Illinois, who had urgently invited him to attend "a mass-meeting of Unconditional Union men" at his old home. In this letter he took occasion to declare his sentiments on various questions paramount at the time. Among these was the subject of a compromise with the South, against which he argued with great force and feeling. Again, he defended the Emancipation Proclamation, a measure with which many Union men were still unreconciled. He referred also to the arming of the negroes as a just and wise expedient; finally concluding with these expressive and felicitous words:

"The signs look better. The Father of Waters again goes unvexed to the sea. Thanks to the great Northwest for it; nor yet wholly to them.

Three hundred miles up they met New England, Empire, Keystone, and Jersey, hewing their way right and left. The sunny South, too, in more colors than one, also lent a helping hand. On the spot, their part of the history was jotted down in black and white. The job was a great national one, and let none be slighted who bore an honorable part in it. And while those who have cleared the great river may well be proud, even that is not all. It is hard to say that anything has been more bravely and well done than at Antietam, Murfreesboro, Gettysburg, and on many fields of less note. Nor must Uncle Sam's web-feet be forgotten. At all the watery margins they have been present, not only on the deep sea, the broad bay, and the rapid river, but also up the narrow, muddy bayou, and wherever the ground was a little damp they have been and made their tracks. Thanks to all. For the great Republic—for the principle it lives by and keeps alive—for man's vast future—thanks to all. Peace does not appear so distant as it did. I hope it will come soon and come to stay; and so come as to be worth the keeping in all future time. It will then have been proved that among freemen there can be no successful appeal from the ballot to the bullet, and that they who take such appeal are sure to lose their case and pay the cost. And there will be some black men who can remember that, with silent tongue, and clinched teeth, and steady eye, and well-poised bayonet, they have helped mankind on to this great consummation; while I fear there will be some white ones unable to forget that with malignant heart and deceitful speech they have striven to hinder it. Still, let us not be over-sanguine of a speedy, final triumph. Let us be quite sober. Let us diligently apply the means, never doubting that a just God, in His own good time, will give us the rightful result."

In a public proclamation, issued October 3, the President more formally expresses his satisfaction and his loyal gratitude:

"The year that is drawing toward its close has been filled with the blessings of fruitful fields and healthful skies. To these bounties, which are so constantly enjoyed that we are prone to forget the source from which they come, others have been added which are of so extraordinary a nature that they cannot fail to penetrate and soften even the heart which is habitually insensible to the ever-watchful providence of Almighty God. In the midst of a civil war of unequalled magnitude and severity, which has sometimes seemed to invite and provoke the aggressions of foreign states, peace has been preserved with all nations, order has been maintained, the laws have been respected and obeyed, and harmony has prevailed everywhere except in the theater of military conflict, while that theater has been greatly contracted by the advancing armies and navies of the Union. The needful diversion of wealth and strength from the fields of peaceful industry to the national defense have not arrested the plow, the shuttle, or the ship. The axe has enlarged the borders of our settlements, and the mines, as well of iron and coal as of the precious metals, have yielded even more abundantly than heretofore. Population has steadily increased, notwithstanding the waste that has been made in the camp, the siege, and the battle-field; and the country, rejoicing in the consciousness of augmented strength and vigor, is permitted to expect a continuance of years with large increase of freedom. No human counsel hath devised, nor hath any mortal hand worked out these great things. They are the gracious gifts of the Most High God, who, while dealing with us in anger for our sins, hath nevertheless remembered mercy. It has seemed to me fit and proper that they should be solemnly, reverently, and gratefully acknowledged, as with one heart and voice, by the whole American people. I do, therefore, invite my fellow-citizens in every part of the United States, and also those who are at sea, and those who are sojourning in foreign lands, to set apart and observe the last Thursday of November next as a day of thanksgiving and prayer to our beneficent Father, who dwelleth in the heavens. And I recommend to them that, while offering up the ascriptions justly due to Him for such singular deliverances and blessings, they do also, with humble penitence for our national perverseness and disobedience, commend to His tender care all those who have become widows, orphans, mourners or sufferers in the lamentable civil strife in which we are unavoidably engaged, and fervently implore the interposition of the Almighty Hand to heal the wounds of the nation, and to restore it, as soon as may be consistent with the divine purposes, to the full enjoyment of peace, harmony, tranquility, and union.''

IMPROVED STATE OF FEELING AT THE NORTH.—THE FALL
ELECTIONS OF 1863.—THE ADMINISTRATION SUSTAINED.

The brightening prospects of the Union cause quickly produced a better state of feeling at the North. In the Fall elections of 1863, every State except New Jersey gave solid majorities on the Republican side; thus strengthening the administration, and giving the President welcome assurances of popular approval. He had awaited with special anxiety the returns from the State of Ohio, where the contest was fraught with peculiar significance. The Democrats had chosen for their candidate the notorious peace-at-any-price Vallandigham, against whom the Republicans had placed John Brough, of Cleveland. On the night of the election, about 10 o'clock, a message clicked on the wires in the telegraph office of the latter city, saying: "Where is John Brough? A. Lincoln." Brough was at hand, and directly the electric voice inquired: "Brough, about what is your majority now?" Brough replied: "Over 30,000." Mr. Lincoln requested Brough to remain at the office during the night. A little past midnight the question came again from Mr. Lincoln: "Brough, what is your majority by this time?" Brough replied: "Over 50,000." And the question was thus repeated and answered several times, with rapidly increasing majorities, till 5 o'clock in the morning, when the question came again: "Brough, what is your majority now?" The latter was able to respond: "Over 100,000." As soon as the words could be flashed back over the wire, they came: *"Glory to God in the highest. Ohio has saved the Nation. A. Lincoln."*

DEDICATION OF THE NATIONAL CEMETERY AT GETTYSBURG.
MR. LINCOLN'S BEAUTIFUL ADDRESS.

After the battle of Gettysburg, a portion of the ground on which the engagement was fought was purchased by the State of Pennsylvania for a burial-place for the Union soldiers who were slain in that bloody encounter. The tract included seventeen and a half acres adjoining the town cemetery. It was planned to consecrate the ground with imposing ceremonies, in which the President, accompanied by his Cabinet and a large body of the military, were invited to assist. The day appointed was the 19th of November; and the chief orator selected was Massachusetts' eloquent son, the Hon. Edward Everett. After him it was expected that the President would add some testimonials in honor of the dead.

Mr. Lincoln and Mr. Everett were representatives of two contrasting phases of American civilization: the one an outgrowth of the rough pioneer life of the West; the other the product of the highest culture of the East. They had met for the first time on this memorable day. Mr. Everett's oration was a finished literary production. Smooth, euphonious and elegant, it was delivered with the silvery tones and the graceful gestures of a trained and consummate speaker. When he had finished, and the applause that greeted him had died away, the multitude called vociferously for an address from Mr. Lincoln. With an unconscious air, the President came forward at the call, put his spectacles on his nose, and read, in a quiet voice, which gradually warmed with feeling, while his careworn face became radiant with the light of genuine emotion, the following brief address :

"Fourscore and seven years ago our fathers brought forth upon this continent a new nation, conceived in liberty, and dedicated to the proposition that all men are created equal. Now we are engaged in a great civil war, testing whether that nation, or any nation so conceived and so dedicated, can long endure. We are met on a great battle-field of that war. We are met to dedicate a portion of it as the final resting-place of those who here gave their lives that that nation might live. It is altogether fitting and proper that we should do this. But, in a larger sense, we cannot dedicate, we cannot consecrate, we cannot hallow this ground. The brave men, living and dead, who struggled here, have consecrated it far above our power to add or detract. The world will little note nor long remember what we *say* here, but it can never forget what they *did* here. It is for us, the living, rather to be dedicated here to the unfinished work that they have thus far so nobly carried on. It is rather for us to be here dedicated to the great task remaining before us, that from these honored dead we take increased devotion to the cause for which they here gave the last full measure of devotion ; that we here highly resolve that the dead shall not have died in vain ; that the nation shall, under God, have a new birth of freedom ; and that government of the people, by the people, and for the people, shall not perish from the earth."

The simple and sublime words of this short address shook the hearts of the listeners, and before the first sentence was ended they were under the spell of a mighty magician. They stood hushed, awed, and melted, as the speaker enforced the solemn lesson of the hour, and brought home to them, in plain, unvarnished terms, the duty which remained for them to do— to finish the work which the dead around them had given their lives to carry on. It was one of the briefest of the many speeches with which Mr. Lincoln had swayed the impulses and opinions of crowds of his fellow men, but it is the one which will be remembered above all others as hallowed by the truest and loftiest inspiration. As the final sentence ended, amid the tears and sobs and cheers of the excited throng, the President turned to Mr. Everett, and, grasping his hand, exclaimed with sincerity: "I congratulate you on your success." Mr. Everett responded in the fervor of his emotion: "Ah, Mr. President, how gladly would I exchange all my hundred pages to have been the author of your twenty lines!"

Of all Mr. Lincoln's public utterances, this is unquestionably the most remarkable. The oration, brief and unpretending as it is, will remain a classic of the English language. The Westminster Review, one of the foremost of the great English quarterlies, said of it: "It has but one equal, in that pronounced upon those who fell in the first year of the Peloponnesian war; and in one respect it is superior to that great speech. It is not only more natural, fuller of feeling, more touching and pathetic, but we know with absolute certainty that *it was really delivered*. Nature here takes precedence of art—even though it be the art of Thucydides."

SCENES AND INCIDENTS AT THE DEDICATION.

Major Harry T. Lee, who was himself a participant in the battle of Gettysburg, and occupied a seat on the platform at the dedication, says that the people listened with marked attention through the two hours of Mr. Everett's noble and scholarly oration; but that when Mr. Lincoln came forward, and, in a voice burdened with emotion, uttered his simple and touching eulogy on "the brave men, living and dead, who struggled here," there was scarcely a dry eye in the whole vast audience.

Mr. John Russell Young, late U. S. Minister to China, was present at the Gettysburg dedication, and says: "I sat behind Mr. Lincoln while Mr. Everett delivered his oration. I remember the great orator had a way of raising and dropping his handkerchief as he spoke. He spoke for two hours, and was very impressive, with his white hair and venerable figure. He was a great orator, but it was like a bit of Greek sculpture—beautiful, but cold as ice. It was perfect art, but without feeling. The art and beauty of it captured your imagination and judgment. Mr. Everett went over the campaign with resonant, clear, splendid rhetoric. There was not a word, or a sentence, or a thought that could be corrected. You felt that every gesture had been carefully studied out beforehand. It was like a great actor playing a great part.

"Mr. Lincoln rose, walked to the edge of the platform, took out his glasses, and put them on. He was awkward. He bowed to the assemblage in his homely manner, and took out of his coat pocket a page of foolscap. In front of Mr. Lincoln was a photographer with his camera, endeavoring to take a picture of the scene. We all supposed that Mr. Lincoln would make rather a long speech—a half-hour at least. He took the single sheet of foolscap, held it almost to his nose, and, in his high tenor voice, without the least attempt at effect, delivered that most extraordinary address which belongs to the classics of literature. The photographer was bustling about, preparing to take the President's picture while he was speaking, but Mr. Lincoln finished before the photographer was ready."

MEETING WITH OLD JOHN BURNS.

It is stated that when President Lincoln reached the town of Gettysburg, on his way to attend the exercises at the cemetery, he inquired for "Old John Burns," the hero of the battle of Gettysburg, who left his farm and fought with the Union soldiers upon that bloody field. The veteran was sent for; and on his arrival the President showed him marked attention, taking him by the arm and walking with him in the procession through the streets to the cemetery.

EDWARD EVERETT'S IMPRESSIONS OF LINCOLN.

Edward Everett, who was associated with Lincoln during these two or three days, says of the impression the President made on him: "I recognized in the President a full measure of the qualities which entitle him to the personal respect of the people. On the only social occasion on which I ever had the honor to be in his company, viz: the Commemoration at Gettysburg, he sat at the table of my friend David Willis, by the side of several distinguished persons, foreigners and Americans; and in gentlemanly appearance, manners, and conversation, he was the peer of any man at the table."

CHAPTER XI.

LINCOLN AND GRANT.——THEIR PERSONAL RELATIONS.——GRANT'S SUCCESSES
AT CHATTANOOGA.——APPOINTED LIEUTENANT-GENERAL. ——GRANT'S FIRST
VISIT TO WASHINGTON.——HIS MEETING WITH LINCOLN.——GRANT COULDN'T
STAY TO DINNER.——LINCOLN'S FIRST IMPRESSIONS OF GRANT.—— "A QUIET
LITTLE FELLOW."——THE FIRST "GENERAL" LINCOLN HAD FOUND.——
LINCOLN'S CONFIDENCE IN GRANT.——"THAT PRESIDENTIAL GRUB."——THE
WHISKEY ANECDOTE.——THE TRUE VERSION.——LINCOLN TELLS GRANT THE
STORY OF SYKES'S DOG.——"WE'D BETTER LET MR. GRANT HAVE HIS OWN
WAY."——GRANT'S OPINION OF LINCOLN.

FROM the hour of Grant's triumph at Vicksburg to the close of the war, Mr. Lincoln never withdrew his confidence from the quiet, persistent, unpretending man who led our armies slowly but surely along the path of victory. As soon as the campaign at Vicksburg was over, Grant's sphere of operations was enlarged by his appointment to the command of the military division of the Mississippi. In November following, he fought the famous battles of Chattanooga, including Lookout Mountain and Missionary Ridge; and, aided by his efficient corps commanders, Sherman, Thomas, and Hooker, gained a succession of brilliant victories for the Union cause. The wisdom of Grant's policy of concentration and "fighting it out" had now become apparent.

GRANT APPOINTED LIEUTENANT-GENERAL.

President Lincoln had watched closely the progress of these events, and had now come to recognize in Grant the master spirit of the war. Accordingly, he determined to give him general command of all the Union armies. In December, 1863, a bill was introduced in the Senate by Hon. E. B. Washburne, of Illinois, and passed both houses of Congress, creating the rank of Lieutenant-General in the army. President Lincoln approved the act, and immediately nominated Grant for the position. The nomination was confirmed; and on the 17th of March Grant issued his first order as Lieutenant-General, assuming command of the armies of the United

States, and announcing that headquarters would be in the field, and until further orders with the Army of the Potomac. Of this army he shrewdly remarked that it seemed to him it "had never fought its battles *through*." He proposed, first of all, to teach that army "not to be afraid of Lee." "I had known him personally," said Grant, "and *knew that he was mortal*." With characteristic energy he formed a simple but comprehensive plan of operations, both East and West; sending Sherman on his great march to Atlanta and the sea, while he, with the Army of the Potomac, pushed straight for Richmond. These operations were vigorously urged, and when they were ended the war was ended. It was but little more than a year from the date of Grant's commission as Lieutenant-General till he received Lee's surrender at Appomattox.

GRANT'S FIRST VISIT TO WASHINGTON.—HIS MEETING WITH LINCOLN.

Immediately upon Grant's appointment as Lieutenant-General, he was summoned to Washington. It was his first visit to the capital since the war began, and he was a stranger to nearly every one from the President down. He arrived in the city on the 8th of March, 1864, taking quarters at Willard's hotel, where, when he went in to dinner, none knew "the quiet, rather stumpy-looking man, who came in leading a little boy—the boy who had ridden by his father's side through all the campaign of Vicksburg." But soon it was whispered about who was in the room, and there was a loud call for three cheers for Ulysses S. Grant, which were given with a will. In the evening General Grant attended a reception at the White House, passing in with the throng, alone and unannounced. The quick eye of the President discovered the identity of the modest soldier, and he was most heartily welcomed. "As soon as it was known that he was present, the pressure of the crowd to see the hero of Vicksburg was so great that he was forced to shelter himself behind a sofa. So irrepressible was the desire to see him that Secretary Seward finally induced him to mount a sofa, that this curiosity might be gratified. When parting from the Presi-

dent, he said, 'This has been rather the warmest campaign I have witnessed during the war.'"

The next day, at noon, the General waited on the President, to receive his commission. The interview took place in the Cabinet room. There were present, besides the members of the Cabinet, General Halleck, a member of Congress, two of General Grant's staff-officers, his eldest son, Frederick D. Grant, and the President's private secretary. The ceremony was simple, the President saying, as he proffered the papers: "The nation's appreciation of what you have done, and its reliance upon you for what remains to be done in the existing great struggle, are now presented with this commission, constituting you Lieutenant-General in the army of the United States. With this high honor devolves upon you also a corresponding responsibility. As the country herein trusts you, so, under God, it will sustain you. I scarcely need to add that with what I here speak for the nation goes my own hearty personal concurrence." The General responded briefly, promising to "accept the commission with gratitude for the high honor conferred. With the aid of the noble armies that have fought on so many fields for our common country, it will be my earnest endeavor not to disappoint your expectations. I feel the full weight of the responsibilities now devolving on me, and I know that if they are met it will be due to those armies, and above all to the favor of that Providence which leads both nations and men."

GRANT COULDN'T STAY TO DINNER.

Before assuming personal command of the Army of the Potomac, as he had determined to do, General Grant found it necessary to return once more to the West. In his parting interview with Mr. Lincoln, he was urged to remain to dinner the next day and meet a brilliant party whom the lady of the White House had invited to do him special honor. The General answered, apologetically: "Mrs. Lincoln must excuse me. I must be in Tennessee at a given time." "But we can't excuse you," said the President. "Mrs. Lincoln's

dinner without you, would be Hamlet with Hamlet left out."
"I appreciate the honor Mrs. Lincoln would do me," said
the General, "but time is very important now. I ought to
be at the front, and a dinner to me means a million dollars a
day lost to the country." Mr. Lincoln was pleased with this
answer, and said cheerfully: "Well, we'll have the dinner
without you."

LINCOLN'S FIRST IMPRESSIONS OF GRANT.—"A QUIET LITTLE
FELLOW."

After Mr. Lincoln's first meeting with General Grant, he
was asked regarding his personal impressions of the new
commander. He replied, "Well, I hardly know what to
think of him. He's the quietest little fellow you ever saw.
He makes the least fuss of any man you ever knew. I believe two or three times he has been in this room a minute or
so before I knew he was here. It's about so all around.
The only evidence you have that he's in any place is that he
makes things *git!* Wherever he is, things move."

THE FIRST "GENERAL" LINCOLN HAD FOUND.

To a subsequent inquiry as to his estimate of Grant's military capacities, Mr. Lincoln responded, with emphasis:
"Grant is the first General I've had. *He's a General.*"
"How do you mean, Mr. Lincoln?" his visitor asked. "Well,
I'll tell you what I mean," replied Lincoln. "You know
how it's been with all the rest. As soon as I put a man in
command of the army, he'd come to me with the plan of a
campaign, and about as much as to say: 'Now I don't believe I can do it, but if you say so I'll try it on,' and so put
the responsibility of success or failure on me. They all wanted
me to be the General. Now, it isn't so with Grant. He hasn't
told me what his plans are. I don't know and I don't want
to know. I am glad to find a man who can go ahead without me. When any of the rest set out on a campaign they'd
look over matters and pick out some one thing they were

short of and they knew I couldn't give them, and tell me they couldn't hope to win unless they had it—and it was most generally cavalry. Now, when Grant took hold, I was waiting to see what his pet impossibility would be, and I reckoned it would be cavalry, of course, for we hadn't horses enough to mount what men we had. There were fifteen thousand or thereabouts up near Harper's Ferry, and no horses to put them on. Well, the other day Grant sent to me about these very men, just as I expected; but what he wanted to know was whether he could make infantry of 'em or disband 'em. He doesn't ask impossibilities of me, and he's the first General I've had that didn't." On another occasion Mr. Lincoln said of Grant: "The great thing about him is his cool persistency of purpose. He is not easily excited, and he has the grip of a bulldog. *When he once gets his teeth in, nothing can shake him off.*"

LINCOLN'S CONFIDENCE IN GRANT.

The President's satisfaction with the new commander was speedily communicated to him in a characteristically frank manner, in a letter dated April 30, 1864:

"LIEUTENANT-GENERAL GRANT:—Not expecting to see you before the Spring campaign opens, I wish to express in this way my entire satisfaction with what you have done up to this time, so far as I understand it. The particulars of your plan I neither know nor seek to know. You are vigilant and self-reliant; and, pleased with this, I wish not to obtrude any restraints or constraints upon you. While I am very anxious that any great disaster or capture of our men in great numbers shall be avoided, I know that these points are less likely to escape your attention than they would be mine. If there be anything wanting which is in my power to give, do not fail to let me know it. And now, with a brave army and a just cause, may God sustain you.

Yours, very truly,   A. LINCOLN."

General Grant himself wrote, on this point: "In my first interview with Mr. Lincoln alone, he stated to me that he had never professed to be a military man, or to know how campaigns should be conducted, and never wanted to interfere in them ; but that procrastination on the part of commanders, and the pressure of the people at the North and of Congress, which, like the poor, he 'had always with him,' had forced him into issuing his well-known series of 'Executive Orders.' He did not know but they were all wrong, and did know that some of them were. All he wanted, or had ever wanted, he said, was that some one would take the responsibility and act, and call on him for all the assistance needed."

General Horace Porter, for some time Grant's chief of staff, says: "The nearest Mr. Lincoln ever came to giving General Grant an order for the movement of troops was during Early's raid upon Washington. On July 10, 1864, he telegraphed a long dispatch from Washington, which contained the following language: 'What I think is that you should provide to retain your hold where you are certainly, and bring the rest with you personally, and make a vigorous effort to defeat the enemy's force in this vicinity. I think there is really a fair chance to do this, if the movement is prompt. This is what I think—upon your suggestion, and is not an order.' Grant replied that on reflection he thought it would have a bad effect for him to leave City Point, then his headquarters, in front of Richmond and Petersburg ; and the President was satisfied with the dispositions which the General made for the repulse of Early without taking command against him in person."

"THAT PRESIDENTIAL GRUB."

A curious incident revealing the intense interest with which Mr. Lincoln watched the career of General Grant, is related by Mr. J. Russell Jones, an old and trusted friend of the President, who joined the army at Vicksburg in time to witness its final triumph. Soon after Mr. Jones's return to Chicago, the President summoned him to Washington. With eager haste, after the first salutations were over, Mr. Lincoln declared the object for which he had secured the interview: " 'I have sent for you, Mr. Jones, to know if that man Grant wants to be

President.' Mr. Jones, although somewhat astonished at the question and the circumstances under which it was asked, replied at once: 'No, Mr. President.' 'Are you sure?' queried the latter. 'Yes,' said Mr. Jones, 'perfectly sure; I have just come from Vicksburg; I have seen General Grant frequently, and talked fully and freely with him about that and every other question, and I know he has no political aspirations whatever, and certainly none for the Presidency. His only desire is to see you re-elected, and to do what he can under your orders to put down the rebellion and restore peace to the country.' 'Ah, Mr. Jones,' said Lincoln, 'you have lifted a great weight off my mind, and done me an immense amount of good; for I tell you, my friend, no man knows how deeply that Presidential grub gnaws till he has had it himself.' "

We cannot believe that Mr. Lincoln cherished any feeling of jealousy of the rising commander, or desired to interfere with whatever political ambition he might nourish. It was rather his desire to be assured of the single-hearted purpose of a military leader whom he had trusted and to whom he wished to confide still more important services in the conduct of the war.

THE WHISKEY ANECDOTE.—THE TRUE VERSION.

It may be remembered that early in the war an anecdote went the rounds of the press to the effect that, in reply to a complaint that Gen. Grant had been guilty of drunkenness in the campaigns in the West, Mr. Lincoln remarked that he would "like to find out what kind of liquor Grant drank," so that he might "send some of it to the other Generals." The true version of that characteristic anecdote is this, as we had it from the lips of the late Judge T. Lyle Dickey, who was a Judge of the Illinois Supreme Court at the time of his death, and who, at the time of Grant's famous Vicksburg campaign, was on the General's staff as chief of cavalry. Judge (then Colonel) Dickey had been sent to Washington with private dispatches for the President and the Secretary of War. Lincoln and Dickey had been intimate friends for years, and during the latter's visit to the former on that occasion, Dickey remarked, "I hear that some one has been trying to poison you against Grant by reporting that he gets drunk; I wish to assure you, Mr. President, that there is not a scintilla of truth in the report." "Oh, Colonel," replied the President, "we get all sorts of reports here, but I'll say this to you: that if those accusing General Grant of getting drunk will tell me *where he gets his whiskey*, I will get a lot of it and send it around to some of the Generals of the army, who are *badly in need* of something of the kind." In view of the fact that the movements and operations of the Army of the Potomac were at that time very unsatisfactory to the President and to the country, and that the only progress that the armies of the Union were making anywhere was at Vicksburg under Grant, the point of the President's remark was very palpable.

LINCOLN TELLS GRANT THE STORY OF SYKES'S DOG.

After Mr. Lincoln and General Grant had become personally intimate, they had many enjoyable conversations and exchanges of anecdotes. Mr. Lincoln especially enjoyed telling the General of the various persons who had come to him with complaints and criticisms about the Vicksburg campaign. "After the place had actually surrendered," said the President, "I thought it was about time to shut down on this sort of. thing. So one day, when a delegation came to see me, and had spent half an hour trying to show me the fatal mistake you had made in paroling Pemberton's army, and insisting that the rebels would violate their paroles and in less than a month confront you again in the ranks and have to be whipped all over again, I thought I could get rid of them best by telling them a story about Sykes's dog. 'Have you ever heard about Sykes's yellow dog?' said I to the spokesman of the delegation. He said he hadn't. 'Well, I must tell you about him,' said I. 'Sykes had a yellow dog he set great store by, but there were a lot of small boys around the village, and that's always a bad thing for dogs, you know. These boys didn't share Sykes's views, and they were not disposed to let the dog have a fair show. Even Sykes had to admit that the dog was getting unpopular ; in fact, it was soon seen that a prejudice was growing up against that dog that threatened to wreck all his future prospects in life. The boys, after meditating how they could get the best of him, finally fixed up a cartridge with a long fuse, put the cartridge in a piece of meat, dropped the meat in the road in front of Sykes's door, and then perched themselves on a fence a good distance off with the end of the fuse in their hands. Then they whistled for the dog. When he came out he scented the bait, and bolted the meat, cartridge and all. The boys touched off the fuse with a cigar, and in about a second a report came from that dog that sounded like a small clap of thunder. Sykes came bouncing out of the house, and yelled: 'What's up! Anything busted?' There was no reply, except a snicker from the small boys roosting on the fence ; but as Sykes looked up he saw the whole air filled with pieces of yellow dog. He picked up the biggest piece he could find—a portion of the back, with a part of the tail still hanging to it, and, after turning it around and looking it all over, he said, 'Well, I guess he'll never be much account again—*as a dog.*' 'And I guess Pemberton's forces will never be much account again—*as an army.*' The delegation began looking around for their hats before I had quite got to the end of the story, and I was never bothered any more about superseding the commander of the Army of the Tennessee.''

"WE'D BETTER LET MR. GRANT HAVE HIS OWN WAY."

When General Grant was ready to begin active operations with the Army of the Potomac, he sent forward all available men from Washington. Secretary Stanton, anxious about the safety of the city, said to Grant one day : "General, I suppose you have left us enough men to strongly garrison the forts?" "No, I can't do that," was Grant's quiet answer. "Why not? Why not? Why not?" repeated the Secretary nervously. "Because I have already sent the men to the front." Said the Secretary, still more nervously: "That won't do. It's contrary to my plans. I cannot allow it. I will order the men back." To this General Grant returned with quiet determination: "I shall need the men there, and you cannot order them back." "Why not? Why not? Why not?" cried the Secretary. "I believe that I rank the Secretary in this matter," remarked General Grant. "Very well, we will see the President about that," responded the Secretary sharply. "I will have to take you to the President." "That is right. The President ranks us both." So they went to the President; and the Secretary, turning to General Grant, said: "Now, General, state your case." But the General calmly replied: "I have no case to state. I am satisfied as it is." This threw the burden of statement on Secretary Stanton, and was excellent strategy. Meanwhile, General Grant had the men. When the Secretary had concluded, Lincoln crossed his legs, rested his elbow on his knee, and said in his quaint way and with a twinkle in his eye: "Now, Mr. Secretary, you know we have been trying to manage this army for nearly three years, and you know we haven't done much with it. We sent over the mountains and brought Mr. Grant, as Mrs. Grant calls him, to manage it for us; and now I guess we'd better let Mr. Grant *have his own way*." And Mr. Grant had it.

GRANT'S OPINION OF LINCOLN.

The favorable opinion which Mr. Lincoln held of General Grant, was strongly reciprocated. A short time before the former's death Grant said: "I regard Lincoln as one of the greatest of men. He is unquestionably the greatest man I have ever encountered. The more I see of him and exchange views with him, the more he impresses me. I admire his courage, and respect the firmness he always displays. Many think from the gentleness of his character that he has a yielding nature; but while he has the courage to change his mind when convinced that he is wrong, he has all the tenacity of purpose which could be desired in a great statesman. His quickness of perception often astonishes me. Long before the statement of a complicated question is finished, his mind will grasp the main points, and he will seem to comprehend the whole subject better than the person who is stating it. He will take rank in history alongside of Washington."

CHAPTER XII.

THROUGHOUT the war, President Lincoln was keenly solic-
itous for the welfare of the Union soldiers. He knew that
upon them all else depended; and he felt bound to them, not
only by official duty, but by the tenderer ties of human interest and love. In all his proclamations and his public utterances, he gave the fullest credit to the brave men in the field,
and claimed for them the country's thanks and gratitude.
His sympathy for the soldiers was as tender as that of a
woman, and his tears were ever ready to start at the mention
of their hardships, their bravery, their sufferings and losses.
Nothing that he could do was left undone, to minister to their
comfort in field or camp or hospital. His most exacting
cares were never permitted to divert his thoughts from them,
and his anxious and tender sympathy included all whom they
held dear. Said Mr. Riddle, in a speech in Congress in
1863: "Let not the distant mother, who has given up a
loved one to fearful death, think that the President does not
sympathize with her sorrow, and would not have been glad,

oh, how glad, to have so shaped events as to have spared the sacrifices. And let not fathers and mothers and wives anywhere think that as he sees the long blue regiments of brave and beautiful ones marching away, stepping to the drum-beat, that he does not contemplate and feel his responsibility as he thinks how many of them shall go to nameless graves, unmarked, save by the down-looking eyes of God's pitying angels." The feeling of the soldiers toward Mr. Lincoln was one of filial respect and love. He was not only the President, the commander-in-chief of all the armies and navies of the United States, but their good "Father Abraham," who loved every man, even the humblest, who wore the Union blue.

ALWAYS GLAD TO SEE THEM AT THE WHITE HOUSE.

Of Mr. Lincoln's personal relations with the soldiers, enough interesting anecdotes could be collected to fill a volume. He saw much of them in Washington, as they marched through that city on their way to the front, or returned on furlough or discharge, or filled the overcrowded hospitals of the capital. Often they called upon him, singly or with companions; and he always had for them a word, however brief, of sympathy and cheer. Mr. Lincoln was always glad to see soldiers at the White House. They were the one class of visitors who seldom came to ask for favors, and never to pester him with advice. It was a real treat for Mr. Lincoln to escape from the politicians and have a quiet talk with a private soldier.

One day in the winter of 1862, two soldiers of the Army of the Potomac, who were in Washington on a furlough, called on the President; and one of them thus describes the interview: "We reached the city early in the morning, and proceeded to see the sights. We took in Congress and the Smithsonian, and at sunset, on our return, called at the White House, where we were politely told that it was after hours and we would have to come again. Quite disappointed, as we were standing on the front steps I saw Mr. Lincoln coming through a side gate from the War Department building and approach us with long strides. We gave the military salute in good shape. Meeting us with a hand outstretched for each and a smiling face, he proceeded to give us a prolonged handshaking. 'How do you do, boys? Come to see my house—excuse me, your house, one I occupy for awhile?' My comrade explained that we were late, to which he said he 'guessed he could fix it,' although he believed there was some such rule for citizens, and addressing me said, laughingly: 'Little Mac, as you call him, won't let you come over here just when you want to always, will he?' 'No,' I replied; 'he thinks Pennsylvania avenue already so crowded with "shoulder straps" that we would be in the way.' Talking with us in this vein for several minutes, it did not seem to us that he felt his responsibility resting upon him with much weight. But on learning where we had been that day, he asked if we had seen Mt. Vernon also, and almost instantly changing in his tone and manner, and putting a hand on each of our shoulders, said: 'I want you soldiers to see it all; it's a great opportunity for you; don't neglect it. To many of you it may never occur again. It all belongs to you boys, for you are going to save the country yet. So visit Congress and the department, and come here; I am always glad to meet you.' And turning to the door he told some one to relax the rule in our case and show us the mansion, and with 'Good-bye, boys,' he grasped the banister and sprung up the steps four at a time. Never shall I forget Mr. Lincoln's sad look, or his paternal manner toward us."

THE WOUNDED SOLDIER AND HIS MOTHER.—SCENE AT A PRESIDENT'S RECEPTION.

Once, at a crowded President's reception, Mr. Lincoln noticed, standing modestly apart as though embarrassed at finding themselves in such a large and brilliant assembly, a young man with a crutch, evidently a wounded soldier, and

his plainly-dressed mother.   Instantly Mr. Lincoln pushed
his way toward them, and taking each by the hand, he spoke

MR. LINCOLN GREETING THE WOUNDED SOLDIER AND HIS MOTHER.—SCENE AT A PRESIDENT'S RECEPTION.

to them kindly, giving them a cordial welcome, and inquiring
their names and residence.   Prominent public men and army

officers were passed by unnoticed, while the President paid his debt of gratitude to the humble soldier who had suffered in the service of his country.

FAVORS TO THE WIVES, MOTHERS, AND FRIENDS OF SOLDIERS.—A HERO REWARDED.

Among the innumerable petitioners for the executive clemency or favor, none were so graciously received as those who appeared in behalf of soldiers. It was half a victory, to say that the person for whom the favor was desired was a member of the Union army. From a great variety of characteristic incidents, a few only may be given here.

A young soldier was one night found sleeping at his post, and according to the inexorable demand of military law, was condemned to be shot. He was a boy in years (only eighteen), though a man in stature, and his immature frame was unfitted for the performance of a soldier's hard duties. The tidings of his dreadful doom were conveyed to his family, and while they sat talking and weeping over the disgraceful death of the son and brother whom they had resigned to the service of the country, a letter was handed in by a neighbor with the simple words: "It is from him." It contained the parting message of the condemned soldier, written in touching, manly words. On his last day's march with his regiment he had carried the knapsack of a sick comrade in addition to his own, and toward the last, when they had to move at double-quick, he had given his arm to his failing companion, although his own strength was greatly overtaxed. When camp was reached, he took the place of his invalid friend on sentinel duty; but now he had gone beyond his power of endurance. Had grim death fronted him he could not have kept off the stupor which benumbed him. The sick lad, whom he befriended at the cost of his life, begged to be shot in his stead. But the doom of the sleeping sentinel was not to be averted; and so he bade his father and mother and little sister a final farewell. The following evening, as the President sat bending over his desk, the child, who had heard her brother's dying message in the far-off country home, stole up to the kind man unannounced. She pleaded for her brother's life in tearful, artful tones, and then placed in Mr. Lincoln's hands the letter of the doomed one which told his story better than she could do. The President's eyes moistened. He wrote a pardon and despatched it at once. Two days after, the young soldier came to the White House with his sister. Lincoln took the youth into his private office, and as he handed him an officer's commission, said: "The soldier who can carry a sick comrade's baggage, and die for the deed without a murmur, deserves well of his country."

"GOD BLESS PRESIDENT LINCOLN."

As he wrote the pardon of another soldier, sentenced to be shot for sleeping while on sentinel duty, the President remarked to a friend standing by: "I could not think of going into eternity with the blood of that poor young man on my hands. It is not to be wondered at that a boy, raised on a farm, probably in the habit of going to bed at dark, should, when required to watch, fall asleep; and I cannot consent to shoot him for such an act." The youth thus restored was afterward found among the slain on the field of Fredericksburg, with a photograph of Mr. Lincoln, on which he had written, "God bless President Lincoln!" worn next to his heart.

"TOO MANY WEEPING WIDOWS."

The Rev. Newman Hall, of London, repeated in a sermon an anecdote told him by a Union officer: "The first week of my command there were twenty-four deserters sentenced by court martial to be shot, and the warrants for their execution were sent to the President to be signed. He refused. I went to Washington and had an interview. I said: 'Mr. President, unless these men are made an example of, the army itself is in danger. Mercy to the few is cruelty to the many.' He replied: 'Mr. General, there are already too many weeping widows in the United States. For God's sake, don't ask me to add to the number, for *I won't do it.*'"

A PARDON SWEETENS SLEEP.

One night Speaker Colfax sought to move the clemency of the President in favor of a deserter who was to be shot. Mr. Lincoln was worn out with the labors of the day; but after patiently listening to the story, he said: "Some of our generals complain that I impair discipline and subordination in the army by my pardons and respites; but it makes me rested, after a hard day's work, if I can find some good excuse for saving a man's life, and I go to bed happy as I think how joyous the signing of my name will make him and his family and friends."

MERCY BEARS RICHER FRUITS THAN STRICT JUSTICE.

Some New Jersey soldiers had deserted, and were recaptured and sentenced to be shot. A delegation of their friends, one of whom was a brother of one of the condemned men, sought the President at the Soldiers' Home, and importuned him for their pardon. It happened that Mr. Lincoln's old Illinois friends, J. F. Speed and Judge Joseph Gillespie, were visiting him at the time, and became greatly interested in the case. After the delegation had stated their errand, the President replied, pointing out that it would be disastrous to the cause if he should pardon men who had deserted their colors, while the armies were confronting each other; he had no right under such circumstances to expect the men who had remained in the ranks to do their duty. "My heart almost sank within me," says Judge Gillespie, "when Mr. Lincoln dismissed them, saying that he would give them a definite answer at the White House at nine o'clock the next morning. I was much afraid that Mr. Lincoln had made up his mind not to pardon the young men. Speed, who I know had more influence with the President than any living being, suggested that we should tackle him and beg for the boys, which we did in good earnest. We plied him with all the reasons we could muster, and still I was afraid we were not gaining ground. When it came to be time to retire, I said to Mr. Lincoln that I did not think I could sleep unless I knew that he was going to pardon the boys. He said: 'Gillespie, I can't tell you." 'Well,' said I, 'you can give me an inkling.' Said he, 'All I can say is that I have always found that *mercy bears richer fruits than strict justice.*' In the morning the delegation were ahead of time, and they were rejoiced beyond measure to receive the pardon for their friends.''

HELPING A MOTHER GET HER SON OUT OF HOSPITAL.

One day, says a visitor at the White House, there were waiting to see the President a couple of plain country people, old and poorly dressed. As the President turned toward them, the husband whispered encouragingly, "Now is your time, dear." The old lady stepped forward, made a low courtesy, and began hesitatingly, "Mr. President —." Mr. Lincoln, looking over his spectacles, fixed those gray, piercing, yet mild eyes upon her; then lifting his head and extending his hand, he said, in the kindest tones: "Well, good lady, what can I do for you?" "Mr. President," she resumed, "I feel so embarrassed I can hardly speak. I never spoke to a President before; but I am a good Union woman down in Maryland, and my son is wounded badly, and in the hospital, and I have been trying to get him out, but somehow couldn't, and they said I had better come right to you. When the war first broke out I gave my son first to God, and then told him he might go fight the rebels; and now if you will let me take him home I will nurse him up, and just as soon as he gets well enough he shall go right back and help put down the rebellion. He is a good boy, and don't want to shirk the service." The tears gathered in Mr. Lincoln's eyes, and his lips quivered, as he replied: "Yes, yes, God bless you! you shall have your son. What hospital did you say?" It seemed a relief to him to turn aside and write a few words, which he handed to the woman, saying: "There, give that to ——; and you will get your son, if he is able to go home with you." "God bless you, Mr. President!" said the father, the only words he had uttered; and the mother, making a low courtesy, fairly sobbed: "O, sir, we are so much obliged to you!"

MAKING GLAD A WIDOW'S HEART.

Mr. Murtagh, of the Washington Republican, relates a tearful incident that occurred in his presence: "I was waiting my turn to speak to the President one day," said Mr. Murtagh, "when my attention was attracted by the sad, patient face of a woman advanced in life, who, in a faded hood and shawl, was among the applicants for an interview. Presently Mr. Lincoln turned to her, saying in his accustomed manner, 'Well, my good woman, what can I do for you this morning?' 'Mr. President,' said she, 'my husband and three sons all went into the army. My husband was killed in battle. I get along very badly since then, living all alone, and I thought I would come and ask you to release to me my oldest son.' Mr. Lincoln looked into her face a moment, and in his kindest accents responded: 'Certainly! certainly! If you have given us *all*, and your prop has been taken away, you are justly entitled to one of your boys!' He immediately made out an order discharging the young man, which the woman took, and thanking him gratefully, went away. I had forgotten the circumstances, when, happening to be in the President's room again, who should come in but the same woman. It appeared that she had gone herself to the front, with the President's order, and found the son she was in search of had been mortally wounded in a recent engagement, and taken to a hospital. She found the hospital, but the boy was dead, or died while she was there. The surgeon in charge made a memorandum of the facts upon the back of the President's order, and, almost broken-hearted, the poor woman had found her way again into Mr. Lincoln's presence. He was much affected by her appearance and story, and said: 'I know what you wish me to do now, and I shall do it without your asking; I shall release to you your second son.' Upon this, he took up his pen and commenced writing the order. While he was writing, the poor woman stood by his side, the tears running down her face, and passed her hand softly over his head, stroking his rough hair, as I have seen a fond mother caress a son. By the time he had finished writing, his own heart and eyes were full. He handed her the paper: 'Now,' said he, '*you* have one and I one of the other two left; that is no more than right.' She took the paper, and reverently placing her hand again upon his head, the tears still upon her cheeks, said: 'The Lord bless you, Mr. Lincoln!'"

COMFORTING A BEREAVED MOTHER.

It came to the knowledge of Mr. Lincoln that a widow living in Boston—a Mrs. Bixby—had lost five sons in the service of their country. Without delay, he addressed the bereaved mother the following touching note:

"I have been shown on the file of the War Department a statement of the Adjutant-General of Massachusetts, that you are the mother of five sons who have died gloriously on the field of battle. I feel how weak and fruitless must be any word of mine which should attempt to beguile you from the grief of a loss so overwhelming; but I cannot refrain from tendering to you the consolation that may be found in the thanks of the Republic they died to save. I pray that our Heavenly Father may assuage the anguish of your bereavements, and leave only the cherished memory of the loved and lost, and the solemn pride that must be yours to have laid so costly a sacrifice upon the altar of freedom.

Yours, very sincerely and respectfully, A. LINCOLN."

THE LITTLE DRUMMER BOY.

The Rev. Mr. Henderson, of Louisville, Ky., was witness of an affecting scene which occurred while he was waiting to speak with Mr. Lincoln. A small, pale, delicate-looking boy, about thirteen years old, was among the number in the antechamber. The President saw him standing there, looking feeble and faint, and said: "Come here, my boy, and tell me what you want." The boy advanced, placed his hand on the arm of the President's chair, and with bowed head and timid accents said: "Mr. President, I have been a drummer in a regiment for two years, and my Colonel got angry with me and turned me off. I was taken sick, and have been a long time in hospital. This is the first time I have been out, and I came to see if you could not do something for me." The President looked at him kindly and tenderly, and asked him where he lived. "I have no home," answered the boy. "Where is your father?" "He died in the army," was the reply. "Where is your mother?" continued the President. "My mother is dead also. I have no mother, no father, no brothers, no sisters, and," bursting into tears, "no friends— nobody cares for me." Mr. Lincoln's eyes filled with tears, and he said to him, "Can't you sell newspapers?" "No," said the boy, "I am too weak; and the surgeon of the hospital told me I must leave, and I have no money, and no place to go." The scene was wonderfully affecting. The President drew forth a card, and addressing on it certain officials to whom his request was law, gave special directions "to care for this poor boy." The wan face of the little drummer lit up with a happy smile as he received the paper, and he went away convinced that he had one good and true friend in the person of the President.

BRAVE WILLIE BRADEN.

Willie Braden, a lad of fourteen, who had served a year on the gun-boat "Ottawa," taking part in two important engagements with the coolness of a veteran,—in the first as a powder-monkey, and the second as captain's messenger,— applied to the President for an appointment to the U. S. Naval School. It was instantly granted. As the boy was on the point of starting for his examination, it was found that he was some months short of the age that would be required for his admission at the time designated in the appointment. The little fellow was so disappointed that he sat down and cried. Some one began explaining the matter to Mr. Lincoln, who quickly interrupted, laying down his spectacles: "Bless me! is that the boy who did so gallantly in those two great battles? Why, I feel that I should bow to him, and not he to me." The President took the papers at once, and as soon as he learned that a postponement until September would suffice, made the order that the lad should report in that month. Then putting his hand on Willie's head, he said: "Now, my boy, go home and have good fun during the two months, for they are about the last holiday you will get."

LINCOLN'S LOVE OF SOLDIERS' HUMOR.

Anything that savored of the wit and humor of the soldiers was especially welcome to Lincoln. Any incident that showed that "the boys" were mirthful and jolly in all their privations seemed to commend itself to him. There was a story of a soldier in the Army of the Potomac, carried to the rear of battle with both legs shot off, who, seeing a pie-woman hovering about, asked, "Say, old lady, are them pies *sewed or pegged?*" And there was another one of a soldier at the battle of Chancellorsville, whose regiment, waiting to be called into the fight, was taking coffee. The hero of the story put to his lips a crockery mug which he had carried, with infinite care, through several campaigns. A stray bullet, just missing the coffee-drinker's head, dashed the mug into fragments and left only its handle on his finger. Turning his head in that direction, the soldier angrily growled, "Johnny, you can't do that again!" Lincoln, relating these two stories together, said, "It seems as if neither death nor danger could quench the grim humor of the American soldier."

WHAT REGIMENT IT WAS.

Captain Mix, at one time the commander of the President's body-guard, relates that, on their way to town from the Soldiers' Home one sultry morning, they came upon a regiment marching into the city. A straggler, very heavily loaded with camp equipage, was accosted by the President with the question: "My lad, what is that?" referring to the designation of his regiment. "It's a regiment," said the soldier curtly, plodding on, his gaze bent steadily upon the ground. "Yes, I see that," rejoined the President, "but I want to know *what* regiment." "—— Pennsylvania," replied the man in the same tone, looking neither to the right nor the left. As the carriage passed on, Mr. Lincoln turned to Captain Mix and said, with a merry laugh, "It is very evident that chap smells no blood of '*royalty*' in this establishment."

THE AUSTRIAN RECRUIT.

Once an Austrian Count applied to President Lincoln for a position in the army. Being introduced by the Austrian Minister, he needed, of course, no further recommendation; but, as if fearing that his importance might not be duly appreciated, he proceeded to explain that he was a Count; that his family were ancient and highly respectable, etc. Here Mr. Lincoln, with a merry twinkle in his eye, tapping the aristocratic lover of titles on the shoulder, in a fatherly way, as if the man had confessed to some wrong, interrupted in a soothing tone, "Never mind; you shall be treated with *just as much consideration* for all that!"

"MAJOR-GENERAL, I RECKON."

A new levy of troops required, on a certain occasion, the appointment of a large additional number of brigadier and major-generals. Among the immense number of applications, Mr. Lincoln came upon one wherein the claims of a certain worthy (not in the service at all) for a generalship were glowingly set forth. But the applicant didn't specify whether he wanted to be brigadier or major-general. The President observed this difficulty, and solved it by a lucid endorsement. The clerk, on receiving the paper again, found written across it: *"Major-General, I reckon. A. Lincoln."*

HORSES MORE VALUABLE THAN BRIGADIERS.

A juvenile "brigadier" from New York, with a small detachment of cavalry, having imprudently gone within the rebel lines near Fairfax Court House, was captured by "guerillas." Upon the fact being reported to Mr. Lincoln, he said that he was very sorry to lose the horses. "What do you mean?" inquired his informant. "Why," rejoined the President, "I can make a better 'brigadier' any day; but those horses cost the government a hundred and twenty-five dollars a head!"

HE WANTED "HARD-TACK," NOT GENERALS.

Mr. Lincoln was especially fond of a joke at the expense of some high military or civil dignitary. He was intensely amused by a story told by Secretary Stanton, of a trip made by him and Gen. Foster up the Broad river in North Carolina, in a tug-boat, when, reaching our outposts on the river bank, a Federal picket yelled out, "Who have you got on board that tug?" The severe and dignified answer was, "The Secretary of War and Major-General Foster." Instantly the picket roared back: "We've got Major-Generals enough up here—*why don't you bring us up some hardtack?*"

LINCOLN'S DESCRIPTION OF "LITTLE PHIL" SHERIDAN.

The first time President Lincoln met General Sheridan was soon after the latter had gained his brilliant successes in the Shenandoah Valley, and everybody was talking about the dashing cavalryman. The President had recently visited the army in the field; and on his return to Washington, at a Cabinet meeting, he was asked, "What kind of a man is this

Sheridan?" "Well," he replied, "he is a little chap, with round head, red face, legs longer than his body, *and not enough neck to hang him by.*"

OPPOSED TO RETALIATION ON REBEL PRISONERS.

Mr. Odell states that when the reports, in an authentic form, first reached Washington of the sufferings of the Union prisoners, Mr. Lincoln was greatly excited and overcome by them. He was told that justice demanded a stern retaliation. He said, with the deepest emotion: "I can never, never starve men like that! Whatever others may say or do, I never can, and I never will, be accessory to such treatment of human beings!"

GENEROUS TRIBUTE TO A FALLEN FOE.

Mr. Lincoln's generous heart was ever ready to recognize the personal worth of rebel soldiers. After the death of Stonewall Jackson, Col. J. W. Forney, editor of the Washington Chronicle, published in his paper a sketch of the brave Confederate leader, praising his high personal character, while regretting his course in fighting against his country's flag. On reading the article, Mr. Lincoln sent a note of thanks to Col. Forney, saying: "I honor you for your generosity to one who, though contending against us in a guilty cause, was nevertheless a gallant man. Let us forget his errors over his fresh-made grave."

OFFICES FOR DISABLED SOLDIERS.

Judge Wm. Johnson, of Ohio, relates that, being in Washington about the middle of President Lincoln's first term, and finding how great was the need of popular confidence in the administration, he suggested to Mr. Lincoln the appointment of disabled soldiers to positions in the Civil Service, as a movement at once just and likely to excite a grateful response in the minds of the people. The idea quickly commended itself to Mr. Lincoln. At the second interview, he said: "I have been thinking about your proposition. Did you ever know Colonel Smith, of Rockford, Ill.? You know he was killed at Vicksburg; that his head was carried off by a shell. He was postmaster of Rockford, and now his wife wants the place."

Thereupon, says Judge Johnson, "Mr. Lincoln wrote a letter to Postmaster-General Blair, directing him to appoint the widow of Colonel Smith postmistress, in the place of her deceased husband, who had fallen in battle, and stating that in consideration of what was due to the men who were fighting our battles, he had made up his mind that the families of those who had fallen, and those disabled in the service, their qualifications being equal, should always have a preference in the Civil Service. The next morning I jumped into an ambulance and went to the convalescing camp, where there were about 7,000 convalescents, a great many of them Ohio men, and when I made my appearance, they called on me for a speech. I got upon a terrace and made them a few remarks, and, coming round to the old saw that 'Republics are always ungrateful,' I told them I could not vouch for the Republic, but I thought I could vouch for the chief man at the head of the administration, and he had already spoken on that subject; and when I read Lincoln's letter the boys flung their hats into the air, and made the welkin ring for a long while. I hurried back to the city, and with a pair of shears cut out Lincoln's letter, and then attached some editorial remarks, and that letter went around, and I believe was published in every friendly newspaper in the United States. About that time Congress passed a resolution to the same effect, that those disabled in the military service of the country, wherever qualified, ought to have a preference over others. This may have been a small matter, but it made a marvellous impression on the army."

"ENCOURAGING THE BOYS."

On one occasion, when the enemy were threatening the defences of Washington, Mr. Lincoln made a personal visit to the men in the trenches, for the purpose, as he stated, of "encouraging the boys." He walked about among them, telling them to hold their ground at every point, and he would soon give them reinforcements. His presence had a most inspiring effect, and the trenches were held by a few hundred soldiers of the Invalid Corps, until the promised help came, and the enemy withdrew.

MR. LINCOLN AMONG THE WOUNDED ON A BATTLE FIELD.

During the campaigns of the Army of the Potomac in the vicinity of the capital, President Lincoln made frequent visits to the front. One of these occasions was after a desperate battle on the Peninsula. It was nightfall, and the dead and wounded were being carried from the battle field. The lanterns of the men who moved among the slain shone out like fireflies as they progressed. As one stretcher was passing Mr. Lincoln he heard the voice of a lad calling to his mother in agonizing tones. His great heart filled. He forgot the crisis of the hour. His very being concentrated itself in the cries of the dying boy. Stopping the carriers he knelt, and bending over him asked: "What can I do for you, my poor child?" "Oh, you will do nothing for me," he replied. "You are a Yankee. I cannot hope that my message to my mother will ever reach her." Mr. Lincoln's tears, his voice, full of the tenderest love, convinced the boy of his sincerity, and he gave his good-bye words without reserve. The President directed them copied, and ordered that they be sent that night, with a flag of truce, into the enemy's lines. He only told the soldier who he was to convince him that his word would be obeyed; and when told that time was precious, as the distant outposts must yet be visited, he arose reluctantly and entered the ambulance.

PASSING THE AMBULANCES.

It seemed that Mr. Lincoln was never to escape the sight of the miseries of war. On his way to his favorite retreat at

"The Soldier's Rest," he often passed long lines of ambulances, laden with the suffering victims of a recent battle. A friend who met him on such an occasion, says: "When I met the President, his attitude and expression spoke the deepest sadness. He paused, and, pointing his hand towards the wounded men, he said: 'Look yonder at those poor fellows. I cannot bear it! This suffering, this loss of life, is dreadful!' Recalling a letter he had written years before to a suffering friend whose grief he had sought to console, I reminded him of the incident, and asked him: 'Do you remember writing to your sorrowing friend these words: "And this too shall pass away. Never fear. Victory will come." 'Yes,' replied he, *victory will come, but it comes slowly.*' "

MAKING THE ROUNDS OF THE HOSPITALS.

On a visit to City Point, Mr. Lincoln called upon the head surgeon at that place, and said he wished to visit all the hospitals under his charge, and shake hands with every soldier. The surgeon asked if he knew what he was undertaking; there were five or six thousand soldiers at that place, and it would be quite a tax upon his strength to visit all the wards and shake hands with every soldier. Mr. Lincoln answered, with a smile, he guessed he was equal to the task; at any rate he would try, and go as far as he could; he should never, probably, see the boys again, and he wanted them to know that he appreciated what they had done for their country. Finding it useless to try to dissuade him, the surgeon began his rounds with the President, who walked from bed to bed, extending his hand to all, saying a few words of sympathy to some, making kind inquiries of others, and welcomed by all with the heartiest cordiality. After some hours the tour of the various hospitals was made, and Mr. Lincoln returned with the surgeon to his office. They had scarcely entered, however, when a messenger came saying that one ward had been omitted, and "the boys" wanted to see the President. The surgeon, who was thoroughly tired, and knew Mr. Lincoln must be, tried to dissuade him from going; but the good man said he must go back; "the boys" would be so disappointed. So he went with the messenger, accompanied by the surgeon, and shook hands with the gratified soldiers, and then returned again to the office. The surgeon expressed the fear that the President's arm would be lamed with so much hand-shaking, saying that it certainly must ache. Mr. Lincoln smiled, and saying something about his "strong muscles," stepped out at the open door, took up a very large, heavy axe which lay there by a log of wood, and chopped vigorously for a few moments, sending the chips flying in all directions; and then, pausing, he extended his right arm to its full length, holding the axe out horizontally, without its even quivering as he held it. Strong men who looked on— men accustomed to manual labor—could not hold the same axe in that position for a moment. Returning to the office, he took a glass of lemonade; and while he was within, the chips he had chopped were gathered up and safely cared for by a hospital steward, because they were "the chips that Father Abraham chopped."

A VISIT TO MR. LINCOLN AT "THE SOLDIER'S REST."

In Summer Mr. Lincoln's favorite home was at "The Soldier's Rest," a place a few miles out of Washington, on the Maryland side, where old and disabled soldiers of the regular army found a refuge. It was a lovely spot, situated on a beautifully wooded hill, reached by a winding road, shaded by thick-set branches. A California lady, who visited Mr. Lincoln there, and went with him to the neighboring cemetery, where were numberless new-made graves of volunteers, says: "While we stood in the soft evening air, watching the faint trembling of the long tendrils of waving willow, and feeling the dewy coolness that was flung out by the old oaks above us, Mr. Lincoln joined us. and stood silent, too, taking in the scene.

" 'How sleep the brave, who sink to rest
By all their country's wishes blest,'—

he said, softly. There was something so touching in the picture opened before us,—the nameless graves, the solemn quiet, the tender twilight air, but more particularly our own feminine disposition to be easily melted, I suppose,—that it made us cry, as if we stood beside the tomb of our own dead, and gave point to the lines which he afterwards quoted:

" 'And women o'er the graves shall weep,
Where nameless heroes calmly sleep.' "

CHAPTER XIII.

VARIOUS SIDES OF PRESIDENT LINCOLN'S CHARACTER.——HIS TASTES, TRAITS, AND HABITS.——FONDNESS FOR THE COMPANIONSHIP OF "LITTLE TAD."—— TAD AT CABINET MEETINGS.——A REPRIEVE FOR A CONDEMNED TURKEY.—— TAD AND MR. LINCOLN REVIEWING THE ARMY OF THE POTOMAC.——LIN- COLN'S LITERARY TASTES.——FONDNESS FOR POETRY AND MUSIC.——HIS REMARKABLE MEMORY.——NOT A LATIN SCHOLAR.——NEVER READ A NOVEL. ——SOLACE IN THEATRICAL REPRESENTATION.——ANECDOTES OF BOOTH, M'CULLOCH, AND HACKETT.——APT DRAMATIC CRITICISMS.——METHODS OF LITERARY WORK.——CAUTION IN IMPROMPTU SPEECHES.——MANAGEMENT OF HIS PRIVATE CORRESPONDENCE.——KNOWLEDGE OF WOODCRAFT.—— TREES AND HUMAN CHARACTER.——EXCHANGING VIEWS WITH PROFESSOR AGASSIZ.——MAGNANIMITY TOWARD OPPONENTS.——RIGHTEOUS INDIGNA- TION.——VIEWS ON THE OBSERVANCE OF THE SABBATH.

OF the two sons left to Mr. Lincoln after the death of Willie in 1862, Robert, the older, was a student in Harvard College, until appointed to service on the staff of General Grant; and "Little Tad," or Thomas, the youngest, was the only one remaining in the White House during the last hard years. He was ten years old in 1863, a bright and lovable child, and his father was associated with him in constant and affectionate companionship. The boy was much with him in his walks and journeys about Washington, and even in his vis- its to the army in the field; and the father would often gain a brief respite from his heavy cares by sharing in the sports and frolics of the light-hearted boy. At the White House Tad was a general favorite, and was free to go and come at will. No matter who was with the President, or how intently he might be absorbed, little Tad was always welcome. "It was an impressive and affecting sight," says Mr. Carpenter, an in- mate of the White House for several months, "to see the burdened President lost for the time being in the affectionate parent, as he would take the little fellow in his arms upon the withdrawal of visitors, and caress him with all the fondness of a mother for the babe upon her bosom." Hon. W. D. Kelley says: "I think no father ever loved his children more fondly than he. The President never seemed grander in my

PRESIDENT LINCOLN AND "LITTLE TAD."

sight than when, stealing upon him in the evening, I would find him with a book open before him, with little Tad beside him. There were, of course, a great many curious books sent to him, and it seemed to be one of the special delights of his life to open those books at such an hour that his boy could stand beside him, and they could talk as he turned over the pages, the father thus giving to the son a portion of that care and attention of which he was ordinarily deprived by the duties of office pressing upon him."

Tad lived to be eighteen years old, dying in Chicago in 1871. It was well said of him that he "gave to the sad and solemn White House the only comic relief it knew."

TAD AT CABINET MEETINGS.

As Tad had great indulgence from every one at the White House, "it sometimes happened that, while the President and his Cabinet were anxiously discussing affairs of state, and were in the midst of questions of great moment, Tad would burst into the room, bubbling with excitement, and insist that his complaint or request should be attended to at once. Sometimes it was the woes of some ill-clad petitioner, repulsed by the ushers, that aroused his childish wrath. At other times he would insist on being allowed to drag before the President of the United States a particularly youthful suitor, whose tale he had heard for himself, and who appeared in the presence with an air of mingled terror and amusement. It may be added that office-seekers generally he regarded with undisguised contempt."

A REPRIEVE FOR A CONDEMNED TURKEY.

"A friend of the Lincoln family," says Noah Brooks, "once sent a fine live turkey to the White House, with the request that it should be served on the President's Christmas table. But Christmas was then several weeks off, and in the interim Tad won the confidence and esteem of the turkey, as he did the affection of every living thing with which he came in contact. 'Jack,' as the fowl had been named, was an object of great interest to Tad, who fed him, petted him, and began to teach him to follow his young master. One day, just before Christmas, 1863, while the President was engaged with one of his Cabinet ministers on an affair of great moment, Tad burst into the room like a bomb-shell, sobbing and crying with rage and indignation. The turkey was about to be killed. Tad had procured from the executioner a stay of proceedings while he flew to lay the case before the President. Jack must not be killed; it was wicked. 'But,' said the President, 'Jack was sent here to be killed and eaten for this very Christmas.' 'I can't help it,' roared Tad, between his sobs. 'He's a good turkey, and I don't want him killed.' The President of the United States, pausing in the midst of his business, took a card and wrote on it an order of reprieve. The turkey's life was spared, and Tad, seizing the precious bit of paper, fled to set him at liberty."

TAD AND MR. LINCOLN REVIEWING THE ARMY OF THE POTOMAC.

When President Lincoln visited General Hooker's headquarters with the Army of the Potomac, just before the battle of Chancellorsville, Little Tad went with him, and rode with his father and General Hooker through the grand reviews that were held. "Over hill and dale," says a member of the Presidential party, "dashed the brilliant cavalcade of the General-in-Chief, surrounded by a company of officers in gay attire and sparkling with gold lace, the party being escorted by the Philadelphia Lancers, a showy troop of soldiers. In the midst, or at the head, rose and fell, as the horses galloped afar, the form of Lincoln, conspicuous by his height and his tall black hat. And ever on the flanks of the hurrying column flew, like a flag or banneret, Tad's little gray riding-cloak. The soldiers soon learned of Tad's presence in the army, and wherever he went on horseback he easily divided the honors with his father. The men cheered and shouted and waved their hats when they saw the dear face and tall figure of the good President, then the best-beloved man in the world; but to these men of war, far away from home and children, the sight of that fresh-faced and laughing boy seemed an inspiration. They cheered like mad.''

LINCOLN'S LITERARY TASTES.—FONDNESS FOR POETRY AND MUSIC.

It has been said of Mr. Lincoln that he lacked imagination. It was certainly not one of the faculties of his mind which had been largely cultivated. He relied more upon the exercise of reason and logic, in all his intellectual processes, than upon fancy or imagination. Still, there are often striking figures of speech to be met with in his writings, and he had a great fondness for poetry and music. He had studied Shakespeare diligently in his youth, and portions of the plays he repeated with singular accuracy. He had a special liking for the minor poems of Thomas Hood and Oliver Wendell Holmes. Dr. Holmes, writing in July, 1885, says that of all the tributes received by him, the one of which he was most proud was from ''good Abraham Lincoln,'' who had a great liking for the poem of ''The Last Leaf,'' and ''repeated it from memory to Governor Andrew, as the Governor himself told me.'' Mr. Arnold says: ''He had a great love for poetry and eloquence, and his taste and judgment were excellent. Next to Shakespeare among the poets was Burns. There was a lecture of his upon Burns full of favorite quotations and sound criticisms.''

N. P. Willis stated that he was pleasantly surprised during a ride with Mr. and Mrs. Lincoln, by the President's referring to his poem of ''Parrhasius,'' and quoting several lines from it.

His musical tastes, says Mr. Brooks, ''were simple and uncultivated, his choice being old airs, songs, and ballads, among which the plaintive Scotch songs were best liked. 'Annie Laurie,' 'Mary of Argyle,' and especially 'Auld Robin Gray,' never lost their charm for him; and all songs which had for their theme the rapid flight of time, decay, the recollections of early days, were sure to make a deep impression. The song which he liked best, above all others, was one called 'Twenty Years Ago'—a simple air, the words to which are supposed to be uttered by a man who revisits the play-ground of his youth. I remember that, one night at the White House, when a few ladies were with the family, singing at the piano-forte, he asked for a little song in which the writer describes his sensations when revisiting the scenes of his boy-hood, dwelling mournfully on the vanished joys and the delightful associations of forty years ago. It is not likely that there was anything in Lincoln's lost youth that he would wish to recall; but there was a certain melancholy and half-morbid strain in that song which struck a responsive chord in his heart. The lines sunk into his memory, and I remember that he quoted them, as if to himself, long afterward."

HIS REMARKABLE MEMORY.

Lincoln's memory was extraordinarily retentive, and without conscious effort he stored in his mind every whimsical or ludicrous narrative which was read or heard. "On several occasions," says Mr. Brooks, "I have held in my hand a printed slip while he was repeating its contents to somebody else, and the precision with which he delivered every word was marvellous." He was fond of the writings of Orpheus C. Kerr and Petroleum V. Nasby, and amused himself and others in the darkest hours by quoting passages from these authors. Nasby's letter from "Wingert's Corners, Ohio," on the threatening prospects of a migration of the negroes from the South, and the President's "evident intenshun of colonizin on 'em in the North," he especially relished. After rehearsing a portion of this letter to his guests at the Soldiers' Home one evening, a sedate New England gentleman expressed surprise that he could find time for memorizing such things. 'Oh,' said Lincoln, 'I don't. If I like a thing, it *just sticks* after once reading it or hearing it.' He once recited a long and doleful ballad, something like 'Vilikins and his Dinah,' the production of a rural Kentucky bard, and when he had finished he added with a laugh, 'I don't believe I have thought of that before for forty years.'" Mr. Arnold testifies: "Although his reading was not extensive, yet his memory was so retentive and so ready, that in history, poetry, and in general literature, few, if any, marked any deficiency. As an illustration of the powers of his memory, may be related the following: A gentleman called at the White House one day, and introduced to him two officers serving in the army, one a Swede and the other a Norwegian. Immediately he repeated, to their delight, a poem of some eight or ten verses descriptive of Scandinavian scenery, and an old Norse legend. He said he had read the poem in a newspaper some years before, and liked it, but it had passed out of his memory until their visit had recalled it. The two books which he read most were the Bible and Shakespeare. With these he was perfectly familiar. From the Bible, as has before been stated, he quoted frequently, and he read it daily, while Shakespeare was his constant companion. He took a copy with him almost always when travelling, and read it at leisure moments."

NOT A LATIN SCHOLAR.

Mr. Lincoln was never ashamed to confess the deficiencies in his early education. A distinguished party, comprising Mr. George Thompson, the English anti-slavery orator, the Rev. John Pierpont, Oliver Johnson, and Hon. Lewis Clephane, once called upon him, and during the conversation Mr. Pierpont turned to Mr. Thompson, and repeated a Latin quotation from the classics. Mr. Lincoln, leaning forward in his chair, looked from one to the other inquiringly, and then remarked, with a smile, "*Which*, I suppose you are both aware, *I* do not understand."

NEVER READ A NOVEL.

While Edwin Forrest was playing an engagement at Ford's Theatre, Mr. Carpenter spoke to the President one day of the actor's fine interpretation of the character of Riche-lieu, and advised him to witness the performance. The conversation occurred in the presence of Senator Harris, of New York. "Who wrote the play?" asked the President of Mr. Carpenter. "Bulwer," was the reply. "Ah!" he rejoined; "well, I knew Bulwer wrote novels, but I did not know he was a play-writer also. It may seem somewhat strange to say," he continued, "but *I never read an entire novel in my life.*" Said Judge Harris, "Is it possible?" "Yes," returned the President, "it is a fact. I once commenced 'Ivanhoe,' but never finished it."

SOLACE IN THEATRICAL REPRESENTATION.—ANECDOTES OF BOOTH, M'CULLOCH, AND HACKETT.

Among the few diversions which Mr. Lincoln allowed himself in Washington, was an occasional visit to the theatre, to witness a representation of some good play by a favorite actor. He felt the absolute necessity of some relaxation from the terrible strain of anxiety; and at least he was secure from the everlasting importunities of politicians and office-seekers, while seated behind the screen in a box at the theatre. Here he could forget himself for the time being, while watching the varied, amusing, stirring scenes on the mimic stage before him. He enjoyed the renditions of Booth with great zest, yet after witnessing "The Merchant of Venice," he remarked on the way home: "It was a good performance, but I had a thousand times rather read it at home, if it were not for Booth's playing. A farce, or a comedy, is best *played;* a tragedy is best *read* at home."

He was much pleased one night with Mr. McCulloch's delineation of the character of "Edgar," which the actor played in support of Edwin Forrest's "Lear." He wished to convey his approval to the young actor, and asked Mr. Brooks, his companion at the moment, with characteristic simplicity: "Do you suppose he would come to the box if we sent word?" Mr. McCulloch was summoned, and, standing at the door of the box in his stage attire, received the thanks of the President, accompanied with words of discriminating praise for the excellence of his delineation.

With his keen sense of humor, the President appreciated to the utmost the inimitable presentation of "Falstaff," by Mr. J. H. Hackett. His desire to accord praise wherever it was merited, led him to express his admiration in a note to the actor. An interchange of slight civilities followed, ending at last in a singular situation. Entering the President's office late one evening, Mr. Brooks noticed Mr. Hackett sitting in the waiting room. Mr. Lincoln inquired anxiously if there were any one outside. On being told, he said, half sadly, "Oh, I can't see him; I can't see him. I was in hopes he had gone away." Then he added, "Now, this illustrates the difficulty of having pleasant friends in this place. You know I liked Hackett as an actor, and how I wrote to tell him so. He sent me that book, and there I thought the matter would end. He is a master of his place in the profession, I suppose, and well fixed in it. But just because we had a little friendly correspondence, such as any two men might have, he wants something. What do you suppose he wants?" I could not guess, and Lincoln added, "Well, he wants to be consul at London. Oh, dear!"

APT DRAMATIC CRITICISMS.

Mr. James E. Murdock, the distinguished Shakespearean scholar and actor, says: "I was charmed, in a conversation with Mr. Lincoln, with the aptness and originality of his remarks and criticisms. His clear insight into characterization was apparent in the expression of his conception of the personalities of 'Falstaff' and old 'Weller,' who seemed to be especial favorites with him. He regarded old Weller as a sort of stage-coach embodiment or type of the Fat Knight, the latter being a tavern reflection, as it were, of the velvet-and-brocade or court side of wit and humor, and the other the familiar or road-side phase or expression of it; but both suggestive of *'the cap-and-bells,'* and furnishing the materials for whole-some merriment. Speaking of Dickens, he said that his works of fiction were so near the reality that the author seemed to him to have picked up his materials from actual life as he el-bowed his way through its crowded thoroughfares, after the manner, in a certain sense, of Shakespeare himself."

METHODS OF LITERARY WORK.—CAUTION IN IMPROMPTU SPEECHES.

Mr. Lincoln was not a ready writer, and when preparing documents or speeches of special importance, he altered and elaborated his sentences with patient care. His public utter-ances were so widely reported and so mercilessly discussed that he acquired caution in expressing himself without due preparation. It is stated, on what seems good authority, that his Gettysburg speech, brief and simple as it is, was rewritten many times before it finally met his approval. He began, also, to be guarded in responding to demands for impromptu speeches, which were constantly being called for. Mr. Brooks relates that "once, being notified that he was to be serenaded, just after some notable military or political event, he asked me to come to dinner, 'so as to be on hand and see the fun afterward,' as he said. He excused himself as soon as we had dined, and, while the bands were playing, the crowds cheering, and the rockets bursting, outside the house, he made his reappearance in the parlor, with a roll of manuscript in his hand. Perhaps, noticing a look of surprise on my face, he said, 'I know what you are thinking about. You think it mighty queer that an old stump-speaker like myself should not be able to address a crowd like this outside without a written speech. But you must remember I am, in a certain way, talking to the country, and I have to be mighty careful. Now, the last time I made an off-hand speech, in answer to a serenade, I used the phrase, as applied to the rebels, 'turned tail and ran.' Some very nice Boston folks, I am grieved to hear, were very much outraged by that phrase, which they thought improper. So I resolved to make no more impromptu speeches, if I could help it.'"

MANAGEMENT OF HIS PRIVATE CORRESPONDENCE.

Mr. Lincoln was a tireless worker, and delegated no duties to others which he could perform himself. His correspondence was enormous, and as a rule he wrote his most important letters with his own hand, frequently going to the trouble of taking copies, which were filed with careful order in a cabinet, the interior of which was divided into pigeon-holes. These pigeon-holes, as Mr. Brooks tells us, "were lettered in alphabetical order, but a few were devoted to individuals. Horace Greeley, I remember, had a pigeon-hole by himself; so did each of several generals who wrote often to him. One compartment, labeled 'W. & W.' excited much curiosity, but I never asked what it meant, and one night, being sent to the cabinet for a letter which the President wanted, he said, 'I see you looking at my 'W. & W.' Can you guess what that stands for?' Of course it was useless to guess. 'Well,' said he, with a roguish twinkle of the eye, 'that's Weed and Wood—Thurlow and Fernandy.' Then he added, with an indescribable chuckle, 'That's a pair of 'em.' When asked why he did not have a letter-book and copying-press, he said, "A letter-book might be easily stolen and carried off, but that stock of filed letters would be a *back-load*."

The work involved in the care of his correspondence imposed a great deal of reading, together with writing. One old friend, living on the Pacific coast, treated him regularly to letters of tedious length, to which the President conscientiously attended. But finally, receiving a communication covering *seventy pages*, "he broke down and never read another."

HIS KNOWLEDGE OF WOODCRAFT.—TREES AND HUMAN CHARACTER.

A lady who once rode with Mr. Lincoln, in the Presidential carriage, to the Soldiers' Home, says: "Around the 'Home' grows every variety of tree, particularly of the evergreen class. Their branches brushed into the carriage as we passed along, and left with us that pleasant woody smell belonging to leaves. One of the ladies, catching a bit of green from one of these intruding branches, said it was cedar, and another thought it spruce.

" 'Let me discourse on a theme I understand,' said the President. 'I know all about trees, in right of being a backwoodsman. I'll show you the difference between spruce, pine and cedar, and this shred of green, which is neither one nor the other, but a kind of illegitimate cypress.' He then proceeded to gather specimens of each, and explain the distinctive formation of foliage belonging to every species. 'Trees,' he said, 'are as deceptive in their likeness to one another as are certain classes of men, amongst whom none but a physiognomist's eye can detect dissimilar moral features until events have developed them. Do you know it would be a good thing if in all the schools proposed and carried out by the improvement of modern thinkers, we could have *a school of events?*' 'A school of events?' repeated the lady he addressed. 'Yes,' he continued, 'since it is only by that active development that character and ability can be tested. Understand me, I now mean men, not trees; *they* can be tried, and an analysis of their strength obtained less expensive to life and human interests than man's. What I say now is a mere whim, you know; but when I speak of a school of events, I mean one in which, before entering real life, students might pass through the mimic vicissitudes and situations that are necessary to bring out their powers and mark the calibre to which they are assigned. Thus, one could select from the graduates an invincible soldier, equal to any position, with no such word as fail; a martyr to right, ready to give up life in the cause; a politician too cunning to be outwitted; and so on. These things have all to be tried, and their sometime failure creates confusion as well as disappointment. There is no

more dangerous or expensive analysis than that which consists
of trying a man.'"

EXCHANGING VIEWS WITH PROFESSOR AGASSIZ.

Among Mr. Lincoln's callers one Sunday evening, was
the distinguished scientist Prof. Agassiz. The two men were
somewhat alike in their simple, shy, and unpretending nature,
and at first felt their way with each other like two school-boys.
Mr. Lincoln began conversation by saying to Prof. Agassiz,
"I never knew how to properly pronounce your name; won't
you give me a little lesson at that, please?" Then he asked
if it were of French or Swiss derivation, to which the Professor
replied that it was partly of each. That led to a discussion of
different languages, the President speaking several words in
different languages which had the same root as similar words
in our own tongue; then he illustrated that by one or two
anecdotes. But he soon returned to his gentle cross-examination of Agassiz, and found out how the Professor studied, how
he composed, and how he delivered his lectures; how he
found different tastes in his audiences in different portions of
the country. When afterwards asked why he put such questions to his learned visitor, he said: "Why, what we got
from him isn't printed in the books; the other things are."
But Lincoln did not do all the questioning. In his turn,
Agassiz asked Lincoln if he had ever engaged in lecturing.
Lincoln gave the outline of a lecture, which he had partly
written years before, to show the origin of inventions, and
prove that there is nothing new under the sun. "I think I
can show," said he, "at least, in a fanciful way, that all the
modern inventions were known centuries ago." Agassiz
begged that Lincoln would finish the lecture some time.
Lincoln replied that he had the manuscript somewhere in his
papers, "and," said he, "when I get out of this place, I'll
finish it up, perhaps."

MAGNANIMITY TOWARD OPPONENTS.

So great was Lincoln's magnanimity, and so keen his

sense of justice, that he never allowed personal considerations to influence his official acts. It is probably true that it was easy for him to forgive an injury; but in any event, he was incapable of using his position as President to gratify his private resentments. It was once represented to him that a recent appointee to an important office had been bitterly opposed to him politically. "I suppose," said he, "the Judge did behave pretty ugly; but that wouldn't make him any less fit for this place, and I have a Scriptural authority for appointing him. You recollect that while the Lord on Mount Sinai was getting out a commission for Aaron, that same Aaron was at the foot of the mountain making a false god, a golden calf, for the people to worship; yet Aaron got his commission, you know." At another time, when remonstrated with upon the appointment to place of one of his former opponents, he said: "Nobody will deny that he is a first-rate man for the place, and I am bound to see that his opposition to me personally shall not interfere with my giving the people a good officer." And on another occasion of similar character, when remonstrated with by members of his Cabinet, he said: "I can't afford to punish every person who has seen fit to oppose my election. We want a competent man in this office; and I know of no one who could perform the duties better than the one proposed."

RIGHTEOUS INDIGNATION.

With all his self-abnegation, Mr. Lincoln could be stern when the occasion warranted it. As an illustration the following incident is related: An officer who had been cashiered from the service, forced himself several times into Mr. Lincoln's presence, to plead for a reversal of his sentence. Each time he read a long argument attempting to prove that he had received unjust treatment. The President listened to him patiently; but the facts, on their most favorable showing, did not seem to him to sanction his interference. In the last interview, the man waxed wroth, and turning abruptly said:

"Well, Mr. President, I see you are fully determined not to do me justice!" This was too aggravating, even for Mr. Lincoln. Manifesting, however, no more feeling than that indicated by a slight compression of the lips, he quietly arose, laid down a package of papers he held in his hand, and then suddenly seizing the disgraced officer by the coat collar, he marched him forcibly to the door, saying, as he ejected him into the passage: "Sir, I give you fair warning never to show yourself in this room again. I can bear censure, but not insult!" In a whining tone the man begged for his papers, which he had dropped. "Begone, sir," said the President, "your papers will be sent to you. I never wish to see your face again!"

VIEWS ON THE OBSERVANCE OF THE SABBATH.

The views and wishes of Mr. Lincoln with respect to the observance of the Sabbath in the army, are well expressed in the following proclamation :

"The President, Commander-in-Chief of the Army and Navy, desires and enjoins the orderly observance of the Sabbath by the officers and men in the military and naval service. The importance to man and beast of the prescribed weekly rest, the sacred rights of Christian soldiers and sailors, a becoming deference to the best sentiment of Christian people, and a due regard for the Divine Will, demand that Sunday labor in the army and navy be reduced to the measure of strict necessity. The discipline and character of the national forces should not suffer, nor the cause they defend be imperiled, by the profanation of the day or name of the Most High. 'At the time of public distress,' adopting the words of Washington in 1776, 'men may find enough to do in the service of their God and their country, without abandoning themselves to vice and immorality.' The first general order issued by the Father of his Country after the Declaration of Independence, indicates the spirit in which our institutions were founded and should ever be defended: 'The General hopes and trusts that every officer and man will endeavor to live and act as becomes a Christian soldier defending the dearest rights and liberties of his country.' "

CHAPTER XIV.

EVENTS IN 1864.——LOOKING TOWARD ANOTHER PRESIDENTIAL TERM.——MR. LINCOLN'S ATTITUDE IN THE MATTER.——A GOOD DEAL PUZZLED.——WILLING TO GO OR STAY.——EXPRESSION OF HIS VIEWS AND FEELINGS. —— RIVAL CANDIDATES FOR THE NOMINATION.——CHASE'S ACHILLEAN WRATH ——LINCOLN'S STRAIGHTFORWARDNESS.——HARMONY RESTORED.——THE BALTIMORE CONVENTION.——ITS DECISION "NOT TO SWAP HORSES WHILE CROSSING A STREAM."——THE BATTLE-SUMMER OF 1864.——WASHINGTON AGAIN THREATENED.——MR. LINCOLN UNDER FIRE.——UNPOPULAR MEASURES.——THE PRESIDENT'S PERPLEXITIES AND TRIALS.——THE FAMOUS LETTER "TO WHOM IT MAY CONCERN."——LITTLE EXPECTATION OF RE-ELECTION.——DANGERS OF ASSASSINATION.——A THRILLING EXPERIENCE. ——LINCOLN'S FORCED SERENITY.——BURDENS TOO GREAT TO BE ENDURED. ——A WELL-NIGH BROKEN-HEARTED MAN.——NEVER HOPED TO BE GLAD AGAIN.——ENVYING THE SOLDIER WHO SLEEPS ON THE GROUND.——"THE SADDEST MAN IN THE WORLD."——SPIRITUALIZED BY SUFFERING.

THE year 1864 witnessed another Presidential election, and one which was attended by the most novel and extraordinary circumstances. It was held while a considerable portion of the people were engaged in armed rebellion against the authority of the National Government, and was not participated in by the voters of several entire States. Aside from these unique features, it marked a most critical epoch in the history of the country, and in that of Abraham Lincoln as well. The policy and acts of the administration, even the question of the further prosecution of the war, were to be submitted to the sovereign tribunal of the people; and with their verdict would be recorded also the popular measure of approval or disapproval of President Lincoln. Those who knew him best during his first official term pronounce him singularly free from plans and calculations regarding his own political future. He was too absorbed in public cares and duties, too nearly crushed by the great burdens resting upon him, to give thought or attention to questions of personal ambition. It had never been his aim during his Presidential life to look far ahead. His purpose was to deal wisely and soberly with questions that arose from day to day and hour to hour; to adapt himself and his actions to the exigencies of the present, and in that way to earn security for the future.   He himself said, using a forcible and apt illustration borrowed from his early life: "The pilots on our Western rivers steer from *point to point*, as they call it—setting the course of the boat no farther than they can see ; and that is all I propose to myself in the great problems that are set before me."

MR. LINCOLN'S ATTITUDE REGARDING A SECOND TERM.

Yet while Mr. Lincoln seemingly gave little heed to the question of a second Presidential term, it must not be inferred that he was indifferent regarding it.   His nature was one of those rare ones which, though desiring approbation, are yet able to live without it.   His whole life had been a schooling in self-reliance and independence, and the last three years especially had rendered him an adept in that stern philosophy. But he was thoroughly human, and deep down in his nature was a craving for human sympathy and support.   Knowing that he had done his best, and was entitled to the full approval of his countrymen, he no doubt felt that it would be a pleasant thing to receive that approval, by being called to serve them for another term.   To one friend he remarked, using his old figure of "the people's attorney," "If the people think I have managed their case for them well enough to trust me to *carry it up to the next term*, I am sure I shall be glad to take it."   He evidently dreaded the rebuke that would be contained in a failure to be re-nominated ; yet it seemed unbecoming to him, in the critical condition of the country, to make any personal effort to that end.   To these considerations were added his extreme weariness, and longing for release from his oppressive burdens.

A GOOD DEAL PUZZLED.—WILLING TO GO OR STAY.—EXPRESSION OF HIS VIEWS AND FEELINGS.

From these various complications, Mr. Lincoln's embarrassment and perplexity, as the time for holding the Republican Convention drew near, were extreme. A journalistic friend (Mr. J. M. Winchell), who had a lengthy conversation with him on the subject, gives what is no doubt a correct idea of his state of mind at that period. "Mr. Lincoln received me," says Mr. Winchell, "kindly and courteously; but his manner was quite changed. It was not now the country about which his anxiety prevailed, but himself. There was an embarrassment about him which he could not quite conceal. I thought it proper to state in the outset that I wished simply to know whatever he was free to tell me in regard to his own willingness or unwillingness to accept a re-nomination. The reply was a monologue of an hour's duration, and one that wholly absorbed me, as it seemed to absorb himself. He remained seated nearly all the time. He was restless, often changing position, and occasionally, in some intense moment, wheeling his body around in his chair and throwing a leg over the arm. This was the only grotesque thing I recollect about him; his voice and manner were very earnest, and he uttered no jokes and told no anecdotes. He began by saying that, as yet, he was not a candidate for re-nomination. He distinctly denied that he was a party to any effort to that end, notwithstanding I knew that there were movements in his favor in all parts of the Northern States. These movements were, of course, without his prompting, as he positively assured me that with one or two exceptions he had scarcely conversed on the subject with his most intimate friends. He was not quite sure whether he desired a re-nomination. Such had been the responsibility of the office—so oppressive had he found its cares, so terrible its perplexities—that he felt as though the moment when he could relinquish the burden and retire to private life would be the sweetest he could possibly experience. But, he said, he would not deny that a re-election would also have its gratification to his feelings. He did not seek it, nor would he do so; he did not desire it for any ambitious or selfish purpose; but, after the crisis the country was passing through under his Presidency, and the efforts he had made conscientiously to discharge the duties imposed upon him, it would be a very sweet satisfaction to him to know that he had secured the approval of his fellow citizens, and earned the highest testimonial of confidence they could bestow. This was the gist of the hour's monologue; and I believe he spoke sincerely. His voice, his manner, armed his modest and sensible words with a power of conviction. He seldom looked me in the face while he was talking; he seemed almost to be gazing into the future. I am sure it was not a pleasant thing for him to seem to be speaking in his own interest. For himself, he affirmed that he should make no promises of office to any one, as an inducement for support. If nominated and elected, he should be grateful to his friends; but the interests of the country must always be first considered."

RIVAL CANDIDATES FOR THE NOMINATION.

The principal candidates talked of as successors to Mr. Lincoln were Secretary Chase, Gen. Fremont, and Gen. Grant. Of the latter, Mr. Lincoln said, with characteristic frankness and generosity: "If he could be more useful as President in putting down the rebellion, I would be content. He is pledged to our policy of emancipation and the employment of negro soldiers; and if this policy is carried out, it will not make much difference who is President." But Gen. Grant's good sense prevailed over his injudicious advisers, and he promptly refused to allow his name to be presented to the convention.

CHASE'S ACHILLEAN WRATH.

The most formidable candidate for the nomination was Secretary Chase. The relations between him and the President had not been latterly very harmonious; and the breach was greatly widened by a bitter personal assault on Mr. Chase, by Gen. F. P. Blair, a newly-elected Congressman from Missouri, made on the floor of the House, about the middle of April, under circumstances which led Mr. Chase to suppose that the President inspired, or at least approved, the attack. Mr. Chase was very angry, and an open rupture between his friends and those of the President was narrowly averted. Mr. Riddle, a Congressman from Mr. Chase's State (Ohio), relates that on the evening after Gen. Blair's offensive speech, he was to accompany Mr. Chase on a visit to Baltimore. "I was shown," says Mr. Riddle, "to the Secretary's private car, where I found him alone, and in a frenzy of rage. A copy of Blair's speech had been shown him at the station, and I was the sole witness of his Achillean wrath. He threatened to leave the train at once, and send the President his resignation; but was persuaded to go on to Baltimore. He wished to forward his resignation from there, but concluded to withhold it till his return to Washington the next day."

LINCOLN'S STRAIGHTFORWARDNESS.—HARMONY RESTORED.

"At Baltimore," continues Mr. Riddle, "I excused myself, and took the return train for Washington. I did not overestimate the danger to the Union cause. It would be a fatal error to defeat Mr. Lincoln at the Baltimore Convention; yet how could he succeed, with the angry resignation of Mr. Chase, and the defection of his friends—the powerful and aggressive radicals? Reaching Washington, I went to the White House direct. I knew the President could not have been a party to Blair's assault, and I wanted his personal assurances to communicate to Mr. Chase at the earliest moment. I was accompanied by Judge Spaulding, an eminent member of the House, fully sharing Mr. Chase's confidence, and somewhat cool toward the President. We found Mr. Lincoln drawn up behind his table, with papers before him, quite grim, evidently prepared for the battle which he supposed awaited him. Without taking a seat, hat in hand, I stated frankly, not without emotion, the condition of affairs, —the public danger, my entire confidence in him, my sole purpose there, the reason of Judge Spaulding's presence, and that we were there in no way as representatives of Mr. Chase. Mr. Lincoln was visibly affected. The tones of confidence, sympathy, personal regard, were strangers to him at that time. Softening, almost melting, he came round to us, shook our hands again and again, returned to his place, and standing there, took up and opened out, from their remote origin, the whole web of matters connected with the present complication. He spoke an hour—calm, clear, direct, simple. He reprehended Blair severely, and stated that he had no knowledge of his speech until after Blair left Washington. We were permitted to communicate this to Mr. Chase. He was satisfied with the President's explanation, and at the Baltimore Convention my large acquaintance enabled me to open the way for Governor Dennison, of Ohio, to become its presiding officer. All recognized the good effect of the organization of that body by the friends of Mr. Chase."

THE BALTIMORE CONVENTION.— ITS DECISION "NOT TO SWAP HORSES WHILE CROSSING A STREAM."

The National Republican Convention which met at Baltimore on the 8th of June, adopted resolutions heartily approving the course of the administration and especially the policy of emancipation, and completed its good work by nominating Abraham Lincoln as its candidate for President for another term. Andrew Johnson, of Tennessee, was nominated for Vice-president.

That Mr. Lincoln was gratified at this proof of confidence and esteem there can be no doubt. In his acceptance of the nomination, he said, with the most delicate modesty: "I view this call to a second term as in no wise more flattering to myself than as an expression of the public judgment that I may better finish a difficult work than could one less severely schooled to the task." And with characteristic humor, he thanked a visiting delegation for their good opinion of him, saying: "I have not permitted myself to conclude that I am the best man in the country; but I am reminded of the old Dutch farmer, who remarked to a companion that *it was not best to swap horses while crossing a stream.*"

THE BATTLE-SUMMER OF 1864.—WASHINGTON AGAIN THREATENED.—MR. LINCOLN UNDER FIRE.

Great excitement and alarm pervaded Washington in the month of July, 1864, when General Early threatened the city, and his rebel cavalry cut off railroad communication with the North, and were ravaging the country roundabout with fire and sword. Mr. Neill says of the imminence of the danger: "I lived in the country, thirteen miles from the city, near the junction of the Baltimore and Washington turnpike with the railroad. After breakfast, on Tuesday, July 12, I went as usual in a railway car to the city, and before noon my house was surrounded by General Bradley Johnson's insurgent cavalry, who had made an attempt to capture the New York express train, and robbed the country store near by of its contents. The presence of the cavalry stopped all travel by railroad; and Senator Ramsey, of Minnesota, who happened to be in Washington, found no way to the North except by descending the Potomac to its mouth, and then ascending Chesapeake bay to the city of Baltimore. While the cavalry was in the fields around my home, the enemy's infantry was marching toward the capital by what was called the Seventh street road, and they set fire to the residence of Hon. Montgomery Blair, who had been Postmaster-General. As I sat in my room at the President's, the smoke of the burning mansion was visible; but business was transacted with as much quietness as if the foe were hundreds of miles distant. Mr. Fox, the assistant Secretary of the Navy, had, in a private note, informed the President that if there was a necessity to leave the city he would find a steamer in readiness at the wharf at the foot of Sixth street. About one o'clock of the afternoon of each day of the skirmishing, the President would enter his carriage, and drive to the forts, in the suburbs, and watch the soldiers repulse the invaders.'' Another account says: ''President Lincoln visited the lines in person, and refused to retire, although urged to do so. He exposed himself freely at Fort Stevens, and a surgeon stànding alongside of him was wounded by a ball which struck a gun and glanced.''

For several days Washington was in great danger of capture. Nearly all its forces had been sent forward to reinforce Gen. Grant, and it was comparatively defenseless. But its slender garrison, mostly raw recruits, held out gallantly under the encouragement of the President, until Gen. Grant sent a column to attack Early, who promptly withdrew, and the crisis was over. This was the last time the enemy threatened the national capital. From that time he had enough to do to defend Richmond.

UNPOPULAR MEASURES.—THE PRESIDENT'S PERPLEXITIES AND TRIALS.

Mr. Lincoln labored under deep depression during the Summer of 1864. The Army of the Potomac achieved apparently very little in return for its enormous expenditure of blood and treasure. Until the victories of Farragut in Mobile Bay, late in August, and Sherman at Atlanta a few days later, the gloom was unrelieved. The people were restless and impatient, and vented their displeasure upon the administration, holding it responsible for all reverses and disappointments, and giving grudging praise for success at any point. The popular displeasure was increased by the President's call for 500,000 additional troops, made July 18th; a measure which some of his strongest friends deprecated, as likely to jeopardize his reelection in November. ''It is not a personal question at all,'' said Mr. Lincoln. ''It matters not what becomes of *me*. *We must have the men.* If I go down, I intend to go like the Cumberland, with my colors flying.'' To the question,

When is the war to end? he said : "Surely I feel as deep an interest in this question as any other can ; but I do not wish to name a day, a month, or a year, when it is to end. We accepted this war *for an object*,—a worthy object; and the war will end *when that object is attained*. Under God, I hope it *never will end until that time*."

Ex-Governor Bross furnishes an account of an interview with Mr. Lincoln during the dark period : "The last time I saw Mr. Lincoln, till, as a pall-bearer, I accompanied his remains to their last resting-place, was in the early part of August, 1864. It was directly after the frightful disaster at Petersburg, and I was on my way to the front, to recover, if possible, the body of my brother, Col. John A. Bross, who fell there at the head of his regiment. I found the President with a large pile of documents before him. He laid down his pen and gave me a cordial but rather melancholy welcome, asking anxiously for news from the West. Neither of us could shut our eyes to the gloom which hung over the entire country. The terrible losses of the Wilderness, and the awful disaster at Petersburg, weighed heavily upon our spirits. To a question, I answered that the people expected a still more vigorous prosecution of the war; more troops and needful appliances would, if called for, be forthcoming. 'I will tell you what the people want,' said the President, 'they want, and must have, *success*. But whether that come or not, I shall stay *right here*, and do my duty. Here I shall be ; and they may come and hang me on that tree (pointing out of the window to one), but, God helping me, I shall never desert my post.' This was said in a way that assured me that these were the sentiments of his inmost soul."

THE FAMOUS LETTER "TO WHOM IT MAY CONCERN."

The President, about this time, was greatly worried by Horace Greeley and others, who importuned him to receive negotiations for peace from the rebel authorities. He at length said to Mr. Greeley: "I not only intend a sincere effort for peace, but you shall be a personal witness that it is made." On the same day that the call for additional troops was made, the President issued, through Mr. Greeley, the famous letter, "To whom it may concern," promising safe conduct to any person or persons authorized to present "any proposition which embraces the restoration of peace, the *integrity of the whole Union*, and the *abandonment of slavery*." Nothing came of the proposed negotiations, except to stop for a time the mischievous fault-finding; which was, of course, the result aimed at by Mr. Lincoln. The act was severely condemned by many Republicans; but Mr. Lincoln only said: "It is hardly fair for them to say the letter amounts to *nothing*. It will shut up Greeley, and satisfy the people who are clamoring for peace. That's *something*, anyhow!"

LITTLE EXPECTATION OF RE-ELECTION.

So much blame was heaped upon the government, and so great the dissatisfaction at the North, that Mr. Lincoln looked upon the election of his competitor, Gen. McClellan, and his own retirement, as not improbable. An incident in evidence of his discouragement is related by Secretary Welles. Entering the Executive office one day, Mr. Welles was asked to write his name across the back of a sealed paper which the President handed him. The names of several other members of the Cabinet were already on the paper, with the dates of signature. After the election, Mr. Lincoln opened the document in the presence of his Cabinet, and read to them its contents, as follows:

"EXECUTIVE MANSION, WASHINGTON, August 23, 1864.

This morning, as for some days past, it seems exceedingly probable that this administration will not be re-elected. Then it will be my duty to co-operate with the President-elect so as to save the Union between the election and the inauguration. A. LINCOLN."

By this careful prevision had Mr. Lincoln pledged himself to give that unselfish and patriotic assistance to his successor, of which he stood so sorely in need during the months previous to his own accession to the Presidency.

DANGERS OF ASSASSINATION.

As the desperation of the rebels and the opposition to Mr. Lincoln at the North increased, fears were entertained by his friends that an attempt might be made upon his life. Mr. Lincoln himself paid but little heed to these forebodings of evil. He said, philosophically: "I long ago made up my mind that if anybody wants to kill me, he will do it. If I wore a shirt of mail and kept myself surrounded by a body-guard, it would be all the same. There are a thousand ways of getting at a man if it is desirable that he should be killed. Besides, in this case, it seems to me, the man who would succeed me would be just as objectionable to my enemies—if I have any." One dark night, as he was going out with a friend, he took along a heavy cane, remarking good-humoredly that "mother" (Mrs. Lincoln) had "got a notion into her head that I shall be assassinated, and to please her I take a cane when I go over to the War Department at nights—when I don't forget it."

A THRILLING EXPERIENCE.

It is probable that the attempts upon the life of President Lincoln were more numerous than even yet is generally known. An incident of a very thrilling character, which might easily have involved a shocking tragedy, is related by Mr. John W. Nichols, who, from the summer of 1862 until 1865, was one of the President's body-guard. "One night, about the middle of August, 1864," says Mr. Nichols, "I was doing sentinel duty at the large gate through which entrance was had to the grounds of the Soldiers' Home, near Washington, where Mr. Lincoln spent much time in summer. About eleven o'clock I heard a rifle-shot in the direction of the city, and shortly afterwards I heard approaching hoof-beats. In two or three minutes a horse came dashing up, and I recognized the belated President. The horse he rode was a very spirited one, and was Mr. Lincoln's favorite saddle-horse. As horse and rider approached the gate, I noticed that the President was bareheaded. As soon as I had assisted him in checking his steed, the President said to me: 'He came pretty near getting away with me, didn't he? He got the bit in his teeth before I could draw the rein.' I then asked him where his hat was; and he replied that somebody had fired a gun off down at the foot of the hill, and that his horse had become scared and had jerked his hat off. I led the animal to the Executive Cottage, and the President dismounted and entered. Thinking the affair rather strange, a corporal and myself started off to investigate. When we reached the place whence the sound of the shot had come— a point where the driveway intersects with the main road— we found the President's hat. It was a plain silk hat, and upon examination we discovered a *bullet-hole* through the crown. We searched the locality thoroughly, but without avail. Next day I gave Mr. Lincoln his hat, and called his attention to the bullet-hole. He made some humorous remark, to the effect that it was made by some foolish marksman, and was not intended for him; but added that he wished nothing said about the matter. We all felt confident it was an attempt to kill the President, and after that he never rode alone."

LINCOLN'S FORCED SERENITY.

Amidst his terrible trials, Mr. Lincoln often exhibited a forced and sorrowful serenity, which many mistook for apathy. Even his oldest and best friends were sometimes deceived in this way. Hon. Leonard Swett relates a touching instance: "In the summer of 1864, when Grant was pounding his way toward Richmond in those terrible battles of the Wilderness, myself and wife were in Washington trying to do what little two persons could do toward alleviating the sufferings of the maimed and dying in the vast hospitals of that city. We tried to be thorough and systematic. We took the first man we came to, brought him delicacies, wrote letters to his friends, or did for him whatever else he most needed; then the next man, and so on. Day after day cars and ambulances were coming in, laden with untold sorrows for thousands of homes. After weeks of this kind of experience my feelings became so wrought up that I said to myself: The country cannot long endure this sacrifice. In mercy, both to North and South, every man capable of bearing arms must be hurried forward to Grant to end this fearful slaughter at the earliest possible moment. I went to President Lincoln at the White House, and poured myself out to him. He was sitting by an open window; and as I paused, a bird lit upon a branch just outside and was twittering and singing most joyously. Mr. Lincoln, imitating the bird, said: '*Tweet, tweet, tweet;* isn't he singing sweetly?' I felt as if my legs had been cut from under me. I rose, took my hat, and said: 'I see the country is safer than I thought.' As I moved toward the door, Mr. Lincoln called out, in his hearty, familiar way: 'Here, Swett, come back and sit down.' Then he went on: 'It is impossible for a man in my position not to have thought of all those things. Weeks ago every man capable of bearing arms was ordered to the front, and everything you have suggested has been done.' ''

BURDENS TOO GREAT TO BE ENDURED.—A WELL-NIGH BROKEN HEART.

The burdens borne by Mr. Lincoln seemed never to tell so seriously on his strength and vitality as in this terrible battle-summer of 1864. For him there had been no respite, no holiday. Others left the heat and dust of Washington, for rest and recuperation; but he remained at his post. The demands upon him were incessant; one anxiety and excitement followed another, and under the relentless strain even his sturdy strength began to give way. "I sometimes fancy," said he, with pathetic good-humor, "that every one of the numerous grist ground through here daily, from a Senator seeking a war with France down to a poor woman after a place in the Treasury Department, darted at me with thumb and finger, picked out *their especial piece of my vitality,* and carried it off. When I get through with such a day's work there is only one word which can express my condition, and that is *flabbiness.*" Once Mr. Brooks "found him sitting in his chair so collapsed and weary that he did not look up or speak when I addressed him. He put out his hand, mechanically, as if to shake hands, when I told him I had come at his bidding. Presently he roused a little, and remarked that he had had '*a mighty hard day.*'" Mr. Riddle, who saw him at this period, after some months' absence, says he was shocked, on gaining admission to the President, "by his appearance—that of a *baited, cornered man,* always on the defence against attacks that he could not openly meet and defy or punish." Mr. Carpenter, an inmate of the White House, says: "Absorbed in his papers, he would become unconscious of my presence, while I intently studied every line and shade of expression in that furrowed face. There were days when I could scarcely look into it without crying. During the first week of the battles of the Wilderness he scarcely slept at all. Passing through the main hall of the domestic apartment on one of these days, I met him, clad in a long morning wrapper, pacing back and forth a narrow passage leading to one of the windows, his hands behind him, great black rings under his eyes, his head bent forward upon his breast,—altogether such a picture of the effects of sorrow, care, and anxiety as would have melted the hearts of the worst of his adversaries, who so mistakenly applied to him the epithets of tyrant and usurper."

Mr. Edward Dicey says: "Never in my knowledge have I seen a sadder face than that of the late President during the time his features were familiar to me. It is so easy to be wise after the event; but it seems to me now that one ought somehow to have foreseen that the stamp of a sad end was impressed by nature on that rugged, haggard face. The exceeding sadness of the eyes and their strange sweetness were the one redeeming feature in a face of unusual plainness, and there was about them that odd, weird look, which some eyes possess, of seeming to see more than the outer objects of the world around.''

NEVER HOPED TO BE GLAD AGAIN.

Mr. Lincoln's family and friends strove to beguile him of his melancholy. They took him to places of amusement; they walked and drove with him in the pleasantest scenes about the capital; and above all, they talked with him of times past, seeking to divert his mind from its present distress by reviving memories of more joyous days. His old friends were, as Mr. Arnold states, ''shocked with the change in his appearance. They had known him at his home, and at the courts in Illinois, with a frame of iron and nerves of steel; as a man who hardly knew what illness was, ever genial and sparkling with frolic and fun, nearly always cheery and bright. Now, they saw the wrinkles on his face and forehead deepen into furrows; the laugh of old days was less frequent, and it did not seem to come from the heart. Anxiety, responsibility, care, thought, disasters, defeats, the injustice of friends, wore upon his giant frame, and his nerves of steel became at times irritable. He said one day, with a pathos which language cannot describe: 'I feel as though I shall *never be glad again.*' ''

ENVYING THE SOLDIER WHO SLEEPS ON THE GROUND.

The Hon. Schuyler Colfax repeats a similarly pathetic expression which fell from the lips of the afflicted President. ''One morning, calling upon him on business, I found him looking more than usually pale and careworn, and inquired the reason. He replied with the bad news he had received at a late hour the previous night, which had not yet been communicated to the press, adding that he had not closed his eyes or breakfasted; and, with an expression I shall never forget, he exclaimed, 'How willingly would I exchange places to-day with the soldier who sleeps on the ground in the Army of the Potomac!'"

"THE SADDEST MAN IN THE WORLD."

A lady who saw Mr. Lincoln in the Summer of 1864 for the first time, and who had expected to see "a very homely man," says: "I was totally unprepared for the impression instantly made upon me. So bowed and sorrow-laden was his whole person, expressing such weariness of mind and body, as he dropped himself heavily from step to step down to the ground. But his face!—oh, the pathos of it!—haggard, drawn into fixed lines of unutterable sadness, with a look of loneliness, as of a soul whose depth of sorrow and bitterness no human sympathy could ever reach. I was so penetrated with the anguish and settled grief in every feature, that I gazed at him through tears, and felt I had stepped upon the threshhold of a sanctuary too sacred for human feet. The impression I carried away was that I had seen, not so much the President of the United States, as *the saddest man in the world.*"

SPIRITUALIZED BY SUFFERING.

The changes in Mr. Lincoln's appearance were noted in the subdued, refined, purified expression of his face, as of one struggling almost against hope, but still patiently enduring. Mr. Brooks says: "I have known impressionable women, touched by his sad face and his gentle bearing, to go away in tears." Another observer, the Rev. C. B. Crane, wrote at the time: "The President looks thin and careworn. His form is bowed as by a crushing load; his flesh is wasted as by incessant solicitude; and his face is thin and furrowed and pale, as though it had become spiritualized by the vicarious pain which he endured in bearing on himself all the calamities of his country."

CHAPTER XV.

THE PRESIDENTIAL ELECTION OF 1864.——LINCOLN CHOSEN FOR A SECOND TERM.
——HOW HE RECEIVED THE NEWS.——KIND WORDS FOR HIS DEFEATED
ADVERSARY.——IMPORTANCE OF LINCOLN'S RE-ELECTION.——COMMENTS BY
GRANT AND SEWARD.——PERSONAL PLANS FOR THE FUTURE.——LINCOLN'S
RELATIONS WITH CHASE.——CHASE'S RETIREMENT FROM THE CABINET.——
LINCOLN APPOINTS HIM CHIEF-JUSTICE.——LINCOLN'S MAGNANIMITY.——
FOURTH ANNUAL MESSAGE.——A CONFIDENTIAL DISCLOSURE.——COLORED
FOLKS' RECEPTION AT THE WHITE HOUSE.——PASSAGE OF THE AMENDMENT
PROHIBITING SLAVERY.——"THIS ENDS THE JOB."——LINCOLN AND THE
SOUTHERN PEACE COMMISSIONERS.——THE MEETING IN HAMPTON ROADS.——
LINCOLN'S IMPRESSIONS OF A. H. STEPHENS.——A "NUBBIN" OF A MAN.——
THE SECOND INAUGURATION.——THE SECOND INAUGURAL ADDRESS.——AN
AUSPICIOUS OMEN.

THE Presidential election of 1864 demonstrated the abiding confidence of the people in Mr. Lincoln and his administration. Every loyal State but three—New Jersey, Delaware, and Kentucky—gave him its electoral vote; and his popular majority over General McClellan, the Democratic candidate, was upwards of 400,000. Mr. Lincoln was cheered but not exultant. Late in the evening of election day, he said, in response to public congratulations: "I am thankful to God for this approval of the people. But while deeply grateful for this mark of their confidence in me, if I know my own heart, my gratitude is free from any taint of personal triumph. It is not in my nature to triumph over any one; but I give thanks to Almighty God for this evidence of the people's resolution to stand by free government and the rights of humanity."

HOW MR. LINCOLN RECEIVED THE ELECTION NEWS.

While the election returns were coming in, early in the evening, Mr. Lincoln was at the War Department. Mr. C. A. Dana, Assistant Secretary of War, who was present on this occasion, says: "General Eckert was coming in continually with telegrams containing election returns. Mr. Stanton would read them, and the President would look at them and comment upon them. Presently there came a lull in the returns, and Mr. Lincoln called me up to a place by his side. 'Dana,' said he, 'have you ever read any of the writings of Petroleum V. Nasby?' 'No, sir,' I said, 'I have only looked at some of them, and they seemed to me funny.' 'Well,' said he, 'let me read you a specimen,' and, pulling out a thin yellow-covered pamphlet from his breast pocket, he began to read aloud. Mr. Stanton viewed this proceeding with great impatience, as I could see; but Mr. Lincoln paid no attention to that. He would read a page or a story, pause to con a new election telegram, and then open the book again and go ahead with a new passage. Finally Mr. Chase came in; and presently Mr. Whitelaw Reid, and then the reading was interrupted. Mr. Stanton went to the door and beckoned me into the next room. I shall never forget his indignation at what seemed to him disgusting nonsense."

KIND WORDS FOR HIS DEFEATED ADVERSARY.

The morning following the election, one of his private secretaries, Mr. Neill, coming to the Executive office earlier than usual, found Mr. Lincoln at his table engaged in his regular routine of official work. "Entering the room," says Mr. Neill, "I took a seat by his side, extended my hand, and congratulated him upon the vote, for the country's sake and for his own sake. Turning away from the papers which had been occupying his attention, he spoke kindly of his competitor, the calm, prudent General, and great organizer."

IMPORTANCE OF LINCOLN'S RE-ELECTION.—COMMENTS BY GRANT AND SEWARD.

The importance of Mr. Lincoln's re-election, to the country and to himself, is forcibly stated by General Grant and Secretary Seward. The former telegraphed from City Point, the day following: "The victory is worth more to the country than a battle won." And the same evening, at a public gathering held to celebrate the event, Mr. Seward said: "The election has placed our President beyond the pale of human envy or human harm, as he is above the pale of human ambition. Henceforth all men will come to see him as we have seen him—a true, loyal, patient, patriotic and benevolent man. Having no longer any motive to malign or injure him, detraction will cease, and Abraham Lincoln will take his place with Washington, and Franklin, and Jefferson, and Adams, and Jackson—among the benefactors of the country and of the human race.''

PERSONAL PLANS FOR THE FUTURE.

Mr. Lincoln evidently felt greatly reassured by the result of what had seemed to him a very doubtful contest; but with the return of cheerfulness came also the dread of continuing his official labors. He began to long and plan for that happy period, at the end of the second term, when he should be free from public burdens. "Mrs. Lincoln desired to go to Europe for a long tour of pleasure," says Mr. Brooks. "The President was disposed to gratify her wish; but he fixed his eyes on California as a place of permanent residence. He had heard so much of the delightful climate and the abundant natural productions of California, that he had become possessed of a strong desire to visit the State, and remain there if he were satisfied with the results of his observations. 'When we leave this place,' he said, one day, 'we shall have enough, I think, to take care of us old people. The boys must look out for themselves. I guess mother will be satisfied with six months or so in Europe. After that I should really like to go to California and take a look at the Pacific coast.' ''

LINCOLN'S RELATIONS WITH CHASE.—CHASE'S RETIREMENT FROM THE CABINET.

When, after the Baltimore Convention, Mr. Chase proposed to resign his position as Secretary of the Treasury, he was persuaded by influential friends of himself and Mr. Lincoln to reconsider his determination. Chief among these friends was Hon. John Brough, the sturdy "War Governor" of Ohio. Later in the summer of 1864, the relations between the President and Secretary Chase again became inharmonious; the latter determined a second time to resign, and communicated that fact in a confidential letter to Gov. Brough. Hon. Wm. Henry Smith, at that time Ohio's Secretary of State, and intimately acquainted with the circumstances as they occurred, says: "Mr. Brough went directly to Washington to bring about another reconciliation. After talking the matter over with Mr. Chase and Mr. Stanton, he called on the President and urged a settlement that would retain the services of Mr. Chase in the Treasury Department. Mr. Lincoln was very kind, and admitted the force of all that was urged; but finally said, with a quiet but impressive firmness, 'Brough, I think you had better *give up the job* this time.' And thereupon he gave reasons why it was unwise for Mr. Chase to continue longer in the Cabinet."

CHASE APPOINTED CHIEF-JUSTICE.—LINCOLN'S MAGNANIMITY.

In the autumn, the Chief-Justiceship became vacant by the death of Judge R. B. Taney; and the friends of Mr. Chase, who was then in retirement, desired his elevation to that honorable seat. Congressman Riddle, who was designated to present the matter to the President, says: "After hearing what I had to say, Mr. Lincoln asked, 'Will this content Mr. Chase?' 'It is said that those bitten of the Presidency die of it,' I replied. His smile showed he would not take that answer. I added: 'Mr. Chase is conscious of ability to serve the country as President. We should expect the greatest from him.' 'He would not disappoint you, were it in his reach. But I should be sorry to see a Chief-Justice anxious to *swap* for it.' I said then what I had already said to Mr. Chase: that I would rather be the Chief-Justice than the President. I urged that the purity and elevation of Mr. Chase's character guaranteed the dignity of the station from all compromise; that momentous questions must arise, involving recent exercises of power, without precedents to guide the court; that the honor of the Government would be safe in the hands of Mr. Chase. 'Would you *pack* the Supreme Court,' he asked, a little sharply. 'Would you have a Judge with no preconceived notions of law?' was my response. 'True, true,' was his laughing reply; 'how could I find any one, fit for the place, who has not some definite notions on all questions likely to arise?'"

The proposed appointment of Mr. Chase as Chief-Justice was severely criticised by certain friends of Mr. Lincoln, who believed Mr. Chase was personally hostile to the President, and could not understand the latter's magnanimity in thus ignoring personal considerations. When told of these criticisms, Mr. Lincoln said: "My friends all over the country are trying to put up the bars between me and Governor Chase. I have a vast number of messages and letters from men who think they are my friends, imploring and warning me not to appoint him. Now I know more about Governor Chase's hostility to me than any of these men can tell me; but *I am going to nominate him.*"

FOURTH ANNUAL MESSAGE.

Early in December the President submitted to Congress his fourth annual message—a brief and business-like statement of the prospects and purposes of the Government. Its first sentence is: "The most remarkable feature in the military operations of the year is General Sherman's attempted march of three hundred miles directly through the insurgent region." Then follows a reference to the important movements that had occurred during the year, "to the effect of moulding society for durability in the Union." The document closes with the following explicit statement: "In presenting the abandonment of armed resistance to the national authority, on the part of the insurgents, as the only indispensable condi-tion to ending the war on the part of the Government, I *retract nothing* heretofore said as to slavery. If the people should, by whatever mode or means, make it an executive duty to re-enslave such persons, *another, and not I,* must be their instrument to perform it. In stating a single condition of peace, I mean simply to say that the war will cease on the part of the Government whenever it shall have ceased on the part of those who began it.''

A CONFIDENTIAL DISCLOSURE.

An intimate friend of the President found him in his office engaged in revising the draft of the above message. With an affectation of confidential secrecy, he said, ''I expect you want to know all about Sherman's raid?'' On being answered in the affirmative, he continued, ''Well, then, I'll read you this paragraph from my message.'' He read the paragraph referring to Sherman's march, as quoted above,— an entirely non-committal statement, giving no indication either of the direction of the march or of the point from which news from Sherman was expected. Laying the paper down, and taking off his spectacles, the President laughed heartily at his friend's disappointment, but added, kindly, ''Well, my dear fellow, that's all that Congress will know about it, anyhow.''

COLORED FOLKS' RECEPTION AT THE WHITE HOUSE.

New Year's day, 1865, was marked by a memorable incident. Among the crowds gathered in the White House grounds stood groups of colored people, watching with eager eyes the tide of people flowing in at the open door to exchange salutations with the President. It was a privilege heretofore reserved for the white race; but now, as the line of visitors thinned, showing that the reception was nearly over, the boldest of the colored men drew near the door with faltering step. Some were in conventional attire, others in fantastic dress, and others again in laborers' garb. The novel procession moved into the vestibule and on into the room where the

President was holding the republican court. Timid and doubting, though determined, they ventured where their oppressed and down-trodden race had never appeared before, and with the keen, anxious, inquiring look on their dark faces, seemed like a herd of wild creatures from the woods, in a strange and dangerous place. The reception had been unusually well attended, and the President was nearly overcome with fatigue. Mrs. Swisshelm, who was present, relates that when her turn came to take his hand she could not forbear exclaiming, "May the Lord have mercy on you, poor man; for the people have none!" He threw up his head and laughed pleasantly, and those around him joined in the laugh. When he saw the dusky faces of his unwonted visitors, he rallied from his fatigue and gave them a hearty welcome. They were wild with joy. Thronging about him, they pressed and kissed his hand, laughing and weeping at once, and exclaiming, "God bless Massa Linkum!" It was a scene not easy to forget: the thanks and adoration of a race paid to their deliverer.

PASSAGE OF THE AMENDMENT PROHIBITING SLAVERY.— "THIS ENDS THE JOB."

Mr. Lincoln had, ever since issuing the Emancipation Proclamation, earnestly desired that that measure should be perfected by a Constitutional amendment forever prohibiting slavery in the territory of the United States. He had discussed the matter fully with his friends in Congress, and repeatedly urged them to press it to an issue. Just before the Baltimore Convention, described in the preceding chapter, he urged Senator Morgan of New York, chairman of the National Republican Committee, to have the proposed amendment made the "key-note of the speeches, and the key-note of the platform." Congressman Rollins, of Missouri, relates that the President said to him, "The passage of the amendment will *clinch the whole matter.*" The subject was already definitely before Congress. In December, 1863, joint resolutions for this great end had been introduced in the House by Hon. James M. Ashley, of Ohio, and in the Senate by Hon. Charles Sumner, of Massachusetts, and Hon. J. B. Henderson, of Missouri. Senator Trumbull, of the Judiciary Committee, to whom the Senate resolutions were referred, reported a substitute for the amendment, which, in April, 1864, passed the Senate by a vote of thirty-eight to six; but reaching the House, June 15, it failed to get the necessary two-thirds vote, and was defeated. At the next session of Congress the resolutions were again presented to the House, and, after a protracted debate, were passed (January 13, 1865,) by a vote of one hundred and nineteen to fifty-six. Illinois was the first State to ratify the amendment; and others promptly followed. Mr. Lincoln was grateful and delighted. He remarked, "This ends the job;" adding, "I feel proud that Illinois is a little ahead."

LINCOLN AND THE SOUTHERN PEACE COMMISSIONERS.—THE MEETING IN HAMPTON ROADS.

Overtures having been made, through General Grant, for a meeting between the President and certain "peace commissioners" representing the belligerents, Mr. Lincoln, anxious that nothing should be left undone that might evidence his desire to bring the war to a close, consented to the interview. On the morning of February 2, 1865, he left Washington, quite privately, in order to accomplish his mission without awakening the gossip and criticism which publicity would excite. At Fortress Monroe he was joined by Secretary Seward. The next morning they received the Southern Commissioners—Messrs. Stephens, Hunter, and Campbell—on board the U. S. steam transport, River Queen, in Hampton Roads. The conference, says Mr. Seward, "was altogether informal. There was no attendance of secretaries, clerks, or other witnesses. Nothing was written or read. The conversation, although earnest and free, was calm and courteous and kind on both sides. The Richmond party approached the subject rather indirectly, and at no time did they either make categorical demands or tender formal stipulations or absolute refusals. Nevertheless, during the conference, which lasted four hours, the several points at issue between the government and the insurgents were distinctly raised and discussed, fully, intelligently, and in an amicable spirit."

The meeting was fruitless. The commissioners asked, as a preliminary step, the recognition of Jefferson Davis as President of the Southern Confederacy. Mr. Lincoln declined, stating that "the only ground on which he could rest the justice of the war—either with his own people or with foreign powers—was that it was not a war of conquest, for the States had never been separated from the Union. Consequently, he could not recognize another government inside of the one of which he alone was President; nor admit the separate independence of States that were yet a part of the Union. 'That,' said he, 'would be doing what you have so long asked Europe to do in vain, and be resigning the only thing the armies of the Union have been fighting for.' Mr. Hunter, one of the commissioners, made a long reply to this, insisting that the recognition of Davis's power to make a treaty was the first and indispensable step to peace, and referred to the correspondence between King Charles I. and his Parliament, as a trustworthy precedent of a constitutional ruler treating with rebels. Mr. Lincoln's face then wore that indescribable expression which generally preceded his hardest hits, and he remarked: 'Upon questions of history I must refer you to Mr. Seward, for he is posted in such things, and I don't pretend to be. My only distinct recollection of the matter is that Charles lost his head.'"

LINCOLN'S IMPRESSIONS OF A. H. STEPHENS.—A "NUBBIN"
OF A MAN.

Alexander H. Stephens, one of the commissioners at the meeting on board the River Queen, and the Vice-president of the waning Southern Confederacy, was a very small man physically, with a complexion so yellow as to suggest an ear of ripe corn. Mr. Lincoln gave the following humorous account of the meeting with him: "Mr. Stephens had on an overcoat about three sizes too big for him, with an old-fashioned high collar. The cabin soon began to get pretty warm, and after a while he stood up and pulled off his big coat. He slipped it off just about as you would husk an ear of corn. I couldn't help thinking, as I looked first at the overcoat and then at the man, 'Well, that's the *biggest shuck* and the *smallest nubbin* I ever laid eyes on.' "

THE SECOND INAUGURATION.

The evening of March 3, 1865, the President had remained with his Cabinet at the Capitol until a late hour, finishing the business pertaining to the last acts of the old Congress. His face had the ineffaceable care-worn look, yet his manner was cheerful, and he appeared to be occupied with the work of the moment, to the exclusion of all thoughts of the future, or of the great event of the morrow.

Rain prevailed during the morning of inauguration day, but before noon it had ceased falling. The new Senate, convened for a special session, was organized, and Andrew Johnson sworn in its presence into the office of Vice-president. Shortly after twelve o'clock, Mr. Lincoln entered the chamber and joined the august procession, which then moved to the eastern portico. As Mr. Lincoln stepped forward to take the oath of office, a flood of sunlight suddenly burst from the clouds, illuminating his face and form as he bowed to the acclamations of the people. Speaking of this incident next day, he said, "Did you notice that sunburst? It made my heart jump."

Cheers and shouts rent the air, as the President prepared to speak his inaugural. He raised his arm, and the crowd hushed to catch his opening words. He paused, as though thronging memories impeded utterance ; then, in a voice clear and strong, but touched with pathos, he read that imperishable composition,

THE SECOND INAUGURAL ADDRESS.

"*Fellow-Countrymen:* At this second appearing to take the oath of the Presidential office, there is less occasion for an extended address than there was at the first. Then, a statement, somewhat in detail, of a course to be pursued, seemed fitting and proper. Now, at the expiration of four years, during which public declarations have been constantly called forth on every point and phase of the great contest which still absorbs the attention and engrosses the energies of the Nation; little that is new could be presented. The progress of our arms, upon which all else chiefly depends, is as well known to the public as to myself ; and it is, I trust, reasonably satisfactory and encouraging to all. With high hope for the future, no prediction in regard to it is ventured.

"On the occasion corresponding to this, four years ago, all thoughts were anxiously directed to an impending civil war. All dreaded it, all sought to avoid it. While the inaugural address was being delivered from this place, devoted altogether to saving the Union without war, insurgent agents were in the city, seeking to destroy it with war,— seeking to dissolve the Union, and divide the effects by negotiation. Both parties deprecated war, but one of them would make war rather than let the Nation survive, and the other would accept war rather than let it perish ; and the war came. One-eighth of the whole population were colored slaves, not distributed generally over the Union, but localized in the southern part of it. These slaves constituted a peculiar and powerful interest. All knew that this interest was somehow the cause of the war. To strengthen, perpetuate, and extend this interest, was the object for which the insurgents would rend the Union by war ; while the Government claimed no right to do more than to restrict the territorial enlargement of it.

"Neither party expected for the war the magnitude or the duration which it has already attained. Neither anticipated that the cause of the conflict might cease with, or even before the conflict itself should cease. Each looked for an easier triumph, and a result less fundamental and astounding. Both read the same Bible, and pray to the same God, and each invokes His aid against the other. It may seem strange that any men should dare to ask a just God's assistance in wringing their bread from the sweat of other men's faces. But let us judge not, that we be not judged. The prayer of both could not be answered. That of neither has been answered fully. The Almighty has his own purposes. 'Woe unto the world because of offenses, for it must needs be that offenses come, but woe to that man by whom the offense cometh.' If we shall suppose that American slavery is one of these offenses, which, in the Providence of God, must needs come, but which, having continued through his appointed time, he now wills to remove, and that he gives to North and South this terrible war, as the woe due to those by whom the offense came, shall we discern therein any departure from those Divine attributes which the believers in a living God always ascribe to him? Fondly do we hope, fervently do we pray, that this mighty scourge of war may soon pass away. Yet, if God wills that it continue until all the wealth piled by the bondman's two hundred and fifty years of unrequited toil shall be sunk, and until every drop of blood drawn by the lash shall be paid by another drawn with the sword, as was said three thousand years ago, so still it must be said: 'The judgments of the Lord are true and righteous altogether.'

"With malice toward none, with charity for all, with firmness in the right, as God gives us to see the right, let us strive on to finish the work we are in; to bind up the nation's wounds; to care for him who shall have borne the battle, and for his widow and for his orphan; to do all which may achieve and cherish a just and lasting peace among ourselves and with all nations."

AN AUSPICIOUS OMEN.

As the procession moved from the Capitol to the White House, at the close of the ceremonies, a bright star was visible in the heavens. The crowds gazing upon the unwonted phenomenon noted it as an auspicious omen, like the baptism of sunshine which had seemed to consecrate the President anew to his exalted office.

CHAPTER XVI.

END OF THE REBELLION.——THE LAST ACTS IN THE GREAT TRAGEDY.——MR.
LINCOLN AT THE FRONT.——A MEMORABLE MEETING.——LINCOLN, GRANT,
SHERMAN, AND PORTER.——SHERMAN'S FAREWELL TO LINCOLN.——THE
LIFE ON SHIPBOARD.——VISIT TO PETERSBURG.——LINCOLN AND THE REBEL
PRISONERS. —— LINCOLN IN RICHMOND. ——THE NEGROES WELCOMING THEIR
"GREAT MESSIAH."——A WARM RECEPTION.——LEE'S SURRENDER.——MR.
LINCOLN RECEIVES THE NEWS.——THE UNIVERSAL REJOICING.——LIN-
COLN'S LAST SPEECH TO THE PUBLIC.——BEHIND THE SCENES.——LINCOLN'S
INTENTIONS TOWARD THE SOUTH.——HIS DESIRE FOR RECONCILIATION.

GREAT EVENTS crowded upon each other in the last few
weeks of the rebellion; and we must pass rapidly over them,
giving special prominence only to those with which President
Lincoln was personally connected. The Army of the Potomac under Grant, which for nearly a year had been incessantly
engaged with the army of General Lee, had forced the latter,
fighting desperately at every step, back through the Wilderness,
into the defences about Richmond; and Lee's early surrender
or retreat southward seemed the only remaining alternatives.
But the latter course, disastrous as it would have been for the
Confederacy, was rendered impracticable by the comprehensive plan of operations that had been adopted a year before.
Interposed between Richmond and the South was now the
powerful army of General Sherman. This daring and self-
reliant officer, after his brilliant triumph at Atlanta the previous Fall, had pushed on to Savannah, and captured that city
also; then turning his veteran columns northward, he had
swept like a dread meteor through South Carolina, destroying
the proud city of Charleston, and then Columbia, the State Capital. General Johnston, with a strong force, vainly tried to stay
his progress through North Carolina; and after a desperate but
unsuccessful battle at Bentonville (March 20), the opposition
gave way, and the Union troops occupied Goldsboro, an important point a hundred miles south of Richmond, commanding the

Southern railway communications of the rebel capital. The situation was singularly dramatic and impressive. In this narrow theatre of war were now being rendered, with all the leading actors on the stage, the closing scenes of that great and bloody tragedy. Grant on the north and Sherman on the south were grinding Lee and Johnston between them like upper and nether millstones.

MR. LINCOLN AT THE FRONT.

The last days of March brought unmistakable signs of the speedy breaking-up of the rebellion. Mr. Lincoln, filled with anticipation not unmixed with anxiety, wished to be at the front. "When we came to the end of the War and the breaking-up of things," says Gen. Grant, "one of Lincoln's friends said to me, 'I think Lincoln would like to come down and spend a few days at City Point, but he is afraid if he does come it might look like interfering with the movements of the army, and after all that has been said about other Generals he hesitates.' I was told, if Lincoln had a hint from me that he would be welcome, he would come by the first boat. Of course I sent word that the President could do me no greater honor than to come down and be my guest. Lincoln came down, and we spent several days riding around the lines. He was a very fine horseman. He talked, and talked, and talked; and the old man seemed to enjoy it, and said: 'How grateful I feel to be with the boys and see what is being done at Richmond.' He never asked a question about the movements. He would say: 'Tell me what has been done; not what is to be done.' He would sit for hours tilted back in his chair, with his hand shading his eyes, watching the movements of the men with the greatest interest." Another account says: "Lincoln made many visits with Grant to the lines around Richmond and Petersburg. On such occasions he usually rode one of the General's fine bay horses, called 'Cincinnati.' He was a good horseman, and made his way through swamps and over corduroy roads as well as the best trooper in the command. The soldiers invariably recognized him, and greeted him, wherever he appeared amongst them, with cheers that were no lip service, but came from the depth of their hearts. He always had a pleasant salute or a friendly word for the men in the ranks.''

A MEMORABLE MEETING.—LINCOLN, GRANT, SHERMAN, AND PORTER.

Much of the time during the President's visit to the army he had his quarters on the steamer River Queen, lying in the James river at City Point. It was the same vessel on which he had received the rebel peace commissioners, a month before; and the one on which he had made the journey from Washington. On the 27th of March a memorable interview occurred in the cabin of this vessel, between President Lincoln, Generals Grant and Sherman, and Admiral Porter. Gen. Sherman thus describes the interview: "I left Goldsboro on the 25th of March, and reached City Point on the afternoon of March 27th. I found General Grant and staff occupying a neat set of log huts, on a bluff overlooking the James river. The General's family was with him. We had quite a long and friendly talk, when he remarked that the President, Mr. Lincoln, was near by in a steamer lying at the dock, and he proposed that we should call at once. We did so, and found Mr. Lincoln on board the River Queen. We had met in the early part of the war, and he recognized me, and received me with a warmth of manner and expression that was most grateful. We then sat some time in the after-cabin, and Mr. Lincoln made many inquiries about the events which attended the march from Savannah to Goldsboro, and seemed to enjoy the humorous stories about 'our bummers,' of which he had heard much. When in lively conversation, his face brightened wonderfully; but if the conversation flagged, his face assumed a sad and sorrowful expression. General Grant and

I explained to him that my next move from Goldsboro would bring my army, increased to 80,000 men by Schofield's and Terry's reinforcements, in close communication with General Grant's army, then investing Lee and Richmond; and that unless Lee could effect his escape, and make junction with Johnston in North Carolina, he would soon be shut up in Richmond with no possibility of supplies, and would have to surrender. Mr. Lincoln was extremely interested in this view of the case, and we explained that Lee's only chance was to escape, join Johnston, and, being then between me in North Carolina and Grant in Virginia, he could choose which to fight. Mr. Lincoln seemed unusually impressed with this; but General Grant explained that at the very moment of our conversation General Sheridan was pressing his cavalry across James river from the north to the south, that he would, with this cavalry, so extend his left below Petersburg as to meet the South Shore Road, and that if Lee should 'let go' his fortified lines, he (Grant) would follow him so close that he could not possibly fall on me alone in North Carolina. I, in like manner, expressed the fullest confidence that my army in North Carolina was willing to cope with Lee and Johnston combined, till Grant could come up. But we both agreed that one more bloody battle was likely to occur before the close of the war. Mr. Lincoln repeatedly inquired as to General Schofield's ability, in my absence, and seemed anxious that I should return to North Carolina, and more than once exclaimed: 'Must more blood be shed? Cannot this last bloody battle be avoided?' We explained that we had to presume that General Lee was a real general; that he must see that Johnston alone was no barrier to my progress, and that if my army of 80,000 veterans should reach Burksville, he was lost in Richmond; and that we were forced to believe he would not await that inevitable conclusion, but make one more desperate effort."

SHERMAN'S FAREWELL TO LINCOLN.

General Sherman adds to the account of the interview on board the River Queen: "When I left Mr. Lincoln I was more than ever impressed by his kindly nature, his deep and earnest sympathy with the afflictions of the whole people, resulting from the war, and by the march of hostile armies through the South; and that his earnest desire seemed to be to end the war speedily, without more bloodshed or devastation, and to restore all the men of both sections to their homes. In the language of his second inaugural address, he seemed to have 'charity for all, malice toward none,' and, above all, an absolute faith in the courage, manliness, and integrity of the armies in the field. When at rest or listening, his legs and arms seemed to hang almost lifeless, and his face was careworn and haggard; but, the moment he began to talk, his face lightened up, his tall form, as it were, unfolded, and he was the very impersonation of good humor and fellowship. The last words I recall as addressed to me were that he 'would feel better when I was back at Goldsboro.' We parted at the gangway of the River Queen, about noon of March 28, and I never saw him again. Of all the men I ever met, he seemed to possess more of the elements of greatness, combined with goodness, than any other."

THE PRESIDENT'S LIFE ON SHIPBOARD.

A few days after the interview described by General Sherman, the President changed his quarters to the cabin of the Malvern, Admiral Porter's flagship. The Admiral says: "The Malvern was a small vessel with poor accommodations, and not at all fitted to receive high personages. She was a captured blockade-runner, and had been given to me as a flag-ship. I offered the President my bed, but he positively declined it, and elected to sleep in a small state-room outside of the cabin occupied by my secretary. It was the smallest kind of a room, six feet long by four and a half feet wide—a small kind of a room for the President of the United States to be domiciled in; but Mr. Lincoln seemed pleased with it. When he came to breakfast the next morning, I inquired how he had slept: 'I slept well,' he answered, 'but you can't put a long sword into a short scabbard. I was *too long* for that berth.' Then I remembered he was over six feet four inches, while the berth was only six feet. That day, while we were out of the ship, all the carpenters were put to work; the state-room was taken down and increased in size to eight feet by six and a half feet. The mattress was widened to suit a berth of four feet width, and the entire state-room remodeled. Nothing was said to the President about the change in his quarters when he went to bed; but next morning he came out smiling, and said: 'A miracle happened last night; I shrank six inches in length and about a foot sideways. I got somebody else's big pillow, and slept in a better bed than I did on the River Queen.' He enjoyed it greatly; but I do think if I had given him two fence-rails to sleep on he would not have found fault. That was Abraham Lincoln, in all things relating to his own comfort. He would never permit people to put themselves out for him, under any circumstances."

VISIT TO PETERSBURG.

On the 2d of April, the stronghold of Petersburg fell into the hands of the Union troops. Mr. Lincoln, accompanied by Admiral Porter, visited the city. They joined Gen. Grant, and sat with him for nearly two hours upon the porch of a comfortable little house with a small yard in front, and crowds of citizens soon gathered at the fence to gaze upon these remarkable men of whom they had heard so much. The President's heart was filled with joy, for he felt that this was "the beginning of the end." Admiral Porter says: "Several regiments passed us *en route*, and they all seemed to recognize the President at once. 'Three cheers for Uncle Abe!' passed along among them, and the cheers were given with a vim which showed the estimation in which he was held by the soldiers. One good-natured fellow sang out, 'We'll get 'em, Abe, *where the boy had the hen;* you go home, and sleep sound to-night; we boys will put you through!' It was not a very courtier-like speech, certainly; but it was homely and honest; and so they cheered us all along the road.''

LINCOLN AND THE REBEL PRISONERS.

"That evening," continues Admiral Porter, "the sailors and marines were sent out to guard and escort in some prisoners, who were placed on board a large transport lying in the stream. There were about a thousand prisoners, more or less. The President expressed a desire to go on shore. I ordered the barge and went with him. We had to pass the transport with the prisoners. They all rushed to the side with eager curiosity. All wanted to see the Northern President. They were perfectly content. Every man had a chunk of meat and a piece of bread in his hand, and was doing his best to dispose of it. 'That's Old Abe,' said one, in a low voice. 'Give the old fellow three cheers,' said another; while a third called out: 'Hello, Abe, your bread and meat's better than pop-corn!' It was all good-natured, and not meant in unkindness. I could see no difference between them and our own men, except that they were ragged and attenuated for want of wholesome food. They were as happy a set of men as ever I saw. They could see their homes looming up before them in the distance, and knew that the war was over. 'They will never shoulder a musket again in anger,' said the President, 'and if Grant is wise he will leave them their guns to shoot crows with. It would do no harm.'''

MR. LINCOLN IN RICHMOND.

The next day (April 3) the Union advance, under Gen. Weitzel, reached and occupied Richmond; Lee being in retreat, with Grant in close pursuit. When the news of the downfall of the rebel capital reached Mr. Lincoln on board the Malvern, he exclaimed fervently: "Thank God that I have lived to see this! It seems to me I have been dreaming a horrid dream for four years, and now the nightmare is gone. *I want to see Richmond.*"

The vessel started up the river, but it was extremely difficult to proceed, as the channel was filled with torpedoes and obstructions, and they were obliged to wait until a passage could be cleared. Admiral Porter thus describes what followed: "When the channel was reported clear of torpedoes (a large number of which were taken up), I proceeded up to Richmond in the 'Malvern,' with President Lincoln. Every vessel that got through the obstructions wished to be the first one up, and pushed ahead with all steam; but they grounded, one after another, the 'Malvern' passing them all, until she also took the ground. Not to be delayed, I took the President in my barge, and, with a tug ahead with a file of marines on board, we continued on up to the city. There was a large bridge across the James about a mile below the landing, and under this a party in a small steamer were caught and held by the current, with no prospect of release without assistance. I ordered the tug to cast off and help them, leaving us in the barge to go on alone. Here we were in a solitary boat, after having set out with a number of vessels flying flags at every mast-head, hoping to enter the conquered capital in a manner befitting the rank of the President of the United States, with a further intention of firing a national salute in honor of the happy result. Mr. Lincoln was cheerful, and had his 'little story' ready for the occasion. 'Admiral, this brings to my mind a fellow who once came to me to ask for an appointment as minister abroad. Finding he could not get that, he came down to some more modest position. Finally he asked to be made a tide-waiter. When he saw he could not get that, he asked me for *an old pair of trousers.* It is sometimes well to be *humble.*'

"I had never been to Richmond before by that route, and did not know where the landing was; neither did the cockswain nor any of the barge's crew. We pulled on, hoping to see some one of whom we could inquire, but no one was in sight. The street along the river-front was as deserted as if this had been a city of the dead. The troops had been in possession some hours, but not a soldier was to be seen. The current was now rushing past us over and among rocks, on one of which we finally stuck; but I backed out and pointed for the nearest landing."

THE NEGROES WELCOMING THEIR "GREAT MESSIAH."

"There was a small house on this landing," continues Admiral Porter, "and behind it were some twelve negroes digging with spades. The leader of them was an old man sixty years of age. He raised himself to an upright position as we landed, and put his hands up to his eyes. Then he dropped his spade and sprang forward. 'Bress de Lord,' he said, 'dere is *de great Messiah!* I knowed him as soon as I seed him. He's bin in my heart fo' long yeahs, an' he's cum at las' to free his chillun from deir bondage! Glory, Hallelujah!' And he fell upon his knees before the President and kissed his feet. The others followed his example, and in a minute Mr. Lincoln was surrounded by these people, who had treasured up the recollection of him caught from a photograph, and had looked up to him for four years as the one who was to lead them out of captivity. It was a touching sight—that aged negro kneeling at the feet of the tall, gaunt-looking man who seemed in himself to be bearing all the grief of the nation, and whose sad face seemed to say, 'I suffer for you all, but will do all I can to help you.' Mr. Lincoln looked down on the poor creatures at his feet; he was much embarrassed at his position. 'Don't kneel to me,' he said, 'that is not right. You must kneel to God only, and thank Him for the liberty you will hereafter enjoy. I am but God's

humble instrument; but you may rest assured that as long as
I live no one shall put a shackle on your limbs, and you shall
have all the rights which God has given to every other free
citizen of this Republic.' It was a minute or two before I
could get the negroes to rise and leave the President. The
scene was so touching I hated to disturb it, yet we could not
stay there all day; we had to move on; so I requested the pa-
triarch to withdraw from about the President with his companions, and let us pass on. 'Yes, Mars,' said the old man, 'but
after bein' so many yeahs in de desert widout water, it's mighty
pleasant to be lookin' at las' on our spring of life. 'Scuse
us, sir; we means no disrepec' to Mars Lincoln; we means
all love and gratitude.' And then, joining hands together in
a ring, the negroes sang a hymn, with melodious and touching voices, only possessed by the negroes of the South. The
President and all of us listened respectfully while the hymn
was being sung. Four minutes at most had passed away since
we first landed at a point where, as far as the eye could reach,
the streets were entirely deserted, but now what a different
scene appeared as that hymn went forth from the negroes'
lips! The streets seemed to be suddenly alive with the colored race. They seemed to spring from the earth. They
came tumbling and shouting, from over the hills and from the
water-side, where no one was seen as we had passed. The
crowd immediately became very oppressive. We needed our
marines to keep them off. I ordered twelve of the boat's
crew to fix bayonets to their rifles and surround the President,
all of which was quickly done; but the crowd poured in so
fearfully that I thought we all stood a chance of being crushed
to death.

A WARM RECEPTION.

"At length the President spoke. He could not move for
the mass of people—he had to do something. 'My poor
friends,' he said, 'you are free—free as air. You can cast off
the name of slave and trample upon it; it will come to you

no more. Liberty is your birthright. God gave it to you as
He gave it to others, and it is a sin that you have been deprived of it for so many years. But you must try to deserve
this priceless boon. Let the world see that you merit it, and
are able to maintain it by your good works. Don't let your
joy carry you into excesses. Learn the laws and obey them ;
obey God's commandments and thank Him for giving you
liberty, for to Him you owe all things. There, now, let me
pass on ; I have but little time to spare. I want to see the
capital, and must return at once to Washington to secure to
you that liberty which you seem to prize so highly.' The
crowd shouted and screeched as if they would split the firma-
ment, though while the President was speaking you might
have heard a pin drop."

Presently the little party were able to move on. "It never
struck me," says Admiral Porter, "there was any one in that
multitude who would injure Mr. Lincoln ; it seemed to me that
he had an army of supporters there who could and would defend him against all the world. Our progress was very slow ;
we did not move a mile an hour, and the crowd was still increasing. It was a warm day, and the streets were dusty,
owing to the immense gathering which covered every part of
them, kicking up the dirt. The atmosphere was suffocating ;
but Mr. Lincoln could be seen plainly by every man, woman,
and child, towering head and shoulders above that crowd ; he
overtopped every man there. He carried his hat in his hand,
fanning his face, from which the perspiration was pouring.
He looked as if he would have given his Presidency for a glass
of water—I would have given my commission for half that.

"Now came another phase in the procession. As we
entered the city every window flew up, from ground to roof,
and every one was filled with eager, peering faces, which
turned one to another, and seemed to ask, 'Is this large man,
with soft eyes, and kind, benevolent face, the one who has
been held up to us as the incarnation of wickedness, the de-

stroyer of the South?' There was nothing like taunt or defiance in the faces of those who were gazing from the windows or craning their necks from the sidewalks to catch a view of the President. The look of every one was that of eager curiosity—nothing more. In a short time we reached the mansion of Mr. Davis, President of the Confederacy, occupied after the evacuation as the headquarters of Generals Weitzel and Shepley. There was great cheering going on. Hundreds of civilians—I don't know who they were—assembled at the front of the house to welcome Mr. Lincoln. General Shepley made a speech and gave us a lunch, after which we entered a carriage and visited the State House—the late seat of the Confederate Congress. It was in dreadful disorder, betokening a sudden and unexpected flight; members' tables were upset, bales of Confederate scrip were lying about the floor, and many official documents of some value were scattered about.

"After this inspection I urged the President to go on board the Malvern. I began to feel more heavily the responsibility resting upon me through the care of his person. The evening was approaching, and we were in a carriage open on all sides. He was glad to go; he was tired out, and wanted the quiet of the flag-ship. I was oppressed with uneasiness until we got on board and stood on deck with the President safe; then there was not a happier man anywhere than myself."

LEE'S SURRENDER.—MR. LINCOLN RECEIVES THE NEWS.

On Sunday, April 9, the President returned to Washington; and there he heard the thrilling news that Lee, with his whole army, had that day surrendered to Grant at Appomattox. Mr. Lincoln's first visit, after reaching the capital, was to the house of Secretary Seward, who had met with a severe accident during his absence, and was a prisoner in a sick room. Lincoln's heart was full of joy, and he entered immediately upon an account of his visit to Richmond and the glorious successes of the Union army; "throwing himself," as Mr. Carpenter says, "in his almost boyish exultation, at full length across the bed, supporting his head upon one hand, and in this manner reciting the story of the collapse of the Rebellion. Concluding, he lifted himself up and said: 'And now for a day of Thanksgiving!'"

THE UNIVERSAL REJOICING.—LINCOLN'S LAST SPEECHES TO THE PUBLIC.

In Washington, as in every city and town in the loyal States, there was the wildest enthusiasm over the good news from the army. Flags were flying everywhere, cannons were sounding, business was suspended, and the people gave themselves up to the impulses of joy and thanksgiving. Monday afternoon the workmen of the navy-yard marched to the White House, joining the thousands already there, and with bands playing and a tumult of rejoicing, called persistently for the President. After some delay, Mr. Lincoln appeared at the window above the main entrance, and was greeted with loud and prolonged cheers and demonstrations of love and respect. He declined to make a formal speech, saying to the excited throng beneath:

"I am very greatly rejoiced that an occasion has occurred so pleasurable that the people can't restrain themselves. I suppose that arrangements are being made for some sort of formal demonstration, perhaps this evening or to-morrow night. If there should be such a demonstration, I, of course, shall have to respond to it, and I shall have nothing to say if I dribble it out before. I see you have a band. I propose now closing up by requesting you to play a certain air, or tune. I have always thought 'Dixie' one of the best tunes I ever heard. I have heard that our adversaries over the way have attempted to appropriate it as a national air. I insisted yesterday that we had fairly captured it. I presented the question to the Attorney-General, and he gave his opinion that it is our lawful prize. I ask the band to give us a good turn upon it."

The band did give "a good turn" not only to "Dixie," but to the whimsical tune of "Yankee Doodle," after which Mr. Lincoln proposed three cheers for Gen. Grant and all under his command; and then "three more cheers for our

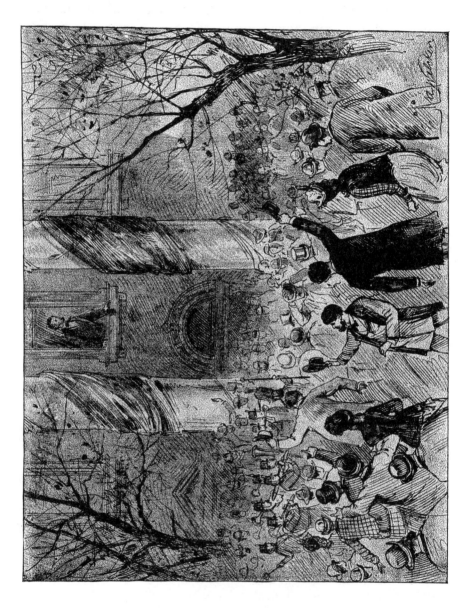

THE REJOICING IN WASHINGTON OVER LEE'S SURRENDER.—PRESIDENT LINCOLN SPEAKING FROM THE WHITE HOUSE.

gallant navy," at the close of which he bowed and retired, amid the inspiring strains of "Hail Columbia," discoursed with vigor by the patriotic musicians.

That same evening, an enthusiastic crowd gathered in front of the White House, and loud calls were made for the President. He responded briefly but pleasantly. A correspondent who was present says of the occasion: "It was my first sight of Mr. Lincoln. He appeared somewhat younger and more off-hand and vigorous than I should have expected. His bright, knowing, somewhat humorous look reminded me of a well practiced country physician who had read men through till he understood them well. There was the humorous kindness of a good-natured doctor who had seen his patients through a most awful siege of sickness, till they were now fairly and fully convalescent, and who was disposed to let the past, whatever it had cost him or them, go by for the time, and have a little cheerful congratulation."

As additional dispatches were received from the army, the joyful excitement in Washington increased. Tuesday evening, April 11, the President's mansion, the Executive Departments, and many of the business places and private residences, were illuminated, bonfires were kindled, and fireworks sent off, in celebration of the great event which stirred the hearts of the people. A vast mass of citizens crowded about the White House, as Mr. Lincoln appeared at the historic East window, and made his last speech to the American public. It was a somewhat lengthy address, and had been prepared and written out for the occasion. "We meet this evening, not in sorrow, but in gladness of heart," began Mr. Lincoln. "No part of the honor or praise is mine. To General Grant, his skillful officers and brave men, all belongs."

BEHIND THE SCENES.

Mr. Brooks, who was in the White House during the delivery of this address, gives the following glimpses behind the scenes: "As Lincoln spoke, the multitude was as silent as if the court-yard had been deserted. Then, as his speech was written on loose sheets, and the candles placed for him were too low, he took a light in his hand and went on with his reading. Soon coming to the end of a page, he found some difficulty in handling the manuscript and holding the candle-stick. A friend who stood behind the drapery of the window reached out and took the candle, and held it until the end of the speech, and the President let the loose pages fall on the floor, one by one, as fast as he was through with them. Presently, Tad, having refreshed himself at the dinner-table, came back in search of amusement. He gathered up the scattered sheets of the President's speech, and then amused himself by chasing the leaves as they fluttered from Lincoln's hand. Anon, growing impatient at his delay to drop another page, he whispered: 'Come, give me another!' The President made a queer motion with his foot toward Tad, but otherwise showed no sign that he had other thoughts than those which he was dropping to the listeners beneath. Without was a vast sea of upturned faces, each eye fixed on the form of the President. Around the tall white pillars of the portico flowed an undulating surface of human beings, stirred by emotion and lighted with the fantastic colors of fireworks. At the window, his face irradiated with patriotic joy, was the much-beloved Lincoln, reading the speech that was to be his last to the people. Behind crept back and forth, on his hands and knees, the boy of the White House, gathering up his father's carefully written pages, and occasionally lifting up his eager face, waiting for more. It was before and behind the scenes. Sometimes I wonder, when I recall that night, how much of a father's love and thought of his boy might have been mingled in Lincoln's last speech to the eager multitude.''

LINCOLN'S INTENTIONS TOWARDS THE SOUTH.—HIS DESIRE
FOR RECONCILIATION.

The last public speech delivered by the President was very largely devoted to the impending problem of reconstruction in the South. It was, he said, "fraught with great difficulty. Unlike the case of a war between independent nations, there is no authorized organ for us to treat with. No one man has authority to give up the rebellion for any other man. We simply must begin with and mould from disorganized and discordant elements. Nor is it a small additional embarrassment, that we, the loyal people, differ amongst ourselves as to the mode, manner and measure of reconstruction. Let us all join in doing the acts necessary to restoring the proper practical relations between these States and the Union."

The problem thus touched upon was one that had long occupied Mr. Lincoln, and especially since the downfall of the Confederacy had been imminent. His practical and far-seeing mind was already addressing itself to the new issues, duties, and responsibilities, which he saw opening before him, and which he well knew would demand all of his wisdom, firmness, and political sagacity. In March he had directed a dispatch from Mr. Stanton to Gen. Grant, saying: "The President wishes you to have no conference with Gen. Lee, unless it be for the capitulation of his army, or on some other minor and purely military matter. He instructs me to say that you are not to decide, discuss, or confer, upon any political question. Such questions the President *holds in his own hands*, and will submit them to no military conferences or conventions." During his meeting with Gen. Grant at Petersburg, the President revealed to the General many of his plans for the rehabilitation of the South, and it could easily be seen that a spirit of magnanimity was uppermost in his heart. And at the conference with Grant, Sherman, and Porter, on board the River Queen, the same subject was broached. "Though I cannot attempt to recall the words spoken by any one of the persons present on that occasion," says Gen. Sherman, "I know we talked generally about what was to be done when Lee's and Johnston's armies were beaten and dispersed. On this point Mr. Lincoln was very full. He said that he had long thought of it, that he hoped this end could be reached without more bloodshed, but in any event he wanted us to get the deluded men of the rebel armies disarmed and back to their homes; that he contemplated no revenge, no harsh measures, but quite the contrary, and that their suffering and hardships during the war would make them the more submissive to law. I cannot say that Mr. Lincoln, or anybody else, used this language; but I know I left his presence with the conviction that he had in his mind, or that his Cabinet had, some plan of settlement ready for application the moment Lee and Johnston were defeated." Says Hon. George Bancroft: "It was the nature of Mr. Lincoln to forgive. When hostilities ceased, he, who had always sent forth the flag with every one of its stars in the field, was eager to receive back his returning countrymen."

His whole feeling toward the Southern people was one of peace and magnanimity. While many were clamoring for the execution of the rebel leaders, and especially Jefferson Davis, Mr. Lincoln said, only a day or two before his death, "This talk about Mr. Davis tires me. I hope he will mount a fleet horse, reach the shores of the Gulf of Mexico, and drive so *far into its waters* that we shall never see him again." And then he told a pat story—perhaps his last—of a boy in Springfield, "who saved up his money and bought a 'coon,' which, after the novelty wore off, became a great nuisance. He was one day leading him through the streets, and had his hands full to keep clear of the little vixen, who had torn his clothes half off him. At length he sat down on the curb-stone, completely fagged out. A man passing was stopped by the lad's disconsolate appearance, and asked the matter. 'Oh,' was the only reply, 'this coon is such a *trouble* to me.' 'Why don't you get rid of him, then?' said the gentleman. '*Hush!*' said the boy, 'don't you see he is gnawing his rope off? I am going to let him do it, and then I will go home and tell the folks *that he got away from me.*'"

CHAPTER XVII.

IT is something to be ever gratefully remembered, that the last day of Mr. Lincoln's life beamed with sunshine. His cares and burdens slipped from him like a garment, and his spirit was filled with a blessed and benignant peace.

On the morning of that fatal Friday, the 14th day of April, the President had a long conversation at breakfast with his son Robert, a member of Grant's staff, who had just arrived from the front with additional particulars of Lee's surrender, of which event he had been a witness. The President listened with close attention to the interesting recital; then, taking up a portrait of General Lee, which his son had brought him, he placed it on the table before him, where he scanned it long and thoughtfully. Presently he said: "It is a good face. It is the face of a noble, brave man. I am glad that the war is over at last." Looking upon Robert, he continued: "Well, my son, you have returned safely from the front. The war is now closed, and we will soon live in peace with the brave men who have been fighting against us. I trust that the era of good feeling has returned, and that henceforth we shall live in harmony together."

After breakfast the President received Speaker Colfax, spending an hour or more in discussing his plans with regard to the adjustment of matters in the South. This was followed by an interview with Hon. John P. Hale, the newly appointed Minister to Spain, and by calls of congratulation from members of Congress and old friends from Illinois. Afterwards,

Mr. Lincoln took a short drive with General Grant, who had just come to the city to consult with him regarding the disbandment of the army and the parole of rebel prisoners. The people were wild with enthusiasm, and wherever the President and General Grant appeared they were greeted with cheers, the clapping of hands, waving of handkerchiefs, and every possible demonstration of delight.

THE LAST CABINET MEETING.—MR. LINCOLN'S SINGULAR DREAM.

At noon, a Cabinet meeting was held, which the President attended, accompanied by General Grant. The meeting is thus described by one who was present, Secretary Welles: "Congratulations were interchanged, and earnest inquiry was made whether any information had been received from General Sherman. General Grant, who was invited to remain, said he was expecting hourly to hear from Sherman, and had a good deal of anxiety on the subject. The President remarked that the news would come soon and come favorably, he had no doubt, for he had last night his usual dream which had preceded nearly every important event of the war. I inquired the particulars of this remarkable dream. He said it was in my department—it related to the water; that he seemed to be in a singular and indescribable vessel, but always the same, and that he was moving with great rapidity toward a dark and indefinite shore; that he had had this singular dream preceding the firing on Sumter, the battles of Bull Run, Antietam, Gettysburg, Stone River, Vicksburg, Wilmington, etc. General Grant remarked, with some emphasis and asperity, that Stone River was no victory—that a few such victories would have ruined the country, and he knew of no important results from it. The President said that perhaps he should not altogether agree with him, but whatever might be the facts, his singular dream preceded that fight. Victory did not always follow his dream, but the event and results were important. He had no doubt that a battle had taken place or was about being fought, 'and Johnston will be beaten, for I had this strange dream again last night. It must relate to Sherman; my thoughts are in that direction, and *I know of no other very important event which is likely just now to occur.*' "

THE LAST DRIVE WITH MRS. LINCOLN.

After the Cabinet meeting, the President took a drive with Mrs. Lincoln, expressing a wish that no one should accompany them. His heart was filled with a solemn joy, which awoke memories of the past to mingle with hopes for the future; and in this subdued moment he desired to be alone with the one who stood nearest to him in human relationship. In the course of their talk together, he said: "Mary, we have had a hard time of it since we came to Washington; but the war is over, and with God's blessing we may hope for four years of peace and happiness, and then we will go back to Illinois and pass the rest of our lives in quiet." "He spoke," says Mr. Arnold, "of his old Springfield home; and recollections of his early days, his little brown cottage, the law office, the court room, the green bag for his briefs and law papers, his adventures when riding the circuit, came thronging back to him. The tension under which he had for so long been kept was removed, and he was like a boy out of school. 'We have laid by,' said he to his wife, 'some money, and during this term we will try and save up more, but shall not have enough to support us. We will go back to Illinois, and I will open a law office at Springfield or Chicago, and practice law, and at least do enough to help give us a livelihood.' Such were the dreams, the day-dreams of Lincoln, on the last day of his life."

INCIDENTS OF THE AFTERNOON.—RIDDANCE TO JACOB THOMPSON.—A FINAL ACT OF PARDON.

Mr. Neill, the President's private secretary, states that between three and four o'clock of this day, he had occasion to seek the President to procure his signature to a paper. "I found," says Mr. Neill, "that he had retired to the private parlor of the house for lunch. While I was looking over the papers on his table, to see if I could find the desired commission, he came back, eating an apple. I told him for what I was looking, and as I talked he placed his hand upon the bell-pull, when I said: 'For whom are you going to ring?' Placing his hand upon my coat, he spoke but two words: 'Andrew Johnson.' 'Then,' I said, 'I will come in again.' As I was leaving the room, the Vice-president had been ushered in, and the President advanced and took him by the hand."

Mr. C. A. Dana, the Assistant Secretary of War, says that his last recollections of President Lincoln are indelibly associated with the seditious Jacob Thompson. "Late in the afternoon," says Mr. Dana, "a dispatch was received at the War Department from the provost marshal of Portland, Maine, saying that he had received information that Jacob Thompson would arrive in Portland during that night, in order to take from there the Canadian steamer which was to sail for Liverpool. On reading this dispatch to Mr. Stanton, the latter said: 'Order him to be arrested—but no; you had better take it over to the President.' I found Mr. Lincoln in the inner room of his business office at the White House, with his coat off, washing his hands preparatory to a drive. 'Hello,' said he, 'what is it?' Listening to the dispatch, he asked: 'What does Stanton say?' 'He thinks he ought to be arrested.' I replied. 'Well,' he continued, drawling his words, 'I rather guess not. When you have an elephant on hand, and he wants to run away, better let him run.'"

During the afternoon the President signed a pardon for a soldier sentenced to be shot for desertion; remarking, as he did so, "Well, I think the boy can do us more good above ground than under ground." He also approved an application for the discharge, on taking the oath of allegiance, of a rebel prisoner, on whose petition he wrote, *"Let it be done."* This act of mercy was his last official order.

THE FATAL EVENING.

It had been decided early in the day that the President and Mrs. Lincoln would attend Ford's Theatre in the evening, to witness the play of "The American Cousin." Mr. Lincoln had invited Gen. Grant to accompany his party to the theatre, saying that the people would expect to see him and should not be disappointed. But the General had declined, as Mrs. Grant was anxious to start that afternoon to visit their children, who were at school in Burlington, New Jersey.

As the hour approached for leaving for the theatre, the President was engaged in a conversation with two friends— Speaker Colfax, and Hon. George Ashmun, of Massachusetts. The business on which they had met not being concluded, the President gave Mr. Ashmun a card, on which he had written these words: "Allow Mr. Ashmun and friend to come in at 9 A. M. to-morrow—A. Lincoln." He then turned to Mr. Colfax, saying: "You are going with Mrs. Lincoln and me to the theatre, I hope." Mr. Colfax pleaded other engagements, when Lincoln remarked: "Mr. Sumner has the gavel of the Confederate Congress, which he got at Richmond to hand to the Secretary of War. But I insisted then that he must give it to you; and you tell him for me to hand it over." He then rose, but seemed reluctant to go, expressing a half-determination to delay a while longer. It was undoubtedly to avoid disappointing the audience, which had been promised his presence, that he went to the play-house that night. At the door he stopped and said to Speaker Colfax, who was about to leave for the Pacific coast, "Colfax, do not forget to tell the people in the mining regions, as you pass through, what I told you this morning about the development when peace comes, and I will telegraph you at San Francisco."

THE VISIT TO THE THEATRE.

It was nine o'clock when the Presidential party reached the theatre. The place was crowded; "many ladies in rich and gay costumes, officers in their uniforms, many well-known citizens, young folks, the usual clusters of gaslights, the usual magnetism of so many people, cheerful, with perfumes, music of violins and flutes—and over all, and saturating all, that vast, vague wonder, Victory, the Nation's victory, the triumph of the Union, filling the air, the thought, the sense, with exhilaration more than all perfumes."

As Mr. Lincoln entered, he was greeted with tremendous cheers, to which he responded with genial courtesy. The box reserved for him, at the right of the stage, a little above the floor, was draped and festooned with flags. As the party were seated, the daughter of Senator Harris, of New York, occupied the corner nearest the stage; next her was Mrs. Lincoln; and behind them sat the President and Major Rathbone, the former being nearest the door.

THE ASSASSIN'S SHOT.

It was half-past ten o'clock, and the audience was absorbed in the progress of the play, when suddenly a pistol shot, loud and sharp, rang through the theatre. All eyes were instantly directed toward the President's box, whence the report proceeded. A moment later, the figure of a man, holding a smoking pistol in one hand and a dagger in the other, appeared at the front of the President's box, and sprang to the stage, some fifteen feet below, shouting as he did so, "*Sic semper tyrannis!*" He fell as he struck the stage; but quickly recovering himself, sprang through the side-wings, and escaped from the theatre by a rear-door.

At the moment of the assassination, a single actor, Mr. Hawk, was on the stage. In his account of the tragical event, he says: "When I heard the shot fired, I turned, looked up at the President's box, heard the man exclaim, '*Sic semper tyrannis!'* saw him jump from the box, seize the flag on the staff and drop to the stage; he slipped when he gained the stage, but he got upon his feet in a moment, brandished a large knife, saying, 'The South shall be free,' turned his face in the direction I stood, and I recognized him as John Wilkes Booth. He ran towards me, and I, seeing the knife, thought I was the one he was after, and ran off the stage and up a flight of stairs. He made his escape out of a door directly in the rear of the theatre, mounted a horse, and rode off. The above all occurred in the space of a quarter of a minute, and at the time I did not know the President was shot."

A SCENE OF HORROR.

Scarcely had the horror-stricken audience witnessed the leap and flight of the assassin, when a woman's shriek pierced through the theatre, recalling all eyes to the President's box. The scene that ensued is described wiu singular vividness by the poet Walt Whitman, who was present: A moment's hush —a scream—the cry of murder—Mrs. Lincoln leaning out of the box, with ashy cheeks and lips, with involuntary cry, pointing to the retreating figure, *'He has killed the President!'* And still a moment's strange, incredulous suspense— and then the deluge!—then that mixture of horror, noises, uncertainty—(the sound, somewhere back, of a horse's hoofs clattering with speed)—the people burst through chairs and railing, and break them up—that noise adds to the queerness of the scene—there is inextricable confusion and terror—women faint—feeble persons fall, and are trampled on—many cries of agony are heard—the broad stage suddenly fills to suffocation with a dense and motley crowd, like some horrible carnival—the audience rush generally upon it—at least the strong men do—the actors and actresses are there in their play costumes and painted faces, with mortal fright showing through the rouge—some trembling, some in tears—the screams and calls, confused talk—redoubled, trebled—two or

THE ASSASSINATION OF PRESIDENT LINCOLN, AT FORD'S THEATRE,
WASHINGTON.

three manage to pass up water from the stage to the President's box—others try to clamber up. Amidst all this, a party of soldiers, two hundred or more, hearing what is done, suddenly appear; they storm the house, inflamed with fury, literally charging the audience with fixed bayonets, muskets, and pistols, shouting, 'Clear out! clear out!' * * And in the midst of that pandemonium of senseless hate—the infuriated soldiers, the audience, the stage, its actors and actresses, its paints and spangles and gaslights,—the life blood from those veins, the best and sweetest of the land, drips slowly down, and death's ooze already begins its little bubbles on the lips.''

PARTICULARS OF THE CRIME.

It appears that Booth, the assassin, had long been plotting the murder of the President, and awaiting a favorable moment for its execution. He had visited the theatre at half-past eleven on the morning of the 14th, and then learned that a box had been taken for Mr. Lincoln that evening. He engaged a fleet horse for a saddle-ride in the afternoon, and left it at a convenient place. In the evening he rode to the theatre, and leaving the animal in charge of an accomplice, entered the house. Making his way to the door of the President's box, and taking a small Derringer pistol in one hand and a double-edged dagger in the other, he thrust his arm into the entrance, where the President, sitting in an arm-chair, presented to his full view the back and side of his head. A flash, a sharp report, a puff of smoke, and the fatal bullet had entered the President's brain.

Major Rathbone, who occupied a seat in the President's box, testifies that he was sitting with his back toward the door, when he heard the discharge of a pistol behind him, and looking around, saw, through the smoke, a man between the door and the President. Major Rathbone instantly sprang toward him and seized him; he wrested himself from his grasp, and made a violent thrust at the Major's breast with a large knife. The Major parried the blow by striking it up, and received a wound in his left arm. The man rushed to the front of the box, and the Major endeavored to seize him again, but only caught his clothes as he was leaping over the railing of the box. Major Rathbone then turned to the President; his position was not changed; his head was slightly bent forward, and his eyes were closed.

THE DYING PRESIDENT.

As soon as the surgeons, who had been summoned, completed their hasty examination, the unconscious form of the President was borne from the theatre to a house across the street, and laid upon his death-bed. Around him were gathered Surgeon-General Barnes, Vice-president Johnson, Senator Sumner, Secretaries Stanton and Welles, Generals Halleck and Meigs, Attorney-General Speed, Postmaster-General Dennison, Mr. McCulloch, Speaker Colfax, and other intimate friends who had been hastily summoned. Mrs. Lincoln sat in an adjoining room, prostrate and overwhelmed, with her son Robert. The examination of the surgeons had left no room for hope. The watchers remained through the night by the bedside of the stricken man, who showed no signs of consciousness; and at seven o'clock in the morning he breathed his last.

THE PEOPLE'S GRIEF.

The news of the President's assassination flashed rapidly over the country, everywhere causing the greatest consternation and grief. The revulsion from the joy which had filled all loyal hearts at the prospects of peace, was sudden and profound. All business ceased, and gave way to mourning and lamentation. The flags, so lately unfurled in exultation, were now dropped at half-mast, and emblems of sorrow were hung from every door and window. Men walked with a dejected air. They gathered together in groups in the street, and spoke of the murder of the President as of a personal calamity. The

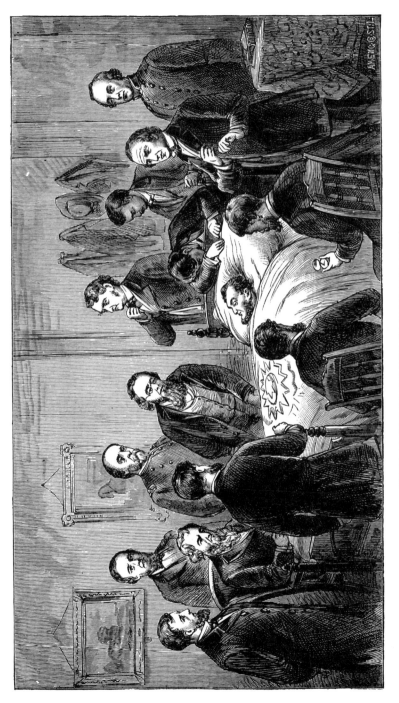

SCENE AT THE DEATH-BED OF PRESIDENT LINCOLN.

nation's heart was smitten, and signs of woe were in every face and every movement.

A scene which transpired in Philadelphia, the morning after the murder, but reflects the picture presented in every city and town in the United States. "We had taken our seats," says the delineator, "in the early car to ride down town, men and boys going to work. The morning papers had come up from town as usual, and the men unrolled them to read as the car started. The eye fell on the black border and ominous column-lines. Before we could speak, a good Quaker at the head of the car broke out in horror: 'My God! What's this? *Lincoln is assassinated.*' The driver stopped the car, and came in to hear the awful tidings. There stood the car, mid-street, as the heavy news was read in the gray dawn of that ill-fated day. Men bowed their faces in their hands, and on the straw-covered floor hot tears fell fast. Silently the driver took the bells from his horses, and we started like a hearse cityward. What a changed city since the day before! Then all was joy over the end of the Civil War; now plunged in a deeper gulf of woe. The sun rose on a city smitten and weeping. All traffic stood still; the icy hand of death lay flat on the heart of commerce, and it gave not a throb. Men stood by their open stores saying, with hands on each other's shoulders: 'Our President is dead.' Over and over, in a dazed way, they said the fateful syllables, as if the bullet that tore through the weary brain at Washington had palsied the nation. The mute news-boy on the corner said never a word as he handed to the speechless buyers the damp sheets from the press; only he brushed, with unwashed hand, from his dirty cheeks the tears till the last paper was gone. Groups stood listening on the pavement with faces to the earth, while one, in choking voice, read the telegrams; then with a look they departed in unworded woe, each cursing bitterly in his breast the 'deep damnation of his taking off.' Mill operatives, clerks, workers, school children, all came home, the faltering voice of the teacher telling the wondering children to 'go home, there will be no school to-day.' The housewife looked up amazed to see husband and children coming home so soon. The father's face frightened her and she cried: 'What is wrong, husband?' He could not speak the news, but the wee girl with the school-books said: 'Mamma, they've killed our President.' Ere noon every house wore crape; it was as if there lay a dead son in every home. For hours a sad group hung around the bulletins, hoping against hope; then, when the last hope died, turned sullenly homeward, saying: 'When all was won, and all was done, then to strike him!' The flags in the harbor fell to half-mast; the streets were rivers of inky streamers; from door-knobs floated crape; and even the unbelled car-horses seemed to draw the black-robed cars more quietly than before."

THE FUNERAL OBSEQUIES.

On Saturday the remains of the President were borne to the White House, where they were embalmed and placed on a grand catafalque in the East room. Tuesday the White House was thrown open to admit the friends of the President who desired to look upon his form as it lay still and restful in death. Wednesday, the 19th, the funeral services took place. Mrs. Lincoln was too ill to be present; but the two sons of the President sat near his coffin in the East room, and next in order were ranged President Andrew Johnson and the members of the Cabinet, and after them the foreign representatives, the chief men of the nation, and a large body of mourning citizens. The services were conducted jointly by the Rev. Dr. Hall, Bishop Simpson, Dr. Gray, and the Rev. Dr. Gurley, the latter delivering the discourse. At two o'clock the funeral cortege started for the Capitol, where the remains were to lie in state until the following morning. The body was borne into the rotunda, amidst funeral dirges and military salutes; and the religious exercises of the occasion

WE MOURN OUR CHIEF.

A NATION'S PALL OF SORROW.

APRIL 15 1865

FAIR FREEDOM STRICKEN LOW.

A PRAYER FOR JUSTICE.

were concluded. A guard was stationed near the coffin, and the public were again admitted to take their farewell of the dead.

While these obsequies were being performed at Washington, similar ceremonies were observed in every part of the country.

THE RETURN TO ILLINOIS.

It had been decided to convey the remains of Mr. Lincoln to the home which he left four years before with such solemn and affectionate words of parting. The funeral cortege left Washington on the 21st. Its passage westward, a distance of nearly two thousand miles, through the principal States and cities of the Union, was a most remarkable and impressive spectacle. The heavily craped train, its sombre engine swathed in black, moved through the land like an eclipse. At every point vast crowds assembled to gain a tearful glimpse as it sped past.

"Over the breast of the spring, the land, amid cities,
   Amid lanes and through old woods, where lately the violets peep'd
     from the ground, spotting the gray debris,
   Amid the grass of the fields each side of the lanes, passing the end-
     less grass,
 ·Passing the yellow-spear'd wheat, every grain from its shroud in the
     dark-brown fields uprisen,
   Passing the apple-tree blows of white and pink in the orchards,
   Carrying a corpse to where it shall rest in the grave,
   Night and day journeys a coffin.

   Coffin that passes through lanes and streets,
   Through day and night with the great cloud darkening the land,
   With the pomp of the inloop'd flags, with the cities draped in black,
   With the show of the States themselves as of crape-veil'd women
     standing,
   With processions long and winding and the flambeaus of the night,
   With the countless torches lit, with the silent sea of faces and the
     unbared heads,
   With the waiting depot, the arriving coffin, and the sombre faces,
   With dirges through the night, with the thousand voices rising strong
     and solemn,
   With all the mournful voices of the dirges pour'd around the coffin,
   The dim-lit churches and the shuddering organs—
   With the tolling, tolling bells' perpetual clang."

At the principal cities delays were made to enable the people to pay their tribute of respect to the remains of their beloved President. Through Baltimore, Harrisburg, Philadelphia, the train passed to New York City, where a magnificent funeral was held; thence along the shore of the Hudson river to Albany, thence westward through the principal cities of New

OAK RIDGE CEMETERY, AT SPRINGFIELD, ILL., SHOWING
LINCOLN'S TOMB AND MONUMENT.

York, Ohio, and Northern Indiana, it wended its solemn way, reaching, on the 1st of May, the city of Chicago. Here very extensive preparations for funeral obsequies had been made by the thousands who had known him in his life, and other thousands who had learned to love him, and now mourned his death.

AT REST IN OAK RIDGE CEMETERY.

On the 3d of May the funeral train reached Springfield, where the old friends and neighbors received reverently back the dust of the beloved dead. Funeral services were held, and for twenty-four hours the catafalque remained in the hall of the House of Representatives, where thousands of tear-dimmed eyes gazed for the last time upon the dear familiar face. Then, on the morning of the 4th of May, a sorrowing procession escorted the remains on their last journey, to the beautiful grounds of Oak Ridge Cemetery. And in that calm retreat, hallowed by Sabbath stillness, he rests from the care and turmoil of his troubled life, while around him Nature spreads her loveliness and peace. And o'er his grave the little children's hands shall scatter flowers, and maidens drop the tear of sweet sincerity, and youth quicken its aspirations for a noble life. And here shall come the gray-haired soldier of that stormy war, to salute reverently his great commander's tomb. And here be paid the loving homage of the dusky race that he redeemed; no fragrance of Summer blooms could be sweeter to him than their prayers, nor the dews of Heaven fall gentler than their tears upon his dust. And pilgrims from every land, who value human worth and human liberty, shall hither bring their tributes of respect. And here, long as our Government endures, shall throng his patriot countrymen, not idly to lament his loss, but to resolve THAT FROM THIS HONORED DEAD THEY TAKE INCREASED DEVOTION TO THE CAUSE FOR WHICH HE GAVE THE LAST FULL MEASURE OF DEVOTION; THAT THE DEAD SHALL NOT HAVE DIED IN VAIN; THAT THE NATION SHALL, UNDER GOD, HAVE A NEW BIRTH OF FREEDOM; AND THAT GOVERNMENT OF THE PEOPLE, BY THE PEOPLE, AND FOR THE PEOPLE, SHALL NOT PERISH FROM THE EARTH.

ABRAHAM LINCOLN.

This man, whose homely face you look upon,
Was one of Nature's masterful great men;
Born with strong arms, that unfought battles won;
Direct of speech and cunning with the pen.

Chosen for large designs, he had the art
Of winning with his humor, and he went
Straight to his mark, which was the human heart;
Wise, too, for what he could not break, he bent.

Upon his back a more than Atlas-load,
The burden of the Commonwealth, was laid;
He stooped, and rose up to it, though the road
Shot suddenly downwards, not a whit dismayed.

Hold, warriors, councilors, kings!—all now give place
To this dear benefactor of the Race.

R. H. STODDARD.

PART IV.

MEMORIES OF LINCOLN.

WALT WHITMAN'S POEM ON PRESIDENT LINCOLN S DEATH.

O CAPTAIN! my Captain! our fearful trip is done;
    The ship has weather'd every rack, the prize we sought is won;
The port is near, the bells I hear, the people all exulting,
      While follow eyes the steady keel, the vessel grim and daring;
        But O heart! heart! heart!
          O the bleeding drops of red,
            Where on the deck my Captain lies
              Fallen cold and dead!

O Captain! my Captain! rise up and hear the bells;
    Rise up—for you the flag is flung—for you the bugle trills;
For you bouquets and ribbon'd wreaths—for you the shores a crowding;
      For you they call, the swaying mass, their eager faces turning:
        Here Captain! dear father!
          This arm beneath your head;
            It is some dream that on the deck
              You've fallen cold and dead.

My Captain does not answer, his lips are pale and still;
    My father does not feel my arm, he has no pulse nor will;
The ship is anchor'd safe and sound, its voyage closed and done;
      From fearful trip the victor ship comes in with object won:
        Exult, O shores, and ring, O bells!
          But I, with mournful tread,
            Walk the deck my Captain lies,
              Fallen cold and dead.

REV. DR. GURLEY'S SERMON AT THE FUNERAL IN WASHINGTON.

The people confided in our lamented President with a firm and loving confidence, which no other man enjoyed since the days of Washington. He deserved it well, and deserved it all. He merited it by his character and by his acts, and by the whole tenor and tone and spirit of his life. He was wise, simple and sincere, plain and honest, truthful and just, benevolent and kind. His perceptions were quick and clear, his judgment was calm and accurate, and his purposes were good and clear beyond a question; always and everywhere he aimed and endeavored to be right and to do right. He gave his personal consideration to all matters, whether great or small. How firmly and well he occupied his position, and met all its grave demands in seasons of trial and difficulty, is known to the country and to the world. He comprehended all the enormity of treason, and rose to the full dignity of the occasion. * * * We admired and loved him on many accounts, for strong and various reasons. We admired his childlike simplicity, his freedom from guile and deceit, his stanch and sterling integrity, his kind and forgiving temper, his industry and patience, his persistent, self-sacrificing devotion to all the duties of his eminent position. From the least to the greatest, his readiness to hear and consider the cause of the poor and the humble, the suffering, the oppressed; his charity toward those who questioned the correctness of his opinions and the wisdom of his policy; his true and enlarged philanthropy, that knew no difference of color or race, but regarded all men as brethren,—all these things commanded and fixed our admiration, and the admiration of the world, and stamped upon his character and life the unmistakable impress of greatness.— [*Extract.*]

FUNERAL ORATION BY REV. PHILLIPS BROOKS, AT PHILADELPHIA.

So let him lie here in our midst to-day, and let our people go and bend with solemn thoughtfulness and look upon his

face and read the lessons of his burial. As he paused here
on his journey from his Western home and told us what by
the help of God he meant to do, so let him pause upon his
way back to his Western grave, and tell us, with a silence
more eloquent than words, how bravely, how truly, by the
strength of God he did it. God brought him up as he brought
David up from the sheep-folds to feed Jacob his people, and
Israel his inheritance. He came up in earnestness and faith,
and he goes back in triumph. As he pauses here to-day, and
from his cold lips bids us bear witness how he has met the
duty that was laid on him, what can we say out of our full
hearts but this—"He fed them with a faithful and true heart,
and ruled them prudently with all his power." The Shepherd of the People! that old name that the best rulers ever
craved. What ruler ever won it like this dead President of
ours? He fed us faithfully and truly. He fed us with counsel when we were in doubt, with inspiration when we sometimes faltered, with caution when we would be rash, with
calm, clear, trustful cheerfulness through many an hour when
our hearts were dark. He fed hungry souls all over the
country with sympathy and consolation. He spread before
the whole land feasts of great duty and devotion and patriotism on which the land grew strong. He fed us with solemn,
solid truths. He taught us the sacredness of government, the
wickedness of treason. He made our souls glad and vigorous
with the love of Liberty that was in his. He showed us how
to love truth, and yet be charitable; how to hate wrong and
all oppression, and yet not treasure one personal injury or insult. He fed all his people, from the highest to the lowest,
from the most privileged down to the most enslaved. "He
fed them with a faithful and true heart." Yes, till the last.
For at the last, behold him standing with hand reached out to
feed the South with Mercy and the North with Charity, and
the whole land with Peace, when the Lord, who had sent
him, called him, and his work was done.—[*Extract.*]

HYMN FOR LINCOLN'S FUNERAL IN NEW YORK CITY.

BY W. C. BRYANT.

O, slow to smite and swift to spare,
   Gentle and merciful and just!
Who, in the fear of God, didst bear
   The sword of power—a nation's trust!

In sorrow by thy bier we stand,
   Amid the awe that hushes all,
And speak the anguish of a land
   That shook with horror at thy fall.

Thy task is done; the bond are free;
   We bear thee to an honored grave,
Whose proudest monument shall be
   The broken fetters of the slave.

Pure was thy life; its bloody close
   Has placed thee with the sons of light,
Among the noble host of those
   Who perished in the cause of Right.

FUNERAL ORATION BY HON. GEORGE BANCROFT.

Those who come after us will decide how much of the wonderful results of his public career is due to his own good common sense, his shrewd sagacity, readiness of wit, quick interpretation of the public mind, his rare combination of fixedness and pliancy, his steady tendency of purpose; how much to the American people, who, as he walked with them side by side, inspired him with their own wisdom and energy; and how much to the overruling laws of the moral world, by which the selfishness of evil is made to defeat itself. But after every allowance, it will remain that members of the government which preceded his administration opened the gates of treason, and he closed them; that when he went to Washington the ground on which he trod shook under his feet, and he left the Republic on a solid foundation; that traitors had seized public forts and arsenals, and he recovered them for the United States, to whom they belonged; that the capital which he found the abode of slaves, is now the home only of the free; that the boundless public domain which was grasped at, and, in a great measure, held for the diffusion of slavery, is now irrevocably devoted to freedom; that then men talked a jargon of a balance of power in a Republic between slave States and free States, and now the foolish words are blown away forever by the breath of Maryland, Missouri, and Tennessee; that a terrible cloud of political heresy rose from the abyss, threatening to hide the light of the sun, and under its darkness a rebellion was rising into indefinable proportions. Through all the mad business of treason, he retained the sweetness of a most placable disposition; and the slaughter of myriads of the best on the battle-field, and the more terrible destruction of our men in captivity by the slow torture of exposure and starvation, had never been able to provoke him into harboring one vengeful feeling or one purpose of cruelty.—[*Extract.*]

HENRY WARD BEECHER'S EULOGY.

Dead, dead, dead, he yet speaketh. Is Washington dead? Is Hampden dead? Is any man, that was ever fit to live, dead? Disenthralled of flesh, risen to the unobstructed sphere where passion never comes, he begins his illimitable work. His life is now grafted upon the infinite, and will be fruitful, as no earthly fruit can be. Your sorrows, O people, are his pæans; your bells and bands and muffled drums sound triumph in his ears. Wail and weep here; God makes it echo joy and triumph there. Pass on! Four years ago, O Illinois, we took from thy midst an untried man, one from among the people; we return him to you a mighty conqueror. Not thine any more, but the nation's; not ours, but the world's. Give him place, O ye prairies! In the midst of this great continent his dust shall rest, a sacred treasure to myriads who shall pilgrim to that shrine, to kindle anew their zeal and patriotism. Ye winds that move over the mighty places of the West, chant his requiem! Ye people, behold the martyr, whose blood, as so many articulate words, pleads for fidelity, for law, for liberty!—[*Extract.*]

JAMES RUSSELL LOWELL'S "COMMEMORATION ODE."

Life may be given in many ways,
And loyalty to Truth be sealed
As bravely in the closet as the field,
So bountiful is Fate;
But then to stand beside her,
When craven churls deride her,
To front a lie in arms and not to yield,
This shows, methinks, God's plan
And measure of a stalwart man,
Limbed like the old heroic breeds,
Who stand self-poised on manhood's solid earth,
Not forced to frame excuses for his birth,
Fed from within with all the strength he needs.

Such was he, our Martyr-Chief
Whom late the Nation he had led,
With ashes on her head,
Wept with the passion of an angry grief.
Nature, they say, doth dote,
And cannot make a man
Save on some worn-out plan,
Repeating us by rote:
For him her Old World moulds aside she threw,
And, choosing sweet clay from the breast
Of the unexhausted West,
With stuff untainted shaped a hero new,
Wise, steadfast in the strength of God, and true.
How beautiful to see
Once more a shepherd of mankind indeed,
Who loved his charge, but never loved to lead;
One whose meek flock the people joyed to be,
Not lured by any cheat of birth,
But by his clear-grained human worth,
And brave old wisdom of sincerity!
They knew that outward grace is dust;
They could not choose but trust
In that sure-footed mind's unfaltering skill,
And supple-tempered will
That bent like perfect steel to spring again and thrust.
His was no lonely mountain-peak of mind,
Thrusting to thin air o'er our cloudy bars,
A sea-mark now, now lost in vapors blind;
Broad prairie rather, genial, level-lined,

Fruitful and friendly for all human kind,
Yet also nigh to heaven and loved of loftiest stars.
Nothing of Europe here,
Or, then, of Europe fronting mornward still
Ere any names of Serf and Peer
Could Nature's equal scheme deface;
Here was a type of the true elder race,
And one of Plutarch's men talked with us face to face.
I praise him not; it were too late;
And some innative weakness there must be
In him who condescends to victory,
Such as the Present gives, and cannot wait,
Safe in himself as in a fate.
So always firmly he:
He knew to bide his time,
And can his fame abide,
Still patient in his simple faith sublime,
Till the wise years decide.
Great captains, with their guns and drums,
Disturb our judgment for the hour,
But at last silence comes;
These all are gone, and, standing like a tower,
Our children shall behold his fame,
The kindly-earnest, brave, foreseeing man,
Sagacious, patient, dreading praise, not blame,
New birth of our new soil, the first American.

[*Extract.*]

ORATION BY HON. CHARLES SUMNER.

In person, Mr. Lincoln was tall and rugged, with little semblance to any historic portrait, unless he might seem, in one respect, to justify the epithet which was given to an early English monarch. His countenance had even more of rugged strength than his person. Perhaps the quality which struck the most, at first sight, was his simplicity of manners and conversation—without form or ceremony of any kind, beyond that among neighbors. His handwriting had the same simplicity. It was as clear as that of Washington, but less florid. He was naturally humane, inclined to pardon, and never remembering the hard things said against him. He was always good to the poor, and in his dealings with them was full of those "kind little words which are of the same blood as great and holy deeds." Such a character awakened instinctively the sympathy of the people. They saw his fellow-feeling with them, and felt the kinship. With him as President, the idea of Republican institutions, where no place is too high for the humblest, was perpetually manifest, so that his simple presence was like a proclamation of the equality of all men.

While social in nature, and enjoying the flow of conversation, he was often singularly reticent. Modesty was natural to such a character As he was without affectation, so he was without pretence or jealousy. No person, civil or military, can complain that he appropriated to himself any honor that belonged to another. To each and all he anxiously gave the credit that was due. His humor has also become a proverb. He insisted, sometimes, that he had no invention, but only a memory. He did not forget the good things that he heard, and was never without a familiar story to illustrate his meaning. When he spoke, the recent West seemed to vie with the ancient East in apologue and fable. His ideas moved, as the beasts entered Noah's ark, in pairs. At times his illustrations had a homely felicity, and with him they seemed to be not less important than the argument, which he always enforced with a certain intensity of manner and voice.

He was original in mind as in character. His style was his own, formed on no model, and springing directly from himself. While failing, often, in correctness, it is sometimes unique in beauty and in sentiment. There are passages which will live always. It is no exaggeration to say that, in weight and pith, suffused in a certain poetical color, they call to mind Bacon's essays. Such passages make an epoch in State papers. No Presidential message or speech from a throne ever had anything of such touching reality. They are harbingers of the great era of humanity. While uttered from the heights of power, they reveal a simple, unaffected trust in Almighty God, and speak to the people as equal to equal.—[*Extract.*]

THE LINCOLN MONUMENT IN OAK RIDGE CEMETERY, SPRINGFIELD, ILL.

This beautiful monument was erected in 1874. It was designed by the American artist, Larkin G. Mead, and cost upwards of $200,000. Its height is one hundred feet. The bronze statue of Lincoln—a remarkably life-like figure—is ten feet high, but from the ground appears life-size. The left hand of the figure holds a scroll, representing the Emancipation Proclamation, and the right hand holds a pen. At the corners of the shaft are bronze groups, representing the infantry, cavalry and artillery branches of the army, with another group for the navy.

RICHARD HENRY STODDARD'S ODE ON LINCOLN.

Not as when some great Captain falls
In battle, where his country calls,
    Beyond the struggling lines
    That push his dread designs

To doom, by some stray ball struck dead;
Or, in the last charge, at the head
    Of his determined men,
    Who *must* be victors then.

Nor as when sink the civic great,
The safer pillars of the State,
    Whose calm, mature, wise words
    Suppress the need of swords.

With no such tears as e'er were shed
Above the noblest of our dead
    Do we to-day deplore
    The Man that is no more.

Our sorrow hath a wider scope,
Too strange for fear, too vast for hope,
    A wonder, blind and dumb,
    That waits—what is to come!

Not more astounded had we been
If Madness, that dark night, unseen,
    Had in our chambers crept,
    And murdered while we slept.

We woke to find a mourning earth,
Our Lares shivered on the hearth,
    The roof-tree fallen, all
    That could affright, appall!

Such thunderbolts, in other lands,
Have smitten the rod from royal hands,
    But spared, with us, till now,
    Each laurelled Cæsar's brow.

No Cæsar he whom we lament,
A man without a precedent,
    Sent, it would seem, to do
    His work, and perish, too.

Not by the weary cares of State,
The endless tasks, which will not wait,
 Which often done in vain,
 Must yet be done again.

Not in the dark, wild tide of war,
Which rose so high, and rolled so far,
 Sweeping from sea to sea
 In awful anarchy.

Four fitful years of mortal strife,
Which slowly drained the nation's life,
 (Yet for each drop that ran
 There sprang an armed man!)

Not then; but when, by measures meet,
By victory, and by defeat,
 By courage, patience, skill,
 The people's fixed "*We will!*"

Had pierced, had crushed Rebellion dead,
Without a hand, without a head,
 At last, when all was well,
 He fell, O how he fell!

The time, the place, the stealing shape,
The coward shot, the swift escape,
 The wife, the widow's scream—
 It is a hideous Dream!

A dream? what means this pageant, then?
These multitudes of solemn men,
 Who speak not when they meet,
 But throng the silent street?

The flags half-mast that late so high
Flaunted at each new victory?
 (The stars no brightness shed,
 But bloody looks the red!)

The black festoons that stretch for miles,
And turn the streets to funeral aisles?
 (No house too poor to show
 The nation's badge of woe.)

The cannon's sudden sullen boom,
The bells that toll of death and doom,

The rolling of the drums,
The dreadful car that comes?

    *   *   *   *   *

Peace! Let the long procession come,
For hark, the mournful muffled drum,
    The trumpet's wail afar,
    And see, the awful car!

Peace! Let the sad procession go,
While cannon boom and bells toll slow.
    And go, thou sacred car,
    Bearing our woe afar!

Go, darkly borne, from State to State,
Whose loyal, sorrowing cities wait
    To honor all they can
    The dust of that good man.

Go, grandly borne, with such a train
As greatest kings might die to gain.
    The just, the wise, the brave,
    Attend thee to the grave.

And you, the soldiers of our wars,
Bronzed veterans, grim with noble scars,
    Salute him once again,
    Your late commander—slain!

Yes, let your tears indignant fall,
But leave your muskets on the wall;
    Your country needs you now
    Beside the forge—the plough.

(When Justice shall unsheath her brand,
If Mercy may not stay her hand,
    Nor would we have it so,
    She must direct the blow).

And you, amid the master-race,
Who seem so strangely out of place,
    Know ye who cometh? He
    Who hath declared ye free.

Bow while the body passes—nay,
Fall on your knees, and weep, and pray!

Weep, weep—I would ye might—
Your poor black faces white.

And, children, you must come in bands,
With garlands in your little hands,
   Of blue, and white, and red,
   To strew before the dead.

So sweetly, sadly, sternly goes
The Fallen to his last repose,
   Beneath no mighty dome,
   But in his modest home;

The churchyard where his children rest,
The quiet spot that suits him best,
   There shall his grave be made,
   And there his bones be laid.

And there his countrymen shall come,
And memory proud, with pity dumb,
   And strangers far and near,
   For many and many a year.

For many a year and many an age,
While History on her ample page
   The virtues shall enroll
   Of that Paternal Soul.

ORATION BY R. W. EMERSON.

The President stood before us a man of the people. He was thoroughly American, had never crossed the sea, had never been spoiled by English insularity or French dissipation; a quiet, native, aboriginal man, as an acorn from the oak; no aping of foreigners, no frivolous accomplishments, Kentuckian born, working on a farm, a flatboatman, a captain in the Black Hawk War, a country lawyer, a representative in the rural Legislature of Illinois—on such modest foundations the broad structure of his fame was laid. How slowly, and yet by happily prepared steps, he came to his place.

   *   *   *   A plain man of the people, extraordinary fortune attended him. Lord Bacon says: "Manifest virtues procure reputation; occult ones, fortune." He offered no shining qualities at the first encounter; he did not offend by superiority. He had a face and manner which disarmed suspicion, which inspired confidence, which confirmed good will. He was a man without vices. He had a strong sense of duty which it was very easy for him to obey. Then he had what farmers call a long head; was excellent in working out the sum for himself; in arguing his case, and convincing you fairly and firmly. Then it turned out that he was a great worker; had prodigious faculty of performance; worked easily. A good worker is so rare; everybody has some disabling quality. In a host of young men that start together, and promise so many brilliant leaders for the next age, each fails on trial; one by bad health, one by conceit or by love of pleasure, or by lethargy, or by a hasty temper—each has some disqualifying fault that throws him out of the career. But this man was sound to the core, cheerful, persistent, all right for labor, and liked nothing so well.

Then he had a vast good nature, which made him tolerant and accessible to all; fair-minded, leaning to the claim of the petitioner; affable, and not sensible to the affliction which the innumerable visits, paid to him when President, would have brought to any one else. And how this good nature became a noble humanity, in many a tragic case which the events of the war brought to him, every one will remember, and with what increasing tenderness he dealt, when a whole race was thrown on his compassion. The poor negro said of him, on an impressive occasion, "Massa Linkum am everywhere."

Then his broad good humor, running easily into jocular talk, in which he delighted, and in which he excelled, was a rich gift to this wise man. It enabled him to keep his secret, to meet every kind of man, and every rank in society; to take off the edge of the severest decisions, to mask his own purpose and sound his companion, and to catch, with true instinct, the temper of every company he addressed. And, more than all, it is to a man of severe labor, in anxious and exhausting crises, the natural restorative, good as sleep, and is the protection of the overdriven brain against rancor and insanity.

He is the author of a multitude of good sayings, so disguised as pleasantries that it is certain they had no reputation at first but as jests; and only later, by the very acceptance and adoption they find in the mouths of millions, turn out to be the wisdom of the hour. I am sure if this man had ruled in a period of less facility of printing, he would have become mythological in a very few years, like Æsop or Pilpay, or one of the Seven Wise Masters, by his fables and proverbs. But the weight and penetration of many passages in his letters, messages, and speeches, hidden now by the very closeness of their application to the moment, are destined hereafter to wide fame. What pregnant definitions; what unerring common sense; what foresight; and, on great occasion, what lofty, and, more than national, what humane tone! His brief speech at Gettysburg will not easily be surpassed by words on any recorded occasion.

It cannot be said there is any exaggeration of his worth. If ever a man was fairly tested, he was. There was no lack of resistance, nor of slander, nor of ridicule. The times have allowed no state secrets; the nation has been in such a ferment, such multitudes had to be trusted, that no secret could be kept. Every door was ajar, and we knew all that befel.

Then, what an occasion was the whirlwind of the war. Here was place for no holiday magistrate, no fair-weather sailor; the new pilot was hurried to the helm in a tornado. In four years,—four years of battle-days,—his endurance, his fertility of resources, his magnanimity, were sorely tried and never found wanting. There, by his courage, his justice, his even temper, his fertile council, his humanity, he stood an heroic figure in the centre of an heroic epoch. He is the true history of the American people in his time. Step by step he walked before them; slow with their slowness, quickening his march to theirs; the true representative of this continent; an entirely public man; father of his country, the pulse of twenty millions throbbing in his heart, the thought of their minds articulated by his tongue.—[*Extract.*]

POEM BY EDWARD ROWLAND SILL.

Were there no crowns on earth,
No evergreen to weave a hero's wreath,
That he must pass beyond the gates of death,
Our hero, our slain hero, to be crowned?
Could there on our unworthy earth be found
    Naught to befit his worth?

    The noblest soul of all!
When was there ever, since our Washington
A man so pure, so wise, so patient,—one
Who walked with this high goal alone in sight,
To speak, to do, to sanction only Right,
    Though very heaven should fall?

    Ah, not for him we weep;
What honor more could be in store for him —
Who would have had him linger in our dim
And troublesome world, when his great work was done,—
Who would not leave that worn and weary one
    Gladly to go to sleep?

    For us the stroke was just;
We were not worthy of that patient heart;
We might have helped him more, not stood apart,
And coldly criticised his works and ways;
Too late now, all too late, our little praise
    Sounds hollow o'er his dust.

    Be merciful, O God!
Forgive the meanness of our human hearts,
That never, till a noble soul departs,
See half the worth, or hear the angel's wings
Till they go rustling heavenward as he springs
    Up from the moulded sod.

    Yet what a deathless crown
Of Northern pine and Southern orange-flower,

For victory, and the land's new bridal-hour,
Would we have wreathed for that beloved brow!
Sadly upon his sleeping forehead now
    We lay our cypress down.

    O martyred one, farewell!
Thou hast not left thy people quite alone;
Out of thy beautiful life there comes a tone
Of power, of love, of trust,—a prophecy,
Whose fair fulfillment all the earth shall be,
    And all the Future tell.

TRIBUTE BY GENERAL GRANT.

I have no doubt that Lincoln will be the conspicuous figure of the war; one of the great figures of history. He was a great man, a very great man. The more I saw of him, the more this impressed me. He was incontestably the greatest man I ever knew. What marked him especially was his sincerity, his kindness, his clear insight into affairs. Under all this, he had a firm will and a clear policy. People used to say that Seward swayed him, or Chase, or Stanton. This was a mistake. He might appear to go Seward's way one day, and Stanton's another; but all the time he was going his own course, and they with him. It was that gentle firmness in carrying out his own will, without apparent force or friction, that formed the basis of his character. He was a wonderful talker and teller of stories. It is said his stories were improper. I have heard of them, but I never heard Lincoln use an improper word or phrase. I have sometimes, when I have heard his memory called in question, tried to recall such a thing, but could not. I always found him preeminently a clean-minded man. I regard these stories as exaggerations. Lincoln's power of illustration, his humor, was inexhaustible. He had a story or an illustration for everything.—[*Extract.*]

Lincoln was the grandest figure of the fiercest civil war. He is the gentlest memory of our world.—[*Robert G. Ingersoll,*

TRIBUTE BY JOHN G. NICOLAY.

President Lincoln was of unusual stature, six feet four inches, and of spare but muscular build; he had been in youth remarkably strong and skillful in the athletic games of the frontier, where, however, his popularity and recognized impartiality oftener made him an umpire than a champion. He had regular and prepossessing features, dark complexion, broad, high forehead, prominent cheek bones, gray, deep-set eyes, and bushy, black hair, turning to gray at the time of his death. Abstemious in his habits, he possessed great physical endurance. He was almost as tender-hearted as a woman. "I have not willingly planted a thorn in any man's bosom," he was able to say. His patience was inexhaustible. He had naturally a most cheerful and sunny temper, was highly social and sympathetic, loved pleasant conversation, wit, anecdote and laughter. Beneath this, however, ran an under-current of sadness; he was occasionally subject to hours of deep silence and introspection that approached a condition of trance. In manner he was simple, direct, void of the least affectation, and entirely free from awkwardness, oddity, or eccentricity. His mental qualities were a quick analytic perception, strong logical powers, a tenacious memory, a liberal estimate and tolerance of the opinions of others, ready intuition of human nature; and perhaps his most valuable faculty was rare ability to divest himself of all feeling or passion in weighing motives of persons or problems of state. His speech and diction were plain, terse, forcible. Relating anecdotes with appreciating humor and fascinating dramatic skill, he used them freely and effectively in conversation and argument. He loved manliness, truth and justice. He despised all trickery and selfish greed. In arguments at the bar he was so fair to his opponent that he frequently appeared to concede away his client's case. He was ever ready to take blame on himself and bestow praise on others. "I claim not to have controlled events," he said, "but confess plainly that events have controlled me." The Declaration of Independence was his political chart and inspiration. He acknowledged a universal. equality of human rights. "Certainly the negro is not our equal in color," he said, "perhaps not in many other respects; still, in the right to put into his mouth the bread that his own hands have earned, he is the equal of every other man, white or black." He had unchanging faith in self-government. "The people," he said, "are the rightful masters of both congresses and courts, not to overthrow the Constitution, but to overthrow the men who pervert the Constitution." Yielding and accommodating in non-essentials, he was inflexibly firm in a principle or position deliberately taken. "Let us have faith that right makes might," he said, "and in that faith let us to the end dare to do our duty as we understand it." The Emancipation Proclamation once issued, he reitterated his purpose never to retract or modify it. "There have been men base enough," he said, "to propose to me to return to slavery our black warriors of Port Hudson and Olustee, and thus win the respect of the masters they fought. Should I do so, I should deserve to be damned in time and eternity. Come what will, I will keep my faith with friend and foe." Benevolence and forgiveness were the very basis of his character; his world-wide humanity is aptly embodied in a phrase of his second inaugural: "with malice toward none, with charity for all." His nature was deeply religious, but he belonged to no denomination; he had faith in the eternal justice and boundless mercy of Providence, and made the Golden Rule of Christ his practical creed. History must accord him a rare sagacity in guiding a great people through the perils of a mighty revolution, an admirable singleness of aim, a skillful discernment and courageous seizure of the golden moment to free his nation from the incubus of slavery, faithful adherence to law, and conscientious moderation in the use of power, a shining personal example of honesty and purity, and finally the possession of that subtle and indefinable magnetism by which he subordinated and directed dangerously disturbed and perverted moral and political forces to the restoration of peace and constitutional authority to his country, and the gift of liberty to four millions of human beings. Architect of his own fortunes, rising with every opportunity, mastering every emergency, fulfilling every duty, he not only proved himself pre-eminently the man for the hour, but the signal benefactor of posterity. As statesman, ruler, and liberator, civilization will hold his name in perpetual honor.

HENRY HOWARD BROWNELL'S ODE ON LINCOLN.

There was tumbling of traitor fort,
　Flaming of traitor fleet,—
Lighting of city and port,
　Clasping in square and street.

There was thunder of mine and gun,
　Cheering by mast and tent,—
When—his dread work all done,
And his high fame full won—
　Died the Good President.

In his quiet chair he sate,
　Pure of malice or guile,
Stainless of fear or hate,—
　And there played a pleasant smile
On the rough and careworn face;
　For his heart was all the while
On means of mercy and grace.

The brave old Flag drooped o'er him,
　(A fold in the hard hand lay,)—
He looked, perchance on the play,—
But the scene was a shadow before him,
　For his thoughts were far away.

'Twas but the morn, (yon fearful
　Death-shade, gloomy and vast,
　Lifting slowly at last,)
　His household heard him say,
" 'Tis long since I've been so cheerful
　So light of heart as to-day."

'Twas dying, the long dread clang,—
  But, or ever the blessed ray
  Of peace could brighten to-day,
  Murder stood by the way,—
Treason struck home his fang!
One throb, and without a pang
  That pure soul passed away.

  * * * * *

Kindly Spirit!—Ah, when did treason
  Bid such a generous nature cease,
Mild by temper and strong by reason,
  But ever leaning to love and peace?

A head how sober! a heart how spacious!
  A manner equal with high or low;
Rough, but gentle; uncouth, but gracious;
  And still inclining to lips of woe.

Patient when saddest, calm when sternest,
  Grieved when rigid for justice's sake;
Given to jest, yet ever in earnest
  If aught of right or truth were at stake.

Simple of heart, yet shrewd therewith;
  Slow to resolve, but firm to hold;
Still with parable and with myth
  Seasoning truth like Them of old;
Aptest humor and quaintest pith!
  (Still we smile o'er the tales he told.)

Yet whoso might pierce the guise
  Of mirth in the man we mourn
Would mark, and with grieved surprise,
  All the great soul had borne,
In the piteous lines, and the kind sad eyes,
  So dreadfully wearied and worn.

  * * * * *

The Land's great lamentations,
  The mighty mourning of cannon,
    The myriad flags half-mast—
The late remorse of the nations,
  Grief from Volga to Shannon!
  (Now they know thee at last.)

How, from gray Niagara's shore
To Canaveral's surfy shoal,—
From the rough Atlantic roar
To the long Pacific roll,—
For bereavement and for dole,
Every cottage wears its weed,
White as thine own pure soul,
And black as the traitor deed!

How, under a nation's pall,
The dust so dear in our sight
To its home on the prairie passed,—
The leagues of funeral,
The myriads morn and night,
Pressing to look their last!

Not alone the State's Eclipse;
But how tears in hard eyes gather,—
And on rough and bearded lips
Of the regiments and the ships,—
"Oh, our dear Father!"

And methinks of all the million
That looked on the dark dead face,
'Neath its sable plumed pavilion,
The crone of a humbler race
Is saddest of all to think on,
And the old swart lips that said,
Sobbing, "Abraham Lincoln!
Oh, he is dead, he is dead!"
        *   *   *   *   *

Perished?—who was it said
Our Leader had passed away?
Dead?   Our President dead?—
He has not died for a day!

We mourn for a little breath,
Such as, late or soon, dust yields;
But the Dark Flower of death
Blooms in the fadeless fields.

We looked on a cold, still brow;
But Lincoln could yet survive;
He never was more alive,
Never nearer than now.

For the pleasant season found him,
  Guarded by faithful hands,
  In the fairest of Summer Lands;
With his own brave Staff around him,
  There our President stands.

There they are all at his side,
  The noble hearts and true,
  That did all men might do,—
Then slept, with their swords, and died.

Gathered home from the grave,
  Risen from sun and rain,
Rescued from wind and wave,
  Out of the stormy main,—
The Legions of our Brave
  Are all in their lines again!

A tenderer green than May
  The Eternal Season wears,—
The blue of our summer's day
  Is thin and pallid to theirs,—
The Horror faded away,
  And 'twas heaven all unawares!

Tents on the Infinite Shore!
  Flags in the azuline sky,
Sails on the seas once more!
  To-day in the heaven on high,
All under arms once more!

The troops are all in their lines,
  The guidons flutter and play:
But every bayonet shines,
  For all must march to-day.

What lofty pennons flaunt?
What mighty echoes haunt,
  As of great guns, o'er the main?
  Hark to the sound again!
The Congress is all-ataunt!
  The Cumberland's manned again!

All the ships and their men
  Are in line of battle to-day,—

All at quarters, as when
  Their last roll thundered away,—
All at their guns, as then,
  For the Fleet salutes to-day.

The armies have broken camp
  On the vast and sunny plain,
  The drums are rolling again;
With steady, measured tramp,
  They're marching all again.

With alignment firm and solemn
  Once again they form
In mighty square and column,—
  But never for charge and storm.

The Old Flag they died under
  Floats above them on the shore,
And on the great ships yonder
  The ensigns dip once more,—
And once again the thunder
  Of the thirty guns and four!

In solid platoons of steel,
  Under's heaven's triumphal arch,
The long lines break and wheel;
  And the word is, "Forward, march!"

The colors ripple o'erhead,
  The drums roll up to the sky,
And with martial time and tread
  The regiments all pass by,—
The ranks of our faithful Dead,
  Meeting their President's eye.

With a soldier's quiet pride
  They smile o'er the perished pain,
  For their anguish was not vain,—
For thee, O Father, we died!
  And we did not die in vain.

March on, your last brave mile!
  Salute him, Star and Lace;
Form around him, rank and file,
  And look on the kind, rough face;

But the quaint and homely smile
Has a glory and a grace
It never has shown erewhile,—
Never, in time and space.

Close around him, hearts of pride!
Press near him side by side,—
Our Father is not alone!
For the Holy Right ye died,
And Christ, the Crucified,
Waits to welcome his own.

TRIBUTES FROM ABROAD.

The death of President Lincoln called out tributes and eulogies, not only from the most eminent poets and orators and statesmen of his own country, but throughout the world. All nations and all peoples vied with each other in expressions of sympathy and grief. The universal outpouring of sorrow was such as never occurred before on the death of any man in any age. As the news flew to the four quarters of the globe, it carried mourning alike to castle and to cottage, which was voiced in world-wide lamentations for the illustrious dead. From Great Britain, France, Germany, Belgium, Italy, Spain, Portugal, Switzerland, the Scandinavian countries, Greece, Russia, Turkey, Egypt, China, Japan, Mexico, Brazil and other countries of South America, and from the islands of the sea, came the official and unofficial tributes. The widowed Queen of England and the Empress Eugenie of France sent, by their own hands, messages of womanly sympathy to the widow of the American President. Prince Bismarck penned and forwarded a note expressing the feelings of his Government. Fitting resolutions were presented in the English House of Lords by Earl Russell, and in the House of Commons by Mr. Disraeli, and adopted, with many eloquent eulogies. Almost every Government in Europe sent, through its diplomatic agents or legislative bodies, its official condolence. In France a popular penny collection was made for a gold medal, inscribed to "Lincoln, the honest man, who abolished slavery, re-established the Union, and saved the Republic, without veiling the statue of Liberty." The most distinguished poets and orators of Europe found in the life and death of Lincoln an inspiring theme. The press, especially that of England, teemed with tributes and eulogies. John Stuart Mill wrote of "the great citizen who has afforded so noble an example of the qualities befitting the first magistrate of a free people." Prof. Goldwin Smith said: "America has gained one more ideal character, the most precious and inspiring of national possessions." The London Times, which had been harshly unjust to Mr. Lincoln, said the news of his death would be "received throughout Europe with sorrow as sincere and profound as it awoke even in the United States," and that "Englishmen learned to respect a man who showed the best characteristics of their race." The Saturday Review said: "During the arduous experience of four years, Mr. Lincoln constantly rose in general estimation, by calmness of temper, by an intuitively logical appreciation of the character of the conflict, and by undisputed sincerity." The London Spectator spoke of Mr. Lincoln as "the noblest President whom America has had since the time of Washington;" and "certainly the best, if not the ablest, man ruling over any country in the civilized world. * * Without the advantages of Washington's education or training, Mr. Lincoln was called from an humble station, at the opening of a mighty civil war, to form a government out of a party in which the habits and traditions of official life did not exist. Finding himself the object of Southern abuse so fierce and so foul that in any man less passionless it would long ago have stirred up an implacable animosity; mocked at for his official awkwardness, and denounced for his steadfast policy by all the Democratic section of the loyal States; tried by years of failure before that policy achieved a single great success; further tried by a series of successes so rapid and brilliant that they would have puffed up a smaller mind and overset its balance; embarrassed by the boastfulness of his people and of his subordinates, no less than by his own inexperience in his relations with foreign States; beset by fanatics of principle on one side, who would pay no attention to his obligations as a constitutional ruler, and by fanatics of caste on the other, who were not only deaf to the claims of justice, but would hear of no policy large enough for a revolutionary emergency,—Mr. Lincoln persevered through all without ever giving way to anger, or despondency, or exultation, or popular arrogance, or sectarian fanaticism, or caste prejudice, visibly growing in force of character, in self-possession, and in magnanimity, till in his last short message to Congress, on the 4th of March, we can detect no longer the rude and illiterate mold of a village lawyer's thought, but find it replaced by a grasp of principle, a dignity of manner, and a solemnity of purpose which would have been unworthy neither of Hampden nor of Cromwell, while his gentleness and generosity of feeling toward his foes are almost greater than we should expect from either of them.''

POEM BY TOM TAYLOR, IN LONDON PUNCH.

One of the most touching and heartfelt of all the foreign tributes to Mr. Lincoln was that of the genial poet Tom Taylor, published in the London Punch—a paper that had used Mr. Lincoln as a convenient subject of caricature and ridicule. The poem appeared a short time after the assassination.

> You lay a wreath on murdered Lincoln's bier,
>   You, who with mocking pencil wont to trace,
> Broad for the self-complacent British sneer,
>   His length of shambling limb, his furrowed face,
>
> His gaunt, gnarled hands, his unkempt, bristling hair,
>   His garb uncouth, his bearing ill at ease,
> His lack of all we prize as debonair,
>   Of power or will to shine, of art to please;
>
> You, whose smart pen backed up the pencil's laugh,
>   Judging each step as though the way were plain;

Reckless, so it could point its paragraph,
  Of chief's perplexity, or people's pain;

Beside this corse, that bears for winding-sheet
  The Stars and Stripes he lived to rear anew,
Between the mourners at his head and feet,
  Say, scurrile jester, is there room for *you?*

Yes; he had lived to shame me from my sneer,
  To lame my pencil, and confute my pen;
To make me own this hind of princes peer,
  This rail-splitter a true-born king of men.

My shallow judgment I had learned to rue,
  Noting how to occasion's height he rose;
How his quaint wit made home-truth seem more true;
  How, iron-like, his temper grew by blows;

How humble, yet how hopeful, he could be;
  How, in good fortune and in ill, the same;
Nor bitter in success, nor boastful he,
  Thirsty for gold, nor feverish for fame.

He went about his work,—such work as few
  Ever had laid on head and heart and hand—
As one who knows, where there's a task to do,
  Man's honest will must heaven's good grace command;

Who trusts the strength will with the burden grow,
  That God makes instruments to work his will,
If but that will we can arrive to know,
  Nor tamper with the weights of good and ill.

So he went forth to battle on the side
  That he felt clear was Liberty's and Right's,
As in his peasant boyhood he had plied
  His warfare with rude Nature's thwarting mights;

The uncleared forest, the unbroken soil,
  The iron bark, that turns the lumberer's ax,
The rapid, that o'erbears the boatman's toil,
  The prairie, hiding the mazed wanderer's tracks,

The ambushed Indian, and the prowling bear,—
  Such were the deeds that helped his youth to train:
Rough culture, but such trees large fruit may bear,
  If but their stocks be of right girth and grain.

So he grew up, a destined work to do,
    And lived to do it: four long-suffering years'
Ill fate, ill feeling, ill report, lived through,
    And then he heard the hisses change to cheers,

The taunts to tribute, the abuse to praise,
    And took both with the same unwavering mood;
Till, as he came on light, from darkling days,
    And seemed to touch the goal from where he stood,

A felon hand, between the goal and him,
    Reached from behind his back, a trigger prest,
And those perplexed and patient eyes were dim,
    Those gaunt, long-laboring limbs were laid to rest!

The words of mercy were upon his lips,
    Forgiveness in his heart and on his pen,
When this vile murderer brought swift eclipse
    To thoughts of peace on earth, good-will to men.

The Old World and the New, from sea to sea,
    Utter one voice of sympathy and shame;
Sore heart, so stopped when it at last beat high;
    Sad life, cut short just as its triumph came!

A deed accurst! Strokes have been struck before
    By the assassin's hand, whereof men doubt
If more of horror or disgrace they bore;
    But thy foul crime, like Cain's, stands darkly out,

Vile hand, that brandest murder on a strife,
    Whate'er its grounds, stoutly and nobly striven;
And with the martyr's crown crownest a life
    With much to praise, little to be forgiven.

THE END.